W9-BVF-517

Oxford
English
THESAURUS
FOR SCHOOLS

Chief Editor: Susan Rennie
Literacy Consultant: John Mannion

OXFORD
UNIVERSITY PRESS

OXFORD
UNIVERSITY PRESS

Great Clarendon Street, Oxford OX2 6DP

Oxford University Press is a department of the University of Oxford.
It furthers the University's objective of excellence in research,
scholarship, and education by publishing worldwide in

Oxford   New York

Auckland Cape Town Dar es Salaam Hong Kong Karachi
Kuala Lumpur Madrid Melbourne Mexico City Nairobi
New Delhi Shanghai Taipei Toronto

With offices in

Argentina Austria Brazil Chile Czech Republic France Greece
Guatemala Hungary Italy Japan Poland Portugal Singapore
South Korea Switzerland Thailand Turkey Ukraine Vietnam

Oxford is a registered trade mark of Oxford University Press
in the UK and in certain other countries

British Library Cataloguing in Publication Data
Data available

ISBN: 978 0 19 275700 5 (hardback)
10 9
ISBN: 978 0 19 275701 2 (paperback)
10 9 8 7 6 5 4 3

Printed in India by Manipal Technologies Ltd, Manipal

Paper used in the production of this book is a natural, recyclable product made from wood
grown in sustainable forests. The manufacturing process conforms to the environmental
regulations of the country of origin.

Contents

Contents

Preface

The *Oxford English Thesaurus for Schools* has been written primarily for secondary school students. It is also designed to complement the *Oxford English Dictionary for Schools* which is aimed at the same age range.

The range of subjects covered in the main entries and topic panels has been chosen to support teaching across the curriculum, and the content of both the thesaurus and appendices reflects the advice of teachers and educational consultants.

The example phrases and sentences given in this thesaurus are based on material in the Oxford Children's Corpus (a database of over **30 million** words of texts written specifically for children), as well as in the larger Oxford English Corpus of over **two billion** words. Selected examples are also given from contemporary and classic literature, to support special panels on descriptive and genre writing. These examples are designed to link with texts currently used in schools.

A special feature of this thesaurus is the Writer's Toolkit section at the back. This offers advice on how to improve key writing skills and is relevant for both creative and non-fiction writing.

Susan Rennie

Introduction

When to use a thesaurus

There are three key reasons to use a thesaurus:

▶ **to find an alternative or more interesting word**
If you find yourself using one word over and over again in your writing, use your thesaurus to find some alternatives. For example, rather than repeating the word *amazing*, you might substitute *astonishing, astounding, staggering,* or *remarkable* (look up **amazing**). A thesaurus can also point you to a more interesting choice of word, such as *amble* or *saunter* instead of simply *walk* (look up **walk**).

▶ **to find the right word**
A thesaurus can tell you the right word to use for a specific person, place, or thing. If you look up **collector**, you will find that someone who collects shells is called a *conchologist*; and the entry for **moon** tells you the difference between a *waxing* and a *waning* moon.

▶ **to give you ideas for writing**
A thesaurus can give you ideas for how to describe a person, place, or thing, or of what details to include in a piece of writing. If you are stuck for ideas for describing a rural landscape, you will find suggestions under **landscape**, **light**, and **weather**, as well as useful lists in **animal**, **bird**, **plant**, and **tree**. A thesaurus can also help you find related words in a topic that you are studying or describing, such as words relating to art, craft, and design (look up **art**), or words used to describe the parts of a book (look up **book**).

What is the difference between a thesaurus and a dictionary?

A dictionary tells you what a word means, whereas a thesaurus tells you what other words have the same meaning, or are related to the word in some way. In other words, a dictionary gives you a *definition* of a word, whereas a thesaurus gives you *synonyms* of a word. For example, if you look up **car** in a dictionary, it will tell you that a car is a vehicle with an engine, designed to carry a small number of people. But a thesaurus will give you synonyms for **car** (*motor car, vehicle, automobile*) and will list some types of car and parts of a car (*convertible, limousine, people carrier; chassis, gearbox, undercarriage*).

You often use a dictionary to check the meaning of something you have read or heard. You use a thesaurus to find ways to write or say something yourself.

Writer's Toolkit

At the back of this thesaurus, you will find a section called the **Writer's Toolkit**. This includes useful tips on how to improve your writing skills. It covers key skills such as using sentences and paragraphs effectively, choosing the appropriate language for formal or informal writing, and putting something into your own words. It also offers advice on how to edit your own work, how to avoid some common mistakes in grammar and punctuation, and how to make your writing more interesting by being creative with language.

Throughout the **Writer's Toolkit**, there are suggestions and tips for how to put your skills into practice. You will also find examples quoted from contemporary and classic literature, which link the topics covered in the **Writer's Toolkit** to the work of a variety of authors.

Thesaurus features

headword

word class or part of speech

fable *NOUN*
the fable of the Tortoise and the Hare
legend, story, tale, parable
❙ SEE ALSO fiction

fabric *NOUN*
1 *windproof fabric*
cloth, material, textile
2 *The fabric of the building is sound.*
structure, framework, make-up

synonyms

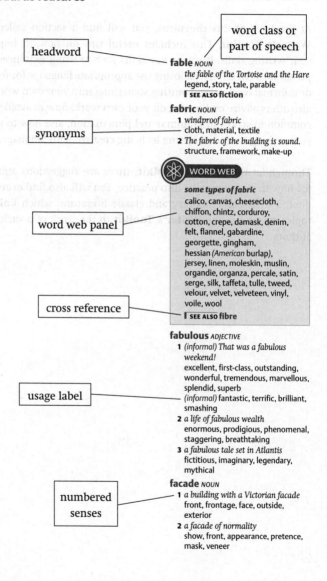

✳ WORD WEB

some types of fabric
calico, canvas, cheesecloth,
chiffon, chintz, corduroy,
cotton, crepe, damask, denim,
felt, flannel, gabardine,
georgette, gingham,
hessian (*American* burlap),
jersey, linen, moleskin, muslin,
organdie, organza, percale, satin,
serge, silk, taffeta, tulle, tweed,
velour, velvet, velveteen, vinyl,
voile, wool
❙ SEE ALSO fibre

word web panel

cross reference

fabulous *ADJECTIVE*
1 *(informal) That was a fabulous
weekend!*
excellent, first-class, outstanding,
wonderful, tremendous, marvellous,
splendid, superb
(informal) fantastic, terrific, brilliant,
smashing
2 *a life of fabulous wealth*
enormous, prodigious, phenomenal,
staggering, breathtaking
3 *a fabulous tale set in Atlantis*
fictitious, imaginary, legendary,
mythical

usage label

facade *NOUN*
1 *a building with a Victorian facade*
front, frontage, face, outside,
exterior
2 *a facade of normality*
show, front, appearance, pretence,
mask, veneer

numbered senses

example phrase or sentence

face NOUN

1 *Donna's face flushed with anger.*
countenance, features, visage
(informal) mug
(formal) physiognomy
► A side view of someone's face is their
profile.

special synonym

2 *Why are you making that funny face?*
expression, look, appearance, aspect
3 *a clock face*
front, facade, cover

❚ OPPOSITE back

opposite (antonym)

4 *the north face of the Eiger*
side, surface, plane

WRITING TIPS

describing faces

It was a gaunt, aquiline face
which was turned towards us,
with piercing dark eyes, which
lurked in deep hollows under
overhung and tufted brows.
— *Sir Arthur Conan Doyle, The Return of Sherlock Holmes*

literary quotation

facial features
beauty spot, bloom, brow,
cheekbones, complexion, crow's
feet, dimple, double chin, ear
lobes, forehead, freckles, jawline,
jowl, laugh-lines, lower lip, mole,
pimple, scar, spot, temples,
upper lip, wrinkles

writing tips panel

facial expressions
beam, frown, glare, glower,
grimace, grin, leer, pout, scowl,
smile, smirk, sneer, wince, yawn

Thesaurus features

▶ The **headword** is the word you look up. Headwords are shown in colour and are given in alphabetical order. Some entries also include headword phrases, such as **fall out** or **be fed up with**, which are listed under the appropriate headword and have their own synonyms and numbered senses.

▶ The **word class** or **part of speech** tells you whether a word is a *noun*, *verb*, *adjective*, *adverb*, or *preposition*.

▶ The **numbered senses** tell you when a word has more than one meaning. Each numbered sense lists synonyms which relate to that sense of the headword.

▶ The **example phrase** or **sentence** show you how you might use a word. Each meaning of a word has a separate example phrase or sentence.

▶ The **synonyms** are words that mean the same, or nearly the same, as the headword. Some synonyms are marked as **idioms**: these are phrases which mean something other than their literal meaning, such as *like a flash* or *go up in smoke*.

▶ A **usage label** tells you that certain synonyms are only for *informal* or *formal* writing. An *old use* label tells you that a word was only used in the past. A regional label, such as *North American* or *Australian*, tells you that a word is used in those countries.

You will find help on using the appropriate language for formal and informal writing in the *Writer's Toolkit* section at the back of this thesaurus.

▶ The **special synonyms** are similar in meaning to the headword, but can only be used in special cases.

▶ The **opposites** are words that are opposite in meaning to the headword. Sometimes, each meaning of a word has its own opposites. Opposites are also known as **antonyms**.

▶ A **cross reference** points you to another headword in the thesaurus where you will find useful words or information.

▶ The **special panels** give extra help or information for certain words. Turn over the page for details about the different types of panel.

Special panels

Throughout this thesaurus, you will see tinted boxes which give extra help on finding and using words.

Usage notes offer advice on common problem areas, such as confusable words. For example, the entry for **famous** has a usage note which tells you that *infamous* is not the opposite of *famous*.

> **Usage Note**
>
> The word **infamous** is not the opposite of **famous**. An **infamous** person has a bad reputation: *Sylvester Fibbs was an infamous liar.*

There are three other types of panel, each marked by a special symbol: **overused word**, **word web**, and **writing tips**.

OVERUSED WORD PANELS

The **overused word** panels offer more interesting alternatives for common words like **bad**, **good**, **happy**, and **sad**. Overused words can make your writing sound dull and repetitive if you use them too often. For example, the **overused word** panel for **say** suggests *snap, snarl, growl, thunder, bark, rasp, rant,* and *rave* as alternatives for to *say something angrily*; and *remark, comment, observe, note,* and *mention* as alternatives for *to say something casually.*

You will find the following **overused word** panels in this thesaurus:

all right	bad	beautiful
big	bit	eat
funny	good	happy
hard	hit	like
little	look	lovely

move	nice	old
sad	say	small
strong	walk	

✳ WORD WEB PANELS

The **word web** panels list words which are related to a particular topic, such as **food**, **fashion**, and **photography**. These can be useful for both non-fiction writing and creative writing. For example, the panel for **bird** lists various types of sea bird, birds of prey, etc; and the panel for **drama** gives terms related to drama, such as *amphitheatre*, *ensemble*, and *monologue*.

Some panels also give definitions for specialized terms which relate to the panel topic. For example, the panel for **amphibian** tells you that the scientific study of amphibians and reptiles is called *herpetology*.

Some **word web** panels list words which belong to a particular category. For example, the **collective noun** panel lists some common collective nouns, such as a *pride* of lions, a *troop* of monkeys, and a *colony* of penguins; and the panel for **phobia** lists some common phobias, such as *acrophobia* (fear of heights), *arachnophobia* (fear of spiders), and *scotophobia* (fear of the dark).

You will find the following **word web** panels in this thesaurus:

abbreviation	accommodation	age
aircraft	amphibian	animal
anniversary	art	athletics
bee	bicycle	bird
blue	boat	body
bone	book	bridge
brown	building	butterfly
camel	car	castle
cat	chess	clock

clothes	coin	collective nouns
collector	communication	computer
cooking	cricket	criminal
crustacean	dance	digestion
dinosaur	dog	drama
drawing	earthquake	energy
environment	eye	fabric
family	fashion	feather
fibre	fiction	figurative language
film	finger	fish
flower	food & nutrition	foot
football	foreign phrases	fortune-telling
fossil	fraction	frog
fruit	fuel	fungi
gem	glasses	green
grey	guitar	hat
herb	horse	ice
illness	injury	insect
jewellery	lens	light
mammal	marsupial	martial arts
mathematics	meal	meat
medicine	metal	mollusc
music	musician	nut
occupation	ocean	paper
pattern	phobia	photography
pink	planet	plant
poetry	politics	pottery
prehistoric	punctuation	purple
rainbow	red	religion
reptile	restaurant	rock
rodent	room	ruler
science	sea	shape
shellfish	shoes	shop

snake	song	space
spice	spider	sport
swimming	television	temperature
tennis	textiles	the Earth
the Moon	the Sun	time
tooth	tower	tree
vegetable	vehicle	volcano
weapon	weights & measures	writer
yellow	zodiac	

WRITING TIPS PANELS

There are two types of panel which offer writing tips: some give help for descriptive writing and others for genre writing.

The **descriptive writing** panels suggest words to use to describe how people or places look, or how things sound, smell, taste, or feel. For example, the **describing clothes** panel lists parts of items of clothing, such as *bodice*, *cuff*, and *lapel*, as well as adjectives used to describe clothes, such as *crumpled*, *stylish*, and *threadbare*.

The **genre** panels suggest vocabulary to use in particular types of creative writing. You can use them to give you ideas at the start of a piece of writing, or to help you refine it at a later stage. There are genre panels for **crime**, **fantasy**, **historical fiction**, **horror**, **science fiction**, and **spy fiction**. For example, the **writing crime fiction** panel includes ideas for characters, such as *criminologist*, *forensic scientist*, and *pathologist*; and the **writing science fiction** panel suggests useful words and phrases, such as *alien life-form*, *cyborg*, and *hyperspace*.

There are also **writing tips** panels for **writing a book review** and **writing about sport**, which offer suggestions for non-fiction writing.

Each **writing tips** panel includes a literary quotation, showing how authors have used words in the panel in either descriptive or genre writing.

You will find the following **writing tips** panels in this thesaurus:

describing animals
describing birds
describing bodies
describing buildings
describing clothes
describing colours
describing faces
describing hair
describing landscape
describing light
describing personality
describing smells
describing sounds
describing taste
describing texture
describing weather
writing crime fiction
writing fantasy fiction
writing historical fiction
writing horror fiction
writing science fiction
writing spy fiction
writing a book review
writing about sport
words in old & poetic use

Aa

aback *ADVERB*

▷ **taken aback**

Ron was taken aback by my question.
surprised, astonished, startled,
shocked, disconcerted,
dumbfounded

abandon *VERB*

1 *Eventually, even his wife abandoned
him.*
desert, leave, leave behind, strand
(informal) dump, ditch
(old use) forsake
┃ **IDIOM** turn your back on

2 *They abandoned their plan to move
to France.*
give up, scrap, drop, cancel, abort,
discard, renounce, relinquish

abbreviate *VERB*

Saint is often abbreviated to St.
shorten, reduce, abridge, contract

abbreviation *NOUN*

 WORD WEB

some common abbreviations
AIDS (acquired immune
deficiency syndrome)
asap (as soon as possible)
ATM (automated teller machine)
awol (absent without leave)
BBC (British Broadcasting
Corporation)
CAD (computer-aided design)
cm (centimetre)

CPR (cardio-pulmonary
resuscitation)
DNA (deoxyribonucleic acid)
EU (European Union)
FA (Football Association)
FAQ (frequently asked questions)
FM (frequency modulation)
GP (general practitioner)
GCSE (General Certificate of
Secondary Education)
HGV (heavy goods vehicle)
ICT (information and
communication technology)
IQ (intelligence quotient)
kg (kilogram)
km (kilometre)
kph (kilometres per hour)
kw (kilowatt)
mm (millimetre)
MP (Member of Parliament)
mph (miles per hour)
NASA (National Aeronautics and
Space Administration)
paye (pay as you earn)
pto (please turn over)
rsvp (répondez s'il vous plaît =
please reply)
TB (tuberculosis)
UN (United Nations)
UNESCO (United Nations
Educational Scientific and
Cultural Organization)

abdomen *NOUN*
SEE **stomach**

abduct *VERB*

*Seth claims he was abducted by
aliens.*
kidnap, seize, capture, carry off
(informal) snatch

abide *VERB*

Vampires cannot abide sunlight.
bear, stand, endure, tolerate,
stomach, put up with
(informal) hack
(British informal) stick

》

a
b
c
d
e
f
g
h
i
j
k
l
m
n
o
p
q
r
s
t
u
v
w
x
y
z

▷ **abide by**
abiding by the rules of the game
obey, observe, comply with, follow,
keep to, adhere to, stick to, heed

ability *NOUN*

1 *the ability to play MP3 files*
capability, capacity, power, facility,
means

2 *a player of exceptional ability*
talent, skill, aptitude, competence,
expertise, proficiency

able *ADJECTIVE*
a very able swimmer
competent, capable, accomplished,
expert, skilful, proficient, talented,
gifted

❙ **OPPOSITE** incompetent

▷ **able to**
*Will you be able to play on
Saturday?*
capable of, in a position to, up to, fit
to, allowed to, permitted to

❙ **OPPOSITE** unable to

abnormal *ADJECTIVE*
*abnormal weather for this time of
year*
unusual, uncommon, atypical,
extraordinary, exceptional, peculiar,
odd, strange, weird, bizarre,
unnatural, freak

❙ **OPPOSITES** normal, typical

abolish *VERB*
the campaign to abolish slavery
get rid of, do away with,
put an end to, eliminate, eradicate,
stamp out

❙ **OPPOSITE** create

abort *VERB*
*The decision was made to abort the
mission.*
terminate, cancel, discontinue, stop,
end, halt, call off

about *PREPOSITION*

1 *The tour takes about an hour.*
approximately, roughly, close to,
around, in the region of, circa

》

> **Usage Note**
>
> The word *circa* (or *c.*) is used
> for approximate dates: *The
> photograph dates from circa 1900.*

2 *a book about Italian cookery*
regarding, relating to, on the subject
of, on

▷ **be about something**
The film is about a teenage spy.
concern, deal with, involve, relate to

about *ADVERB*

1 *rats scurrying about in the attic*
around, here and there, in all
directions

2 *There were not many people about.*
near, nearby, around, hereabouts

above *PREPOSITION*

1 *flying above the clouds*
over, higher than

2 *a crowd of above a thousand*
more than, larger than, over

abridged *ADJECTIVE*
an abridged encyclopedia
concise, shortened, reduced, cut
down, condensed, edited

abroad *ADVERB*
spending a year abroad
overseas, in a foreign country

abrupt *ADJECTIVE*

1 *The riders came to an abrupt halt.*
sudden, hurried, hasty, quick, rapid,
unexpected, precipitate

❙ **OPPOSITE** gradual

2 *I was put off by his abrupt manner.*
curt, blunt, rude, brusque, terse,
short, brisk, sharp, impolite, uncivil

❙ **OPPOSITE** polite

absence *NOUN*

1 *absence from school*
non-attendance, absenteeism,
truancy, leave

❙ **OPPOSITE** presence

2 *an absence of noise*
lack, want, non-existence, deficit,
shortage, dearth

OPPOSITE presence

absent *ADJECTIVE*
absent from home
away, missing
► To be absent from school without a good reason is to **play truant**.
► Someone who is absent is an **absentee**.
OPPOSITE present

absent-minded *ADJECTIVE*
an absent-minded inventor
forgetful, inattentive, distracted, scatterbrained
IDIOM with a memory like a sieve

absolute *ADJECTIVE*
1 *a look of absolute terror*
complete, total, utter, outright, pure, sheer
2 *a ruler with absolute power*
unlimited, total, unrestricted, supreme, infinite
OPPOSITE limited

absolutely *ADVERB*
The stench was absolutely disgusting.
completely, totally, utterly, thoroughly, wholly, entirely, quite

absorb *VERB*
1 *Let the rice absorb all the water.*
soak up, suck up, take in, draw in, mop up
2 *The TV absorbed his attention for a while.*
engage, engross, captivate, occupy, preoccupy, hold, grip, rivet

absorbed *ADJECTIVE*
▷ **be absorbed in**
Meg was completely absorbed in her knitting.
be engrossed in, be interested in, be preoccupied with, be immersed in, concentrate on, focus on

absorbent *ADJECTIVE*
an absorbent cloth
porous, spongy, sponge-like

absorbing *ADJECTIVE*
an absorbing book

interesting, fascinating, intriguing, gripping, enthralling, engrossing, captivating, riveting, spellbinding

abstain *VERB*
▷ **abstain from**
I'm abstaining from junk food for a month.
go without, give up, forgo, refrain from, eschew, avoid, reject, renounce, deny yourself, desist from
OPPOSITE indulge in

abstract *ADJECTIVE*
Beauty and truth are abstract ideas.
theoretical, intellectual, philosophical
OPPOSITE concrete

absurd *ADJECTIVE*
That's an absurd idea!
ridiculous, ludicrous, nonsensical, senseless, irrational, illogical, preposterous, stupid, foolish, silly, laughable
(British informal) daft
OPPOSITES sensible, reasonable

abundance *NOUN*
an abundance of food
plenty, profusion, plethora
OPPOSITES scarcity, lack, shortage

abundant *ADJECTIVE*
an abundant supply of food
ample, plentiful, generous, profuse, lavish, liberal
OPPOSITES meagre, scarce

abuse *VERB*
1 *a doctor who abused his position*
misuse, exploit, take advantage of
2 *The dog had been abused by its owner.*
mistreat, maltreat, ill-treat, hurt, injure, beat
3 *He was booked for abusing the referee.*
insult, be rude to, swear at
IDIOM call someone names

abuse *NOUN*
1 *the abuse of power*

misuse, exploitation

2 *campaigning against the
abuse of animals*
mistreatment, maltreatment,
ill-treatment, harm, injury

3 *shouting abuse in public*
insults, name-calling, swear words,
expletives

abusive ADJECTIVE

*an email containing abusive
language*
insulting, rude, offensive,
derogatory, hurtful, impolite,
slanderous, libellous, pejorative,
vituperative
▎**OPPOSITE** polite

abysmal ADJECTIVE

1 *The service in the restaurant was
abysmal.*
poor, very bad, awful, appalling,
dreadful, disgraceful, terrible,
worthless, woeful
(informal) rotten, dire

2 *showing an abysmal lack of good
taste*
profound, extreme, utter, complete,
deep

abyss NOUN

I felt as if I were falling into an abyss.
chasm, pit, void, gulf, crater, rift,
fissure

academy NOUN

an academy of music and drama
college, school, university, institute,
conservatory, conservatoire

accelerate VERB

1 *The bus accelerated to its top speed.*
go faster, speed up, pick up speed
▎**OPPOSITES** decelerate, slow down

2 *a treatment to accelerate healing*
make faster, hasten, quicken,
expedite

accent NOUN

1 *speaking with a slight Welsh accent*
pronunciation, intonation, tone

2 *The accent is on the first syllable.*
beat, stress, emphasis,

rhythm, pulse

accept VERB

1 *Will you accept my apology?*
take, receive, welcome
▎**OPPOSITES** reject, refuse

2 *He accepted my decision as final.*
go along with, abide by, defer to, put
up with, resign yourself to
(informal) swallow

acceptable ADJECTIVE

an acceptable standard of living
satisfactory, adequate,
good enough, sufficient, suitable,
tolerable, passable
▎**OPPOSITE** unacceptable

accepted ADJECTIVE

*Galileo challenged the accepted view
of the universe.*
recognized, established,
acknowledged, agreed, approved,
customary, orthodox, standard
▎**OPPOSITE** unorthodox

access NOUN

*The access to the house is through the
garden.*
entrance, entry, way in, approach

access VERB

*Can I access my email on this
computer?*
get at, obtain, reach, make use of

accessory NOUN

1 *a mobile phone with accessories*
attachment, fitting, extra, addition,
appendage, extension

2 *an accessory to the crime*
accomplice, associate,
collaborator (in)

accident NOUN

1 *accidents in the home*
misfortune, mishap, disaster,
calamity, catastrophe
▶ Someone who is always having
accidents is **accident-prone**.

2 *a road accident*
crash, collision, smash
▶ An accident involving a lot of

vehicles is a **pile-up**.

▶ A railway accident may involve a **derailment**.

▷ **by accident**

I found the letter by accident.

by chance, accidentally, coincidentally, unintentionally

accidental ADJECTIVE

1 *causing accidental damage*
unintentional, unintended, unwitting, incidental

2 *an accidental discovery*
unexpected, unforeseen, unplanned, chance, fortuitous

▎**OPPOSITES** deliberate, intentional

acclaim VERB

The album was acclaimed by music critics.

praise, applaud, commend, cheer, welcome

acclaim NOUN

It won the acclaim of audiences worldwide.

praise, applause, commendation, approval, congratulations

accommodate VERB

1 *The tent can accommodate two people.*
house, shelter, lodge, put up, take in, hold, sleep, have room for

2 *The staff tried to accommodate our needs.*
serve, assist, help, cater for, oblige, supply, satisfy

accommodation NOUN

The price includes food and accommodation.

housing, lodging, living quarters, residence, dwelling, shelter, home

▎**IDIOM** a roof over your head

WORD WEB

some types of accommodation
apartment, barracks, bed and breakfast, bedsit, boardinghouse, chalet,

(informal) digs, flat, guest house, hall of residence, hostel, hotel, house, inn, motel, *(informal)* pad, studio, timeshare, villa, youth hostel

▎**SEE ALSO** building

accompany VERB

1 *I'll accompany you to the door.*
escort, go with, show, conduct, usher, attend

▎**IDIOM** keep someone company

2 *a drink to accompany the meal*
go along with, complement, partner

accomplice NOUN

We believe the murderer had an accomplice.

partner, collaborator, associate, accessory, confederate, conspirator

accomplish VERB

The team had accomplished their mission.

achieve, succeed in, realize, attain, fulfil, carry out, perform, complete

accomplished ADJECTIVE

an accomplished musician
skilled, talented, able, expert, gifted, capable, clever, competent, proficient

accomplishment NOUN

1 *Reaching the Moon was a remarkable accomplishment.*
achievement, feat, success, effort, exploit

2 *one of her many accomplishments*
talent, ability, gift, skill

accord NOUN

▷ **of your own accord**

Did the guests leave of their own accord?

voluntarily, willingly, by choice

accord VERB

▷ **accord with**

His story does not accord with yours.

correspond to, agree with, concur with, be compatible with   **»** *(informal)* square with

account NOUN

1 *a vivid account of life in Russia*
report, record, description, history,
narrative, story, chronicle, log
(informal) write-up

2 *Your opinion is of no account to me.*
importance, significance,
consequence, interest, value

▷ **on account of**
*He gave up work on account of ill
health.*
because of, owing to, due to

account VERB

▷ **account for**
*How do you account for the missing
money?*
explain, give reasons for, justify,
make excuses for

accumulate VERB

1 *He had accumulated a fortune by the
age of twenty.*
collect, gather, amass, assemble,
heap up, pile up, hoard
❙ **OPPOSITES** disperse, lose

2 *Greenhouse gases are accumulating
faster than before.*
build up, grow, increase, accrue
❙ **OPPOSITE** decrease

accuracy NOUN

*We've increased the accuracy of our
search engine.*
correctness, precision, exactness,
validity, reliability

accurate ADJECTIVE

*Is the story based on
accurate information?*
correct, precise, exact, true, truthful,
reliable, authentic
❙ **IDIOMS** on the mark
(informal) spot on, bang on
❙ **OPPOSITES** inaccurate, inexact, false

accusation NOUN

a false accusation of witchcraft
allegation, charge, indictment,
imputation, claim

accuse VERB

▷ **accuse of**
*Two contestants were accused of
cheating.*
charge with, blame for, condemn for,
denounce for
❙ **OPPOSITE** defend

accustomed ADJECTIVE

▷ **accustomed to**
eyes not accustomed to daylight
used to, acclimatized to,
familiar with
❙ **OPPOSITE** unaccustomed to

ache NOUN

a dull ache in the joints
pain, soreness, throbbing,
discomfort, pang, twinge

ache VERB

Our legs ached from the long walk.
hurt, be painful, be sore, throb,
pound, smart

achieve VERB

1 *She achieved her lifelong ambition to
win an Oscar.*
accomplish, attain, succeed in,
carry out, fulfil

2 *He achieved the highest score in the
test.*
acquire, win, gain, earn, get, score

achievement NOUN

the achievement of a lifetime
accomplishment, attainment,
success, feat, triumph

acid ADJECTIVE

1 *the acid taste of lemon juice*
sour, acidic, sharp, tart, vinegary
❙ **OPPOSITES** alkali, sweet

2 *an acid tone of voice*
sharp, sarcastic, scathing, cutting,
biting, stinging, caustic, acerbic

acknowledge VERB

1 *Do you acknowledge that there is a
problem?*
admit, accept, concede, grant, allow,
recognize
❙ **OPPOSITE** deny

2 *She didn't even acknowledge my email.*
answer, reply to, respond to
❙ **OPPOSITE** ignore

acquaintance *NOUN*
1 *an old acquaintance of mine*
associate, contact, colleague
2 *a passing acquaintance with the law*
knowledge of, familiarity with, understanding of, awareness of

acquainted *ADJECTIVE*
▷ **acquainted with**
I'm not acquainted with the area myself.
familiar with, aware of, knowledgeable about
❙ **OPPOSITE** ignorant of

acquire *VERB*
Her family acquired the land years ago.
get, get hold of, obtain, come by, gain, secure
❙ **IDIOM** get your hands on
❙ **OPPOSITE** lose

acquisition *VERB*
The motorbike is his latest acquisition.
purchase, addition, investment

across *PREPOSITION*
the building across the road
on the other side of, over

act *NOUN*
1 *an act of courage*
action, deed, feat, exploit, operation, gesture
2 *His friendliness was just an act.*
pretence, show, pose, charade, masquerade
3 *a song-and-dance act*
performance, sketch, turn, routine, number

act *VERB*
1 *Rose had only a second in which to act.*
do something, take action, make a move

2 *Just try to act normally.*
behave, conduct yourself, react
3 *The beaver's tail acts as a rudder.*
function, operate, serve, work
4 *Have you acted in a musical before?*
perform, play, appear

action *NOUN*
1 *worn smooth by the action of the waves*
operation, working, effect, mechanism
2 *the actions of the main character in the play*
deed, act, exploit, feat, undertaking, measure, step
3 *killed in action in the First World War*
battle, fighting, combat

activate *VERB*
Press any key to activate the screen.
switch on, turn on, start, trigger, set off
❙ **OPPOSITES** deactivate, switch off

active *ADJECTIVE*
1 *leading an active lifestyle*
energetic, lively, busy, vigorous, dynamic, mobile
❙ **IDIOM** *(informal)* on the go
❙ **OPPOSITES** inactive, sedentary
2 *an active member of the community*
hard-working, dedicated, tireless, industrious
3 *Is this email account still active?*
functioning, working, operational, in operation, live
❙ **IDIOM** up and running
❙ **OPPOSITES** inactive, dormant

activity *NOUN*
1 *a street bustling with activity*
action, life, busyness, liveliness, excitement, movement, animation
❙ **IDIOM** hustle and bustle
2 *sports and other leisure activities*
hobby, interest, pastime, pursuit, recreation, occupation, task

actor, actress *NOUN*
a well-known TV actor

performer, player, star
(formal) thespian

▶ The main actor in a play or film is the **leading actor** or **lead**.

▶ The other actors are the **supporting actors**.

▶ All the actors in a play or film are the **cast** or the **company**.

❙ SEE ALSO drama

actual *ADJECTIVE*

This photograph shows the actual size.
real, true, genuine, authentic
❙ OPPOSITES imaginary, supposed

actually *ADVERB*

Just tell me what actually happened.
really, truly, definitely, in fact,
in reality, for real
❙ IDIOMS as a matter of fact, if truth be told

acute *ADJECTIVE*

1 an acute pain
intense, strong, piercing, agonizing, searing
❙ OPPOSITES mild, slight

2 an acute shortage of food
severe, serious, urgent, critical

3 an acute sense of hearing
keen, sharp, quick, astute, shrewd, perceptive, intelligent, alert
❙ OPPOSITE dull

adapt *VERB*

1 The play has been adapted for television.
modify, adjust, change, alter,
convert, remodel, customize

2 adapting to a different climate
become accustomed, adjust,
acclimatize

add *VERB*

adding an extension to the house
attach, join on, append, tack on,
insert

▷ **add to**
The sound effects add to the
atmosphere.
increase, enhance, intensify,

magnify, heighten, deepen

▷ **add up**

1 adding up the total cost
count up, tally
(informal) tot up

2 (informal) His story just doesn't add up.
be convincing, make sense

▷ **add up to**
The angles in a triangle add up to 180°.
total, amount to, come to, run to, make

addict *NOUN*

1 a drug addict
(informal) user, junkie

2 a football addict
fan, fanatic, enthusiast, lover, devotee
(informal) nut, freak, buff

addicted *ADJECTIVE*

▷ **addicted to**
addicted to TV soap operas
dependent on, obsessed with,
fanatical about
(informal) hooked on

addition *NOUN*

1 the addition of sound to the video
adding, incorporation, inclusion, introduction
❙ OPPOSITES subtraction, removal, deletion

2 an addition to the menu
add-on, supplement, adjunct, extra, appendage, afterthought

▷ **in addition**
In addition, I would like to say thanks.
also, as well, too, moreover,
furthermore

▷ **in addition to**
In addition to fiction, she also wrote poetry.
as well as, besides, apart from,
on top of, over and above

additional *ADJECTIVE*
an additional change of clothes

a
b
c
d
e
f
g
h
i
j
k
l
m
n
o
p
q
r
s
t
u
v
w
x
y
z

extra, further, more, added,
supplementary, spare

address NOUN

1 *Is this your usual address?*
home, residence, dwelling
2 *Lincoln's famous address at Gettysburg*
speech, lecture, talk, presentation, sermon

address VERB

Dr Garvey rose to address the audience.
speak to, talk to, make a speech to, lecture to

adept ADJECTIVE

adept at swimming underwater
skilled, skilful, expert, accomplished, proficient, talented, gifted, competent, deft
OPPOSITE inept

adequate ADJECTIVE

1 *The room was barely adequate for one person.*
enough, sufficient
2 *an adequate standard of living*
satisfactory, acceptable, tolerable, passable
OPPOSITE inadequate

adhere VERB

▷ **adhere to**
1 *dust adhering to the lens*
stick to, cling to, bond with
2 *adhering to the rules*
abide by, comply with, follow, heed, observe, stick to, stand by, respect

adjacent ADJECTIVE

a room with an adjacent kitchen
adjoining, connecting, neighbouring, next-door
▷ **adjacent to**
playing fields adjacent to the school
next to, next-door to, beside, alongside, bordering

adjoining ADJECTIVE

We stayed in adjoining rooms.
adjacent, connecting, neighbouring,

next-door, side-by-side

adjust VERB

adjusting the height of your seat
modify, alter, change, customize, rearrange, regulate, tune, set
(informal) tweak
▷ **adjust to**
adjusting to life in the city
adapt to, get used to, get accustomed to, become acclimatized to, come to terms with

adjustable ADJECTIVE

an adjustable headrest
modifiable, adaptable, variable, alterable, changeable, flexible, movable
OPPOSITE fixed

adjustment NOUN

some minor adjustments to the script
change, alteration, modification, amendment, edit
(informal) tweak

administer VERB

1 *The island is administered by its own council.*
manage, run, regulate, govern, direct, preside over, control, supervise, command, oversee
2 *learning how to administer first aid*
dispense, distribute, give out, hand out, issue, provide, supply, dole out, deal out

admirable ADJECTIVE

Does Macbeth have any admirable qualities?
commendable, praiseworthy, laudable, creditable, exemplary, worthy, honourable, deserving, pleasing
OPPOSITE deplorable

admiration NOUN

I'm full of admiration for her music.
respect, appreciation, approval, high regard, esteem
OPPOSITES contempt, scorn

a b c d e f g h i j k l m n o p q r s t u v w x y z

admire *VERB*

1 *I admire your honesty.*
respect, think highly of, look up to, have a high opinion of, hold in high regard, applaud, approve of, esteem
┃ OPPOSITE despise

2 *We stopped to admire the view.*
enjoy, appreciate, be delighted by

admirer *NOUN*

He is a great admirer of Charlie Chaplin.
fan, devotee, enthusiast, follower, supporter, adherent

admission *NOUN*

1 *an admission of guilt*
confession, declaration, acknowledgement, acceptance
┃ OPPOSITE denial

2 *the price of admission to the museum*
entrance, entry, access, admittance

admit *VERB*

1 *He was admitted to hospital last night.*
take in, receive, accept, allow in, let in
┃ OPPOSITE exclude

2 *I admit that I was wrong.*
acknowledge, confess, concede, accept, grant, allow
┃ OPPOSITE deny

admittance *NOUN*

There is no admittance to the park after dark.
entry, entrance, admission, access

adolescence *NOUN*

a film about the trials of adolescence
puberty, teens, youth

adolescent *NOUN*

a clothing range for adolescents
teenager, youth, juvenile
(informal) teen

adolescent *ADJECTIVE*

a group of adolescent girls
teenage, juvenile
(informal) teen

adopt *VERB*

1 *adopting a stray animal*
foster, take in

2 *adopting a healthy eating plan*
take on, take up, espouse, embrace, assume, choose, follow

adorable *ADJECTIVE*

an adorable smile
lovable, delightful, charming, appealing, enchanting

adore *VERB*

Iris adored both her grandchildren.
love, be devoted to, dote on, cherish, treasure, worship
┃ IDIOM think the world of

adorn *VERB*

a tree adorned with fairy lights
decorate, embellish, ornament, array, trim

adult *ADJECTIVE*

the size of an adult gorilla
grown-up, mature, full-size, fully grown
┃ OPPOSITES young, immature

advance *NOUN*

1 *the advance of technology*
progress, development, growth, evolution

2 *recent advances in medicine*
improvement, breakthrough, step forward

▷ **in advance**
We knew about the test in advance.
beforehand, ahead of time

advance *VERB*

1 *The army advanced towards the capital.*
move forward, go forward, proceed, press on, make progress, gain ground, make headway
┃ OPPOSITE retreat

2 *Computer animation has advanced rapidly.*
progress, develop, grow, improve, evolve

advantage NOUN

> *one of the advantages of living here*
> benefit, strong point, asset, plus, bonus, blessing, boon
>
> ❘ OPPOSITES disadvantage, drawback, downside

advantageous ADJECTIVE

> *in an advantageous position*
> beneficial, helpful, favourable, useful, fruitful, worthwhile, profitable, valuable

advent NOUN

> *the advent of the mobile phone*
> arrival, appearance, emergence, invention

adventure NOUN

> 1 *the story of our adventures on holiday*
> exploit, venture, escapade
> 2 *travelling the world in search of adventure*
> excitement, thrills, action

adventurous ADJECTIVE

> *She lead an adventurous life as a secret agent.*
> exciting, bold, daring, intrepid, challenging, eventful
>
> ❘ OPPOSITE unadventurous

adverse ADJECTIVE

> *the adverse effects of global warming*
> harmful, disadvantageous, detrimental, damaging, unfavourable, bad, unfortunate
>
> ❘ OPPOSITE favourable

advertise VERB

> *a poster advertising the concert*
> publicize, promote, announce, make known
> (informal) plug

advertisement NOUN

> *an advertisement in the local paper*
> announcement, notice, promotion, commercial, write-up
> (informal) ad, advert, plug

advice NOUN

> *offering advice on coping with stress*
> guidance, help, directions, recommendations, suggestions, tips, hints, pointers

advise VERB

> 1 *The doctor advised me to rest.*
> counsel, recommend, suggest, advocate, urge
> 2 *We will advise you of the result.*
> inform, notify, give notice

adviser NOUN

> *talking to a careers adviser*
> counsellor, consultant, confidant or confidante, aide, mentor

advocate VERB

> *advocating changes to the law*
> recommend, prescribe, advise, urge, support, back

advocate NOUN

> *an advocate of animal rights*
> champion, supporter, upholder, exponent, proponent

aeroplane NOUN

> SEE **aircraft**

affair NOUN

> *Their wedding was an elaborate affair.*
> event, incident, happening, occasion, occurrence, episode
>
> ▷ **affairs**
> *an interest in world affairs*
> business, matters, concerns, questions, subjects, topics, activities

affect VERB

> 1 *the area affected by the drought*
> influence, have an effect on, have an impact on, change, modify, alter
> 2 *Her story affected me deeply.*
> move, touch, make an impression on, disturb, upset, concern, trouble, distress

affected ADJECTIVE

> *an affected look of surprise*
> assumed, put on, feigned, pretended, false, insincere
>
> ❘ OPPOSITE genuine

a
b
c
d
e
f
g
h
i
j
k
l
m
n
o
p
q
r
s
t
u
v
w
x
y
z

affection NOUN
feelings of affection for one another
fondness, liking, love, friendship,
friendliness, attachment, devotion,
warmth
OPPOSITE dislike

affectionate ADJECTIVE
an affectionate kiss
loving, tender, caring,
fond, friendly, warm
OPPOSITES unfriendly, cold

affiliated ADJECTIVE
▷ **affiliated to**
an organization affiliated to the UN
associated with, allied to, connected
with

affirm VERB
*The police affirmed that they had a
suspect.*
declare, confirm, assert, state,
pronounce, attest
OPPOSITE deny

affirmative ADJECTIVE
an affirmative answer
positive, agreeing, consenting,
assenting, concurring, confirming
OPPOSITE negative

affluent ADJECTIVE
an affluent neighbourhood
prosperous, wealthy, rich, well off,
well-to-do
(informal) flush, well-heeled
OPPOSITES poor, impoverished

afford VERB
1 *I can't afford a new phone.*
have enough money for, pay for,
run to
2 *How much time can you afford?*
spare, allow

afraid ADJECTIVE
1 *Megan was too afraid to move.*
frightened, scared, terrified,
petrified, alarmed, fearful,
intimidated, cowardly
IDIOMS frightened out of your wits,
scared to death, scared stiff

OPPOSITE brave
2 *Don't be afraid to ask.*
hesitant, reluctant, unwilling, shy,
slow
▷ **be afraid of**
Aren't you afraid of ghosts?
be frightened of, be scared of, fear,
dread

aftermath NOUN
the aftermath of the hurricane
after-effects, consequences,
repercussions, results, outcome,
upshot

afterwards ADVERB
Shortly afterwards, the phone rang.
later, later on, subsequently, in due
course, thereafter

again ADVERB
Can I see you again next week?
another time, once more, once
again, over again, afresh, anew

against PREPOSITION
1 *leaning against the wall*
touching, up against, in contact with
2 *taking a stand against bullying*
in opposition to, opposed to, hostile
to, averse to

Usage Note
Words which include 'against' in
their meaning often begin with
anti-, for example *anticlockwise*
and *antiseptic*.

age NOUN
1 *Ada's eyesight had dimmed with age.*
old age, maturity
2 *in the age of the dinosaurs*
period, time, era, epoch, days

 WORD WEB

names for people's ages
pre-teen, teenager (13-19 years)
sexagenarian (60-69 years)
septuagenarian (70-79 years)
octogenarian (80-89 years)

nonagenarian (90-99 years)
▶ Informal words for people aged twenty and over are **twenty-something**, **thirty-something**, etc.

age VERB
1 *Dogs age faster than humans.*
become older, grow old
2 *The cheese is left to age for six months.*
mature, mellow, ripen

aged ADJECTIVE
an aged relative
elderly, old, senior

agency NOUN
a recruitment agency
office, business, department, service, bureau

agenda NOUN
What's on the agenda for today?
programme, plan, schedule, timetable

agent NOUN
1 *a literary agent*
representative, spokesperson, negotiator, intermediary, mediator
2 *a CIA agent*
spy, secret agent, operative, mole
FOR TIPS ON WRITING SPY FICTION SEE spy

aggression NOUN
an act of mindless aggression
hostility, violence, aggressiveness, confrontation, militancy, belligerence, warmongering

aggressive ADJECTIVE
1 *an aggressive tone of voice*
hostile, violent, confrontational, antagonistic, argumentative, quarrelsome, bullying, warlike, belligerent
❙ **OPPOSITES** peaceful, peaceable
2 *an aggressive sales pitch*
forceful, assertive
(informal) pushy, in-your-face

❙ **OPPOSITE** laid-back

agile ADJECTIVE
as agile as a mountain goat
nimble, graceful, sure-footed, sprightly, acrobatic, supple, lithe
❙ **OPPOSITES** clumsy, stiff

agitated ADJECTIVE
As time passed, I grew more and more agitated.
upset, nervous, anxious, flustered, unsettled, edgy, restless, disturbed, ruffled
❙ **OPPOSITES** calm, cool

agonizing ADJECTIVE
an agonizing decision
painful, excruciating, torturous, harrowing, distressing

agony NOUN
The creature writhed in agony.
pain, suffering, torture, torment, anguish, distress

agree VERB
1 *I'm glad that we agree.*
concur, be unanimous
❙ **IDIOM** see eye to eye
❙ **OPPOSITE** disagree
2 *I agree that you are right.*
accept, acknowledge, admit, grant, allow, assent
❙ **OPPOSITE** deny
3 *I agreed to pay my share.*
consent, promise, be willing, undertake, acquiesce
❙ **OPPOSITE** refuse
4 *The two stories don't agree.*
match, correspond, tally
(informal) square
▷ **agree on**
Can we agree on a price?
decide, fix, settle, choose, establish
▷ **agree with**
1 *Do you agree with animal testing?*
support, advocate, subscribe to, back
2 *Spicy food doesn't agree with me.*
suit

a
b
c
d
e
f
g
h
i
j
k
l
m
n
o
p
q
r
s
t
u
v
w
x
y
z

agreeable ADJECTIVE
> *the agreeable task of choosing the menu*
pleasant, enjoyable, pleasing, delightful, congenial
OPPOSITES disagreeable, unpleasant

agreement NOUN
1 *nodding their heads in agreement*
accord, consensus, assent, consent, unanimity, harmony
OPPOSITE disagreement
2 *signing an agreement*
contract, treaty, pact, settlement, understanding, bargain, deal
► An agreement to end fighting is an **armistice** or **truce**.

agriculture NOUN
SEE **farming**

ahead ADVERB
1 *A car pulled out just ahead of us.*
in advance, in front, before
2 *Keep looking straight ahead.*
forwards, to the front

aid NOUN
1 *with the aid of a calculator*
help, assistance, support, backing, cooperation
2 *aid for the victims of the earthquake*
relief, support, funding, subsidy, donations, contributions

aid VERB
aiding the police in their enquiries
help, assist, support, back, collaborate with, cooperate with
IDIOM lend a hand to

aide NOUN
an aide to the vice president
assistant, helper, adviser
IDIOM right-hand man or woman

ailing ADJECTIVE
1 *her ailing mother*
ill, sick, sickly, poorly, infirm
2 *the country's ailing economy*
failing, weak, poor, fragile
IDIOM in a bad way
OPPOSITE healthy

ailment NOUN
SEE **illness**

aim NOUN
> *What is the aim of the experiment?*
objective, purpose, object, goal, intention, end, target, ambition, wish, dream, hope

aim VERB
1 *aiming a rifle*
point, direct, train, line up, focus, take aim
2 *a book aimed at teenagers*
target, direct, design, tailor, pitch
3 *aiming to go to drama school*
intend, mean, plan, propose, want, wish, seek

aimless ADJECTIVE
leading an aimless life
purposeless, meaningless, pointless, without direction

air NOUN
1 *the air we breathe*
atmosphere
► The word **aerial** means 'in or from the air', as in **aerial photograph** and **aerial archaeology**.
2 *a gust of fresh air*
breeze, draught, ventilation
3 *The words are set to a traditional air.*
song, tune, melody
4 *The castle had an air of menace about it.*
appearance, look, atmosphere, aura, impression, mood, tone, feeling

air VERB
1 *airing a room*
ventilate, freshen, refresh
2 *a chance to air your views*
express, voice, make known, make public, articulate, declare, state

aircraft NOUN

WORD WEB

some types of aircraft
aeroplane (*North American* airplane),
air-ambulance, airliner, airship,
biplane, bomber, delta-wing,
fighter, glider, hang-glider,
helicopter, hot-air balloon,
jet, jumbo jet, microlight,
monoplane, seaplane, spy plane,
(*historical*) Zeppelin

parts of an aircraft
cabin, cargo hold, cockpit,
engine, fin, flap, flight deck,
fuselage, joystick, passenger
cabin, propeller, rotor, rudder,
tail, tailplane, undercarriage,
wing

▶ The flying of aircraft is **aviation**.
▶ A person who flies aircraft is an **aviator** or **pilot**.
▶ The pilot of a hot-air balloon is a **balloonist**.
▶ The study of aircraft and aviation is **aeronautics**.

airy ADJECTIVE
a light and airy room
well-ventilated, fresh, breezy, cool
❚ **OPPOSITES** airless, stuffy

aisle NOUN
a seat next to the aisle
passageway, passage, gangway, lane

alarm NOUN
1 *a fire alarm*
signal, warning, alert, siren
2 *Maria's eyes widened in alarm.*
fear, fright, panic, anxiety,
apprehension, distress, terror

alarm VERB
The sudden noise alarmed the horses.
frighten, scare, panic, agitate, upset,
distress, unnerve, startle, shock
❚ **IDIOM** (*informal*) put the wind up

❚ **OPPOSITE** reassure

alarming ADJECTIVE
Wetlands are being destroyed at an alarming rate.
frightening, terrifying, shocking,
startling, disturbing
(*informal*) scary
❚ **OPPOSITE** reassuring

alert NOUN
▷ **be on the alert**
Police are warning residents to be on the alert.
be vigilant, be on your guard, be on the lookout
❚ **IDIOMS** (*informal*) stay on your toes, keep your eyes peeled

alert ADJECTIVE
After my nap, I woke up fresh and alert.
vigilant, watchful, attentive,
observant, wide awake, on the alert,
on the lookout
❚ **IDIOM** (*informal*) on the ball
❚ **OPPOSITE** inattentive

alert VERB
Dial 999 to alert the emergency services.
warn, notify, inform, make aware,
forewarn
(*informal*) tip off

alien NOUN
1 *a film about aliens who invade the Earth*
extraterrestrial, alien life-form
FOR TIPS ON WRITING SCIENCE FICTION
SEE **science fiction**
2 *an illegal alien*
foreigner, immigrant

alien ADJECTIVE
1 *in an alien country*
foreign, strange, unfamiliar,
exotic
❚ **OPPOSITES** native, familiar
2 *Scientists are searching for alien life.*
extraterrestrial

a
b
c
d
e
f
g
h
i
j
k
l
m
n
o
p
q
r
s
t
u
v
w
x
y
z

alienate VERB

1 *He managed to alienate my whole family.*
antagonize, make an enemy of, offend, upset, set at odds

2 *feeling alienated from society*
isolate, distance, cut off, estrange

alight ADJECTIVE

1 *One of the sparks set the grass alight.*
burning, on fire, in flames, blazing, ablaze

2 *Adil's eyes were alight with excitement.*
lit up, illuminated, fired up

align VERB

1 *Align the text with the left-hand margin.*
line up, even up

2 *He chose to align himself with the rebels.*
ally, affiliate, associate, side, team up
▌ IDIOM throw in your lot

alike ADJECTIVE

The twins look exactly alike.
similar, the same, identical, indistinguishable, uniform
▌ IDIOM (informal) much of a muchness
▌ OPPOSITES dissimilar, different

alive ADJECTIVE

Do you think that cactus is still alive?
living, live, existing, in existence, surviving, flourishing
▌ OPPOSITE dead

▷ **alive to**
being alive to new ideas
receptive to, open to, alert to, aware of, conscious of
▌ OPPOSITES unreceptive to, unaware of

allay VERB

The doctor tried to allay our fears.
relieve, calm, soothe, alleviate, reduce, lessen, diminish

allege VERB

It is alleged that he worked for MI5.
claim, assert, contend, accuse, charge

allegiance NOUN

They were forced to pledge allegiance to the King.
loyalty, faithfulness, obedience, fidelity, devotion
▌ OPPOSITES disloyalty, treachery

alley NOUN

He disappeared around a corner into an alley.
passage, passageway, lane, backstreet

alliance NOUN

The two countries formed an alliance.
partnership, association, union, confederation, league, coalition

allocate VERB

The school is allocating more time for sports.
allot, assign, set aside, reserve, earmark

allow VERB

1 *Do you allow calculators in the exam?*
permit, let, authorize, approve of, consent to, agree to, give permission for, put up with, stand, tolerate
▌ OPPOSITE forbid

2 *We've allowed three hours for the journey.*
allocate, set aside, assign, allot, designate, earmark

allowance NOUN

an annual allowance of £500
payment, contribution, grant, subsidy, handout

alloy NOUN

an alloy of two metals
blend, combination, composite, compound, amalgam, fusion, mixture

all right ADJECTIVE

saying that something is all right
satisfactory, acceptable,
adequate, reasonable, passable,
tolerable, not bad
(informal) OK or okay
The food on the plane was
tolerable.

❙ OPPOSITES unsatisfactory,
unacceptable, below standard

being all right to do something
permissible, permitted,
acceptable, allowed
It is not **permissible** to
download these files.

feeling, looking all right
well, unhurt, unharmed,
uninjured, in good health, safe,
fine

❙ IDIOM in one piece
The stunt man was **uninjured**,
apart from a few bruises.

ally NOUN
The two countries work together as
allies.
friend, partner
❙ OPPOSITE enemy

almost ADVERB
I've almost finished my homework.
nearly, practically, just about,
virtually, all but, well-nigh, as good
as, not quite

alone ADVERB
Did you go to the party alone?
on your own, by yourself,
unaccompanied

alone ADJECTIVE
Jacqui had no friends and felt very
alone.
lonely, friendless, isolated,
solitary, lonesome

also ADVERB
Some flowers can also be used in
cooking.
in addition, besides, too,
additionally, furthermore, further,
moreover
(old use) to boot

alter VERB
We had to alter our plans for the
weekend.
change, adjust, adapt, modify,
amend, revise, redo, work,
transform, vary

alternate ADJECTIVE
The club meets on alternate
Tuesdays.
every other, every second

alternative ADJECTIVE
Do you have an alternative plan?
different, other, second, substitute,
standby, reserve, backup, fallback

alternative NOUN
I had no alternative but to pay the
fine.
choice, option, substitute,
replacement

altogether ADVERB
1 I have six cousins altogether.
in all, in total, all told
2 I'm not altogether convinced.
completely, entirely, absolutely,
quite, totally, utterly, wholly, fully,
perfectly, thoroughly, one hundred
per cent

always ADVERB
1 The planets are always in motion.
continually, continuously,
constantly, endlessly, all the
time, day and night, unceasingly,
perpetually, eternally, for ever
2 My bus is always late.
consistently, invariably, persistently,
regularly, repeatedly, habitually,
unfailingly, without fail, every time

amateur NOUN
All the players in the team

a
b
c
d
e
f
g
h
i
j
k
l
m
n
o
p
q
r
s
t
u
v
w
x
y
z

35

are amateurs.
non-professional

OPPOSITE professional

amaze VERB

Katie amazed everyone with her performance.
astonish, astound, surprise, stun, stagger, dumbfound, startle, shock
(informal) flabbergast, bowl over

IDIOM (informal) knock for six

amazed ADJECTIVE

I was amazed by the number of emails I received.
astonished, astounded, stunned, surprised, dumbfounded, speechless, staggered, thunderstruck, at a loss for words
(informal) flabbergasted
(British informal) gobsmacked

amazement NOUN

Izzy was staring at the sky in amazement.
astonishment, surprise, shock, awe, wonder

amazing ADJECTIVE

98 per cent is an amazing score!
astonishing, astounding, staggering, stunning, extraordinary, remarkable, incredible, unbelievable, breathtaking, awesome, phenomenal, sensational, stupendous, tremendous, wonderful
(informal) mind-boggling, jaw-dropping
(literary) wondrous

ambition NOUN

1 *At that age, he was full of ambition.*
drive, determination, enterprise, initiative, motivation
(informal) get-up-and-go

2 *Her ambition is to go to art college.*
goal, aim, aspiration, dream, desire, intention, objective, target, wish, hope

ambitious ADJECTIVE

1 *a very ambitious young woman*
enterprising, determined,

motivated, purposeful, committed, keen
(informal) go-ahead, go-getting

OPPOSITES unambitious, laid-back

2 *I think your plan is too ambitious.*
demanding, challenging, formidable, difficult, grand, large-scale

OPPOSITES modest, low-key

ambush VERB

Highwaymen used to ambush wealthy travellers.
waylay
(North American) bushwhack

amend VERB

I amended the last paragraph to make it clearer.
revise, change, alter, adjust, modify, adapt, edit, rewrite, reword

amends PLURAL NOUN

▷ **make amends for**
He's trying to make amends for what he did.
make up for, atone for

among PREPOSITION

We spotted a deer among the trees.
amid, in the middle of, surrounded by, in, between

amount NOUN

1 *a large amount of salt in the water*
quantity, measure, supply, volume, mass, bulk

2 *a cheque for the correct amount*
sum, total, quota, number, aggregate

amount VERB

▷ **amount to**
The bill amounted to 40 euros.
add up to, come to, run to, total, equal, make

amphibian NOUN

 WORD WEB

some animals which are amphibians
axolotl, bullfrog, frog,

natterjack toad, newt,
salamander, toad, tree frog

▶ Amphibians are described as
cold-blooded because their body
temperature is the same as the
surrounding environment.

▶ The scientific study of amphibians
and reptiles is **herpetology**.

▶ A related adjective is
amphibious.

❙ SEE ALSO **frog**

ample *ADJECTIVE*

1 *There is ample space for parking.*
enough, sufficient, adequate, plenty
of, lots of, more than enough
(informal) loads of
❙ OPPOSITES insufficient,
inadequate

2 *an ample supply of water*
plentiful, abundant, copious,
profuse, generous,
lavish, liberal
❙ OPPOSITES meagre, scanty

amuse *VERB*

1 *I think this story will amuse you.*
make you laugh, entertain, please,
divert, cheer up
(informal) tickle
❙ OPPOSITE bore

2 *We were left to amuse ourselves.*
entertain, occupy, busy, engage

amusement *NOUN*

1 *Our favourite amusement was
catching tadpoles.*
pastime, activity, recreation,
entertainment, diversion, game,
hobby, interest, sport

2 *a source of much amusement*
mirth, merriment, hilarity, laughter,
glee

3 *He built the boat for his own
amusement.*
entertainment, pleasure, enjoyment,
fun, delight

amusing *ADJECTIVE*

*an amusing story about a pig who
can talk*
funny, humorous, comical, witty,
hilarious, diverting, entertaining,
jocular, droll
❙ OPPOSITES solemn, serious

analogy *NOUN*

*the analogy between a computer and
the human brain*
comparison, parallel, similarity,
correspondence, correlation

analyse *VERB*

*analysing the results of the
experiment*
examine, study, inspect, investigate,
scrutinize, evaluate, interpret

analysis *NOUN*

the analysis of your data
examination, study, inspection,
investigation, scrutiny, evaluation,
interpretation

analytical *ADJECTIVE*

Holmes used an analytical approach.
methodical, logical, systematic,
scientific

anarchy *NOUN*

*The country was descending into
anarchy.*
lawlessness, disorder, chaos,
pandemonium

anatomy *NOUN*
SEE **body**

ancestor *NOUN*

*His maternal ancestors came from
Russia.*
forebear, forefather, predecessor,
antecedent, progenitor
❙ OPPOSITE descendant

Usage Note

The ancestors on your mother's
side are your *maternal ancestors*,
and those on your father's side are
your *paternal ancestors*.

a
b
c
d
e
f
g
h
i
j
k
l
m
n
o
p
q
r
s
t
u
v
w
x
y
z

ancestry NOUN

Sofia was proud of her Polish ancestry.
descent, origins, heredity, heritage, lineage, extraction, roots, blood

ancient ADJECTIVE

1 *the pyramids of ancient Egypt*
early, prehistoric, primeval, primordial

▌ OPPOSITE modern

2 *Honey is an ancient remedy for wounds.*
old, age-old, archaic, time-honoured

▌ OPPOSITES new, recent

3 *That old computer game looks ancient now.*
antiquated, old-fashioned, dated, archaic
(humorous) antediluvian

▌ IDIOMS out of the ark, *(informal)* past its sell-by date

▌ OPPOSITES contemporary, up to date

anecdote NOUN

an anecdote about his childhood
story, tale, narrative, reminiscence
(informal) yarn

angelic ADJECTIVE

an angelic smile
innocent, virtuous, pure, saintly, cherubic

▌ OPPOSITES devilish, demonic

anger NOUN

Mrs Perry flushed pink with anger.
rage, fury, wrath, rancour, indignation, vexation, outrage
(literary) ire

▶ An outburst of anger is a **tantrum** or **temper**.

▶ To express anger is to **vent your anger** or **vent your spleen**.

anger VERB

Hamlet was angered by his father's murder.
enrage, infuriate, incense, inflame, madden, outrage, annoy, vex, irk, exasperate, antagonize, provoke

▌ IDIOMS make your blood boil, make you see red

▌ OPPOSITE pacify

angle NOUN

1 *the angle between two walls*
corner, point, nook

2 *She wore a beret set at a slight angle.*
slope, slant, tilt, gradient

3 *seeing things from a different angle*
perspective, point of view, viewpoint, standpoint, view, outlook, aspect, approach, slant, tack

angry ADJECTIVE

Hayden was angry at his parents for lying to him.
cross, furious, irate, enraged, infuriated, incensed, outraged, annoyed, vexed, irked, exasperated, in a temper, fuming, indignant, raging, seething, apoplectic
(informal) mad, livid
(Australian & NZ informal) snaky

▌ IDIOMS up in arms, foaming at the mouth, seeing red

▌ OPPOSITE calm

▷ **get angry**

Mr Ellis never gets angry in public.
lose your temper, fly into a rage, go berserk

▌ IDIOMS *(informal)* blow a fuse, blow your top, flip your lid, fly off the handle, hit the roof, lose your rag, go off the deep end

anguish NOUN

a cry of anguish
agony, pain, distress, torment, suffering, misery, woe, sorrow, heartache

animal NOUN

the wild animals of Africa
creature, beast, brute

▶ A word for wild animals in general is **wildlife**.

▶ The animals of a particular place or time are its **fauna**.

WORD WEB

types of animal
amphibian, arachnid, bird, fish, insect, mammal, marsupial, mollusc, reptile, rodent

▶ Animals with a backbone are **vertebrates** and those without a backbone are **invertebrates**.

▶ Animals that eat meat are **carnivores** and those that eat plants are **herbivores**

▶ Animals that eat both meat and plants are **omnivores**.

▶ Animals that are kept by people are **domestic animals** and those kept on a farm are **livestock**.

▶ Animals that sleep most of the winter are **hibernating animals**.

▶ Animals that are active at night are **nocturnal animals**.

▶ Animals that live in the sea are **marine** animals.

▶ The scientific study of animals is **zoology**.

▶ The study of plants and animals is **natural history** and a person who studies them is a **naturalist**.

▶ The medical treatment of animals is **veterinary medicine**.

SEE ALSO amphibian, bird, cat, dog, fish, horse, insect, mammal, marsupial, reptile, rodent

FOR GROUPS OF ANIMALS SEE collective noun

WRITING TIPS

describing animals
The woolly-coated orange-eyed mongoose lemurs bound from branch to branch, wagging their long thick tails like dogs, and calling to each other in a series of loud and astonishingly pig-like grunts.
— *Gerald Durrell, Menagerie Manor*

body parts
antler, coat, fang, fin, fleece, flipper, fluke, foreleg, forelimbs, fur, hide, hind leg, hoof, horn, mandible, mane, muzzle, paw, pelt, snout, tail, tentacle, trotter, trunk, tusk, whisker

skin or coat
camouflaged, coarse, drab, furry, glossy, hairy, leathery, matted, mottled, patchy, piebald, prickly, scaly, shaggy, shiny, silky, sleek, slimy, smooth, spiky, spotted, striped, wiry, woolly

movement
bound, canter, crouch, dart, gallop, gambol, leap, lumber, nuzzle, pad, paw, pounce, range, roam, scuttle, skip, skulk, slink, slither, spring, stalk, stamp, stampede, trot

sounds
bark, bay, bellow, bleat, bray, buzz, cluck, croak, gabble, growl, grunt, hiss, howl, jabber, low, mew, neigh, pipe, purr, roar, snap, snarl, snort, snuffle, squeak, trumpet, whimper, whine, whinny, yap, yelp, yowl

animated *ADJECTIVE*
an animated discussion about our favourite films
lively, spirited, energetic, enthusiastic, vibrant, vivacious, exuberant, perky
OPPOSITES lifeless, lethargic

animation *NOUN*
FOR TYPES OF FILM SEE film

animosity *ADJECTIVE*
I could sense the animosity between them.
hostility, enmity, antipathy, antagonism, ill will, ill feeling

»

IDIOM bad blood
OPPOSITES friendship, goodwill

annihilate VERB

Deforestation threatens to annihilate whole species.
destroy, wipe out, eradicate, obliterate

anniversary NOUN

 WORD WEB

special anniversaries
centenary (100 years)
sesquicentenary (150 years)
bicentenary (200 years)
tercentenary (300 years)
quatercentenary (400 years)
quincentenary (500 years)
millenary (1000 years)

wedding anniversaries
silver wedding (25 years)
ruby wedding (40 years)
golden wedding (50 years)
diamond wedding (60 years)

announce VERB

announcing the football results
make known, make public, declare, broadcast, state, report, present, proclaim, give out, release

announcement NOUN

1 *an announcement over the intercom*
statement, declaration, pronouncement, proclamation, bulletin, communiqué

2 *the announcement of the results*
declaration, notification, publication, broadcasting

annoy VERB

1 *It annoys me to see people mistreat animals.*
irritate, displease, exasperate, anger, antagonize, upset, vex, irk, nettle
(informal) rile, aggravate
OPPOSITES please, gratify

2 *Wes is always annoying me in class.*
pester, bother, trouble, harass,

badger, nag, plague
(informal) bug, hassle

annoyance NOUN

1 *Much to my annoyance, the DVD was scratched.*
irritation, exasperation, indignation, anger, vexation, displeasure, chagrin

2 *Junk mail is a constant annoyance.*
nuisance, bother, trouble, worry

annoyed ADJECTIVE

He sounded quite annoyed on the phone.
irritated, exasperated, vexed, irked, antagonized, nettled
(informal) riled, aggravated

annoying ADJECTIVE

an annoying habit
irritating, exasperating, maddening, provoking, tiresome, trying, vexing, irksome, troublesome, bothersome

annual ADJECTIVE

our annual holiday
yearly, once-a-year
► A **biannual** event happens twice a year, and a **biennial** event happens every two years.
SEE ALSO anniversary

annually ADVERB

The guidebook is updated annually.
every year, once a year, per annum

anomaly NOUN

I spotted an anomaly in the figures.
inconsistency, oddity, peculiarity, quirk, aberration

anonymous ADJECTIVE

1 *an anonymous donation*
unnamed, nameless, unidentified, unknown

2 *an anonymous letter*
unsigned

answer NOUN

1 *an answer to your email*
reply, response, acknowledgement, reaction
► A quick or angry answer is a **retort** and a sharp or witty answer is a

a b c d e f g h i j k l m n o p q r s t u v w x y z

rejoinder or **riposte**.

2 *the answers to the quiz*
solution, explanation
❙ **OPPOSITE** question

answer *VERB*

1 *I spent the morning answering emails.*
reply to, respond to, react to, acknowledge

2 *'I don't know,' she answered.*
reply, respond, return

▶ To answer quickly or angrily is to **retort**.

▷ **answer for**
He's old enough to answer for his actions.
be accountable for, explain, pay for, make up for

antagonize *VERB*

trying to antagonize the guards
provoke, anger, annoy, exasperate
(informal) aggravate
❙ **OPPOSITE** pacify

anthology *NOUN*

an anthology of science fiction
collection, compilation, compendium, miscellany
FOR OTHER TYPES OF BOOK SEE **book**

anticipate *VERB*

1 *No one anticipated that the harvest would fail.*
expect, predict, foresee, foretell, bargain on

2 *eagerly anticipating the arrival of spring*
look forward to, await, long for

anticipation *NOUN*

nearly bursting with anticipation
expectation, expectancy, suspense

anticlimax *NOUN*

After all the hype, the match was an anticlimax.
let-down, disappointment
(informal) wash-out

antidote *NOUN*

SEE **poison**

antiquated *ADJECTIVE*

an antiquated law
out of date, outdated, outmoded, old-fashioned, ancient, obsolete
❙ **IDIOMS** behind the times, out of the ark
❙ **OPPOSITES** modern, up to date

antique *ADJECTIVE*

a piece of antique furniture
old, vintage, antiquarian
❙ **OPPOSITES** modern, contemporary

antisocial *ADJECTIVE*

1 *antisocial behaviour*
objectionable, offensive, disruptive, disorderly, discourteous

2 *feeling a bit antisocial*
unsociable, unfriendly
❙ **OPPOSITES** sociable, gregarious

anxiety *NOUN*

1 *a growing sense of anxiety*
apprehension, concern, worry, fear, nervousness, nerves, unease, disquiet
(informal) the jitters
❙ **IDIOM** butterflies in your stomach
❙ **OPPOSITES** calmness, confidence

2 *the anxieties of today's teenagers*
worry, fear, trouble, care

anxious *ADJECTIVE*

1 *feeing anxious before the exam*
nervous, worried, apprehensive, concerned, uneasy, fearful, edgy, fraught, tense, troubled
(informal) uptight, jittery, twitchy
❙ **OPPOSITES** calm, confident

2 *We were all anxious to hear what happened.*
eager, keen, impatient, itching
❙ **IDIOM** on tenterhooks

anyhow *ADVERB*

1 *Anyhow, it doesn't matter.*
anyway, in any case

2 *(informal) boxes piled anyhow on the floor*
carelessly, haphazardly, randomly

apart ADVERB
▷ **apart from**
No one knows, apart from us.
except for, aside from, besides,
other than, excepting,
with the exception of

apartment NOUN
a self-catering holiday apartment
flat, suite, rooms
▌ SEE ALSO **accommodation**

aperture NOUN
Smoke escaped through an aperture
in the roof.
hole, opening, gap

apologetic ADJECTIVE
An apologetic email arrived the next
day.
sorry, repentant, remorseful,
regretful, penitent, contrite
▌ OPPOSITE **unrepentant**

apologize VERB
Ryan apologized for his mistake.
say you are sorry, repent, be
penitent

appal VERB
appalled by the number of casualties
horrify, shock, dismay, distress,
outrage, scandalize, revolt, disgust,
sicken

appalling ADJECTIVE
1 the appalling living conditions in the
trenches
shocking, horrifying, horrific,
dreadful, horrendous, atrocious,
abominable, horrible, terrible,
distressing, sickening, revolting
2 (informal) My handwriting is
appalling.
very bad, awful, terrible, deplorable,
disgraceful, lamentable
(informal) abysmal

apparatus NOUN
apparatus for breathing underwater
equipment, tackle
(informal) gear

apparent ADJECTIVE
1 She quit her job for no apparent
reason.
obvious, evident, clear, noticeable,
detectable, perceptible,
recognizable, conspicuous, visible
▌ OPPOSITE **unclear**
2 an apparent lack of interest
seeming, outward, ostensible

apparently ADVERB
Apparently you did not receive my
email.
evidently, seemingly, ostensibly

appeal VERB
appealing for international aid
ask, request, call, entreat, plead,
beg, implore
▷ **appeal to**
a film that will appeal to all ages
attract, interest, please, fascinate,
tempt, draw in

appeal NOUN
1 an appeal for funding
request, call, cry, entreaty
▶ An appeal signed by a lot of people is
a **petition**.
2 the appeal of a good mystery
attraction, interest, fascination,
allure, charm, attractiveness

appealing ADJECTIVE
an appealing new cover design
attractive, engaging, alluring,
captivating, charming, tempting,
enticing, irresistible
▌ OPPOSITES **off-putting, repellent**

appear VERB
1 cracks appearing on the surface
become visible, come into view,
emerge, develop, occur, show up,
surface, arise, crop up, spring up
2 At first, the room appeared to be
empty.
seem, look
3 appearing in a new film
act, perform, take part, feature

appearance NOUN
1 the sudden appearance of symptoms

a b c d e f g h i j k l m n o p q r s t u v w x y z

occurrence, manifestation, emergence, onset, arrival

2 *his rather dishevelled appearance*
look, air, aspect, bearing, mien

3 *the appearance of normality*
impression, air, semblance, show

appease VERB
an offering to appease the gods
placate, pacify, mollify, win over
❚ OPPOSITES antagonize, provoke

appendix NOUN
the authors listed in the appendix
supplement, addendum, afterword
FOR OTHER PARTS OF A BOOK SEE **book**

appetite NOUN
1 *I've lost my appetite.*
hunger

2 *an appetite for adventure*
desire, eagerness, enthusiasm, passion, keenness, wish, urge, taste, thirst, longing, yearning, craving, lust, zest

appetizing ADJECTIVE
the appetizing smell of baking
delicious, tasty, tempting, mouth-watering
FOR TIPS ON DESCRIBING TASTE SEE **taste**

applaud VERB
1 *The spectators applauded loudly.*
clap, cheer
❚ OPPOSITE boo

2 *I applaud your honesty.*
praise, commend, admire, welcome
❚ OPPOSITES condemn, criticize

applause NOUN
The audience burst into applause.
clapping, cheering, ovation

appliance NOUN
kitchen appliances
device, machine, gadget, instrument, apparatus, contraption
(informal) gizmo

application NOUN
1 *your application for a refund*
request, claim, appeal, petition

2 *a job that requires patience and application*
effort, hard work, diligence, commitment, dedication, perseverance, persistence, devotion

apply VERB
1 *applying a moisturizer*
put on, lay on, spread

2 *applying all your concentration*
use, employ, exercise, utilize

3 *applying for a grant*
make an application for, ask for, request, bid, petition

▷ **apply to**
Answer all the questions that apply to you.
be relevant to, relate to, refer to, pertain to, concern, affect, cover

appoint VERB
appointing a new team captain
choose, select, elect, vote for, decide on, settle on

appointed ADJECTIVE
at the appointed place and time
scheduled, prearranged, arranged, agreed, specified, designated, set, fixed

appointment NOUN
1 *an appointment to see the doctor*
arrangement, engagement, date

2 *the appointment of a new coach*
nomination, naming, selection, choice, choosing, election

3 *seeking a university appointment*
job, post, position, situation, office

appreciate VERB
1 *learning to appreciate music*
enjoy, like, love, admire, respect, esteem
❚ OPPOSITES disparage, disdain

2 *I appreciate your help with this.*
value, be grateful for, be glad of

3 *I appreciate that this is a difficult time.*
recognize, realize, understand, comprehend, be aware

》

4 *Antique jewellery will appreciate in value.*
grow, increase, go up, mount, rise
❙ **OPPOSITES** depreciate, decrease

appreciation *NOUN*

1 *the appreciation of poetry*
enjoyment, love, admiration
❙ **OPPOSITES** disparagement, disdain (for)

2 *a token of our appreciation*
gratitude, thanks

3 *They had no appreciation of the danger.*
recognition, acknowledgement, realization, awareness

4 *a slight appreciation in value*
growth, increase, rise
❙ **OPPOSITES** depreciation, decrease

appreciative *ADJECTIVE*

an appreciative audience
admiring, enthusiastic, approving, complimentary

apprehend *VERB*

1 *Police have apprehended a third suspect.*
arrest, capture, seize
❙ **OPPOSITE** release

2 *(formal) I fail to apprehend your meaning.*
understand, comprehend

apprehension *NOUN*

1 *a voice filled with apprehension*
anxiety, worry, concern, unease, disquiet, nervousness, trepidation

2 *a clear apprehension of the subject*
understanding, comprehension, grasp

3 *the apprehension of the murderer*
arrest, capture, seizure
❙ **OPPOSITE** release

apprehensive *ADJECTIVE*

She gave an apprehensive glance over her shoulder.
anxious, worried, nervous, tense, agitated, edgy, uneasy, unsettled, troubled, frightened, fearful
❙ **OPPOSITES** calm, untroubled

apprentice *NOUN*

a plumber's apprentice
trainee, learner, novice, probationer
(informal) rookie

approach *VERB*

1 *We approached the campsite on foot.*
move towards, draw near to, come near to, near, advance on, close in on, gain on

2 *They approached me with an offer to join the squad.*
speak to, talk to, go to, contact, sound out

3 *She approaches her work in a creative way.*
tackle, undertake, set about, go about, embark on, address

approach *NOUN*

1 *the approach of footsteps*
arrival, advance, coming

2 *making a formal approach to the school*
application, appeal, proposal, submission, request

3 *a sensible approach to life*
attitude, manner, style, method, system, way

4 *The best approach to the house is from the west.*
access, entry, entrance, way in, driveway

approachable *ADJECTIVE*

The staff are always very approachable.
friendly, pleasant, agreeable, welcoming, sympathetic
❙ **OPPOSITES** unapproachable, aloof

appropriate *ADJECTIVE*

an appropriate style of dress
suitable, proper, fitting, apt, right, well-judged, relevant, pertinent, apposite
❙ **OPPOSITE** inappropriate

approval *NOUN*

We nodded our heads in approval.
agreement, consent, support, acceptance, assent, permission,

authorization, go-ahead, blessing

❙ OPPOSITES disapproval, refusal

approve *VERB*

A majority voted to approve the plan.

agree to, consent to, authorize, allow, accept, pass, permit, support, back

❙ IDIOMS give the green light to, give the thumbs-up to

❙ OPPOSITES refuse, give the thumbs-down to

▷ **approve of**

Her family did not approve of the marriage.

agree with, be in favour of, favour, welcome, support, endorse, like, think well of, take kindly to, admire, commend, applaud

❙ OPPOSITE condemn

approximate *ADJECTIVE*

the approximate length of the journey

estimated, rough, broad, loose, inexact

(informal) ballpark

❙ OPPOSITE exact

approximately *ADVERB*

starting at approximately ten o'clock

roughly, about, around, round about, close to, nearly, more or less

❙ OPPOSITE precisely

apt *ADJECTIVE*

1 *He is apt to forget things.*

inclined, likely, liable, prone, given

2 *Each chapter begins with an apt quotation.*

appropriate, suitable, proper, fitting, right, well-judged, relevant, pertinent, apposite

(informal) spot on

❙ OPPOSITE inappropriate

aptitude *NOUN*

an aptitude for music

talent, gift, ability, skill, flair, expertise, inclination, bent

arbitrary *ADJECTIVE*

an apparently arbitrary decision

illogical, irrational, random, subjective, capricious, wanton

❙ OPPOSITE rational

arc *NOUN*

the arc of a rainbow

arch, bow, curve, crescent

arch *NOUN*

the arch of a eyebrow

curve, arc, bow, crescent

arch *VERB*

a cat arching its back

curve, bend, bow, hunch

architecture *NOUN*

FOR TERMS USED IN ARCHITECTURE SEE building

archive *NOUN*

a book containing the family archives

records, annals, history

arctic *ADJECTIVE*

SEE **polar**

ardent *ADJECTIVE*

an ardent supporter of the club

enthusiastic, passionate, fervent, keen, eager, avid, wholehearted, zealous

arduous *ADJECTIVE*

an arduous climb to the summit

tough, difficult, hard, laborious, strenuous, taxing, back-breaking, demanding, challenging, gruelling, punishing

area *NOUN*

1 *a vast area of desert*

expanse, stretch, tract, space

▶ A small area is a **patch**.

▶ An area of water or ice is a **sheet**.

2 *an inner-city area*

district, locality, neighbourhood, region, zone, vicinity

3 *a fascinating area of research*

field, sphere, province, domain

arena *NOUN*

an indoor sports arena

a
b
c
d
e
f
g
h
i
j
k
l
m
n
o
p
q
r
s
t
u
v
w
x
y
z

stadium, amphitheatre, ground
(*North American*) bowl, park
▌ SEE ALSO **sport**

argue VERB

1 *Those two are always arguing about
something.*
quarrel, disagree, fight, have an
argument, squabble, wrangle, bicker
▌ IDIOMS cross swords, lock horns

► To argue about the price of
something is to **haggle**.
▌ OPPOSITE agree

2 *I argued that it was my turn to use
the computer.*
claim, assert, maintain, contend,
reason, allege

argument NOUN

1 *an argument over who should pay
for the meal*
disagreement, quarrel, dispute, row,
clash, fight, squabble, altercation,
contretemps

2 *summing up both sides of the
argument*
reasoning, justification, evidence,
case, thesis

arid ADJECTIVE

the arid surface of Mars
dry, barren, parched, waterless,
lifeless, infertile, sterile,
unproductive
▌ OPPOSITES fertile, lush

arise VERB

1 *a list of problems that may arise*
occur, emerge, develop, ensue,
appear, come about, come up, crop
up, happen, come to light, surface

2 *(old use) Arise, Sir knight.*
stand up, get up

aristocrat NOUN

a Spanish aristocrat
noble, nobleman or noblewoman,
peer
▌ OPPOSITE commoner

aristocratic ADJECTIVE

an aristocratic family
noble, titled,

upper-class, blue-blooded

arm NOUN

FOR PARTS OF YOUR BODY SEE body

arm VERB

a gang armed with sticks
equip, supply, provide, furnish,
fit out

armour NOUN

a knight in armour
chain-mail
► An outfit of armour is a **suit of
armour**.
► Something fitted with armour is
armoured or **armour-plated**.

arms PLURAL NOUN

a display of arms
weapons, weaponry, guns, firearms,
armaments, fire-power
► A store of arms is an **armoury** or
arsenal.

army NOUN

1 *He served with the army in France.*
armed force, military, militia, troops,
soldiery, infantry
► A body of troops defending a town
or fort is a **garrison**.
► A country's army, navy, and air force
are its **armed services**.
▌ SEE ALSO **soldier**

2 *an army of volunteers*
mass, horde, mob, swarm, throng

aroma NOUN

the rich aroma of coffee
smell, scent, odour, fragrance,
perfume
**FOR TIPS ON DESCRIBING SMELLS SEE
smell NOUN**

aromatic ADJECTIVE

cooking with aromatic herbs
fragrant, scented, perfumed,
fragranced
**FOR TIPS ON DESCRIBING SMELLS SEE
smell NOUN**

around PREPOSITION

1 *wearing a necklace around her neck*
about, round, encircling,

surrounding

2 *There were around a hundred people in the audience.*
about, approximately, roughly, more or less

arouse VERB

1 *without arousing any suspicions*
cause, generate, lead to, evoke, produce, provoke, set off, excite, stimulate, incite, stir up, whip up
┃ OPPOSITES calm, quell

2 *aroused from sleep*
wake up, waken, awaken, rouse

arrange VERB

1 *The books are arranged in alphabetical order.*
sort, order, organize, set out, lay out, display, group, categorize, classify, collate

2 *We arranged to meet outside the cinema.*
plan, agree, determine, organize, set up, schedule

arrangement NOUN

1 *the arrangement of the furniture*
layout, positioning, organization, grouping, display, design

2 *the arrangements for our holiday*
plan, preparation, planning, provision

3 *an arrangement to share the costs*
agreement, deal, bargain, contract

array NOUN

an array of dials on the control panel
range, display, line-up, arrangement

arrest VERB

1 *A man has been arrested for murder.*
seize, capture, apprehend, detain, take prisoner, take into custody
(British informal) nick

2 *trying to arrest the spread of disease*
stop, halt, check, curb, block, prevent, obstruct

arrest NOUN

the arrest of the main suspect
seizure, capture, apprehension

arrival NOUN

1 *the arrival of our guests*
coming, appearance, entrance, approach

2 *the arrival of autumn*
onset, advent, emergence, beginning

arrive VERB

When is the train due to arrive?
come, appear, turn up, get in
(informal) show up

▷ **arrive at**

1 *We arrived at our hotel before noon.*
get to, reach

2 *Have you arrived at a decision?*
make, reach, settle on, decide on

arrogant ADJECTIVE

an arrogant belief in his own superiority
boastful, conceited, proud, haughty, self-important, pompous, superior, supercilious, bumptious
(informal) big-headed, cocky
┃ IDIOMS full of yourself
(informal) too big for your boots
┃ OPPOSITE modest

art NOUN

1 *a class in art and design*
artwork, fine art

2 *the art of writing well*
skill, craft, technique, talent, knack, trick

WORD WEB

terms used in art, craft, and design

2D, 3D, abstract, applied art, artefact, artist, artwork, ceramics, collage, composition, crafts, craftsperson, design, designer, drawing, expressive arts, fine art, form, graphic design, illustration, image, installation, jewellery, materials, media, modelling, montage, painter, painting, pattern, plastic arts, printmaking, process,　　》

a
b
c
d
e
f
g
h
i
j
k
l
m
n
o
p
q
r
s
t
u
v
w
x
y
z

sculptor, sculpture, shape, technique, textile art, textiles, texture, visual arts

SEE ALSO drawing, film, photography, textiles

FOR PERFORMING ARTS SEE dance, drama, music

article NOUN
1 *an article for sale*
item, object, thing
2 *an article in a magazine*
essay, report, piece, feature

articulate ADJECTIVE
an articulate speaker
fluent, eloquent, lucid
OPPOSITE inarticulate

articulate VERB
able to articulate your feelings
express, communicate, voice, put into words

artificial ADJECTIVE
1 *an artificial flower*
man-made, synthetic, imitation, unreal, unnatural, manufactured, fake, false
OPPOSITES real, natural
2 *an artificial smile*
pretended, sham, affected, assumed, simulated
(informal) put on
OPPOSITES genuine, natural

artistic ADJECTIVE
a room decorated in an artistic style
creative, imaginative, aesthetic, attractive, tasteful
(informal) arty

ascend VERB
1 *footsteps ascending the stairs*
climb, go up, mount, move up, scale
2 *a kite ascending into the air*
fly up, rise, soar
OPPOSITE descend

ascent NOUN
1 *the ascent of Everest*
climbing, mounting, scaling

2 *The trail follows a steep ascent.*
slope, gradient, incline, rise
OPPOSITES descent, drop

ashamed ADJECTIVE
feeling ashamed for what he had done
sorry, remorseful, regretful, repentant, shamefaced, embarrassed, contrite, mortified, penitent
(informal) red-faced
OPPOSITES unashamed, unrepentant

ask VERB
1 *She asked us to be quiet.*
request, entreat, appeal to, beg, implore
2 *I asked him where he came from.*
enquire, demand, query, question
3 *Who are you asking to the party?*
invite
(formal) request the pleasure of your company
▷ **ask for**
1 *I asked for their advice.*
request, appeal for, call for, seek, solicit
2 *They were asking for trouble!*
encourage, attract, cause, provoke, stir up

asleep ADJECTIVE
My brother is still fast asleep.
sleeping, dozing, having a nap, napping
(informal) snoozing
(formal) slumbering
IDIOMS (informal) dead to the world
(humorous) in the land of Nod
► An animal asleep for the winter is **hibernating**.
OPPOSITE awake
▷ **fall asleep**
falling asleep on the couch
go to sleep, doze, drop off, nod off
► To fall asleep quickly is to **go out like a light**.

a b c d e f g h i j k l m n o p q r s t u v w x y z

aspect *NOUN*

1 *the negative aspects of modern life*
part, feature, element, angle, detail, side, facet

2 *Today the park has a gloomy aspect.*
appearance, look, manner, air, expression, face, countenance

3 *a room with a southern aspect*
outlook, view, prospect

aspire *VERB*

▷ **aspire to**
those who aspire to be Olympic champions
aim for, hope for, dream of, long for, desire, seek

┃ IDIOMS set your heart on, set your sights on

assault *NOUN*

the victim of a serious assault
attack, mugging

assault *VERB*

charged with assaulting a policeman
attack, strike, hit, beat up, mug

assemble *VERB*

1 *A crowd assembled to watch the rescue.*
gather, come together, congregate, convene, converge, meet, rally

┃ OPPOSITE disperse

2 *Inspector Pym had assembled all the evidence.*
collect, gather, bring together, put together, round up, marshal, muster

3 *assembling a model aeroplane*
construct, build, put together, fit together

assembly *NOUN*

1 *the assembly of the car*
construction, building, fabrication, manufacture

2 *a large assembly in the market square.*
gathering, meeting, convention, congregation, crowd
(informal) get-together

▶ An assembly to show support for

something, often out of doors, is a **rally**.

assent *NOUN*

She has already given us her assent.
agreement, approval, consent, go-ahead, permission

┃ OPPOSITES refusal, dissent

assert *VERB*

1 *The accused man asserts that he is innocent.*
state, claim, contend, declare, argue, maintain, proclaim, insist

2 *Mary asserted her claim to the English throne.*
insist on, stand up for, uphold, defend

assertive *ADJECTIVE*

trying to be more assertive in class
confident, self-confident, bold, forceful, insistent, commanding

assess *VERB*

a quiz to assess your fitness level
evaluate, determine, judge, rate, appraise, measure, gauge, estimate, calculate, work out, value, weigh up
(informal) size up

assessment *NOUN*

What is your assessment of the situation?
judgement, estimation, rating, appraisal, valuation

asset *NOUN*

She has proved a real asset to the team.
advantage, benefit, blessing, help, strength, good point

┃ OPPOSITE liability

assign *VERB*

1 *I was assigned the job of guarding the door.*
allocate, allot, give, consign, hand over, delegate, charge with, entrust with

2 *An experienced detective was assigned to the case.*
appoint, nominate, co-opt

assignment *NOUN*
> *a homework assignment*
> task, project, exercise, piece of work, job, mission, undertaking

assist *VERB*
> *assisting the crew with their duties*
> help, aid, support, back up, cooperate with, collaborate with
>
> **IDIOM** lend a hand to
> **OPPOSITE** hinder

assistance *NOUN*
> *Can I be of any assistance?*
> help, aid, support, backing, cooperation, collaboration, reinforcement
>
> **IDIOM** a helping hand

assistant *NOUN*
> *an assistant to the producer*
> helper, aide, partner, colleague, associate, supporter

associate *VERB*
> ▷ **associate with**
> 1 *Black cats are often associated with witchcraft.*
> connect with, identify with, link with, relate to
> 2 *He used to associate with members of the band.*
> be friends with, go about with, mix with

association *NOUN*
> 1 *a junior tennis association*
> club, society, organization, group, league, fellowship, partnership, union, alliance
> ▶ A political association is a **party**.
> 2 *Our association goes back a long way.*
> relationship, partnership, friendship, relation, connection, link, bond

assorted *ADJECTIVE*
> *assorted flavours of ice cream*
> various, different, mixed, diverse, miscellaneous, several, sundry

assortment *NOUN*
> *an assortment of sandwiches*
> variety, selection, mixture, array, choice, collection, medley, miscellany

assume *VERB*
> 1 *I assume that you agree with me.*
> presume, suppose, take for granted, believe, fancy, think, understand, gather
> 2 *assuming more responsibility*
> accept, take on, undertake, shoulder, bear
> 3 *assuming a false identity*
> adopt, put on, affect

assumed *ADJECTIVE*
> *an assumed identity*
> false, fake, fictitious, bogus, invented, made-up
> *(informal)* phoney

assumption *NOUN*
> *the basic assumption that the Earth is a sphere*
> belief, presumption, supposition, theory, hypothesis

assurance *NOUN*
> 1 *You have my assurance.*
> promise, guarantee, pledge, vow
> 2 *projecting an air of calm assurance*
> confidence, self-confidence, self-assurance, self-possession

assure *VERB*
> 1 *He assured us that he was telling the truth.*
> promise, reassure, give your word to, vow to
> 2 *to assure the success of the mission*
> ensure, make certain of, secure, guarantee

assured *ADJECTIVE*
> *an air of quiet, assured strength*
> confident, self-confident, self-assured, poised, composed, imperturbable
> *(informal)* unflappable

astonish *VERB*

They were astonished at the size of the crater.
amaze, astound, surprise, stagger, shock, dumbfound, startle, stun, take aback, take by surprise
(informal) flabbergast

❙ **IDIOMS** leave you speechless, take your breath away, bowl you over *(informal)* knock you for six

astonishing *ADJECTIVE*

capable of reaching astonishing speeds
amazing, astounding, staggering, stunning, remarkable, surprising, extraordinary, incredible, breathtaking, phenomenal, sensational, stupendous, tremendous, dazzling
(informal) mind-boggling

astound *VERB*
SEE **astonish**

astounding *ADJECTIVE*
SEE **astonishing**

astrology *NOUN*
SEE **zodiac**

astronomy *NOUN*
FOR TERMS USED IN ASTRONOMY SEE **space**

astute *ADJECTIVE*

an astute businesswoman
shrewd, sharp, acute, smart, clever, canny

asylum *NOUN*

seeking political asylum
refuge, sanctuary, protection, immunity

athletic *ADJECTIVE*

He is tall with an athletic build.
muscular, fit, strong, sturdy, powerful, strapping, well-built, brawny, burly
(informal) sporty

❙ **OPPOSITES** puny, weedy
FOR TIPS ON DESCRIBING PEOPLE'S BODIES SEE **body**

athletics *PLURAL NOUN*

 WORD WEB

some athletic events

cross-country, decathlon, discus, heptathlon, high jump, hurdles, javelin, long jump, marathon, pentathlon, pole vault, relay, shot put, sprint, steeplechase, triathlon, triple jump

FOR TIPS ON WRITING ABOUT SPORT SEE **sport**

atmosphere *NOUN*

1 *The atmosphere on Mars is unbreathable.*
air, sky

2 *There was a relaxed atmosphere at the end of term.*
feeling, feel, mood, spirit, air, ambience, aura
(informal) vibe

atrocious *ADJECTIVE*

1 *a series of atrocious murders*
wicked, brutal, barbaric, cruel, vicious, savage, monstrous, inhuman, vile, fiendish, horrifying, abominable, terrible, dreadful

2 *atrocious weather conditions*
very bad, terrible, dreadful, awful
❙ SEE ALSO **bad**

atrocity *NOUN*

atrocities committed during the war
crime, violation, horror, outrage

attach *VERB*

1 *Attach this label to the parcel.*
fasten, fix, join, tie, bind, secure, connect, link, couple, stick, affix, add, append
❙ **OPPOSITE** detach

2 *attaching importance to education*
ascribe, assign, give

attached *ADJECTIVE*
▷ **attached to**
Some people get very attached to their pets.

a
b
c
d
e
f
g
h
i
j
k
l
m
n
o
p
q
r
s
t
u
v
w
x
y
z

fond of, close to, devoted to, keen on, loyal to, affectionate towards, friendly towards

attachment NOUN
1 *an attachment for a hairdryer*
accessory, fitting, extension, add-on, part
2 *a strong attachment to her native country*
closeness, connection, devotion, loyalty, bond

attack NOUN
1 *an attack by an armed gang*
assault, strike, charge, raid, ambush, invasion, onslaught, offensive
▶ An attack from the air is an **air raid** or **blitz**, and a continuous attack with guns or missiles is a **bombardment**.
2 *an attack on your reputation*
criticism, censure, condemnation, outburst, tirade
3 *an attack of coughing*
bout, fit, spasm, episode
(informal) turn

attack VERB
1 *They were attacked by a mob armed with sticks.*
assault, set on, beat up, mug, charge, pounce on, assail, raid, storm, bombard
▶ To attack someone from a hidden place is to **ambush** them.
▶ If an animal attacks you, it might **savage** you.
2 *attacking the author's reputation*
criticize, censure, denounce, condemn
(informal) knock, rubbish, slate
❙ **OPPOSITES** defend, praise

attacker NOUN
He managed to escape his attacker.
assailant, assaulter, mugger, raider, invader
❙ **OPPOSITE** defender

attain VERB
after attaining a degree in History
get, obtain, reach, achieve, accomplish, gain, secure, realize, fulfil

attempt VERB
She will attempt to beat the world record.
try, endeavour, strive, seek, aim, venture, make an effort, have a go at
(informal) have a shot at, have a bash at

attempt NOUN
my first attempt at writing a novel
try, effort, go
(informal) shot, bash

attend VERB
Over a hundred people attended the rally.
be present at, go to, appear at, take part in, turn up at
(informal) show up at
▷ **attend to**
1 *attending to the lesson*
listen to, pay attention to, follow, heed, mark, mind, note
2 *attending to the baby*
take care of, care for, look after, mind, tend, deal with, see to

attendance NOUN
1 *the attendance of several celebrities*
presence, appearance, participation
❙ **OPPOSITE** non-attendance
2 *The attendance was low because of the rain.*
audience, turnout, gate, crowd

attendant NOUN
the personal attendant of Queen Victoria
assistant, aide, companion, escort, retainer, servant

attention NOUN
1 *The work requires my full attention.*
concentration, consideration, study, focus, observation, scrutiny, thought, awareness, heed
2 *needing urgent medical attention*

treatment, care

attentive _ADJECTIVE_

a most attentive audience
alert, observant, watchful, heedful,
aware, vigilant, on the alert,
on the lookout

attic _NOUN_

boxes stored in the attic
loft, garret

attitude _NOUN_

a positive attitude towards life
outlook, approach, stance, position,
view, manner, disposition, frame of
mind

attract _VERB_

The show continues to attract a wide
audience.
interest, appeal to, captivate, charm,
entice, lure, draw in, pull in
❙ **OPPOSITES** repel, put off

attraction _NOUN_

1 What is the attraction of living in
New York?
appeal, desirability, charm, allure,
pull
❙ **OPPOSITE** repulsion

2 a major tourist attraction
place of interest, sight, draw

attractive _ADJECTIVE_

1 an attractive young woman
beautiful, pretty, good-looking,
handsome, gorgeous, glamorous,
striking, fetching, fascinating,
captivating, enchanting, arresting
❙ **OPPOSITES** unattractive, ugly,
repulsive
❙ **SEE ALSO beautiful**

2 an attractive offer
appealing, interesting, agreeable,
desirable, pleasing, tempting,
inviting
❙ **OPPOSITES** unattractive, uninviting

attribute _VERB_

The lines are attributed to
Shakespeare.
ascribe, assign, credit

attribute _NOUN_

He has all the attributes of a top
striker.
quality, characteristic, trait,
property, feature, element, aspect,
mark, hallmark

audible _ADJECTIVE_

a voice that was barely audible
perceptible, detectable, discernible,
distinct
❙ **OPPOSITE** inaudible
FOR TIPS ON DESCRIBING SOUNDS SEE
sound❶

audience _NOUN_

Some members of the audience
cheered.
crowd, spectators
▶ The audience for a TV programme is
the **viewers**.
▶ The audience for a radio programme
is the **listeners**.

aura _NOUN_

creating an aura of calm
atmosphere, feeling, feel, mood,
spirit, air, ambience
(informal) vibe

austere _ADJECTIVE_

the tall, austere figure of Dr Murray
severe, stern, dour, unadorned,
spartan

authentic _ADJECTIVE_

1 an authentic Roman coin
genuine, real, actual, bona fide
❙ **OPPOSITES** imitation, fake

2 an authentic account of what
happened
accurate, truthful, reliable, true,
honest, dependable, factual
❙ **OPPOSITES** false, inaccurate

author _NOUN_

a book signed by the author
writer, novelist, poet, playwright

authoritarian _ADJECTIVE_

an authoritarian regime
dictatorial, autocratic, despotic,
tyrannical, undemocratic

》

OPPOSITES democratic, liberal

authority NOUN

1 I need your authority to access the
   files.
   permission, authorization, consent,
   approval, sanction, clearance

2 challenging the authority of the
   Church
   power, command, control,
   domination, rule, charge

3 a leading authority on handwriting
   expert, specialist, pundit,
   connoisseur

authorize VERB

Has this payment been authorized?
approve, agree to, consent to,
sanction, clear, allow

automatic ADJECTIVE

1 an automatic car wash
   automated, mechanical,
   programmed, computerized

2 an automatic response
   instinctive, involuntary, impulsive,
   spontaneous, reflex, unconscious,
   unthinking

autonomous ADJECTIVE

an autonomous state
independent, self-governing,
sovereign

OPPOSITE dependent

auxiliary ADJECTIVE

an auxiliary engine
supplementary, secondary, reserve,
back-up

OPPOSITE primary

available ADJECTIVE

1 Is the Internet available in the
   library?
   accessible, obtainable, at hand,
   within reach

   OPPOSITES unavailable, inaccessible

2 There are no more seats available.
   unoccupied, unsold, free
   (informal) up for grabs

   OPPOSITES unavailable, taken

average ADJECTIVE

It was just an average day at school.
ordinary, normal, typical,
standard, usual, regular, everyday,
commonplace

OPPOSITES unusual, extraordinary

averse ADJECTIVE

▷ **averse to**
I'm not averse to the idea.
against, opposed to, hostile to

OPPOSITES keen on, for

aversion NOUN

▷ **aversion to**
Some mammals have an aversion to
water.
dislike of, distaste of, antipathy to,
hostility to

OPPOSITE liking for

avert VERB

1 Nina averted her eyes from the glare.
   turn away, turn aside, redirect

2 taking steps to avert a crisis
   prevent, avoid, ward off, stave off,
   pre-empt, forestall

avid ADJECTIVE

an avid reader of science fiction
keen, eager, enthusiastic,
passionate, ardent, fervent

avoid VERB

1 I swerved to avoid the lamp post.
   get out of the way of, keep clear of,
   steer clear of, dodge, fend off

2 He has to avoid eating fried foods.
   refrain from, abstain from, shun

3 Go out the back way to avoid being
   seen.
   prevent, preclude, avert, pre-empt,
   forestall

await VERB

We are awaiting further instructions.
wait for, look out for, expect, look
forward to, anticipate

awake VERB

Our guests awoke early.
wake up, wake, awaken, rise, stir

awake *ADJECTIVE*

> *lying awake all night worrying*
> wide awake, sleepless, restless,
> conscious, astir
> ▶ Not being able to sleep is to be
>   suffering from **insomnia**.
> ❙ **OPPOSITE** asleep

awaken *VERB*

> **1** *I was awakened by birds singing.*
>   wake up, waken, wake, rouse
> **2** *a song which awakens memories of
>   her youth*
>   arouse, stir up, stimulate, evoke,
>   kindle, revive

award *VERB*

> *They awarded her the Nobel Peace
> Prize.*
> give, grant, accord, bestow on,
> confer on, present to

award *NOUN*

> *the award for best band*
> prize, trophy, medal

aware *ADJECTIVE*

> ▷ **aware of**
> *Were you aware of the danger?*
> acquainted with, conscious of,
> familiar with, informed about
> ❙ **OPPOSITE** ignorant of

awareness *NOUN*

> *an awareness of time passing*
> consciousness, recognition,
> perception, realization

awe *NOUN*

> *The audience listened in awe.*
> wonder, amazement, admiration,
> reverence

awesome *ADJECTIVE*

> *the awesome power of a hurricane*
> awe-inspiring, amazing,
> breathtaking, spectacular, stunning,
> staggering, formidable
> *(informal)* mind-boggling

awful *ADJECTIVE*

> **1** *an awful performance*

> very bad, dreadful, terrible, dire,
> abysmal
> *(informal)* rubbish, lousy, pathetic
> **2** *an awful crime*
>   horrifying, shocking, appalling,
>   atrocious, abominable
> **3** *an awful thing to say*
>   unpleasant, disagreeable, nasty,
>   horrid, detestable
> **4** *I feel awful about forgetting your
>   birthday.*
>   sorry, ashamed, embarrassed, guilty,
>   remorseful
>   ❙ **SEE ALSO** bad

awkward *ADJECTIVE*

> **1** *an awkward shape to carry*
>   difficult, cumbersome,
>   unmanageable, unwieldy
>   *(informal)* fiddly
>   ❙ **OPPOSITES** easy, handy
> **2** *You've arrived at an awkward time.*
>   inconvenient, inappropriate,
>   inopportune, difficult
>   ❙ **OPPOSITES** convenient, opportune
> **3** *an awkward silence*
>   uncomfortable, embarrassing,
>   uneasy, tense
>   ❙ **OPPOSITES** comfortable, relaxed
> **4** *Why are you being so awkward?*
>   uncooperative, unhelpful,
>   unreasonable, stubborn, obstinate
>   ❙ **OPPOSITES** cooperative, amenable
> **5** *an awkward movement*
>   clumsy, graceless, unskilful,
>   ungainly, inept, blundering
>   ❙ **OPPOSITES** graceful, skilful,
>   dexterous

axe *NOUN*

> *an axe for splitting wood*
> hatchet, cleaver, chopper

axe *VERB*

> *a decision to axe the TV series*
> cancel, drop, scrap, abolish,
> discontinue, cut, end
> *(informal)* ditch
> ❙ **IDIOM** *(informal)* pull the plug on

a
b
c
d
e
f
g
h
i
j
k
l
m
n
o
p
q
r
s
t
u
v
w
x
y
z

Bb

babble *VERB*
What was that man babbling about?
chatter, prattle, gabble, jabber,
burble
(British informal) natter, witter

baby *NOUN*
a mother and her baby
infant, child, newborn
(poetic) babe
(Scottish) bairn
▶ A baby just learning to walk is a
toddler.
▶ The time when someone is a baby is
their **babyhood**.

baby *ADJECTIVE*
baby carrots
miniature, mini, tiny
(informal) teeny, titchy
(Scottish) wee
⏐**SEE ALSO small**

babyish *ADJECTIVE*
Teenagers may find the film babyish.
childish, immature, infantile
⏐**OPPOSITES grown-up, mature**

back *NOUN*
1 sitting at the back of the bus
rear, tail end
(North American) tag end
▶ The back end of an animal is its
hindquarters, **rear**, or **rump**.
▶ The back of a ship is the **stern**.
⏐**OPPOSITES front, head**
2 on the back of an envelope
reverse, underside
(informal) flip-side

⏐**OPPOSITES front, face**
3 carrying a bag on your back
FOR PARTS OF YOUR BODY SEE body

back *ADJECTIVE*
1 the back door of the house
rear, tail, rearmost, posterior
▶ The back legs of an animal are its
hind legs.
⏐**OPPOSITES front, anterior**
2 a back massage
lumbar
▶ The fin on the back of a fish is its
dorsal fin.
3 a back issue of a magazine
past, previous, earlier, old
⏐**OPPOSITES future, forthcoming**

back *ADVERB*
1 leaning back in your chair
backwards, rearwards
⏐**OPPOSITE forwards**
2 It happened a few months back.
ago, previously, earlier, before now
⏐**OPPOSITE ahead**
3 Please write back soon.
in return, in response

back *VERB*
1 Joel began backing towards the door.
go backwards, reverse, retreat,
step back, draw back
⏐**OPPOSITE advance**
2 backing the bid to host the Games
support, endorse, favour, sanction,
advocate, promote
⏐**IDIOMS give your blessing to,
throw your weight behind**
⏐**OPPOSITE oppose**
3 backing a team to win the cup
bet on, put money on
▷ **back down**
We've come too far to back down
now.
give in, surrender, concede defeat
▷ **back off**
backing off at the sight of blood
retreat, withdraw, retire, recoil,
give way

▷ **back out of**

backing out of the deal
withdraw from, pull out of, renege on, fail to honour

▷ **back up**

1 *backing up your friends*
support, stand by, second

2 *The new evidence backs up his story.*
confirm, substantiate, corroborate, bear out

backfire *VERB*

His plan backfired spectacularly.
fail, go wrong, go awry
ⅼ IDIOMS blow up in your face
(informal) go pear-shaped

background *NOUN*

1 *a background of dense forest*
backdrop, setting, scene
ⅼ OPPOSITE foreground

2 *the background to the Civil War*
circumstances surrounding, lead-up to

3 *people from different backgrounds*
family circumstances, environment, upbringing, tradition, culture, class

backing *NOUN*

The new manager has the backing of the players.
support, endorsement, approval, blessing, sponsorship

backup *NOUN*

providing backup for the crew
support, assistance, reinforcements, reserves

backward or **backwards** *ADJECTIVE*

1 *a backward glance*
towards the rear, rearward
ⅼ OPPOSITE forward

2 *an economically backward country*
underdeveloped, undeveloped
ⅼ OPPOSITES advanced, progressive

backwards *ADVERB*

1 *taking a step backwards*
towards the rear, rearwards
ⅼ OPPOSITE forwards

2 *spelling your name backwards*

in reverse order

▷ **backwards and forwards**

running backwards and forwards
to and fro

bad *ADJECTIVE*

OVERUSED WORD

bad in quality, bad at doing something

poor, inferior, unsatisfactory, substandard, second-rate, inadequate, weak, incompetent, imperfect, awful, hopeless, terrible, dreadful, useless, worthless, abysmal, woeful, pathetic, lousy, shoddy, slipshod *(informal)* rubbish, duff

*The film was spoilt by the **second-rate** dialogue.*

ⅼ OPPOSITES excellent, fine

a bad experience, bad news

unpleasant, unwelcome, disagreeable, upsetting, horrific, horrendous, disastrous, horrible, awful, terrible, dreadful, appalling, shocking, hideous, ghastly, frightful, abominable

► Another word for a bad experience is an **ordeal**.

*Some patients experienced **unwelcome** side-effects.*

ⅼ OPPOSITES good, excellent

a bad accident, bad illness

severe, serious, grave, profound, critical, acute

*On opening night, I suffered from **severe** stage fright.*

ⅼ OPPOSITES minor, slight

a bad habit, something that is bad for you

harmful, damaging, detrimental, dangerous, hazardous, injurious

*The sun's rays are **damaging** to your eyes.*   »

a
b
c
d
e
f
g
h
i
j
k
l
m
n
o
p
q
r
s
t
u
v
w
x
y
z

a bad smell, bad taste
disgusting, revolting, repulsive, sickening, nauseating, repugnant, foul, loathsome, offensive, vile
A **sickening** smell invaded our nostrils.

OPPOSITES pleasant, appetizing

bad timing, a bad moment
inconvenient, unsuitable, unfortunate, inappropriate, inopportune, inauspicious
Is this an **inconvenient** time to call?

OPPOSITES convenient, opportune

bad weather, a bad reception
harsh, hostile, unfavourable, adverse, miserable
(formal) inclement
The **adverse** weather is forecast to continue.

OPPOSITES fine, favourable

a bad person, bad deed
wicked, evil, malevolent, malicious, villainous, cruel, vicious, corrupt, sinful, nefarious, monstrous, diabolical, immoral, detestable, hateful, mean, nasty
▶ A bad person is a **scoundrel**, **rogue**, or **rascal.**
▶ A bad character in a story or film is a **villain** or (informal) **baddy.**
He played a **monstrous** villain in one of the Bond films.

OPPOSITES good, virtuous

a bad mood, bad temper
angry, ill-humoured, foul
The director arrived in a **foul** temper.

OPPOSITE good-humoured
SEE ALSO bad-tempered

bad behaviour
disobedient, naughty, mischievous, unruly, undisciplined, wayward, disgraceful, deplorable
A player has been suspended for **unruly** conduct.

OPPOSITES exemplary, angelic

feeling bad about something
guilty, ashamed, sorry, remorseful, repentant
Claudius feels **guilty** about murdering King Hamlet.

OPPOSITES unashamed, unrepentant

food going bad
mouldy, rotten, off, decayed, sour, spoiled, rancid, putrid
Eat the bananas before they go **mouldy**.

OPPOSITE fresh

not bad
acceptable, adequate, reasonable, passable, tolerable, all right
The prices are **reasonable** if you book early.

badge NOUN
a membership badge
brooch, pin, emblem, insignia
(North American) button

badly ADVERB
1 a wall which is badly painted
not well, poorly, unsatisfactorily, inadequately, incorrectly, shoddily
OPPOSITES well, properly
2 animals being badly treated
ill, unkindly, harshly, cruelly, unfairly
OPPOSITES well, humanely, fairly
3 A rescue worker has been badly injured.
seriously, severely, gravely, critically
OPPOSITE slightly
4 The children badly need a rest.

very much, desperately, urgently

bad-tempered *ADJECTIVE*

At first, Scrooge is a bad-tempered miser.

cross, grumpy, grouchy, irritable, moody, quarrelsome, fractious, ill-tempered, short-tempered, cantankerous, crotchety, curmudgeonly, snappy, testy, tetchy, sullen, peevish

(North American) cranky, ornery

❙ **OPPOSITES** good-humoured, affable

baffle *VERB*

Ben shook his head, looking totally baffled.

puzzle, confuse, perplex, bewilder, mystify, stump

(informal) flummox, fox, flabbergast

bag *NOUN*

a reusable plastic bag

sack, carrier, holdall, satchel, handbag, shoulder bag

▶ A bag you carry on your back is a **backpack** or **rucksack**.

baggage *NOUN*

We loaded our baggage onto a trolley.

luggage, bags, cases, suitcases, belongings, things

(informal) gear, stuff

baggy *ADJECTIVE*

a pair of baggy jeans

loose, loose-fitting, roomy, voluminous

bait *NOUN*

Some people fell for the bait and answered the email.

lure, enticement, trap, decoy, inducement

bake *VERB*

SEE **cook**

balance *NOUN*

1 *Erin lost her balance and fell on the ice.*

stability, equilibrium, footing

2 *paying the balance of your fees*

remainder, residue, amount outstanding

balance *VERB*

balancing a tray on each hand

steady, stabilize, poise

bald *ADJECTIVE*

a bald patch on the head

bare, hairless

❙ **OPPOSITE** hairy

FOR TIPS ON DESCRIBING HAIR SEE hair

ball *NOUN*

1 *a ball of string*

sphere, globe, orb

▶ A small ball of something is a **pellet** or **globule**.

2 *a bouncy ball*

FOR GAMES PLAYED WITH A BALL SEE sport

ballot *NOUN*

holding a secret ballot

vote, poll, election, referendum, plebiscite

ban *VERB*

1 *Mobile phones are banned in school.*

forbid, prohibit, bar, veto, proscribe, exclude, outlaw, banish

❙ **OPPOSITES** allow, permit

2 *banned from international competition*

exclude, bar, banish, outlaw, expel

❙ **OPPOSITE** admit

ban *NOUN*

a ban on exporting ivory

prohibition, bar, veto, proscription

▶ A temporary ban is a **moratorium**.

▶ To end a ban on something is to **lift** it.

❙ **OPPOSITE** permission

banal *ADJECTIVE*

a disappointingly banal ending

unoriginal, commonplace, predictable, hackneyed, trite, unimaginative, uninspiring

band⁰ *NOUN*

an arm band

strip, stripe, ring, line, belt, hoop

a
b
c
d
e
f
g
h
i
j
k
l
m
n
o
p
q
r
s
t
u
v
w
x
y
z

band❷ NOUN

1 *a band of followers*
gang, group, company, party, body, troop, crew, mob, team, set
(informal) bunch

2 *a jazz band*
group, ensemble, orchestra, consort

bandage NOUN

a bandage round your knee
dressing, plaster, gauze, lint

bandit NOUN

a gang of armed bandits
robber, brigand, thief, outlaw, desperado, highwayman, pirate, buccaneer

bang NOUN

1 *a loud bang*
blast, boom, crash, crack, thud, thump, pop, explosion, report
FOR TIPS ON DESCRIBING SOUNDS SEE **sound❶**

2 *a bang on the head*
bump, knock, blow, hit, bash, thump, punch, smack, crack
(informal) whack, wallop, clout

bang VERB

banging your fist on the table
hit, strike, beat, bash, thump, knock, hammer, pound, rap, slam
(informal) whack, wallop, wham

banish VERB

banished from his native country
exile, expel, deport, send away, eject

bank NOUN

1 *the banks of the River Ganges*
edge, side, shore, embankment, margin, verge, brink

2 *a grassy bank*
slope, mound, ridge, rise, knoll

3 *a bank of dials and switches*
array, row, line, series

banner NOUN

1 *streets decorated with banners*
flag, standard, streamer, pennant

2 *demonstrators carrying banners*
placard, sign, notice, poster

banquet NOUN

a state banquet
dinner, feast
(informal) spread

bar NOUN

1 *bars across a window*
rod, rail, spar, strut, beam, pole

2 *a bar of chocolate*
block, slab, wedge, tablet, cake
▶ A bar of gold or silver is an **ingot**.

3 *a bar to progress*
obstacle, barrier, hindrance, obstruction, block

bar VERB

1 *The door had been barred on the inside.*
bolt, fasten, secure, barricade

2 *A fallen tree barred the way ahead.*
block, hinder, impede, obstruct, stop, check

3 *barred from entering the country*
ban, prohibit, exclude, keep out

barbaric ADJECTIVE

the barbaric treatment of slaves
cruel, brutal, inhuman, inhumane, barbarous, savage, brutish

bare ADJECTIVE

1 *in your bare feet*
naked, nude, exposed, uncovered, unclothed, undressed
OPPOSITES clothed, covered

2 *a bare mountain slope*
barren, treeless, leafless
OPPOSITES fertile, lush

3 *The room was bare except for a single bed.*
empty, clear, unfurnished, undecorated
OPPOSITE furnished

4 *the bare facts of the case*
plain, simple, unembellished, bald, stark

5 *Only pack the bare essentials.*
basic, minimum

barely ADVERB

We barely had time to get changed.
hardly, scarcely, only just

bargain *NOUN*

  1 *I'll make a bargain with you.*
  deal, agreement, arrangement,
  promise, contract, pact

  2 *looking for bargains in the sales*
  good buy, special offer
  (informal) snip, steal

bargain *VERB*

  bargaining over the price
  haggle, do a deal, negotiate

  ▷ **bargain on**
  *I hadn't bargained on sleeping in a
  tent.*
  expect, anticipate, envisage, foresee,
  count on, reckon on, allow for

barge *VERB*

  ▷ **barge into**
  1 *People were running around and
  barging into each other.*
  bump into, collide with, veer into

  2 *Don't just barge into my room
  without knocking.*
  push into, rush into, storm into

bark *VERB*

  the sound of dogs barking
  woof, yap, yelp, growl
  FOR TIPS ON DESCRIBING ANIMALS SEE
  animal

barrage *NOUN*

  1 *a tidal barrage*
  dam, weir, barrier

  2 *a heavy artillery barrage*
  bombardment, volley, gunfire

  3 *facing a barrage of questions*
  mass, stream, flood, torrent, deluge,
  onslaught, avalanche

barrel *NOUN*

  a barrel of gunpowder
  cask, drum, tub, keg, butt

barren *ADJECTIVE*

  a barren landscape
  arid, dry, bare, infertile, sterile,
  unproductive, unfruitful
  OPPOSITES fertile, lush

barricade *NOUN*

  building a barricade of sandbags

barrier, blockade, obstacle,
obstruction

barrier *NOUN*

  1 *Spectators must stay behind the
  barrier.*
  fence, railing, barricade, blockade

  ▶ A barrier across a road is a
  roadblock.

  2 *a barrier to achieving peace*
  obstacle, obstruction, bar,
  hindrance, impediment, hurdle,
  stumbling block

base *NOUN*

  1 *the base of the pyramid*
  bottom, foot, foundation, support,
  stand

  ▶ A base under a statue is a **pedestal**
  or **plinth**.

  2 *The decimal system has 10 as its
  base.*
  basis, foundation, root, starting
  point, bedrock

  3 *The lifeboat crew returned to base
  safely.*
  headquarters, camp, station, post,
  depot

base *VERB*

  1 *a study based on new data*
  found, build, construct, establish,
  form, ground

  2 *a company based in Wales*
  locate, site, situate, position

basement *NOUN*

  steps leading down to the basement
  cellar, vault

  ▶ A room underneath a church is a
  crypt.

  ▶ An underground cell in a castle is a
  dungeon.
  FOR TIPS ON DESCRIBING BUILDINGS SEE
  building

bashful *ADJECTIVE*

  too bashful to ask for a dance
  shy, reserved, timid, diffident

basic *ADJECTIVE*

  1 *The basic ingredients of bread are
  flour, yeast, and water.*

a
b
c
d
e
f
g
h
i
j
k
l
m
n
o
p
q
r
s
t
u
v
w
x
y
z

fundamental, essential, main,
primary, principal, chief, key, central,
cardinal
OPPOSITES secondary, extra

2 *a campsite with basic facilities*
plain, simple, minimal, rudimentary,
limited, unsophisticated
OPPOSITES elaborate, advanced

basically ADVERB
Basically, I think you're right.
fundamentally, essentially, in
essence, at heart, at bottom

basics PLURAL NOUN
learning the basics of algebra
fundamentals, essentials, first
principles, foundations, groundwork
IDIOM nuts and bolts

basin NOUN
a basin of soapy water
bowl, dish, sink

basis NOUN
What is the basis of your argument?
base, foundation, grounds, rationale

basket NOUN
a picnic basket
► A basket of food is a **hamper**.
► A basket on a bicycle is a **pannier**.
► A small basket of fruit is a **punnet**.

bass ADJECTIVE
in a loud, bass voice
low, deep, sonorous
OPPOSITES high-pitched, high
FOR TIPS ON DESCRIBING SOUNDS SEE
sound❶

bat NOUN
a heavy, wooden bat
club, stick

batch NOUN
a fresh batch of pancakes
group, quantity, set, lot, bunch,
bundle

bathe VERB
1 *bathing in the sea*
swim, go swimming, take a dip
2 *bathing a wound*
clean, wash, rinse, cleanse

▷ **bathed in**
a scene bathed in moonlight
flooded with, covered with, suffused
with, enveloped in

baton NOUN
a conductor's baton
stick, wand, truncheon

batter VERB
the sound of hail battering a tin roof
beat, pound, thump, pummel,
buffet, rain blows on

battle NOUN
1 *a battle between neighbouring
countries*
fight, conflict, action, engagement,
hostilities, skirmish, armed struggle
► A place where a battle takes place
is a **battlefield**, **battleground**, or
field of battle.
SEE ALSO fight, fighting

2 *caught in a legal battle*
argument, dispute, struggle, clash,
conflict

bawl VERB
1 *I heard someone bawl out
my name.*
shout, cry, yell, roar, bellow, bark
(informal) holler
2 *the sound of a baby bawling*
cry, wail, howl, sob

bay NOUN
anchored in a sheltered bay
cove, inlet, gulf, sound

bazaar NOUN
1 *a Turkish bazaar*
market, souk
2 *a church bazaar*
sale, fête, fair

be VERB
1 *I'll be at home all morning.*
stay, continue, remain
2 *The concert will be in March.*
take place, happen, come about,
occur
3 *She wants to be a famous writer.*
become, develop into

beach *NOUN*

  a sandy beach
  sands, seashore, seaside, shore,
  strand

bead *NOUN*

  1 *a string of beads*
  ball, pellet

  2 *wiping beads of sweat from his brow*
  drop, droplet, drip, blob, pearl

beam *NOUN*

  1 *a wooden beam*
  bar, timber, plank, post, joist, rafter,
  boom, spar, strut, support

  2 *a beam of sunlight*
  ray, shaft, stream, streak, gleam
  FOR TIPS ON DESCRIBING LIGHT SEE
  light❶

  3 *A huge beam spread across her face.*
  smile, grin

beam *VERB*

  1 *In the photo, we are all beaming at*
  the camera.
  smile, grin

  2 *The satellite will beam a signal back*
  to Earth.
  transmit, send out, broadcast, emit

bear *VERB*

  1 *a messenger bearing news*
  carry, bring, convey, transport, take,
  transfer

  2 *The rope won't bear my weight.*
  support, hold, take, sustain

  3 *The gravestone bears an old*
  inscription.
  display, show, exhibit, carry

  4 *unable to bear the heat*
  endure, tolerate, put up with,
  stand, withstand, cope with, abide,
  stomach
  (informal) hack
  (British informal) stick
  (formal) brook

  5 *Queen Victoria bore nine children.*
  give birth to, have, produce

  6 *a tree bearing fruit*
  produce, yield, give, supply

▷ **bear out**
  This bears out everything I said.
  confirm, support, substantiate,
  corroborate, back up

▷ **bear up**
  How are you bearing up?
  cope, manage, get by

▷ **bear with**
  Please bear with me a little longer.
  be patient with, put up with, tolerate

bearable *ADJECTIVE*

  making the pain more bearable
  tolerable, endurable, acceptable
  ❙ OPPOSITE unbearable

bearer *NOUN*

  the bearer of bad news
  bringer, carrier, conveyor, porter,
  messenger, emissary
  ❙ OPPOSITE unbearable

bearings *PLURAL NOUN*

  We lost our bearings in the fog.
  sense of direction, orientation,
  position, whereabouts

beast *NOUN*

  1 *beasts of the forest*
  animal, creature, brute
  FOR MYTHOLOGICAL BEASTS SEE
  fantasy

  2 *acting like a cruel beast*
  villain, monster, brute, fiend, swine

beat *VERB*

  1 *beating an animal with a stick*
  hit, strike, thrash, thump, batter,
  whip, lash, flog, lay into, rain blows
  on
  (informal) whack, wallop
  ❙ SEE ALSO hit

  2 *Spain beat Germany in the final.*
  defeat, conquer, win against,
  vanquish, get the better of,
  overcome, overwhelm, rout,
  trounce, trash
  (informal) hammer, lick

  3 *Beat the eggs, milk, and sugar*
  together.
  whisk, whip, blend, mix, stir

  4 *Is his heart still beating?*

pound, thump, palpitate

▷ **beat someone up**
The bully threatened to beat us up.
assault, attack, mug
(informal) rough up

beat NOUN

1 *the beat of a heart*
pulse, throb, palpitation, pounding, thumping

2 *music with a strong beat*
rhythm, accent, stress

beautiful ADJECTIVE

OVERUSED WORD

a beautiful person

attractive, good-looking, pretty, gorgeous, glamorous, radiant, elegant, enchanting, dazzling, stunning, magnificent, resplendent
(Scottish) bonny
*Guinevere looked **radiant** in a red silk gown.*

► A man who is pleasing to look at is **good-looking** or **handsome**.

OPPOSITES ugly, unattractive

a beautiful day, beautiful weather

fine, excellent, glorious, marvellous, sunny, superb, splendid, wonderful
*The festival organizers are hoping for **fine** weather.*

OPPOSITES dull, gloomy, drab

a beautiful sight, beautiful view

picturesque, scenic, charming, delightful, splendid, glorious, magnificent, spectacular
*I chose a postcard with a **scenic** view of the Alps.*

a beautiful sound, beautiful voice

harmonious, mellifluous, melodious, sweet-sounding

*Their debut CD features twelve **melodious** tracks.*

OPPOSITE grating

beautiful technique, beautiful workmanship

skilful, skilled, accomplished, well executed, masterly, expert, deft, dexterous
*Ronaldo flicked a **masterly** header into the net.*

beauty NOUN

1 *a film star famous for her beauty*
attractiveness, prettiness, loveliness, charm, allure, magnificence, radiance, splendour

OPPOSITE ugliness

2 *The beauty of living here is the climate.*
advantage, benefit, strong point, plus, bonus

OPPOSITES disadvantage, downside

because CONJUNCTION

I came here because I was invited.
since, as, seeing that, in view of the fact that

▷ **because of**
Play was stopped because of bad light.
as a result of, on account of, thanks to, owing to, due to, by virtue of

beckon VERB

The old man beckoned me to come forward.
gesture, signal, motion, wave, gesticulate

become VERB

1 *Women's football is becoming more popular.*
begin to be, turn, get

2 *In later life, she became a recluse.*
grow into, change into, develop into, turn into

3 *Just wear what becomes you.*
suit, flatter, look good on

▷ **become of**
Whatever became of your plan to go abroad?
happen to, come of

bed *NOUN*
1 *a room with a double bed*
bunk, mattress
▶ A bed for a baby is a **cot**, **cradle**, or **crib**.
▶ A bed on a ship or train is a **berth**.
2 *a flower bed*
plot, patch, border
3 *the bed of the ocean*
bottom, floor
❙ **OPPOSITE** surface
▷ **go to bed**
Is it time to go to bed yet?
retire, turn in
❙ **IDIOM** (informal) hit the sack

bedraggled *ADJECTIVE*
We carried the wet and bedraggled kitten into the house.
dishevelled, disordered, untidy, unkempt, scruffy, tousled
❙ **OPPOSITES** smart, spruce

bee *NOUN*

 WORD WEB

some types of bee
bumblebee, drone, honeybee, queen, worker
▶ A young bee after it hatches is a **larva**.
▶ A group of bees is a **swarm** or a **colony**.
▶ A place where bees live is a **hive**.
▶ The practice of farming bees for their honey is **beekeeping** or **apiculture**.
▶ The scientific study of honeybees is **apiology**.
❙ **SEE ALSO insect**

before *ADVERB*
1 *Those people were before us in the queue.*

in front of, ahead of, in advance of
❙ **OPPOSITES** after, behind
2 *Please switch off the lights before you leave.*
prior to, previous to, earlier than, preparatory to
❙ **OPPOSITE** after
3 *Have you seen this film before?*
previously, in the past, earlier, sooner
❙ **OPPOSITE** later

beg *VERB*
1 *begging for mercy*
ask, plead, call
2 *They begged her not to leave.*
implore, plead with, entreat, beseech, appeal to

begin *VERB*
1 *The builders began work yesterday.*
start, commence, embark on, set about
❙ **OPPOSITES** end, finish, conclude
2 *When did the trouble begin?*
appear, arise, emerge, originate, start, commence, spring up
❙ **OPPOSITES** end, stop, cease

beginner *NOUN*
a class for beginners
learner, starter, novice
(informal) rookie
▶ A beginner in a trade or a job is an **apprentice** or **trainee**.
▶ A beginner in the police or armed services is a **cadet** or **recruit**.

beginning *NOUN*
1 *I missed the beginning of the film.*
start, opening, commencement, introduction, preamble
▶ A piece of music at the beginning of a musical or opera is a **prelude** or **overture**.
▶ A piece of writing at the beginning of a book is a **preface** or **prologue**.
❙ **OPPOSITES** end, conclusion
2 *the beginning of life on Earth*
starting point, origin, inception, genesis, onset, establishment,

a
b
c
d
e
f
g
h
i
j
k
l
m
n
o
p
q
r
s
t
u
v
w
x
y
z

foundation, emergence, birth,
launch, dawn

behalf NOUN
▷ **on behalf of**
writing on behalf of a friend
in the name of, in place of, on the
authority of

behave VERB
1 *Our neighbour is behaving very
oddly.*
act, conduct yourself, react, perform
2 *My little brother promised to behave.*
be good, be on your best behaviour,
behave yourself
OPPOSITE misbehave

behaviour NOUN
a reward for good behaviour
conduct, manners, actions,
performance

behind PREPOSITION
1 *hiding behind a door*
at the back of, on the other side of
2 *Phil was walking just behind us.*
after, following
IDIOMS hard on the heels of, in the
wake of
OPPOSITES in front of, ahead of
3 *I guessed who was behind the
practical joke.*
responsible for, to blame for, the
cause of, at the bottom of
4 *Everyone got behind the team.*
on the side of, in support of,
supporting, backing
(informal) rooting for

behind ADVERB
I'm a bit behind with the payments.
late, behindhand, overdue, in arrears

being NOUN
beings from another planet
creature, individual, person, entity

belief NOUN
1 *a woman of strong religious beliefs*
faith, principle, creed, doctrine
2 *It is my belief is that he stole the
money.*

opinion, view, conviction, feeling,
notion, theory

believable ADJECTIVE
a believable plot
credible, plausible
OPPOSITES unbelievable,
implausible

believe VERB
1 *I don't believe anything he says.*
accept, have faith in, have
confidence in, rely on, trust
OPPOSITES disbelieve, doubt
2 *I believe you know my parents.*
think, understand, assume,
presume, gather
(informal) reckon

belittle VERB
people who try to belittle your ideas
disparage, run down, decry,
denigrate, deprecate
(informal) pooh-pooh

belligerent ADJECTIVE
adopting a belligerent tone
hostile, antagonistic, aggressive,
confrontational, combative, warlike,
militant, pugnacious, bellicose
(British informal) bolshie

bellow VERB
a sergeant bellowing out orders
shout, roar, bawl, yell, bark, boom,
thunder

belly NOUN
SEE **stomach**

belong VERB
1 *This ring belonged to my
grandmother.*
be owned by, be the property of,
be in the hands of
2 *I never felt that I belonged in my old
school.*
fit in, be suited to
(informal) click
3 *Do you belong to a sports club?*
be a member of, be in, be associated
with

a
b
c
d
e
f
g
h
i
j
k
l
m
n
o
p
q
r
s
t
u
v
w
x
y
z

belongings *PLURAL NOUN*
> Put any personal belongings in a locker.
> possessions, property, goods, things, effects, bits and pieces *(informal)* gear, stuff

beloved *ADJECTIVE*
> Ailsa returned to her beloved island.
> much loved, adored, dear, darling, cherished, treasured, precious
> **❙ OPPOSITE** hated

below *PREPOSITION*
> 1 swimming just below the surface
> under, underneath, beneath
> **❙ OPPOSITE** above
>
> 2 The temperature never fell below 20 degrees.
> less than, lower than
> **❙ OPPOSITES** above, over

belt *NOUN*
> 1 a leather belt
> girdle, sash, strap, band
> ▶ A broad sash worn round the waist is a **cummerbund**.
>
> 2 a belt of thick fog
> band, strip, line, stretch, zone, area

bench *NOUN*
> sitting on a bench in the park
> seat, form
> ▶ A long seat in a church is a **pew**.

bend *VERB*
> 1 The fire had bent the railings out of shape.
> curve, curl, coil, loop, hook, twist, crook, angle, flex, arch, warp
> ▶ Things which bend easily are **flexible** or **pliable**.
> **❙ OPPOSITE** straighten
>
> 2 bending down to tie a shoelace
> stoop, bow, crouch, lean over
>
> 3 a road that bends to the right
> turn, swing, veer, wind

bend *NOUN*
> a sharp bend in the road
> curve, turn, angle, corner, twist, kink

beneath *PREPOSITION*
> 1 sitting beneath an cherry tree
> under, underneath, below, at the foot of
> **❙ OPPOSITES** above, on top of
>
> 2 It was beneath her dignity to appear on a chat show.
> unworthy of, unbecoming to, ill-suited to

beneficial *ADJECTIVE*
> the beneficial effects of eating fruit
> favourable, advantageous, helpful, useful, valuable, salutary
> **❙ OPPOSITES** harmful, detrimental

benefit *NOUN*
> the benefits of regular exercise
> advantage, reward, gain, good point, blessing, boon
> *(informal)* perk
> **❙ OPPOSITES** disadvantage, drawback

benefit *VERB*
> The rainy weather will benefit gardeners.
> be good for, be of service to, help, aid, assist, serve, profit
> **❙ OPPOSITES** hinder, harm

benevolent *ADJECTIVE*
> Chinese dragons are benevolent creatures.
> kind, kindly, kind-hearted, good-natured, well-meaning, well-disposed, sympathetic, charitable, compassionate, caring
> **❙ OPPOSITES** malevolent, unkind

benign *ADJECTIVE*
> 1 a benign expression on her face
> kindly, friendly, kind-hearted, good-natured, genial, sympathetic, well-disposed, benevolent
> **❙ OPPOSITES** unfriendly, hostile
>
> 2 a benign climate
> mild, temperate, balmy, favourable
> **❙ OPPOSITE** hostile
>
> 3 a benign tumour
> non-cancerous
> **❙ OPPOSITE** malignant

a
b
c
d
e
f
g
h
i
j
k
l
m
n
o
p
q
r
s
t
u
v
w
x
y
z

bent *ADJECTIVE*

a pair of bent wire spectacles
curved, looped, twisted, buckled,
crooked, arched, bowed, warped,
misshapen, out of shape, deformed,
contorted
(British informal) wonky
❘ OPPOSITE straight

▷ **bent on**
Are you still bent on going?
intent on, determined on, set on

bent *NOUN*

She has a definite artistic bent.
talent, gift, flair, aptitude, inclination

berry *NOUN*
SEE **fruit**

berserk *ADJECTIVE*

▷ **go berserk**
*The crowd went berserk when the
band appeared.*
go mad, go crazy, go wild
❘ IDIOMS *(informal)* go off your head,
go bananas

beside *PREPOSITION*

sitting beside each other on the bus
next to, alongside, abreast of,
adjacent to, next door to, close to,
near, by

▷ **beside the point**
*The fact that I'm a girl is beside the
point.*
irrelevant, unimportant, neither
here nor there

▷ **beside yourself**
She was beside herself with grief.
distraught, frantic, overcome
❘ IDIOMS at your wits' end, out of
your mind

besides *PREPOSITION*

*No one knows the password, besides
you and me.*
as well as, in addition to, apart from,
other than, aside from

besides *ADVERB*

Besides, it's too late to phone now.
also, in addition,

furthermore, moreover

besiege *VERB*

1 *The Roman army besieged and took
the city.*
blockade, lay siege to

2 *besieged by adoring fans*
surround, mob, harass, plague

3 *besieged with offers of help*
overwhelm, bombard, inundate,
swamp, flood, snow under

best *ADJECTIVE*

1 *the best player in the squad*
finest, foremost, greatest, leading,
top, premier, supreme, pre-eminent,
outstanding, unequalled, unrivalled,
unsurpassed, second to none
(informal) star, top-drawer
❘ OPPOSITE worst

2 *I did what I thought was best.*
most suitable, most appropriate,
most advisable

best *ADVERB*

Which song did you like best?
most, the most
❘ OPPOSITE least

bestow *VERB*

▷ **bestow on**
*The ring is said to bestow power on
the wearer.*
confer on, give to, grant to, present
with

bet *NOUN*

placing a bet on the winner
wager, gamble, stake
(informal) flutter

bet *VERB*

1 *betting on the lottery*
wager, gamble, stake
(informal) have a flutter

2 *(informal) I bet we'll miss the bus.*
feel sure, be certain, be convinced,
expect, predict

betray *VERB*

1 *Wallace was betrayed by one of his
own men.*
be disloyal to, be unfaithful to,

inform on, conspire against,
double-cross, play false
❙IDIOMS stab someone in the back,
sell someone down the river
► Someone who betrays you is a
traitor.
► To betray your country is to commit
treason.
2 *Her face betrayed no emotion.*
reveal, show, indicate, disclose,
divulge, expose, tell

betrayal *NOUN*
a classic story of love and betrayal
treachery, disloyalty, breach of faith,
breach of trust, faithlessness

better *ADJECTIVE*
1 *This computer is much better than
my old one.*
superior, finer, preferable
❙IDIOM a cut above
❙OPPOSITES worse, inferior
2 *I hope you feel better soon.*
recovered, cured, healed, well, fitter,
stronger
❙OPPOSITE worse

between *PREPOSITION*
1 *a path between the house and the
garden*
connecting, joining, linking, uniting
2 *We divided the food between us.*
among, amongst

beware *VERB*
Beware! There are thieves about.
be careful, watch out, look out, take
care, be on your guard
▷ **beware of**
Beware of the bull.
watch out for, avoid, mind, heed,
keep clear of

bewilder *VERB*
a bewildering set of instructions
puzzle, confuse, perplex, mystify,
baffle, bemuse
(informal) flummox, fox, flabbergast

beyond *PREPOSITION*
1 *extending beyond the perimeter*
past, behind, after, on the far side of,

further away than
❙OPPOSITES in front of, before
2 *far beyond our capabilities*
greater than, superior to, exceeding,
above
❙OPPOSITES beneath, within

bias *NOUN*
*Does the author show signs
of bias?*
prejudice, partiality, one-sidedness,
favouritism, discrimination,
unfairness, imbalance
❙OPPOSITE impartiality

biased *ADJECTIVE*
an example of biased reporting
prejudiced, partial, one-sided,
partisan, discriminatory, bigoted,
unbalanced, skewed
❙OPPOSITE impartial

bicycle *NOUN*
a rack for parking bicycles
push bike
(informal) bike
► A person who rides a bicycle is a
cyclist.

 WORD WEB

types of bicycle
BMX bike, mountain bike, racing
bicycle, reclining or recumbent
bicycle, road bicycle, tandem,
trailer bike, touring bicycle, track
bicycle,
(historical) penny-farthing
► A cycle with one wheel is a
monocycle.
► A cycle with three wheels is a
tricycle or *(informal)* **trike**.
► A cycle without pedals is a
scooter.

parts of a bicycle
brakes, brake lever, chain,
crossbar, derailleur, frame,
(North American) gearshift,
handlebars, mudguard, pedals,
saddle, sprockets, tyre, wheel **》**

a
b
c
d
e
f
g
h
i
j
k
l
m
n
o
p
q
r
s
t
u
v
w
x
y
z

▶ An arena for track cycling is a **velodrome**.

▶ The main group of cyclists in a road bicycle race is the **peloton**.

bid *NOUN*

1 *a bid of several thousand dollars*
offer, tender, proposal
2 *a bid to beat the world record*
attempt, effort, try, endeavour

bid *VERB*

The club bid over a million pounds for the player.
offer, tender, propose, put up

big *ADJECTIVE*

OVERUSED WORD

big in size, scale
large, huge, great, massive, immense, enormous, gigantic, giant, colossal, mammoth, monstrous, monumental, titanic, outsize
(informal) whopping, humongous, mega
(literary) gargantuan
*Our class made a **giant** model of a human ear.*
❙ OPPOSITES small, little, tiny

big in area, distance
vast, immense, expansive, considerable, sweeping
*Some day spaceships will be able to travel **vast** distances.*

big inside
spacious, roomy, capacious, extensive, sizeable, palatial, cavernous
*The **spacious** front pocket has room for all your valuables.*
❙ OPPOSITES cramped, confined, poky

big and heavy, awkward
weighty, hefty, voluminous

*The alchemist carried a **ponderous** volume marked with ancient symbols.*

big and strong, tall
well built, hulking, hefty, strapping, burly, beefy, brawny, sturdy, mighty, towering, mountainous, giant
*His **strapping** physique is perfect for an action hero.*

a big part, big portion
ample, considerable, substantial, sizeable, generous, lavish, bumper, princely
(informal) tidy
*Each character gets an **ample** share of the treasure.*
❙ OPPOSITES meagre, paltry

a big decision, big moment
important, serious, grave, weighty, significant, key, momentous, historic, far-reaching, crucial, vital, major
*This year's final promises to be a **momentous** occasion.*
❙ OPPOSITES insignificant, minor

a big brother, big sister
elder, older
*Did you know that Vera has two **elder** sisters?*
❙ OPPOSITES younger, little

bill *NOUN*

1 *Please send us the bill by email.*
account, invoice, statement, charges
(North American) check, tab
2 *the last act on the bill this evening*
programme, line-up

bill *VERB*

1 *We will bill you for any damage.*
invoice, charge
(North American) check, tab
2 *She is billed as the player to watch.*
advertise, announce, proclaim, label, style, dub

billow VERB

1 *smoke billowing from the chimney*
pour, swirl, spiral, roll

2 *a huge sail billowing in the wind*
swell, fill out, puff out, bulge, balloon

bind VERB

1 *His hands were bound with a rope.*
tie up, fasten together, secure, make fast, lash, tether
OPPOSITES release, loose

2 *The leaves can be used to bind wounds.*
bandage, wrap, strap up
OPPOSITES untie, unwrap

3 *bound by ties of friendship*
unite, connect, join, attach
OPPOSITE separate

binding ADJECTIVE

a binding agreement
fixed, unalterable, unbreakable, inescapable

bird NOUN

the conservation of wild birds

WORD WEB

some common British birds
blackbird, blue tit, bullfinch, bunting, chaffinch, crow, cuckoo, dove, greenfinch, jackdaw, jay, linnet, magpie, martin, nightingale, pigeon, raven, robin, rook, skylark, sparrow, starling, swallow, swift, thrush, tit, wagtail, waxwing, woodpecker, wren, yellowhammer

birds of prey
buzzard, eagle, falcon, hawk, kestrel, kite, merlin, osprey, owl, sparrowhawk, vulture

farm and game birds
capercaillie, chicken, duck, goose, grouse, guinea fowl, partridge, pheasant, ptarmigan, quail, turkey

▶ Birds kept by farmers are called **poultry**.

seabirds and water birds
albatross, auk, bittern, coot, cormorant, crane, curlew, duck, gannet, goose, guillemot, gull, heron, kingfisher, kittiwake, lapwing, mallard, moorhen, oystercatcher, peewit, pelican, penguin, puffin, seagull, snipe, stork, swan, teal

birds from other countries
bird of paradise, budgerigar, canary, cockatoo, flamingo, humming bird, ibis, kookaburra, macaw, mynah bird, parakeet, parrot, peacock or peafowl, toucan

birds which cannot fly
emu, kiwi, ostrich, penguin

▶ A female bird is a **hen** and a male bird is a **cock**.

▶ A young bird is a **chick**, **fledgling**, or **nestling**, and a family of chicks is a **brood**.

▶ A group of birds is a **colony** or **flock**, and a group of flying birds is a **flight** or **skein**.

▶ The scientific study of birds is **ornithology**.

▶ A person who observes birds in their natural habitat is a **birdwatcher**.

FOR GROUPS OF BIRDS SEE **collective noun**

WRITING TIPS

describing birds

A fish-hawk, which, secure on the topmost branches of a dead pine, had been a distant spectator of the fray, now stooped from his high and ragged perch, and   》

soared, in wide sweeps, above his prey.
— James Fenimore Cooper, *The Last of the Mohicans*

body parts
beak, bill, breast, claw, comb, crest, crop, feathers, plumage, tail, talon, wattle, wing

❙ SEE ALSO feather

plumage
bedraggled, downy, drab, feathery, fluffy, ruffled, speckled, spotted

movement
circle, dart, flap, flit, flutter, fly, glide, perch, soar, swoop, waddle, wheel

sounds
caw, chirp, cluck, coo, gabble, honk, hoot, quack, screech, squawk, trill, twitter, warble

bit *NOUN*

 OVERUSED WORD

a bit of a whole
piece, part, section, portion, fraction, share, segment, slice
The first **section** of the film is shot in black and white.

a large, heavy bit
chunk, lump, hunk, wedge, slab, brick
Saturn's rings are made of **lumps** of ice and rock.

a small, light bit
fragment, scrap, shaving, shred, sliver, snippet, chip, speck, spot, particle, atom, mite, jot, modicum, pinch, touch, dab, daub, trace, hint, suggestion
(informal) smidgen, tad

The map was drawn on a **scrap** of old paper.

a bit of food
morsel, crumb, bite, nibble, taste, mouthful, soupçon
We ate every last **morsel** of breakfast.

a bit of liquid
drop, dash, dribble, drizzle, dollop, blob, splash, swig
Add a **dash** of lemon juice to the sauce.

a bit
slightly, rather, fairly, somewhat, quite, vaguely, faintly, a little, a shade
I found the whole evening **slightly** dull.

not a bit
not at all, not in any way, not a jot, not one iota, not a whit
Hannah is **not at all** like her sisters.

to bits
to pieces
(informal) to smithereens
The raft will surely be pounded **to pieces**.

bite *VERB*

1 *biting into a sandwich*
munch, nibble, chew, crunch, gnaw, sink your teeth into
(informal) chomp
❙ SEE ALSO eat

2 *bitten all over by midges*
nip, pinch, sting, pierce, wound, snap at
▶ A fierce animal **mauls** or **savages** its prey.

3 *Higher petrol prices are beginning to bite.*
take effect, kick in

bite *NOUN*

1 *Can I have a bite of your sandwich?*
mouthful, nibble, taste, morsel

2 *the bite of a black widow spider*
nip, sting, wound

biting *ADJECTIVE*

1 *a biting wind from the north*
freezing, bitter, piercing, raw,
wintry, icy
(informal) perishing

2 *biting criticism*
sharp, critical, scathing, cutting,
savage, caustic

bitter *ADJECTIVE*

1 *the bitter taste of olives*
sour, sharp, acid, acrid, tart
▌OPPOSITE sweet
FOR TIPS ON DESCRIBING TASTE SEE
taste

2 *I still feel bitter about what
happened.*
resentful, embittered, disgruntled,
aggrieved
▌OPPOSITE contented

3 *a bitter disappointment*
upsetting, hurtful, distressing, cruel
▌OPPOSITES mild, slight

4 *a bitter wind*
freezing, biting, piercing, raw,
wintry, icy
(informal) perishing

bizarre *ADJECTIVE*

a bizarre coincidence
strange, odd, peculiar, weird,
uncanny, extraordinary, outlandish
(informal) freaky

black *ADJECTIVE*

1 *black ink*
jet-black, pitch-black, ebony, inky,
raven, charcoal, sooty
FOR TIPS ON DESCRIBING COLOURS SEE
colour

2 *in a black mood*
bad-tempered, ill-humoured, angry,
foul
▌OPPOSITES bright, cheerful

blame *VERB*

*Nobody blames you for what
happened.*
hold responsible, accuse, condemn,
reproach, scold

▷ **to blame**
*Who do you think was most to
blame?*
responsible, culpable, guilty, at fault,
in the wrong

blame *NOUN*

taking the blame for the accident
responsibility, culpability, guilt, fault

bland *ADJECTIVE*

1 *a bland flavour*
mild, weak, insipid, flavourless,
tasteless
(informal) wishy-washy
▌OPPOSITES strong, pungent

2 *a bland remake of a classic film*
dull, uninteresting, unexciting,
lacklustre, monotonous, boring
▌OPPOSITES exciting, thrilling

blank *ADJECTIVE*

1 *a blank sheet of paper*
empty, bare, clean, plain, unmarked,
unused

2 *The assistant gave me a blank look.*
expressionless, vacant, stony,
impassive, deadpan

blank *NOUN*

filling in the blanks
space, break, gap

blanket *NOUN*

1 *wrapped in a woollen blanket*
cover, sheet, quilt, rug, throw

2 *a blanket of snow on the ground*
covering, layer, film, sheet, carpet,
mantle, veil

blare *VERB*

cars blaring their horns
FOR TIPS ON DESCRIBING SOUNDS SEE
sound❶

blast *NOUN*

1 *a blast of cold air*
gust, rush, draught, burst

》

a
b
c
d
e
f
g
h
i
j
k
l
m
n
o
p
q
r
s
t
u
v
w
x
y
z

2 *the blast of a toy trumpet*
blare, honk, toot

3 *Several people were injured in the blast.*
explosion, detonation, shock

blast *VERB*

1 *Dynamite was used to blast through the rock.*
explode, blow up, burst

2 *a radio blasting out music*
blare, boom

blatant *ADJECTIVE*

a blatant lie
obvious, flagrant, glaring, shameless, barefaced, brazen, unabashed

blaze *NOUN*

1 *Firefighters fought the blaze for hours.*
fire, flames, inferno, conflagration

2 *a blaze of light*
glare, burst, flare, flash

blaze *VERB*

1 *Soon the campfire was blazing.*
burn, be alight, be in flames

2 *warships with their guns blazing*
fire, shoot, blast, discharge

bleach *VERB*

In the old days, linen was bleached in the sun.
turn white, whiten, blanch, make pale

bleak *ADJECTIVE*

1 *a bleak mountainside*
bare, barren, desolate, empty, exposed, stark

2 *The future looks bleak for the club.*
gloomy, hopeless, depressing, dismal, grim, miserable
OPPOSITES bright, promising

blemish *NOUN*

a slight blemish on the surface
flaw, defect, imperfection, mark, spot, stain

blend *VERB*

1 *Blend the ingredients together.*
mix, combine, stir, whisk

2 *The colours blend well with each other.*
go together, match, fit, be compatible, harmonize, coordinate
OPPOSITE clash

blend *NOUN*

a blend of powdered spices
mixture, mix, combination, compound, amalgam, fusion

blessing *NOUN*

1 *The project has the blessing of local people.*
approval, backing, support, consent, permission
OPPOSITE disapproval

2 *The new coach has been a blessing to the club.*
benefit, advantage, asset, plus, bonus, boon, godsend
OPPOSITES curse, evil

blight *NOUN*

1 *a potato crop ruined by blight*
disease, rot

2 *Their marriage was seen as a blight on the family.*
curse, evil, plague, menace, affliction
OPPOSITES blessing, boon

blight *VERB*

an area blighted by unemployment
afflict, plague, menace, curse, ruin, spoil, mar

blind *ADJECTIVE*

Polar bear cubs are born blind.
sightless, unsighted, unseeing, visually impaired
OPPOSITES sighted, seeing

▷ **blind to**
remaining blind to the danger around them
ignorant of, unaware of, oblivious to, indifferent to, heedless of
OPPOSITES aware of, mindful of

blindly *ADVERB*

blindly following orders
mindlessly, unthinkingly,

unquestioningly, uncritically

bliss *NOUN*
> the sheer bliss of being in love
> joy, delight, pleasure, happiness,
> heaven, ecstasy
> **❙ OPPOSITE** misery

blissful *ADJECTIVE*
> a blissful week of sunshine
> joyful, delightful, pleasurable,
> heavenly, ecstatic
> **❙ OPPOSITE** miserable

bloated *ADJECTIVE*
> a pale face with bloated features
> swollen, bulging, puffy, distended,
> dilated, inflated

blob *NOUN*
> a blob of glue
> drop, lump, spot, dollop, daub,
> globule

block *NOUN*
> 1 a block of ice
> chunk, hunk, lump, piece, wedge,
> slab, brick
> 2 a block in the drainpipe
> blockage, jam, obstacle,
> obstruction, impediment

block *VERB*
> 1 A mass of leaves had blocked the
> drain.
> clog, choke, jam, plug, stop up,
> congest
> (informal) bung up
> **❙ OPPOSITE** clear
> 2 The new building will block our view.
> obstruct, interfere with, hamper,
> hinder, impede

blockage *NOUN*
> a blockage in the main pipe
> block, jam, obstruction, congestion

blond or **blonde** *ADJECTIVE*
> a blonde wig
> fair-haired, fair, golden, flaxen
> **❙ OPPOSITE** dark
> **FOR TIPS ON DESCRIBING HAIR** SEE **hair**

blood *NOUN*
> Do you have any Spanish blood?
> ancestry, family, lineage, roots

bloodshed *NOUN*
> a scene of ancient bloodshed
> killing, massacre, slaughter,
> butchery, carnage

bloodthirsty *ADJECTIVE*
> the bloodthirsty cries of an angry
> mob
> murderous, vicious, barbaric,
> savage, brutal

bloody *ADJECTIVE*
> 1 a bloody handkerchief
> bloodstained, blood-soaked, gory
> 2 the bloody battle of the Somme
> gory, bloodthirsty, brutal, barbaric,
> savage, murderous

bloom *NOUN*
> the shape of a lotus bloom
> flower, blossom, bud

bloom *VERB*
> 1 The cactus are blooming now that
> summer is here.
> blossom, flower, open
> **❙ OPPOSITES** fade, wither
> 2 New ideas began to bloom.
> develop, grow, flourish, thrive,
> burgeon

blossom *NOUN*
> cherry blossom
> blooms, buds, flowers

blossom *VERB*
> 1 The seeds we've sown will blossom
> next year.
> bloom, flower, open
> **❙ OPPOSITES** fade, wither
> 2 She has blossomed into a fine young
> actress.
> develop, grow, mature, progress,
> evolve

blot *NOUN*
> an ink blot
> spot, blotch, mark, blob, splodge,
> smudge, smear, stain

a
b
c
d
e
f
g
h
i
j
k
l
m
n
o
p
q
r
s
t
u
v
w
x
y
z

blot VERB

▷ **blot out**

1 *A huge cloud of ash blotted out the sun.*
obscure, obliterate, block out, hide, mask, conceal

2 *trying to blot out the memory of the accident*
erase, delete, wipe out, eradicate

blotch NOUN

blotches of lichen on a wall
patch, blot, spot, mark, blob, splodge, splash, stain

blow VERB

1 *a wind blowing from the east*
blast, gust, bluster, puff, fan

2 *leaves blowing across the road*
drift, flutter, waft, float, glide, whirl, swirl

3 *The wind nearly blew my hat off.*
sweep, force, drive, carry, toss

4 *a car blowing its horn*
sound, play, blast, honk, hoot

5 *(informal) I think I've blown my chance of being in the team.*
ruin, wreck, spoil, mess up, dash, scotch
(informal) scupper

▷ **blow out**

blowing out a match
extinguish, put out, snuff

▷ **blow over**

The storm will soon blow over.
die down, abate, subside, ease off, let up

▷ **blow up**

watching fireworks blow up in the sky
explode, go off, detonate, ignite

▷ **blow something up**

1 *blowing up a tyre*
inflate, pump up, swell, fill out, expand

2 *Guy Fawkes planned to blow up Parliament.*
blast, bomb, destroy

3 *blowing up a photograph*
enlarge, magnify

4 *The problem has been blown up out of all proportion.*
exaggerate, overstate

blow NOUN

1 *a blow on the head*
knock, bang, bash, hit, punch, clout, slap, smack, swipe, thump
(informal) wallop, whack

2 *Losing the match was a terrible blow.*
shock, upset, setback, disappointment, catastrophe, misfortune, disaster, calamity

blue ADJECTIVE, NOUN

 WORD WEB

some shades of blue
aquamarine, azure, baby blue, cobalt, cyan, indigo, lapis, navy, sapphire, sky blue, turquoise, ultramarine
FOR TIPS ON DESCRIBING COLOURS SEE colour

blueprint NOUN

1 *the blueprint of a building*
plan, design, sketch, diagram, layout

2 *a blueprint for tackling climate change*
model, template, pattern, guide, prototype, example

bluff VERB

Max tried to bluff his way through the interview.
deceive, trick, fake, fool, hoodwink
(informal) con, kid

blunder NOUN

I spotted a few blunders in the spelling.
mistake, error, fault, slip, slip-up, gaffe, faux pas
(informal) howler
(British informal) clanger

blunder VERB

1 *The goalkeeper blundered and let in the goal.*
make a mistake, err, miscalculate,

slip up

2 *someone blundering about in the dark*
stumble, stagger, founder, lurch

blunt *ADJECTIVE*

1 *a blunt knife*
dull, worn, unsharpened
OPPOSITES sharp, pointed

2 *a blunt reply*
plain-spoken, frank, candid, abrupt, direct, brusque, curt

blur *VERB*

eyes blurred with tears
obscure, cloud, dim, smudge, fog
OPPOSITES sharpen, focus

blurred *ADJECTIVE*

The old photo was blurred at the edges.
indistinct, hazy, fuzzy, unclear, vague, out of focus
OPPOSITES sharp, clear

blush *VERB*

Holly felt her face start to blush.
flush, redden, go red, colour, burn

blustery *ADJECTIVE*

a blustery day in autumn
gusty, windy, blowy, stormy, squally, wild
OPPOSITE calm

board *NOUN*

1 *a wooden board*
plank, panel, beam, timber

2 *a board of directors*
committee, panel, council

board *VERB*

1 *boarding an aircraft*
get on, go on board, enter, embark

2 *boarding with a host family*
lodge, stay, live, reside, be housed, be put up
(North American) room

boast *VERB*

1 *My father never boasted about his success.*
brag, show off, crow, gloat, swagger
IDIOM blow your own trumpet

2 *The film boasts an impressive cast.*
feature, possess, enjoy, pride yourself on

boastful *ADJECTIVE*

Beowulf gives a boastful account of his past deeds.
arrogant, big-headed, conceited, vain, bumptious
(informal) cocky, swanky
OPPOSITES modest, humble

boat *NOUN*

a fishing boat
ship, craft, vessel

 WORD WEB

some types of boat or ship
barge, canoe, catamaran, cruise liner, dhow, dinghy, dugout, ferry, freighter, gondola, hovercraft, hydrofoil, junk, launch, lifeboat, motor boat, oil tanker, punt, raft, rowing boat, schooner, skiff, speedboat, steamship, tanker, trawler, tug, yacht

military boats or ships
aircraft carrier, battleship, destroyer, frigate, gunboat, minesweeper, submarine, warship

some boats used in the past
brigantine, clipper, coracle, cutter, galleon, galley, man-of-war, paddle steamer, schooner, trireme, windjammer

parts of a boat or ship
boom, bridge, bulwark, cabin, crow's nest, deck, engine room, fo'c'sle or forecastle, funnel, galley, helm, hull, keel, mast, poop, porthole, propeller, quarterdeck, rigging, rudder, sail, tiller

► The front part of a boat is the **bow** or **prow**, and the back part is the **stern**.   »

a
b
c
d
e
f
g
h
i
j
k
l
m
n
o
p
q
r
s
t
u
v
w
x
y
z

a
b
c
d
e
f
g
h
i
j
k
l
m
n
o
p
q
r
s
t
u
v
w
x
y
z

▶ The left-hand side of a boat when you are facing forward is called **port** and the right-hand side is called **starboard**.

bob *VERB*
bobbing up and down in the water
bounce, toss, dance, wobble, jiggle

bodily *ADJECTIVE*
bodily exercise
physical, corporeal, corporal

body *NOUN*

 WORD WEB

outer parts of the human body
abdomen, ankle, arm, armpit, breast, buttocks, calf, cheek, chest, chin, ear, elbow, eye, finger, foot, forehead, genitals, groin, hand, head, heel, hip, instep, jaw, knee, kneecap, knuckle, leg, lip, mouth, navel, neck, nipple, nose, pores, shin, shoulder, skin, stomach, temple, thigh, throat, waist, wrist

inner parts of the human body
arteries, bladder, bowels, brain, eardrum, glands, gullet, gums, guts, heart, intestines, kidneys, larynx, liver, lungs, muscles, nerves, ovaries, pancreas, prostate, sinews, stomach, tendons, tongue, tonsils, tooth, uterus, veins, windpipe, womb

┃ SEE ALSO **digestion**

▶ The study of the human body is **anatomy**.
▶ The main part of your body except your head, arms, and legs is your **trunk** or **torso**.
▶ The shape of your body is your **build**, **figure**, or **physique**.
▶ The dead body of a person is a **corpse** or *(formal)* **cadaver** and

the dead body of an animal is a **carcass**.

FOR BONES IN YOUR BODY SEE **bone**

 WRITING TIPS

describing people's bodies

Behind him walked his opposite, a huge man, shapeless of face, with large, pale eyes, with wide, sloping shoulders; and he walked heavily, dragging his feet a little, the way a bear drags his paws.
— *John Steinbeck, Of Mice and Men*

big or strong
athletic, beefy, brawny, bulky, burly, hefty, hulking, muscular, sinewy, statuesque, tall, wiry

overweight
chubby, corpulent, dumpy, fat, flabby, heavyset, obese, plump, podgy, portly, rotund, round, stocky, stout, tubby, well-rounded

small or thin
bony, diminutive, gangling or gangly, gaunt, lanky, lean, petite, puny, scraggy, scrawny, short, skeletal, skinny, slender, slight, spindly, squat, svelte, thin, trim, weedy, willowy

bog *NOUN*
Midges thrive in bogs and wet grassland.
swamp, marsh, mire, quagmire, wetland, fen

bog *VERB*
The novel is bogged down with historical details.
overwhelm, swamp, mire, ensnare, entangle, embroil

bogus *ADJECTIVE*
a series of bogus emails
fake, fraudulent, counterfeit, spurious, sham

(informal) phoney
> **OPPOSITES** genuine, authentic

boil *VERB*

1 *Let the water boil before you add the pasta.*
bubble, simmer, seethe, steam

2 *Would you like your egg boiled or fried?*
SEE **cook**

boisterous *ADJECTIVE*

a group of boisterous sports fans
lively, high-spirited, noisy, rowdy, unruly, wild, uproarious, riotous
> **OPPOSITES** restrained, calm

bold *ADJECTIVE*

1 *a bold attempt to rescue a comrade*
brave, courageous, daring, heroic, adventurous, audacious, fearless, dauntless, valiant, intrepid, plucky, daredevil
> **OPPOSITES** timid, cowardly

2 *painted in bold colours*
striking, strong, vivid, bright, eye-catching, prominent, showy, loud, gaudy, garish
> **OPPOSITES** pale, subtle

bolster *VERB*

foods which bolster your immune system
strengthen, reinforce, boost, fortify, shore up

bolt *NOUN*

1 *held together with a metal bolt*
pin, bar, peg, rivet

2 *a bolt of lightning*
shaft, streak, flash, beam

bolt *VERB*

1 *Did you remember to bolt the door?*
fasten, bar, latch, lock, secure

2 *He saw us coming and bolted out of the shop.*
run away, dash away, dart, flee, sprint, rush off

3 *I just had time to bolt down a sandwich.*
gobble, gulp, guzzle, wolf down

(informal) scoff
> **SEE ALSO** eat

bombard *VERB*

1 *Napoleon's forces bombarded the harbour.*
shell, pound, bomb, blast, blitz

2 *The station has been bombarded with emails.*
overwhelm, besiege, inundate, swamp, flood, snow under

bond *NOUN*

1 *strengthening the bonds between our countries*
relationship, association, connection, tie, link

2 *Gulliver finds himself tied in bonds.*
rope, restraint, chain, fetter, shackle

bone *NOUN*

 WORD WEB

> *some bones in the human body*
> backbone or spine, collarbone, cranium or skull, pelvis, ribs, shoulder blade, vertebrae
> ► The bones of your body are your **skeleton**.
> ► The branch of medicine concerned with treating bones and muscles is **orthopaedics**.
> ► A practitioner who specializes in manipulating bones and muscles is an **osteopath**.

bonus *NOUN*

1 *a cash bonus*
handout, supplement, reward, gratuity, tip

2 *The climate here is certainly a bonus.*
advantage, benefit, strong point, plus, blessing
> **OPPOSITES** disadvantage, downside

bony *ADJECTIVE*

The zombies stretched their bony arms towards us.
skinny, lean, skeletal, emaciated, gaunt

a
b
c
d
e
f
g
h
i
j
k
l
m
n
o
p
q
r
s
t
u
v
w
x
y
z

book NOUN

 WORD WEB

parts of a book

appendix, binding, blurb, chapter, contents, cover, design, end pages, epilogue, illustrations, index, introduction, jacket, layout, preface, spine, title page, typeface, volume

types of book

anthology, audiobook, booklet, e-book, edition, hardback, manuscript, pamphlet, paperback, prequel, reprint, sequel, serial, trilogy

▌ SEE ALSO **fiction**

people involved in producing books

author, bookseller, co-author, designer, editor, illustrator, proofreader, reader, reviewer, typesetter

▶ The study of books and their history is **bibliography**.

▶ A person who loves or collects books is a **bibliophile**.

 WRITING TIPS

writing a book review

In my view, stories and novels consist of three parts: narration, which moves the story from point A to point B and finally to point Z; description, which creates a sensory reality for the reader; and dialogue, which brings characters to life through their speech.

— *Stephen King, On Writing*

useful words & phrases

atmosphere, bestseller, caricature, character, characterization, cliché, cliffhanger, climax, conclusion, critique, denouement, description, dialogue, excerpt, finale, genre, hero, heroine, imagery, jargon, metaphor, mood, narration, narrator, passage, pen name or nom de plume, plot, prose, protagonist, quotation, page-turner, setting, stereotype, structure, style, sub-plot, symbolism, synopsis, technique, text, theme, tone, turning point, twist, villain

adjectives

absorbing, action-packed, derivative, descriptive, edgy, engaging, far-fetched, fast-paced, fictional, fictitious, figurative, florid, flowery, gripping, hard-boiled, humorous, imaginative, lacklustre, literary, melodramatic, nail-biting, naturalistic, original, ornate, picturesque, plodding, poetic, prosaic, realistic, (*informal*) rip-roaring, sentimental, sharp, sketchy, slow-moving, spellbinding, sprawling, stilted, stylistic, surreal, symbolic, thin, thought-provoking, trite, uneven, unimaginative, unrealistic, visual, well-crafted, well-drawn, well-rounded, witty, wooden, wordy

▶ A person who writes reviews is a **reviewer** or **critic**.

▌ SEE ALSO **drama**, **fiction**

book VERB

1 *Have you booked a seat on the train?*
order, reserve

2 *I've booked the disco for the party.*
arrange, engage, organize, lay on, line up

▷ **book in**
You need to book in at the front desk.
register, check in, enrol

boom VERB

1 *A voice boomed along the corridor.*

roar, bellow, shout, blast, thunder, resound, reverberate
FOR TIPS ON DESCRIBING SOUNDS SEE **sound❶**

2 *Business was booming in the restaurant.*
flourish, thrive, prosper, do well, expand, progress

boom NOUN

1 *A loud boom shook the building.*
blast, roar, rumble, thunder, reverberation, resonance

2 *the recent boom in teenage fiction*
growth, increase, escalation, expansion, upsurge
OPPOSITE slump

boost VERB

I need something to boost my energy.
increase, enhance, improve, strengthen, bolster, help, encourage, raise, uplift
OPPOSITES lower, dampen

boost NOUN

1 *a boost in sales*
increase, growth, rise, upsurge, upturn

2 *giving your confidence a boost*
lift, uplift, encouragement, spur

boot NOUN

a pair of leather boots
FOR TIPS ON DESCRIBING CLOTHES SEE **clothes**

boot VERB

The goalkeeper booted the ball to midfield.
kick, strike, drive, propel, punt

booth NOUN

a ticket booth
kiosk, stall, stand, cubicle, cabin

border NOUN

1 *the border between France and Germany*
boundary, frontier

2 *a decorative border*
edge, margin, perimeter, rim, fringe, verge, periphery

border VERB

a meadow bordered by trees
surround, enclose, encircle, edge, fringe, bound

bore❶ VERB

boring a hole through the wall
drill, pierce, perforate, puncture, burrow, tunnel, sink

bore❷ VERB

That computer game bores me now.
weary, tire, pall on
IDIOM send you to sleep
OPPOSITE interest

bore NOUN

Filling in forms is such a bore.
bother, nuisance, pest, trial
(informal) drag, hassle
OPPOSITE interest

bored ADJECTIVE

sitting at home feeling bored
weary, uninterested
(informal) fed up

boring ADJECTIVE

The film was so boring I fell asleep.
dull, dreary, tedious, unexciting, uninteresting, dry, monotonous, uninspiring, insipid, unimaginative, uneventful, humdrum, tiresome, wearisome, mind-numbing
OPPOSITES interesting, exciting

borrow VERB

borrowing large sums of money
get on loan, lease, hire
(informal) scrounge, cadge
OPPOSITE lend

boss NOUN

the boss of a film studio
head, chief, manager, leader, director, chair, president, principal
(British informal) gaffer

bossy ADJECTIVE

The new receptionist is a bit bossy.
domineering, bullying, overbearing, officious, imperious, pushy

a
b
c
d
e
f
g
h
i
j
k
l
m
n
o
p
q
r
s
t
u
v
w
x
y
z

bother VERB

1 *Would it bother you if I played some music?*
disturb, trouble, inconvenience, annoy, irritate, pester, vex, exasperate
(informal) bug, hassle

2 *I can see that something is bothering you.*
worry, trouble, concern, perturb
▎**IDIOM** prey on your mind

3 *Bryan didn't bother to change his shirt.*
make an effort, take trouble, concern yourself, care, mind

bother NOUN

1 *I went to a lot of bother to get your present.*
trouble, fuss, effort, care

2 *It's such a bother to remember the password.*
nuisance, annoyance, irritation, inconvenience, pest, trouble, difficulty, problem
(informal) hassle, drag

bottle NOUN

Bring a bottle of water with you.
flask, flagon, jar, pitcher
▶ A bottle for serving water or wine is a **carafe** or **decanter**.
▶ A small bottle for perfume or medicine is a **phial**.

bottle VERB

▷ **bottle something up**
keeping your feelings bottled up
hold in, cover up, conceal, suppress
▎**OPPOSITES** show, express

bottom NOUN

1 *We camped at the bottom of the mountain.*
foot, base, foundation
▎**OPPOSITES** top, peak

2 *the bottom of the sea*
bed, floor
▎**OPPOSITE** surface

3 *the bottom of the garden*
end, far end, extremity

4 *sitting on your bottom*
buttocks, rear, rump, seat
(informal) behind, backside, bum

bottom ADJECTIVE

on the bottom shelf
lowest, last, bottommost
▎**OPPOSITES** top, highest

bough NOUN

the bough of a tree
branch, limb

bought PAST TENSE

SEE **buy**

bounce VERB

1 *The ball bounced twice before it reached the net.*
rebound, ricochet

2 *bouncing up and down on a trampoline*
jump, spring, leap, bound, bob, prance

bounce NOUN

1 *an awkward bounce of the ball*
rebound, ricochet, spring, leap

2 *The ball has lost its bounce.*
springiness, elasticity

3 *She came back from her holiday full of bounce.*
vitality, liveliness, vivacity, energy, vigour, spirit, sparkle
(informal) pep, zip

bound❶ VERB

Finty came bounding down the stairs.
leap, bounce, jump, spring, vault, skip, hop, prance

bound NOUN

A kangaroo can cover 10 metres in a single bound.
leap, jump, spring, vault, skip, hop

bound❷ ADJECTIVE

▷ **bound for**
a ship bound for the West Indies
going to, heading for, making for, travelling towards, off to

bound ADJECTIVE

1 *It's bound to rain at the weekend.*
certain, sure, destined, fated

2 *I felt bound to invite them to the party.*
obliged, duty-bound, committed, compelled, forced, required

bound❸ VERB

1 *a field bounded by a ditch*
enclose, surround, encircle, border, edge, hem in

2 *bounded by rules and regulations*
limit, restrict, confine, circumscribe

boundary NOUN

Some animals use scent to mark the boundary of their territory.
border, frontier, edge, end, limit, perimeter, dividing line

bounds PLURAL NOUN

beyond the bounds of our imagination
limits, boundary, perimeter, extent

bouquet NOUN

a bouquet of fresh flowers
bunch, posy, sprig, spray
▌ SEE ALSO **flower**

bout NOUN

1 *a fencing bout*
contest, match, round, fight, encounter

2 *a short bout of exercise*
period, session, spell, stint, burst

3 *recovering from a bout of flu*
attack, fit, dose, spasm

bow❶ VERB

1 *The conductor bowed to the audience.*
stoop, bend, nod

2 *The branch bowed under my weight.*
lower, bend, duck, dip, buckle

3 *bowing to pressure from the government*
give in, submit, yield, succumb, surrender

bow NOUN

with a slight bow of his head
nod, bend, lowering, dip, duck, stoop
▶ A deep bow showing respect is an **obeisance**.

bow❷ NOUN

at the bow of the ship
front, prow, nose, head
▌ SEE ALSO **boat**

bowels PLURAL NOUN

1 *food passing through your bowels*
intestines, entrails, innards
(informal) guts

2 *The path lead us down into the bowels of the cave.*
interior, inside, depths, recesses

bowl❶ NOUN

a bowl of fresh fruit
basin, dish, pot, vessel
▶ A large bowl for serving soup is a **tureen**.

bowl❷ VERB

bowling the last ball of the match
throw, pitch, fling, hurl, toss
▌ SEE ALSO **sport**

box NOUN

a box full of junk
case, chest, carton, packet, crate, trunk, casket, coffer

boxer NOUN

a heavyweight boxer
prizefighter
(formal) pugilist

boy NOUN

a boy of ten or eleven
lad, youngster, youth
(informal) kid

boyfriend NOUN

Have you met Lisa's new boyfriend?
partner, lover, sweetheart
(informal) flame

bracing ADJECTIVE

a bracing walk along the beach
refreshing, invigorating, stimulating, energizing, restorative

a
b
c
d
e
f
g
h
i
j
k
l
m
n
o
p
q
r
s
t
u
v
w
x
y
z

brag *VERB*

Riley was still bragging about the goal he scored.
boast, gloat, crow, show off
❚ **IDIOM** blow your own trumpet
► A person who is always bragging is a **braggart**.

brain *NOUN*

I racked my brain, trying to remember.
mind, reason, sense, wit, intellect, intelligence, brainpower
❚ **IDIOM** (humorous) grey matter

brainy (informal) *ADJECTIVE*

Aiden is the brainy one in the family.
clever, intelligent, smart, bright

branch *NOUN*

1 *the topmost branch of the tree*
bough, limb, arm
2 *the local branch of the Kennel Club*
section, division, department, wing

branch *VERB*

1 *Follow the road until it branches into two.*
divide, fork, split
2 *At this point, the railway branches south.*
turn, bend, veer, fork

brand *NOUN*

my favourite brand of shampoo
make, kind, sort, type, variety, label
► The sign of a particular brand of goods is a **trademark**.

brand *VERB*

1 *a letter branded on an animal*
mark, stamp, sear
2 *I didn't want to be branded as a coward.*
identify, mark out, label, stigmatize

brandish *VERB*

a mob brandishing sticks and shovels
flourish, wield, wave, flaunt

brave *ADJECTIVE*

a brave rescue attempt
courageous, heroic, valiant, bold, fearless, daring, gallant, intrepid, plucky
❚ **OPPOSITE** cowardly

bravery *NOUN*

awarded a medal for bravery
courage, heroism, valour, fearlessness, daring, nerve, gallantry, grit, pluck
(informal) guts, bottle
❚ **OPPOSITE** cowardice

brawl *NOUN*

We could hear a brawl on the street outside.
fight, quarrel, skirmish, scuffle, tussle, fracas, melee
(informal) scrap

brawny *ADJECTIVE*

a big and brawny wrestler
muscular, athletic, well built, strapping, burly, beefy, hulking
❚ **OPPOSITES** puny, scrawny
FOR TIPS ON DESCRIBING BODIES SEE body

breach *NOUN*

1 *Handling the ball is a breach of the rules.*
breaking, violation, infringement, infraction
2 *The storm caused a breach in the sea wall.*
break, rupture, split, crack, opening, fracture, fissure

breach *VERB*

1 *The website has been accused of breaching copyright.*
break, violate, infringe, contravene, flout
2 *The river breached its banks and swamped the village.*
burst, break through, rupture

breadth *NOUN*

1 *the breadth of a human hair*
width, broadness, thickness, span
2 *the breadth of human knowledge*
range, extent, scope, reach, scale

break *VERB*

1 *Break the chocolate bar into small pieces.*
divide, split, snap, crack

2 *The vase fell off the shelf and broke.*
smash, shatter, burst, fracture, crack, split, splinter, snap, chip
(informal) bust

3 *The flash on my camera has broken again.*
stop working, go wrong, malfunction, fail, crash, break down
(informal) pack in, conk out

4 *breaking the law*
disobey, contravene, violate, breach, infringe, flout

5 *I tried to break the news gently.*
tell, announce, reveal, disclose, divulge

6 *breaking the world record*
beat, better, exceed, surpass, top, outdo, outstrip

7 *No one has yet managed to break the code.*
solve, decode, decipher
(informal) crack

▷ **break down**

1 *Our car broke down on the motorway.*
stop working, go wrong, malfunction, fail, crash, break
(informal) pack in, conk out

2 *The peace talks have broken down.*
fail, fall through, collapse, founder

3 *breaking down the figures*
itemize, separate, split, divide

▷ **break in**

1 *breaking into a building*
force your way in

2 *breaking into a conversation*
interrupt, cut in, butt in
(informal) chip in

▷ **break off**

1 *breaking off for lunch*
have a rest, pause, stop

2 *breaking off communications*
end, stop, cease, terminate, call a halt to
▌IDIOM pull the plug on

▷ **break out**

A flu epidemic broke out last winter.
begin, spread, start

▷ **break out of**

breaking out of jail
escape from, break loose from, abscond from

▷ **break up**

1 *After the speeches, the crowd began to break up.*
disperse, scatter, disband

2 *The couple broke up after only two years.*
separate, split up

break *NOUN*

1 *Can you see any breaks in the chain?*
breach, crack, hole, gap, opening, split, rift, rupture, fracture, fissure

2 *making a break for freedom*
escape, dash, bid

3 *taking a break for lunch*
interval, pause, rest, lull, time-out
(informal) breather

breakable *ADJECTIVE*

Does the parcel contain anything breakable?
fragile, delicate, brittle, frail
▌OPPOSITE unbreakable

breakdown *NOUN*

1 *a breakdown in the computer network*
malfunction, failure, fault, crash

2 *a breakdown in the peace talks*
failure, collapse

3 *Can you give me a breakdown of the figures?*
analysis

break-in *NOUN*

a break-in at the local bank
burglary, robbery, theft, raid

breakthrough *NOUN*

a breakthrough in the treatment of cancer
advance, step forward, discovery, development, revolution, progress, innovation
▌OPPOSITE setback

a
b
c
d
e
f
g
h
i
j
k
l
m
n
o
p
q
r
s
t
u
v
w
x
y
z

a
b
c
d
e
f
g
h
i
j
k
l
m
n
o
p
q
r
s
t
u
v
w
x
y
z

breast NOUN

a baby at a mother's breast
bosom, bust, chest

breath NOUN

1 Take a deep breath.
inhalation
OPPOSITE exhalation

2 There wasn't a breath of wind in
the air.
breeze, puff, waft, whiff, whisper,
sigh

breathe VERB

1 breathing in and out
▶ To breathe in is to **inhale** and to
breathe out is to **exhale**.
▶ The formal word for breathing is
respiration.
▶ To breathe heavily is to **pant** or **puff**.
▶ To breathe with difficulty is to **gasp**
or **wheeze**.

2 Don't breathe a word of this to
anyone.
speak, say, relate, pass on

breathless ADJECTIVE

I was breathless after running for
the bus.
out of breath, gasping, panting,
puffing, wheezing
(informal) out of puff

breathtaking ADJECTIVE

the breathtaking view from the
summit
spectacular, stunning,
staggering, astonishing, amazing,
overwhelming, awe-inspiring,
awesome

breed VERB

1 Salmon swim upstream to breed
every year.
reproduce, have young, procreate,
multiply, spawn

2 I was born and bread in the city.
bring in, rear, raise, nurture

3 Bad hygiene breeds disease.
cause, produce, generate,
encourage, promote, cultivate,
induce

breed NOUN

1 a rare breed of cattle
variety, stock, strain
▶ The evidence of how a dog has been
bred is its **pedigree**.

2 a new breed of supercomputers
type, sort, kind, variety, class,
generation

breeze NOUN

a cool breeze from the ocean
wind, draught, gust
(poetic) zephyr
FOR TIPS ON DESCRIBING THE WEATHER
SEE **weather**

breezy ADJECTIVE

1 a bright and breezy morning
windy, blowy, blustery, gusty, fresh,
brisk

2 Dr Bell had a gruff voice and a
breezy manner.
cheerful, cheery, carefree, jaunty
(informal) upbeat

brew VERB

1 I'm just going to brew some tea.
make, prepare, infuse
▶ When you brew beer it **ferments**.

2 It looks like a storm is brewing.
develop, form, loom, build up,
gather, threaten

brew NOUN

The witches in Macbeth concoct an
evil brew.
mixture, mix, concoction, blend,
amalgam, cocktail

bridge NOUN

 WORD WEB

some types of bridge
cantilever bridge, flyover,
footbridge, pontoon bridge, rope
bridge, suspension bridge, swing
bridge
▶ A bridge to carry water is an
aqueduct and a long bridge
carrying a road or railway is a
viaduct.

brief *ADJECTIVE*

1 *a brief excursion to the shops*
short, quick, hasty, fleeting, flying, short-lived, temporary, cursory

2 *a brief account of what happened*
concise, succinct, short, abbreviated, condensed, compact, potted, pithy
⸀ **OPPOSITES** long, lengthy

bright *ADJECTIVE*

1 *a bright light*
shining, brilliant, blazing, dazzling, glaring, gleaming
⸀ **OPPOSITES** dim, weak

2 *The day was cold, but bright.*
sunny, fine, fair, clear, cloudless
⸀ **OPPOSITES** dull, cloudy, overcast

3 *a bright shade of pink*
strong, intense, vivid, vibrant, bold, lurid, garish
▶ Colours that glow in the dark are **luminous** colours.
⸀ **OPPOSITES** dull, faded, muted

4 *a bright student*
clever, intelligent, sharp, quick-witted, smart, astute
(informal) brainy
⸀ **OPPOSITES** stupid, dull-witted

5 *a bright smile*
cheerful, happy, lively, merry, jolly, radiant
⸀ **OPPOSITES** sad, gloomy

brighten *VERB*

1 *Her eyes brightened and she began to smile.*
light up, lighten

2 *some ways to brighten your day*
cheer up, enliven, perk up, brighten up

brilliant *ADJECTIVE*

1 *burning with a brilliant light*
bright, blazing, dazzling, glaring, gleaming, glittering, glorious, shining, splendid, vivid
⸀ **OPPOSITES** dim, dull

2 *Brunel was a brilliant engineer.*
clever, exceptional, outstanding, gifted, talented
⸀ **OPPOSITES** incompetent, talentless

3 *(informal) I saw a brilliant film last week.*
excellent, marvellous, outstanding, wonderful, superb
(informal) fantastic, fabulous
⸀ **SEE ALSO** good

brim *NOUN*

My glass was full to the brim.
rim, edge, brink, lip

bring *VERB*

1 *Did you remember to bring the sandwiches?*
carry, bear, deliver, transport, fetch

2 *This road will bring you to the centre of town.*
lead, conduct, escort, guide, take

3 *The drought brought famine and disease.*
cause, produce, lead to, result in, give rise to, generate, occasion

▷ **bring something about**
The friction brings about a rise in temperature.
cause, effect, create, generate, lead to

▷ **bring something off**
The author manages to bring off a surprise ending.
accomplish, carry out, pull off, achieve

▷ **bring someone up**
a story about a boy who is brought up by wolves
rear, raise, care for, foster, look after, nurture

▷ **bring something up**
I tried to bring up the subject of pocket money.
mention, raise, introduce, broach, air

brink *NOUN*

1 *We stood on the brink of a deep crater.*
edge, lip, rim, verge, brim

2 *on the brink of a great discovery*
verge, threshold, point

a
b
c
d
e
f
g
h
i
j
k
l
m
n
o
p
q
r
s
t
u
v
w
x
y
z

brisk *ADJECTIVE*

1 *The runners set off at a brisk pace.*
quick, fast, rapid, swift, energetic, invigorating, vigorous, refreshing, bracing
❙ **OPPOSITES** slow, leisurely

2 *A brisk, business-like voice answered the phone.*
curt, abrupt, blunt, short, terse, brusque

3 *The shops do a brisk trade in the summer.*
busy, lively, bustling, hectic
❙ **OPPOSITES** quiet, slack, slow

bristle *NOUN*

Shrimps have fine bristles on their legs.
hair, whisker, spine, pickle, barb, quill
▶ Short hairs that grow on a person's chin are **stubble**.

bristle *VERB*

1 *I felt the hairs bristle on the back of my neck.*
rise, stand on end

2 *Clare bristled at the idea of being left behind.*
take offence, bridle, take umbrage

3 *The new model bristles with technology.*
be full of, be packed with, overflow with

brittle *ADJECTIVE*

The mixture will become brittle as it cools.
breakable, fragile, crisp, crumbly
❙ **OPPOSITE** flexible

broach *VERB*

He seemed unwilling to broach the subject.
mention, bring up, raise, introduce, air

broad *ADJECTIVE*

1 *a broad expanse of blue sky*
wide, extensive, vast, open, large, spacious, expansive, sweeping
❙ **OPPOSITE** narrow

2 *Give me a broad outline of the plot.*
general, rough, vague, loose, indefinite, imprecise
❙ **OPPOSITES** specific, detailed

3 *She spoke with a broad Australian accent.*
strong, distinct, marked, obvious
❙ **OPPOSITE** slight

broadcast *VERB*

The concert will be broadcast live on TV.
transmit, relay, beam, air, screen, televise

broadcast *NOUN*

watching a live TV broadcast
transmission
▶ A broadcast on the Internet is a **webcast** or **podcast**.

broaden *VERB*

1 *The band are hoping to broaden their fan base.*
expand, increase, enlarge, extend, develop, diversify

2 *The river broadens as it nears the ocean.*
widen, expand, open out, spread out, stretch out

broad-minded *ADJECTIVE*

a broad-minded approach towards art
liberal, tolerant, open-minded, enlightened, permissive
❙ **OPPOSITES** narrow-minded, reactionary

brochure *NOUN*

a holiday brochure
leaflet, pamphlet, booklet, catalogue
▶ A brochure advertising a school or university is a **prospectus**.

broke *PAST TENSE*
SEE **break**

broken *ADJECTIVE*

1 *a broken vase*
smashed, shattered, cracked, splintered, in pieces, in bits

(informal) in smithereens
OPPOSITES intact, whole

2 *Which of these computers is broken?*
faulty, defective, malfunctioning, damaged, out of order
OPPOSITE working

3 *a night of broken sleep*
disturbed, interrupted, fitful, restless

4 *From that day on, he was broken in spirit.*
crushed, defeated, beaten, shattered

brood *VERB*
Are you still brooding over what I said?
worry, fret, mope, dwell on, agonize over

brother *NOUN*
an elder brother
▶ A formal name for a brother or sister is a **sibling**.
FOR OTHER MEMBERS OF A FAMILY SEE **family**

brought *PAST TENSE*
SEE **bring**

brown *ADJECTIVE, NOUN*

WORD WEB

some shades of brown
beige, bronze, buff, camel, caramel, chestnut, chocolate, coffee, dun, fawn, hazel, khaki, mahogany, russet, sandy, sepia, tan, tawny, toffee
FOR TIPS ON DESCRIBING COLOURS SEE **colour**

brown *VERB*
Brown the meat in the oven.
SEE **cook** *VERB*

browse *VERB*
1 *browsing through a magazine*
look through, leaf through, scan, skim, peruse

2 *Deer often browse on young trees.*
graze, feed

bruise *NOUN, VERB*
SEE **injury**

brush *VERB*
1 *brushing your teeth*
scrub, clean, polish

2 *brushing your hair*
groom, comb, tidy, smooth

3 *brushing the crumbs off the table*
sweep, flick

4 *Something soft brushed against my cheek.*
touch, stroke, graze, scrape, sweep

▷ **brush aside**
My question was just brushed aside.
dismiss, disregard, shrug off, make light of

▷ **brush up**
I have two weeks to brush up my French.
revise, improve, go over, refresh your memory of
(informal) mug up on
(British informal) swot up on

brutal *ADJECTIVE*
a series of brutal murders
savage, vicious, violent, cruel, barbaric, ferocious, bloodthirsty, inhuman, merciless, pitiless, ruthless, callous, sadistic
OPPOSITES gentle, humane

brutality *NOUN*
the brutality of the military regime
savagery, viciousness, violence, cruelty, barbarity, ferocity, inhumanity
OPPOSITE humanity

bubble *NOUN*
soap bubbles
lather, suds, foam, froth
▶ The bubbles in a fizzy drink are called **effervescence**.

bubble *VERB*
Heat the water until it starts to bubble.
boil, seethe, gurgle, froth, foam

a
b
c
d
e
f
g
h
i
j
k
l
m
n
o
p
q
r
s
t
u
v
w
x
y
z

bubbly *ADJECTIVE*
> **1** *a bubbly drink*
> fizzy, sparkling, effervescent, gassy, carbonated, aerated
> **2** *a bright and bubbly personality*
> cheerful, lively, vivacious, bouncy, high-spirited, spirited, animated, ebullient
> *(informal)* chirpy

bucket *NOUN*
> *a bucket and spade*
> pail, can

buckle❶ *NOUN*
> *a belt with a large silver buckle*
> clasp, fastener, fastening, clip, catch

buckle *VERB*
> *Please buckle your seat belts.*
> fasten, secure, clasp, clip, do up, hook up

buckle❷ *VERB*
> *The bridge buckled under our weight.*
> bend, warp, twist, crumple, cave in, collapse

bud *NOUN*
> *Buds are appearing on the apple trees.*
> shoot, sprout

budding *ADJECTIVE*
> *a budding actress*
> aspiring, promising, potential, would-be, up-and-coming, rising
> *(informal)* wannabe

budge *VERB*
> *The lock on the door refused to budge.*
> move, shift, give way, stir

budget *NOUN*
> *a budget of £50 to spend on clothes*
> allowance, allocation, funds, resources

budget *VERB*
> *How much have you budgeted for the holidays?*
> allocate, set aside, allow, allot, earmark

buffer *NOUN*
> *The atmosphere acts as a buffer between the Earth and the Sun.*
> barrier, cushion, bulwark, shield, guard

buffet❶ *NOUN*
> *You can buy a sandwich in the buffet.*
> cafeteria, snack bar, cafe, bar
> ⌐ SEE ALSO **restaurant**

buffet❷ *VERB*
> *a coast buffeted by strong winds*
> batter, pound, beat, lash, pummel

bug *NOUN*
> **1** *collecting bugs from the garden*
> insect, minibeast
> *(informal)* creepy-crawly
> **2** *Someone had planted a bug in the room.*
> hidden microphone, wire, tap
> **3** *a bug in a computer program*
> fault, error, defect, flaw
> *(informal)* glitch, gremlin
> **4** *(informal) a stomach bug*
> infection, virus, disease, germ, illness
> **5** *(informal) We've all caught the blogging bug.*
> enthusiasm, craze, mania, fad, obsession, fixation

bug *VERB*
> **1** *Our conversations were being bugged.*
> tap, record, monitor, intercept
> **2** *(informal) Please stop bugging me with questions.*
> bother, annoy, pester, trouble, harass

build *VERB*
> **1** *building a shed in the garden*
> construct, erect, put together, put up, set up, assemble
> **2** *building a sense of community*
> develop, grow, establish
> **3** *Traffic has been building steadily.*
> increase, accumulate, grow, build up

▷ **build up**

Pressure builds up inside the volcano.
increase, intensify, grow, rise, mount, escalate

▷ **build something up**

1 *building up your strength*
increase, improve, strengthen, develop, boost

2 *building up a collection of DVDs*
accumulate, collect, gather, amass

build *NOUN*

a woman of slender build
body, form, frame, figure, physique
FOR TIPS ON DESCRIBING BODIES SEE **body**

building *NOUN*

the tallest building in New York
construction, structure, dwelling

▶ A person who designs buildings is an **architect** and the process of designing buildings is **architecture**.

WORD WEB

some types of building
apartment block, bungalow, cabin, castle, cinema, cottage, folly, fort, hut, lighthouse, mansion, mill, observatory, palace, school, shed, skyscraper, stadium, tenement, terrace, theatre, tower, tower block, townhouse, villa
FOR RELIGIOUS BUILDINGS SEE **religion**

WRITING TIPS

describing buildings

The house was low, was once white with a deep front porch and green shutters, but had long ago darkened to the colour of the slate-grey yard around it. Rain-rotted shingles drooped over the eaves of the veranda.
— *Harper Lee, To Kill a Mockingbird*

outside features
arch, balcony, balustrade, bay window, bow window, buttress, chimney, colonnade, column, courtyard, cupola, dome, dormer window, drainpipe, eaves, foundations, gable, gutter, masonry, parapet, pediment, pillar, pipes, porch, quadrangle, roof, shutter, spire, storey, terrace, tower, turret, vault, veranda, wall, window, windowsill, wing

inside features
attic, basement, ceiling, cellar, conservatory, corridor, crypt, dungeon, foyer, gallery, garret, lobby, mezzanine, room
(old use chamber*)*, staircase, stairwell

adjectives
airy, compact, cramped, crumbling, forbidding, grand, imposing, ramshackle, rickety, ruined, run-down, solid, spacious, spartan, sprawling, squalid, stark, stately, towering, tumbledown

bulge *NOUN*

Asian elephants have two bulges on their foreheads.
bump, hump, lump, swelling, protuberance

bulge *VERB*

The Earth bulges slightly at the Equator.
stick out, swell, protrude, balloon, curve outwards

bulk *NOUN*

1 *the massive bulk of a blue whale*
size, dimensions, magnitude, mass, largeness

2 *We did the bulk of the work ourselves.*
main part, most part, majority
▍**IDIOM** the lion's share

a
b
c
d
e
f
g
h
i
j
k
l
m
n
o
p
q
r
s
t
u
v
w
x
y
z

》

OPPOSITE minority

bulky ADJECTIVE
The parcel is too bulky to post.
unwieldy, cumbersome, awkward,
unmanageable, ponderous
OPPOSITE compact
SEE ALSO big

bulletin NOUN
1 a news bulletin
report, announcement, broadcast
2 The society publishes a quarterly
bulletin.
newsletter, review, magazine,
gazette

bully NOUN
acting like a big bully
persecutor, tormentor, tyrant, thug

bully VERB
1 being bullied in the playground
persecute, intimidate, torment,
terrorize
(informal) push around
2 I felt bullied into saying yes.
pressurize, coerce, force, push,
browbeat, dragoon

bump VERB
1 bumping your head on the ceiling
hit, strike, knock, bang
2 bumping along an unpaved road
bounce, shake, jerk, jolt
▷ **bump into**
1 I nearly bumped into a lamp-post.
collide with, bang into, run into,
crash into
2 We bumped into some friends in
town.
meet, come across, run into

bump NOUN
1 We felt a bump as the plane landed.
thud, thump, bang, blow, knock
2 How did you get that bump on your
head?
lump, swelling, bulge, protuberance

bumpy ADJECTIVE
1 a bumpy road
rough, uneven, irregular, lumpy

OPPOSITES smooth, even
2 a bumpy ride in the back of a truck
bouncy, jerky, jolting, jarring, bone-
shaking, lurching, choppy

bunch NOUN
1 a bunch of keys
bundle, collection, set, cluster,
clump
2 a bunch of flowers
bouquet, posy, spray, nosegay
3 (informal) They're a friendly bunch
of people.
group, set, circle, band, gang, crowd

bundle NOUN
a bundle of old newspapers
bunch, batch, pile, stack, collection,
pack, bale

bundle VERB
1 They bundled their clothes into
blankets.
pack, tie, fasten, bind, wrap, roll,
swathe
2 The hostages were bundled into a
car.
shove, push, jostle, thrust,
manhandle

buoyant ADJECTIVE
in a buoyant mood
light-hearted, cheerful, cheery,
happy, carefree
(informal) upbeat
OPPOSITE gloomy

burden NOUN
1 carrying a heavy burden
load, weight, cargo
2 the burden of deciding what to do
responsibility, obligation, duty,
pressure, stress, trouble, worry

burden VERB
1 burdened with shopping bags
load, weigh down, encumber,
lumber
2 I won't burden you with my
problems.
bother, worry, trouble, distress,
afflict, oppress
(informal) saddle

burgeon *VERB*
> *Fox populations are burgeoning in urban areas.*
> grow, expand, increase, swell, mushroom, rocket, boom

burglar *NOUN*
> *The burglars got in through the window.*
> robber, thief, housebreaker

burglary *NOUN*
> *There have been reports of burglaries in the area.*
> robbery, theft, break-in, stealing

burly *ADJECTIVE*
> *the burly figure of a weightlifter*
> well built, strapping, sturdy, muscular, beefy

burn *VERB*
> **1** *Forest fires are burning out of control.*
> be alight, be on fire, blaze, flame, flare
> ► To burn without flames is to **glow** or **smoulder**.
> **2** *They tried to cover up by burning the evidence.*
> set fire to, incinerate, reduce to ashes
> *(informal)* torch
> ► To start something burning is to **ignite**, **kindle**, or **light** it.
> ► To burn a dead body is to **cremate** it.
> **3** *The match had burnt a hole in the carpet.*
> scorch, singe, sear, char, blacken
> ► To burn yourself with hot liquid is to **scald** yourself.
> ► To burn a mark on an animal is to **brand** it.

burning *ADJECTIVE*
> *a burning ambition to become an actor*
> strong, intense, extreme, acute, eager, fervent, passionate

burrow *NOUN*
> *a rabbit burrow*
> hole, tunnel

> ► A piece of ground with many burrows is a **warren**.
> ► A fox's burrow is called an **earth**.
> ► A badger's burrow is called an **earth** or a **sett**.

burrow *VERB*
> *Rabbits had burrowed under the fence.*
> tunnel, dig, excavate, mine, bore

burst *VERB*
> **1** *the noise of people bursting balloons*
> break, rupture, split, tear, pop
> *(informal)* bust
> **2** *A huge meteor had burst in the sky.*
> break apart, split apart, fall to pieces, rupture, explode
> **3** *Doug burst into the room without knocking.*
> charge, barge, rush, dash, hurtle, plunge

burst *NOUN*
> **1** *a burst in the front tyre*
> rupture, puncture, split, break, tear, fracture
> **2** *a burst of applause*
> outbreak, outburst, rush, wave, explosion

bury *VERB*
> **1** *They were buried in an unmarked grave.*
> inter, entomb
> ❙ **OPPOSITES** disinter, exhume, unearth
> **2** *The letter was buried under a pile of papers.*
> cover, conceal, hide, secrete

bush *NOUN*
> *a rhododendron bush*
> shrub, thicket

bushy *ADJECTIVE*
> *bushy eyebrows*
> thick, dense, hairy, shaggy, bristly

business *NOUN*
> **1** *What kind of business are you in?*
> trade, trading, commerce, industry, work, occupation

»

a
b
c
d
e
f
g
h
i
j
k
l
m
n
o
p
q
r
s
t
u
v
w
x
y
z

2 *information for small businesses*
company, firm, organization

3 *The whole business was a mystery to me.*
matter, issue, affair, point, concern, question

bustle *VERB*

The square was full of people bustling about.
rush, dash, hurry, scurry, scuttle
(informal) buzz

busy *ADJECTIVE*

1 *I've been busy all afternoon.*
occupied, engaged, employed, working, hard-pressed
(informal) hard at it
❚ **IDIOMS** up to your eyes, run off your feet
❚ **OPPOSITE** idle

2 *We've got a busy day ahead of us.*
hectic, active, full, eventful, frantic
❚ **OPPOSITES** quiet, restful

3 *The town is always busy on Saturdays.*
crowded, bustling, lively, teeming
❚ **OPPOSITES** quiet, peaceful

4 *I tried the number but it's busy.*
unavailable, engaged
❚ **OPPOSITES** available, free

but *CONJUNCTION*

It was morning but it was still dark.
however, nevertheless

but *PREPOSITION*

No one spoke but me.
except, except for, other than

butt *VERB*

The ship had to butt its way through the ice.
ram, shove, push, thrust, bump, knock

▷ **butt in**

Someone butted in with a question.
interrupt, cut in, break in
(informal) chip in
❚ **IDIOM** *(informal)* put your oar in

butterfly *NOUN*

⬡ **WORD WEB**

the life cycle of a butterfly
egg, larva or caterpillar, pupa
▶ The hard case surrounding a pupa is a **chrysalis**.
▶ The process whereby a caterpillar develops into a butterfly is **metamorphosis**.
▶ The scientific study of butterflies is **lepidoptery**.
❚ **SEE ALSO insect**

buttocks *PLURAL NOUN*

an exercise to strengthen the buttocks
rear, bottom, seat, rump
(informal) behind, backside, glutes
(humorous) posterior
(North American informal) butt

buy *VERB*

Where did you buy your trainers?
purchase, pay for, obtain, acquire
❚ **OPPOSITE** sell

buzz *NOUN*

1 *the buzz of conversation*
hum, drone
FOR TIPS ON DESCRIBING SOUNDS SEE sound❶

2 *(informal) I always get a buzz from going to the cinema.*
thrill, excitement, tingle, frisson
(informal) kick

Cc

cabin *NOUN*
1 *a log cabin*
hut, shack, shed, lodge, chalet, shelter
2 *the captain's cabin*
berth, compartment, quarters

cable *NOUN*
1 *an anchor cable*
rope, cord, line
2 *an electric cable*
flex, lead, wire, cord

cache *NOUN*
a cache of stolen goods
hoard, store, stockpile
(informal) stash

cadet *NOUN*
a cadet in the police force
recruit, trainee

cafe *NOUN*
a pavement cafe
coffee shop, cafeteria, tea-room, bistro, brasserie
❙ SEE ALSO restaurant

cage *NOUN*
a cage for a hamster
enclosure, pen, pound, hutch
▶ A large cage or enclosure for birds is an **aviary**.
▶ A cage or enclosure for poultry is a **coop**.

cage *VERB*
a prisoner caged in a cell
enclose, pen, confine, coop up

cake *ADJECTIVE*
1 *a birthday cake*
sponge, flan, gateau, pastry
2 *a cake of soap*
bar, block, tablet, slab

caked *ADJECTIVE*
boots caked with mud
coated, covered, plastered, mired, encrusted

calamity *NOUN*
The earthquake was a national calamity.
disaster, catastrophe, tragedy, misfortune, mishap, blow

calculate *VERB*
1 *calculating your carbon footprint*
compute, work out, reckon, add up, count up, tally, total
(informal) tot up
▶ To calculate something roughly is to **estimate**.
2 *The attack was calculated to cause injury.*
intend, mean, design

calendar *NOUN*
a busy social calendar
timetable, schedule, diary, agenda

call *VERB*
1 *'Stop that infernal noise!' I called.*
cry out, shout, yell, exclaim
(informal) holler
❙ SEE ALSO say
2 *I'll call you tonight.*
phone, ring, telephone, give someone a call
(informal) give someone a ring, give someone a bell
3 *The website is called 'News4U'.*
name, dub, title, entitle, term
4 *She called us all for a meeting.*
summon, send for, order
▷ **call at**
calling at the shops on the way home
visit, pay a visit to, drop in on, drop by

》

a
b
c
d
e
f
g
h
i
j
k
l
m
n
o
p
q
r
s
t
u
v
w
x
y
z

▷ **call for**

1 *This calls for a celebration.*
require, need, necessitate, justify, warrant, be grounds for

2 *calling for a ban on fireworks*
request, demand, appeal for, ask for, seek

▷ **call something off**
The race was called off at the last minute.
cancel, abandon, scrap
(informal) scrub

call *NOUN*

1 *a loud call from the kitchen*
cry, shout, yell, exclamation

2 *a quick call at the post office*
visit, stop

3 *I'll give you a call at the weekend.*
phone call
(informal) ring, buzz, bell

4 *a call for action on climate change*
demand, request, appeal, plea

5 *There's no call for that kind of language.*
need, necessity, reason, justification

callous *ADJECTIVE*
a callous and mindless attack
cold-hearted, hard-hearted, heartless, unfeeling, insensitive, unsympathetic
❙ **OPPOSITES** compassionate, kind

calm *ADJECTIVE*

1 *Please try to stay calm.*
composed, cool, level-headed, relaxed, serene, sedate, unruffled, unflustered, unperturbed, unemotional, unexcitable
❙ **OPPOSITES** anxious, nervous

2 *calm weather conditions*
still, quiet, peaceful, tranquil, windless, smooth
❙ **OPPOSITES** stormy, windy, rough

camel *NOUN*

 WORD WEB

▶ Camels, alpacas, and llamas are all types of **camelid**.

▶ A **dromedary** camel has one hump and a **bactrian** camel has two humps.

camera *NOUN*
SEE **photography**

camouflage *VERB*
We used branches to camouflage our tent.
disguise, mask, screen, cover up, conceal

camp *NOUN*

1 *a camp in the woods*
campsite, camping ground, base
▶ A military camp is an **encampment**.

2 *leaders of the two opposite camps*
faction, wing, group, lobby

campaign *NOUN*

1 *a military campaign*
operation, offensive, action, war

2 *the campaign to end child poverty*
movement, crusade, drive, fight, effort, struggle

campaign *VERB*

1 *campaigning for world peace*
fight, battle, push, lobby, agitate

2 *campaigning in an election*
canvass, electioneer

cancel *VERB*

1 *the decision to cancel the match*
call off, abandon, scrap, drop
(informal) scrub, ditch, axe
▶ To cancel something after it has already begun is to **abort** it.
▶ To put something off until later is to **postpone** it.

2 *cancelling a credit card*
invalidate, annul, revoke, rescind, retract, withdraw
❙ **OPPOSITES** validate, verify

candid ADJECTIVE
> *a candid answer*
> frank, direct, open, honest, straightforward, forthright
> *(informal)* upfront
> **OPPOSITE** guarded

candidate NOUN
> *a candidate for a job*
> applicant, contender, entrant, interviewee

canopy NOUN
> *The trees formed a canopy overhead.*
> covering, awning, shade

canyon NOUN
> *a river canyon*
> ravine, gorge, gully, valley, glen
> *(North American)* gulch

cap NOUN
> 1 *a baseball cap*
> SEE **hat**
> 2 *a twist-off cap*
> lid, top, stopper
> 3 *a cap on spending*
> limit, ceiling, check, curb

cap VERB
> 1 *a mountain capped with snow*
> top, crown, cover, tip
> 2 *The budget will be capped for two years.*
> limit, restrict, curb, control

capability NOUN
> *the capability to perform well*
> ability, capacity, power, potential, aptitude, competence, skill

capable ADJECTIVE
> *a capable student*
> competent, able, accomplished, proficient, skilful, talented, gifted
> **OPPOSITE** incompetent

capacity NOUN
> 1 *the capacity of the lecture theatre*
> size, volume, space, extent, room
> 2 *her capacity to inspire others*
> capability, ability, power, potential, aptitude, competence, skill
> 3 *in his capacity as head teacher*

position, function, role, office

cape❶ NOUN
> *a woollen cape*
> cloak, shawl, wrap, robe
> *(old use)* mantle

cape❷ NOUN
> *Gibraltar is situated on a narrow cape.*
> headland, promontory, point, head, horn, peninsula

capital NOUN
> 1 *Kingston is the capital of Jamaica.*
> capital city
> 2 *the capital to start a business*
> funds, money, finance, cash, assets, means, resources

capitalize VERB
> ▷ **capitalize on**
> *capitalizing on their recent success*
> take advantage of, profit from, make the most of, exploit

capsize VERB
> *The boat struck a rock and capsized.*
> overturn, tip over, turn over, keel over
> **IDIOM** turn turtle

capsule NOUN
> 1 *a vitamin capsule*
> pill, tablet, lozenge, pastille
> 2 *a lunar capsule*
> module, craft, pod

captain NOUN
> 1 *the ship's captain*
> commander, commanding officer, master
> *(informal)* skipper
> 2 *the team captain*
> leader, head, chief
> *(informal)* skipper

caption NOUN
> *Write a caption for the picture.*
> title, heading, legend, description

captive NOUN
> *the release of the captives*
> prisoner, convict, detainee, hostage
> ► Someone who holds a person or

a
b
c
d
e
f
g
h
i
j
k
l
m
n
o
p
q
r
s
t
u
v
w
x
y
z

animal captive is their **captor**.

captive ADJECTIVE

They were held captive for ten days.
imprisoned, captured, in captivity,
arrested, detained, jailed

❙ IDIOM behind bars

❙ OPPOSITES free, released

captivity NOUN

spending years in captivity
imprisonment, confinement,
detention, incarceration

❙ OPPOSITE freedom

capture VERB

1 *capturing a master criminal*
catch, arrest, apprehend, seize, take
prisoner
(informal) nab
(British informal) nick

2 *The city of York was captured by the
Vikings.*
occupy, seize, take, conquer

car NOUN

a fuel-efficient car
motor car, motor, vehicle
(North American) automobile

▶ An informal name for an old, noisy
car is a **banger**.

WORD WEB

some types of car
convertible, coupé, estate, four-
wheel drive or 4x4, hatchback,
limousine *(informal* limo*)*,
MPV (multi-purpose vehicle),
people carrier, racing car, saloon,
sports car, SUV (sports utility
vehicle)

▶ Very early cars are **veteran** or
vintage cars.

parts of a car
accelerator, bonnet, brake,
boot *(North American* trunk*)*,
bumper *(North American* fender*)*,
chassis, choke, clutch, doors,
engine, exhaust pipe, fuel tank,
gearbox, gear lever, handbrake,
headlamps, ignition, lights,
mirrors, mudguards, roof,
steering wheel, tyres,
undercarriage, wheels,
windscreen, windscreen wipers,
wings

❙ SEE ALSO vehicle

carcass NOUN

the carcass of an antelope
dead body, corpse, remains
(formal) cadaver

care NOUN

1 *taking care with your work*
attention, concentration,
thoroughness, thought,
meticulousness

❙ OPPOSITE carelessness

2 *choosing your words with care*
caution, discretion, thought,
consideration, regard, sensitivity

❙ OPPOSITE disregard

3 *leaving our cat in the care of a
relative*
charge, keeping, protection, safe
keeping, supervision

4 *all the cares of the world*
worry, anxiety, trouble, concern,
burden, responsibility, sorrow, stress

▷ **take care**
Please take care crossing the road.
be careful, be on your guard, look
out, watch out

▷ **take care of**
Who will take care of my plants?
care for, look after, mind, watch
over, attend to, tend

care VERB

I don't care which film we see.
mind, bother, be interested, be
bothered, be worried

▷ **care about**
caring about the planet
be concerned about, be interested
in, be worried about, be bothered
about

▷ **care for**

1 *They obviously care for each other.*
love, be fond of, cherish, adore, hold dear, dote on
⌐ IDIOM think the world of

2 *I don't really care for broccoli.*
like, be fond of, be keen on, be partial to

3 *caring for sick animals*
look after, take care of, attend to, tend, nurse

career NOUN
a career as a journalist
job, occupation, profession, trade, business, employment, calling
⌐ SEE ALSO job

carefree ADJECTIVE
spending a carefree weekend
easy-going, relaxing, untroubled, stress-free, peaceful, restful
(informal) laid-back
⌐ OPPOSITES stressful, hectic

careful ADJECTIVE

1 *keeping a careful eye on things*
attentive, cautious, watchful, alert, wary, vigilant
⌐ OPPOSITES careless, inattentive

2 *being careful with your spelling*
diligent, conscientious, thoughtful, meticulous, painstaking, thorough, precise
⌐ OPPOSITES careless, negligent

▷ **be careful**
Please be careful with those scissors.
take care, be on your guard, look out, watch out

careless ADJECTIVE

1 *a careless piece of work*
messy, untidy, thoughtless, inaccurate, slapdash, shoddy, scrappy, sloppy, slovenly, slipshod
⌐ OPPOSITES careful, thoughtful

2 *the danger of careless driving*
inattentive, thoughtless, absent-minded, heedless, irresponsible, negligent, reckless
⌐ OPPOSITES careful, attentive

caress VERB
a mother caressing her baby
stroke, touch, fondle, pet

cargo NOUN
a ship carrying cargo
goods, freight, merchandise

carnage NOUN
the carnage of the trenches
slaughter, bloodshed, massacre, bloodbath, butchery

carnival NOUN
a carnival for Mardi Gras
festival, fair, fête, gala, parade, procession, pageant

carp VERB
carping on about the good old days
complain, grumble, grouse, whine
(informal) gripe, moan
(British informal) whinge

carpenter NOUN
a carpenter's tools
woodworker, joiner, cabinetmaker

carpet NOUN
a carpet of snow
covering, blanket, mantle, expanse

carriage NOUN
SEE **vehicle**

carry VERB

1 *carrying a tray into the kitchen*
transport, convey, transfer, move, take, bring, fetch
(informal) cart, lug

2 *carrying a signal from outer space*
transmit, relay, conduct, convey, send, beam

3 *The bridge can safely carry 40 tonnes.*
bear, support, hold up

4 *Her voice carried to the back of the hall.*
be audible, be heard, reach, travel

5 *The vote was carried by a huge majority.*
approve, accept, pass, endorse, ratify

》

▷ **carry on**

We carried on in spite of the rain.
continue, go on, persevere, persist,
keep on
(informal) stick with it, stick at it

▷ **carry something out**

Did you carry out my instructions?
perform, execute, accomplish,
achieve, complete, finish

cart NOUN
SEE **vehicle**

carton NOUN

a carton of juice
box, pack, packet, package, case,
container

cartoon NOUN

1 *a cartoon of the Prime Minister*
caricature, lampoon
(informal) send-up

2 *Batman first appeared in a cartoon.*
cartoon strip, comic strip, comic,
graphic novel

3 *watching a Bugs Bunny cartoon*
animation, animated film
▎SEE ALSO **film**

carve VERB

1 *carving a statue out of marble*
sculpt, chisel, hew, shape, fashion

2 *carving your initials on a wall*
engrave, incise, score, cut

3 *carving a turkey*
cut up, slice

cascade NOUN

*the upper cascades of the Columbia
River*
torrent, waterfall

case❶ NOUN

1 *a case for a camera*
box, container, holder, covering,
casing, canister, carton, casket

2 *Put your cases on the trolley.*
suitcase, bag, trunk, valise, baggage,
luggage

case❷ NOUN

1 *a case of mistaken identity*
instance, example,

occurrence, illustration

2 *a famous murder case*
inquiry, investigation

3 *the case against animal testing*
argument, line of reasoning,
exposition, thesis

cash NOUN

1 *Can I pay by cash?*
currency, change, coins, notes

2 *plenty of cash in the bank*
money, finance, funds, resources,
wherewithal

cast VERB

1 *casting a pebble into the sea*
throw, toss, pitch, fling, sling, lob

2 *casting a dark shadow*
emit, send out, give off, shed

3 *casting a glance backwards*
direct, send, shoot

4 *a statue cast in bronze*
form, mould, shape, fashion

cast NOUN

1 *a plaster cast*
mould, form, shape, model

2 *a star-studded cast*
actors, performers, players,
company, troupe, dramatis personae

3 *The last line gives the poem a sinister
cast.*
character, aspect, feeling,
atmosphere, mood

castle NOUN

a twelfth-century Norman castle
fortress, fort, fortification, citadel,
chateau, stronghold

 WORD WEB

parts of a castle
bailey, barbican, battlements,
buttress, courtyard, donjon,
drawbridge, dungeon, gate,
gateway, keep, magazine, moat,
motte, parapet, portcullis,
postern, rampart, tower, turret,
wall, watchtower

casual *ADJECTIVE*

1 *a casual meeting*
accidental, chance, unexpected,
unintentional, unplanned
▌OPPOSITES deliberate, premeditated

2 *a casual remark*
unthinking, off-hand, unconsidered,
impromptu, throwaway
(informal) off-the-cuff
▌OPPOSITES considered, thoughtful

3 *a casual atmosphere*
easy-going, informal, relaxed
(informal) laid-back, chilled-out,
chilled
▌OPPOSITES formal, uptight

4 *casual clothing*
informal, everyday, leisure
▌OPPOSITE formal

casualty *NOUN*

reports of heavy casualties
victim, sufferer, death, loss, fatality

cat *NOUN*

a cat with long whiskers
(informal) puss, pussy cat, kitty,
moggy

 WORD WEB

some breeds of domestic cat
Abyssinian, Burmese, chinchilla,
Manx, Persian, Siamese
► A male cat is a **tom** or **tomcat**.
► A young cat is a **kitten**.
► A cat with streaks in its fur is a
tabby.
► A cat with mottled brown fur is a
tortoiseshell.
► A related adjective is **feline**.
FOR TIPS ON DESCRIBING ANIMALS
SEE **animal**

wild animals of the cat family
bobcat, cheetah, cougar, jaguar,
leopard, lion, lynx, mountain
lion, ocelot, panther, puma, tiger,
wild cat

catalogue *NOUN*

1 *a library catalogue*
list, listing, index, register, directory,
inventory, archive

2 *a mail-order catalogue*
brochure, pamphlet, leaflet

catastrophe *NOUN*

the catastrophe that befell Pompeii
disaster, calamity, tragedy,
cataclysm, debacle

catch *VERB*

1 *catching a ball*
seize, grab, grasp, grip, clutch, seize,
snatch, receive, intercept, get
▌OPPOSITES drop, miss

2 *catching fish*
hook, net, trap

3 *catching the culprits*
capture, apprehend, arrest, seize,
take prisoner
(informal) nab, collar
▌OPPOSITE release

4 *catching a cold*
contract, pick up, get, develop,
be taken ill with
(informal) go down with, come
down with

5 *being caught listening at the door*
discover, surprise, find out

6 *a foot caught in a stirrup*
get stuck, snag, jam, wedge, lodge

▷ **catch on**

1 *Do you think e-books will catch on?*
become popular, do well, succeed,
thrive, flourish
(informal) take off

2 *It took me a while to catch on.*
understand, comprehend
(informal) cotton on, latch on

catch *NOUN*

1 *a large catch of shrimp*
haul, yield, net

2 *There must be a catch somewhere.*
disadvantage, drawback, snag,
hitch, problem, trap, trick

3 *a safety catch*
fastening, latch, lock, bolt, clasp

a
b
c
d
e
f
g
h
i
j
k
l
m
n
o
p
q
r
s
t
u
v
w
x
y
z

catching *ADJECTIVE*
(informal) Chickenpox is catching.
infectious, contagious, communicable
OPPOSITE non-infectious

catchy *ADJECTIVE*
a catchy tune
memorable, unforgettable, appealing

categorical *NOUN*
a categorical denial
definite, clear, absolute, positive, unequivocal, unqualified, emphatic, out-and-out
OPPOSITES qualified, equivocal

category *NOUN*
first prize in the under-18s category
class, group, grouping, section, division, set, grade, rank

cater *VERB*
▷ **cater for**
1 *catering for the wedding guests*
cook for, provide food for, feed, serve
2 *catering for all types of user*
provide for, serve, accommodate, meet the needs of

cattle *PLURAL NOUN*
cattle grazing in a meadow
cows, herd, livestock
▶ Male cattle are **bulls**, **steers**, or **oxen**.
▶ Young male cattle are **calves** or **bullocks**.
▶ Young female cattle are **calves** or **heifers**.
▶ A related adjective is **bovine**.

caught *PAST TENSE*
SEE **catch**

cause *NOUN*
1 *the cause of the accident*
source, root, origin, starting point
2 *There is no cause for alarm.*
reason, grounds, need, justification, call
3 *raising money for a good cause*

purpose, object, aim, objective

cause *VERB*
A single spark caused the fire.
bring about, give rise to, lead to, result in, create, generate, engender, produce, prompt, induce, provoke, trigger

caution *NOUN*
1 *proceeding with caution*
care, attention, alertness, watchfulness, wariness, vigilance, discretion, prudence
2 *receiving a caution from the police*
warning, reprimand, admonishment, rebuke
(informal) telling-off

cautious *ADJECTIVE*
a cautious driver
careful, attentive, alert, watchful, wary, vigilant, prudent
OPPOSITES careless, reckless

cave *NOUN*
a limestone cave
cavern, pothole, chamber
▶ A man-made cave with decorative walls is a **grotto**.
▶ The entrance to a cave is the **mouth**.
▶ The hobby of exploring caves is **caving** or **potholing**.
▶ The scientific study of caves is **speleology**.
▶ Prehistoric people who lived in caves were **troglodytes**.

cave *VERB*
▷ **cave in**
1 *The whole roof had caved in.*
collapse, fall in
2 *caving in under pressure*
give in, yield, capitulate, surrender

cavity *NOUN*
a hidden cavity in the wall
hole, hollow, space, chamber, pocket, gap

cease *VERB*
1 *The fighting ceased at midnight.*
come to an end, end, finish, stop, halt, conclude

a
b
c
d
e
f
g
h
i
j
k
l
m
n
o
p
q
r
s
t
u
v
w
x
y
z

OPPOSITES begin, resume, continue

2 *The firm ceased trading last year.*
bring to an end, stop, discontinue, terminate, suspend, wind up

celebrate *VERB*

1 *Let's celebrate!*
enjoy yourself, have fun, have a good time
(informal) party

2 *celebrating the festival of Eid*
commemorate, observe, mark, keep, honour

celebrated *ADJECTIVE*

a celebrated novelist
famous, well-known, acclaimed, renowned, eminent, notable, prominent, esteemed, exalted, vaunted

OPPOSITES little-known, unsung

celebration *NOUN*

1 *a birthday celebration*
party, function, festivity, festival, jamboree

2 *the celebration of Thanksgiving*
commemoration, observance, marking, keeping

celebrity *NOUN*

1 *the trappings of celebrity*
fame, renown, stardom, popularity, prominence

2 *a TV celebrity*
famous person, personality, VIP, star, superstar, idol, big name
(informal) celeb

cell *NOUN*

1 *a prison cell*
room, chamber, dungeon, lock-up

2 *a terrorist cell*
group, unit, squad

cellar *NOUN*

a coal cellar
basement, vault

▶ A room underneath a church is a **crypt**.

cemetery *NOUN*

an old gravestone in the cemetery

graveyard, burial ground, churchyard

▶ A place where dead people are cremated is a **crematorium**.

▶ A large ancient burial ground is a **necropolis**.

central *ADJECTIVE*

1 *the central part of the building*
middle, core, inner, innermost, interior

OPPOSITES outer, peripheral

2 *the central characters in the novel*
main, chief, principal, major, primary, foremost, key, core, essential, vital, fundamental

OPPOSITES minor, lesser

centre *NOUN*

the centre of the labyrinth
middle, heart, core, hub

▶ The edible part in the centre of a nut is the **kernel**.

▶ The central part of an atom or cell is the **nucleus**.

▶ The centre of a storm or hurricane is the **eye**.

OPPOSITES edge, periphery

centre *VERB*

▷ **centre on**

The story centres on the quest for the Ring.

focus on, concentrate on, revolve around, be concerned with

ceramics *NOUN*

SEE **pottery**

ceremony *NOUN*

1 *an annual ceremony of remembrance*
rite, ritual, formalities, service, observance

▶ A ceremony where someone is given a special honour is an **investiture**.

▶ A ceremony to celebrate something new is an **inauguration** or **opening**.

▶ A ceremony to make a church or other building sacred is a **dedication**.

▶ A ceremony to remember a dead person or a past event is

》

a **commemoration**.

2 *a presentation made with a great deal of ceremony*
formality, pomp, pageantry, spectacle

certain *ADJECTIVE*

1 *I'm certain we'll get tickets.*
confident, convinced, positive, sure, determined
OPPOSITE uncertain

2 *certain proof of your theory*
definite, clear, convincing, absolute, unquestionable, reliable, trustworthy, undeniable, infallible, genuine, valid
OPPOSITE unreliable

3 *facing certain disaster*
inevitable, unavoidable
OPPOSITE possible

4 *certain to be a success*
bound

▷ **for certain**
I'll give you the money tomorrow for certain.
certainly, definitely, for sure, without doubt

▷ **make certain**
Please make certain that you have enough money.
make sure, ensure

certainly *ADVERB*
I'd certainly like to meet her.
definitely, undoubtedly, unquestionably, assuredly, without a doubt

certainty *NOUN*

1 *a certainty to win the election*
inevitability, foregone conclusion
(informal) sure thing, dead cert
OPPOSITE possibility

2 *answering with certainty*
confidence, conviction, assurance, sureness
OPPOSITE doubt

certificate *NOUN*
a pass certificate
diploma, document, licence,

guarantee, testimonial

chain *NOUN*

1 *holding hands to form a chain*
line, row, cordon

▶ A decorative chain of flowers or ribbons is a **festoon**.

2 *a chain of unfortunate events*
series, sequence, succession, string

chain *VERB*
Some suffragettes chained themselves to railings.
secure, fasten, tie, hitch, tether, shackle, fetter

chair *NOUN*
SEE **seat**

challenge *NOUN*

1 *Learning to swim has been a real challenge.*
test, trial

2 *Do you accept my challenge?*
dare

challenge *VERB*

1 *I challenge you not to eat chips for a week.*
dare, defy
IDIOM throw down the gauntlet to

2 *a part that will challenge any actor*
test, stretch, tax, make demands on

3 *challenging the existence of black holes*
question, dispute, call into question

challenging *ADJECTIVE*
a challenging new job
demanding, testing, taxing, exacting
OPPOSITE undemanding

champion *NOUN*

1 *the current Paralympic champion*
title-holder, prizewinner, victor, winner, conqueror
(informal) champ

2 *a champion of civil rights*
advocate, proponent, promoter, supporter, upholder, defender, backer, patron

champion *VERB*
championing the rights of children

advocate, support, promote, uphold, defend, back, espouse, stand up for

championship NOUN
a hockey championship
competition, contest, tournament

chance NOUN
1 *There's a chance of rain tomorrow.*
possibility, prospect, likelihood, probability, danger, threat, risk
OPPOSITE certainty

2 *my one big chance for fame*
opportunity, time, occasion, opening, window

3 *Are you prepared to take a chance?*
gamble, risk
(informal) punt
IDIOM leap in the dark

▷ **by chance**
We found the place purely by chance.
by accident, accidentally, unintentionally, fortuitously, by coincidence
OPPOSITE intentionally

change VERB
1 *changing all our plans*
alter, modify, rearrange, reorganize, adjust, adapt, amend, revise, transform, vary
OPPOSITES preserve, retain

2 *The town has changed since Victorian times.*
alter, become different, develop, evolve, move on, metamorphose

3 *changing places with each other*
exchange, replace, switch, substitute
(informal) swap

▷ **change into**
Tadpoles change into frogs.
become, turn into, metamorphose into, be transformed into

change NOUN
1 *a last-minute change of plan*
alteration, modification, variation, revision, amendment, adjustment, adaptation, metamorphosis

2 *a change of clothes*
exchange, replacement, switch, substitution
(informal) swap

changeable ADJECTIVE
changeable weather
variable, unsettled, unpredictable, unreliable, inconsistent, erratic, unstable
▶ If your loyalty is changeable you are **fickle**.
OPPOSITE steady

channel NOUN
1 *the English Channel*
strait, passage, sound
2 *a TV channel*
station
3 *a channel for rainwater*
duct, conduit, gutter, drain, ditch, trough, sluice

channel VERB
aid channelled through the UN
convey, transmit, relay, conduct, transfer, pass on

chaos NOUN
a scene of chaos and panic
disorder, disorganization, confusion, mayhem, turmoil, tumult, pandemonium, anarchy, lawlessness, bedlam, muddle, a shambles
OPPOSITES order, orderliness

chaotic ADJECTIVE
a chaotic mix of musical styles
disorderly, disorganized, confused, muddled, topsy-turvy, in turmoil, anarchic, unruly, riotous, lawless
(informal) shambolic
OPPOSITES orderly, organized

chapter NOUN
1 *the longest chapter in the book*
section, part, division
▶ One section of a play is an **act** or **scene**.
▶ One part of a serial is an **episode** or **instalment**.
▶ The first chapter of a book is the **opening chapter** and the last one is

a
b
c
d
e
f
g
h
i
j
k
l
m
n
o
p
q
r
s
t
u
v
w
x
y
z

the **closing chapter**.

2 *a new chapter in my life*
period, phase, stage, era, epoch

character NOUN

1 *a woman with a strong character*
personality, temperament, nature, disposition, mentality, make-up, manner, spirit, identity

2 *He's a bit of an odd character.*
person, individual, figure, personality, creature

3 *the character of Lady Macbeth*
part, role

4 *written in Chinese characters*
letter, figure, symbol, hieroglyph

characteristic NOUN

the characteristics of medieval art
feature, attribute, trait, property, quality, peculiarity, idiosyncrasy, quirk

characteristic ADJECTIVE

a characteristic feature of this area
typical, distinctive, recognizable, representative, particular, special, peculiar, idiosyncratic, singular

characterize VERB

1 *His films are characterized by nail-biting action.*
distinguish, typify, mark

2 *How would you characterize the author's style?*
portray, depict, describe, present, represent, categorize, brand

charade NOUN

The investigation was just a charade.
pretence, show, act, façade, masquerade

charge NOUN

1 *an admission charge of six euros*
price, payment, fee, rate, fare, tariff, toll, levy

2 *facing criminal charges*
accusation, allegation, indictment

3 *a cavalry charge*
attack, assault, offensive, onslaught, drive, push

4 *leaving the house in your charge*
care, keeping, protection, custody, trust

▷ **be in charge of**
Who is in charge of the catering?
manage, supervise, oversee, direct, lead, command, run
(informal) head up

charge VERB

1 *How much do you charge for lessons?*
ask for, make someone pay, invoice

2 *being charged with attempted robbery*
accuse (of), indict

3 *charging into the room unannounced*
rush, storm, barge, push, drive, stampede, go headlong

4 *I'm charging you with buying the tickets.*
entrust, give responsibility for

charismatic ADJECTIVE

a charismatic performer
charming, captivating, inspiring, compelling, magnetic, alluring

charitable ADJECTIVE

a charitable gesture
compassionate, benevolent, philanthropic, altruistic, humanitarian, unselfish, considerate, kind, caring, generous, magnanimous
OPPOSITES selfish, uncaring

charity NOUN

charity towards the poor
compassion, generosity, kindness, benevolence, consideration, caring, goodwill, altruism, philanthropy
OPPOSITE selfishness

charm NOUN

1 *the grace and charm of a romantic heroine*
appeal, attraction, charisma, allure, magnetism

2 *a magic charm*
spell, incantation, formula

3 *a lucky charm*
talisman, trinket, mascot, amulet, fetish

a b c d e f g h i j k l m n o p q r s t u v w x y z

charm VERB

She charmed the audience with her humour and wit.
delight, please, captivate, enchant, entrance, fascinate, beguile, bewitch, win over

charming ADJECTIVE

a charming film about friendship and adolescence
delightful, endearing, appealing, likeable, pleasing, attractive, captivating

chart NOUN

1 *a chart of the Pacific*
map
2 *a chart showing average rainfall*
diagram, graph, table

chart VERB

a TV series charting the rise of ancient Rome
follow, track, trace, map, outline, record, document

charter NOUN

the UN charter on human rights
constitution, treaty, code, agreement

charter VERB

chartering a minibus for our trip
hire, lease, rent

chase VERB

I dreamt I was being chased by a werewolf.
pursue, run after, follow, track, trail, hunt

▷ **chase something away**
1 *a candle to chase away midges*
drive away, drive off, scare off
(informal) send packing
2 *music to chase away the blues*
drive out, dispel, dismiss, banish, put out of your mind

chase NOUN

a high-speed car chase
pursuit, hunt, trail

chasm NOUN

a deep chasm in the hillside
opening, gulf, fissure, rift, ravine, crevasse, canyon, gorge, pit, abyss

chat NOUN

Do you have time for a quick chat?
talk, conversation, gossip
(informal) confab
(British informal) natter, chinwag

chat VERB

chatting on the phone
talk, converse, gossip
(British informal) natter, have a chinwag

chatter VERB

1 *chattering on about his favourite subject*
prattle, babble
(British informal) natter, rabbit on
2 *teeth chattering with the cold*
rattle, jangle

chatter NOUN

I don't engage in idle chatter.
prattle, babble
(informal) chit-chat
(British informal) nattering

chatty ADJECTIVE

a chatty neighbour
talkative, communicative, loquacious, garrulous, gossipy
(informal) mouthy
❙ OPPOSITES uncommunicative, taciturn

cheap ADJECTIVE

1 *a cheap flight to Paris*
inexpensive, low-priced, low-cost, affordable, reasonable, economical, budget, bargain, cut-price, discount
2 *a cheap plastic interior*
inferior, poor-quality, second-rate, substandard, shoddy, trashy
(informal) rubbishy, cheapo, tacky
❙ OPPOSITES superior, good-quality

cheat VERB

The bank is accused of cheating its customers.
deceive, defraud, trick, swindle, dupe, double-cross, hoodwink
(informal) con, diddle, fleece,

rip off, sucker

cheat NOUN

calling the umpire a cheat
cheater, swindler, fraudster,
fraud, charlatan, double-crosser,
confidence trickster
(informal) con artist

check VERB

1 *Remember to check your spelling.*
examine, inspect, look over,
scrutinize

┃ **IDIOM** *(informal)* give the once-over

2 *checking that the door is locked*
make sure, confirm, verify

3 *Fire-breaks are used to check the
spread of forest fires.*
halt, stop, arrest, block, obstruct,
curb, hold back, hamper, hinder,
slow, slow down

check NOUN

1 *running some checks on my computer*
test, examination, inspection,
check-up, study, scrutiny, perusal

2 *Parliament acts as a check on the
power of the sovereign.*
control, curb, limitation, restraint,
restriction, constraint

cheeky ADJECTIVE

*My little sister has a cheeky answer
for everything!*
impudent, impertinent, insolent,
disrespectful, rude, irreverent,
flippant
(informal) brass-necked, lippy, fresh
(North American informal) sassy

┃ **OPPOSITE** respectful

cheer NOUN

a loud cheer from the crowd
applause, ovation, hurray, hurrah,
whoop

cheer VERB

1 *cheering the team from the sidelines*
applaud, clap, shout, yell

┃ **OPPOSITES** jeer, boo

2 *Even the sunshine failed to cheer me.*
SEE **cheer up**

▷ **cheer up**
*Everyone had cheered up by the
afternoon.*
brighten up, perk up, rally, revive,
take heart, bounce back
(informal) buck up

▷ **cheer someone up**
What can I do to cheer you up?
raise your spirits, brighten, hearten,
gladden, uplift, buoy up, perk up
(informal) buck up

┃ **OPPOSITES** sadden, depress

cheerful ADJECTIVE

1 *Gemma arrived in a cheerful mood.*
happy, good-humoured,
light-hearted, cheery, merry, jolly,
joyful, bright, sunny, chirpy, perky,
lively, animated, elated, buoyant,
jovial, gleeful
(informal) upbeat

┃ **IDIOM** *(informal)* full of beans
┃ **OPPOSITES** sad, gloomy

2 *a sunny and cheerful room*
pleasant, agreeable, attractive,
bright, welcoming, friendly

┃ **OPPOSITES** dark, dismal

cheerless ADJECTIVE

a cheerless empty house
dreary, gloomy, dismal, bleak,
mirthless, joyless

chemist NOUN

an all-night chemist
pharmacist
(old use) apothecary, alchemist

▶ A chemist's shop is a **dispensary** or
pharmacy.

cherish VERB

1 *a gift to cherish forever*
treasure, prize, value, hold dear, care
for, keep safe

2 *We have lost a dear and cherished
friend.*
love, adore, dote on, be devoted to,
revere

┃ **IDIOM** think the world of

chess NOUN

WORD WEB

names of chess pieces
bishop, castle or rook, king,
knight, pawn, queen

other terms used in chess
castling, check, checkmate,
chessboard, endgame, gambit,
grandmaster, mate, move,
opening, queening, sacrifice,
stalemate, tournament

chest NOUN

1 *a pain in your chest*
breast, torso, front

2 *a chest full of old clothes*
box, crate, case, trunk, casket, coffer

chew VERB

chewing a piece of gum
munch, gnaw, chomp
(*formal*) masticate
SEE ALSO eat

chic ADJECTIVE

a chic new outfit
stylish, elegant, sophisticated,
smart, fashionable
(*informal*) swish

chicken NOUN

free-range chickens
▶ A female chicken is a **hen**.
▶ A male chicken is a **rooster** or **cock**.
▶ A young chicken is a **chick**.
▶ A group of chickens is a **brood**.
▶ A farm which keeps chickens is a
poultry farm.

chief NOUN

1 *Sitting Bull was chief of the Lakota.*
leader, ruler, commander, captain,
chieftain, master

2 *the chief of NASA*
head, chief executive, director,
president, governor, principal, CEO
(*informal*) boss

chief ADJECTIVE

1 *The chief ingredients are butter*
and icing sugar.
main, principal, primary, prime,
major, foremost, key, central,
basic, essential, vital, fundamental,
predominant, prominent
▶ A chief rival or enemy is an **arch
rival** or **arch enemy**.
OPPOSITES minor, secondary

2 *the chief editor of the magazine*
head, senior, top, leading, principal,
premier, supreme, highest
OPPOSITE subordinate

chiefly ADVERB

*Kangaroos are found chiefly in
Australia.*
mainly, mostly, primarily, principally,
predominantly, generally, usually,
typically, in the main, on the whole

child NOUN

1 *a book which appeals to children of
all ages*
boy or girl, infant, juvenile,
youngster, youth, lad or lass
(*informal*) kid, tot, nipper

2 *How many children do you have?*
son or daughter, descendant,
offspring
▶ A child whose parents are dead is an
orphan.
▶ A child looked after by a guardian is
a **ward**.
SEE ALSO baby

childhood NOUN

Neil spent his childhood by the sea.
boyhood or girlhood, youth, early
life, infancy
▶ The time when someone is a baby is
their **babyhood**.
▶ The time when someone is a
teenager is their **adolescence** or
teens.
OPPOSITE adulthood

childish ADJECTIVE

*a childish obsession with
anything pink*
immature, babyish, juvenile,
infantile, puerile
OPPOSITE mature

a
b
c
d
e
f
g
h
i
j
k
l
m
n
o
p
q
r
s
t
u
v
w
x
y
z

chill NOUN

1 *feeling a chill in the air*
coldness, chilliness, coolness, nip

2 *Watch you don't catch a chill.*
cold, fever

chill VERB

1 *Chill the pudding before serving it.*
cool, refrigerate, freeze
OPPOSITES warm, heat

2 *The look in his eyes chilled me to my core.*
frighten, scare, terrify, petrify
IDIOMS make your blood run cold, give you goosebumps

▷ **chill out**
(informal) chilling out at the weekend
relax, unwind, take it easy
(informal) chill
IDIOM put your feet up

chilly ADJECTIVE

1 *a chilly evening*
cold, cool, frosty, icy, crisp, fresh, raw, wintry
(informal) nippy
OPPOSITE warm

2 *They gave us a very chilly reception.*
unfriendly, unwelcoming, cold, cool, frosty
OPPOSITES friendly, warm

chime VERB

The hall clock chimes every hour.
ring, sound, strike, peal, toll

chimney NOUN

smoke from a chimney
▶ A chimney on a ship or steam engine is a **funnel**.
▶ A pipe to take away smoke and fumes is a **flue**.

chin NOUN

FOR TIPS ON DESCRIBING FACES SEE **face** NOUN

china NOUN

pieces of broken china
crockery, dishes, plates, tableware, cups and saucers, porcelain

chink NOUN

1 *a chink in the wall*
gap, space, crack, crevice, hole, opening, aperture, fissure, split, slit, rift, cleft

2 *the chink of glass bottles*
clink, jingle, jangle, tinkle
FOR TIPS ON DESCRIBING SOUNDS SEE **sound❶**

chip NOUN

1 *chips of broken glass*
bit, piece, fragment, scrap, sliver, splinter, flake, shaving
SEE ALSO bit

2 *This teapot has a chip on the lid.*
crack, nick, notch, flaw

chip VERB

1 *Someone has chipped my favourite mug.*
crack, nick, notch

2 *chipping away at the paintwork*
cut, hack, chisel, carve, whittle

choice NOUN

1 *I'm afraid you have no choice.*
alternative, option

2 *a good choice of DVDs*
range, selection, variety, assortment, array

3 *your own choice of music*
selection, preference, choosing, pick

choice ADJECTIVE

We use only choice ingredients.
superior, first-class, first-rate, top-quality, best, finest, prime, premier, select, prize
(informal) top-notch
OPPOSITES inferior, second-rate

choke VERB

1 *being choked by fumes*
suffocate, smother, stifle, asphyxiate, throttle

2 *choking on a fish bone*
gag, cough, retch

3 *a drain choked with leaves*
block, clog, obstruct, congest, bung up, stop up

choose *VERB*

  1 *choosing this year's winner*
  select, decide on, pick out, opt for,
  plump for, settle on, vote for, elect

  2 *I would never chose to live there.*
  decide, determine, prefer, resolve

chop *VERB*

  chopping wood for the fire
  cut, split, hew, hack, slash, cleave

  ▶ To chop down a tree is to **fell** it.

  ▷ **chop something off**
  chopping off the lower branches
  cut off, lop off, sever, shear, truncate

  ▶ To chop off an arm or leg is to
  amputate it.

  ▷ **chop something up**
  chopping up some vegetables
  cut up, cube, dice, mince

choppy *ADJECTIVE*

  The sea had grown choppy.
  rough, turbulent, stormy, squally,
  tempestuous

chronicle *NOUN*

  a chronicle of her early life
  story, history, narrative, account,
  record, journal, annals, saga

chubby *ADJECTIVE*

  SEE **fat**

chuck (*informal*) *VERB*

  1 *chucking your bag on the floor*
  throw, fling, sling, toss, hurl,
  pitch, cast
  (*informal*) bung, dump

  2 *chucking a bad habit*
  give up, drop, discard, abandon,
  reject
  (*informal*) quit, pack in

chuckle *VERB*

  chuckling at a funny story
  laugh, giggle, snigger, chortle, titter

chunk *NOUN*

  biting a chunk out of an apple
  piece, portion, lump, block, hunk,
  slab, wedge
  (*informal*) wodge

church *NOUN*

  an old parish church
  chapel, cathedral, minster, abbey
  FOR OTHER RELIGIOUS BUILDINGS SEE
  religion

churn *VERB*

  a paddle steamer churning the water
  agitate, disturb, stir up, beat

circle *NOUN*

  1 *We arranged the chairs in a circle.*
  ring, round, hoop, loop, band, circlet

  ▶ A flat, solid circle is a **disc**.

  ▶ A three-dimensional round shape is
  a **sphere**.

  ▶ An egg shape is an **oval** or **ellipse**.

  ▶ The distance round a circle is the
  circumference.

  ▶ The distance across a circle is the
  diameter.

  ▶ The distance from the centre to the
  circumference is the **radius**.

  ▶ A circular movement is a **revolution**
  or **rotation**.

  ▶ A circular trip round the world is a
  circumnavigation.

  ▶ A circular trip of a satellite round a
  planet is an **orbit**.

  2 *Erin has a wide circle of friends.*
  group, set, crowd
  (*informal*) gang, bunch

  ▶ A small group of friends who keep
  others out is a **clique** or **coterie**.

circle *VERB*

  Vultures were circling overhead.
  go round, wheel, revolve, rotate,
  whirl, spiral

  ▶ To sail completely round something
  is to **circumnavigate** it.

circuit *NOUN*

  a single circuit of the race track
  lap, round, circle, revolution, orbit

circular *ADJECTIVE*

  Most of Saturn's rings are circular.
  round, ring-shaped, disc-shaped

circulate *VERB*

  1 *blood circulating in your veins*
  pass round, move round

》

a
b
c
d
e
f
g
h
i
j
k
l
m
n
o
p
q
r
s
t
u
v
w
x
y
z

2 *circulating the latest news*
distribute, send round, broadcast, communicate, publicize, disseminate

circumference NOUN

the circumference of a pond
perimeter, border, boundary, edge, rim

circumstances PLURAL NOUN

the circumstances surrounding the murder
situation, conditions, background, context, state of affairs, factors, particulars, details
▌ IDIOM lie of the land

citizen NOUN

1 *the citizens of Beijing*
resident, inhabitant, city-dweller, townsman or townswoman
(formal) denizen

2 *an Australian citizen*
national, passport holder, subject

city NOUN

the city of Nairobi
▶ The chief city of a country or region is the **metropolis**.
▶ An area of houses outside the central part of a city is the **suburbs**.
▶ Related adjectives are **urban**, **municipal**, and **metropolitan**.
▌ SEE ALSO **town**

civil ADJECTIVE

1 *Please try to be civil.*
polite, courteous, well-behaved, well-mannered
▌ OPPOSITES uncivil, rude

2 *civil aircraft*
civilian, non-military
▌ OPPOSITE military

civilization NOUN

1 *the civilization of ancient Egypt*
culture, society, way of life

2 *reaching a certain level of civilization*
development, progress, advancement, enlightenment, sophistication, refinement

civilized ADJECTIVE

behaving in a civilized manner
polite, courteous, well-behaved, well-mannered, civil, sophisticated, cultured, polished, refined
▌ OPPOSITES uncivilized, rude

claim VERB

1 *claiming a refund for your ticket*
ask for, apply for, request, demand

2 *He claims that he can speak Russian.*
declare, assert, allege, maintain, contend, argue, insist

clamour NOUN

the rising clamour of angry voices
noise, din, racket, uproar, commotion, rumpus, hubbub

clamp VERB

The rack is clamped onto the car roof.
fasten, attach, fix, secure, screw, bolt

clap VERB

1 *clapping loudly at the end of the concert*
applaud, cheer, give a round of applause
▌ IDIOMS give a big hand (to), put your hands together (for)

2 *Suddenly, a hand clapped me on the shoulder.*
slap, hit, pat, smack

clarify VERB

Can you clarify the situation for me?
explain, make clear, elucidate, illuminate
▌ IDIOMS throw light on, spell out
▌ OPPOSITE confuse

clarity NOUN

1 *I was impressed by the clarity of the image.*
sharpness, clearness, crispness, definition

2 *explaining everything with absolute clarity*
clearness, coherence, lucidity, transparency, precision
▌ OPPOSITE confusion

clash *VERB*

1 *cymbals clashing*
crash, resound

2 *Demonstrators clashed with the police.*
argue, fight, contend, squabble
❙ **IDIOMS** come to blows, lock horns

3 *Do these colours clash?*
conflict, jar, be incompatible
❙ **IDIOM** be at odds
❙ **OPPOSITES** harmonize, go together

clash *NOUN*

1 *the clash of cymbals*
crash, bang, ringing

2 *a clash between rival supporters*
fight, confrontation, argument, conflict, scuffle
(informal) scrap

clasp *NOUN*

1 *an ornamental hair clasp*
clip, pin, fastener, brooch, buckle

2 *in the clasp of my arms*
grasp, grip, hold, embrace

clasp *VERB*

clasping the baby in her arms
grasp, grip, hold, embrace

class *NOUN*

1 *There are 24 children in our class.*
form, set, stream
▶ The other pupils in your class are your **classmates**.

2 *the discovery of a new class of planets*
category, group, classification, division, grade, set, sort, type, kind, species

3 *people from different social classes*
level, rank, status, stratum, echelon

class *VERB*

Our books are classed according to size.
classify, categorize, group, rank, grade, designate

classic *ADJECTIVE*

1 *That was a classic tennis final this year.*
outstanding, exceptional, excellent, first-class, first-rate, fine, great, admirable, masterly
(informal) top-notch
❙ **OPPOSITES** ordinary, second-rate

2 *a classic example of Dutch painting*
typical, representative, characteristic, perfect, textbook, model, archetypal, quintessential
❙ **OPPOSITE** atypical

> ### Usage Note
>
> The words **classic** and **classical** are not synonyms. A *classical concert* is a concert of classical music; but a *classic concert* is an outstanding concert of any style.

classify *VERB*

All living things can be classified into species.
categorize, class, group, grade, rank, sort, order, bracket
▶ The science of classifying and naming species is **taxonomy**.

claw *NOUN*

1 *the claws of a wild animal*
talon, nail

2 *a lobster claw*
pincer

claw *VERB*

The tree had been clawed by a grizzly bear.
scratch, scrape, tear, rip, lacerate

clean *ADJECTIVE*

1 *a clean pair of socks*
washed, cleaned, laundered, scrubbed, swept, tidy, immaculate, spotless, unstained, unsullied, hygienic, sanitary
❙ **OPPOSITE** dirty

2 *keeping a wound clean*
sterile, sterilized, disinfected, uninfected
❙ **OPPOSITES** infected, septic

3 *the clean air of the mountains*
pure, clear, fresh, unpolluted, uncontaminated

»

a
b
c
d
e
f
g
h
i
j
k
l
m
n
o
p
q
r
s
t
u
v
w
x
y
z

OPPOSITES polluted, contaminated

4 *a clean sheet of paper*
blank, unused, unmarked, empty, bare, fresh, new, pristine
OPPOSITES used, marked

5 *Keep the fight clean.*
fair, honest, honourable, sporting, sportsmanlike
OPPOSITE unfair

clean VERB

1 *cleaning the house from top to bottom*
wash, wipe, mop, swab, sponge, scour, scrub, dust, sweep, vacuum, shampoo, swill
▶ To clean clothes is to **launder** them.
OPPOSITES dirty, mess up

2 *cleaning a wound with antiseptic*
cleanse, bathe, disinfect, sterilize, sanitize
OPPOSITES infect, contaminate

cleanse VERB

1 *cleansing a wound*
clean, bathe, rinse, disinfect, sterilize, sanitize
OPPOSITES infect, contaminate

2 *cleansing the air in the house*
purify, clear, refine, filter, purge

clear ADJECTIVE

1 *a clear mountain stream*
clean, pure, transparent, translucent
OPPOSITES opaque, muddy

2 *a beautiful clear day*
bright, sunny, cloudless, unclouded
▶ A clear night is a **moonlit** or **starlit** night.
OPPOSITES cloudy, overcast

3 *The address on the envelope is not clear.*
legible, recognizable, visible
OPPOSITE illegible

4 *Your camera takes very clear pictures.*
sharp, well defined, focused
OPPOSITE blurred

5 *speaking in a clear voice*
distinct, audible
OPPOSITES indistinct, muffled

6 *giving clear instructions*
understandable, intelligible, comprehensible, lucid, coherent, plain, explicit, straightforward, unambiguous
OPPOSITES ambiguous, confusing

7 *a clear case of plagiarism*
definite, unambiguous, indisputable, incontrovertible, unmistakable, evident, obvious, patent, manifest, noticeable, distinct, overt, conspicuous, perceptible, pronounced, glaring
OPPOSITE imperceptible

8 *Is the road clear ahead?*
open, unobstructed, passable, empty, free
OPPOSITES blocked, obstructed

9 *a clear conscience*
innocent, untroubled, blameless
OPPOSITE guilty

clear VERB

1 *clearing the weeds from the path*
get rid of, remove, eliminate, strip

2 *clearing a blocked drain*
unblock, unclog, unstop, open up
▶ To clear a channel is to **dredge** it.

3 *Clear the building by the nearest exit.*
evacuate, empty

4 *The fog cleared slowly.*
disappear, go away, vanish, evaporate, disperse, dissipate, shift, lift, melt away, fade

5 *He was cleared of all the charges against him.*
acquit, free, absolve, exonerate *(informal)* let off

6 *The runners cleared the first hurdle.*
go over, get over, jump over, pass over, vault

▷ **clear up**

1 *The weather should clear up by the afternoon.*
become clear, brighten, fair up

2 *The symptoms often clear up by themselves.*
heal, get better, recover, mend

▷ **clear something up**

1 *I'll clear up the mess later.*
clean up, tidy up, put right, put straight, put in order

2 *clearing up the mystery of her disappearance*
explain, answer, solve, resolve
▐ **IDIOM** get to the bottom of

clearly ADVERB

1 *Speak slowly and clearly.*
distinctly, plainly, intelligibly, audibly, legibly

2 *Clearly, we need to talk.*
obviously, evidently, plainly, patently, undoubtedly, unquestionably, without question

cleft NOUN

a cleft in the rock face
crack, split, fissure, crevice

clench VERB

1 *clenching your teeth*
close tightly, squeeze together, grit, clamp

2 *clenching an umbrella in her hand*
grip, clasp, grasp, hold

clergyman or clergywoman NOUN
SEE **religion**

clever ADJECTIVE

1 *an exceptionally clever student*
intelligent, bright, smart, quick-witted, astute, able, capable, competent, gifted, talented
(informal) brainy
▐ **OPPOSITE** unintelligent

2 *a clever scheme to make money*
ingenious, crafty, cunning, canny, shrewd, artful, wily
▐ **OPPOSITE** stupid

3 *Jean has always been clever with her hands.*
skilful, dexterous, adroit, nimble, deft, adept, handy
▐ **OPPOSITES** unskilful, clumsy

cliché NOUN

Saying 'have a nice day' is such a cliché.
stock phrase, banality, platitude, truism

click NOUN, VERB

FOR TIPS ON DESCRIBING SOUNDS SEE **sound❶**

client NOUN

The firm has a number of overseas clients.
customer, user, consumer, buyer, shopper

cliff NOUN

a village perched on the top of a cliff
crag, rock face, precipice, ridge, bluff, escarpment, scar

climate NOUN

1 *the effects of pollution on our climate*
weather conditions, weather patterns

▶ The scientific study of the Earth's climate is **climatology**.
▐ **SEE ALSO weather**

2 *the current economic climate*
situation, environment, conditions, atmosphere, ethos

climax NOUN

The climax of the film is a stunning car chase.
high point, highlight, height, culmination, peak, pinnacle
▐ **OPPOSITE** anticlimax

climb VERB

1 *climbing a steep hill*
ascend, go up, scale, mount, clamber up
▐ **OPPOSITE** descend

2 *We watched the balloons climb into the sky.*
rise, soar, ascend, mount, rocket

3 *The road climbs steeply up to the village.*
go uphill, rise, slope, incline

》

a
b
c
d
e
f
g
h
i
j
k
l
m
n
o
p
q
r
s
t
u
v
w
x
y
z

▷ **climb down**

1 *climbing down from the summit*
descend, go down

2 *You'll never get him to climb down.*
back down, give in, surrender, admit
defeat

IDIOMS eat your words, do a U-turn

climb NOUN

*It's a steep climb to the cave
entrance.*
ascent, rise, slope, gradient, incline

clinch VERB

*A late goal clinched the victory for
the home team.*
secure, seal, settle, decide, confirm,
conclude, finalize, close
(informal) sew up

cling VERB

1 *a rider clinging tightly to the reins*
clasp, clutch, grasp, hold on

2 *limpets clinging to the rocks*
stick, adhere

clip❶ NOUN

a hair clip
pin, clasp, fastener, hook, catch

clip VERB

The two sheets were clipped together.
pin, staple, fasten, attach, tack

clip❷ VERB

1 *clipping a hedge*
cut, trim, prune, crop

2 *The back wheel just clipped the kerb.*
hit, strike, scrape, nudge

clip NOUN

showing a clip from the new film
extract, excerpt, snippet, trailer

cloak NOUN

*wearing a long cloak, like a
highwayman*
cape, coat, wrap
(old use) mantle

cloak VERB

a night cloaked in darkness
cover, envelop, swathe, surround,
shroud, veil, cloud, obscure, conceal,
mask

clock NOUN

 WORD WEB

parts of a clock or watch
dial, escapement, face,
pendulum, spring

*instruments used to measure
time*
atomic clock, chronograph,
cuckoo clock, digital clock,
hourglass, pocket watch, quartz
clock, stopwatch, sundial, water
clock or hydrochronometer,
wristwatch

▶ The study of clocks and
timekeeping is **horology**.

▶ A person who makes clocks or
watches is a **clockmaker** or
watchmaker.

clog VERB

dead leaves clogging the drain
block, choke, congest, obstruct,
bung up, stop up, jam, plug

close ADJECTIVE

1 *Our house is close to the shops.*
near, nearby, not far (from)

▶ To be actually by the side of
something is to be **adjacent**.
OPPOSITES far, distant

2 *Catriona and I are close friends.*
intimate, dear, devoted, firm,
faithful, inseparable, bosom,
close-knit
OPPOSITES distant, casual

3 *a close examination of the evidence*
careful, detailed, thorough,
painstaking, minute, meticulous,
rigorous
OPPOSITES casual, cursory

4 *a man bearing a close resemblance to
the prime minister*
strong, firm, distinct, marked,
noticeable, unmistakable
OPPOSITES slight, passing

a
b
c
d
e
f
g
h
i
j
k
l
m
n
o
p
q
r
s
t
u
v
w
x
y
z

5 *a very close race*
equal, even, level, well-matched

⎹ **IDIOM** neck and neck

⎹ **OPPOSITE** one-sided

6 *The air is very close in this room.*
humid, muggy, stuffy, clammy, heavy, airless, stifling, sticky, sultry

⎹ **OPPOSITES** fresh, airy

close VERB

1 *Don't forget to close the lid.*
shut, fasten, seal, secure

2 *The road is now closed to traffic.*
block, seal off, barricade, obstruct

3 *They closed the concert with my favourite song.*
finish, end, conclude, stop, terminate, complete
(informal) wind up

close NOUN

What was the score at the close of play?
finish, end, stop, conclusion, termination, completion

clot VERB

Blood will clot when exposed to the air.
coagulate, solidify, thicken, congeal

cloth NOUN

1 *fine woollen cloth*
fabric, material, textile
FOR TYPES OF CLOTH SEE fabric

2 *a cloth to wipe the windows*
rag, duster, flannel, wipe
(Australian) washer

clothe VERB

▷ **be clothed in**
The bridesmaids were clothed in white.
be dressed in, be wearing, be clad in, be decked in, be fitted out in

clothes PLURAL NOUN

What clothes are you taking on holiday?
clothing, garments, outfits, dress, attire, garb, finery
(informal) gear, get-up, togs
(old use) raiment

▶ A set of clothes to wear is a **costume**, **outfit**, or **suit**.

▶ An official set of clothes worn for school or work is a **uniform**.

▶ A collection of clothes or costumes is a **wardrobe**.

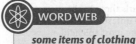 **WORD WEB**

some items of clothing
anorak, apron, ball gown, bandanna, bikini, blazer, blouse, bow tie, boxer shorts *(informal* boxers*)*, bra, briefs, cagoule *(North American* windbreaker*)*, camisole, cape, cardigan, cloak, coat, cowl, cravat, cummerbund, dinner jacket *(North American* tuxedo*)*, dress, dressing gown, dungarees, gloves, gown, Hawaiian shirt, headscarf, hoody, jacket, jeans, jersey, jodhpurs, jumper, kaftan, kilt, knickerbockers, knickers, leggings, leotard, mackintosh *(informal* mac*)*, miniskirt, mittens, nightdress *(informal* nightie*)*, overalls, overcoat, petticoat, pinafore, plus fours, polo shirt, pullover, pyjamas *(informal* PJs*)*, raincoat, robe, rugby shirt, sari, sarong, scarf, shawl, shirt, shorts, shrug, skirt, slip, socks, stockings, stole, suit, sweater, sweatshirt, swimsuit, tails, tank top, three-piece suit, tie, tights, top, tracksuit, trousers *(North American* pants*)*, trunks, T-shirt, tunic, twinset, underpants, underwear *(informal* undies*)*, veil, vest, waistcoat, wetsuit, wrap

⎹ **SEE ALSO hat**

FOR CLOTHES WORN IN THE PAST SEE historical »

WRITING TIPS

describing clothes

She was not elegantly dressed, but a noble-looking woman, and the girls thought the grey cloak and unfashionable bonnet covered the most splendid mother in the world.
— *Louisa May Alcott, Little Women*

parts & accessories

belt, bodice, braces (North American suspenders), braid, buckle, buttons, collar, cuff, flounce, frill, fringe, hem, hood, lapel, leg, lining, pintucks, pocket, ruffle, seam, sleeve, top-stitching, trim, turn-ups (North American cuffs), waist, waistband, zip

adjectives

baggy, casual, chic, creased, crumpled, dapper, designer, dingy, drab, elegant, fashionable, frayed, frilly, frumpy, grubby, ill-fitting, in good or bad repair, patched, printed, ragged, scruffy, shabby, slovenly, sporty, stylish, tailored, tattered, tatty, threadbare, unfashionable, waterproof, windproof, worn

▶ Someone who wears smart clothes is **well dressed** or **well groomed**.

SEE ALSO fabric, fashion

cloud NOUN
a cloud of steam from the kettle
billow, puff, haze, mist

cloud VERB
Don't let anger cloud your judgement.
obscure, confuse, muddle

cloudy ADJECTIVE
1 a cloudy sky
overcast, dull, grey, dark, dismal, gloomy, sunless, leaden
OPPOSITES cloudless, clear

FOR TIPS ON DESCRIBING WEATHER SEE weather

2 cloudy pond water
muddy, murky, milky, dirty
OPPOSITES clear, transparent

club NOUN
1 a wooden club
stick, bat, baton, truncheon, cudgel
2 a book club
group, society, association, organization, circle, union

club VERB
The victim was clubbed over the head with a blunt instrument.
hit, strike, beat, batter, bludgeon (informal) clout, clobber
SEE ALSO hit

clue NOUN
1 Can you give me a clue?
hint, suggestion, indication, pointer, tip, idea
2 The police are still looking for clues.
piece of evidence, lead
SEE ALSO crime

clump NOUN
a clump of trees
group, thicket, cluster, mass
▶ A clump of grass or hair is a **tuft**.

clumsy ADJECTIVE
1 My fingers were clumsy with the cold.
awkward, graceless, ungainly, inelegant, lumbering
OPPOSITE graceful
2 their clumsy handling of the situation
unskilful, inept, incompetent
OPPOSITE skilful

cluster NOUN
clusters of holly berries
bunch, clump, mass, knot, collection, gathering

cluster VERB
people clustering around a shop window

crowd, huddle, gather, collect, group

clutch VERB
In her hand, she clutched a handkerchief.
grip, grasp, clasp, cling to, hang on to, hold on to

clutches PLURAL NOUN
Van Helsing escapes from the clutches of Dracula.
grasp, power, control

clutter NOUN
clearing up the clutter in my room
mess, muddle, disorder, untidiness, junk, litter, rubbish

coach NOUN
1 *travelling by coach*
bus
SEE ALSO vehicle
2 *a swimming coach*
trainer, instructor, teacher, tutor

coach VERB
He was coached by a former champion.
train, teach, instruct, drill, school

coarse ADJECTIVE
1 *a coarse woollen blanket*
rough, harsh, scratchy, bristly, hairy
OPPOSITES soft, fine
2 *coarse table manners*
rude, impolite, uncouth, improper, crude, vulgar
OPPOSITES polite, refined

coast NOUN
the rocky coast of Alaska
shore, coastline, shoreline, seaside, seashore

coast VERB
coasting downhill on a bike
cruise, freewheel, glide

coat NOUN
1 *a thick woollen coat*
FOR ITEMS OF CLOTHING SEE clothes
2 *the colour of a horse's coat*
hair, fur, hide, pelt, skin
▶ A sheep's coat is a **fleece**.

3 *a new coat of paint*
layer, coating, covering, film, skin

coat VERB
raisins coated with chocolate
cover, spread, smear, plaster, daub, glaze, enrobe

coax VERB
coaxing a kitten out of a tree
persuade, cajole, wheedle, inveigle, tempt, entice
(informal) sweet-talk

code NOUN
1 *a message written in a secret code*
cipher, encryption
▶ To put a message in code is to **encode** or **encrypt** it.
▶ To understand a message in code is to **decode**, **decipher**, or *(informal)* **crack** it.
▶ The study of codes is **cryptography** or **cryptology**.
2 *a strict code of conduct*
rules, regulations, laws

coerce VERB
The leaders were coerced into signing the treaty.
force, compel, constrain, pressure, press, push, bully, browbeat
IDIOM twist someone's arm

coherent ADJECTIVE
Try to write a coherent answer.
articulate, intelligible, cogent, lucid, logical, rational, reasoned
OPPOSITES incoherent, muddled

coil NOUN
a coil of rope
spiral, twist, curl, twirl, screw, corkscrew, whirl, whorl, roll, scroll
▶ A coil of wool or thread is a **skein**.

coil VERB
a snake coiled round a branch
curl, loop, wind, wrap, roll, twist, twirl, twine, spiral

coin NOUN
Do you have a pound coin?
piece, bit

》

WORD WEB

some historical coins
denarius, doubloon, ducat,
farthing, florin, groat, guinea,
halfpenny, shilling, sixpence,
sovereign

▶ A series of coins used for currency
is **coinage**.

▶ The making of coins for currency
is **minting**.

▶ The study of coins is
numismatics, and a person
who studies or collects coins is a
numismatist.

coin VERB

The phrase 'brave new world' was
coined by Shakespeare.
invent, make up, think up, dream up,
conceive, create, devise

coincide VERB

1 This year, the school holidays coincide
with Easter.
co-occur, fall together, happen
together, clash

2 Our opinions rarely coincide.
agree, correspond, tally, accord, be
in accord, be compatible, match up

coincidence NOUN

By a strange coincidence, we have
the same birthday.
chance, accident, luck, fortune,
fluke, happenstance

cold ADJECTIVE

1 a spell of cold weather
chilly, chill, frosty, freezing, icy, raw,
arctic, bitter, cool, crisp, snowy,
wintry
(informal) perishing, nippy
❙ OPPOSITES hot, warm
FOR TIPS ON DESCRIBING WEATHER SEE
weather

2 feeling cold all over
chilled, chilly, frozen, shivering,
shivery

▶ Someone with an abnormally low

body temperature is suffering from
hypothermia.

3 I gave the shop assistant a cold stare.
unfriendly, unkind, unfeeling,
distant, cool, indifferent,
stony, uncaring, unemotional,
unsympathetic
❙ OPPOSITES warm, friendly

collaborate VERB

1 Several zoos collaborated on the
rhino project.
work together, cooperate, join
forces, pool resources

2 They were accused of collaborating
with the enemy.
cooperate, collude, consort,
fraternize

collapse VERB

1 Many buildings collapsed in the
earthquake.
fall down, fall in, cave in, give way,
crumple, buckle, disintegrate,
tumble down

2 Some of the runners collapsed in the
heat.
faint, pass out, black out, fall over,
keel over

colleague NOUN

a present from her colleagues at
the BBC
co-worker, workmate, teammate,
partner, associate, collaborator

collect VERB

1 collecting shells on the beach
gather, accumulate, amass, hoard,
pile up, store up, stockpile

2 collecting money for charity
raise, take in

3 collecting a parcel from the post
office
fetch, pick up, get, call for
❙ OPPOSITES drop off, hand in

4 A crowd collected at the stage door.
assemble, gather, come together,
congregate, convene, converge,
muster
❙ OPPOSITES scatter, disperse

collection NOUN

a collection of old photographs
hoard, store, stock, pile,
accumulation, set, assortment, array

▶ A collection of books, CDs, or DVDs
is a **library**.

▶ A collection of stories or poems is an
anthology.

collective ADJECTIVE

the collective efforts of many people
common, shared, joint, mutual,
communal, combined

collective noun NOUN

WORD WEB

▶ an **army** or **colony** of ants
▶ a **flock** of birds
▶ a **herd** of cattle
▶ a **brood** of chicks
▶ a **pod** of dolphins
▶ a **herd** of elephants
▶ a **shoal** of fish
▶ a **gaggle** or **skein** of geese
▶ a **band** of gorillas
▶ a **swarm** of insects
▶ a **troop** of kangaroos
▶ a **pride** of lions
▶ a **troop** of monkeys
▶ a **covey** of partridges
▶ a **colony** of penguins
▶ a **litter** of piglets, or kittens,
  or puppies
▶ a **pack** of rats
▶ a **flock** of sheep
▶ a **colony** of penguins
▶ a **school** of whales
▶ a **pack** of wolves

collector NOUN

WORD WEB

*names for collectors and
enthusiasts*
ornithologist (birds)

bibliophile (books)
lepidopterist (butterflies)
numismatist (coins)
palaeontologist (fossils)
entomologist (insects)
deltiologist (postcards)
audiophile (recorded music)
conchologist (shells)
philatelist (stamps)
arctophile (teddy bears)

college NOUN

studying at a music college
academy, school, university,
institute

collide VERB

▷ **collide with**
meteors colliding with the Earth
crash into, smash into, bump into,
run into, hit, strike

collision NOUN

a collision on the motorway
crash, accident, smash, bump, knock

▶ A collision involving a lot of vehicles
is a **pile-up**.

colloquial ADJECTIVE

*Her books are written in a colloquial
style.*
informal, conversational, casual,
everyday, idiomatic, vernacular
❙ OPPOSITE formal

colony NOUN

1 *New Zealand was once a British
colony.*
territory, dependency, protectorate,
settlement

2 *a colony of ants*
SEE **collective noun**

colossal ADJECTIVE

the skeleton of a colossal creature
huge, enormous, gigantic, immense,
massive, giant, mammoth,
monumental, towering, vast
(informal) whopping, humongous
❙ OPPOSITES small, tiny
❙ SEE ALSO big

a
b
c
d
e
f
g
h
i
j
k
l
m
n
o
p
q
r
s
t
u
v
w
x
y
z

colour *NOUN*

the colours of the rainbow
hue, shade, tint, tone, tinge

WRITING TIPS

describing colours

Then the green things began to show buds and the buds began to unfurl and show colour, every shade of blue, every shade of purple, every tint and hue of crimson.
— *Frances Hodgson Burnett, The Secret Garden*

light colours
delicate, faded, muted, neutral, opalescent, pale, pastel, soft, subtle, washed-out

dark or strong colours
bold, bright, deep, fiery, flaming, fluorescent, garish, gaudy, intense, iridescent, *(informal)* jazzy, loud, luminous, lurid, neon, radiant, vibrant, vivid, *(informal)* zingy

▶ The colours red, blue, and yellow are known as **primary colours**.

▶ A colour made by mixing two primary colours is a **secondary colour**.

▶ The pattern of colours seen in a rainbow is called a **spectrum**.

mixed colours
marbled, mottled, muddy, multicoloured, patchwork, piebald, rainbow, variegated

FOR TIPS ON DESCRIBING HAIR COLOUR SEE hair

colour *VERB*

1 *colouring your hair green*
tint, dye, stain, tinge, paint

2 *The experience coloured his whole childhood.*
affect, influence, have an impact on, skew

colourful *ADJECTIVE*

1 *a colourful design*
multicoloured, vibrant, vivid, bright, showy, garish, gaudy
(informal) jazzy
❙ OPPOSITE colourless

2 *She gave a colourful account of her trip.*
vivid, lively, interesting, exciting, striking, rich, picturesque
❙ OPPOSITE dull

colourless *ADJECTIVE*

1 *a colourless liquid*
uncoloured, clear, transparent, neutral

▶ Something which has lost its colour is **bleached** or **faded**.

2 *a book full of colourless characters*
dull, boring, uninteresting, unexciting, drab, dreary, lacklustre
❙ OPPOSITES colourful, interesting

column *NOUN*

1 *a stone column*
pillar, post, support, upright, shaft, pile

2 *reading the sports column*
article, piece, report, feature

3 *walking in a column*
line, file, procession, row, convoy

comb *VERB*

1 *combing your hair*
groom, brush, tidy, arrange, untangle

2 *combing the crime scene for evidence*
search, scour, sweep, ransack, rummage through

combat *NOUN*

a memorial for soldiers killed in combat
battle, war, warfare, fighting, action, hostilities
❙ SEE ALSO fight

combat *VERB*

a campaign to combat street crime
fight, oppose, counter, resist, stand up to, tackle, battle against, grapple with

a b c d e f g h i j k l m n o p q r s t u v w x y z

combination NOUN

  a combination of talent and hard work
  mixture, mix, union, fusion, merger, amalgamation, marriage, synthesis

combine VERB

  1 *Combine all the ingredients in a saucepan.*
  mix, blend, fuse, bind, merge, marry, integrate, amalgamate
  | **OPPOSITES** separate, divide

  2 *Three schools combined to stage the event.*
  unite, join forces, get together

come VERB

  1 *My parents will be coming tomorrow.*
  arrive, appear, visit, turn up
  (informal) show up
  | **OPPOSITES** leave, go

  2 *Summer is coming at last.*
  advance, draw near

  3 *How did you come to write the novel?*
  happen, chance

▷ **come about**
  How did the accident come about?
  happen, occur, take place, arise, result

▷ **come across**
  I came across some old letters.
  find, discover, chance upon, meet, bump into

▷ **come from**
  Where does your family come from?
  originate from, hail from, be from

▷ **come of**
  That's what comes of trying to be helpful!
  result from, follow on from, stem from, arise from

▷ **come round** or **come to**
  coming round after an operation
  become conscious, revive, wake up

▷ **come to**
  1 *We came to the end of the road.*
  reach, get to, arrive at

  2 *The hotel bill came to a hundred euros.*
  add up to, amount to, total

comfort NOUN

  1 *some words of comfort*
  consolation, support, encouragement, sympathy, condolence

  2 *living in relative comfort*
  ease, contentment, well-being, prosperity, luxury, affluence
  | **OPPOSITE** discomfort

comfort VERB

  some ways to comfort a crying baby
  console, soothe, calm, reassure, cheer up, hearten
  | **OPPOSITES** distress, upset

comfortable ADJECTIVE

  1 *a comfortable sofa*
  cosy, snug, relaxing, soft, roomy, padded, plush
  (informal) comfy
  | **OPPOSITE** uncomfortable

  2 *comfortable clothes for travelling*
  casual, informal, loose-fitting
  | **OPPOSITES** restrictive, tight-fitting

  3 *leading a comfortable life*
  contented, pleasant, agreeable, well-off, prosperous, luxurious, affluent
  | **OPPOSITES** hard, spartan

comic ADJECTIVE

  The act opens with a comic scene.
  humorous, funny, amusing, comical, comedic, light-hearted
  | **OPPOSITES** serious, tragic

comical ADJECTIVE

  Her impersonation of the queen is quite comical.
  funny, amusing, humorous, hilarious, witty, droll

▶ To be comical in a silly way is to be **absurd**, **farcical**, **ludicrous**, or **ridiculous**.

▶ To be comical in a hurtful way is to be **sarcastic**.
  | **SEE ALSO** funny

a
b
c
d
e
f
g
h
i
j
k
l
m
n
o
p
q
r
s
t
u
v
w
x
y
z

command *NOUN*

1 *giving the command to advance*
order, instruction, direction, commandment, edict

2 *Who has command of the ship?*
control, charge, authority, dominion, jurisdiction, leadership, management, supervision, power

3 *The job requires a good command of German.*
knowledge, mastery, grasp, understanding, comprehension, ability (in)

command *VERB*

1 *commanding a robot to move forwards*
order, instruct, direct, tell, bid

2 *Nelson commanded the British fleet.*
be in charge of, control, direct, govern, head, lead, manage, supervise, oversee
(informal) head up

commander *NOUN*

the commander of the task force
leader, head, chief, director, manager, officer-in-charge
(informal) boss, skipper

commemorate *VERB*

a stamp to commemorate the Moon landing
celebrate, remember, mark, observe, pay tribute to, be a memorial to, honour, salute

commence *VERB*

Let the battle commence.
begin, start, get going, get under way
(informal) kick off
⌐**IDIOM** get off the ground

commend *VERB*

My photo was commended in the under-18 category.
praise, compliment, congratulate, applaud
⌐**OPPOSITE** criticize

comment *NOUN*

1 *making a sarcastic comment*

remark, statement, observation, opinion, pronouncement, mention
▶ A hostile comment is a **criticism**.

2 *a comment written in the margin*
note, annotation, footnote, gloss, reference

comment *VERB*

▷ **comment on**
Several people commented on my dress.
remark on, mention, make mention of, notice, discuss, talk about

commentary *NOUN*

1 *listening to the match commentary*
narration, description, voice-over, report, review

2 *This edition includes a commentary on the play.*
criticism, analysis, interpretation, explanation, notes, review

commerce *NOUN*

international commerce
business, trade, trading, dealing

commit *VERB*

1 *committing a double murder*
carry out, do, perform, execute, accomplish, perpetrate
(informal) pull off

2 *committing your time and energy to a project*
allocate, devote, dedicate, make available, assign, consign, pledge

commitment *NOUN*

1 *her total commitment to her sport*
dedication, devotion, allegiance, loyalty, passion

2 *making a commitment to lose weight*
promise, pledge, vow, undertaking, resolution

committee *NOUN*

a committee of volunteers
board, panel, council, body

common *ADJECTIVE*

1 *Hurricanes are a common occurrence in Florida.*
frequent, regular, commonplace, everyday, normal, routine, ordinary,

familiar, usual, customary, habitual

OPPOSITES rare, unusual

2 *Falconry was common in Europe in the Middle Ages.*
widespread, general, popular, universal, prevalent, rife, conventional, established, accepted

3 *Humans and apes share a common ancestor.*
shared, mutual, joint, communal, collective

commonplace ADJECTIVE

a city where cycling is commonplace
common, everyday, regular, routine, normal, ordinary, frequent, familiar, usual

OPPOSITES rare, unusual

commotion NOUN

causing a commotion in the street
disturbance, row, uproar, racket, rumpus, fuss, stir, unrest, disorder, furore, fracas, hullabaloo, brouhaha, pandemonium, bedlam, hue and cry

communal ADJECTIVE

a communal changing room
shared, joint, public, common, collective

OPPOSITES private, individual

communicate VERB

1 *communicating the good news*
convey, relay, transmit, relate, pass on, report, tell, impart

2 *We usually communicate by email.*
contact each other, correspond, be in touch, liaise

3 *Malaria is communicated by mosquitoes.*
transmit, transfer, pass on, spread

communication NOUN

1 *Dolphins use sound for communication.*
communicating, contact, dialogue, conversation

2 *a communication from outer space*
message, dispatch, statement, announcement, letter, report, communiqué

 WORD WEB

some forms of communication
advertising, blog, body language, Braille, broadcast, bulletin board, email, fax, junk mail, letter, mailshot, memo or memorandum, Morse code, newspaper, podcast, postcard, radio, satellite, semaphore, sign language or signing, social networking, telegram, telepathy, telephone, television, texting, video conference, webcast, website, wiki

communicative ADJECTIVE

I'm not feeling very communicative today.
talkative, expressive, vocal, chatty, forthcoming

OPPOSITES uncommunicative, taciturn

community NOUN

a small farming community
society, population, people, populace, residents, inhabitants

compact➊ NOUN

a compact between two nations
treaty, pact, agreement, contract, settlement, accord

compact➋ ADJECTIVE

1 *fabric with a compact weave*
dense, tight, close, firm, solid, compressed

OPPOSITE loose

2 *a compact camera*
small, portable, handy, neat, petite

OPPOSITE bulky

companion NOUN

looking for a travelling companion
friend, partner, comrade, associate *(informal)* pal, buddy, chum *(British informal)* mate

company NOUN

1 *a company selling mobile phones*
firm, business, corporation,

a
b
c
d
e
f
g
h
i
j
k
l
m
n
o
p
q
r
s
t
u
v
w
x
y
z

organization, establishment,
enterprise, agency, office

2 *enjoying the company of friends*
fellowship, companionship, society

compare VERB
comparing two sets of figures
contrast, juxtapose, set side by side,
weigh up

▷ **compare with something**
It doesn't compare with the original version.
be as good as, rival, emulate, equal,
match up to, come close to, be on a
par with

comparison NOUN
1 *We put the signatures side by side for comparison.*
comparing, contrast, juxtaposition

2 *There's no comparison between their team and ours.*
resemblance, similarity, likeness,
correspondence

compartment NOUN
The money was hidden in a secret compartment.
section, division, cell, cubicle,
cubbyhole

compassion NOUN
showing compassion for all living creatures
sympathy, empathy, fellow
feeling, concern, consideration,
understanding, kindness, charity
❙ OPPOSITE indifference

compassionate ADJECTIVE
a gentle and compassionate soul
sympathetic, caring, considerate,
warm, loving, kind, charitable
❙ OPPOSITES unsympathetic, uncaring

compatible ADJECTIVE
Apparently, our star signs are not compatible.
well suited, well matched,
like-minded
❙ IDIOMS on the same wavelength,
in tune

❙ OPPOSITE incompatible

compel VERB
Villagers were compelled to leave their homes.
force, make, coerce, press, push
(informal) lean on

compelling VERB
1 *a compelling story of love and revenge*
captivating, enthralling, absorbing,
gripping, riveting, spellbinding,
mesmerizing

2 *a compelling argument*
convincing, persuasive, powerful,
strong, irresistible

compensate VERB
to compensate you for your loss of earnings
recompense, repay, reimburse,
remunerate

▷ **compensate for**
compensating for changes in water temperature
make up for, counteract, balance
out, cancel out

compensation NOUN
a claim for compensation
recompense, repayment,
reimbursement, remuneration,
damages

compete VERB
competing in a hockey tournament
participate, take part, enter, play,
go in (for)

▷ **compete against**
competing against a strong team
oppose, play against, contend with,
vie with, challenge
❙ IDIOM go head to head with

competence NOUN
showing a high degree of competence
ability, capability, skill, proficiency,
expertise, prowess
(informal) know-how
❙ OPPOSITE incompetence

competent *ADJECTIVE*
a competent swimmer
able, capable, skilful, skilled,
accomplished, proficient, expert
❙ **OPPOSITE** incompetent

competition *NOUN*
1 *first prize in a poetry competition*
contest, quiz, championship,
tournament, match, game, trial, race
FOR TIPS ON WRITING ABOUT SPORT SEE
sport

2 *the competition between the two
teams*
rivalry, competitiveness

3 *eyeing up the competition*
opposition, rivals, opponents,
other side

competitive *ADJECTIVE*
a competitive marketplace
aggressive, combative, fierce,
cut-throat
(informal) dog-eat-dog

competitor *NOUN*
1 *The competitors lined up for the start
of the race.*
contestant, contender, participant,
player, entrant

2 *Who are your main competitors?*
rival, opponent, challenger

compile *VERB*
compiling a list of suspects
assemble, put together, make up,
compose, gather, collect, collate

complacent *ADJECTIVE*
a complacent smirk
self-satisfied, smug

complain *VERB*
*Hal spent most of the weekend
complaining.*
protest, grumble, grouse, carp,
bleat, whine, make a fuss
(informal) gripe, moan
(British informal) whinge
▶ Someone who is always complaining
is **querulous**.

▷ **complain about something**
complaining about the noise
protest about, object to, criticize,
find fault with
❙ **OPPOSITE** praise

complaint *NOUN*
1 *writing a letter of complaint*
criticism, objection, protest,
grievance, grouse, grumble
(informal) gripe
(British informal) whinge

2 *a nasty stomach complaint*
disease, illness, ailment, sickness,
disorder, infection, condition,
problem, upset

complement *NOUN*
1 *The music is a perfect complement to
the film.*
accompaniment, accessory,
supplement, companion, partner
❙ **OPPOSITES** contrast, foil

2 *We had our full complement of
players for the match.*
quota, contingent, amount,
allowance, capacity

complement *VERB*
a drink to complement your meal
accompany, go with, suit, set off,
enhance
❙ **OPPOSITES** contrast with, clash with

complementary *ADJECTIVE*
a skirt with a complementary jacket
matching, compatible,
corresponding, harmonious

complete *ADJECTIVE*
1 *a complete set of cards*
whole, entire, full, intact
❙ **OPPOSITES** incomplete, partial

2 *The new building is not yet complete.*
finished, completed, ended,
concluded
❙ **OPPOSITE** unfinished

3 *My audition was a complete disaster.*
total, absolute, thorough, utter,
pure, sheer, downright, unqualified,
unmitigated, out-and-out

a
b
c
d
e
f
g
h
i
j
k
l
m
n
o
p
q
r
s
t
u
v
w
x
y
z

complete VERB

  1 *She has another year to complete her training.*
  finish, end, conclude, finalize
  (informal) wind up, wrap up

  2 *a pair of shoes to complete my outfit*
  finish off, round off, top off, crown, cap

completely ADVERB

  I'm not completely convinced.
  totally, wholly, entirely, thoroughly, utterly, fully, absolutely

complex ADJECTIVE

  1 *the complex structure of a plant cell*
  composite, compound

  2 *Defusing a bomb is a complex task.*
  complicated, intricate, difficult, elaborate, detailed, involved
  (informal) fiddly
  ❙ **OPPOSITES** simple, straightforward

complexion NOUN

  an olive complexion
  skin, skin tone, colour, colouring
  FOR TIPS ON DESCRIBING FACES SEE **face**

complicated ADJECTIVE

  1 *a complicated task*
  complex, intricate, difficult
  (informal) fiddly
  ❙ **OPPOSITES** simple, straightforward

  2 *a complicated plot*
  involved, elaborate, convoluted, multilayered

compliment NOUN

  an unexpected compliment
  commendation, tribute, accolade
  ❙ **IDIOM** pat on the back
  ❙ **OPPOSITES** criticism, insult

  ▷ **compliments**
  receiving compliments on my cooking
  praise, acclaim, admiration, appreciation, congratulations

complimentary ADJECTIVE

  1 *a complimentary remark*
  appreciative, approving, admiring, positive, favourable, flattering, congratulatory

  ❙ **OPPOSITES** critical, insulting, negative

  2 *complimentary tickets for the film*
  free, gratis, courtesy
  ❙ **IDIOM** on the house

comply VERB

  ▷ **comply with**
  complying with the new regulations
  obey, observe, follow, abide by, conform to, adhere to, go along with
  ❙ **OPPOSITES** disobey, flout

component NOUN

  the main components of a computer
  part, piece, bit, element, ingredient, constituent, module

compose VERB

  Beethoven composed nine symphonies.
  create, devise, write, pen, produce, make up, think up, invent

  ▷ **be composed of**
  This quilt is composed of pieces of patchwork.
  be made of, consist of, comprise

  ▷ **compose yourself**
  I needed a few minutes to compose myself.
  calm down, control yourself, regain your composure
  ❙ **IDIOMS** get a grip on yourself, pull yourself together

composed ADJECTIVE

  Ian arrived, looking composed and confident.
  calm, cool, level-headed, relaxed, serene, sedate, unruffled, unflustered, unperturbed, unemotional
  ❙ **OPPOSITES** nervous, excited

composition NOUN

  1 *Is the song your own composition?*
  creation, work, piece, study
  (formal) opus
  FOR TYPES OF MUSICAL COMPOSITION SEE **music**

  2 *studying the composition of rocks*
  make-up, structure, formation,

constitution, anatomy

3 *the composition of the photograph*
arrangement, layout, design,
configuration

compound NOUN

*Steel is a compound of iron and
carbon.*
amalgam, alloy, mixture, mix, blend

comprehend VERB

*It is hard to comprehend the size of
the universe.*
understand, make sense of, grasp,
appreciate, perceive, follow, fathom,
take in
(informal) figure out, get

comprehension NOUN

*testing your comprehension of the
chapter*
understanding, knowledge,
awareness, conception, grasp,
mastery
❙ **OPPOSITE** ignorance

comprehensive ADJECTIVE

a comprehensive summary of the plot
complete, full, thorough, detailed,
extensive, exhaustive, inclusive,
all-inclusive, all-embracing,
wide-ranging, encyclopedic,
sweeping, wholesale
❙ **OPPOSITES** selective, narrow

compress VERB

compressing tin cans for recycling
press, squeeze, crush, compact,
squash, flatten

comprise VERB

*The team comprised athletes from
several countries.*
be composed of, consist of, be made
up of, include, contain

compromise VERB

1 *Neither side is willing to compromise.*
come to an understanding, make
a deal
❙ **IDIOMS** meet each other halfway,
find a happy medium

2 *compromising the future of*

the planet
undermine, weaken, jeopardize,
damage, harm

compulsive ADJECTIVE

1 *a compulsive urge to laugh*
irresistible, uncontrollable,
compelling, overwhelming,
overpowering

2 *a compulsive liar*
obsessive, habitual, chronic,
incurable, persistent

3 *The new series is compulsive viewing.*
compelling, gripping, engrossing,
absorbing, enthralling, captivating

compulsory ADJECTIVE

*The wearing of seat belts is
compulsory.*
obligatory, mandatory, required,
necessary, prescribed
❙ **OPPOSITE** optional

computer NOUN

 WORD WEB

some types of computer
desktop, handheld, laptop,
mainframe, netbook, notebook,
palmtop, PC, server, tablet

parts of a computer system
CD-ROM drive, DVD drive, hard
disk, hub, keyboard, memory
stick, microchip, microprocessor,
modem, monitor, motherboard,
mouse, processor, screen,
terminal, touchpad, USB port

other terms used in computing
back-up, bit, broadband,
browser, bug, byte, cursor,
cybercrime, data, database,
default, digital, download, email,
ethernet, firewall, gigabyte,
hacker, hardware, ICT, input,
interface, Internet
(informal Net*)*, malware,
megabyte, memory, menu,
network, offline, online,
operating system, peripheral, »

phishing, printout, program, reboot, software, spam, spreadsheet, spyware, start-up, surfing, upload, virus, Web, wi-fi, window, wireless, word processor

concave ADJECTIVE
a concave lens
diverging
OPPOSITES convex, converging

conceal VERB
1 The prisoners concealed the entrance to the tunnel.
hide, cover up, screen, disguise, mask, camouflage
OPPOSITES uncover, reveal
2 He managed to conceal the truth for years.
keep quiet about, keep secret, hush up, suppress
IDIOM keep a lid on
OPPOSITES disclose, confess

conceited ADJECTIVE
Justin walked off with a conceited swagger.
arrogant, proud, vain, self-satisfied, self-important, boastful, overbearing, supercilious (informal) big-headed, cocky
IDIOMS full of yourself
(informal) too big for your boots
OPPOSITES modest, self-effacing

conceive VERB
1 Darwin conceived the idea of natural selection.
originate, think up, devise, invent, formulate, design, develop (informal) dream up
2 I cannot conceive what life would be like on Mars.
imagine, envisage, see, visualize, grasp

concentrate VERB
1 This term, we are concentrating on biology.
focus, centre, pinpoint

2 Be quiet! I'm trying to concentrate.
think hard, focus, pay attention
3 The shops are concentrated in the centre of town.
collect, gather, cluster, mass, converge

concentrated ADJECTIVE
1 a concentrated effort to escape
strenuous, forceful, determined, spirited, all-out
2 a concentrated solution
condensed, reduced
OPPOSITE diluted

concept NOUN
I find the concept of time travel fascinating.
idea, thought, notion, theory

conception NOUN
Einstein changed our conception of time..
idea, image, perception, view, notion

concern VERB
1 I was told that the matter did not concern me.
affect, involve, be relevant to, apply to, be important to, matter to
2 The melting of the ice caps concerns me deeply.
worry, trouble, disturb, distress, upset, bother
3 The play concerns the love between Romeo and Juliet.
be about, deal with, relate to, pertain to

concern NOUN
1 People are too wrapped up in their own concerns.
affair, business, responsibility, interest
2 A new virus is causing concern among bee-keepers.
anxiety, worry, apprehension, unease, disquiet
3 the head of a large banking concern
company, business, firm, enterprise, establishment, corporation

concerned *ADJECTIVE*

1 *Many scientists are concerned about global warming.*
worried, anxious, troubled, upset, distressed, bothered

2 *We will be emailing all those concerned.*
involved, affected, interested, implicated

concerning *PREPOSITION*

a letter concerning your application
about, regarding, relating to, with reference to, referring to, relevant to, with regard to, in connection with, touching

concert *NOUN*

a concert of jazz music
recital, performance, show

concise *ADJECTIVE*

a concise account of what happened
brief, short, condensed, succinct, abridged, abbreviated, compact, pithy

▶ A concise account of something is a **précis** or **summary**.

▌OPPOSITES lengthy, expanded

conclude *VERB*

1 *This concludes our tour of the library.*
bring to an end, complete, close, finish, terminate, round off, wind up
(informal) wrap up

2 *The festival concluded with some fireworks.*
come to an end, finish, close, terminate, culminate, draw to a close

3 *The jury concluded that she was guilty.*
decide, judge, deduce, infer, gather

conclusion *NOUN*

1 *the conclusion of Tolkien's trilogy*
end, ending, close, finale, finish, completion, culmination

2 *Have you reached a conclusion yet?*
decision, judgement, opinion, verdict, deduction

concrete *ADJECTIVE*

looking for concrete evidence
real, actual, definite, conclusive, firm, solid, substantial, physical, material, tangible

▌OPPOSITE abstract

condemn *VERB*

1 *The club condemned the players involved.*
criticize, censure, denounce, deplore, disapprove of

▌OPPOSITES praise, condone

2 *a ghost condemned to wander the Earth forever*
doom, sentence, bind

condemnation *NOUN*

There was widespread condemnation of the violence.
criticism, censure, denunciation

▌OPPOSITES approval, praise

condense *VERB*

Try to condense the story into a hundred words.
shorten, abridge, reduce, compress, abbreviate, summarize, edit

▌OPPOSITE expand

condescending *ADJECTIVE*

a condescending attitude
superior, patronizing, snobbish
(informal) snooty, stuck-up

condition *NOUN*

1 *Is the guitar in good condition?*
state, order, repair, shape, form, fitness

2 *living in overcrowded conditions*
circumstances, environment, situation

3 *a condition of joining the library*
requirement, obligation, term, constraint, prerequisite, proviso

▷ **on condition that**
You can come on condition that you keep quiet.
provided, providing that, on the understanding that, only if

a
b
c
d
e
f
g
h
i
j
k
l
m
n
o
p
q
r
s
t
u
v
w
x
y
z

condone *ADJECTIVE*

Our company has never condoned whaling.

accept, allow, disregard, let pass, pardon, excuse

❙ **IDIOM** turn a blind eye to

❙ **OPPOSITE** condemn

conduct *VERB*

1 Marianne usually conducts our meetings.

direct, manage, preside over, organize, coordinate, run, control, administer, supervise, orchestrate, handle

2 A guide conducted us round the site.

guide, lead, escort, accompany, usher, take

▷ **conduct yourself**

The visitors conducted themselves with dignity.

behave, act, acquit yourself

conduct *NOUN*

an award for good conduct

behaviour, manners, actions, deeds

confer *VERB*

1 conferring a knighthood

bestow, award (to), grant (to), present (to)

2 You are allowed to confer with your team-mates.

consult, have a discussion, converse, deliberate, talk things over

conference *NOUN*

hosting a scientific conference

meeting, congress, convention, forum, summit, discussion

confess *VERB*

1 Dixon confessed that he had stolen the money.

admit, own up, acknowledge, reveal, divulge

(informal) come clean

❙ **OPPOSITE** deny

2 I confess I don't know the answer.

acknowledge, admit, concede, grant, allow, own

confide *VERB*

Ewan was afraid to confide the secret to anyone.

reveal, disclose, tell, divulge, confess

confidence *NOUN*

1 The team had lost all confidence in the manager.

trust, faith, belief, credence

2 I wish I had her confidence.

self-assurance, self-confidence, assertiveness, boldness, self-reliance, conviction

confident *ADJECTIVE*

1 I am confident that we will win.

certain, sure, positive, convinced, satisfied, in no doubt

❙ **OPPOSITE** doubtful

2 Abby is more confident than her sister.

self-assured, self-confident, bold, assertive, self-reliant

confidential *ADJECTIVE*

The details of the plan are confidential.

private, secret, classified, restricted

(informal) hush-hush

❙ **OPPOSITE** public

confine *VERB*

1 They confined their discussion to the weather.

limit, restrict

2 Our chickens are not confined indoors.

enclose, shut in, coop up, incarcerate

confirm *VERB*

1 The sighting confirmed his belief in UFOs.

prove, substantiate, corroborate, justify, verify, vindicate, bear out, back up

❙ **OPPOSITE** disprove

2 Please phone to confirm your booking.

verify, make official

❙ **OPPOSITE** cancel

confiscate VERB
One of the teachers confiscated my phone.
take possession of, seize, impound

conflict NOUN
1 *There's a lot of conflict in their family.*
disagreement, quarrelling, hostility, friction, antagonism, opposition, discord, strife, unrest
2 *the Balkan conflict of the 1990s*
war, warfare, combat, fighting, engagement, hostilities

conflict VERB
▷ **conflict with**
Her statement conflicts with the evidence.
disagree with, differ from, contradict, contrast with, clash with, be at odds with

conflicting ADJECTIVE
My brother and I have conflicting tastes in music.
contrasting, incompatible, contradictory, opposite, contrary, irreconcilable

conform VERB
▷ **conform to** or **with**
This website conforms to W3C guidelines.
obey, observe, abide by, keep to, submit to, comply with, fit in with, follow
❙ OPPOSITES disobey, flout

confront VERB
1 *the scene in which Macbeth confronts the witches*
come face to face with, challenge, stand up to, accost, tackle
2 *the difficulties which confront us*
face, stand in your way, threaten, beset

confrontation NOUN
a confrontation between rival fans
conflict, clash, encounter, fight, battle, disagreement, quarrel

confuse VERB
1 *I was confused by Lauren's message.*
puzzle, bewilder, mystify, baffle, perplex, bemuse
(informal) flummox, fox
2 *You must be confusing me with someone else.*
mix up, muddle

confusing ADJECTIVE
a confusing set of instructions
puzzling, perplexing, baffling, bewildering, unclear, misleading, ambiguous
❙ OPPOSITES clear, unambiguous

confusion NOUN
1 *a look of confusion on your face*
bewilderment, perplexity, bafflement, puzzlement, befuddlement
❙ OPPOSITES certainty, clarity
2 *a scene of utter confusion*
chaos, disorder, disarray, mayhem, pandemonium, bedlam
❙ OPPOSITES order, calm

congenial ADJECTIVE
the congenial company of our hosts
friendly, sociable, hospitable, convivial, amiable, pleasant, agreeable
❙ OPPOSITES unsociable, unfriendly

congested ADJECTIVE
The roads are congested during the rush hour.
blocked, jammed, choked, clogged, obstructed, crowded
(informal) snarled up, jam-packed, gridlocked
❙ OPPOSITE clear

congratulate VERB
We congratulated the winners.
praise, applaud, compliment, pay tribute to, salute
❙ IDIOMS pat someone on the back, take your hat off to
❙ OPPOSITE criticize

a b c d e f g h i j k l m n o p q r s t u v w x y z

133

congregate VERB

The guests congregated in the hall.
gather, assemble, collect, convene, come together, muster, cluster
┃ OPPOSITE disperse

connect VERB

a cable to connect two PCs
join, attach, fasten, link, couple, fix together, tie together
┃ OPPOSITE separate

▷ **connect with**
an old custom connected with Halloween
associate with, relate to, identify with

connection NOUN

There is a connection between the Moon and the tides.
relationship, link, association, interconnection, interdependence, bond, tie

conquer VERB

1 The Romans used people they had conquered as slaves.
defeat, beat, vanquish, subjugate, overcome, overwhelm, crush

2 Alexander the Great conquered Egypt in 332 BC.
seize, capture, take, win, occupy, possess

3 first woman to conquer Mount Everest
climb, ascend, scale

conquest NOUN

the Mongol conquest of China
capture, seizure, invasion, occupation, possession, takeover, subjugation

conscientious ADJECTIVE

a very conscientious worker
hard-working, diligent, industrious, careful, attentive, meticulous, painstaking, thorough, dedicated, dutiful, responsible
┃ OPPOSITES careless, irresponsible

conscious ADJECTIVE

1 The patient was conscious throughout the operation.
awake, alert, aware
┃ OPPOSITES unconscious, unaware

2 making a conscious effort to save energy
deliberate, intentional, planned, calculated, premeditated
┃ OPPOSITES accidental, unintentional

consecutive ADJECTIVE

It rained for three consecutive days.
successive, succeeding, running, straight, in a row, in succession
┃ IDIOM (informal) on the trot

Usage Note

You can say three days straight or three straight days but only three days running.

consent NOUN

They acted without my consent.
agreement, sanction, authorization, permission, approval, acceptance, acquiescence, assent
(informal) go-ahead

consent VERB

▷ **consent to**
The head has consented to our request.
agree to, grant, approve, authorize, sanction, go along with, acquiesce in
┃ IDIOM give the green light to
┃ OPPOSITE refuse

consequence NOUN

1 the long-term consequences of a poor diet
result, effect, outcome, upshot, repercussion, ramification
┃ OPPOSITE cause

2 Her wealth was of no consequence to him.
importance, significance, import, account, value

conservation NOUN

the conservation of natural resources

preservation, protection,
maintenance, upkeep
❙ **OPPOSITE** destruction

conservative ADJECTIVE

1 *a very conservative taste in music*
old-fashioned, conventional,
unadventurous, traditional,
restrained
❙ **OPPOSITES** progressive, up-to-date

2 *800 years is a conservative estimate
of the age of this tree.*
cautious, moderate, modest
❙ **OPPOSITE** extreme

conserve VERB

*You can conserve electricity by
switching off lights.*
save, preserve, be sparing with,
safeguard, look after, protect,
sustain
❙ **OPPOSITE** waste

consider VERB

1 *considering all the options*
think about, examine, contemplate,
ponder on, reflect on, study,
evaluate, meditate on, weigh up,
mull over
(informal) size up

2 *His first novel is considered to be his
best.*
reckon, judge, deem, regard as, rate

considerable ADJECTIVE

*1000 pounds is a considerable sum
of money.*
large, sizeable, substantial,
significant
❙ **OPPOSITES** negligible, paltry

considerate ADJECTIVE

*How considerate of you to offer me
a lift.*
thoughtful, kind, helpful, obliging,
unselfish, neighbourly
❙ **OPPOSITE** selfish

consist VERB

▷ **consist of**
*A comet consists largely of ice and
dust.*

be made up of, be composed of,
comprise, contain, include, involve

consistency NOUN

*a paste with the consistency of
porridge*
texture, thickness, density
FOR TIPS ON DESCRIBING TEXTURE SEE
texture

consistent ADJECTIVE

*The greenhouse is kept at a
consistent temperature.*
steady, constant, regular, stable,
even, unchanging, uniform
❙ **OPPOSITES** variable, fluctuating

▷ **be consistent with**
*The injuries are consistent with a
crocodile attack.*
be compatible with, be in keeping
with, be in line with
❙ **OPPOSITE** be inconsistent with

consolation NOUN

*A late goal provided some
consolation for the losers.*
comfort, solace, sympathy,
commiseration, support

console VERB

*I tried everything I could to console
her.*
comfort, sympathize with,
commiserate with, support, soothe,
cheer up

conspicuous ADJECTIVE

The castle is a conspicuous landmark.
noticeable, prominent, obvious,
clear, unmistakable, eye-catching,
visible, evident, apparent, glaring
❙ **OPPOSITE** inconspicuous

conspiracy NOUN

a conspiracy to assassinate Hitler
plot, intrigue, scheme, ploy, plan

conspire VERB

1 *Guy Fawkes conspired to
blow up Parliament.*
plot, intrigue, scheme, plan

2 *Everything seemed to conspire
against me.*

»

unite, combine, join forces

constant ADJECTIVE

1 *the constant noise of traffic outside*
continual, continuous, non-stop, ceaseless, incessant, persistent, perpetual, interminable, endless, unending, never-ending, everlasting, permanent
OPPOSITE intermittent

2 *running at a constant pace*
steady, consistent, regular, stable, even, unchanging, uniform
OPPOSITE variable

3 *a constant friend for many years*
faithful, loyal, devoted, dependable, reliable, firm, true, trustworthy
OPPOSITE unreliable

constitute VERB

1 *Eleven players constitute a hockey team.*
make up, compose, comprise, form

2 *The oil spill constitutes a danger to wildlife.*
amount to, represent, be equivalent to, be tantamount to

constitution NOUN

1 *the constitution of a molecule*
composition, make-up, structure, configuration, formation, anatomy

2 *She is blessed with a strong constitution.*
health, condition, strength, build, stamina

constraint NOUN

There are no constraints on word length.
restriction, limitation, limit, restraint, curb, check, control

construct VERB

constructing a tent in the garden
build, erect, assemble, put together, put up, set up
OPPOSITE demolish

construction NOUN

1 *before the construction of the Great Wall of China*
building, erecting, erection,

assembly, setting-up

2 *The bridge is a temporary construction.*
structure, edifice, building, work

3 *putting a new construction on the poem*
interpretation, explanation, meaning, reading, analysis

consult VERB

1 *You should consult a doctor first.*
seek advice from, speak to, ask, talk things over with

2 *consulting an encyclopedia*
refer to, look up, check

consume VERB

1 *An adult penguin consumes up to 500g of fish a day.*
eat, devour, swallow
SEE ALSO eat

2 *Refrigerators consume a vast amount of energy.*
use up, go through, spend, exhaust, deplete

3 *The building was consumed by fire.*
destroy, devastate, lay waste, gut, raze

▷ **be consumed with**
Othello was consumed with jealousy.
be filled with, be overwhelmed by, be gripped by

contact NOUN

1 *Rugby is a sport which involves physical contact.*
touch, touching, handling

2 *Have you had any contact with him lately?*
communication, correspondence, connection, dealings

3 *a list of personal contacts*
acquaintance, associate, friend

contact VERB

I'll contact you when I have some news.
get in touch with, communicate with, notify, speak to, talk to, correspond with, write to, call, phone, ring

contagious ADJECTIVE

Measles is a very contagious disease.
infectious, communicable
(informal) catching
┃ **OPPOSITE** non-infectious

contain VERB

1 The packet contained a number of old letters.
have inside, hold, include, incorporate, comprise, consist of

2 I tried hard to contain my annoyance.
restrain, hold back, suppress, control, curb, rein in, bottle up

container NOUN

Put the left-over sauce in a container.
receptacle, vessel, holder, repository, box, case, canister, carton, pot, tub, tin

contaminate VERB

The beach has been contaminated by sewage.
pollute, poison, defile, taint, soil, corrupt
┃ **OPPOSITE** purify

contemplate VERB

1 contemplating your reflection in a mirror
look at, view, regard, observe, gaze at, stare at, survey, study

2 I am contemplating a change of career.
think about, consider, ponder, reflect on, meditate on, weigh up, mull over

contemporary ADJECTIVE

1 an exhibition of contemporary art
modern, current, recent, present-day

2 a contemporary hairstyle
up-to-date, fashionable, the latest, cutting-edge
(informal) trendy
┃ **OPPOSITES** old-fashioned, out-of-date

contempt NOUN

Vivian gave a snort of contempt.
scorn, disdain, derision, disrespect
┃ **OPPOSITES** admiration, respect

contemptuous ADJECTIVE

a contemptuous wave of her hand
scornful, disdainful, derisive, disrespectful
┃ **OPPOSITES** admiring, respectful

contend VERB

1 Four teams are contending for a place in the final.
compete, vie, battle, strive, struggle

2 The witness contends that he heard a noise.
assert, declare, claim, maintain, argue, insist

▷ **contend with**
We had to contend with bad weather and midges!
cope with, deal with, put up with, grapple with, face, confront, take on

content ADJECTIVE

Larry was content to sit and wait.
happy, contented, satisfied, pleased, willing
┃ **OPPOSITE** unwilling

contented ADJECTIVE

Grace sank into the bath with a contented sigh.
happy, pleased, content, satisfied, fulfilled, serene, peaceful, relaxed, comfortable, tranquil, untroubled
┃ **OPPOSITE** discontented

contents PLURAL NOUN

to understand the contents of the human genome
constituents, ingredients, components, elements

contest NOUN

a contest between humans and computers
competition, challenge, tournament, match, game, encounter, bout, fight, battle, struggle, tussle

contest VERB

1 Six parties will be contesting the election.

»

a
b
c
d
e
f
g
h
i
j
k
l
m
n
o
p
q
r
s
t
u
v
w
x
y
z

compete for, fight for, contend for, vie for

2 *No one contested the referee's decision.*
challenge, disagree with, object to, dispute, oppose, call into question

contestant NOUN

a contestant on a TV quiz show
competitor, participant, contender, player, entrant

continual ADJECTIVE

It was a day of continual interruptions.
recurrent, repeated, constant, frequent, perpetual
OPPOSITE occasional

Usage Note

The words **continual** and **continuous** are not synonyms. *Continual noises* happen repeatedly, whereas a *continuous noise* never stops.

---

continue VERB

1 *We continued our search until it got dark.*
keep up, prolong, sustain, persevere with, pursue
(informal) stick at

2 *This rain can't continue for long.*
carry on, last, persist, endure, extend, keep on, go on, linger, drag on

3 *We'll continue the lesson after lunch.*
resume, carry on with, proceed with, return to, pick up

continuous ADJECTIVE

She has continuous pain in her ankle.
persistent, uninterrupted, unbroken, never-ending, non-stop, incessant, unceasing
▶ An illness which continues for a long time is a **chronic** illness.
OPPOSITE intermittent
SEE ALSO continual

contract NOUN

signing a contract for a new film
agreement, deal, compact, bargain, undertaking
▶ A contract between two countries is an **alliance** or **treaty**.
▶ A contract to end a dispute about money is a **settlement**.

contract VERB

1 *Metal contracts when it gets colder.*
shrink, constrict, tighten, draw in, reduce, lessen
OPPOSITE expand

2 *The crew contracted a mysterious disease.*
catch, pick up, get, develop
(informal) go down with, come down with

contradict VERB

1 *No one dared to contradict the soothsayer.*
challenge, disagree with, speak against, oppose

2 *Her statement contradicts the evidence.*
go against, be at odds with, counter, dispute

contradiction NOUN

There is a contradiction between what he says and what he does.
conflict, disagreement, dispute, clash, mismatch, inconsistency

contradictory ADJECTIVE

two contradictory statements
conflicting, inconsistent, incompatible, irreconcilable, at variance
OPPOSITE compatible

contraption NOUN

a room full of weird contraptions
machine, device, gadget, invention, apparatus, contrivance, mechanism
(informal) gizmo

contrary ADJECTIVE

1 *presenting a contrary view*
opposite, opposing, conflicting, contradictory, antithetical

OPPOSITES similar, parallel

2 *Zoe had always been a contrary child.*
awkward, difficult, stubborn, disobedient, obstinate, uncooperative, unhelpful, wilful, perverse
OPPOSITE cooperative

▷ **contrary to**
contrary to popular belief
in opposition to, at odds with

contrast NOUN

1 *Can you see the contrast between the two paintings?*
difference, distinction, dissimilarity, disparity, variance
OPPOSITE similarity

2 *Alvin is a complete contrast to his father.*
opposite, antithesis, complement, foil
OPPOSITE match

contrast VERB

1 *Contrast the language of the two poems.*
compare, juxtapose, distinguish between, differentiate

2 *The title of the book contrasts with its theme.*
differ (from), conflict, be at variance, be at odds, clash, disagree
OPPOSITES match, suit

contribute VERB

Many people contributed blankets and clothing.
donate, give, provide, supply, grant
(informal) chip in

▷ **contribute to**
The music contributed to the overall mood.
add to, enhance, play a part in, be conducive to

contrive VERB

The three of us contrived a brilliant plan.
devise, come up with, create, concoct, hatch, invent,
manufacture, engineer

▷ **contrive to**
He somehow contrived to lose my address.
manage to, find a way to, succeed in

control VERB

1 *No single body controls the Internet.*
be in control of, be in charge of, run, direct, command, manage, lead, guide, govern, administer, regulate, rule, superintend, supervise

2 *Please try to control your temper.*
restrain, contain, hold back, check, curb

control NOUN

1 *Spain once had control over a rich empire.*
authority, power, command, rule, government, management, direction, leadership, dominance, supremacy

2 *imposing tighter controls on cyber-crime*
restriction, limit, restraint, regulation, curb, check

controversial ADJECTIVE

a controversial decision by the umpire
debatable, questionable, arguable, contentious

controversy NOUN

the controversy over the election results
disagreement, dispute, debate, argument, quarrelling, contention, storm
(informal) row

convalescence VERB

a month's convalescence in hospital
recovery, recuperation, rehabilitation

convene VERB

We must convene an emergency meeting.
summon, call, order

a
b
c
d
e
f
g
h
i
j
k
l
m
n
o
p
q
r
s
t
u
v
w
x
y
z

convenient ADJECTIVE

1 *Is this a convenient time to call?*
suitable, appropriate, fitting, favourable, opportune, timely
OPPOSITE inconvenient

2 *a convenient piece of software*
handy, helpful, useful, labour-saving, practical, accessible

convention NOUN

1 *a film which breaks the conventions of science fiction*
custom, tradition, practice, protocol, norm

2 *a convention of leading scientists*
conference, congress, meeting, forum

conventional ADJECTIVE

the conventional way of cooking a turkey
customary, traditional, usual, accepted, prevailing, common, normal, ordinary, everyday, routine, standard, regular, habitual, orthodox
OPPOSITES unconventional, unorthodox

converge VERB

the point where two lines converge
come together, join, meet, merge, combine, coincide
OPPOSITE divide

conversation NOUN

My mum overheard our conversation.
discussion, talk, chat, gossip, tête-à-tête
(informal) confab
(British informal) natter, chinwag
▶ Conversation in a play, film, or novel is **dialogue**.

convert VERB

1 *They converted their attic into a bedroom.*
adapt, turn, change, alter, transform, modify, redevelop

2 *My sister converted me into becoming a vegetarian.*
win over, reform, persuade

convex ADJECTIVE

a convex lens
converging
OPPOSITES concave, diverging

convey VERB

1 *a craft to convey astronauts to the Moon*
transport, carry, bring, deliver, take, fetch, bear, transfer
▶ To convey something by sea is to **ferry** or **ship** it.

2 *The symbols convey a secret meaning.*
communicate, relay, transmit, pass on, carry, tell, relate, impart

convict VERB

Three of the men were convicted of fraud.
find guilty, condemn, sentence
OPPOSITE acquit

convict NOUN

an escaped convict
prisoner, inmate, criminal, offender, felon
(informal) jailbird, con

convince VERB

How can I convince you that I am not lying?
persuade, assure, satisfy, prove to, win over

convincing ADJECTIVE

1 *I tried to think of a convincing excuse.*
believable, credible, plausible, likely

2 *The books makes a convincing argument for evolution.*
persuasive, powerful, strong, compelling, telling, conclusive

cook VERB

cooking a simple meal
prepare
(informal) rustle up
▶ To cook food for guests or customers is to **cater** for them.
▶ To cook food for too long is to **overcook** it, and to cook it for too short a time is to **undercook** it.

WORD WEB

some ways to cook food
bake, barbecue, boil, braise, brew, broil, casserole, chargrill, deep-fry, fry, grill, microwave, poach, roast, sauté, scramble, sear, simmer, steam, stew, stir-fry, toast

other ways to prepare food
baste, blend, chop, dice, grate, grind, infuse, knead, liquidize, marinade, mince, mix, peel, purée, sieve, sift, stir, whisk

▌ SEE ALSO food

equipment used in cooking
baking tin, blender, casserole, chopping board, colander, food grill, ladle, liquidizer, microwave, mincer, oven, roasting tin, rolling pin, saucepan, sieve, skewer, spatula, tagine, tandoor, whisk, wok

measurements used in cooking
cup or cupful, dessertspoon, pinch, spoonful, teaspoon, tablespoon

cook NOUN
training as a ship's cook
► The chief cook in a restaurant or hotel is the **chef**.
► A person who cooks food as a business is a **caterer**.

cookery NOUN
a book about Mexican cookery
cooking, cuisine

cool ADJECTIVE
1 *a cool breeze*
chilly, coldish, fresh, bracing, brisk
(informal) nippy
▌ OPPOSITE warm
FOR TIPS ON DESCRIBING WEATHER SEE
weather

2 *a cool glass of lemonade*

chilled, iced, refreshing
3 *Can everybody please stay cool?*
calm, composed, collected, level-headed, relaxed, poised, at ease, unflustered, unruffled, unperturbed
(informal) unflappable, laid-back
▌ OPPOSITES frantic, stressed
4 *getting a cool reception*
unfriendly, unwelcoming, distant, remote, aloof, frosty, chilly
(informal) stand-offish
▌ OPPOSITE warm
5 *a cool response to my idea*
unenthusiastic, half-hearted, indifferent, lukewarm, tepid
▌ OPPOSITE enthusiastic
6 *(informal) Your new phone is really cool!*
impressive, fashionable, chic, smart
(informal) trendy, fab

cool VERB
Cool the mixture in the fridge overnight.
chill, refrigerate, freeze
▌ OPPOSITES warm, heat up

cooperate VERB
▷ **cooperate with**
refusing to cooperate with the authorities
work with, collaborate with, aid, assist, support, be of service to
▌ IDIOM *(informal)* play ball with

cooperation NOUN
The game was developed with the cooperation of NASA.
collaboration, assistance, participation, teamwork

cooperative ADJECTIVE
1 *a cooperative effort to protect the waterfront*
collaborative, collective, united, shared, joint
▌ OPPOSITE single-handed
2 *I found him surprisingly cooperative.*
supportive, helpful, obliging, accommodating, willing

»

a
b
c
d
e
f
g
h
i
j
k
l
m
n
o
p
q
r
s
t
u
v
w
x
y
z

OPPOSITE uncooperative

coordinate VERB

the job of coordinating the fireworks
organize, arrange, synchronize,
orchestrate, bring together

cope VERB

How are you coping on your own?
manage, carry on, get by, make do,
survive

▷ **cope with**

I can't cope with all this homework!
deal with, handle, manage, tackle,
face

IDIOM get to grips with

copy NOUN

a copy of a Roman mosaic floor
replica, reproduction, duplicate,
imitation, likeness

► A copy made to deceive someone is
a **fake**, **forgery**, or **counterfeit**.

► A living organism which is identical
to another is a **clone**.

copy VERB

1 The passage is copied from a
manuscript.
duplicate, reproduce, replicate

► To copy something in order to
deceive is to **fake**, **forge**, or
counterfeit it.

2 Lots of bands tried to copy the
Beatles.
imitate, mimic, impersonate,
emulate

cord NOUN

a thick cord of blue silk
string, rope, cable, thread, twine,
flex

core NOUN

1 the Earth's core
centre, interior, middle, heart,
nucleus

2 the core of her argument
essence, basis, nub, heart, crux, gist
(informal) nitty-gritty

corner NOUN

1 the corner of the road

turn, turning, bend, curve, junction,
intersection

► The place where two lines meet is
an **angle**.

2 in a remote corner of Asia
area, region, district, quarter, nook

IDIOM neck of the woods

corny ADJECTIVE

a corny joke
overused, clichéd, stale, banal, trite,
hackneyed

corporation NOUN

a multinational corporation
company, business, firm, concern,
conglomerate

corpse NOUN

The pathologist examined the corpse.
dead body, remains, carcass
(formal) cadaver
(informal) stiff

correct ADJECTIVE

1 Your answers are all correct.
right, accurate, true, exact, precise,
faultless, perfect

2 the correct way to eat a boiled egg
proper, right, acceptable, accepted,
regular, appropriate, suitable

correct VERB

1 correcting a spelling mistake
rectify, amend, put right, remedy,
repair, fix, sort

2 correcting exam papers
mark

correspond VERB

▷ **correspond to**

Each symbol corresponds to a sound.
equate to, relate to, be equivalent
to, match

▷ **correspond with**

1 The paint doesn't correspond with
the colour on the tin.
agree with, match, be similar to, be
consistent with, tally with

2 I correspond with my friends by text.
write to, communicate with, send
letters to

a
b
c
d
e
f
g
h
i
j
k
l
m
n
o
p
q
r
s
t
u
v
w
x
y
z

correspondent NOUN

> a BBC correspondent
> reporter, journalist, columnist, commentator

corresponding ADJECTIVE

> a picture with its corresponding caption
> equivalent, matching, related, parallel, comparable, analogous

corrode VERB

> an acid which corrodes metal
> eat away, erode, rot, rust

corrupt ADJECTIVE

> a revolution against the corrupt government
> dishonest, fraudulent, criminal, illegal, unlawful, unethical, unscrupulous, untrustworthy
> (informal) bent, crooked
> **OPPOSITES** honest, ethical

corrupt VERB

> trying to corrupt the minds of teenagers
> pervert, deprave, lead astray

cost NOUN

> 1 the total cost of the holiday
> price, charge, payment, fee, tariff, fare, toll, levy, outlay, expense, expenditure, spend
> (humorous) damage
> 2 the appalling cost to human life
> loss, sacrifice, toll, damage

cost VERB

> 1 How much did your camera cost?
> sell for, go for, come to, amount to
> (informal) set you back
> 2 The work has been costed at $5000.
> price, value

costly ADJECTIVE

> 1 dresses made from costly silks
> dear, expensive, high-cost
> (informal) pricey
> **OPPOSITE** cheap
> 2 a costly mistake
> disastrous, catastrophic, calamitous, damaging, harmful

costume NOUN

> The guards wear the Greek national costume.
> outfit, dress, clothing, suit, attire, garment, garb
> (informal) get-up
> ▶ An official set of clothes worn for school or work is a **uniform**.
> **SEE ALSO clothes**

cosy ADJECTIVE

> 1 a cosy new jumper
> snug, comfortable, warm
> (informal) comfy
> **OPPOSITE** uncomfortable
> 2 a cosy atmosphere
> homely, welcoming, friendly, intimate, secure

couch NOUN

> an old leather couch
> settee, sofa

cough VERB

> The fumes made us all cough.
> clear your throat, hack, hawk, hem

council NOUN

> the members of the school council
> committee, board, panel

counsel VERB

> Merlin counselled King Arthur to look after his sword.
> advise, guide, direct, recommend, urge, warn, caution

count VERB

> 1 counting the days until the end of term
> add up, calculate, compute, estimate, reckon, figure out, work out, total
> 2 It's what you do that counts.
> matter, be important, be significant, carry weight
> 3 I would count it an honour to be asked.
> regard, consider, judge, deem, rate
> ▷ **count on**
> You can count on my support.
> depend on, rely on, trust, bank on, be sure of

a
b
c
d
e
f
g
h
i
j
k
l
m
n
o
p
q
r
s
t
u
v
w
x
y
z

counter VERB

countering an enemy attack
defend against, hit back at, parry, respond to, answer, challenge, contest

countless ADJECTIVE

the lights of countless stars
innumerable, numerous, numberless, incalculable, untold
❙ **OPPOSITE** finite

country NOUN

1 *England and Wales are separate countries.*
nation, state, land, territory
▶ A country ruled by a king or queen is a **kingdom**, **monarchy**, or **realm**.
▶ A country governed by leaders elected by the people is a **democracy**.
▶ A democratic country with a president is a **republic**.
2 *buying a house in the country*
countryside, provinces, outdoors
(informal) the sticks
▶ A related adjective is **rural** and its opposite is **urban**.
▶ Country life can also be described as **bucolic** or **pastoral**.
❙ **OPPOSITES** town, city
3 *a vast area of open country*
terrain, territory, landscape, environment, scenery, surroundings

coupon NOUN

a coupon for a free sandwich
voucher, token, ticket

courage NOUN

the courage shown by the firefighting crew
bravery, valour, fearlessness, boldness, daring, audacity, heroism, gallantry, nerve, pluck, grit
(informal) guts
❙ **OPPOSITE** cowardice

courageous ADJECTIVE

her courageous fight against cancer
brave, valiant, fearless, bold, daring, audacious, heroic, gallant, intrepid, plucky
❙ **OPPOSITE** cowardly

course NOUN

1 *The spacecraft could drift off its course.*
route, path, track, way, trajectory, bearing
2 *The best course is to wait and watch.*
plan of action, procedure, approach, strategy
3 *some changes to the geography course*
syllabus, programme, curriculum
▷ **of course**
Of course you can come to my party.
naturally, certainly, definitely, undoubtedly, needless to say, it goes without saying

courteous ADJECTIVE

I received a courteous reply to my letter.
polite, respectful, well-mannered, civil, gracious, considerate, obliging
❙ **OPPOSITES** rude, impolite

cover VERB

1 *The entrance was covered by a hanging tapestry.*
obscure, conceal, disguise, hide, mask, blot out
2 *Wear googles to cover your eyes.*
shield, screen, protect, shade, veil
3 *My new shoes were covered with mud.*
cake, coat, plaster, encrust
4 *The book covers the various branches of science.*
deal with, include, incorporate, take in, embrace
5 *The cyclists will cover 150 km over two days.*
progress, travel

cover NOUN

1 *Leave the cover of the jar loose.*
lid, top, cap
2 *The cover of the book was torn.*
wrapper, binding, jacket, envelope
3 *seeking cover from the storm*

shelter, protection, shield, refuge, sanctuary

covering *NOUN*

a light covering of snow on the hills
coating, coat, layer, blanket, carpet, film, veneer, skin, sheet, veil, mantle, shroud

coward *NOUN*

Only a coward would run away.
mouse, baby
(informal) chicken, yellow-belly, scaredy-cat

❚ **OPPOSITES** hero, heroine

cowardly *ADJECTIVE*

making a cowardly retreat
faint-hearted, spineless, lily-livered, craven, timid, timorous, fearful
(informal) gutless, yellow, chicken

❚ **OPPOSITES** brave, courageous, heroic

cower *VERB*

A tiny creature was cowering in the corner.
cringe, shrink, crouch, flinch, quail

crack *NOUN*

1 *There's a crack in this cup.*
break, chip, fracture, flaw, chink, split

2 *peering through a crack in the rock*
gap, space, opening, crevice, fissure, rift, cleft, cranny

3 *the crack of a rifle*
bang, explosion, report, pop

4 *a crack on the head*
blow, knock, hit, bash, bang, thump, smack
(informal) whack, wallop, clout

crack *VERB*

1 *The fall must have cracked the vase.*
break, fracture, chip, split, rupture, shatter, splinter

2 *Travis was beginning to crack under the strain.*
break down, lose control
(informal) lose it

❚ **IDIOM** go to pieces

3 (informal) *a difficult code to crack*
decipher, decode, interpret, solve

cradle *NOUN*

1 *a baby's cradle*
cot, crib

2 *the cradle of civilization*
birthplace, origin, source

craft *NOUN*

1 *the craft of hand-weaving*
art, skill, technique, expertise, handicraft

► A person who is skilled in a particular craft is a **craftsman** or **craftswoman**.
FOR TERMS USED IN ART, CRAFT, AND DESIGN SEE art

2 *a wooden sailing craft*
vessel, boat, ship, aircraft, spacecraft

❚ **SEE ALSO aircraft, boat**

crafty *ADJECTIVE*

a crafty plan to deceive the guards
cunning, shrewd, canny, artful, devious, sly, tricky, wily, scheming

cram *VERB*

1 *cramming clothes into a rucksack*
stuff, pack, squeeze, squash, force, jam, thrust, push, shove, compress, crush

2 *We all crammed into the back of the car.*
crowd, push, pile, squeeze, squash

3 *cramming for an exam*
revise, study
(British informal) swot

cramped *ADJECTIVE*

The seating on the plane was cramped.
confined, restricted, tight, narrow, uncomfortable, crowded
(informal) poky

❚ **OPPOSITE** roomy

crash *NOUN*

1 *There was a loud crash from the kitchen.*
bang, clash, clatter, racket

► A crash of thunder is a **peal**.
FOR TIPS ON DESCRIBING SOUNDS SEE sound❶

》

a
b
c
d
e
f
g
h
i
j
k
l
m
n
o
p
q
r
s
t
u
v
w
x
y
z

2 *a crash on the motorway*
collision, accident, smash, bump
▶ A crash involving a lot of vehicles is a **pile-up**.
▶ A train crash may involve a **derailment**.

3 *the stock-market crash*
collapse, failure, ruin, fall

crash VERB
1 *Their car crashed into the back of a lorry.*
bump, smash, collide, knock, plough
2 *The satellite may crash to Earth soon.*
fall, drop, plunge, plummet, dive, tumble
3 *Several banks crashed in the Great Depression.*
fail, collapse, fold, go under
(informal) go bust
❙ IDIOM go to the wall

crate NOUN
a crate of bananas
box, case, chest, packing case, container

crater NOUN
craters on the surface of Mercury
pit, hollow, hole, dip, depression, bowl, basin, cavity

craving NOUN
a craving for chocolate
desire, longing, yearning, hankering, hunger, appetite, thirst

crawl VERB
a caterpillar crawling along a leaf
creep, edge, inch, slither, wriggle

craze NOUN
the latest craze in footwear
fad, trend, vogue, fashion, obsession, mania, rage
(informal) thing

crazy ADJECTIVE
1 *It's enough to drive you crazy!*
mad, insane, demented, deranged, unbalanced, unhinged, hysterical, frantic, frenzied, wild, berserk

(informal) nuts, bonkers, loopy
(British informal) crackers, potty
❙ IDIOMS (informal) off your head, round the bend, round the twist
❙ OPPOSITE sane
2 *Everyone told me it was a crazy idea.*
absurd, ridiculous, ludicrous, idiotic, senseless, silly, stupid, foolhardy, preposterous, hare-brained, half-baked
(informal) crackpot, cockeyed, wacky, zany
(British informal) daft, barmy
❙ OPPOSITE sensible
3 *(informal) Alison is crazy about shoes.*
fanatical, enthusiastic, passionate, fervent, wild
(informal) mad, nuts

creamy ADJECTIVE
a creamy sauce
rich, smooth, thick, velvety, buttery

crease NOUN
ironing the creases out of a shirt
wrinkle, crinkle, pucker, fold, furrow, line, ridge, groove
▶ A crease made deliberately in a garment is a **pleat**.

crease VERB
Try not to crease the paper.
wrinkle, crinkle, crumple, crush, pucker, scrunch up

create VERB
1 *creating a new work of art*
make, produce, generate, originate, fashion, build, construct
❙ OPPOSITE destroy
2 *plans to create a new website*
establish, set up, start up, launch, institute, initiate, found
❙ OPPOSITE abolish

creation NOUN
1 *the creation of life on Earth*
beginning, origin, birth, generation, initiation
2 *money for the creation of a sports centre*
establishment, foundation,

institution, setting up, construction

3 *This pasta sauce is my own creation.*
work, invention, concoction, concept
(informal) brainchild

creative ADJECTIVE
a writer with a creative mind
imaginative, inventive, innovative, original, experimental, artistic, inspired
OPPOSITE unimaginative

creator NOUN
Walt Disney was the creator of Mickey Mouse.
inventor, maker, originator, producer, designer, deviser, author, architect

creature NOUN
A hideous creature emerged from the swamp.
animal, beast, being, brute
FOR MYTHOLOGICAL CREATURES SEE fantasy

credentials PLURAL NOUN
the right credentials for the job
qualifications, suitability, eligibility, attributes

credible ADJECTIVE
Did you find the plot credible?
believable, plausible, conceivable, likely, possible, probable, feasible, reasonable, persuasive, convincing
OPPOSITES incredible, implausible

credit NOUN
She is finally getting the credit she deserves.
recognition, honour, praise, distinction, fame, glory, reputation
OPPOSITE dishonour

credit VERB
1 *It's hard to credit that we are alone in the universe.*
believe, accept, have faith in,

give credence to, trust
(informal) swallow, buy
OPPOSITE doubt

2 *Edison is credited with inventing the light bulb.*
recognize, attribute, identify, associate

creed NOUN
Pupils of all races and creeds attend the school.
faith, religion, belief, ideology, principle

creep VERB
1 *The snail crept halfway out of its shell.*
crawl, edge, inch, slither, wriggle

2 *I crept out of bed without waking the others.*
tiptoe, sneak, slip, slink, steal

creepy (informal) ADJECTIVE
The graveyard was creepy at night.
frightening, eerie, ghostly, sinister, uncanny, unearthly, weird
(informal) spooky, scary

crest NOUN
1 *Some dinosaurs had unusual head crests.*
comb, crown, plume, tuft

2 *the view from the crest of the hill*
summit, top, peak, crown, ridge, head, brow

3 *a carving of the family crest*
emblem, insignia, coat of arms, regalia, badge

crevice NOUN
moss growing in a rock crevice
crack, split, gap, fissure, rift, cleft, chink, cranny
▶ A deep crack in a glacier is a **crevasse**.

crew NOUN
1 *an aircraft crew*
company, corps, squad, hands

2 *a film crew*
team, unit, party, band, gang

a
b
c
d
e
f
g
h
i
j
k
l
m
n
o
p
q
r
s
t
u
v
w
x
y
z

cricket NOUN

WORD WEB

terms used in cricket

bails, batsman, batting average, boundary, bowler, century, crease, cricketer, declaration, dismissal, duck, fielder or fieldsman, googly, innings, LBW, leg spin, maiden over, not out, over, run, six, spin bowler, stump, test match, umpire, wicket, wicketkeeper

FOR TIPS ON WRITING ABOUT SPORT SEE **sport**

crime NOUN

1 *Identity theft is a serious crime.*
offence, violation, felony, misdemeanour

2 *a crackdown on crime*
lawbreaking, wrongdoing, criminality, illegality

▶ The scientific study of crime is **criminology** and a person who specializes in this is a **criminologist**.

▶ The use of scientific methods to solve crime is **forensic science** or **forensics**.
Sherlock Holmes was an expert in forensics.

WRITING TIPS

writing crime fiction

Poirot locked the door on the inside, and proceeded to a minute inspection of the room. He darted from one object to another with the agility of a grasshopper. I remained by the door, fearing to obliterate any clues.
— *Agatha Christie, The Mysterious Affair at Styles*

characters

criminologist, detective inspector, forensic scientist, master criminal, murderer,

pathologist, police officer, private detective, private eye, sleuth, toxicologist

useful words & phrases

accessory, accomplice, alibi, bloodstain, case history, circumstantial evidence, clue, confession, corroborate, crime scene, cross-examine, CSI, deduction, DNA sample, dusting for fingerprints, evidence, examination, expert witness, false identity, fingerprint analysis, forensics, forgery, homicide, hunch, hypothesis, incriminate, in custody, inquiry, investigation, lead, line of enquiry, manhunt, morgue, motive, perpetrator, post-mortem, prime suspect, profiling, proof, reconstruction, questioning, sequence of events, statement, suspect, testimony, *(informal)* tip-off, whodunnit, witness, victim

FOR FINGERPRINT ANALYSIS SEE **finger**

criminal NOUN

a gang of hardened criminals
lawbreaker, offender, felon, wrongdoer, malefactor, miscreant *(informal)* crook

▶ A criminal who has been sent to prison is a **convict**.

WORD WEB

some types of criminal

assassin, bandit, blackmailer, burglar, cat burglar, *(informal)* con man, cybercriminal, forger, gangster, hacker, highwayman, hijacker, identity thief, kidnapper, money launderer, mugger, murderer, outlaw, pickpocket, pirate, poacher, robber, shoplifter, smuggler, terrorist, thief, thug, vandal

a
b
c
d
e
f
g
h
i
j
k
l
m
n
o
p
q
r
s
t
u
v
w
x
y
z

criminal *ADJECTIVE*

> *Police have uncovered a criminal network.*
> illegal, unlawful, corrupt, dishonest
> *(informal)* crooked
> ▌**OPPOSITES** lawful, honest, above board

cringe *VERB*

> *cringing with embarrassment*
> shrink, flinch, wince, cower

cripple *VERB*

> **1** *The fall may have crippled the horse.*
> disable, handicap, maim, lame
> **2** *a country crippled by war and famine*
> ruin, destroy, crush, wreck, damage, weaken, paralyse, immobilize, incapacitate

crisis *NOUN*

> *the crisis caused by the Wall Street crash*
> emergency, calamity, catastrophe, disaster, predicament, extremity, meltdown, turning point
> *(informal)* crunch

crisp *ADJECTIVE*

> **1** *a crisp coating of chocolate*
> crunchy, crispy, brittle, hard
> ▌**OPPOSITES** soft, soggy
> **2** *a crisp winter morning*
> fresh, brisk, bracing, refreshing, invigorating

critic *NOUN*

> **1** *a film critic*
> reviewer, commentator, columnist, analyst, pundit, expert
> **2** *a lifelong critic of racism*
> opponent, attacker, detractor

critical *ADJECTIVE*

> **1** *making critical remarks*
> negative, disapproving, derogatory, uncomplimentary, unfavourable, scathing, disparaging, censorious
> ▌**OPPOSITES** complimentary, positive
> **2** *a critical point in the match*
> crucial, important, vital, essential, pivotal, key, paramount,

decisive, serious
> ▌**OPPOSITE** unimportant

criticism *NOUN*

> **1** *a scathing criticism of the media*
> condemnation, censure, fault-finding, disparagement, disapproval, reproach
> *(informal)* flak
> ▌**OPPOSITE** praise
> **2** *a piece of literary criticism*
> analysis, evaluation, assessment, appraisal, commentary, critique

criticize *VERB*

> *The film has been criticized for its poor script.*
> condemn, find fault with, censure, attack, denigrate, disparage, reproach, berate
> *(informal)* knock, pan, slam, slate
> ▌**OPPOSITE** praise

crockery *NOUN*

> *a shelf full of crockery*
> china, dishes, plates

crooked *ADJECTIVE*

> **1** *a crooked tree trunk*
> bent, twisted, warped, contorted, misshapen, deformed, gnarled
> ▌**OPPOSITE** straight
> **2** *(informal) a crooked banker*
> criminal, dishonest, corrupt, illegal, unlawful
> ▌**OPPOSITE** honest

crop *NOUN*

> *a heavy crop of apples*
> harvest, yield, produce

crop *VERB*

> *cropping the edges of a picture*
> cut, trim, clip, snip, shear, shave, chop
> ▷ **crop up**
> *Several problems have cropped up.*
> arise, occur, appear, emerge, surface, come up, turn up, pop up
> ▌**IDIOM** come to light

cross *VERB*

> **1** *Cross the road at the traffic lights.*

a
b
c
d
e
f
g
h
i
j
k
l
m
n
o
p
q
r
s
t
u
v
w
x
y
z

go across, travel across, pass over, traverse, span
▶ To cross a river or stream is to **ford** it.

2 *The two sets of footprints cross here.*
intersect, meet, join, connect
▶ To form a pattern of crossing lines is to **criss-cross**.

3 *No one dared to cross Caesar.*
oppose, defy, argue with, contradict

▷ **cross out**
My name had been crossed out on the list.
delete, score out, strike out, cancel

cross *ADJECTIVE*
The coach will be cross if we miss training.
angry, annoyed, irate, upset, vexed, irked, bad-tempered, ill-tempered, irritable, grumpy, testy, surly, snappy
(British informal) shirty
(North American informal) sore, ticked off
▌ OPPOSITE pleased

crossroads *NOUN*
Turn left at the crossroads.
intersection, junction
▶ A junction of two motorways is an **interchange**.

crouch *VERB*
You need to crouch to get into the cave.
squat, stoop, duck, bend, bob down, hunch, cower

crowd *NOUN*
1 *A crowd formed outside the gates.*
gathering, assembly, throng, multitude, horde, swarm, mob, mass, crush, rabble

2 *The show attracted a huge crowd.*
audience, spectators, gate, attendance

3 *one of the trendy crowd*
set, gang, circle, clique
(informal) bunch

crowd *VERB*
1 *People crowded outside to*

watch the fireworks.
gather, collect, cluster, assemble, congregate, mass, flock, throng, muster

2 *Hundreds of people crowded into the hall.*
push, pile, squeeze, pack, cram, crush, jam, bundle, herd

crowded *ADJECTIVE*
The shops are always crowded at the weekend.
full, packed, busy, teeming, swarming, overflowing, jammed, congested
(informal) chock-a-block, jam-packed, mobbed
(Australian & NZ informal) chocker
▌ OPPOSITES empty, deserted

crown *NOUN*
1 *a crown of solid gold*
coronet, circlet, diadem, tiara

2 *a servant of the Crown*
monarch, sovereign, king, queen, royalty

3 *The church sits on the crown of the hill.*
top, crest, summit, peak, brow

crown *VERB*
1 *Queen Victoria was crowned in 1837.*
▶ A ceremony at which a monarch is crowned is a **coronation**.

2 *mountain peaks crowned with snow*
top, cap, tip, surmount

3 *They crowned a remarkable season with another win.*
round off, cap, complete

crucial *ADJECTIVE*
Copernicus made a crucial discovery about the universe.
important, critical, decisive, vital, pivotal, key, momentous, all-important
▌ OPPOSITE unimportant

crude *ADJECTIVE*
1 *the processing of crude oil*
raw, natural, unprocessed, unrefined, untreated

OPPOSITES refined, treated

2 *crude workmanship*
rough, clumsy, makeshift, primitive, rudimentary, rough and ready
OPPOSITES skilful, sophisticated

3 *a crude joke*
rude, obscene, indecent, dirty, smutty, vulgar, coarse, lewd
OPPOSITE clean

cruel ADJECTIVE

1 *banning the cruel treatment of animals*
brutal, savage, inhumane, barbaric, barbarous, heartless, ruthless, merciless, callous
OPPOSITES compassionate, humane

2 *a cruel blow to all our hopes*
severe, harsh, bitter, painful, agonizing

cruelty NOUN

exposing the cruelty of the slave trade
brutality, inhumanity, heartlessness, ruthlessness, barbarity, savagery
OPPOSITES compassion, humanity

crumb NOUN

cake crumbs on the carpet
bit, fragment, scrap, morsel, particle
SEE ALSO bit

crumble VERB

1 *The plasterwork is beginning to crumble.*
disintegrate, break up, fall apart, fall to pieces, collapse, decay, decompose

2 *Crumble the dried leaves between your fingers.*
crush, grind, pulverize

crumpled ADJECTIVE

a crumpled t-shirt
creased, wrinkled, crinkled, rumpled, crushed

crunch VERB

1 *a dog crunching on a bone*
chew, munch, chomp, grind
SEE ALSO eat

2 *footsteps crunching through the snow*
FOR TIPS ON DESCRIBING SOUNDS SEE **sound❶**

crush VERB

1 *I crushed my jumper into my school bag.*
squash, squeeze, mangle, pound, press, bruise, crunch, scrunch
▶ To crush something into a soft mess is to **mash** or **pulp** it.
▶ To crush something into a powder is to **grind** or **pulverize** it.
▶ To crush something out of shape is to **crumple** or **smash** it.

2 *The Jacobite army was crushed at Culloden.*
defeat, conquer, vanquish, overcome, overwhelm, quash, trounce, rout

crush NOUN

a crush of people in the dining hall
crowd, throng, mob, press, jam, congestion

crust NOUN

The liquid rock cooled to form a crust.
skin, shell, coating, film, exterior
▶ A crust that forms over a cut or graze is a **scab**.

crustacean NOUN

WORD WEB

some animals which are crustaceans
barnacle, crab, crayfish, langoustine, lobster, prawn, sea slater, shrimp, woodlouse
(Scottish, Australian & NZ slater)
SEE ALSO shellfish

cry NOUN

1 *a cry of pain*
call, shout, yell, roar, howl, exclamation, bellow, scream, screech, shriek, yelp

»

2 *the cry of a whooping crane*
sound, call
**FOR SOUNDS MADE BY ANIMALS AND
BIRDS** SEE **animal**, **bird**

cry *VERB*
1 *Babs looked like she was going to cry.*
weep, sob, shed tears, wail,
whimper, snivel
(informal) blubber
▶ When someone starts to cry, their
eyes **well up with tears**.
2 *We heard someone crying for help.*
call, shout, yell, exclaim, roar, bawl,
bellow, scream, screech, shriek
(informal) holler

cuddle *VERB*
cuddling a hot-water bottle
hug, clasp, embrace, caress, fondle,
nestle against, snuggle against

cue *NOUN*
*When I nod, that is your cue to
speak.*
signal, sign, prompt, reminder

culminate *VERB*
▷ **culminate in**
*The film culminates in a tense
shoot-out.*
finish with, conclude with, close
with, build up to, lead up to

culprit *NOUN*
*Police are still searching for the
culprits.*
offender, wrongdoer, criminal, felon

cult *NOUN*
1 *an obscure religious cult*
sect, group, movement
2 *the cult of celebrity*
worship, veneration, obsession,
fixation

cultivate *VERB*
1 *cultivating a piece of land*
farm, work, till, plough,
grow crops on
2 *cultivating good habits*
develop, encourage, promote,
further, foster, nurture

cultural *ADJECTIVE*
the cultural life of the city
artistic, intellectual, aesthetic,
creative

culture *NOUN*
1 *a woman of culture*
cultivation, refinement, taste,
sophistication
2 *the culture of ancient Greece*
civilization, society, traditions,
customs, heritage

cunning *ADJECTIVE*
1 *as cunning a criminal as you'll ever
meet*
crafty, devious, artful, scheming, sly,
tricky, wily, sneaky
2 *Agent Lewis had devised a cunning
plan.*
clever, shrewd, ingenious, inventive,
creative, inspired, brilliant

cup *NOUN*
a cup and saucer
mug, beaker, tumbler, tankard
▶ A decorative drinking cup is a **goblet**
or **chalice**.

cupboard *NOUN*
a cupboard under the stairs
cabinet, dresser, sideboard
▶ A cupboard for food is a **larder**.

curb *VERB*
I tried hard to curb my anger.
control, restrain, hold back,
suppress, contain, check, limit,
restrict, rein in, keep in check
▌**IDIOM** keep a lid on

curb *NOUN*
curbs on violent video games
control, restraint, check, limit,
restriction, rein

cure *VERB*
1 *A good night's rest will cure your
headache.*
heal, ease, improve, make better,
relieve
▌**OPPOSITE** aggravate
2 *curing the problem of child poverty*
remedy, put right, sort, solve, repair,

mend, fix, put an end to, eliminate

cure NOUN

an effective cure for malaria
remedy, treatment, antidote, therapy, medicine, medication

▶ A cure for all kinds of diseases or troubles is a **panacea**.

curiosity NOUN

1 *Babies are full of curiosity about the world.*
inquisitiveness, interest
▶ Uncomplimentary synonyms are **nosiness**, **prying**, and **snooping**.

2 *His first film is something of a curiosity.*
oddity, novelty, rarity, curio

curious ADJECTIVE

1 *We were all curious about the visitors.*
intrigued, interested (in), agog, inquisitive
▶ An uncomplimentary word is **nosy**.
┃ **OPPOSITES** uninterested (in), indifferent (to)

2 *What is that curious smell?*
odd, strange, peculiar, abnormal, unusual, extraordinary, funny, mysterious, puzzling, weird, bizarre

curl NOUN

1 *Her hair was a mass of raven curls.*
wave, ringlet, lock

2 *a curl of paper*
coil, twist, scroll, spiral, swirl

curl VERB

1 *The snake curled itself around a branch.*
wind, twist, loop, coil, wrap, twine

2 *smoke curling from the chimney*
coil, spiral, twirl, swirl, furl, snake, writhe, ripple

curly ADJECTIVE

a boy with curly black hair
wavy, curled, curling, frizzy, crinkly, ringletted
┃ **OPPOSITE** straight
FOR TIPS ON DESCRIBING HAIR SEE **hair**

currency NOUN
SEE **money**

current ADJECTIVE

1 *all the current teenage fashions*
modern, contemporary, present-day, up to date, topical, prevailing, prevalent
┃ **OPPOSITES** past, old-fashioned

2 *Have you got a current passport?*
valid, usable, up to date
┃ **OPPOSITE** out of date

3 *Who is the current president?*
present, existing, reigning, incumbent
┃ **OPPOSITES** past, former

current NOUN

drifting along with the current
flow, tide, stream
▶ A current of air is a **draught**.

curse NOUN

1 *There is an ancient curse on the family of Ravenswood.*
jinx, hex

2 *I could hear him muttering curses.*
swear word, oath, expletive, profanity

cursed ADJECTIVE

It seemed to me that our voyage was cursed.
doomed, damned, jinxed, ill-fated, ill-starred

curt ADJECTIVE

I received a very curt reply.
abrupt, terse, blunt, brusque, short

curve NOUN

plotting a curve on a graph
bend, turn, loop, arch, arc, bow, bulge, curvature
▶ A curve on a road surface is a **camber**.

curve VERB

The road ahead curves round to the right.
bend, turn, wind, loop, curl, arc, arch, swerve, veer, snake, meander

a
b
c
d
e
f
g
h
i
j
k
l
m
n
o
p
q
r
s
t
u
v
w
x
y
z

a
b
c
d
e
f
g
h
i
j
k
l
m
n
o
p
q
r
s
t
u
v
w
x
y
z

curved ADJECTIVE

a pattern of curved lines
curving, curvy, bent, looped,
arched, bowed, bulging, winding,
meandering, serpentine, undulating

▶ A surface curved like the inside
of a circle is **concave**, and one
curved like the outside of a circle is
convex.

cushion NOUN

1 *a chair cushion*
pillow, pad, bolster

2 *a cushion against rising prices*
protection, shield, buffer,
bulwark

cushion VERB

The mat will cushion your fall.
soften, lessen, alleviate, absorb,
deaden, dampen

custody NOUN

▷ **in custody**
Two men are being held in custody.
in jail, in prison
(informal) inside
IDIOMS under lock and key,
behind bars

custom NOUN

1 *the custom of giving presents at
Christmas*
tradition, practice, convention,
habit, routine, observance, ritual

2 *We need to attract more custom.*
customers, buyers, clients, trade,
business

customary ADJECTIVE

*It is customary to leave the waiter
a tip.*
traditional, conventional,
usual, normal, common, typical,
expected, habitual, routine, regular,
everyday, ordinary, prevailing,
prevalent
OPPOSITE unusual

customer NOUN

a queue of angry customers
buyer, shopper, client, purchaser,
consumer

cut VERB

1 *Cut the vegetables into chunks.*
chop, slice, carve, split, slit, sever,
cleave

▶ To cut food into cubes is to **dice** it.
▶ To cut something up to examine it is
to **dissect** it.
▶ To cut down a tree is to **fell** it.
▶ To cut something with an axe is to
hew it.

2 *a name cut into the stone*
carve, score, incise, engrave, notch,
chisel, chip

3 *You've had your hair cut!*
trim, clip, crop, snip, shave

▶ To cut grass is to **mow** it.
▶ To cut twigs off a plant is to **prune** it.
▶ To cut wool off a sheep is to **shear** it.

4 *Hank fell and cut his knee.*
gash, slash, wound, lacerate, scratch,
graze, nick

5 *I had to cut my essay to make it fit
the page.*
shorten, condense, edit, abbreviate,
abridge, truncate

6 *We are cutting our prices by ten per
cent.*
lower, reduce, decrease, drop, slash

▶ If you cut something by half, you
halve it.

▷ **cut something off**

1 *cutting off the lower branches*
chop off, lop, sever

▶ To cut off a limb is to **amputate** it.

2 *cutting off the electricity*
discontinue, shut off, suspend

cut NOUN

1 *Make a small cut in the fabric.*
slash, slit, incision, snip, nick, gash

2 *a nasty cut on my forehead*
gash, wound, injury, laceration,
scratch, graze

3 *a cut in the price of fuel*
fall, reduction, decrease, lowering,
drop

4 *(informal) Each of the gang took
their cut.*
share, portion, percentage, quota

cutting ADJECTIVE
> He made a cutting remark about
> my tie.
> hurtful, wounding, scathing, biting,
> caustic, barbed

cycle NOUN
> **1** a special lane for cycles
> SEE **bicycle**
> **2** the cycle of the seasons
> round, circle, rotation, succession,
> sequence

Dd

a
b
c
d
e
f
g
h
i
j
k
l
m
n
o
p
q
r
s
t
u
v
w
x
y
z

dab *NOUN*
a dab of glue
spot, drop, bit, blob, daub, dollop
▌**SEE ALSO bit**

dab *VERB*
Lily dabbed her eyes with a handkerchief.
pat, touch, press, wipe, daub

dad *NOUN*
SEE **father**

daily *ADJECTIVE*
a daily exercise routine
everyday, day-to-day, regular

daily *ADVERB*
The rooms are cleaned daily.
every day, each day, once a day

dainty *ADJECTIVE*
a dainty little ribbon
delicate, neat, charming, elegant, fine, exquisite, bijou
(informal) cute, dinky
▌**OPPOSITE clumsy**

dam *NOUN*
a dam built by beavers
barrage, barrier, embankment, dyke, weir

damage *NOUN*
the damage caused by the floods
harm, destruction, devastation, injury, ruin

damage *VERB*
Many paintings were damaged in the fire
harm, spoil, mar, break, impair, weaken, disfigure, deface, mutilate, scar
▶ To damage something beyond repair is to **destroy**, **ruin**, or **wreck** it.
▶ To damage something deliberately is to **sabotage** or **vandalize** it.

damaging *ADJECTIVE*
Litter has a damaging effect on wildlife.
harmful, detrimental, injurious, negative
▌**OPPOSITE beneficial**

damning *ADJECTIVE*
damning new evidence of his crimes
incriminating, implicating, conclusive, incontrovertible, irrefutable

damp *ADJECTIVE*
1 *These clothes are still damp.*
moist, wettish, dank, soggy, clammy
▌**OPPOSITE dry**
2 *a cold and damp morning*
drizzly, foggy, misty, rainy, wet
▶ Weather which is both damp and warm is **humid** or **muggy**.

dampen *VERB*
1 *Dampen the cloth with a little water.*
moisten, wet
▶ To wet something completely is to **soak** it.
2 *Nothing could dampen my enthusiasm.*
lessen, decrease, diminish, reduce, stifle, suppress

dance *VERB*
I could have danced for joy.
caper, cavort, skip, prance, gambol, leap, hop, whirl, twirl, gyrate, pirouette

dance *NOUN*

 WORD WEB

some kinds of dance or dancing
ballet, ballroom dancing, barn dance, belly-dancing, bolero, 》

> break-dancing, cancan, disco,
> flamenco, folk dance, Highland
> dancing, hornpipe, jazz dance,
> jig, jive dancing, limbo dancing,
> line-dancing, mazurka, morris
> dance, quadrille, reel, rumba,
> samba, Scottish country dancing,
> square dance, step dancing,
> street dance, tap dancing,
> tarantella
> ▶ A person who writes the steps for
> a dance is a **choreographer**.

danger NOUN

1 *Is the crew in any danger?*
peril, jeopardy, menace, threat,
trouble, crisis
❙ **OPPOSITE** safety

2 *the dangers of sunbathing*
risk, hazard, problem, pitfall, trap

3 *There is a danger that the volcano
may erupt.*
chance, possibility, risk

dangerous ADJECTIVE

1 *a dangerous rescue attempt*
hazardous, perilous, risky, unsafe,
precarious, treacherous, menacing,
threatening
(informal) hairy, dicey

2 *arrested for dangerous driving*
careless, reckless

3 *a highly dangerous chemical*
harmful, destructive, poisonous,
deadly, toxic
❙ **OPPOSITES** harmless, safe

dangle VERB

keys dangling from a chain
hang, swing, sway, wave, droop,
flap, trail

dank ADJECTIVE

a cold and dank dungeon
damp, musty, clammy

dare VERB

1 *Who dares to enter the mummy's
tomb?*
have the courage, be brave enough,
have the nerve, venture

2 *My friends dared me to ring the
doorbell.*
challenge, defy, provoke, goad

daring ADJECTIVE

*a daring attempt to swim Niagara
Falls*
bold, brave, courageous, audacious,
fearless, valiant, intrepid, plucky
(informal) gutsy
▶ A daring person is a **daredevil**.
❙ **OPPOSITES** timid, cowardly

dark ADJECTIVE

1 *a dark winter night*
black, murky, dim, gloomy, dingy,
inky, shadowy, louring
❙ **OPPOSITES** bright, moonlit

2 *a dark blue scarf*
❙ **OPPOSITES** pale, light

3 *long dark hair*
black, brunette, sable, raven, ebony
❙ **OPPOSITE** fair
FOR TIPS ON DESCRIBING HAIR SEE **hair**

4 *a dark period of my life*
bleak, unhappy, miserable, grim,
gloomy, dismal, negative
❙ **OPPOSITE** happy

5 *This peaceful island holds a dark
secret.*
mysterious, sinister, ominous,
disturbing
(informal) shady

6 *creatures from the dark side*
evil, wicked, malevolent, demonic,
ungodly, unholy

dark NOUN

1 *I can't see you in the dark.*
darkness, blackout, gloom
❙ **OPPOSITES** light, brightness

2 *No one was allowed out after dark.*
nightfall, night-time
❙ **OPPOSITES** daytime, daybreak

▷ **in the dark**
*I was completely in the dark about
the party.*
uninformed, ignorant, clueless,
unaware (of)
❙ **OPPOSITE** in the know

a
b
c
d
e
f
g
h
i
j
k
l
m
n
o
p
q
r
s
t
u
v
w
x
y
z

darken *VERB*
> *Suddenly, the sky darkened.*
> grow dark, grow dim, blacken, cloud over
>
> ❙ **OPPOSITES** brighten, lighten

darkness *NOUN*
> **1** *a light shining in the darkness*
> blackness, dimness, gloom, murk, shade, shadow
>
> ❙ **OPPOSITES** brightness, light
>
> **2** *the forces of darkness*
> evil, wickedness, the dark side

darling *NOUN*
> SEE **love**

dart *VERB*
> **1** *A rabbit darted out of the bushes.*
> run, dash, race, sprint, speed, rush, tear, pelt, scurry, scamper
>
> ❙ **SEE ALSO** run
>
> **2** *Mr Ames darted a glance at his wife.*
> direct, throw, cast, shoot

dash *VERB*
> **1** *We dashed home in time for tea.*
> hurry, run, rush, race, hasten, speed, sprint, tear, fly, zoom
>
> **2** *Cleopatra dashed the goblet to the ground.*
> throw, hurl, fling, toss, smash
> (informal) sling, chuck
>
> **3** *They dashed our hopes of winning a medal.*
> destroy, wreck, ruin, shatter, scotch
> (informal) scupper
>
> ❙ **IDIOM** put paid to

dash *NOUN*
> **1** *making a dash for shelter*
> run, rush, race, sprint, bolt, charge
>
> **2** *Add a dash of milk.*
> drop, splash, spot, swig, dribble, drizzle

dashing *ADJECTIVE*
> *Craig looked very dashing in a kilt.*
> stylish, elegant, dapper, spruce, debonair
> (informal) natty

data *PLURAL NOUN*
> *entering data into a computer*
> information, details, facts, figures, statistics

date *NOUN*
> *When is your lunch date?*
> meeting, appointment, engagement

date *VERB*
> **1** *Some films never seem to date.*
> age, become dated, show its age
>
> **2** *(informal) Is she dating someone just now?*
> go out with, see, be involved with

dated *ADJECTIVE*
> *The special effects look dated now.*
> old-fashioned, outdated, outmoded, antiquated, behind the times, passé
> (informal) old hat
>
> ❙ **IDIOM** out of the ark
>
> ❙ **OPPOSITES** modern, cutting-edge

daunting *ADJECTIVE*
> *An audition can be a daunting prospect.*
> formidable, challenging, forbidding, unnerving, discouraging, off-putting

dawdle *VERB*
> *Don't dawdle—we haven't got all day!*
> linger, dally, drag your feet, delay, lag behind, straggle
> (informal) dilly-dally
>
> ❙ **OPPOSITE** hurry

dawn *NOUN*
> **1** *We were woken at dawn by birdsong.*
> daybreak, sunrise, first light
> (North American) sunup
>
> ❙ **OPPOSITES** dusk, sunset
>
> **2** *the dawn of a new era*
> beginning, start, birth, origin, genesis, onset, rise

dawn *VERB*
> *A new era in medicine is dawning.*
> begin, start, emerge, arise, develop, unfold
>
> ❙ **OPPOSITE** end

▷ **dawn on someone**
The truth was beginning to dawn on me.
become clear to, occur to, register with, strike, hit

day *NOUN*

1 *Badgers sleep during the day.*
daytime, daylight
┃ **OPPOSITES** night, night-time

2 *Things were different in your day.*
age, era, time, period, epoch

daze *VERB*
She was dazed by the contents of the letter.
stun, shock, stupefy, stagger, bewilder, perplex, take aback
(informal) flabbergast

daze *NOUN*
walking around in a daze
stupor, trance, daydream

dazzle *VERB*

1 *My eyes were dazzled by the light.*
blind, disorient

2 *She dazzled the audience with her performance.*
amaze, astonish, stun, impress, overwhelm, awe
(informal) bowl over, blow away, knock out

dead *ADJECTIVE*

1 *Lyra thinks her parents are dead.*
deceased, departed
▶ You can describe a person who is recently dead as **the late**.
a tribute to the late actor
┃ **OPPOSITES** alive, living

2 *Zombies are dead bodies which can move.*
lifeless, inanimate
▶ A dead body is a **carcass** or **corpse**.

3 *The town centre is dead at this time of night.*
quiet, dull, boring, lifeless, sleepy, flat, slow
┃ **OPPOSITES** lively, animated

4 *This phone is completely dead.*
not working, broken, inoperative,

defective, worn out
(informal) kaput
(British informal) knackered
▶ A battery which is dead is **flat**.

5 *Latin is a dead language.*
extinct, obsolete, defunct, disused
┃ **OPPOSITE** living

deaden *VERB*

1 *an injection to deaden the pain*
anaesthetize, lessen, reduce, suppress
┃ **OPPOSITE** increase

2 *deadening the noise of traffic*
dampen, muffle, quieten
┃ **OPPOSITE** amplify

deadly *ADJECTIVE*

1 *the deadly sting of a scorpion*
lethal, fatal, mortal, life-threatening, poisonous, toxic, noxious
┃ **OPPOSITE** harmless

2 *The Joker is Batman's deadly enemy.*
mortal, bitter, sworn, implacable

3 *A deadly hush descended on the room.*
complete, total, absolute, utter

deafening *ADJECTIVE*
the deafening sound of heavy metal music
loud, blaring, booming, thunderous, ear-splitting, penetrating

deal *VERB*

1 *Who is going to deal the cards?*
give out, distribute, share out, hand out, pass round, dispense

2 *a company dealing in software*
do business, trade

▷ **deal with something**

1 *I'll deal with the catering.*
cope with, sort out, attend to, see to, handle, manage, look after, take charge of, take in hand

2 *The book deals with the history of art.*
be concerned with, cover, discuss, explore, examine

deal *NOUN*
signing a deal with a

a
b
c
d
e
f
g
h
i
j
k
l
m
n
o
p
q
r
s
t
u
v
w
x
y
z

record company
agreement, contract, bargain,
settlement, arrangement

▷ **a good deal** or **a great deal**
*It is a good deal colder than last
year.*
a lot, considerably, markedly,
noticeably, substantially

dear *ADJECTIVE*

1 *a very dear friend of mine*
close, loved, beloved, valued,
cherished, treasured
❙ **OPPOSITE** distant

2 *Their prices are far too dear for me.*
expensive, costly, high-priced,
exorbitant
(informal) pricey
❙ **OPPOSITE** cheap

dearly *ADVERB*

I would dearly love to visit New York.
very much, greatly, deeply,
profoundly

dearth *NOUN*

a dearth of new ideas
lack, scarcity, shortage, deficiency,
want, absence

death *NOUN*

1 *the death of the pharaoh*
dying, end, passing, decease
▶ A death caused by an accident or war
is a **fatality**.

2 *the death of all our hopes*
end, extinction, destruction,
annihilation

deathly *ADJECTIVE*

*From his deathly pallor, I knew he
was a vampire.*
deathlike, ghostly, ghastly, ashen,
cadaverous

debate *NOUN*

a debate about animal rights
discussion, argument, dispute
▶ Something which people argue
about a lot is a **controversy**.

debate *VERB*

1 *The panel debated the existence
of God.*

discuss, argue about, talk through,
thrash out

2 *I debated what to do next.*
consider, ponder, deliberate, weigh
up, reflect on, mull over

debris *NOUN*

debris from the shipwreck
remains, wreckage, fragments,
waste, detritus, flotsam and jetsam

decay *VERB*

1 *a pile of decaying vegetation*
decompose, rot, disintegrate,
putrefy, spoil, perish

2 *Ancient Greek civilization eventually
decayed.*
decline, degenerate, deteriorate
❙ **IDIOMS** go downhill, go to seed, go
to the dogs

decay *NOUN*

the decay of the Roman Empire
decline, degeneration, deterioration,
collapse, crumbling

deceit *NOUN*

*Claudius obtains the throne through
deceit.*
deception, trickery, dishonesty,
fraud, duplicity, double-dealing,
pretence, bluff, cheating,
deceitfulness, lying
❙ **OPPOSITE** honesty

deceitful *ADJECTIVE*

*Foxes are often portrayed as deceitful
in stories.*
dishonest, underhand, insincere,
duplicitous, untruthful, false,
cheating, hypocritical, lying,
treacherous, two-faced, sneaky
❙ **OPPOSITE** honest

deceive *VERB*

Emile had deceived all of us.
fool, trick, delude, dupe, hoodwink,
cheat, double-cross, mislead,
swindle
(informal) con, take in
❙ **IDIOMS** pull the wool over
someone's eyes, take someone for
a ride

decency NOUN

1 *a comedy show that pushes the bounds of decency*
propriety, respectability, modesty, decorum, good taste

2 *He had the decency to admit he was wrong.*
courtesy, politeness, good manners, thoughtfulness, consideration

decent ADJECTIVE

1 *The ancient skeleton is to get a decent burial.*
proper, honourable, appropriate, respectable, decorous, modest, seemly
⌐ OPPOSITES indecent, improper

2 *getting a decent night's sleep*
satisfactory, adequate, sufficient, reasonable, tolerable, acceptable, fair
⌐ OPPOSITE inadequate

deception NOUN
SEE **deceit**

deceptive ADJECTIVE

The blurb on the back of the book is deceptive.
misleading, deceiving, unreliable, false, distorted

decide VERB

1 *Have you decided what to wear yet?*
choose, make a decision, make up your mind, opt, elect, resolve

2 *The umpire decided that the ball was in play.*
conclude, judge, rule, pronounce, adjudicate

3 *There will be a play-off to decide the medals.*
determine, settle

decision NOUN

awaiting the judges' decision
judgement, verdict, ruling, conclusion, findings

decisive ADJECTIVE

1 *a decisive piece of evidence*
conclusive, deciding, irrefutable, critical, key

2 *A referee needs to be decisive.*
firm, forceful, strong-minded, resolute, quick-thinking
⌐ OPPOSITES indecisive, hesitant

declaration NOUN

a declaration of war
announcement, pronouncement, proclamation, statement, assertion

declare VERB

1 *She declared her intention to retire next year.*
announce, make known, state, express, reveal, voice, proclaim

2 *He declared that he was innocent.*
assert, affirm, profess, state, maintain, contend, insist

decline VERB

1 *I declined her invitation to dinner.*
refuse, reject, rebuff, turn down, say no to, pass up
⌐ OPPOSITE accept

2 *The band's popularity declined rapidly.*
decrease, diminish, lessen, dwindle, wane, shrink, subside, tail off
⌐ OPPOSITE increase

decline NOUN

1 *a sharp decline in sales*
fall, drop, lowering, decrease, reduction, downturn, slump

2 *the country's decline into poverty*
descent, slide, fall, degeneration

decode VERB
SEE **code**

decorate VERB

1 *We decorated the tree with tinsel.*
ornament, adorn, furnish, trim, beautify, prettify, deck, festoon, garnish

2 *some ideas for decorating your bedroom*
refurbish, renovate, paint, wallpaper *(informal)* do up, make over

3 *a firefighter decorated for bravery*
award a medal to, honour, reward

a
b
c
d
e
f
g
h
i
j
k
l
m
n
o
p
q
r
s
t
u
v
w
x
y
z

decoration NOUN

1 *the rich decoration inside the dome*
ornamentation, embellishment,
adornment, furnishing

2 *putting up the Christmas decorations*
ornament, bauble, garland, trinket,
knick-knack

3 *a decoration for bravery*
medal, award

decorative ADJECTIVE

fabric with a decorative design
ornamental, elaborate, fancy,
ornate, colourful, attractive, pretty
❚ OPPOSITES plain, functional

> **Usage Note**
>
> The word **decorous** is not a
> synonym of **decorative**. A
> *decorative dress* is ornate, but a
> *decorous dress* is appropriate for
> the occasion.

decrease VERB

1 *My energy decreased as the day
went on.*
decline, diminish, lessen, weaken,
dwindle, flag, wane, shrink, subside,
tail off

2 *decreasing your carbon footprint*
reduce, cut, lower, lessen, minimize
(*informal*) slash
FOR OPPOSITES SEE increase

decrease NOUN

a decrease in the use of plastic bags
decline, drop, fall, cut, reduction,
downturn
❚ OPPOSITE increase

decree NOUN

issuing a royal decree
order, command, declaration,
pronouncement, proclamation,
edict, ruling

decree VERB

*Caesar decreed that a new calendar
be adopted.*
order, command, declare,
pronounce, proclaim, ordain, dictate

dedicate VERB

*a woman who dedicated her life to
helping others*
commit, devote, pledge, set aside,
sacrifice

dedicated ADJECTIVE

1 *a dedicated fan of jazz music*
committed, devoted, keen,
enthusiastic, faithful, staunch, firm

2 *a dedicated phone line*
exclusive, special, private,
purpose-built

dedication NOUN

*It requires years of dedication to
master kung fu.*
commitment, devotion, application,
resolve, effort

deduce VERB

*Hubble deduced that the universe is
expanding.*
conclude, work out, infer, reason,
gather

deduct VERB

*Points are deducted for each
incorrect answer.*
subtract, take away, take off,
knock off, debit
❚ OPPOSITE add

deed NOUN

a heroic deed
act, action, feat, exploit, effort,
achievement

deep ADJECTIVE

1 *Loch Ness is deep, dark, and murky.*
▶ A very deep pit or lake may be
described as **bottomless** or
fathomless.
❚ OPPOSITE shallow

2 *a deep cave filled with prehistoric art*
extensive, cavernous, yawning,
gaping

3 *a deep feeling of unease*
intense, strong, extreme, profound,
deep-seated
❚ OPPOSITE slight

4 *I owe you a deep apology.*
wholehearted, earnest, genuine,

sincere, heartfelt

❙ OPPOSITE superficial

5 *Angelina fell into a deep sleep.*
heavy, sound, profound

❙ OPPOSITE light

6 *A deep voice answered the phone.*
low, low-pitched, bass, throaty,
husky, sonorous

❙ OPPOSITE high

▷ **deep in**
I found Grant deep in thought.
absorbed in, immersed in,
preoccupied by, lost in

deer *NOUN*

a herd of red deer

▶ A male deer is a **buck**, **hart**,
roebuck, or **stag**.

▶ A female deer is a **doe** or **hind**.

▶ A young deer is a **fawn**.

▶ Deer's flesh used as food is **venison**.

defeat *VERB*

*The British forces were defeated at
Yorktown.*
beat, conquer, vanquish, triumph
over, get the better of, overcome,
overpower, subjugate, crush, rout,
trounce
(informal) lick

defeat *NOUN*

*Our team suffered a humiliating
defeat.*
conquest, loss, subjugation, rout,
trouncing
(informal) drubbing

❙ OPPOSITE victory

defect *NOUN*

surgery to correct a heart defect
fault, flaw, imperfection, deformity,
shortcoming, failure, weakness

▶ A defect in a computer program is
a **bug**.

defective *ADJECTIVE*

a disease caused by a defective gene
faulty, flawed, imperfect, unsound,
malfunctioning, damaged,
out of order

❙ OPPOSITES perfect, intact

defence *NOUN*

1 *a weak point in the enemy's defences*
protection, barricade, fortification,
shield, guard, safeguard

2 *The speaker gave a defence of
multiculturalism.*
justification, vindication, excuse,
explanation, argument, case

defend *VERB*

1 *defending ourselves against the
enemy*
protect, guard, fortify, shield,
secure, safeguard, keep safe

❙ OPPOSITE attack

2 *He gave a speech defending his
actions.*
justify, vindicate, support, back,
stand up for, make a case for

❙ OPPOSITE accuse

defender *NOUN*

a lifelong defender of human rights
supporter, backer, advocate,
champion, upholder, apologist

❙ OPPOSITE opponent

defensive *ADJECTIVE*

taking defensive action
protective, guarding, defending

❙ OPPOSITES offensive, attacking

defer *VERB*

*We deferred our departure until the
weekend.*
delay, put off, put back, postpone

❙ IDIOMS put on ice, put on the back
burner

defiant *ADJECTIVE*

The prisoner gave a defiant answer.
rebellious, uncooperative,
non-compliant, obstinate,
mutinous, insubordinate
(British informal) stroppy

❙ OPPOSITES cooperative, compliant

deficiency *NOUN*

a vitamin deficiency
lack, shortage, want, inadequacy,
insufficiency

❙ OPPOSITE sufficiency

deficient *ADJECTIVE*
> *a diet deficient in vitamins*
lacking (in), short (of), wanting, inadequate, insufficient, unsatisfactory
> **OPPOSITE** sufficient

define *VERB*
> *How would you define this word?*
explain, give the meaning of, interpret, clarify

definite *ADJECTIVE*
1 *Have you made a definite decision?*
certain, sure, fixed, settled, decided
> **OPPOSITES** uncertain, undecided
2 *showing definite signs of improvement*
clear, distinct, noticeable, obvious, marked, positive, pronounced, unmistakable
> **OPPOSITES** indistinct, vague

definitely *ADVERB*
> *That is definitely the paw print of a bear.*
certainly, for certain, surely, unquestionably, undoubtedly, absolutely, positively, without doubt, without fail

definition *NOUN*
1 *Give a definition of the following words.*
explanation, interpretation, meaning, sense
2 *a photograph that lacks definition*
clarity, focus, sharpness, resolution

definitive *ADJECTIVE*
1 *a definitive answer*
conclusive, final, categorical
2 *the definitive history of British cinema*
authoritative, classic, standard, unrivalled, ultimate, best

deflect *VERB*
> *The player deflected a corner into his own net.*
divert, turn aside, avert, fend off, ward off, stave off, parry

deft *ADJECTIVE*
> *a few deft strokes of a brush*
skilful, agile, nimble, dexterous, expert, proficient, adept
(informal) nifty
> **OPPOSITE** clumsy

defy *VERB*
1 *The building appears to defy the laws of gravity.*
disobey, contravene, violate, flout, breach, challenge, confront
> **OPPOSITE** obey
2 *I defy you to come up with a better idea.*
challenge, dare
3 *Rick's hair defied all efforts to keep it tidy.*
resist, withstand, defeat, prevent, frustrate

degenerate *VERB*
> *The TV series degenerated into a soap opera.*
deteriorate, decline, descend
> **IDIOMS** go downhill, go to the dogs
> **OPPOSITE** improve

degrading *ADJECTIVE*
> *Manual labour was seen as degrading to the Romans.*
shameful, humiliating, demeaning, undignified

degree *NOUN*
> *Playing the oboe requires a high degree of skill.*
level, standard, grade, measure, amount, extent, proportion

dejected *ADJECTIVE*
> *I felt dejected after we lost the game.*
depressed, dispirited, disheartened, downhearted, downcast, despondent, disconsolate, crestfallen, miserable, forlorn
> **IDIOMS** *(informal)* down in the mouth, down in the dumps
> **OPPOSITES** cheerful, upbeat
> **SEE ALSO** sad

delay *VERB*
1 *My bus was delayed again this morning.*
detain, hold up, keep waiting, make late, hinder, slow down
2 *They had to delay the start of the race.*
postpone, put off, defer, hold over
▶ To beak off a meeting until a later time is to **adjourn** it.
3 *We cannot delay any longer.*
hesitate, hold back, dawdle, shilly-shally, stall, linger, loiter
(informal) dilly-dally
| IDIOM drag your feet

delay *NOUN*
There has been an unexpected delay.
hold-up, wait, stoppage, postponement, adjournment

delete *VERB*
I deleted your email by mistake.
remove, erase, cancel, cross out, strike out, excise, cut
| OPPOSITES add, insert

deliberate *ADJECTIVE*
1 *a deliberate attempt to sink the ship*
intentional, planned, calculated, conscious, premeditated
| OPPOSITES accidental, unintentional
2 *She walked slowly, taking small, deliberate steps.*
careful, steady, cautious, unhurried, measured
| OPPOSITES hasty, careless

deliberately *VERB*
Are you ignoring me deliberately?
on purpose, intentionally, knowingly, wittingly, by design
| OPPOSITES accidentally, unintentionally

delicacy *NOUN*
1 *the delicacy of lace*
fineness, fragility, flimsiness
2 *a matter requiring some delicacy*
tact, sensitivity, diplomacy, subtlety, care

3 *Frogs' legs are a delicacy in France.*
treat, luxury, speciality

delicate *ADJECTIVE*
1 *a piece of delicate embroidery*
fine, dainty, intricate, exquisite
| OPPOSITES coarse, crude
2 *a delicate glass ornament*
fragile, frail, flimsy
| OPPOSITE sturdy
3 *a delicate shade of lilac*
subtle, soft, muted, pale, light
| OPPOSITES garish, lurid
4 *a child with a delicate constitution*
frail, weak, feeble, sickly, unhealthy, tender
| OPPOSITES strong, hardy, robust
5 *his delicate handling of the situation*
tactful, sensitive, careful, considerate, discreet, diplomatic
| OPPOSITE insensitive
6 *This is rather a delicate issue.*
awkward, embarrassing, tricky, ticklish
7 *her delicate playing of the piano concerto*
sensitive, gentle, light, soft
| OPPOSITE clumsy

delicious *ADJECTIVE*
A delicious smell wafted from the kitchen.
appetizing, mouth-watering, delectable, flavoursome, tasty, tempting
(informal) scrumptious, yummy, moreish
| OPPOSITE unappetizing
FOR TIPS ON DESCRIBING TASTE SEE **taste**

delight *VERB*
The magic of this book never fails to delight me.
please, charm, amuse, divert, entertain, enchant, entrance, fascinate, captivate, thrill
| IDIOM *(informal)* tickle you pink
| OPPOSITE dismay

》

a
b
c
d
e
f
g
h
i
j
k
l
m
n
o
p
q
r
s
t
u
v
w
x
y
z

▷ **delight in**
Conor delights in teasing his little sister.
enjoy, get pleasure from, relish, savour, lap up, revel in

delight NOUN
Nadia's eyes lit up with delight.
happiness, joy, pleasure, enjoyment, bliss, ecstasy, glee
❙ **OPPOSITE** displeasure

delighted ADJECTIVE
My friend was delighted with her present.
pleased, happy, glad, joyful, gleeful, thrilled, ecstatic, overjoyed, elated, exultant
❙ **IDIOMS** on cloud nine, in seventh heaven
(informal) over the moon, tickled pink

delightful ADJECTIVE
What a delightful surprise!
lovely, pleasant, pleasing, enjoyable, appealing, attractive, charming, endearing

delirious ADJECTIVE
He was raving in his sleep, as if delirious.
feverish, frenzied, frantic, deranged, mad, crazy, wild, beside yourself
❙ **OPPOSITE** calm

deliver VERB
1 delivering a parcel
convey, carry, transport, hand over, present, supply, distribute, dispatch, ship
2 delivering an important speech
give, make, read out, pronounce, utter, broadcast
3 delivering a blow to the head
strike, deal, administer, inflict, give
(informal) land

delivery NOUN
1 goods ready for delivery
conveyance, carriage, transportation, distribution, dispatch, shipping

2 A good speech requires a strong delivery.
articulation, enunciation, diction

delude VERB
You're deluding yourself as usual.
deceive, fool, trick, mislead, hoax, bluff
(informal) con

delusion NOUN
People were under the delusion that the Earth was flat.
misconception, misapprehension, false impression, fantasy, self-deception

demand VERB
1 I demanded a refund for my ticket.
insist on, claim, call for, push for, seek, request
2 'What do you want?' a voice demanded.
ask, enquire
3 Archery demands skill and concentration.
require, need, necessitate, call for, involve, entail

demand NOUN
1 King John agreed to the demands of his barons.
request, requirement, call, claim, dictate
2 the increasing demand for green energy
desire, call, need, appetite, market

demanding ADJECTIVE
1 Acting is a demanding profession.
difficult, challenging, exhausting, hard, tough, testing, taxing, onerous, arduous
❙ **OPPOSITE** easy
2 Toddlers can be very demanding.
difficult, trying, tiresome, insistent

demise NOUN
What caused the demise of the dinosaurs?
end, death, passing, failure, fall, collapse, downfall

a b c d e f g h i j k l m n o p q r s t u v w x y z

demolish VERB

1 *The building was demolished in the 1960s.*
knock down, pull down, tear down, flatten, level, destroy, bulldoze
OPPOSITES build, construct

2 *Simon proceeded to demolish my theory.*
destroy, pull apart, tear to pieces, ruin, wreck, overturn, explode

demonstrate VERB

1 *Einstein demonstrated that time is relative.*
prove, indicate, verify, establish, confirm

2 *The crew demonstrated how to use a life jacket.*
show, exhibit, illustrate, exemplify

3 *Campaigners were demonstrating in the street.*
protest, march, parade

demonstration NOUN

1 *a software demonstration*
show, display, presentation

2 *a demonstration against world poverty*
protest, rally, march, parade
(informal) demo

demote VERB

The club were demoted to the second division.
put down, relegate
OPPOSITE promote

den NOUN

1 *the winter den of a polar bear*
lair, burrow, hole

2 *This room is my private den.*
hideout, shelter, hiding place

denial NOUN

their continuing denial of the truth
repudiation, contradiction, refutation, rebuttal
OPPOSITES admission, confirmation

denote VERB

What does this symbol denote?
indicate, signify, stand for, mean, express, symbolize, represent

denounce VERB

1 *The idea was denounced as mad.*
attack, condemn, censure, criticize, disparage, decry

2 *The key witness was denounced as a liar.*
expose, accuse, incriminate, condemn, betray

dense ADJECTIVE

1 *a blanket of dense fog*
thick, heavy, murky, opaque

2 *a rainforest with dense undergrowth*
compact, thick, impenetrable, solid, packed, crowded

3 *(informal) I'm being rather dense today!*
stupid, slow, foolish, simple-minded
(informal) dim, thick

dent NOUN

a large dent in the car door
indentation, depression, hollow, dip, dimple

dent VERB

A football hit the door and dented it.
make a dent in, knock in, push in

dentist NOUN

a check-up at the dentist
► A dentist who specializes in straightening teeth is an **orthodontist**.
► A dental assistant who helps you look after your teeth is a **hygienist**.
SEE ALSO tooth

deny VERB

1 *Popov denied that he was a spy.*
repudiate, contradict, refute, dispute, challenge, contest
OPPOSITES admit, confirm

2 *He denied our request for an interview.*
refuse, reject, rebuff, decline, dismiss, turn down
IDIOM give the thumbs down to
OPPOSITES accept, agree to, allow

depart VERB

1 *Our guests departed after breakfast.*
leave, set off, get going, set out, go away, exit, withdraw, decamp
IDIOM make tracks
OPPOSITES arrive, get in

2 *The book departs from the usual style of horror fiction.*
diverge, deviate, digress, stray, differ, vary
OPPOSITES follow, conform to

department NOUN

Mr Lloyd works in the sales department.
section, branch, division, sector, unit, office, agency

departure NOUN

1 *The weather delayed our departure.*
leaving, leave-taking, going, exit, withdrawal
OPPOSITES arrival, entrance

2 *a departure from the norm*
divergence, deviation, digression, variation, shift, innovation

depend VERB

▷ **depend on someone**
You can depend on me.
rely on, count on, bank on, trust
IDIOM pin your hopes on

▷ **depend on something**
Good health depends on many different things.
be decided by, be determined by, be dependent on, rest on, hinge on

dependable ADJECTIVE

Are these friends of yours dependable?
reliable, trustworthy, loyal, faithful, trusty, honest, sound, steady
OPPOSITE unreliable

dependent ADJECTIVE

▷ **dependent on**
Our plans are dependent on the weather.
determined by, decided by, subject to, controlled by, reliant on

depict VERB

1 *Picasso often depicted bulls and horses.*
portray, illustrate, picture, represent reproduce, paint, draw, sketch

2 *The film depicts the horror of war.*
describe, present, show, outline, detail, relate, set forth

deplete VERB

depleting the Earth's resources
reduce, diminish, exhaust, drain, run down, consume, expend, use up

deplorable ADJECTIVE

a deplorable lack of good taste
disgraceful, shameful, scandalous, shocking, unforgivable, lamentable, reprehensible, inexcusable
OPPOSITE admirable

deplore VERB

We deplore the testing of products on animals.
condemn, denounce, disapprove of, find unacceptable, frown on
(formal) abhor
IDIOM take a dim view of

depose VERB

The last Roman emperor was deposed in 476 AD.
overthrow, dethrone, unseat, topple, oust

deposit NOUN

1 *paying the deposit on a new computer*
down payment, first instalment, prepayment

2 *large deposits of oil and natural gas*
layer, seam, vein, stratum, sediment

deposit VERB

1 *Tim deposited his bag on the floor.*
put down, set down, place, rest, drop
(informal) dump, plonk

2 *rocks and sand deposited by a glacier*
leave behind, cast up, wash up

depress VERB

1 *The long, dark nights were depressing me.*
sadden, dispirit, dishearten, demoralize, get you down, weigh down on you
OPPOSITE cheer

2 *Depress the control key on the keyboard.*
press down, push down, hold down

depressed ADJECTIVE

1 *The argument left me feeling depressed.*
downhearted, dispirited, disheartened, unhappy, sad, miserable, gloomy, glum, melancholy, morose, despondent, dejected, desolate, downcast, low, down, blue
IDIOMS (informal) down in the dumps, down in the mouth
OPPOSITE cheerful

2 *a depressed inner-city area*
run-down, poverty-stricken, poor, deprived, underprivileged, disadvantaged
OPPOSITE prosperous

depressing ADJECTIVE

I found the ending of the book depressing.
disheartening, dispiriting, gloomy, sad, dismal, dreary, sombre, bleak, cheerless
OPPOSITE cheerful

depression NOUN

1 *Sophie sank into a state of depression.*
despair, sadness, gloom, unhappiness, low spirits, melancholy, misery, dejection, despondency
OPPOSITE cheerfulness

2 *the Great Depression of the 1930s*
recession, slump, downturn
OPPOSITE boom

3 *a depression in the ground*
hollow, indentation, dent, dip, pit, cavity, crater, basin, bowl

deprive VERB

▷ **to deprive someone of something**
Heart failure deprives the brain of oxygen.
deny, refuse, divest of, strip of, rob
OPPOSITE provide with

deprived ADJECTIVE

a charity which helps deprived families
poor, needy, underprivileged, disadvantaged, destitute
OPPOSITES wealthy, privileged

depth NOUN

▷ **in depth**
Let's examine the poem in depth.
in detail, thoroughly, comprehensively
OPPOSITE superficially

deputy NOUN

The Sheriff's Office has two deputies.
second-in-command, assistant, aide, stand-in, substitute, reserve

---

Usage Note

The prefix ***vice-*** can also be used to mean a deputy, for example a *vice-captain* or a *vice-president*.

---

derelict ADJECTIVE

a derelict building
dilapidated, run-down, neglected, disused, deserted, abandoned, tumbledown, ramshackle

derision NOUN

His idea was greeted with shouts of derision.
scorn, ridicule, mockery, disdain, taunts, jeers

derive VERB

1 *Bill derives a lot of pleasure from his garden.*
get, gain, obtain, receive, procure

2 *She derives many of her ideas from books.*
borrow, draw, pick up, acquire, take, extract
(informal) lift

derogatory ADJECTIVE

His email was full of derogatory remarks.

critical, uncomplimentary, insulting, disparaging, scornful, pejorative, negative

❚ OPPOSITES complimentary, positive

descend VERB

1 *descending a steep path*
go down, come down, climb down, move down

❚ OPPOSITES ascend, climb

2 *The road descends gradually into the valley.*
drop, fall, slope, slant, incline, dip, sink

▷ **be descended from**
Humans are descended from apes.
come from, originate from, be related to, spring from, stem from

descendant NOUN

the descendants of Queen Victoria
successor, heir

❚ OPPOSITE ancestor

descent NOUN

1 *at the bottom of a steep descent*
drop, fall, dip, incline, gradient, slide

❚ OPPOSITE ascent

2 *a family of Polish descent*
ancestry, lineage, origin, extraction, roots, stock, blood

describe VERB

1 *Can you describe what you saw?*
report, recount, relate, tell about, narrate, detail, outline

2 *Friends described him as a modest man.*
portray, characterize, represent, present, depict, define, label, brand

description NOUN

1 *a detailed description of what happened*
report, account, narrative, story

2 *Write a description of your favourite character.*
portrait, portrayal, characterization, representation, sketch

3 *We sell antiques of every description.*
kind, type, sort, variety

descriptive ADJECTIVE

The author writes in a very descriptive style.
expressive, colourful, detailed, graphic, vivid

desert NOUN

The surface of Mars is a cold and dry desert.
wasteland, wilderness, wastes

desert VERB

Gauguin deserted his wife and family.
abandon, leave, jilt
(informal) walk out on, ditch
(old use) forsake

❚ IDIOMS leave high and dry, leave in the lurch

▶ To leave someone in a place from which they cannot escape is to **maroon** or **strand** them.

deserted ADJECTIVE

By midnight, the streets were deserted.
empty, unoccupied, uninhabited, vacant, desolate, abandoned

▶ An uninhabited island is a **desert** island.

❚ OPPOSITES crowded, inhabited

deserve VERB

You deserve a break after all that work.
be entitled to, be worthy of, have earned, merit, warrant

design NOUN

1 *the design for the new art gallery*
plan, drawing, outline, blueprint, sketch

▶ A first version of something, from which others are made, is a **prototype**.

2 *The mosaic tiles form a geometric design.*
style, pattern, motif, arrangement, composition, layout

design VERB

1 *Ada Byron designed the first computer language.*
create, develop, invent, devise, conceive, think up

2 *The book is designed to make you think.*
intend, plan, devise, aim (at), mean

designate VERB

1 *The city has been designated a World Heritage Site.*
name, classify, label, term, dub

2 *Designate your preferred email address.*
nominate, appoint, assign, identify, elect

desirable ADJECTIVE

1 *a house with many desirable features*
appealing, attractive, sought-after, tempting
(informal) must-have
❙ OPPOSITE unappealing

2 *It is desirable to phone in advance.*
advisable, sensible, prudent, wise, recommended, preferable
❙ OPPOSITE unwise

desire NOUN

a burning desire to travel
wish, want, longing, yearning, craving, ambition, aspiration, fancy, hankering, yen, urge, hunger, itch

desire VERB

whatever your heart desires
wish for, long for, want, aspire to, crave, fancy, hanker after, yearn for, pine for, have a yen for, hunger for
❙ IDIOM set your heart on
▶ To desire something that belongs to someone else is to **covet** it.

desolate ADJECTIVE

1 *feeling desolate and utterly alone*
depressed, dejected, miserable, sad, melancholy, hopeless, wretched, forlorn
❙ OPPOSITE cheerful

2 *a desolate landscape*
bleak, barren, stark, bare, deserted, uninhabited, inhospitable, godforsaken, dismal, cheerless
❙ OPPOSITE pleasant

despair NOUN

Pearson threw his hands up in despair.
desperation, anguish, wretchedness, hopelessness, misery, despondency, unhappiness, gloom
❙ OPPOSITE hope

despair VERB

There are many reasons not to despair.
lose hope, be discouraged, be despondent, lose heart
❙ OPPOSITE hope

despatch NOUN, VERB
SEE **dispatch** NOUN, VERB

desperate ADJECTIVE

1 *The crew were in a desperate situation.*
difficult, critical, grave, serious, severe, drastic, dire, urgent, extreme

2 *We were desperate for news.*
anxious, frantic, eager, impatient, longing, itching

3 *a band of desperate outlaws*
dangerous, reckless, rash, impetuous

despicable ADJECTIVE

a despicable act of cruelty
disgraceful, hateful, shameful, contemptible, loathsome, vile

despise VERB

I despise people who cheat.
hate, loathe, deplore, disdain, feel contempt for, have a low opinion of, look down on, scorn, sneer at
(formal) abhor
❙ OPPOSITES admire, respect

despite PREPOSITION

We went for a walk despite the rain.
in spite of, regardless of, notwithstanding, undeterred by, in the face of
❙ OPPOSITE because of

dessert NOUN

There is plum crumble for dessert.
pudding, sweet
(informal) afters

destined ADJECTIVE

1 *Macbeth is destined to become king.*
fated, doomed, preordained,
intended, meant, certain

2 *This parcel is destined for Japan.*
bound, directed, intended, headed,
en route

destiny NOUN

The crystal ball shows your destiny.
fate, fortune, future, doom, lot

destroy VERB

1 *An avalanche destroyed the village.*
demolish, devastate, crush, smash,
shatter, flatten, level, knock down,
sweep away

2 *The injury has destroyed her chances
of a medal.*
ruin, wreck, spoil, sabotage, thwart,
undo

3 *One of the horses had to be
destroyed.*
put down, kill, put to sleep

destruction NOUN

1 *The hurricane caused widespread
destruction.*
devastation, damage, demolition,
ruin, wreckage, havoc
❙ OPPOSITE creation

2 *The species is threatened by the
destruction of its habitat.*
eradication, obliteration,
elimination, annihilation,
extermination, extinction
❙ OPPOSITES preservation,
conservation

destructive ADJECTIVE

*Tornadoes have a great destructive
power.*
damaging, devastating,
catastrophic, disastrous, harmful,
injurious, ruinous, violent

detach VERB

*The lens can be detached
for cleaning.*
remove, separate, disconnect,
disengage, take off, split off, release,
undo, unfasten, part, isolate
▶ To detach a trailer from a vehicle is
to **unhitch** it.
▶ To detach railway carriages is to
uncouple them.
❙ OPPOSITE attach

detached ADJECTIVE

1 *The stables are detached from the
main building.*
separated, separate, unconnected
(to)
❙ OPPOSITE involved

2 *trying to remain a detached observer*
objective, disinterested, impartial,
unbiased, neutral
❙ OPPOSITES involved, partial

detail NOUN

*Her account was accurate in every
detail.*
fact, particular, feature,
characteristic, aspect, respect,
element, item, point, specific

detailed ADJECTIVE

*a detailed description of Victorian
London*
precise, exact, specific,
full, thorough, elaborate,
comprehensive, exhaustive, minute
❙ OPPOSITES rough, vague

detain VERB

1 *I'll try not to detain you for long.*
delay, hold up, keep, keep waiting

2 *Police have detained two suspects.*
hold, imprison, confine, take into
custody
❙ OPPOSITE release

detect VERB

1 *They have detected evidence of snow
on Mars.*
discover, find, uncover, unearth,
reveal, identify, track down

2 *I could detect a note of fear in her
voice.*
perceive, discern, be aware of,

notice, spot, recognize, make out, catch

detective NOUN
Hercule Poirot is a fictional detective.
investigator, sleuth
(informal) private eye
(North American informal) gumshoe
FOR TIPS ON WRITING CRIME FICTION
SEE **crime**

deter VERB
ways to deter slugs from eating your vegetables
discourage, dissuade, prevent, stop, avert, put off, scare off
| OPPOSITE encourage

deteriorate VERB
Her sight has begun to deteriorate.
worsen, decline, fail, degenerate, get worse
| IDIOM go downhill
| OPPOSITES improve, get better

determination NOUN
All of the players showed great determination.
resolve, commitment, will-power, courage, dedication, drive, grit, perseverance, persistence, spirit
(informal) guts

determine VERB
1 *I determined to follow their advice.*
resolve, decide, make up your mind
2 *Your genes determine your body size.*
dictate, decide, control, regulate, govern
3 *determining the speed at which sound travels*
calculate, compute, establish, ascertain, work out, figure out

determined ADJECTIVE
1 *My grandmother was a very determined woman.*
resolute, decisive, purposeful, strong-minded, persistent, tenacious, adamant
| OPPOSITES weak-minded, irresolute
2 *making a determined effort to lose weight*

resolved, committed, unswerving, dogged
| OPPOSITES feeble, half-hearted

detest VERB
I detest the smell of tobacco smoke.
dislike, hate, loathe, despise, be unable to bear, be unable to stand
(formal) abhor
| OPPOSITES love, adore

detour NOUN
We wasted time by taking a detour.
diversion, indirect route, roundabout route

detrimental ADJECTIVE
Too much water can be detrimental to plants.
damaging, harmful, destructive, adverse
| OPPOSITE beneficial

devastate VERB
1 *The tsunami devastated the island.*
destroy, wreck, ruin, demolish, flatten, level, lay waste
2 *We were devastated by the news.*
shock, stun, daze, overwhelm, shatter, traumatize

develop VERB
1 *We are developing our sports programme.*
expand, extend, enlarge, enhance, improve, broaden, diversify
2 *Their fan base has developed over the years.*
grow, spread, expand, build up
3 *The symptoms developed quickly.*
emerge, arise, break out, grow, spread
4 *Her piano playing has developed this year.*
improve, progress, evolve, get better, advance, refine, mature
5 *I've developed a taste for jazz.*
get, acquire, pick up, cultivate

development NOUN
1 *the future development of our website*
growth, evolution, expansion,

improvement, progress, spread

2 *Have there been any new developments?*
event, happening, occurrence, incident, change

deviate VERB

This deviates from our original plan.
diverge, differ, vary, depart, digress, stray

device NOUN

a remote control device
tool, implement, instrument, appliance, apparatus, gadget, contraption
(informal) gizmo

devious ADJECTIVE

1 *a devious plan to make money*
deceitful, underhand, dishonest, furtive, scheming, cunning, sly, sneaky, treacherous, wily

2 *The bus took a devious route.*
indirect, roundabout, circuitous, winding, meandering, tortuous
OPPOSITE direct

devise VERB

devising a strategy for the match
conceive, form, invent, contrive, formulate, make up, come up with, plan, prepare, map out, think out, think up

devoid ADJECTIVE

▷ **devoid of**
a singer who is completely devoid of talent
lacking in, wanting, bereft of, without, deficient in

devote VERB

She devotes her spare time to the garden.
dedicate, allocate, set aside, allot, assign, commit

devoted ADJECTIVE

a devoted fan
loyal, faithful, dedicated, committed, staunch, steadfast, true

devotion NOUN

the story of a dog's devotion to his master
loyalty, fidelity, commitment, dedication, attachment, fondness, allegiance

devour VERB

Declan devoured a plateful of sandwiches.
eat, consume, gobble up, bolt down, gulp down, swallow
(informal) guzzle, scoff, wolf down
SEE ALSO eat

devout ADJECTIVE

a devout Catholic
dutiful, committed, loyal, pious, sincere, reverent

diagnose VERB

No one could diagnose the cause of her illness.
identify, determine, detect, recognize, name, pinpoint

diagram NOUN

a diagram of the digestive system
chart, plan, sketch, drawing, representation, outline

dialogue NOUN

The play consists of a series of dialogues.
conversation, talk, discussion, exchange, debate, chat
SEE ALSO drama

diary NOUN

Pepys wrote about the Fire of London in his diary.
journal, memoir, chronicle, record, annal
(North American) daybook

▶ A diary describing a voyage or mission is a **log** or **logbook**.

▶ A diary which includes pictures and souvenirs is a **scrapbook**.

▶ A diary published on a website is a **blog**.

dictate VERB

▷ **dictate to someone**

You have no right to dictate to me!
order about, give orders to,
command, bully
(informal) boss about, push around
⎸ IDIOM lord it over

dictator NOUN

Hitler became a ruthless dictator.
autocrat, absolute ruler, tyrant,
despot

▶ The rule of a dictator is a
dictatorship.

die VERB

1 *A giant tortoise has died at the age
of 176.*
expire, perish, pass away, pass on
(informal) snuff it, croak
⎸ IDIOMS give up the ghost
(informal) kick the bucket, pop your
clogs

▶ To die of hunger is to **starve**.

2 *My computer has died on me again.*
fail, crash, break down, malfunction
(informal) pack up, conk out

▷ **die down**

The wind should die down soon.
lessen, decrease, decline, subside,
abate, ease off, let up, peter out,
wane, ebb

▷ **die out**

When did the dinosaurs die out?
become extinct, cease to exist,
disappear, vanish

diet NOUN

*including fruit and vegetables in
your diet*
food, nourishment, nutrition

▶ A diet which does not include meat
is a **vegetarian** diet.

▶ A diet which does not include any
animal products is a **vegan** diet.
⎸ SEE ALSO food

differ VERB

*The statements differ on a number
of points.*
disagree, conflict, clash,
contradict each other

⎸ IDIOM be at odds
⎸ OPPOSITE agree

▷ **differ from**

*How do the poems differ from each
other?*
be different to, contrast with, vary
from, run counter to
⎸ OPPOSITE resemble

difference NOUN

1 *the difference between two colours*
contrast, distinction, dissimilarity,
disparity, variation, divergence
⎸ OPPOSITE similarity

2 *I see a real difference in my energy
levels.*
change, alteration, modification,
improvement

3 *We've had our differences in the
past.*
disagreement, argument, quarrel,
dispute

different ADJECTIVE

1 *The twins have very different
personalities.*
dissimilar, unlike, differing,
contrasting, varying, disparate
⎸ IDIOMS like chalk and cheese,
poles apart
⎸ OPPOSITES identical, similar

2 *There are two different types of
rugby.*
separate, distinct, distinctive,
distinguishable, individual

3 *people of different faiths*
various, assorted, several, diverse,
numerous

4 *Your hair looks different today.*
changed, altered, unfamiliar

5 *Let's do something different this
weekend.*
unusual, original, fresh, new, novel,
out of the ordinary

difficult ADJECTIVE

1 *a difficult crossword puzzle*
hard, complicated, complex,
involved, intricate, baffling,
perplexing, puzzling, tricky
(informal) thorny, knotty

》

a
b
c
d
e
f
g
h
i
j
k
l
m
n
o
p
q
r
s
t
u
v
w
x
y
z

175

OPPOSITE simple

2 *a difficult climb to the top of the hill*
challenging, arduous, demanding,
taxing, exhausting, formidable,
gruelling, laborious, strenuous,
tough

OPPOSITE easy

3 *a difficult person to work with*
troublesome, awkward, demanding,
uncooperative, obstinate, stubborn,
trying, tiresome

OPPOSITES cooperative,
accommodating

difficulty NOUN

1 *One of the climbers got into real
difficulty.*
trouble, adversity, hardship, distress,
problems, challenges
(informal) hassle

2 *We ran into one difficulty after
another.*
problem, complication, hitch,
obstacle, snag, stumbling block

dig VERB

1 *digging the garden*
cultivate, fork over, turn over

2 *digging a hole in the ground.*
burrow, excavate, tunnel, bore,
gouge out, hollow out, scoop out

3 *I felt someone dig me in the ribs.*
poke, prod, jab, stab

▷ **dig into**
digging into our family history
investigate, research, delve into,
look into, enquire into, probe

▷ **dig up**

1 *Body-snatchers used to dig up
corpses.*
unearth, exhume, disinter

OPPOSITES bury, inter

2 *digging up facts about the suspect*
discover, uncover, find, reveal,
expose, turn up

digest VERB

I haven't had time to digest the news.
take in, assimilate, absorb,
understand, comprehend, grasp

digestion NOUN

WORD WEB

parts of the digestive system
appendix, bile, colon,
duodenum, epiglottis, gall
bladder, gastric acid, large
intestine, liver, oesophagus,
pancreas, rectum, salivary
glands, small intestine, stomach

▶ A doctor who specializes
in digestive disorders is a
gastroenterologist.

SEE ALSO food, stomach

digital ADJECTIVE

a digital photograph
computerized

OPPOSITE analogue

dignified ADJECTIVE

*A state banquet is a dignified
occasion.*
stately, distinguished, grand, noble,
majestic, august, imposing, formal,
solemn, sedate

OPPOSITE undignified

dignity NOUN

1 *The joke spoilt the dignity of the
occasion.*
formality, seriousness, solemnity,
propriety, decorum

2 *instilling a sense of dignity and pride*
self-respect, self-esteem, self-worth

dilemma NOUN

*Hamlet faces the dilemma of whether
or not to kill Claudius.*
quandary, predicament

IDIOMS tight spot, vicious circle,
catch-22

diligent ADJECTIVE

1 *a diligent worker*
hard-working, conscientious,
industrious

2 *a diligent search of the crime scene*
careful, attentive, painstaking,
meticulous, rigorous, thorough

dilute VERB

1 *Dilute the juice before serving.*
thin, water down, weaken
OPPOSITE concentrate

2 *The original deal has been diluted.*
weaken, tone down, moderate, compromise
OPPOSITE beef up

dim ADJECTIVE

1 *the dim light of a single candle*
faint, muted, subdued
OPPOSITE bright

2 *a long, dim corridor*
dark, dull, dingy, murky, gloomy, badly lit
OPPOSITE bright

3 *I have a dim memory of hearing the story before.*
vague, indistinct, faint, blurred, fuzzy, hazy, sketchy
OPPOSITE clear

dimension NOUN

1 *measuring the dimensions of the room*
measurements, size, extent, capacity
SEE ALSO measurement

2 *Podcasts have added a new dimension to radio.*
aspect, feature, element, side, angle, facet

diminish VERB

1 *plans to diminish the use of fossil fuel*
lessen, reduce, decrease, minimize, cut back on, curtail

2 *Our water supply was diminishing rapidly.*
become less, decrease, decline, subside, dwindle, wane
OPPOSITE increase

din NOUN

I can't hear above that din!
noise, racket, row, rumpus, clatter, clangour, commotion, uproar, hullabaloo, hubbub, cacophony

dine VERB

We will be dining at eight o'clock.
eat, have dinner, have lunch
(old use) sup

dingy ADJECTIVE

brightening up a dingy room
dull, drab, dreary, dowdy, colourless, dismal, gloomy, murky
OPPOSITE bright

dinosaur NOUN

WORD WEB

some types of dinosaur
apatosaurus, archaeopteryx, brachiosaurus, diplodocus, gallimimus, iguanodon, megalosaurus, pterodactylus, stegosaurus, triceratops, tyrannosaurus rex, velociraptor

▶ The study of dinosaurs and other fossils is **palaeontology**.
SEE ALSO fossil, prehistoric

dip VERB

1 *I dipped my hand in the water.*
immerse, lower, submerge, plunge, dunk

2 *The road dips down into the valley.*
descend, go down, slope down, drop down, fall away, sink

3 *Sales have dipped again this month.*
decrease, decline, diminish, fall, drop, dwindle, slump

dip NOUN

1 *a dip in the road ahead*
slope, slide, decline, hollow, depression

2 *taking a dip in the sea*
swim, bathe, paddle

3 *a dip in popularity*
decrease, decline, fall, drop, downturn, slump

dire ADJECTIVE

1 *They warned us of dire consequences.*
dreadful, terrible, awful, appalling, severe, grave

2 *The ground is in dire need of rain.*
urgent, desperate, drastic, extreme, pressing

direct ADJECTIVE

1 *Which is the most direct route?*

straight, short, quick

OPPOSITES indirect, roundabout

2 *a direct flight*
non-stop

3 *Please give me a direct answer.*
straightforward, frank, honest,
sincere, blunt, plain, candid,
unambiguous, unequivocal

OPPOSITE evasive

4 *the direct opposite*
exact, complete

direct VERB

1 *Can you direct me to the station?*
guide, point, show the way, give
directions to

2 *He directed his criticism at the
government.*
aim, target, point, train

3 *Dr Knox will direct the experiment.*
manage, run, be in charge of,
control, administer, govern,
superintend, supervise,
take charge of

▶ To direct an orchestra is to **conduct**
it.

4 *Officers directed the crowd to move
back.*
instruct, command, order, tell

direction NOUN

1 *Which direction did they go in?*
way, route, course, path, bearing

2 *The company is under new direction.*
management, command, control,
administration, leadership,
supervision

▷ **directions**
Follow the directions on the packet.
instructions, guidance, guidelines

director NOUN

the director of a large museum
manager, head, chief, chief
executive, leader, governor,
president
(informal) boss

dirt NOUN

1 *a floor covered in dirt*
filth, grime, mess, muck, mud, dust

2 *playing football in the dirt*

earth, soil, clay, ground

dirty ADJECTIVE

1 *a pile of dirty washing*
unclean, unwashed, soiled, stained,
grimy, grubby, filthy, messy, mucky,
muddy, squalid
(British informal) manky, grotty

OPPOSITE clean

2 *It's dangerous to drink dirty water.*
impure, polluted, foul, contaminated

OPPOSITE pure

3 *That was a dirty trick!*
unfair, dishonest, underhand, mean,
unsporting

OPPOSITE honest

4 *telling dirty jokes*
rude, obscene, indecent, coarse,
crude, smutty, filthy

OPPOSITE decent

disability NOUN

*The Paralympics are open to athletes
with disabilities.*
handicap, incapacity, impairment,
infirmity

disable VERB

*I managed to disable the smoke
alarm.*
deactivate, turn off, switch off,
disconnect, defuse

OPPOSITE activate

disabled ADJECTIVE

*He has been disabled since the
accident.*
handicapped, incapacitated

▶ An animal which is injured and
cannot walk is **lame**.

▶ A person who cannot move part of
their body is **paralysed**.

OPPOSITE able-bodied

disadvantage NOUN

*Being short is a disadvantage for
basketball.*
drawback, handicap, hindrance,
inconvenience, downside, snag,
catch

IDIOM fly in the ointment

OPPOSITES advantage, plus

disagree VERB

We often disagree about music.
argue, differ, clash, quarrel, be of a different opinion
> **IDIOMS** be at odds, be at loggerheads
> **OPPOSITE** agree

▷ **disagree with**

1 *He disagrees with everything I say.*
argue with, contradict, oppose, object to, dispute, contest, challenge, take issue with

2 *Broccoli disagrees with me.*
make you ill, upset your stomach, have a bad effect on you

disagreeable ADJECTIVE

1 *The water had a disagreeable taste.*
unpleasant, offensive, disgusting, revolting, repellent, repulsive, objectionable, obnoxious
> **OPPOSITE** pleasant

2 *What a disagreeable man!*
bad-tempered, rude, impolite, unfriendly, churlish, irritable, peevish
> **OPPOSITE** charming

disagreement NOUN

There was some disagreement over the bill.
argument, dispute, difference of opinion, conflict, discord, quarrel, row, clash, squabble, contretemps
> **OPPOSITE** agreement

disappear VERB

1 *The scar has nearly disappeared.*
vanish, fade away, melt away, clear, recede
> **OPPOSITES** appear, materialize

2 *a way of life that has disappeared*
die out, cease to exist, come to an end, vanish, pass away
> **OPPOSITES** emerge, arise

disappoint VERB

The announcement will disappoint some fans.
let down, fail, dissatisfy, displease, dismay, upset, sadden
> **OPPOSITES** please, satisfy

disappointed ADJECTIVE

I was disappointed with my score.
displeased, unhappy, upset, unsatisfied, saddened, downhearted, disheartened, discouraged, let down
(British informal) gutted
> **OPPOSITES** pleased, satisfied

disapprove VERB

▷ **disapprove of**

Her family disapproved of her marriage.
object to, take exception to, dislike, deplore, condemn, criticize, denounce, frown on
> **IDIOM** take a dim view of
> **OPPOSITE** approve of

disaster NOUN

1 *The country was rocked by a series of disasters.*
catastrophe, calamity, tragedy, misfortune, setback, blow
▶ Events such as earthquakes and floods are called **natural disasters**.

2 *The show was a complete disaster.*
failure, fiasco, shambles
(informal) flop, washout

disastrous ADJECTIVE

the disastrous effects of the war
catastrophic, devastating, calamitous, destructive, dire, dreadful, terrible, ruinous

disbelief NOUN

We stared at the TV screen in disbelief.
incredulity, doubt, distrust, mistrust, scepticism

disc NOUN

the disc of the full moon
SEE **circle**

discard VERB

discarding some old clothes
get rid of, throw away, throw out, reject, cast off, dispose of, dump, scrap, toss out
(informal) ditch, bin

discharge VERB

1 *He was found not guilty and discharged.*
free, release, let go, liberate

2 *Burning coal discharges carbon dioxide.*
emit, expel, eject, give out, give off, produce

disciple NOUN

Confucius had many disciples.
follower, supporter, adherent, admirer, devotee

▶ In Christianity, the disciples of Jesus are called the **apostles**.

discipline NOUN

1 *maintaining discipline in the classroom*
control, order, good behaviour, obedience

2 *Genetics is a relatively new discipline.*
field, subject, area of study, speciality

disclose VERB

disclosing top-secret information
reveal, divulge, make known, pass on, tell, impart, make public
┃ OPPOSITE conceal

discomfort NOUN

1 *Is your tooth still giving you discomfort?*
pain, soreness, aching

2 *I could sense her discomfort at my question.*
uneasiness, unease, embarrassment, awkwardness, distress, discomfiture

disconnect VERB

disconnecting a computer cable
detach, unplug, unhook, cut off, disable

discontented ADJECTIVE

feeling discontented with life
dissatisfied, disgruntled, displeased, unhappy, miserable
(informal) fed up
┃ OPPOSITES contented, satisfied

discount NOUN

a discount of 20 per cent
reduction, deduction, cut, concession, markdown

discount VERB

1 *I'll have to discount your answer.*
ignore, dismiss, disregard, pay no attention to, overlook
┃ OPPOSITE acknowledge

2 *Prices have been discounted by 20 per cent.*
reduce, mark down, cut, lower
┃ OPPOSITE increase

discourage VERB

1 *Don't let her words discourage you.*
dishearten, demoralize, depress, intimidate, unnerve
┃ OPPOSITE encourage

2 *software to discourage spammers*
deter, dissuade, prevent, restrain, hinder
(informal) put off

discover VERB

1 *I discovered some fossils on the beach.*
find, come across, spot, stumble across, track down, uncover, unearth

2 *We discovered the truth years later.*
find out, learn, realize, recognize, ascertain, work out

discovery NOUN

1 *the discovery of the body*
finding, location, uncovering, unearthing, revelation, disclosure

2 *an important scientific discovery*
find, breakthrough, innovation

discreet ADJECTIVE

I made a few discreet enquiries.
tactful, sensitive, delicate, careful, cautious, diplomatic, judicious
┃ OPPOSITE tactless

discrepancy NOUN

a clear discrepancy between the two scores
difference, disparity, disagreement,

variation, inconsistency, mismatch
OPPOSITE correspondence

discretion NOUN

1 *You can count on my discretion.*
tact, sensitivity, delicacy, diplomacy
OPPOSITE tactlessness

2 *at the discretion of the judges*
option, choice, preference,
inclination, will

discriminate VERB

*discriminating between fact and
fiction*
distinguish, differentiate, tell
the difference, tell apart, draw a
distinction

▷ **discriminate against**
*a policy which discriminates against
older people*
be biased against, be prejudiced
against, treat unfairly, victimize

discrimination NOUN

1 *showing a complete lack of
discrimination*
good taste, good judgement

2 *a policy against racial discrimination*
prejudice, bias, intolerance, bigotry,
unfairness, favouritism

► Discrimination against people
because of their sex is **sexism**.

► Discrimination against people
because of their race is **racism**.

discuss VERB

1 *I discussed the idea with my friends.*
talk about, confer about, debate

2 *This topic is discussed in the next
chapter.*
examine, explore, deal with, analyse,
consider, tackle

discussion NOUN

a discussion about Internet safety
conversation, talk, dialogue,
exchange of views

► A formal discussion is a **conference**
or **debate**.

disdain NOUN

*He treated the new recruits with
disdain.*

contempt, disrespect, scorn,
derision

disease NOUN

*a doctor specializing in tropical
diseases*
illness, sickness, ailment, disorder,
complaint, affliction, condition
(informal) bug

► An outbreak of disease that spreads
quickly is an **epidemic**.

► The scientific study of diseases is
pathology.
SEE ALSO illness

diseased ADJECTIVE

the replacement of a diseased organ
unhealthy, sickly, ailing, infected
OPPOSITE healthy

disgrace NOUN

1 *the disgrace of being caught cheating*
humiliation, shame, dishonour,
scandal, ignominy, disrepute
IDIOM loss of face

2 *The litter on the streets is a disgrace.*
outrage, scandal, affront, atrocity

disgrace VERB

*The behaviour of some fans has
disgraced the club.*
dishonour, shame, discredit, bring
shame on, blacken, stain, taint,
tarnish, sully

disgraceful ADJECTIVE

the disgraceful state of the city centre
shameful, shocking, appalling,
outrageous, scandalous,
contemptible, reprehensible
OPPOSITES honourable, admirable

disguise VERB

1 *a woman who disguised herself as a
soldier*
dress up, be in disguise, camouflage

2 *I tried to disguise my feelings.*
conceal, hide, cover up, camouflage,
mask, screen, veil
OPPOSITES reveal, expose

disguise NOUN

wearing a wig as a disguise

a
b
c
d
e
f
g
h
i
j
k
l
m
n
o
p
q
r
s
t
u
v
w
x
y
z

costume, camouflage, mask

disgust NOUN

A shiver of disgust ran down my spine.

revulsion, repugnance, repulsion, aversion, abhorrence, distaste, dislike, loathing, detestation

| **OPPOSITES** delight, liking

disgust VERB

The sight of blood disgusts me.

repel, revolt, repulse, sicken, appal, offend, distress, horrify

| **IDIOM** turn your stomach

| **OPPOSITES** delight, please

disgusting ADJECTIVE

Ginkgo fruit has a disgusting smell.

repulsive, revolting, horrible, nasty, loathsome, repellent, repugnant, offensive, sickening, nauseating, stomach-turning

(informal) yucky, icky, gross

| **OPPOSITES** delightful, pleasing

FOR TIPS ON DESCRIBING SMELL AND TASTE SEE smell NOUN**, taste** NOUN

dish NOUN

1 *an earthenware dish*

bowl, basin, plate, platter, pot

► A dish to serve soup from is a **tureen**.

2 *What's your favourite dish?*

food, recipe, meal, course

dish VERB

▷ **dish out**

Mr Elliot began dishing out sheets of paper.

distribute, hand out, dole out, dispense, allocate

dishevelled ADJECTIVE

Lester arrived looking flushed and dishevelled.

messy, untidy, scruffy, unkempt, bedraggled, slovenly, ruffled

| **OPPOSITES** neat, tidy

dishonest ADJECTIVE

1 *a dishonest lawyer*

deceitful, corrupt, untrustworthy,

immoral, disreputable, cheating, lying, swindling, thieving

(informal) bent, crooked, dodgy, shady

2 *The website makes some dishonest claims.*

false, fraudulent, misleading, untruthful

| **OPPOSITE** honest

dishonesty NOUN

Plagiarism is a form of dishonesty.

deceit, cheating, lying, insincerity, fraud, corruption

(informal) crookedness

| **OPPOSITE** honesty

disinfect VERB

Lavender was used to disinfect wounds.

cleanse, sterilize, decontaminate

► To disinfect a room with fumes is to **fumigate** it.

| **OPPOSITE** infect

disintegrate VERB

Most meteorites disintegrate before reaching Earth.

break up, fall apart, break into pieces, crumble, decay, decompose

disinterested ADJECTIVE

Referees have to remain disinterested.

impartial, neutral, unbiased, unprejudiced, detached, fair

| **OPPOSITE** biased

Usage Note

The word **uninterested** is not a synonym of **disinterested**. A *disinterested* referee is unbiased, but an *uninterested* referee is bored.

---

disk NOUN

SEE **disc**

dislike NOUN

We have a mutual dislike of rap music.

hatred, loathing, detestation,

antipathy, distaste, disgust,
disapproval, revulsion
OPPOSITE liking

dislike *VERB*

I dislike people who lie to me.
hate, loathe, detest, disapprove
of, object to, be averse to, take
exception to
OPPOSITE like

disloyal *ADJECTIVE*

*They were accused of being disloyal
to the king.*
unfaithful, treacherous, faithless,
false, unreliable, untrustworthy
OPPOSITES loyal, faithful

dismal *ADJECTIVE*

1 *The graveyard was a dismal place
at night.*
dull, drab, dreary, mournful, doleful,
dingy, colourless, cheerless, gloomy,
murky
OPPOSITES bright, cheerful

2 *(informal) It was a dismal
performance by our team.*
dreadful, awful, terrible, feeble,
useless, hopeless
(informal) pathetic
OPPOSITES bright, cheerful

dismantle *VERB*

*It took all day to dismantle the
exhibition.*
take apart, take down,
break up, disassemble
▶ To dismantle a tent is to **strike** it.
OPPOSITES assemble, put together

dismay *NOUN*

*We watched the news reports with
dismay.*
distress, alarm, shock, concern,
anxiety, disquiet, consternation

dismayed *ADJECTIVE*

*We were dismayed by the recent
news.*
distressed, disturbed, discouraged,
disconcerted, depressed, taken
aback, shocked, alarmed
OPPOSITES pleased, encouraged

dismiss *VERB*

1 *Mrs Owen dismissed her class.*
send away, discharge, free, let go,
release

2 *The firm dismissed ten workers.*
sack, give the sack, discharge, let go,
give notice to, make redundant
(informal) fire

3 *I dismissed the idea of selling my
bike.*
discard, drop, reject, banish, set
aside, brush aside, wave aside, put
out of your mind

disobedient *ADJECTIVE*

a disobedient class
badly behaved, insubordinate,
naughty, undisciplined,
uncontrollable, unmanageable,
unruly, ungovernable, troublesome,
defiant, disruptive, rebellious,
mutinous
OPPOSITE obedient

disobey *VERB*

1 *Prometheus disobeyed the gods.*
be disobedient to, defy, rebel against
▶ To refuse to obey orders from a
commanding officer is to **mutiny**.
OPPOSITE obey

2 *disobeying the rules the game*
break, disregard, ignore, violate,
infringe, flout, contravene

disorder *NOUN*

1 *Sandie stared at the disorder of her
desk.*
untidiness, mess, muddle, chaos,
confusion, clutter, jumble
OPPOSITE order

2 *The meeting broke up in disorder.*
disturbance, uproar, commotion,
quarrelling, rioting, brawling,
fighting, lawlessness, anarchy

3 *suffering from an eating disorder*
disease, condition, complaint,
affliction, illness, ailment, sickness

disorderly *ADJECTIVE*

1 *books arranged in a disorderly
fashion*
untidy, disorganized, chaotic,

messy, in disarray
(informal) higgledy-piggledy

OPPOSITE orderly

2 *disorderly behaviour*
disobedient, unruly, uncontrollable,
undisciplined, ungovernable,
unmanageable

dispatch *VERB*

*The parcel has already been
dispatched.*
post, send, transmit, forward

dispatch *NOUN*

sending an urgent dispatch
message, communication, report,
letter, bulletin, communiqué

dispel *VERB*

1 *Open a window to dispel the smoke.*
clear away, drive away, scatter,
eliminate

2 *dispelling the myth that girls dislike
computer games*
do away with, get rid of, set aside,
dismiss, banish, debunk

dispense *VERB*

1 *dispensing aid to the refugees*
distribute, hand out, dole out, pass
round, supply, provide

2 *a feudal lord dispensing justice*
administer, issue, deliver, deal out,
mete out

▷ **dispense with**
*We are dispensing with fees
altogether.*
get rid of, dispose of, do without,
forego, waive, drop, omit

IDIOM *(informal)* give something
a miss

disperse *VERB*

1 *Dandelion seeds are dispersed by the
wind.*
scatter, spread, distribute,
disseminate

2 *The crowd dispersed quickly after the
match.*
break up, scatter, disband, separate,
split up, go in different directions

OPPOSITE gather

3 *The morning fog soon dispersed.*
dissipate, dissolve, melt away,
vanish, clear, lift

displace *VERB*

1 *The gales displaced some roof tiles.*
dislodge, put out of place, shift,
dislocate

OPPOSITE replace

2 *MP3 players have displaced CDs and
tapes.*
replace, take the place of, succeed,
supersede, supplant

display *VERB*

1 *The students' work was displayed in
the foyer.*
exhibit, present, show, set out, put
on show, show off, parade, showcase

▶ To display something boastfully is to
flaunt it.

2 *displaying great skill with the ball*
show, demonstrate, reveal, show
evidence of, manifest

display *NOUN*

a display of recent artwork
exhibition, show, presentation,
demonstration, parade, spectacle,
showcase

displease *VERB*

*I must have done something to
displease her.*
annoy, irritate, upset, put out,
anger, irk, exasperate, vex

dispose *VERB*

▷ **dispose of something**
disposing of an old sofa
get rid of, discard, throw away,
throw out, jettison, scrap
(informal) dump, ditch, chuck out

▷ **be disposed to do something**
No one seems disposed to help us.
be willing to, be inclined to, be ready
to, be likely to

disposition *NOUN*

*Our dog has a very friendly
disposition.*
temperament, nature, character,
make-up, personality, mentality

disprove VERB

There is no evidence to disprove her story.

refute, rebut, prove false, demolish, debunk

IDIOM shoot full of holes

OPPOSITE prove

dispute VERB

Some disputed her claim to the throne.

disagree with, object to, challenge, contest, call into question, take issue with

dispute NOUN

a dispute over who should pay

argument, disagreement, debate, controversy, difference of opinion, quarrel, row, squabble, clash

disregard VERB

I disregarded the doctor's advice.

ignore, pay no attention to, take no notice of, discount, reject, brush aside, shrug off

IDIOM turn a blind eye to

OPPOSITE heed

disrespectful ADJECTIVE

It's disrespectful to walk on someone's grave.

rude, bad-mannered, insulting, impolite, insolent, cheeky

OPPOSITE respectful

disrupt VERB

The roadworks are disrupting bus services.

interrupt, disturb, upset, unsettle, interfere with, play havoc with, throw into confusion

disruptive ADJECTIVE

disruptive behaviour

unruly, undisciplined, uncontrollable, unmanageable, ungovernable, troublesome, rebellious, rowdy

dissatisfaction NOUN

a frown of deep dissatisfaction

displeasure, discontentment,

disappointment, disgruntlement, annoyance, frustration

OPPOSITES satisfaction, contentment

dissatisfied ADJECTIVE

I felt dissatisfied with my score.

displeased, discontented, disappointed, disgruntled, unhappy, frustrated, annoyed, aggrieved

OPPOSITES satisfied, contented

dissolve VERB

1 *Stir the mixture until the sugar dissolves.*

disperse, disintegrate, melt

2 *Damien felt his strength dissolve.*

weaken, lessen, fade, dissipate, break down, collapse

dissuade VERB

▷ **dissuade someone from**

I tried to dissuade her from leaving.

discourage from, persuade not to, talk out of, deter from, warn against

OPPOSITES persuade to, encourage to

distance NOUN

What is the distance from the Earth to the Sun?

measurement, space, extent, reach, mileage

▶ The distance across something is the **breadth** or **width**.

▶ The distance along something is the **length**.

▶ The distance between two points is a **gap** or **interval**.

SEE ALSO measurement

distant ADJECTIVE

1 *travelling to distant countries*

faraway, far-off, remote, out-of-the-way, outlying

OPPOSITES nearby, close

2 *in the distant past*

old, ancient, bygone, remote

OPPOSITE recent

3 *His distant manner puts me off.*

unfriendly, unapproachable, formal, reserved, withdrawn, cool,

haughty, aloof
OPPOSITES friendly, warm

distinct *ADJECTIVE*

1 *I can see a distinct improvement.*
definite, evident, noticeable, obvious, perceptible
OPPOSITE imperceptible

2 *The image is quite distinct.*
clear, well defined, distinguishable, recognizable, sharp, unmistakable, visible, plain to see
OPPOSITE indistinct

3 *divided into distinct sections*
separate, discrete, different, individual

distinction *NOUN*

1 *the distinction between good and evil*
difference, contrast, distinctiveness, discrepancy, differentiation

2 *the distinction of captaining the squad*
honour, glory, merit, credit, prestige

distinctive *ADJECTIVE*

the distinctive markings of a rattlesnake
characteristic, recognizable, unmistakable, particular, special, peculiar, unique, exclusive

distinctly *ADVERB*

1 *We could hear the music distinctly from upstairs.*
clearly, audibly, plainly, sharply
OPPOSITE faintly

2 *There was something distinctly odd about Igor.*
definitely, decidedly, markedly, particularly, unmistakably, patently, manifestly

distinguish *VERB*

1 *distinguishing one twin from the other*
tell apart, differentiate, discriminate between, tell the difference between, tell

2 *distinguishing a face in the crowd*
identify, recognize, detect, make out, single out, discern, perceive

distinguished *ADJECTIVE*

1 *a distinguished academic record*
excellent, first-rate, outstanding, exceptional
OPPOSITE ordinary

2 *a distinguished Hollywood actor*
famous, celebrated, well-known, eminent, notable, prominent, renowned, acclaimed
OPPOSITES unknown, obscure

distort *VERB*

1 *The crash distorted the front wheel.*
bend, buckle, twist, warp, contort, disfigure, deform, put out of shape

2 *The newspaper distorted the facts of the story.*
misrepresent, twist, slant, falsify, garble

distract *VERB*

Don't distract the bus driver.
divert the attention of, disturb, put off, sidetrack, lead astray

distraught *ADJECTIVE*

Milly was too distraught to think clearly.
distressed, upset, overcome, overwrought, beside yourself, desperate, frantic

distress *NOUN*

Eva let out a cry of distress.
suffering, torment, anguish, pain, misery, dismay, disquiet, anxiety, grief, sadness, sorrow, wretchedness, heartache

distress *VERB*

I could see that my words distressed her.
upset, disturb, trouble, worry, dismay, perturb, alarm, agitate, torment, pain
OPPOSITE comfort

distribute *VERB*

1 *distributing leaflets*
give out, hand round, circulate, dispense, issue, deal out, share out, dole out, dish out

2 *Distribute the seeds evenly.*
scatter, spread, disperse

a b c d e f g h i j k l m n o p q r s t u v w x y z

distribution NOUN

the distribution of international aid
delivery, dispersal, allocation,
issuing, handing out, giving out

district NOUN

a mountainous district of Nepal
area, region, territory, locality,
vicinity, neighbourhood, quarter,
sector, zone

distrust NOUN

*Hank had a deep distrust of
grown-ups.*
suspicion, mistrust, wariness,
chariness, scepticism,
misgivings (about)

OPPOSITE trust

distrust VERB

*I distrusted him from the moment I
met him.*
doubt, mistrust, be suspicious of,
be wary of, be chary of, question,
suspect, be sceptical about, have
misgivings about

OPPOSITE trust

disturb VERB

1 *Please don't let me disturb you.*
interrupt, intrude on, disrupt,
bother, pester, trouble, distract

2 *Some of the pictures may disturb
you.*
distress, trouble, upset, unsettle,
disconcert, worry, perturb

3 *Someone had disturbed the papers
on my desk.*
rearrange, move around, mix up,
muddle up, mess up, interfere with

disturbance NOUN

1 *We apologize for the disturbance to
pedestrians.*
disruption, inconvenience, upset,
interference, intrusion

2 *a disturbance in the street outside*
fight, commotion, quarrel, row, riot,
brawl, fracas

disturbing ADJECTIVE

*The film contains disturbing images
of war.*

distressing, upsetting, unsettling,
disconcerting, troubling,
disquieting, worrying

ditch NOUN

at the bottom of a muddy ditch
trench, channel, trough, drain,
gutter, gully

dither VERB

I'm still dithering over what to do.
hesitate, waver, be in two minds,
vacillate
(informal) shilly-shally

dive VERB

1 *A group of penguins dived into the
water.*
plunge, jump, leap
▶ A dive in which you land flat on your
front is a **bellyflop**.

2 *A small plane dived suddenly out of
the clouds.*
fall, drop, plummet, pitch, nosedive,
swoop

3 *We dived into the nearest doorway.*
leap, bound, duck, lunge, throw
yourself, run headlong

diverse ADJECTIVE

a rich and diverse culture
varied, mixed, diversified, assorted,
miscellaneous, different, differing,
varying, divergent

diversion NOUN

1 *a traffic diversion*
detour, alternative route,
re-direction, re-routing

2 *the diversions on offer at the theme
park*
entertainment, amusement,
recreation

diversity NOUN

*the diversity of flower species in the
area*
variety, assortment, range, array,
multiplicity

divert VERB

1 *Our train was diverted to another
station.*
redirect, re-route, switch

》

a
b
c
d
e
f
g
h
i
j
k
l
m
n
o
p
q
r
s
t
u
v
w
x
y
z

2 *She diverted herself by browsing the Internet.*
entertain, amuse, occupy, interest, distract, keep happy

divide VERB

1 *We divided the class into two teams.*
separate, split, split up, break up, part, partition
❙ OPPOSITE combine

2 *We divided the chocolate between us.*
distribute, share out, ration, give out, deal out, dish out, dispense

3 *The river divides into several channels.*
diverge, branch off, fork, split, part
❙ OPPOSITE converge

4 *Divide the remaining number by ten.*
▶ The result of dividing one number by another is the **quotient**.
❙ OPPOSITE multiply

divination NOUN
SEE **fortune telling**

divine ADJECTIVE

1 *a service of divine worship*
religious, sacred, holy, spiritual, devotional

2 *Do you believe in a divine being?*
godly, godlike, immortal, heavenly, celestial

3 *(informal) These muffins taste divine!*
excellent, wonderful, superb

division NOUN

1 *the division of Europe after the war*
dividing, splitting, break-up, separation, partition, dividing up, carving up

2 *the deep division within the family*
disunity, disagreement, discord, conflict, split, feud

3 *a job in the sales division*
branch, department, section, arm, unit, wing

divulge VERB

He refused to divulge any more details.
disclose, make known, reveal, tell, impart, pass on, give away, let slip

dizzy ADJECTIVE

Roller coasters make me feel dizzy.
light-headed, giddy, dazed, faint, reeling, unsteady, wobbly
(informal) woozy

do VERB

1 *Kim didn't know what to do.*
act, behave, conduct yourself

2 *I have a lot of work to do this morning.*
attend to, cope with, deal with, handle, look after, perform, undertake

3 *It took half an hour to do the dishes.*
accomplish, achieve, carry out, complete, execute, finish

4 *I need to do all of these sums.*
answer, puzzle out, solve, work out

5 *Sunbathing can do damage to your skin.*
bring about, cause, produce, result in

6 *If you don't have milk, water will do.*
be acceptable, be enough, be satisfactory, be sufficient, serve

▷ **do away with**
doing away with homework
get rid of, abolish, eliminate, end, put an end to, discontinue
(informal) scrap

▷ **do something up**

1 *doing up your shoelaces*
fasten, tie, lace

2 *doing up an old cottage*
redecorate, make over, refurbish, renovate, restore

docile ADJECTIVE

a docile pet
tame, gentle, meek, obedient, manageable, submissive
❙ OPPOSITE fierce

dock ❶ NOUN

a ferry pulling in to the dock
harbour, quay, jetty, wharf, landing stage, dockyard, pier, port, marina

dock VERB

The ferry docks at 8 a.m.
moor, berth, tie up, anchor

dock[2] VERB

docking ten points from the final score
deduct, take away, subtract, remove, cut

doctor NOUN

a prescription from the doctor
physician, general practitioner, GP, consultant
(informal) doc, medic
SEE ALSO medicine

document NOUN

a box containing old documents
paper, record, certificate, deed, report

dodge VERB

1 *Jud managed to dodge the snowball.*
avoid, evade, sidestep

2 *He managed to dodge the police for seven months.*
elude, evade, escape from, shake off
IDIOM *(informal)* give someone the slip

3 *dodging in and out of the line of cars*
dart, dive, slip, duck, wriggle

dog NOUN

a dog with a shaggy coat
hound
(informal) mutt, pooch
► An uncomplimentary word for a dog is **cur**.

✺ WORD WEB

some breeds of dog

Afghan hound, Alsatian, basset hound, beagle, bloodhound, boxer, bulldog, bull terrier, cairn terrier, chihuahua, cocker spaniel, collie, corgi, dachshund, Dalmatian, Dobermann, foxhound, fox terrier, golden retriever, Great Dane, greyhound, husky, Irish setter, Labrador, mastiff, Pekinese or Pekingese, Pomeranian, poodle, pug, Rottweiler, St Bernard, Schnauzer, setter, sheepdog,

spaniel, terrier, West Highland terrier, whippet, wolfhound, Yorkshire terrier
(informal Yorkie)

► A female dog is a **bitch**.
► A young dog is a **pup**, **puppy**, or **whelp**.
► A dog of pure breed with known ancestors has a **pedigree**.
► A dog of mixed breeds is a **mongrel**.
► A related adjective is **canine**.
FOR TIPS ON DESCRIBING ANIMALS
SEE **animal**

dole VERB

▷ **dole out**
doling out free samples
give out, distribute, dispense, hand out, dish out, deal out

domestic ADJECTIVE

1 *doing domestic chores*
household, family

2 *Cats and dogs are domestic animals.*
domesticated, tame, pet
OPPOSITE wild

dominant ADJECTIVE

1 *playing a dominant role in the team*
leading, main, chief, major, powerful, principal, important, influential
OPPOSITE minor

2 *The archway is a dominant feature of the house.*
conspicuous, prominent, obvious, large, imposing, eye-catching
OPPOSITE insignificant

dominate VERB

1 *Our opponents dominated the first half.*
control, direct, monopolize, govern, take control of, take over

2 *Mount Kilimanjaro dominates the landscape.*
tower over, loom over, overlook, command, dwarf

a
b
c
d
e
f
g
h
i
j
k
l
m
n
o
p
q
r
s
t
u
v
w
x
y
z

donate VERB
donating money to charity
give, contribute, grant, present, endow

donation NOUN
We rely on donations from the public.
contribution, gift, grant, offering, handout

done ADJECTIVE
1 *My thank-you letters are all done now.*
finished, complete, over
2 *The cake will rise when it's done.*
cooked, ready

donor NOUN
the gift of an anonymous donor
benefactor, contributor, sponsor, patron, backer

doomed ADJECTIVE
The mission was doomed from the start.
ill-fated, ill-starred, fated, cursed, jinxed, damned

door NOUN
Please shut the door behind you.
entrance, exit, doorway, portal
▶ A door in a floor or ceiling is a **hatch** or **trapdoor**.
▶ The plank or stone underneath a door is the **threshold**.
▶ The beam or stone above a door is the **lintel**.

dose NOUN
a dose of medicine
measure, dosage, portion, draught

dot NOUN
dots of paint on the carpet
spot, speck, fleck, point, mark, speckle

▷ **on the dot**
(informal) The bus leaves at nine on the dot.
exactly, precisely, on time

dot VERB
a blue sky dotted with clouds
spot, fleck, mark, spatter, scatter, sprinkle, pepper

dote VERB
▷ **dote on someone**
Edie dotes on her grandchildren.
adore, be devoted to, love dearly, worship, idolize, cherish, treasure

double ADJECTIVE
a double set of doors
dual, twofold, paired, twin, matching, duplicate
▶ Two stars that revolve round each other form a **binary star**.

double NOUN
Stacey is the double of her sister.
twin, duplicate, exact likeness, look-alike
IDIOMS spitting image, dead ringer
▶ A living organism created as an exact copy of another one is a **clone**.

doubt NOUN
1 *Have you any doubt about his story?*
distrust, suspicion, mistrust, hesitation, reservation, scepticism, wariness, misgivings
OPPOSITE confidence
2 *There is no doubt that you will pass your exam.*
question, uncertainty, ambiguity, controversy, confusion
OPPOSITE certainty

doubt VERB
There is no reason to doubt his story.
distrust, feel uncertain about, feel unsure about, question, disbelieve, mistrust, suspect, be sceptical about, be suspicious of, be wary of, have misgivings about
OPPOSITE trust

doubtful ADJECTIVE
1 *I was doubtful about the idea at first.*
unsure, uncertain, unconvinced, hesitant, distrustful, sceptical, suspicious, wary, chary, in a quandary
IDIOM in two minds
OPPOSITE certain

2 *Our plans for the weekend are looking doubtful.*
unlikely, improbable, in doubt

3 *a doubtful decision by the referee*
questionable, debatable, arguable, open to question
(informal) iffy

downfall NOUN

the downfall of the Aztec empire
collapse, fall, ruin, overthrow, crash, failure, undoing

downward ADJECTIVE

a steep downward slope
downhill, descending
❙ OPPOSITE upward

drab ADJECTIVE

1 *a room painted in drab colours*
dull, dingy, dreary, cheerless, colourless, dismal, gloomy, sombre
(Scottish) dreich
❙ OPPOSITES bright, cheerful

2 *leading a drab existence*
uninteresting, uneventful, dull, boring, tedious, monotonous, dry
❙ OPPOSITES interesting, colourful

draft NOUN

I wrote a first draft of my essay.
outline, plan, sketch, rough version

draft VERB

I began to draft my first chapter.
outline, plan, prepare, sketch, work out

drag VERB

dragging a suitcase behind you
pull, tow, haul, draw, tug, trail, heave, lug
❙ OPPOSITE push

dragon NOUN

FOR CREATURES FOUND IN FANTASY FICTION SEE **fantasy**

drain NOUN

a drain to catch surplus water
ditch, channel, drainpipe, gutter, pipe, sewer

drain VERB

1 *using a pump to drain a well*

dry out, empty out, clear out, void

2 *draining oil from the engine*
draw off, empty, extract, siphon off, bleed, filter, tap

3 *The water slowly drained away.*
flow, stream, trickle, seep, leak, dribble, ooze

4 *The tough climb drained my energy.*
use up, consume, exhaust, deplete, expend, sap

5 *I waited till everyone had drained their glass.*
drink up, swallow, quaff
(informal) knock back, swig

drama NOUN

1 *a television drama*
play, piece, dramatization

2 *studying drama at college*
acting, the theatre, the stage, stagecraft

3 *witnessing the drama of a real robbery*
action, excitement, suspense, spectacle

 WORD WEB

some types of drama
ballet, comedy, comic sketch, dance theatre, improvisation, melodrama, mime, musical, music theatre, mystery play, one-act play, opera, pantomime
(informal panto), review, situation comedy (informal sitcom), soap opera (informal soap), tragedy

parts of a play
act, scene, prologue, intermission, finale, script or playscript, dialogue, monologue, soliloquy

parts of a theatre
apron, auditorium, balcony or circle, box office, curtain, dressing room, foyer, front of house, green room, orchestra pit, proscenium, stage, stalls, wings 》

a
b
c
d
e
f
g
h
i
j
k
l
m
n
o
p
q
r
s
t
u
v
w
x
y
z

> **people involved in drama**
> actor (formal thespian), actress,
> audience, cast, director,
> dramatis personae, dramatist or
> playwright, producer, prompter,
> set designer, stagehand, stage
> manager, voice coach
>
> **other terms relating to drama**
> acting, amphitheatre, aside,
> audition, backdrop, backstage,
> blocking, casting, characters,
> chorus, cue, downstage, dress
> rehearsal, ensemble, entrance,
> exit, lines, off-stage, on-stage,
> premiere, props, protagonist,
> read-through, rehearsal, scenery,
> set design, stage directions,
> stage set, tableau, theatre in the
> round, upstage

dramatic ADJECTIVE
1 the dramatic arts
  theatrical, stage, thespian
2 The ending of the film is very
  dramatic.
  exciting, thrilling, action-packed,
  sensational, spectacular, eventful,
  gripping, riveting, suspenseful,
  tense, nail-biting, hair-raising
3 a dramatic change in her
  appearance
  noticeable, considerable,
  substantial, remarkable, exceptional,
  phenomenal, extreme

drastic ADJECTIVE
  time to take drastic action
  desperate, extreme, radical, harsh,
  severe, serious, far-reaching
  ❙ OPPOSITE moderate

draught NOUN
  a cold draught from the window
  breeze, current of air, gust, puff, waft

draw VERB
1 Rembrandt drew several self-
  portraits.
  sketch, trace, doodle, outline,
  illustrate, depict, portray, render

2 Draw you chair towards the table.
  pull, drag, haul, tow, tug, lug, heave
3 The train drew slowly into the
  station.
  move, progress, proceed, roll, inch,
  cruise, glide
4 The samurai warrior drew his
  sword.
  pull out, take out, withdraw,
  unsheathe
5 Where did you draw your
  information from?
  take, extract, derive
6 The concert should draw a big
  crowd.
  attract, bring in, pull in
7 The two teams drew 1-1.
  finish equal, tie

▷ **draw near**
  A shadowy figure drew near us.
  approach, advance, come near

▷ **draw on**
  drawing on all our ingenuity
  call on, make use of, use, employ,
  have recourse to

▷ **draw something out**
  The ending of the book is rather
  drawn out.
  extend, lengthen, prolong, protract,
  drag out, spin out

▷ **draw something up**
  drawing up a new plan
  compose, write out, formulate,
  devise, design, frame, invent

draw NOUN
1 The game ended in a draw.
  tie, dead heat
2 a prize draw
  lottery, raffle

drawback NOUN
  The only real drawback is the cost.
  disadvantage, downside, difficulty,
  handicap, obstacle, inconvenience,
  hindrance, snag, catch, hitch
  ❙ IDIOM fly in the ointment
  ❙ OPPOSITES advantage, plus

drawing NOUN

a drawing of a bowl of fruit
sketch, illustration, design, study,
cartoon, doodle, scribble

 WORD WEB

**terms used in drawing and
painting**
acrylics, airbrush, background,
brushwork, canvas, chalk,
charcoal, complementary
colours, composition,
crayon, easel, figure drawing,
foreground, foreshortening,
freehand, fresco, gouache,
graffiti, hatching, impasto, ink,
landscape, life drawing, mural,
oils, op art, palette, pastel,
pencil, perspective, pigment,
portrait, portraiture,
self-portrait, shading, sketching,
still life, stippling, study, tone,
wash, watercolour

SEE ALSO art

dread NOUN

*The thought of entering the crypt
filled me with dread.*
fear, terror, trepidation, alarm,
apprehension, anxiety, disquiet,
unease

dread VERB

Nina was dreading her aunt's visit.
fear, be afraid of, worry about,
be anxious about

OPPOSITE look forward to

dreadful ADJECTIVE

1 *a dreadful accident at sea*
terrible, appalling, horrendous,
horrible, distressing, shocking,
upsetting, tragic, grim

2 *They thought the acting was
dreadful.*
bad, awful, terrible, abysmal,
atrocious, abominable, deplorable,
disgraceful, dire
(informal) rotten, rubbish, lousy

OPPOSITES good, excellent

dream NOUN

1 *woken by a bad dream*
▶ A bad dream is a **nightmare**.
▶ A dreamlike experience you have
while awake is a **daydream**,
fantasy, or **reverie**.
▶ Something you see in a dream or
daydream is a **vision**.
▶ The dreamlike state when you are
hypnotized is a **trance**.
▶ Something you think you see that
is not real is a **hallucination** or
illusion.

2 *Her dream is to be on the stage.*
ambition, hope, wish, desire,
longing, yearning, aspiration, goal

dream VERB

I dreamed I was lost in a labyrinth.
imagine, fancy, fantasize, daydream

▷ **dream of**
*I've always dreamt of being on
television.*
wish to, hope to, aspire to, long to,
yearn to, hanker after

▷ **dream something up**
Who dreamt up this mad idea?
think up, come up with, invent,
devise, concoct, hatch

dreary ADJECTIVE

1 *an announcer with a dreary voice*
dull, boring, tedious, flat,
monotonous, unexciting,
uninteresting, uninspiring

OPPOSITE lively

2 *a day of dreary weather*
dull, dismal, depressing, gloomy,
cheerless, murky, overcast
(Scottish) dreich

OPPOSITES bright, sunny

drench VERB

The rain drenched me to the skin.
soak, saturate, wet through, steep,
douse, drown

dress NOUN

1 *a party dress*
frock, gown, robe

2 *Please wear evening dress.*

》

a
b
c
d
e
f
g
h
i
j
k
l
m
n
o
p
q
r
s
t
u
v
w
x
y
z

clothes, clothing, attire, outfit, costume, garments, wear
∎ SEE ALSO clothes

dress *VERB*

1 *I woke and dressed quickly.*
get dressed, put clothes on
∎ OPPOSITE undress

2 *Samantha was dressed in a smart suit.*
clothe, attire, deck out, garb, enrobe

3 *dressing a wound*
bandage, bind, wrap, put a dressing on

dribble *VERB*

1 *a baby dribbling down its chin*
drool, slobber, slaver

2 *Water dribbled out of the tap.*
drip, trickle, drizzle, leak, ooze, seep

drift *VERB*

1 *a raft drifting downstream*
float, be carried, be borne, glide, cruise, waft

2 *My mind had already begun to drift.*
wander, stray, meander, be diverted, digress

drift *NOUN*

1 *the drift of populations across Europe*
movement, moving, flow, transfer, shift, glide

2 *a car stuck in a snow drift*
bank, heap, mound, pile, ridge

3 *I don't get your drift.*
meaning, point, gist, sense, import

drill *NOUN*

1 *a weekly fire drill*
practice, training

2 *You all know the drill by now.*
procedure, routine, system

drill *VERB*

1 *drilling a hole in the wall*
bore, penetrate, pierce, puncture, perforate

2 *drilling the new cadets*
train, instruct, coach, discipline, exercise

drink *VERB*

Spud drank the potion in one go.
swallow, gulp, quaff, drain, sip, slurp
(informal) swig, knock back, down
(formal) imbibe

drink *NOUN*

1 *a selection of soft drinks*
beverage

2 *He took a long drink from his flask.*
swallow, draught, gulp, sip
(informal) swig, slug

3 *a talk on the dangers of drink*
alcohol, spirits
(informal) booze

drip *VERB*

Water was dripping from the ceiling.
drop, dribble, splash, trickle, leak

drip *NOUN*

a bucket to catch the drips of water
drop, dribble, spot, splash, trickle

drive *VERB*

1 *learning to drive a car*
control, operate, handle, manage, steer, work

2 *Can you drive us to the airport?*
run, give someone a lift, take, transport, convey, ferry

3 *an engine driven by wind power*
power, propel, move, push

4 *What drove you to write the song?*
compel, lead, force, oblige, prompt, spur

5 *You must drive a stake through the vampire's heart.*
push, thrust, plunge, sink, ram, hammer

▷ **drive someone out**
Many crofters were driven out of their homes.
eject, throw out, expel, evict

▶ To drive people out of their country is to **banish** or **exile** them.

drive *NOUN*

1 *We went for a drive in the country.*
ride, trip, journey, outing, excursion, jaunt
(informal) spin

2 *the drive to succeed*
ambition, determination, commitment, motivation, keenness, energy, tenacity, zeal

3 *an annual charity drive*
campaign, initiative, effort, push, crusade

driver NOUN
the number of drivers on our roads
motorist
► A person who drives someone's car as a job is a **chauffeur**.

droop VERB
The roses have begun to droop.
wilt, sag, hang down, bend, flop, slump

drop NOUN

1 *heavy drops of rain*
drip, droplet, spot, bead, blob, globule

2 *Add a drop or two of milk.*
dash, dribble, splash, trickle, spot

3 *a drop in the price of oil*
decrease, reduction, cut, fall, slump

4 *a drop of two metres*
descent, drop, plunge

drop VERB

1 *Suddenly a hawk dropped out of the sky.*
descend, dive, swoop, dip, plunge, plummet

2 *I dropped to the ground exhausted.*
collapse, fall, sink, subside, slump, tumble

3 *Harry dropped the ball and ran.*
let fall, let go of, release, lose your grip on

4 *Temperatures have dropped sharply.*
decrease, decline, reduce, fall, dip, slump

5 *The road drops away to the right.*
descend, fall away, drop, slope

6 *Let's drop the idea altogether.*
abandon, discard, reject, give up, scrap, relinquish
(informal) ditch, dump

7 *He's been dropped from the team.*
omit, eliminate, exclude, leave out

▷ **drop off**
I felt myself starting to drop off.
fall asleep, doze off, drift off
(informal) nod off

▷ **drop in**
Do drop in on your way home.
visit, call, pay a call

▷ **drop out**
Three contestants have now dropped out.
withdraw, back out, pull out
(informal) quit
❙ IDIOM fall by the wayside

drowsy ADJECTIVE
By midnight, I was starting to feel drowsy.
sleepy, tired, weary

drug NOUN
a new drug for cancer
medicine, remedy, treatment
► A drug which relieves pain is an **analgesic** or **painkiller**.
► A drug which calms you down is a **sedative** or **tranquillizer**.
► Drugs which make you more active are **stimulants**.

drum NOUN
FOR MUSICAL INSTRUMENTS SEE **music**

dry ADJECTIVE

1 *Nothing will grow in this dry soil.*
acrid, parched, waterless, moistureless, dehydrated, desiccated, barren, shrivelled, wizened
❙ OPPOSITES wet, moist

2 *Dr Boyle gave rather a dry speech.*
dull, boring, uninteresting, dreary, tedious, unimaginative, uninspiring
❙ OPPOSITES interesting, lively

3 *a dry sense of humour*
ironic, wry, subtle, laconic

dry VERB

1 *hanging clothes out to dry*
get dry, dry out

2 *The earth had been dried by the desert sun.*
parch, scorch, dehydrate,

a
b
c
d
e
f
g
h
i
j
k
l
m
n
o
p
q
r
s
t
u
v
w
x
y
z

desiccate, shrivel, wither

dual ADJECTIVE

a building with a dual purpose
double, twofold, twin, combined

dubious ADJECTIVE

1 *I'm a bit dubious about the idea.*
doubtful, uncertain, unsure, hesitant, sceptical, suspicious
OPPOSITES certain, sure

2 *a firm with a dubious reputation*
unreliable, untrustworthy, questionable, suspect
(informal) shady, dodgy

duck NOUN

a yellow-billed duck
▶ A male duck is a **drake**.
▶ A young duck is a **duckling**.

duck VERB

1 *Marsha ducked to avoid the snowball.*
bend down, bob down, crouch, stoop

2 *They threatened to duck me in the pool.*
dip, immerse, plunge, submerge

3 *trying to duck the question*
avoid, evade, dodge, shirk, sidestep

due ADJECTIVE

1 *The train is due this morning.*
expected, anticipated, scheduled for

2 *Your subscription is now due.*
owed, owing, payable, outstanding, unpaid

3 *treating animals with due respect*
proper, suitable, appropriate, fitting, adequate, sufficient, deserved

dull ADJECTIVE

1 *a dull shade of green*
drab, dingy, dreary, sombre, muted, subdued
OPPOSITE bright

2 *a dull morning*
cloudy, overcast, grey, sunless, murky, dreary
OPPOSITE clear

3 *The film was so dull that I fell asleep.*
uninteresting, boring, tedious,
unexciting, unimaginative, monotonous, flat, lacklustre, lifeless, uneventful
OPPOSITE interesting

4 *I heard a dull thud from upstairs.*
indistinct, muffled, muted, stifled
OPPOSITES distinct, sharp

5 *He's rather a dull student.*
stupid, slow, unintelligent, unimaginative, obtuse
(informal) dim, dense
OPPOSITES clever, bright

dumb ADJECTIVE

1 *We were all struck dumb with amazement.*
silent, mute, speechless, tongue-tied
IDIOM at a loss for words

2 *(informal) What a dumb question!*
stupid, silly, unintelligent, brainless, idiotic
(British informal) daft

dumbfounded ADJECTIVE

I was dumbfounded when I heard the news.
amazed, astonished, astounded, stunned, staggered, thunderstruck, speechless, struck dumb
(informal) flabbergasted
(British informal) gobsmacked

dump NOUN

1 *a rubbish dump*
tip, dumping ground, scrapheap

2 *(informal) This place is a bit of a dump.*
tip, hovel, pigsty, mess
(informal) hole

dump VERB

1 *dumping some of your old clothes*
get rid of, throw away, throw out, discard, dispose of, scrap, bin

2 *Just dump your things in the bedroom.*
put down, set down, place, drop, deposit, throw down
(informal) plonk, bung

duplicate NOUN

an exact duplicate of the letter
copy, reproduction, replica
▶ An exact copy of a document is a
facsimile.
▶ A person who looks like you is your
double or **twin**.
▶ A living organism which is a
duplicate of another one is a **clone**.

durable ADJECTIVE

Denim is a very durable material.
hard-wearing, lasting, strong, tough,
robust
❙ **OPPOSITE** flimsy

duration NOUN

*We'll be away for the duration of the
holidays*
length, period, extent, term, span

dusk NOUN

Bats begin to emerge at dusk.
twilight, nightfall, sunset, close of
day
(North American) sundown
(poetic) gloaming
❙ **OPPOSITE** dawn

dust NOUN

1 *sweeping the dust from the floor*
dirt, grime, particles, powder, grit
2 *giving the shelves a dust*
wipe, clean, brush, sweep

dust VERB

1 *dusting the bookshelves*
wipe, clean, brush, sweep
2 *dusting a cake with icing sugar*
sprinkle, dredge, sift, powder

dusty ADJECTIVE

a pile of dusty old books
dirty, grimy, grubby, unswept

❙ **OPPOSITE** clean

dutiful ADJECTIVE

*a reward for dutiful service to his
country*
faithful, loyal, obedient, devoted,
conscientious, reliable, responsible,
trustworthy
❙ **OPPOSITES** irresponsible, lazy

duty NOUN

1 *It's our duty to help those in need.*
responsibility, obligation, mission
2 *a list of your daily duties*
job, task, assignment, chore
3 *increasing the duty on petrol*
tax, charge

dwell VERB

▷ **dwell on**
Try not to dwell on the past.
keep thinking about, worry about,
brood over

dwelling NOUN
SEE **house**

dwindle VERB

Our supplies are dwindling fast.
diminish, decrease, decline, lessen,
shrink, subside, wane
❙ **OPPOSITE** increase

dye VERB

Sadie has dyed her hair red.
colour, tint, stain

dynamic ADJECTIVE

a dynamic new head teacher
energetic, lively, spirited,
enthusiastic, vigorous, forceful,
active, enterprising
(informal) go-ahead
❙ **OPPOSITES** apathetic, laid-back

a
b
c
d
e
f
g
h
i
j
k
l
m
n
o
p
q
r
s
t
u
v
w
x
y
z

Ee

a
b
c
d
e
f
g
h
i
j
k
l
m
n
o
p
q
r
s
t
u
v
w
x
y
z

each *ADVERB*
> The tickets cost five dollars each.
apiece, per person, per head

eager *ADJECTIVE*
> Vicky is always eager to help.
keen, enthusiastic, anxious, impatient, desperate, willing
(informal) itching
❙ **OPPOSITE** unenthusiastic

ear *NOUN*
> **FOR TIPS ON DESCRIBING FACES**
> SEE **face**

early *ADJECTIVE*
> 1 *The bus was early today.*
ahead of time, ahead of schedule
❙ **OPPOSITE** late
> 2 *the early death of both her parents*
premature, untimely, unseasonable
> 3 *the early attempts at manned flight*
first, initial, preliminary, advance
❙ **OPPOSITES** recent, latest
> 4 *an example of early cave painting*
old, primitive, ancient
❙ **OPPOSITES** modern, later

earn *VERB*
> 1 *How much do you earn each week?*
be paid, receive, get, make, bring in, collect
(informal) pocket
❙ **OPPOSITES** lose, waste
> 2 *She has earned her celebrity status.*
deserve, merit, warrant, justify, be worthy of

earnest *ADJECTIVE*
> He greeted me with an earnest handshake.
serious, sincere, solemn, thoughtful, grave, sober
❙ **OPPOSITES** casual, flippant

earnings *PLURAL NOUN*
> the average earnings of employees
income, pay, wages, salary, revenue, yield, takings, proceeds

earth *NOUN*
> 1 *Four-fifths of the Earth's surface is covered by water.*
world, globe, planet
> 2 *an area of hard, parched earth*
ground, land, soil, dirt, clay
▶ Rich, fertile earth is **loam**.
▶ The top layer of fertile earth is **topsoil**.
▶ Rich earth consisting of decayed plants is **humus**.

 WORD WEB

the Earth

▶ The inner part of the Earth is called the **core**; the layer above the core is the **mantle**, and the hard, outer layer is the **crust**.
▶ The scientific study of the Earth's crust is **tectonics**.
▶ A related adjective is **terrestrial**.
  terrestrial sciences
▶ The layer of gases which surrounds the Earth is its **atmosphere**.
▶ Parts of the atmosphere are the **troposphere**, the **stratosphere**, and the **ozone layer**.
▶ The scientific study of the Earth's climate is **climatology**.
❙ SEE ALSO **planet**, **space**

earthquake NOUN

 WORD WEB

▸ When there is an earthquake, you feel a **shock** or **tremor**.

▸ A smaller tremor that occurs after an earthquake is an **aftershock**.

▸ An instrument which detects and measures earthquakes is a **seismograph**.

▸ The scientific study of earthquakes is **seismology**.

SEE ALSO volcano

ease NOUN

1 *Rhona can swim twenty lengths with ease.*
effortlessness, no trouble, no difficulty, simplicity
OPPOSITE difficulty

2 *Wealthy Romans led lives of ease.*
comfort, contentment, leisure, well-being, relaxation, rest, tranquillity
OPPOSITE stress

ease VERB

1 *some pills to ease the pain*
relieve, lessen, reduce, soothe, alleviate, moderate, dull, deaden
OPPOSITE aggravate

2 *We eased the piano into position.*
edge, guide, manoeuvre, inch, slide, slip

3 *My headache slowly began to ease.*
decrease, lessen, abate, subside, let up, die down, slacken
OPPOSITES increase, intensify

easily ADVERB

The rules of the game are easily understood.
without difficulty, effortlessly, comfortably, readily
OPPOSITE with difficulty

east NOUN, ADJECTIVE, ADVERB

Queensland is in the east of Australia.

▸ The parts of a country or continent in the east are the **eastern** parts.

▸ To travel towards the east is to travel **eastward** or **eastwards**.

▸ A wind from the east is an **easterly** wind.

▸ In the past, the countries of east Asia, east of the Mediterranean, were called **oriental** countries.

easy ADJECTIVE

1 *Tonight's homework is really easy.*
undemanding, effortless, light
(informal) a cinch, a doddle
IDIOMS *(informal)* a piece of cake, plain sailing

2 *The instructions were easy to understand.*
simple, straightforward, uncomplicated, clear, plain, elementary

3 *Our cat has an easy life.*
carefree, comfortable, peaceful, relaxed, leisurely, restful, tranquil, untroubled
OPPOSITES difficult, hard

eat VERB

1 *Seals eat their own weight in fish every day.*
consume, devour, swallow, feed on, dine on
(informal) put away
(formal) partake of, ingest

2 *Let's eat out tonight.*
have a meal, have dinner, dine, feed

Usage Note

The synonyms **feed** and **feed on** are used mainly about animals: *Bats typically feed around dusk and dawn.*

▷ **eat away at** or **eat into**

1 *Salt water had eaten away at the timbers.*
corrode, erode, wear away, decay, rot

2 *All these bills are eating into our savings.*

»

use up, exhaust, deplete, go through, consume, expend

📎 **OVERUSED WORD**

to eat quickly, greedily
bolt down, gobble, gulp, demolish
(informal) guzzle, scoff, wolf down
Todd and his friends **demolished** a whole pizza each.

to eat noisily
chomp, crunch, gnash, gnaw, munch, slurp
The contestants were dared to **munch** live insects.

to eat large amounts
feast, gorge
❙ IDIOM (informal) eat like a horse
The guests **gorged** themselves on roasted meats.

to eat too much
overeat
(informal) stuff yourself, pig out
❙ IDIOM (informal) make a pig of yourself
Uncle Amos had **overeaten** and had to lie down.

to eat small amounts
nibble, peck, pick at, pick away at, taste, snack on
Nicole **nibbled** nervously on a cracker.

to eat something completely
eat up, gobble up
(informal) polish off
I **ate up** every last crumb on my plate.

to eat with pleasure
relish, savour
(informal) tuck into, get stuck into

The cheese is best eaten slowly to **savour** the taste.

❙ SEE ALSO bite, chew

ebb VERB
1 waiting for the tide to ebb
recede, go out, retreat, flow back
2 She felt her strength began to ebb.
decline, weaken, lessen, diminish, dwindle, fade, wane

eccentric ADJECTIVE
an eccentric style of dress
odd, peculiar, strange, weird, bizarre, abnormal, unusual, curious, unconventional, unorthodox, outlandish, quirky, zany
(informal) way-out, oddball
❙ OPPOSITES conventional, orthodox

echo VERB
1 The sound echoed across the valley.
resound, reverberate, ring
2 Her words echoed my own feelings.
repeat, reproduce, restate, imitate, mimic, parrot

ecological ADJECTIVE
an ecological campaigner
environmental, green, conservation, eco-
❙ SEE ALSO environment

economic ADJECTIVE
1 a global economic crisis
financial, fiscal, monetary, budgetary
2 The theatre is no longer economic to run.
profitable, lucrative, fruitful, productive
❙ OPPOSITE unprofitable

economical ADJECTIVE
1 being economical with your money
careful, prudent, thrifty, frugal
▶ If you are economical with money in a selfish way, you are **mean**, **miserly**, or **parsimonious**.
❙ OPPOSITES wasteful, profligate

2 *a car that is economical to run*
cheap, inexpensive, low-cost, reasonable

OPPOSITES expensive, costly

economize VERB
trying to economize on petrol
cut back, save money, cut costs, scrimp

ecstatic ADJECTIVE
Mandy was ecstatic when she won the lottery.
elated, delighted, overjoyed, gleeful, joyful, blissful, rapturous, euphoric, exultant

IDIOMS *(informal)* over the moon, tickled pink

edge NOUN
1 *a house on the edge of a lake*
border, margin, side, fringe, brink, verge, perimeter, boundary
2 *The edge of this cup is chipped.*
brim, rim, lip
3 *Her writing always has an edge to it.*
sharpness, keenness, intensity, bite, sting

edge VERB
1 *A narrow footpath edges the cliff.*
border, fringe, skirt
2 *a bonnet edged with black lace*
trim, hem
3 *Silas edged slowly away from the door.*
creep, inch, work your way, sidle, steal, slink

edgy ADJECTIVE
Sitting there all alone, I began to feel edgy.
nervous, restless, anxious, agitated, excitable, tense, jumpy, fidgety
(informal) jittery, uptight

OPPOSITE calm

edible ADJECTIVE
Are these toadstools edible?
safe to eat, harmless, non-toxic, non-poisonous

OPPOSITE poisonous

Usage Note

The words **edible** and **eatable** do not mean the same thing. An *edible* mushroom is safe to eat, whereas an *eatable* mushroom is good to eat.

---

edit VERB
The letters were edited before publication.
revise, correct, adapt, modify, rework, rewrite, rephrase
▶ To edit a work so as to shorten it is to **abridge** it.

edition NOUN
a special holiday edition of the magazine
issue, number, version, volume, publication

educate VERB
The job of a school is to educate young people.
teach, train, inform, instruct, tutor, school

educated ADJECTIVE
Her mother came from an educated family.
knowledgeable, learned, literate, well informed, well read, cultivated, cultured, intellectual, scholarly

education NOUN
a school for the education of local children
schooling, teaching, training, instruction, tuition, tutoring, coaching
▶ A programme of education is a **curriculum** or **syllabus**.
▶ Education beyond secondary school is known as **further**, **higher**, or **tertiary** education.

eerie ADJECTIVE
The deserted fairground had an eerie atmosphere.
uncanny, sinister, weird, mysterious, ghostly, unearthly, other-worldly, unnatural, freakish

»

a b c d e f g h i j k l m n o p q r s t u v w x y z

(informal) scary, spooky, creepy

effect NOUN

1 *the harmful effects of smoking*
result, consequence, outcome, sequel, upshot

2 *The music had a strange effect on me.*
impact, influence

3 *The lighting gives an effect of warmth.*
feeling, impression, sense, illusion

effective ADJECTIVE

1 *an effective treatment for spots*
successful, effectual, powerful, potent
OPPOSITES ineffective, weak

2 *an effective leader*
competent, able, capable, proficient, skilled

3 *building an effective case against whaling*
convincing, persuasive, compelling, impressive, strong, powerful, telling
OPPOSITE unconvincing

efficient ADJECTIVE

1 *Hyenas are supremely efficient hunters.*
competent, capable, able, proficient, skilled, effective, productive

2 *an efficient method of transport*
economic, cost-effective, streamlined, organized, orderly
OPPOSITE inefficient

effort NOUN

1 *A lot of effort went into making the film.*
work, trouble, exertion, application, industry, labour, toil
IDIOM *(humorous)* elbow grease

2 *I made an effort to be friends with her.*
attempt, try, endeavour, go
(informal) shot, stab, bash

egg NOUN

Crocodiles bury their eggs in sand.
▶ Eggs laid by fish, frogs, or toads are called **spawn**.

▶ Objects which are egg-shaped are described as **ovoid**.

eject VERB

1 *Lava is ejected from volcanoes.*
discharge, emit, send out, vent, belch, spew out

2 *The protesters were ejected from the meeting.*
remove, expel, evict, banish, throw out, turn out
(informal) kick out

elaborate ADJECTIVE

an absorbing book with an elaborate plot
complicated, complex, detailed, intricate, involved, convoluted
OPPOSITE simple

elaborate VERB

▷ **elaborate on**
Please elaborate on your answer.
expand on, enlarge on, give details of, amplify, flesh out

elated ADJECTIVE

We were elated when we won the match.
delighted, pleased, thrilled, joyful, ecstatic, gleeful, exultant, delirious
IDIOMS *(informal)* over the moon, tickled pink

elbow VERB

Jan elbowed her way to the front of the queue.
push, shove, nudge, jostle

elder ADJECTIVE

My elder brother is at college now.
older, senior, big
OPPOSITE younger

elderly ADJECTIVE

I helped an elderly lady onto the bus.
aged, ageing, old, senior
OPPOSITE young

elect VERB

We elected a new team captain.
vote for, vote in, appoint, choose, pick, select

election NOUN
> *a parliamentary election*
> vote, ballot, poll

electric ADJECTIVE
> **1** *an electric cable*
> electrical, power
> **2** *The atmosphere in the hall was electric.*
> exciting, electrifying, charged, tense, dramatic, thrilling

elegant ADJECTIVE
> *Chloe always wears elegant clothes.*
> graceful, stylish, fashionable, chic, smart, tasteful, sophisticated
> **OPPOSITE** inelegant

element NOUN
> *We discussed various elements of the play.*
> part, feature, aspect, factor, facet, component, constituent, ingredient, strand
> ▷ **be in your element**
> *Rob is in his element in a guitar shop.*
> be at home, be comfortable, be happy, enjoy yourself

elementary ADJECTIVE
> *a course in elementary maths*
> basic, simple, easy, fundamental, rudimentary, straightforward, uncomplicated
> **OPPOSITES** advanced, complex

eligible ADJECTIVE
> *Children under twelve are not eligible to enter.*
> qualified, allowed, authorized, permitted, entitled, able
> **OPPOSITE** ineligible

eliminate VERB
> *a spray to eliminate bad odours*
> get rid of, put an end to, do away with, eradicate, stamp out
> ► To be eliminated from a competition is to be **knocked out**.

eloquent ADJECTIVE
> *The winning author gave an eloquent speech.*
> articulate, fluent, well expressed, expressive, lucid

elude VERB
> *Geronimo eluded capture for several years.*
> avoid, evade, escape from, get away from, dodge, shake off
> **IDIOM** (informal) give someone the slip

embark VERB
> *Passengers may embark at any port.*
> board, go aboard
> **OPPOSITE** disembark
> ▷ **embark on something**
> *embarking on a new space mission*
> begin, start, commence, undertake, set out on, venture into, launch into

embarrass VERB
> *I didn't mean to embarrass you in front of your friends.*
> humiliate, shame, mortify, make you blush

embarrassed ADJECTIVE
> *I feel embarrassed when I speak in public.*
> humiliated, ashamed, awkward, uncomfortable, bashful, mortified, self-conscious, shamefaced, red-faced

embarrassing ADJECTIVE
> *The show was so bad it was embarrassing.*
> humiliating, mortifying, shameful (informal) cringe-making, toe-curling

emblem NOUN
> *The dove is an emblem of peace.*
> symbol, sign, representation, image, token, mark, badge, crest, insignia

embrace VERB
> **1** *a mother embracing her baby*
> hug, clasp, cuddle, hold, caress, enfold
> **2** *The exhibition embraces both modern and traditional art.*

》

a
b
c
d
e
f
g
h
i
j
k
l
m
n
o
p
q
r
s
t
u
v
w
x
y
z

include, incorporate, take in, cover, encompass

3 *willing to embrace new ideas*
welcome, accept, adopt, take up
❙ **IDIOM** take on board

embrace *NOUN*
holding each other in a fond embrace
hug, clasp, cuddle, hold, caress

emerge *VERB*
1 *Zak emerged gingerly from his hiding place.*
appear, issue, come out, come into view, materialize, surface
2 *Gradually more details began to emerge.*
become known, be revealed, come out, come to light, unfold

emergency *NOUN*
trying to keep calm in an emergency
crisis, disaster, catastrophe, calamity

emigrant *NOUN*
Shiploads of emigrants left from Ireland.
❙ **OPPOSITE** immigrant

emigrate *VERB*
Thousands were forced to emigrate to America.
leave the country, move abroad, relocate, resettle
❙ **OPPOSITE** immigrate

eminent *ADJECTIVE*
a group of eminent scientists
renowned, celebrated, famous, great, well known, distinguished, notable, prominent, respected, acclaimed, esteemed, illustrious
❙ **OPPOSITE** unknown

emission *NOUN*
reducing carbon emissions
discharge, outpouring, outflow

emit *VERB*
1 *a chimney emitting clouds of smoke*
discharge, expel, vent, belch, blow out, give off
2 *a satellite emitting radio signals*
transmit, broadcast,

give out, send out
❙ **OPPOSITE** receive

emotion *NOUN*
His performance was full of emotion and energy.
feeling, passion, sentiment, heart, fervour, strength of feeling

emotional *ADJECTIVE*
1 *He gave an emotional farewell speech.*
moving, touching, stirring, affecting, impassioned, poignant, sentimental (*informal*) tear-jerking
2 *She's a very emotional woman.*
passionate, intense, excitable, sensitive, temperamental, hot-blooded
❙ **OPPOSITES** unemotional, cold

emphasis *NOUN*
1 *giving more emphasis to diet and exercise*
importance, prominence, weight, attention, priority
2 *Put the emphasis on the first syllable.*
stress, accent, weight, beat

emphasize *VERB*
emphasizing the key points in the story
highlight, stress, focus on, draw attention to, spotlight, foreground, underline

employ *VERB*
1 *The new centre will employ 100 workers.*
hire, recruit, engage, take on, sign up, appoint
2 *The software employs the latest technology.*
use, utilize, make use of, apply, practise, exercise

employee *NOUN*
100 employees will work at the new centre.
worker, member of staff
▶ All the employees of an organization are its **staff**, **personnel**, or **workforce**.

employment NOUN
>   *looking for suitable employment*
>   work, a job, an occupation,
>   a profession, a trade
>   ☞ SEE ALSO **job**

empty ADJECTIVE
>   1 *This bottle is empty.*
>   ☞ OPPOSITE full
>
>   2 *The building has been empty for*
>   *years.*
>   unoccupied, uninhabited, vacant,
>   deserted
>   ☞ OPPOSITE occupied
>
>   3 *There's an empty space in the corner.*
>   free, clear, blank, bare, unused
>
>   4 *making empty threats*
>   meaningless, idle, hollow,
>   ineffectual

empty VERB
>   1 *Empty the dirty water from the sink.*
>   drain, pour out, tip out, remove,
>   extract
>   ☞ OPPOSITE fill
>
>   2 *She emptied her handbag onto the*
>   *table.*
>   unload, unpack
>
>   3 *The building emptied when the*
>   *alarm went off.*
>   clear, evacuate, vacate

enable VERB
>   1 *The money will enable us to build a*
>   *sports centre.*
>   allow, make it possible for
>
>   2 *A passport enables you to travel*
>   *abroad.*
>   permit, allow, entitle, authorize,
>   qualify
>   ☞ OPPOSITE prevent (from)

enchanting ADJECTIVE
>   *Sirens were said to lure sailors with*
>   *their enchanting voices.*
>   captivating, charming, delightful,
>   attractive, appealing, engaging,
>   bewitching, spellbinding

enchantment NOUN
>   1 *The island had an air of*
>   *enchantment.*
>   magic, wonder, delight, pleasure
>
>   2 *a book of ancient enchantments*
>   spell, incantation
>   ☞ SEE ALSO **fantasy**

enclose VERB
>   1 *The Imperial Palace is enclosed by an*
>   *earthen wall.*
>   surround, encircle, bound, close in,
>   fence in, shut in
>
>   2 *The documents were enclosed in a*
>   *brown envelope.*
>   contain, insert, wrap, bind, sheathe

enclosure NOUN
>   *the new chimpanzee enclosure at*
>   *the zoo*
>   compound, pen, cage
>   ▶ An enclosure for chickens is a **coop**
>   or **run**.
>   ▶ An enclosure for horses is a
>   **paddock**.
>   ▶ An enclosure for sheep is a **fold**.

encounter VERB
>   1 *I have yet to encounter a real ghost.*
>   meet, come across, run into, come
>   face to face with
>   *(informal)* bump into
>
>   2 *The space crew encountered some*
>   *problems.*
>   experience, come upon, confront,
>   be faced with

encounter NOUN
>   1 *an encounter with an alien species*
>   meeting, contact
>
>   2 *the most violent encounter of the war*
>   battle, engagement, fight, struggle,
>   confrontation

encourage VERB
>   1 *We went along to encourage our*
>   *team.*
>   support, motivate, inspire, cheer,
>   spur on, egg on
>
>   2 *She encouraged me to try the*
>   *audition.*
>   persuade, urge, press, coax
>
>   3 *a scheme to encourage new research*
>   stimulate, promote, boost, further,
>   strengthen, foster, nurture, cultivate
>   ☞ OPPOSITE discourage

encouragement NOUN

My coach gave me a lot of encouragement.

support, inspiration, motivation, morale-boosting, incitement, stimulation, urging, incentive, stimulus, reassurance

encouraging ADJECTIVE

The results of the trials were encouraging.

hopeful, positive, promising, reassuring, optimistic, cheering, favourable

end NOUN

1 *There is a surprise twist at the end of the film.*

ending, finish, close, conclusion, culmination, termination, finale

▶ A section added at the end of a letter is a **postscript**.

▶ A section added at the end of a story is an **epilogue**.

▶ The outcome of a plot or story, which is revealed at the end, is a **denouement**.

OPPOSITES start, beginning

2 *At last we had reached the end of our journey.*

termination, destination

3 *The fence marks the end of the garden.*

boundary, limit, extremity, bottom

OPPOSITE top

4 *We found ourselves at the end of the queue.*

back, rear, tail

OPPOSITE head

5 *What end did you have in mind?*

aim, purpose, intention, objective, plan, outcome, result

end VERB

1 *The concert ended with a firework display.*

close, conclude, come to an end, finish, stop, cease, terminate, culminate

(informal) round off, wind up

2 *Britain ended its slave trade in 1807.*

abolish, do away with, get rid of, put an end to, discontinue, terminate, eliminate, cancel

endanger VERB

Bad driving endangers other people.

put at risk, put in danger, jeopardize, threaten, imperil

OPPOSITES protect, safeguard

endeavour VERB

We will endeavour to respond within 24 hours.

try, attempt, aim, seek, strive, make an effort

endeavour NOUN

Despite our best endeavours, things can go wrong.

attempt, effort, try, bid

ending NOUN

The ending of the film was the best part.

end, finish, close, conclusion, culmination, finale

endless ADJECTIVE

1 *a job that requires endless patience*

unending, limitless, infinite, inexhaustible, unlimited

2 *an endless round of dull speeches*

continual, continuous, constant, incessant, interminable, perpetual, unbroken, uninterrupted, everlasting, ceaseless

endorse VERB

A number of celebrities are endorsing the campaign.

support, back, subscribe to, champion, sanction, give your backing to, put your name to

endurance NOUN

The climb was a test of our endurance.

perseverance, persistence, determination, resolution, stamina, fortitude, staying power

endure VERB

1 *Many mill workers endured harsh conditions.*

bear, stand, suffer, cope with,

experience, go through, put up with, tolerate, face, undergo

2 *a tradition which has endured for centuries*
survive, continue, last, persist, abide, carry on, live on, keep going

enemy NOUN
The families of Romeo and Juliet are bitter enemies.
opponent, antagonist, adversary, rival
(literary) foe
❙ **OPPOSITES** friend, ally

energetic ADJECTIVE
1 *My mum has always been an energetic person.*
dynamic, active, animated, spirited, zestful, sprightly, tireless, indefatigable
❙ **IDIOM** *(informal)* full of beans
❙ **OPPOSITES** inactive, lethargic

2 *Bhangra is an energetic dance style.*
lively, vigorous, brisk, fast, quick moving, strenuous
❙ **OPPOSITES** slow-paced, sluggish

energy NOUN
1 *The dancers had tremendous energy.*
liveliness, vitality, spirit, vigour, life, drive, zest, verve, gusto, enthusiasm, dynamism
(informal) get-up-and-go, zip, punch, oomph
❙ **OPPOSITE** lethargy

2 *Wind power is a renewable source of energy.*
power, fuel

✳ **WORD WEB**

renewable energy sources
biomass, geothermal power, hydropower or water power, solar power, wave power, wind power

non-renewable energy sources
fossil fuels, nuclear power
❙ **SEE ALSO** fuel

enforce VERB
Umpires have to enforce the rules.
impose, apply, administer, carry out, implement, put into effect, insist on

engage VERB
1 *The plot failed to engage my attention.*
capture, catch, grab, gain, hold, arrest, grip, absorb, occupy

2 *engaging in conversation*
take part, participate, partake, join

3 *engaging the powers of darkness*
attack, encounter, clash with, do battle with, take on, fight

4 *engaging extra staff for Christmas*
employ, hire, recruit, take on, appoint

engaged ADJECTIVE
1 *I'll be engaged all afternoon.*
busy, occupied, employed, immersed (in), preoccupied (with)
(informal) tied up

2 *I tried phoning but the line was engaged.*
busy, being used, unavailable
❙ **OPPOSITES** free, available

engagement NOUN
1 *a business engagement*
meeting, appointment, commitment, date

2 *a fierce engagement between the two fleets*
battle, encounter, fight, action, confrontation, clash

engine NOUN
a wind-powered engine
motor, mechanism, turbine
▶ A railway engine is a **locomotive**.

engrave VERB
The following words were engraved on the tombstone.
carve, cut, etch, inscribe

engrossed ADJECTIVE
Nina was still engrossed in her novel.
absorbed, busy, occupied, preoccupied, engaged, immersed

a
b
c
d
e
f
g
h
i
j
k
l
m
n
o
p
q
r
s
t
u
v
w
x
y
z

a
b
c
d
e
f
g
h
i
j
k
l
m
n
o
p
q
r
s
t
u
v
w
x
y
z

engulf *VERB*

The tsunami engulfed several villages.
flood, swamp, drown, immerse, inundate, overwhelm, submerge, swallow up

enhance *VERB*

The award will enhance the author's reputation.
improve, strengthen, boost, further, increase, heighten, amplify

enjoy *VERB*

I always enjoy going to the cinema.
like, love, be fond of, be keen on, relish, revel in, delight in, take pleasure in
(informal) get a kick out of
▌ OPPOSITES dislike, hate

enjoyable *ADJECTIVE*

I hope you find the show enjoyable.
pleasant, agreeable, entertaining, amusing, pleasing, delightful, pleasurable, satisfying
▌ OPPOSITE unpleasant

enjoyment *NOUN*

reading purely for enjoyment
pleasure, entertainment, fun, amusement, delight, satisfaction

enlarge *VERB*

The zoo is enlarging its lion enclosure.
expand, extend, develop, make bigger, broaden, widen, elongate, stretch
▶ To make something seem larger is to **magnify** it.
▌ OPPOSITE reduce

enormity *NOUN*

1 Does Macbeth realize the enormity of his crimes?
wickedness, vileness, depravity, baseness

2 New reports reveal the enormity of the disaster.
immensity, magnitude, vastness, size, extent, scale
▌ OPPOSITES smallness, insignificance

enormous *ADJECTIVE*

the enormous skeleton of a T-Rex
huge, gigantic, immense, colossal, massive, monstrous, monumental, mountainous, towering, tremendous, vast, mighty mammoth
(informal) whopping, humongous
(literary) gargantuan
▌ OPPOSITES small, tiny
▌ SEE ALSO **big**

enough *ADJECTIVE*

We have enough food for thirty guests.
sufficient, adequate, ample

enquire *VERB*

▷ **enquire about**
I enquired about train times to York.
ask for, make enquiries about, request

▷ **enquire into**
enquiring into the effects of advertising on children
investigate, examine, look into, probe
(informal) check out

enquiry *NOUN*

1 Please send your enquiries by email.
question, query, request

2 an official enquiry into a series of UFO sightings
investigation, examination, probe, hearing, inquest

enrage *VERB*

I was enraged by their stupidity.
anger, infuriate, madden, incense, inflame, exasperate, provoke
▌ IDIOMS make you see red, make your blood boil
▌ OPPOSITES placate, pacify
▌ SEE ALSO **angry**

enrol *VERB*

1 I enrolled in the local swimming club.
join, sign up, register, put your name down, apply, volunteer

2 The club is now enrolling new members.

admit, sign up, take on, engage

ensure VERB

How can you ensure that no one is cheating?
make certain, make sure, guarantee, see to it

entail VERB

What exactly does the job entail?
involve, require, demand, call for, need, occasion

enter VERB

1 *Silence fell as Gandalf entered the room.*
come in, walk in, go into, gain access to
IDIOM set foot in
OPPOSITE leave

2 *The bullet entered his left shoulder.*
go into, penetrate, pierce, puncture, perforate

3 *I'll enter your name on the guest list.*
insert, record, register, log, put down, set down, sign, write
OPPOSITE cancel

4 *Four teams are entering the competition.*
take part in, enrol in, sign up for, go in for, join in, participate in, compete in
OPPOSITE withdraw from

enterprise NOUN

1 *All the contestants showed enterprise and enthusiasm.*
resourcefulness, initiative, drive, ambition, imagination, creativity, ingenuity

2 *Deep-sea diving is still a hazardous enterprise.*
undertaking, activity, venture, task, business, exercise, project, scheme, mission

enterprising ADJECTIVE

The website was created by an enterprising group of students.
resourceful, imaginative, creative, ambitious, entrepreneurial, intrepid, bold, adventurous, industrious

(informal) go-ahead

entertain VERB

1 *We entertained ourselves by telling ghost stories.*
amuse, divert, keep amused, please, interest, occupy
OPPOSITE bore

2 *You can entertain guests in the private dining room.*
receive, welcome, cater for, give hospitality to

3 *She would never entertain such a foolish idea.*
consider, contemplate, countenance, hear of, think of

entertainer NOUN

FOR MUSICIANS AND OTHER PERFORMING ARTISTS SEE **music**, **performance**

entertainment NOUN

Gladiators fought for the entertainment of huge crowds.
amusement, recreation, diversion, enjoyment, fun

enthusiasm NOUN

The young cast showed plenty of enthusiasm.
keenness, commitment, drive, passion, fervour, zeal, zest, energy, vigour, gusto
OPPOSITE apathy

enthusiast NOUN

My brother is a cricket enthusiast.
fan, fanatic, devotee, lover, supporter, admirer, addict
(informal) freak, nut

enthusiastic ADJECTIVE

1 *an enthusiastic supporter of the club*
keen, passionate, avid, devoted, energetic, fervent, zealous
IDIOM *(humorous)* bright-eyed and bushy-tailed
OPPOSITE apathetic

2 *The crowd burst into enthusiastic applause.*
eager, excited, lively, vigorous,

a
b
c
d
e
f
g
h
i
j
k
l
m
n
o
p
q
r
s
t
u
v
w
x
y
z

exuberant, hearty

entire ADJECTIVE

Douglas spent the entire morning in bed.
whole, complete, total, full

entirely ADVERB

1 *I'm not entirely sure that I agree with you.*
completely, absolutely, totally, utterly, fully, perfectly, quite

2 *Is this entirely your own work?*
solely, only, wholly, exclusively, purely

entitle VERB

1 *The voucher entitles you to claim a discount.*
permit, allow, enable, authorize, qualify

2 *The sequel is entitled 'The Return of Godzilla'.*
name, title, call, label, designate, dub

entity NOUN

A mysterious alien entity is threatening the planet.
being, creature, life-form, organism, body, individual

entrance NOUN

1 *Please pay at the main entrance.*
entry, way in, access, approach, door, gate
► The entrance to a cave is the **mouth**.
► An entrance hall is a **foyer** or **lobby**.
► When you go through the entrance to a building, you cross the **threshold**.
OPPOSITE exit

2 *Entrance to the museum is free.*
admission, access, entry, admittance

3 *Hermione made a dramatic entrance.*
entry, arrival, appearance

entrance VERB

Narcissus was entranced by his own reflection.
enchant, captivate, enthral, transfix, mesmerize, spellbind, bewitch,

delight, charm

entrant NOUN

A prize will be awarded to the winning entrant.
contestant, competitor, contender, candidate, participant

entry NOUN

1 *A van was blocking the entry to the school.*
entrance, way in, access, approach, door, gate

2 *an entry in my diary*
item, note, memo, record, log

envelop VERB

A thick mist enveloped the whole city.
cover, surround, encircle, hide, mask, conceal, cloak, shroud, veil, swathe

envious ADJECTIVE

He was envious of his brother's success.
jealous, resentful, grudging
IDIOM green with envy (at)

environment NOUN

studying gorillas in their natural environment
habitat, surroundings, setting, conditions, situation

▷ **the environment**
the impact of humans on the environment
the natural world, nature, the earth, the world, the ecosystem

 WORD WEB

terms relating to the environment

acid rain, biodegradable, carbon emissions, carbon footprint, climate change, conservation, eco-friendly (or -unfriendly), ecological, environmentalist, environmentally friendly (or unfriendly), global warming, green, greenhouse effect, greenhouse gases,

non-renewable energy, organic,
ozone-friendly (or -unfriendly),
ozone layer, pollution, recycling,
renewable energy, sustainability,
toxic waste

SEE ALSO energy

envisage *VERB*
1 *We did not envisage any problems.*
expect, anticipate, foresee, predict
2 *Can you envisage a world without polar bears and tigers?*
imagine, picture, conceive of, contemplate

envy *NOUN*
Walter was consumed with envy and rage.
jealousy, resentment, bitterness

envy *VERB*
Nadia had never envied her sister's fame.
be jealous of, begrudge, grudge, resent

episode *NOUN*
1 *an embarrassing episode in his career*
event, incident, occurrence, occasion, experience, exploit, adventure
2 *the first episode of the new series*
instalment, part, programme, show, section, chapter

equal *ADJECTIVE*
1 *Make the portions of equal size.*
equivalent, identical, matching, corresponding, uniform, the same
2 *The scores were equal at half-time.*
even, level, tied, drawn
IDIOMS all square, level pegging, neck and neck
▶ To make the scores equal is to **equalize**.

equal *VERB*
1 *Six plus five equals eleven.*
be equal to, come to, add up to, total, amount to, make

2 *Her time equals the Olympic record.*
match, be level with, be the same as, parallel

equip *VERB*
Each classroom is equipped with a computer.
provide, supply, furnish, stock, provision
▶ To equip soldiers with weapons is to **arm** them.

equipment *NOUN*
The shed is full of gardening equipment.
apparatus, tools, implements, materials, machinery, gadgetry, hardware, paraphernalia, tackle, kit *(informal)* gear

equivalent *ADJECTIVE*
A mile is equivalent to 1609 metres.
matching, the same as, identical, corresponding, parallel, analogous, similar

era *NOUN*
Shakespeare lived in the Elizabethan era.
age, period, time, epoch

erase *VERB*
Someone had erased the message.
delete, remove, rub out, wipe out, obliterate

erect *ADJECTIVE*
The bear sat up with its ears erect.
upright, vertical, perpendicular, bristling, standing on end

erect *VERB*
The town hall was erected in 1890.
build, construct, raise, put up, set up
▶ To erect a tent is to **pitch** it.
OPPOSITE demolish

erode *VERB*
1 *a valley eroded by a glacier*
wear away, eat away, grind down
2 *The whole experience eroded my confidence.*
destroy, undermine, weaken, diminish, damage

a b c d e f g h i j k l m n o p q r s t u v w x y z

errand NOUN

going on an errand to the shops
task, job, assignment, mission, trip,
journey

erratic ADJECTIVE

*Their performance has been erratic
this season.*
inconsistent, irregular, uneven,
variable, changeable, fluctuating,
unpredictable, unreliable, unstable
┃ OPPOSITE consistent

error NOUN

1 *a grammatical error*
mistake, fault, lapse, blunder, slip,
slip-up
▶ The error of leaving something out is
an **omission** or **oversight**.
▶ A spelling error is a **misspelling**.
▶ A error made during printing is a
misprint.
2 *I think there is an error in your
argument.*
flaw, inaccuracy, misunderstanding,
misconception, inconsistency

erupt VERB

*Ash continued to erupt from the
volcano.*
be discharged, be emitted, pour out,
issue, spout, gush, spurt, belch

escape VERB

1 *Few prisoners ever escaped from
Devil's Island.*
get away, run away, break free, break
out, slip away, make a getaway
┃ IDIOM *(informal)* do a runner
▶ A person who escapes from prison or
confinement is an **escapee**.
▶ A performer who escapes from
chains, etc., is an **escape artist** or
escapologist.
2 *They help a runaway slave to escape
his pursuers.*
elude, get away from, dodge,
shake off
┃ IDIOM *(informal)* give someone the
slip
3 *The driver narrowly escaped injury.*
avoid, sidestep
┃ IDIOM steer clear of

escape NOUN

1 *a daring escape from a
prisoner-of-war camp*
getaway, breakout, flight
2 *an explosion caused by a gas escape*
leak, leakage, spill, seepage,
discharge

escort NOUN

*The mayor always travels with a
police escort.*
bodyguard, guard, convoy,
entourage, minder, attendant,
chaperone

escort VERB

*A man was escorted outside by
security guards.*
accompany, conduct, take, usher,
guide, shepherd

especially ADVERB

I love shopping, especially for shoes.
above all, chiefly, particularly,
primarily, most of all

espionage NOUN

SEE **spy**

essential ADJECTIVE

1 *Water is an essential part of our diet.*
important, necessary, crucial, vital,
key, all-important, indispensable
┃ OPPOSITES unimportant, trivial
2 *the essential aspects of his character*
basic, fundamental, primary, main,
key, intrinsic
┃ OPPOSITES secondary, incidental

establish VERB

1 *establishing a new business*
set up, start, create, found, initiate,
institute, inaugurate, launch
2 *establishing a motive for the crime*
determine, prove, demonstrate,
confirm, verify

estate NOUN

1 *a new housing estate*
area, development, scheme
2 *The castle is sited on a large estate.*

land, grounds, park

3 *The millionaire left his estate to charity.*
property, fortune, wealth, possessions

estimate NOUN

an estimate of the age of the universe
assessment, calculation, evaluation, guess, judgement, opinion

▶ An estimate of the value of something is a **valuation**.

▶ An estimate of what a job is going to cost is a **quotation** or **tender**.

estimate VERB

Scientists estimate that the Earth is 4.5 billion years old.
calculate, assess, work out, compute, count up, evaluate, judge, reckon, deem

eternal ADJECTIVE

1 *The elixir was believed to give eternal life.*
everlasting, unending, never-ending, permanent, perpetual, infinite, undying, immortal
❚ **OPPOSITES** transitory, transient

2 *(informal) I'm tired of her eternal complaining.*
constant, continual, continuous, never-ending, non-stop, perpetual, endless, persistent, incessant, unbroken, uninterrupted
❚ **IDIOM** round the clock
❚ **OPPOSITES** occasional, intermittent

evacuate VERB

1 *Hundreds of residents were evacuated.*
remove, send away, move out

2 *We were told to evacuate the building.*
leave, vacate, abandon, withdraw from, clear, empty, quit

evade VERB

1 *He evaded capture by dressing as a woman.*
elude, avoid, escape, steer clear of, fend off

2 *Stop trying to evade my question!*
avoid, dodge, bypass, sidestep, skirt around, shirk
(informal) duck
❚ **OPPOSITES** confront, tackle

evaporate VERB

1 *The waterhole had completely evaporated.*
dry up

2 *Our courage soon evaporated.*
vanish, fade, wear off, melt away, peter out, fizzle out

even ADJECTIVE

1 *You need an even surface for ice-skating.*
level, flat, smooth, plane
❚ **OPPOSITE** uneven

2 *The runners kept up an even pace.*
regular, steady, unvarying, constant, uniform
❚ **OPPOSITE** irregular

3 *Miss Bartlett has an even temper.*
calm, cool, placid, unexcitable
(informal) unflappable
❚ **OPPOSITE** excitable

4 *The scores were even at half time.*
equal, level, tied, drawn
❚ **IDIOMS** all square , level pegging , neck and neck

5 *2, 4, and 6 are even numbers.*
❚ **OPPOSITE** odd

even VERB

▷ **even something up**
We need another player to even up the numbers.
equalize, balance, match, level out, square up

evening NOUN

By evening, the temperature had dropped.
dusk, nightfall, sunset, twilight
(North American) sundown

event NOUN

1 *The biography gives the main events of her life.*
happening, incident, occurrence

2 *an event to mark the bicentenary*

a
b
c
d
e
f
g
h
i
j
k
l
m
n
o
p
q
r
s
t
u
v
w
x
y
z

function, occasion, ceremony, reception

3 *a major sporting event*
competition, contest, fixture, game, match, tournament

eventful *ADJECTIVE*
It has been an eventful two weeks.
interesting, exciting, busy, action-packed, lively, hectic
▎**OPPOSITES** uneventful, dull

eventual *ADJECTIVE*
Who was the eventual winner?
final, ultimate, overall, resulting, ensuing

eventually *ADVERB*
The sun will eventually run out of fuel.
finally, ultimately, in the end, at last
▎**IDIOMS** at the end of the day, in the long run

evergreen *ADJECTIVE*
Most pine trees are evergreen.
▎**OPPOSITE** deciduous
▎**SEE ALSO** tree

everlasting *ADJECTIVE*
Peter Pan has an everlasting childhood.
never-ending, unending, endless, ceaseless, eternal, infinite, perpetual, undying
▶ Everlasting life is **immortality**.
▎**OPPOSITES** transitory, transient

everyday *ADJECTIVE*
Just wear your everyday clothes.
ordinary, normal, day-to-day, usual, regular, standard, customary, routine, commonplace, run-of-the-mill

evict *VERB*
Thousands were evicted from their farms.
expel, eject, remove, throw out, turn out, put out

evidence *NOUN*
This letter is evidence of his guilt.
proof, confirmation,

verification, substantiation
▶ Evidence given in a law court is a **testimony**.
▶ To give evidence in court is to **testify**.

evident *ADJECTIVE*
It was evident that someone was lying.
clear, obvious, apparent, plain, certain, unmistakable, undeniable, noticeable, conspicuous, patent, manifest

evidently *ADVERB*
The woman was evidently upset.
clearly, obviously, plainly, undoubtedly, unmistakably, patently, manifestly

evil *ADJECTIVE*
1 *a charm to ward off evil spirits*
malevolent, malign, sinister, fiendish, diabolical
▎**OPPOSITES** good, benign
2 *Who would do such an evil deed?*
wicked, immoral, cruel, sinful, villainous, malicious, foul, hateful, vile

evil *NOUN*
1 *The message of the film is that good triumphs over evil.*
wickedness, malevolence, badness, wrongdoing, sin, immorality, villainy, malice, the dark side
▎**OPPOSITE** good
2 *the twin evils of famine and drought*
disaster, misfortune, suffering, pain, affliction, curse, woe

evolve *VERB*
Life evolved on Earth over millions of years.
develop, grow, progress, emerge, mature, advance

exact *ADJECTIVE*
1 *an exact copy of your signature*
accurate, precise, correct, true, faithful, perfect
▎**OPPOSITES** inaccurate, rough

2 *She gave us exact instructions.*
specific, clear, detailed, meticulous, strict
OPPOSITE vague

exactly ADVERB

1 *The room was exactly as I remembered it.*
precisely, strictly, in every respect, absolutely, just
OPPOSITES roughly, more or less

2 *The bus leaves at 9 a.m. exactly.*
specifically, precisely, strictly
IDIOM on the dot

3 *I copied down her words exactly.*
accurately, correctly, perfectly, faithfully, literally
IDIOM word for word

exaggerate VERB
He tends to exaggerate his problems.
magnify, inflate, overstate, make too much of, embellish, embroider
IDIOM blow out of all proportion
OPPOSITES minimize, understate

examination NOUN

1 *We sit our examinations in June.*
test, assessment
(informal) exam

2 *an appointment for an eye examination*
check-up, test
► A medical examination of a dead person is a **post-mortem**.

3 *a thorough examination of the evidence*
investigation, inspection, scrutiny, study, analysis, survey, review, appraisal

examine VERB

1 *You will be examined on your chosen subject.*
question, interrogate, quiz
► To examine someone rigorously is to **grill** them.

2 *The detective examined all the evidence.*
inspect, study, investigate, analyse, look closely at, pore over, scrutinize,

probe, survey, review, weigh up, sift

example NOUN

1 *an example of Shakespeare's use of imagery*
instance, illustration, sample, specimen, case

2 *setting a good example to others*
precedent, model, ideal, standard, benchmark

exasperate VERB
All these delays were beginning to exasperate us.
annoy, irritate, upset, frustrate, anger, infuriate, madden, vex

exceed VERB
Her performance exceeded all our expectations.
surpass, better, outdo, go beyond, beat, top

excel VERB
a player who excels at running with the ball
do best, stand out, shine
IDIOM be second to none

excellent ADJECTIVE
a guitarist with an excellent technique
first-class, first-rate, outstanding, exceptional, tremendous, marvellous, wonderful, superb, great, fine, superior, superlative, top-notch
(informal) brilliant, fantastic, terrific, fabulous, sensational, super
OPPOSITES bad, awful, second-rate
SEE ALSO good

except PREPOSITION
Everyone knew the answer except me.
apart from, aside from, other than, with the exception of, excluding, not counting, barring, bar, but

exception NOUN
an exception to the usual spelling rule
oddity, peculiarity, deviation, special

a
b
c
d
e
f
g
h
i
j
k
l
m
n
o
p
q
r
s
t
u
v
w
x
y
z

case, anomaly

▷ **take exception to something**
I took exception to what he said.
dislike, object to, be averse to,
disapprove of, take issue with

exceptional ADJECTIVE

1 *a period of exceptional turmoil*
unusual, uncommon, abnormal,
atypical, unexpected,
unprecedented, unheard-of,
surprising
❙ OPPOSITES normal, usual

2 *a performer with exceptional talent*
extraordinary, outstanding,
phenomenal, amazing, rare, special,
uncommon, remarkable, prodigious
❙ OPPOSITE average

excerpt NOUN

*He read an excerpt from his new
novel.*
extract, passage, quotation, citation,
section

► An excerpt from a newspaper is a
cutting.

► An excerpt from a film is a **clip**.

excess NOUN

an excess of fat in their diet
surplus, superfluity, glut

▷ **in excess of**
speeds in excess of 60 mph
more than, greater than, over,
beyond

excessive ADJECTIVE

1 *I find their prices excessive.*
too great, too high, outrageous,
extortionate, exorbitant,
extravagant, unreasonable
❙ IDIOM *(informal)* over the top

2 *Police were accused of using excessive
force.*
extreme, superfluous, unreasonable,
disproportionate

exchange VERB

The shop will exchange faulty goods.
change, replace, substitute, swap,
switch, trade

► To exchange goods for other goods

without using money is to **barter**.

excite VERB

1 *The first episode failed to excite me.*
thrill, enthuse, exhilarate, stimulate,
animate, enliven, rouse, electrify
❙ OPPOSITE calm

2 *News of the discovery excited great
interest.*
arouse, provoke, incite, stir up,
trigger, kindle, spark

excited ADJECTIVE

Bethan was too excited to sleep.
agitated, lively, enthusiastic,
exuberant, thrilled, elated, eager,
animated
❙ OPPOSITE calm

excitement NOUN

*There was an air of real excitement
in the crowd.*
suspense, tension, drama, thrill,
eagerness, anticipation
(informal) buzz

exciting ADJECTIVE

*The last ten minutes of the match
were the most exciting.*
dramatic, eventful, thrilling,
gripping, compelling, sensational,
stirring, rousing, stimulating,
electrifying, exhilarating
(informal) rip-roaring
❙ OPPOSITES dull, boring

exclaim VERB

'Run for your lives!' he exclaimed.
call, shout, cry out, yell
❙ SEE ALSO **say** VERB

exclamation NOUN

*Alan let out a sudden exclamation
of pain.*
cry, shout, yell

► An exclamation using swear words is
an **oath** or **expletive**.

exclude VERB

1 *Adults are excluded from our club.*
ban, bar, prohibit, keep out, banish,
reject

OPPOSITE admit (to)

2 *excluding dairy products from your diet*
leave out, omit, rule out
OPPOSITE include

excluding PREPOSITION
The zoo is open every day excluding Christmas.
except, except for, with the exception of, apart from, aside from, other than, barring, bar, but

exclusive ADJECTIVE
1 *staying at an exclusive hotel*
select, upmarket, high-class, elite
(informal) posh, fancy, swish, classy
OPPOSITE downmarket
2 *The room is for your exclusive use.*
private, personal, individual, sole
OPPOSITES shared, joint
▷ **exclusive of**
The price is exclusive of tax.
not including, minus, omitting
OPPOSITE inclusive of

excursion NOUN
an excursion to the seaside
trip, journey, outing, expedition, jaunt, day out

excuse VERB
I can't excuse his behaviour.
forgive, overlook, disregard, pardon, condone, justify
OPPOSITE condemn
▷ **be excused from**
being excused from schoolwork
be exempt from, be let off, be relieved from, be freed from

excuse NOUN
I had a perfect excuse for being late.
reason, explanation, defence, justification, pretext

execute VERB
1 *The tsar and his family were executed in 1918.*
put to death
► Someone who executes people is an **executioner**.

► To execute someone unofficially without a proper trial is to **lynch** them.
2 *She executed a perfect dive.*
perform, carry out, implement, complete, accomplish, bring off

execution NOUN
1 *The square was once a place of public execution.*
capital punishment, the death penalty
2 *the execution of a penalty kick*
performance, implementation, carrying out, completion, accomplishment

exempt ADJECTIVE
▷ **exempt from**
Some students will be exempt from fees.
free from, not liable to, not subject to
OPPOSITES subject to, liable to

exercise NOUN
1 *a programme of daily exercise*
physical activity, working out, workouts, keep-fit, training
2 *a guitar exercise to improve technique*
drill, practice, lesson, task

exercise VERB
1 *exercising to keep fit*
do exercises, work out, train
2 *exercising the neighbour's dog*
take for a walk, take out, walk
3 *I suggest you exercise caution.*
use, make use of, employ, practise, apply

exert VERB
He exerted a huge influence on younger artists.
bring to bear, exercise, apply, use, employ

exertion NOUN
Allow your body recover from all the exertion.
effort, hard work, labour, toil

a
b
c
d
e
f
g
h
i
j
k
l
m
n
o
p
q
r
s
t
u
v
w
x
y
z

exhale *VERB*

> *Please exhale slowly.*
> breathe out
> **OPPOSITE** inhale

exhaust *VERB*

> **1** *Walking in the midday heat had exhausted me.*
> tire, tire out, wear out, fatigue, weary, drain, take it out of you
> *(informal)* do you in
> *(British informal)* knacker
> **2** *exhausting the Earth's supply of energy*
> use up, go through, consume, deplete, erode, drain

exhausted *ADJECTIVE*

> *The climb had left us all exhausted.*
> tired, weary, worn out, fatigued, breathless, gasping, panting
> *(informal)* all in, done in, bushed, zonked
> *(British informal)* knackered

exhausting *ADJECTIVE*

> *Digging the garden is exhausting work.*
> tiring, demanding, hard, laborious, strenuous, difficult, gruelling, wearisome
> **OPPOSITE** easy

exhaustion *NOUN*

> *being overcome by sheer exhaustion*
> tiredness, fatigue, weariness, weakness

exhibit *VERB*

> **1** *Her work is currently being exhibited in New York.*
> display, show, present, put on display
> **2** *The patient is exhibiting signs of stress.*
> show, demonstrate, reveal, display, demonstrate, manifest
> **OPPOSITE** hide

exhibition *NOUN*

> *an exhibition of Japanese art*
> display, show, exposition

exile *VERB*

> *Thousands were exiled from their own country.*
> banish, expel, deport, eject, drive out

exile *NOUN*

> **1** *returning home after years in exile*
> banishment, expulsion, deportation
> **2** *the return of political exiles*
> refugee, deportee, displaced person

exist *VERB*

> **1** *Do you think that vampires really exist?*
> be real, be found, occur
> **2** *Plants cannot exist without sunlight.*
> live, stay alive, survive, subsist, keep going, last, continue, endure

existence *NOUN*

> **1** *the existence of life on other planets*
> occurrence, reality
> **2** *eking out a harsh existence on a desert island*
> life, way of life, subsistence, survival, lifestyle
> ▷ **in existence**
> *the only known copy in existence of the film*
> existing, surviving, remaining, extant, living, alive

existing *ADJECTIVE*

> **1** *There are two existing species of elephants.*
> surviving, living, remaining
> **2** *a change to the existing rules*
> present, current

exit *NOUN*

> **1** *I'll wait for you by the exit.*
> door, way out, doorway, gate, barrier
> **OPPOSITE** entrance
> **2** *The robbers made a hurried exit.*
> departure, escape, retreat, withdrawal, exodus
> *(formal)* egress
> **OPPOSITES** entrance, arrival

exit VERB

Please exit by the main door.
go out, leave, depart, withdraw
▌ OPPOSITE enter

exotic ADJECTIVE

1 *a marketplace filled with exotic sights and smells*
unusual, unfamiliar, alien, exciting, romantic
▌ OPPOSITES familiar, commonplace

2 *an exotic holiday destination*
faraway, far-off, far-flung, remote, distant
▌ OPPOSITE nearby

expand VERB

1 *Wood expands when it gets wet.*
swell, enlarge, extend, stretch, lengthen, broaden, widen, thicken, fill out
▌ OPPOSITE contract

2 *Their business is expanding rapidly.*
increase, enlarge, grow, build up, develop, branch out
▌ OPPOSITES decrease, reduce

expanse NOUN

a vast expanse of desert
area, stretch, tract
▶ An expanse of water or ice is a **sheet**.

expect VERB

1 *I expect you'd like something to eat.*
suppose, presume, imagine, surmise, assume
(informal) guess, reckon
(North American informal) figure

2 *They are expecting a lot of interest in the sale.*
anticipate, envisage, predict, foresee, look forward to

3 *Do you expect me to work on Saturdays?*
require, want, count on, insist on, demand

expedition NOUN

a geography expedition to Iceland
voyage, exploration, mission, quest
▶ An expedition to worship at a holy place is a **pilgrimage**.

▶ An expedition to watch or hunt wild animals is a **safari**.

expel VERB

1 *Whales expel air through their blowholes.*
send out, force out, eject

2 *The entire team was expelled from the tournament.*
dismiss, throw out, send away, ban, evict, deport, banish, exile
(informal) chuck out
▶ To expel evil spirits is to **exorcize** them.

expense NOUN

worried about the expense of fuel
cost, price, charges, expenditure, outlay, outgoings

expensive ADJECTIVE

an expensive designer sports shop
dear, costly, high-priced, exorbitant, extortionate, overpriced
(informal) pricey
▌ OPPOSITE cheap

experience NOUN

1 *the result of years of experience and training*
practice, involvement, participation, knowledge, know-how, track record

2 *the most terrifying experience of my life*
happening, event, occurrence, incident, adventure
▶ An unpleasant experience is an **ordeal**.

experienced ADJECTIVE

an experienced stage actor
skilled, qualified, expert, knowledgeable, trained, professional, seasoned, practised
▌ OPPOSITE inexperienced

experiment NOUN

the results of a scientific experiment
test, trial, examination, investigation, observation, research

a
b
c
d
e
f
g
h
i
j
k
l
m
n
o
p
q
r
s
t
u
v
w
x
y
z

experiment *VERB*

▷ **experiment with**
experimenting with some new software
try out, test out, trial, sample
(*informal*) check out

experimental *ADJECTIVE*

an experimental design for a robot
exploratory, preliminary, tentative, trial, test, pilot

expert *NOUN*

an expert in web design
specialist, authority, pundit, genius, ace, wizard, master, maestro
(*informal*) whizz, hotshot
(*British informal*) dab hand

expert *ADJECTIVE*

The trip is led by expert mountaineers.
skilful, skilled, capable, competent, experienced, knowledgeable, professional, proficient, qualified, trained

OPPOSITES amateur, unskilful

expertise *NOUN*

She has wide expertise in teaching ICT.
skill, competence, knowledge, ability, know-how, proficiency, prowess

expire *VERB*

1 *Your library card has expired.*
run out, come to an end, become invalid, lapse

2 *I had the feeling that I was about to expire.*
die, pass away
SEE ALSO die

explain *VERB*

1 *My teacher explained how to tune a guitar.*
make clear, describe, elucidate, clarify

IDIOMS throw light on, spell out

2 *Your theory does not explain the footprints.*

account for, give reasons for, excuse, justify

explanation *NOUN*

1 *an explanation of how electricity works*
account, description, demonstration, clarification

2 *They found no explanation for the accident.*
reason, excuse, justification

explode *VERB*

1 *The firework exploded with a bang.*
blow up, go off, detonate, burst, erupt

2 *They exploded the dynamite in the tunnel.*
detonate, set off, let off

3 *Internet usage has exploded in recent years.*
increase, grow, escalate, boom, burgeon, mushroom

exploit *NOUN*

The book records the exploits of a teenage girl.
adventure, deed, feat, act, escapade, stunt

exploit *VERB*

1 *exploiting the area as a tourist attraction*
make use of, make the most of, capitalize on, develop, profit by
(*informal*) cash in on

2 *a company accused of exploiting its workers*
take advantage of, abuse, misuse, ill-treat

exploration *NOUN*

the exploration of deep space
investigation, survey, study, inspection, observation, research, reconnaissance

explore *VERB*

1 *The vehicle will explore the surface of Mars.*
travel through, survey, inspect, search, probe, reconnoitre

2 *We must explore all the possibilities.*

examine, investigate, look into, research, analyse, scrutinize

explorer NOUN

a team of undersea explorers
voyager, traveller, discoverer, researcher

explosion NOUN

1 We heard the explosion several streets away.
blast, bang, boom, eruption, detonation
▸ An explosion of laughter is an **outburst**.
▸ The sound of a gun going off is a **report**.

2 an explosion in the birth rate
increase, growth, escalation, boom, burgeoning, mushrooming

explosive ADJECTIVE

1 an explosive chemical
volatile, unstable, inflammable, combustible

2 an explosive temper
violent, fiery, stormy, irascible, passionate, touchy, volatile

3 an explosive situation
highly charged, heated, overwrought, tense, unstable, volatile

export VERB

China exports many of its goods to the US.
sell abroad, send abroad, ship overseas
❙ **OPPOSITE** import

expose VERB

1 The vampire smiled, exposing his fangs.
uncover, reveal, unmask, unveil, lay bare

2 The fraud was exposed in the newspaper.
make known, publish, reveal, disclose
❙ **IDIOM** (informal) blow the whistle on

exposure NOUN

1 the exposure of the Gunpowder Plot
uncovering, revelation, discovery, detection, disclosure, unmasking

2 receiving a lot of exposure in the press
publicity, coverage, attention, interest

express VERB

He's always quick to express his opinions.
declare, voice, state, convey, communicate, air, put into words, put across, give vent to

expression NOUN

1 An expression of horror flooded his face.
look, face, appearance, countenance, visage
FOR FACIAL EXPRESSIONS SEE **face**

2 'Cheesed off' is a colloquial expression.
phrase, saying, idiom, term
▸ A colloquial expression is also called a **colloquialism**.
▸ An expression that people use too much is a **cliché**.

3 the expression of your opinions
declaration, utterance, voicing, communication, articulation

4 She plays the piano with great expression.
feeling, emotion, passion, intensity, spirit

expressive ADJECTIVE

1 Becky gave me an expressive nudge.
meaningful, significant, revealing, telling

2 Try to be more expressive in your playing.
passionate, emotional, moving, stirring
❙ **OPPOSITES** expressionless, flat

exquisite ADJECTIVE

1 Notice the exquisite stitching on the quilt.
beautiful, fine, delicate, intricate,

dainty

2 *She always dresses with exquisite taste.*
discerning, refined, discriminating

extend *VERB*

1 *Mr Burns sat back and extended his legs.*
stretch out, hold out, put out, reach out, stick out
OPPOSITES pull back, withdraw

2 *We extended our visit by a couple of days.*
lengthen, prolong, protract, delay, draw out, spin out
OPPOSITES shorten, cut

3 *They have recently extended their website.*
enlarge, expand, increase, build up, develop, enhance, add to, widen the scope of
OPPOSITES reduce, cut back

4 *We extended a warm welcome to the visitors.*
give, offer, proffer
(formal) accord

5 *The road extends as far as the border.*
continue, carry on, reach, stretch

extension *NOUN*

1 *the extension of the Roman empire*
expansion, enlargement, development, enhancement, growth

2 *building an extension to the school*
addition, annex, add-on

extensive *ADJECTIVE*

1 *The rainforest covers an extensive area.*
large, great, substantial, considerable, vast, broad, wide, spread out
OPPOSITE small

2 *an extensive knowledge of the film industry*
wide, wide-ranging, comprehensive, thorough, broad
OPPOSITE narrow

extent *NOUN*

1 *The map shows the extent of the island.*
area, expanse, spread, breadth, length, dimensions, proportions, measurement

2 *No one guessed the full extent of the damage.*
amount, degree, level, size, scope, magnitude, range

exterior *ADJECTIVE*
an exterior wall
outside, external, outer, outward, outermost
OPPOSITE interior

exterior *NOUN*
The exterior of the house has been repainted.
outside, external surface
► The front of a building is the **facade**.
OPPOSITE interior

exterminate *VERB*
Zeus planned to exterminate the human race.
destroy, kill, get rid of, annihilate, wipe out

external *ADJECTIVE*
In external appearance, the house was shabby.
exterior, outside, outer, outward, outermost
OPPOSITE internal

extinct *ADJECTIVE*
Dodos became extinct in the seventeenth century.
died out, wiped out, vanished
► An extinct volcano is an **inactive** volcano.

extinguish *VERB*

1 *extinguishing a forest fire*
put out, quench, douse, smother, snuff out, stamp out
OPPOSITE ignite

2 *extinguishing any hope of escape*
put an end to, destroy, crush, stifle

extra ADJECTIVE

1 *an extra charge for baggage*
additional, further, added, supplementary, excess

2 *We brought extra clothes just in case.*
more, spare, surplus, reserve

extract VERB

1 *extracting a tooth*
take out, remove, pull out, draw out, withdraw
(informal) whip out

2 *a passage extracted from a novel*
excerpt, quote, cite, select

extract NOUN

an extract from her latest novel
excerpt, quotation, citation, passage, section

▶ An extract from a newspaper is a **cutting**.

▶ An extract from a film is a **clip**.

extraordinary ADJECTIVE

an ordinary woman who led an extraordinary life
amazing, astonishing, astounding, remarkable, exceptional, incredible, outstanding, phenomenal, sensational, marvellous, miraculous, rare, special, unheard of, unusual
❙ **OPPOSITE** ordinary

extravagant ADJECTIVE

1 *They planned a large and extravagant wedding.*
lavish, expensive, showy, ostentatious, fancy
(informal) flashy

▶ Someone who spends money in an extravagant way is a **spendthrift**.
❙ **OPPOSITES** modest, low-key

2 *charging extravagant fees*
excessive, immoderate, unrestrained, exaggerated
❙ **IDIOM** *(informal)* over the top
❙ **OPPOSITE** modest

extreme ADJECTIVE

1 *Polar bears can withstand extreme cold.*
great, intense, severe, acute, exceptional, excessive, utmost, maximum
❙ **OPPOSITE** slight

2 *an island in the extreme north of Canada*
farthest, furthest, remotest
❙ **OPPOSITE** near

3 *holding extreme views on religion*
radical, immoderate, extremist, fanatical
❙ **OPPOSITE** moderate

4 *the popularity of extreme sports*
dangerous, hazardous, adventurous, high-risk

extremely ADVERB

Crows are extremely intelligent birds.
very, exceptionally, especially, highly, extraordinarily, immensely, hugely, tremendously, supremely
(informal) awfully, terribly
(North American informal) mighty

eye NOUN

 WORD WEB

parts of an eye
cornea, eyeball, eyebrow, eyelash, eyelid, iris, lens, pupil, retina

▶ Related adjectives are **ocular**, **optic** and **ophthalmic**.

▶ A person who tests your eyesight is an **optician** or **ophthalmic optician**.

FOR TIPS ON DESCRIBING FACES SEE **face**

eye VERB

The two strangers eyed each other warily.
look at, regard, watch, observe, scrutinize, view, survey, gaze at, stare at, contemplate
(informal) size up
(North American informal) eyeball

a
b
c
d
e
f
g
h
i
j
k
l
m
n
o
p
q
r
s
t
u
v
w
x
y
z

fable NOUN
the fable of the Tortoise and the Hare
legend, story, tale, parable
❙ SEE ALSO fiction

fabric NOUN
1 *windproof fabric*
cloth, material, textile
2 *The fabric of the building is sound.*
structure, framework, make-up

 WORD WEB

> **some types of fabric**
> calico, canvas, cheesecloth,
> chiffon, chintz, corduroy,
> cotton, crepe, damask, denim,
> felt, flannel, gabardine,
> georgette, gingham,
> hessian (*American* burlap),
> jersey, linen, moleskin, muslin,
> organdie, organza, percale, satin,
> serge, silk, taffeta, tulle, tweed,
> velour, velvet, velveteen, vinyl,
> voile, wool
> **❙ SEE ALSO fibre**

fabulous ADJECTIVE
1 (*informal*) *That was a fabulous
weekend!*
excellent, first-class, outstanding,
wonderful, tremendous, marvellous,
splendid, superb
(*informal*) fantastic, terrific, brilliant,
smashing
2 *a life of fabulous wealth*
enormous, prodigious, phenomenal,

staggering, breathtaking
3 *a fabulous tale set in Atlantis*
fictitious, imaginary, legendary,
mythical

facade NOUN
1 *a building with a Victorian facade*
front, frontage, face, outside,
exterior
2 *a facade of normality*
show, front, appearance, pretence,
mask, veneer

face NOUN
1 *Donna's face flushed with anger.*
countenance, features, visage
(*informal*) mug
(*formal*) physiognomy
▶ A side view of someone's face is their
profile.
2 *Why are you making that funny
face?*
expression, look, appearance, aspect
3 *a clock face*
front, facade, cover
❙ OPPOSITE back
4 *the north face of the Eiger*
side, surface, plane

 WRITING TIPS

> **describing faces**
>
> It was a gaunt, aquiline face
> which was turned towards us,
> with piercing dark eyes, which
> lurked in deep hollows under
> overhung and tufted brows.
> — *Sir Arthur Conan Doyle, The Return of
> Sherlock Holmes*
>
> **facial features**
> beauty spot, bloom, brow,
> cheekbones, complexion, crow's
> feet, dimple, double chin, ear
> lobes, forehead, freckles, jawline,
> jowl, laugh-lines, lower lip, mole,
> pimple, scar, spot, temples,
> upper lip, wrinkles
>
> **facial expressions**
> beam, frown, glare, glower,

grimace, grin, leer, pout, scowl, smile, smirk, sneer, wince, yawn

adjectives
bloated, chinless, chiselled, clean-shaven, craggy, drawn, fine-boned, florid, flushed, freckled, gaunt, haggard, heart-shaped, heavy-set, lined, livid, olive, pallid, pasty, pimply, pinched, pockmarked, rosy, ruddy, sallow, scarred, spotless, spotty, sunburned, tanned, unshaven, wan, wasted, weather-beaten, weathered, wizened, wrinkled

chin
jutting, lantern, pointed, square, stubbly, weak

ears
earringed, flappy, lobed, pendulous, pierced, sticking-out (informal jug)

eyebrows
arched, beetling, bushy, knitted, shaggy, tufted, unruly

eyes
baggy, beady, bleary, bloodshot, bulging, close-set, cross-eyed, deep-set, downcast, glassy, heavy-lidded, hollow, hooded, piercing, protuberant, puffy, steely, sunken, swollen, tearful, twinkling, watery

lips
full, pouting, puckered, pursed, thin

nose
aquiline, beaked, bulbous, button, classical, crooked, hooked, Roman

❙ SEE ALSO hair

face VERB

1 *a room facing the sea*
be opposite to, look towards, overlook, give on to

2 *We had to face some tough questions.*
stand up to, face up to, deal with, cope with, tackle, meet, encounter, confront

❙ OPPOSITE avoid

3 *a wall faced with marble*
cover, surface, coat, front, veneer

facet NOUN

1 *gemstones cut with facets*
side, surface, plane, face

2 *the many facets of Indian culture*
aspect, feature, element, dimension, strand, component

facilitate VERB
papers to facilitate travel abroad
ease, assist, make easier, help along

❙ IDIOM smooth the path for

fact NOUN

1 *the fact of the matter*
reality, truth, certainty

❙ OPPOSITE fiction

2 *facts and figures*
detail, particular, point, finding, information, data

▷ **in fact**
In fact, rhubarb is not a fruit.
actually, as a matter of fact, in reality

factor NOUN
Many factors affect your body weight.
element, component, feature, aspect, dimension

factory NOUN
an old tyre factory
works, plant, mill

factual ADJECTIVE
a factual account of life in China
true, truthful, accurate, authentic, faithful, genuine, correct, exact

❙ OPPOSITES fictitious, made-up

faculty NOUN
the faculty of speech
power, capacity, capability

fad NOUN
the latest fad in computer games

a
b
c
d
e
f
g
h
i
j
k
l
m
n
o
p
q
r
s
t
u
v
w
x
y
z

craze, trend, vogue, fashion

fade *VERB*

1 *The colours will fade over time.*
become paler, become dim, bleach, blanch
❙ **OPPOSITE** brighten

2 *Her memory is beginning to fade.*
decline, diminish, dwindle, weaken, die away, wane, ebb
❙ **OPPOSITE** grow

fail *VERB*

1 *Their first attempt to climb Everest failed.*
be unsuccessful, go wrong, fall through, founder, come unstuck, come to grief, miscarry, misfire
(informal) flop, bomb
❙ **OPPOSITE** succeed

2 *The computer failed during a test flight.*
break down, stop working, cut out, malfunction
(informal) pack in, conk out

3 *By late afternoon, the light was failing.*
weaken, decline, diminish, dwindle, fade, deteriorate, peter out
❙ **OPPOSITE** improve

4 *You failed to warn us of the danger.*
neglect, forget, omit
❙ **OPPOSITE** remember

5 *My brother failed his driving test.*
be unsuccessful in
(informal) flunk
❙ **OPPOSITE** pass

fail *NOUN*

▷ **without fail**
Deliver this message without fail.
for certain, assuredly, without exception

failing *NOUN*
Vanity is one of his failings.
fault, flaw, imperfection, weakness, defect
❙ **OPPOSITE** strength

failure *NOUN*

1 *a power failure*

breakdown, fault, malfunction, crash, loss, collapse, stoppage

2 *Our first experiment was a failure.*
defeat, disappointment, disaster, fiasco
(informal) flop, wash-out
❙ **OPPOSITE** success

faint *ADJECTIVE*

1 *a faint line*
indistinct, unclear, ill-defined, dim, vague, faded, blurred, hazy, pale, shadowy, misty
❙ **OPPOSITES** clear, distinct

2 *a faint smell of burning*
delicate, slight
❙ **OPPOSITE** strong

3 *a faint cry for help*
weak, feeble, muted, subdued, muffled, hushed, soft, low, distant
❙ **OPPOSITE** loud

4 *Are you feeling faint?*
dizzy, giddy, light-headed, unsteady, weak, feeble
(informal) woozy

faint *VERB*
I nearly fainted in the midday heat.
become unconscious, collapse, pass out, black out, keel over
(old use) swoon

faintly *ADVERB*

1 *Lights glimmered faintly in the distance.*
indistinctly, unclearly, dimly, hazily, weakly
❙ **OPPOSITES** clearly, distinctly

2 *His face seemed faintly familiar.*
slightly, vaguely, somewhat, a little, a bit

fair❶ *ADJECTIVE*

1 *a fair trial*
just, equitable, even-handed, impartial, unbiased, honest, honourable, fair-minded, unprejudiced, disinterested
❙ **OPPOSITE** unfair

2 *a boy with fair hair*
blond, blonde, light, golden, yellow, flaxen

OPPOSITE dark

3 *a creature with fair skin*
light, pale, white, creamy

4 *The forecast is for fair weather.*
fine, dry, sunny, bright, clear, cloudless

OPPOSITE inclement

5 *We have a fair chance of winning.*
reasonable, moderate, average, acceptable, adequate, satisfactory, passable, respectable, tolerable

OPPOSITE poor

fair² NOUN

1 *a village fair*
fête, gala, festival, carnival

2 *a book fair*
show, exhibition, display, market, bazaar

fairly ADVERB

1 *The race will be judged fairly.*
justly, equitably, impartially, honestly, properly

IDIOM fair and square

OPPOSITE unfairly

2 *The stew is fairly spicy.*
quite, rather, somewhat, slightly, moderately

3 *I'm fairly certain he's lying.*
reasonably, up to a point, tolerably, passably, adequately

fairy NOUN

Tinker Bell is a mischievous fairy.
pixie, elf, imp, brownie, sprite, leprechaun

SEE ALSO fantasy

faith NOUN

1 *having faith in your abilities*
trust, belief, confidence, conviction

OPPOSITES doubt, mistrust

2 *people of many faiths*
religion, belief, creed, doctrine, ideology

SEE ALSO religion

faithful ADJECTIVE

1 *a faithful friend*
loyal, constant, devoted, true, reliable, dependable, firm,

staunch, steadfast, trusty

OPPOSITE disloyal

2 *a faithful copy of the original*
accurate, exact, precise, true

OPPOSITE inaccurate

fake NOUN

1 *It's not a real Leonardo: it's a fake.*
imitation, copy, reproduction, replica, forgery, sham

2 *That fortune-teller was a fake.*
charlatan, fraud, impostor

fake ADJECTIVE

1 *a fake passport*
false, forged, counterfeit, bogus
(informal) phoney, dud

2 *a fake diamond*
imitation, artificial, pretend, simulated, mock, sham

OPPOSITES real, genuine, authentic

fake VERB

1 *Someone managed to fake my signature.*
forge, copy, counterfeit, fabricate, falsify, imitate, reproduce

2 *I tried to fake interest in the topic.*
feign, pretend, put on, simulate, affect

fall VERB

1 *Thousands of meteorites fall to Earth each year.*
drop, descend, come down, plunge, plummet, nosedive

2 *The athlete fell and sprained her ankle.*
tumble, topple, trip, stumble

3 *The temperature fell to below freezing.*
go down, become lower, decrease, decline, lessen, diminish, dwindle

4 *Sea levels have fallen dramatically.*
go down, subside, recede, sink, ebb

5 *Edinburgh fell to the Jacobites without any fighting.*
give in, surrender, yield, capitulate

6 *a memorial to those who fell in the war*
die, be killed, perish
(old use) be slain

»

7 *My birthday falls on a Saturday this year.*
happen, occur, take place

▷ **fall apart**
The paper fell apart in my hands.
break up, go to pieces, disintegrate, shatter

▷ **fall back**
The rescue team were forced to fall back.
retreat, withdraw, draw back, pull back

▷ **fall for**
1 *Years ago, I fell for the girl next door.*
fall in love with, be attracted to, take a fancy to

2 *How did you fall for that old trick?*
be fooled by, be taken in by, be duped by

▷ **fall in**
The roof fell in during the storm.
collapse, cave in, give way

▷ **fall out**
Those two are always falling out.
argue, disagree, quarrel, squabble, bicker

▷ **fall through**
Our holiday plans have fallen through.
fail, come to nothing, collapse, founder

fall NOUN

1 *a fall from a great height*
tumble, topple, trip, plunge, dive, descent

2 *a sharp fall in temperature*
drop, lowering
❙ OPPOSITE rise

3 *a fall in the number of pupils*
decrease, reduction, decline, slump
❙ OPPOSITE increase

4 *a story about the fall of Troy*
downfall, defeat, overthrow, surrender, capitulation

false ADJECTIVE

1 *We were given false information.*
wrong, incorrect, untrue, inaccurate, mistaken, erroneous, faulty, invalid, misleading, deceptive
❙ OPPOSITE correct

2 *travelling under a false identity*
fake, bogus, sham, counterfeit, forged, fraudulent
❙ OPPOSITES genuine, authentic

3 *wearing false eyelashes*
artificial, imitation, synthetic, simulated, fake, mock, pretend
❙ OPPOSITES real, natural

4 *a false friend*
unfaithful, disloyal, unreliable, untrustworthy, deceitful, dishonest, treacherous
❙ OPPOSITES faithful, loyal

falsify VERB
accused of falsifying the test results
alter, tamper with, doctor, forge, counterfeit

falter VERB
The actor faltered slightly over his lines.
hesitate, stumble, pause, waver, vacillate, stammer, stutter

fame NOUN
the fame of being a pop star
celebrity, stardom, renown, glory, reputation, name, standing, stature, prominence
▶ Fame that you get for doing something bad is **notoriety**.

famed ADJECTIVE
▷ **famed for**
Amsterdam is famed for its canals.
famous for, well-known for, celebrated for, renowned for, noted for

Usage Note

The words *famed* and *famous* are not always interchangeable. You would say *a film star famed for* or *famous for her beauty* but *a famous film star*.

familiar *ADJECTIVE*

1 *Bicycles are a familiar sight in Beijing.*
common, everyday, normal, ordinary, usual, regular, customary, frequent, mundane, routine
┃ OPPOSITE rare

2 *on familiar terms with some celebrities*
informal, friendly, intimate, relaxed, close
┃ OPPOSITES formal, unfriendly

▷ **familiar with**
Are you familiar with the legend of Sinbad?
acquainted with, aware of

familiarity *NOUN*

1 *There was an air of familiarity between them.*
friendship, closeness, intimacy, friendliness

2 *I have some familiarity with Latin.*
knowledge of, acquaintance with, experience of, understanding of

family *NOUN*

Most of her family live in South Africa.
relations, relatives, kin, clan
┃ IDIOMS flesh and blood, kith and kin

✺ WORD WEB

members of a family
ancestor, forebear, forefather, descendant (*literary* scion), father, mother, husband, wife, spouse, parent, child, daughter, son, brother, sister, sibling, aunt, uncle, nephew, niece, cousin, second cousin, grandparent, great- grandparent, grandfather, grandmother, granddaughter, grandson, great-aunt, great-uncle, father-in-law, mother-in-law, daughter-in-law, son-in-law, brother-in-law, sister- in-law, stepfather, stepmother, stepchild, stepdaughter, stepson, stepbrother, stepsister, half-brother, half-sister, foster-parent, foster-child

▶ The study of family history and ancestors is **genealogy**. A **family tree** is a diagram which shows how people in a family are related.
┃ SEE ALSO father, mother

famine *NOUN*

years of drought and famine
starvation, hunger

famous *ADJECTIVE*

Mark Twain is a famous American author.
well-known, celebrated, renowned, acclaimed, admired, distinguished, revered, eminent, exalted, illustrious, noted, notable

▶ A **notorious** person or place is famous for a bad reason.
a notorious accident blackspot
┃ OPPOSITES unknown, obscure

Usage Note

The word **infamous** is not the opposite of **famous**. An **infamous** person has a bad reputation: *Sylvester Fibbs was an infamous liar.*

fan❶ *NOUN*

a ceiling fan
ventilator, blower, extractor, air-conditioner

fan❷ *NOUN*

a football fan
enthusiast, admirer, devotee, follower, supporter

fanatic *NOUN*

a fitness fanatic
enthusiast, addict, devotee (*informal*) freak, nut

a b c d e f g h i j k l m n o p q r s t u v w x y z

fanatical *ADJECTIVE*

fanatical about football
enthusiastic, passionate, obsessive, extreme, fervent, over-enthusiastic, rabid, zealous
❙ OPPOSITE moderate

fanciful *ADJECTIVE*

a fanciful tale set in ancient Japan
imaginary, fictitious, made-up, fantastic, fabulous, whimsical
❙ OPPOSITE realistic

fancy *VERB*

1 *(informal) Which film do you fancy seeing?*
feel like, want, wish for, desire, prefer
2 *I fancied I heard a noise upstairs.*
imagine, think, believe, suppose *(informal)* reckon

fancy *NOUN*

1 *Painting is more than a passing fancy for me.*
whim, urge, desire, caprice
2 *The author is given to strange flights of fancy.*
imagination, fantasy, dreaming, creativity

fancy *ADJECTIVE*

The guitarist wore a fancy waistcoat.
elaborate, decorative, ornate, ornamented, showy
(informal) flashy, snazzy
❙ OPPOSITE plain

fantastic *ADJECTIVE*

1 *The rock had been carved into fantastic shapes.*
fanciful, extraordinary, strange, odd, weird, outlandish, incredible, imaginative, far-fetched
❙ OPPOSITE realistic
2 *(informal) You missed a fantastic concert!*
excellent, first-class, outstanding, superb, wonderful, tremendous, marvellous
(informal) brilliant, fabulous, smashing

fantasy *NOUN*

1 *a fantasy about being a movie star*
dream, daydream, reverie, wish, hope
2 *The book is a mixture of science fiction and fantasy.*
make-believe, invention, imagination, fancy

 **WRITING TIPS**

writing fantasy fiction

It appeared that Gandalf had been to a great council of the white wizards, masters of lore and good magic; and that they had at last driven the Necromancer from his dark hold in the south of Mirkwood.
— *J. R. R. Tolkien, The Hobbit*

characters

alchemist, apprentice, changeling, dragon-master, druid, enchanter, enchantress, gatekeeper, magus, seer, shaman, shape-shifter, soothsayer, sorcerer, sorceress, warlock, witch, witchfinder, wizard

creatures

banshee, basilisk, boggart, bunyip, centaur, chimera, cyclops, dragon, dwarf, elf, fairy, faun, genie, giant, goblin, gorgon, gryphon, harpie, kelpie, mermaid, merman, ogre, phoenix, sasquatch, selkie, sphinx, troll, unicorn, yeti

setting

castle, cave or cavern, den, dungeon, empire, era, enchanted forest, fortress, island, kingdom, labyrinth, lair, maze, realm, stronghold, underworld

useful words & phrases

amulet, augury, bewitch, charm, chronicle, clairvoyance, coven, crucible, curse, dark arts, divination, elixir, enchantment, hex, immortality, incantation, invisibility, legend, lore, mace, magic, nemesis, omen, oracle, portal, potion, prophecy, quest, riddle, rune, sorcery, spell, spirit guide, spirit quest, staff, superhuman, talisman, vision, wand, witchcraft, wizardry

SEE ALSO fortune telling

far *ADJECTIVE*
1 *in the far north of Canada*
distant, faraway, far-off, far-flung, remote, outlying
2 *on the far side of the bay*
opposite, other
OPPOSITE near

▷ **by far**
They are by far the best team.
far and away, easily
IDIOMS by a long shot, by a mile

far *ADVERB*
1 *We were still far from sight of land.*
far away, a long way, at a distance
(informal) miles
2 *The road is far more dangerous in winter.*
much, considerably, significantly, markedly, decidedly, greatly, a good deal

fare *NOUN*
How much is the train fare?
charge, cost, price, fee, toll

farewell *NOUN*
Anna bade a tearful farewell to her sister.
goodbye, adieu

far-fetched *ADJECTIVE*
Her story sounds far-fetched to me.
unbelievable, unlikely, improbable, unconvincing, unrealistic, incredible
OPPOSITES likely, believable

farm *NOUN*
a sheep farm

farmstead, holding, ranch
(Australia & New Zealand) station

farm *VERB*
This land has been farmed for centuries.
cultivate, work, till, plough

farming *NOUN*
organic methods of farming
agriculture, cultivation, husbandry

fascinate *VERB*
Wells was fascinated by the idea of time travel.
interest (in), captivate, enthral, engross, absorb, attract, beguile, entrance, charm, enchant
OPPOSITES bore, repel

fascinating *ADJECTIVE*
I found the programme fascinating.
interesting, absorbing, enthralling, captivating, engrossing, riveting, gripping, entertaining, intriguing, diverting, engaging, stimulating
OPPOSITES boring, dull

fascination *NOUN*
Sharks have always held a fascination for me.
attraction, charm, allure, captivation, interest, appeal, draw
OPPOSITE repulsion

fashion *NOUN*
1 *Dale was behaving in a peculiar fashion*
manner, way, style, method
2 *the latest fashion in footwear*
trend, vogue, craze, fad, style, look

 WORD WEB

some terms used in fashion
accessories, bias cut, boutique, bust, cap sleeve, catwalk, cut, designer, drape, drop waist, empire line, fashion icon, fashion shoot, fashion show, gathering, godet, haute couture, hemline, high waist, inseam, model,   **»**

a b c d e f g h i j k l m n o p q r s t u v w x y z

neckline, off-the-shoulder,
pintuck, placket, polo neck,
raglan sleeve, runway, scoop
neck, seam, season, shirring,
spaghetti strap, stitching,
strapless, stretch, style, tailoring,
top-stitching, trend, turtleneck,
V-neck, waistline, wing collar

▶ Someone who slavishly folllows
fashion is a **fashion victim** or
fashionista.

SEE ALSO clothes, fabric

fashionable *ADJECTIVE*
a fashionable new hairstyle
stylish, chic, up-to-date, popular,
elegant, smart
(informal) trendy, hip, in
IDIOM all the rage
OPPOSITES unfashionable,
out-of-date

fast *ADJECTIVE*
1 *a fast lap around the track*
quick, rapid, speedy, swift, brisk,
hurried, hasty, high-speed,
headlong, breakneck
(informal) nippy
OPPOSITES slow, unhurried
2 *Be sure to make the rope fast.*
secure, fastened, firm, tight
OPPOSITE loose

fast *ADVERB*
1 *skiing fast down the slope*
quickly, speedily, swiftly, rapidly,
briskly
(informal) flat out
IDIOMS at full tilt, like a shot, like
the wind
2 *The jeep was stuck fast in the mud.*
firmly, securely, tightly
3 *fast asleep*
deeply, sound, completely

fasten *VERB*
1 *Fasten one end of the rope around
your waist.*
tie, fix, attach, connect, join, link,
bind, hitch, tether, clamp, pin,

clip, tack, stick
OPPOSITES unfasten, untie
2 *Please fasten your seat-belts.*
secure, lock, bolt, make fast, seal
OPPOSITES unfasten, release

fat *ADJECTIVE*
1 *foods that will make you fat*
overweight, obese, plump, chubby,
podgy, dumpy, tubby, round,
rotund, portly, stout, heavy, beefy,
corpulent, flabby
▶ Someone with a fat stomach is
pot-bellied.
OPPOSITES thin, skinny
**FOR TIPS ON DESCRIBING PEOPLE'S
BODIES SEE body**
2 *a large fat envelope*
thick, bulky, chunky, weighty,
substantial
(informal) stuffed
OPPOSITE thin
3 *writing a fat cheque*
large, substantial, sizeable, generous

fatal *ADJECTIVE*
1 *a fatal wound*
deadly, lethal, mortal, incurable,
terminal
2 *a fatal error*
disastrous, catastrophic, dreadful,
dire, calamitous, ruinous

fate *NOUN*
1 *I didn't know what fate had in store
for me.*
fortune, destiny, providence, chance,
luck, future, lot
IDIOM the lap of the gods
2 *Each of the crew met with a grisly
fate.*
death, demise, end, doom

father *NOUN*
1 *My father grew up in South Africa.*
(informal) dad, daddy, pa, old man
(North American informal) pop
▶ A related adjective is **paternal**.
**FOR OTHER MEMBERS OF A FAMILY SEE
family**
2 *Galileo is considered the father of
astronomy.*

founder, originator, inventor, creator, architect

fatigue NOUN
The climbers were overcome with fatigue.
exhaustion, tiredness, weariness, weakness

fatty ADJECTIVE
Try to cut down on fatty foods.
fat, greasy, oily
OPPOSITE lean

fault NOUN
1 *a fault in the electrical wiring*
defect, flaw, malfunction, snag, problem, weakness
(informal) glitch, bug
2 *It's not my fault that you slept in.*
responsibility, liability, culpability
▷ **at fault**
Both the drivers were at fault.
to blame, guilty, responsible, culpable

faultless ADJECTIVE
a faultless performance
perfect, flawless, immaculate, impeccable, spotless
OPPOSITES imperfect, flawed

faulty ADJECTIVE
a faulty DVD
broken, not working, malfunctioning, defective, out of order, unusable, damaged
IDIOM *(informal)* on the blink
OPPOSITES working, in good order

fauna NOUN
SEE **animal**

favour NOUN
1 *Would you do me a favour?*
good turn, good deed, kindness, service, courtesy
2 *The idea found favour with the public.*
approval, support, liking, goodwill
▷ **be in favour of**
Are you in favour of banning whaling?

approve of, support, be on the side of, be for, be pro
OPPOSITES be against, disapprove of

favour VERB
Which team do you favour to win the cup?
approve of, support, back, advocate, choose, like, opt for, prefer
(informal) fancy, go for
OPPOSITE oppose

favourable ADJECTIVE
1 *The weather is favourable for flying.*
advantageous, beneficial, helpful, good, suitable, auspicious, encouraging
OPPOSITE unfavourable
2 *The film received favourable reviews.*
positive, complimentary, good, glowing, approving, agreeable, enthusiastic, sympathetic
(informal) rave
OPPOSITES critical, hostile, negative

favourite ADJECTIVE
What's your favourite colour?
preferred, favoured, best-loved, treasured, dearest, special, top

favourite NOUN
1 *Of all cities in Europe, Paris is my favourite.*
preference, first choice, pick
2 *Ruth had always been the teacher's favourite.*
pet, darling
IDIOM the apple of your eye

fear NOUN
1 *shaking with fear*
fright, terror, horror, alarm, panic, dread, anxiety, apprehension, trepidation
OPPOSITE courage
SEE ALSO afraid
2 *a fear of snake and spiders*
phobia, dread
FOR SPECIAL TYPES OF PHOBIA SEE **phobia**

a
b
c
d
e
f
g
h
i
j
k
l
m
n
o
p
q
r
s
t
u
v
w
x
y
z

a
b
c
d
e
f
g
h
i
j
k
l
m
n
o
p
q
r
s
t
u
v
w
x
y
z

fear *VERB*

1 *As a child, I used to fear the dark.*
be frightened of, be afraid of, be
scared of, dread

2 *I fear we may be too late.*
suspect, expect, anticipate

fearful *ADJECTIVE*

1 *with a fearful look in his eyes*
frightened, afraid, scared, terrified,
petrified, nervous, apprehensive,
anxious, timid, panicky
(informal) jittery
| OPPOSITE brave

2 *We came across a fearful sight.*
frightening, terrifying, shocking,
ghastly, dreadful, appalling, terrible,
awful, frightful, fearsome, gruesome

fearless *ADJECTIVE*

a fearless enemy
brave, courageous, audacious,
daring, bold, heroic, valiant,
intrepid, plucky, unafraid
| OPPOSITES cowardly, timid

feasible *ADJECTIVE*

*Is it feasible to fly there and back in
a day?*
possible, practicable, practical,
achievable, realistic, workable,
viable
(informal) doable
| OPPOSITES impractical, impossible

feast *NOUN*

1 *a wedding feast*
banquet, dinner
(informal) spread

2 *the feast of Saint Valentine*
festival, holiday

feast *VERB*

*a band of hyenas feasting on
their prey*
gorge, feed, dine

feat *NOUN*

*The Great Wall of China was an
incredible feat of engineering.*
act, action, deed, exploit,
achievement, performance

feather *NOUN*

a goose feather
plume, quill

 WORD WEB

▶ The body, wings, and tail of a bird
are covered by **contour feathers**.
The smaller, softer feathers under
these are **down feathers**. All
the feathers on a bird are its
plumage.

▶ When a bird **preens** its feathers,
it smooths them with its beak.
When a bird **moults**, it sheds and
replaces its feathers.

parts of a feather
barbs, barbules, shaft, vane

feature *NOUN*

1 *a feature of Roman architecture*
characteristic, attribute, property,
aspect, quality, peculiarity, trait,
facet, factor, element, hallmark

2 *a feature in the school magazine*
article, report, story, item, piece,
column

▷ **features**

a tall, thin man with fine features
face, countenance, visage
(formal) physiognomy
FOR TIPS ON DESCRIBING FACES SEE **face**

feature *VERB*

1 *The film features an original
soundtrack.*
present, promote, highlight,
spotlight, showcase

2 *Holmes features in over fifty short
stories.*
appear, participate, take part,
figure, star

federation *NOUN*

a federation of states
confederation, confederacy,
alliance, league, coalition, union,
commonwealth

fed up (informal) ADJECTIVE
   Erin sat at her desk looking fed up.
   depressed, unhappy, annoyed,
   discontented, dissatisfied, bored
   (informal) cheesed off, brassed off,
   browned off, hacked off
▷ **be fed up with**
   I'm fed up with doing all the work.
   be tired of, have had enough of, be
   disgusted with
   (informal) be sick and tired of

fee NOUN
   an annual membership fee
   charge, cost, payment, price, tariff,
   toll

feeble ADJECTIVE
1 *looking old and feeble*
   weak, frail, infirm, poorly, sickly,
   puny, weedy, debilitated, decrepit
   ▌OPPOSITES strong, powerful
2 *a feeble attempt*
   ineffective, inadequate,
   unconvincing, unsatisfactory, poor,
   weak, flimsy, lame

feed VERB
1 *enough food to feed everyone*
   provide for, cater for, give food to,
   nourish, supply, sustain
2 *Bats usually feed at night.*
   eat, take food
▷ **feed on**
   *Chameleons feed on a variety of
   insects.*
   eat, consume, devour, live on

feed NOUN
   a sack of animal feed
   fodder, food, foodstuff

feel VERB
1 *Feel how soft this material is.*
   touch, stroke, caress, fondle, handle
   ▌SEE ALSO texture
2 *feeling your way in the dark*
   grope, fumble
3 *The animal won't feel any pain.*
   experience, undergo, endure,
   suffer from
4 *I usually don't feel the cold.*

   perceive, sense, notice, detect,
   be aware of, be conscious of
5 *I feel that I've met you before.*
   think, believe, consider, maintain
   (informal) reckon
6 *It feels warmer today.*
   appear, seem, strike you as
▷ **feel for**
   I feel for the people who live there.
   sympathize with, pity
▷ **feel like**
   Do you feel like something to eat?
   fancy, want, desire, wish for

feel NOUN
1 *the feel of sand between your toes*
   feeling, sensation, touch, texture
2 *The film captures the feel of wartime
   France.*
   atmosphere, mood, feeling, spirit,
   ambience, aura
   (informal) vibe

feeling NOUN
1 *a loss of feeling in your toes*
   sense of touch, sensation, sensitivity
2 *I didn't mean to hurt your feelings.*
   emotion, passion, sentiment
3 *I had a feeling that something was
   wrong.*
   suspicion, notion, inkling, idea,
   impression, fancy, intuition, hunch
4 *the strength of public feeling*
   opinion, belief, view, attitude, mood

feign VERB
   feigning interest in the conversation
   pretend, simulate, put on, affect,
   fake

fell VERB
1 *felling a tree with a saw*
   cut down, chop down, clear
2 *Ali felled his opponent with one
   punch*
   knock down, strike down, knock out
   (informal) flatten

fellow NOUN
   an odd-looking fellow with a squint
   man, person, character
   (informal) guy

   》

(British informal) bloke, chap

fellowship NOUN
in the spirit of good fellowship
friendship, companionship,
comradeship, camaraderie

female ADJECTIVE
a female friend
❙ **OPPOSITE** male
FOR FEMALE ANIMALS SEE **animal**

feminine ADJECTIVE
a feminine style of dress
womanly, ladylike, girlish
(informal) girlie
❙ **OPPOSITE** masculine

fence NOUN
a perimeter fence
railing, barrier, barricade, paling,
stockade
► A fence made of pointed sticks is a
palisade.

fence VERB
a field fenced by hedgerows
enclose, surround, bound, encircle

fend VERB
▷ **fend for yourself**
We were left to fend for ourselves.
look after yourself, take care of
yourself, shift for yourself
❙ **IDIOM** stand on your own two feet
▷ **fend off**
fending off the enemy
repel, resist, ward off, fight off,
hold off, repulse

ferment NOUN
All Europe was in a state of ferment.
turmoil, unrest, upheaval, agitation,
excitement, commotion, turbulence,
confusion, disorder, tumult

ferocious ADJECTIVE
1 a ferocious fight to the death
vicious, savage, violent, bloody,
brutal, barbaric
❙ **OPPOSITES** gentle, tame
2 the ferocious heat of the sun
fierce, intense, relentless
❙ **OPPOSITE** mild

ferret VERB
ferreting around in my rucksack
rummage, search, hunt, forage,
go through, scour

ferry VERB
a bus ferrying people to the station
transport, convey, take, carry, run,
shuttle, ship

fertile ADJECTIVE
1 planted in fertile soil
fruitful, productive, rich, lush,
fecund
❙ **OPPOSITES** barren, sterile
2 a fertile imagination
inventive, creative, rich, prolific,
teeming

fertilize VERB
1 a good compost to fertilize the soil
manure, feed, enrich
2 How do frogs fertilize their eggs?
inseminate, pollinate

fervent ADJECTIVE
It was her fervent wish to return to
Ireland.
eager, keen, avid, ardent, intense,
wholehearted, heartfelt, passionate
❙ **OPPOSITES** indifferent, lukewarm

festival NOUN
a summer music festival
celebration, carnival, fiesta, fête,
gala, fair, jubilee, jamboree
(informal) fest
FOR RELIGIOUS FESTIVALS SEE **religion**

festive ADJECTIVE
Chinese New Year is a festive
occasion.
cheerful, happy, merry, jolly, cheery,
joyful, joyous, jovial, light-hearted,
celebratory
❙ **OPPOSITES** gloomy, sombre

fetch VERB
1 going to fetch a doctor
get, bring, collect, transport, pick
up, retrieve, obtain, carry, convey
2 How much will the painting fetch?
sell for, go for, make, raise, bring in,
earn

fetching *ADJECTIVE*
> *wearing a very fetching hat*
> attractive, appealing, flattering,
> becoming, charming

feud *NOUN*
> *a feud between two families*
> vendetta, quarrel, dispute, conflict,
> hostility, enmity, rivalry, strife,
> antagonism

fever *NOUN*
> **1** *a fever of 39 degrees Celsius*
> temperature
> **2** *a fever of activity*
> frenzy, excitement, agitation, mania,
> passion, fervour

feverish *ADJECTIVE*
> **1** *feeling feverish with the cold*
> hot, burning, flushed, delirious
> **2** *There was feverish activity in the*
> *kitchen.*
> frenzied, frantic, excited, agitated,
> hectic, frenetic, busy, hurried,
> restless

few *ADJECTIVE*
> *on a few occasions*
> not many, hardly any, a small
> number of, a handful of, one or two
> ▌ **OPPOSITE** many

fiasco *NOUN*
> *the fiasco of the cancelled concert*
> failure, disaster, catastrophe, mess,
> farce, debacle
> *(informal)* shambles
> ▌ **OPPOSITE** success

fibre *NOUN*
> **1** *Nylon is a synthetic fibre.*
> thread, strand, hair, filament
> **2** *a diet lacking in fibre*
> roughage

 WORD WEB

> ***natural fibres***
> bamboo, cotton, hemp, jute,
> linen, ramie, silk, sisal, wool

> ***synthetic fibres***
> acetate, acrylic, microfibre,
> nylon, polypropylene, polyester,
> rayon, viscose
> ▌ **SEE ALSO** fabric

fickle *ADJECTIVE*
> *the fickle support of the public*
> changeable, erratic, unreliable,
> unsteady, unpredictable, inconstant,
> capricious, mercurial
> ▌ **OPPOSITES** constant, steady

fiction *NOUN*
> **1** *The 'Lord of the Rings' is a work of*
> *fiction.*
> creative writing, storytelling
> ▌ **OPPOSITE** non-fiction
> **2** *Some of the news story was pure*
> *fiction.*
> fantasy, invention, fabrication, lies
> ▌ **IDIOMS** pack of lies, flight of fancy
> ▌ **OPPOSITE** fact

 WORD WEB

> ***formats for fiction***
> drama or play, epistolary novel
> (told through letters), graphic
> novel, narrative poem, novel,
> novelization, novella, screenplay,
> short story
> ▌ **SEE ALSO** book, drama

> ***genres of fiction***
> adventure story,*(informal)* chick
> lit, crime or detective fiction,
> epic, fable, fairy story, fantasy,
> ghost story, gothic, historical
> fiction, horror, mystery, myth,
> picaresque, pulp fiction,
> romance, science fiction
> *(informal* sci-fi), spy fiction,
> thriller

> ***types of non-fiction***
> autobiography, biography, diary
> or journal, documentary,   **»**

a
b
c
d
e
f
g
h
i
j
k
l
m
n
o
p
q
r
s
t
u
v
w
x
y
z

essay, history, journalism, manual, memoir, monograph, report, review, textbook, travelogue

FOR TIPS ON WRITING A BOOK REVIEW SEE **book**

fictional *ADJECTIVE*
Middle-earth is a fictional realm.
imaginary, made-up, invented, fanciful
❙ **OPPOSITES** factual, real

fictitious *ADJECTIVE*
travelling under a fictitious name
false, fake, fabricated, fraudulent, bogus, assumed, spurious, unreal
❙ **OPPOSITES** genuine, real

> **Usage Note**
>
> The words **fictional** and **fictitious** do not mean the same thing. A *fictional* character exists only in fiction, whereas a *fictitious* identity is created to deceive others.

fiddle *VERB*
1 *fiddling with the control panel*
adjust, tinker, meddle, tamper, twiddle, play about, mess about
2 *(informal) fiddling a bank account*
falsify, manipulate, massage, alter, rig, doctor
❙ **IDIOM** *(informal)* cook the books

fiddly *(informal) ADJECTIVE*
Wiring a plug can be a fiddly job.
intricate, complicated, awkward, involved
❙ **OPPOSITE** simple

fidelity *NOUN*
1 *They promised fidelity to each other.*
faithfulness, loyalty, constancy
❙ **OPPOSITE** infidelity
2 *fidelity to the original document*
accuracy, exactness, closeness, adherence
❙ **OPPOSITE** inaccuracy

fidget *VERB*
children fidgeting in their chairs
be restless, move about, wriggle, squirm

field *NOUN*
1 *cattle grazing in the field*
meadow, pasture, grassland, green, paddock
2 *a football field*
ground, pitch, playing field
3 *advances in the field of genetics*
area, sphere, speciality, discipline, territory, province, domain

fiend *NOUN*
1 *like a fiend from Hell*
demon, devil, evil spirit
2 *(informal) a fresh-air fiend*
enthusiast, fanatic, devotee
(informal) freak, nut

fierce *ADJECTIVE*
1 *a fierce attack by armed robbers*
vicious, ferocious, savage, brutal, violent, wild, cruel, merciless, ruthless, pitiless
2 *facing fierce competition*
strong, intense, keen, eager, fervent, passionate, vehement, aggressive, relentless, cut-throat

fiery *ADJECTIVE*
1 *the fiery heat of the midday sun*
burning, blazing, flaming, red-hot
❙ **OPPOSITES** cool, mild
2 *the fiery taste of chilli pepper*
hot, spicy, peppery
❙ **OPPOSITE** mild
3 *a fiery temper*
passionate, excitable, volatile, violent, raging, explosive
❙ **OPPOSITES** calm, mild

fight *NOUN*
1 *the fight to capture the island*
battle, conflict, action, engagement, hostilities
2 *a fight in the street*
brawl, scuffle, skirmish, tussle, fracas, set-to
(informal) scrap, punch-up
(old use) fisticuffs

► A fight arranged between two people is a **duel**.

3 *a heavyweight fight*
boxing match, contest, bout

4 *a fight with your girlfriend*
argument, quarrel, squabble, row, dispute

5 *the fight to save the rainforest*
campaign, crusade, struggle, action, effort

fight VERB

1 *caught fighting in the playground*
brawl, exchange blows, come to blows, scuffle, grapple, wrestle *(informal)* scrap, have a punch-up

2 *fighting over who should go first*
argue, quarrel, squabble, row, bicker, wrangle

3 *The two countries fought each other in the war.*
do battle with, wage war with, attack

4 *fighting the plan to build a motorway*
protest against, oppose, resist, contest, make a stand against, campaign against

fighter NOUN

a guerrilla fighter
soldier, warrior, combatant
SEE ALSO **boxer**

fighting NOUN

soldiers killed during the fighting
combat, hostilities, war, battle, conflict

figurative ADJECTIVE

the poet's use of figurative language
metaphorical, symbolic
OPPOSITE literal

 WORD WEB

figures of speech based on sound
alliteration, assonance (repeated vowel sounds),

consonance (repeated consonants), onomatopoeia

figures of speech based on meaning
hyperbole, metaphor, metonymy, personification, simile
FOR TIPS ON USING FIGURATIVE LANGUAGE SEE **Writer's Toolkit**

figure NOUN

1 *adding up the figures*
number, numeral, digit, integer, statistic

2 *Can you put a figure on it?*
price, value, amount, sum, cost

3 *See the figure on page 22.*
diagram, graph, illustration, drawing

4 *having the figure of an athlete*
body, build, frame, physique

5 *an important figure in Irish history*
person, character, individual

6 *a clay figure of a bird*
statue, carving, sculpture

figure VERB

Wolves often figure in fairy tales.
appear, feature, be mentioned, be referred to

▷ **figure out**

figuring out what it all means
work out, make out, understand, comprehend, make sense of, see, grasp, fathom
IDIOM get to the bottom of

file❶ VERB

a kit for filing your nails
smooth, grind down, rub down, rasp, hone, whet

file❷ NOUN

1 *keeping your notes in a file*
folder, binder, portfolio

2 *The agency kept a secret file on her.*
dossier, report, record, archive

3 *walking in a single file*
line, row, column, queue, string, chain, procession

file VERB

1 *The cards are filed alphabetically.*
organize, arrange, categorize, classify, catalogue, store

2 *filing out of the classroom*
walk in a line, march, troop, parade

fill VERB

1 *filling the cupboard with junk*
load, pack, stuff, cram, top up, stock, supply

▶ To fill something with air is to **inflate** it.
OPPOSITE empty

2 *filling a hole with cement*
close up, plug, seal, block up, stop up, clog

3 *The scent of roses filled the room.*
permeate, suffuse

4 *Hundreds of protesters filled the streets.*
crowd, throng, cram

5 *That job has already been filled.*
take up, occupy

filling NOUN

a sandwich filling
stuffing, insides, innards, contents, filler, padding, wadding

filling ADJECTIVE

That meal was very filling!
substantial, hearty, ample, generous, heavy

film NOUN

1 *the latest James Bond film*
movie, picture, video, DVD

2 *a career in film*
cinema, movies
IDIOMS the big screen, the silver screen

3 *a film of grease on the wall*
coat, coating, layer, covering, sheet, skin, membrane

WORD WEB

types of film
action picture, animation, (informal) biopic, (informal) buddy movie, (informal) chic flick, costume drama, disaster movie, documentary, epic, feature film, film noir, horror film, road movie, (informal) romcom, short, silent film, thriller, (informal) weepie, western

people involved in films
actor, animator, camera crew, cast, co-star, cinematographer, director, editor, extras, film crew, film star, film studio, producer, projectionist, screenwriter, sound engineer, stunt artist, voice coach

other terms relating to film
3-D, adaptation, BAFTA, CGI, cinematography, clip, costumes, credits, cut, dubbing, editing, fade-out, film score, flashback, footage, Hollywood, IMAX, leading role, lighting, mise en scène, montage, nomination, off-set, on-set, Oscar, premiere, release date, remake, rushes, scene, screenplay, screen test, script, sequence, slow motion (informal slo-mo), sound effects, soundtrack, special effects, storyboard, subtitles, supporting role, titles, trailer, voice-over, wide-screen

▶ A list of films by a particular actor or director is a **filmography**.

▶ A person who enjoys watching films is a **cinephile** or (informal) **film buff**.

SEE ALSO television

filter VERB

1 *The water must be filtered before drinking.*
strain, sieve, sift, purify, refine

2 *Rain began to filter through the roof.*
pass, trickle, leak, seep, ooze, percolate

filth NOUN

The beach was covered in filth.
dirt, grime, muck, mess, mud,
sludge, scum, sewage, refuse

filthy ADJECTIVE

1 *Those trainers are filthy!*
dirty, mucky, messy, grimy, grubby,
muddy, soiled, stained, unwashed,
sordid, foul, polluted, contaminated
❙ OPPOSITES clean, pure

2 *telling filthy jokes*
obscene, rude, dirty, vulgar, crude,
bawdy, lewd

final ADJECTIVE

1 *the final moments of the film*
last, closing, finishing, concluding,
terminal
❙ OPPOSITE opening

2 *What was the final result?*
eventual, ultimate, definite,
conclusive, decisive

finale NOUN

The show led up to a grand finale.
end, ending, close, conclusion,
climax, culmination, denouement

finally ADVERB

1 *I've finally managed to finish my book.*
eventually, at last, in the end
❙ IDIOM at long last

2 *Finally, I'd like to say a few words.*
lastly, in conclusion

finance NOUN

1 *a company dealing in finance*
financial affairs, money matters,
economics, investment, commerce,
banking, accounting

2 *Our finances are in the red.*
money, bank account, funds,
resources, assets, wealth

finance VERB

They needed money to finance their film.
pay for, fund, subsidize, invest in,
sponsor, back

financial ADJECTIVE

chaos in the financial markets
monetary, money, economic, fiscal,
commercial, banking
(formal) pecuniary

find VERB

1 *Did you ever find your keys?*
locate, spot, track down, trace,
recover, retrieve, detect, identify
❙ OPPOSITE lose

2 *We found a perfect place for a picnic.*
come across, discover, encounter,
stumble on, unearth, uncover

3 *You might find that you feel tired.*
become aware, realize, learn,
recognize, notice, observe

findings PLURAL NOUN

the findings of the police investigation
conclusions, judgement, verdict,
decision

fine① ADJECTIVE

1 *a fine example of Dutch painting*
excellent, first-class, superb,
splendid, admirable, commendable,
good
❙ OPPOSITE bad

2 *a day of fine weather*
sunny, fair, dry, bright, clear,
cloudless, pleasant
❙ OPPOSITE dull

3 *woven from fine silk*
delicate, lightweight, thin, fragile,
flimsy, slender, slim
❙ OPPOSITE thick

4 *a layer of fine sand*
fine-grained, dusty, powdery
❙ OPPOSITE coarse

5 *You're looking fine today.*
well, healthy, all right, in good shape
❙ IDIOM in the pink

6 *That all sounds fine to me.*
all right, acceptable, passable,
satisfactory
(informal) OK

fine② NOUN

a fine for speeding

a
b
c
d
e
f
g
h
i
j
k
l
m
n
o
p
q
r
s
t
u
v
w
x
y
z

penalty, forfeit, charge, damages

finger NOUN

wearing a ring on her finger
digit

WORD WEB

the fingers on a hand (in order)
thumb, index finger, middle
finger, ring finger, little finger
(Scottish & North American pinkie)

► The forensic study of fingerprints
is **fingerprinting** or **fingerprint
analysis**.

► The patterns used to classify
fingerprints are **arc**, **loop**, and
whorl.

finger VERB

*Kurt fingered his moustache
nervously.*
touch, feel, handle, fondle, caress,
play with, toy with

fingerprint NOUN
SEE **finger**

finicky ADJECTIVE

Cats can be finicky about their food.
fussy, hard to please, particular
(informal) choosy, picky

finish VERB

1 *Have you finished your homework?*
complete, reach the end of,
accomplish, discharge, round off
(informal) wrap up

2 *I've already finished my coffee.*
consume, use up, get through,
exhaust, empty, drain
(informal) polish off

3 *The concert finishes at ten o'clock.*
end, stop, conclude, come to a stop,
cease, terminate
(informal) wind up
OPPOSITES start, begin

finish NOUN

1 *We watched the film until the finish.*
end, close, conclusion, completion,
result, termination

OPPOSITE start

2 *furniture with a glossy finish*
surface, polish, shine, gloss, glaze,
sheen, lustre, patina

fire NOUN

warming our toes at the fire
blaze, flames, bonfire, burning,
conflagration, combustion, inferno

▷ **catch fire**
The leaves caught fire quickly.
catch light, ignite, kindle
IDIOMS burst into flames, go up in
smoke

▷ **on fire**
The forest was soon on fire.
burning, flaming, blazing, alight,
in flames, aflame, ablaze

▷ **set fire to**
They tried to set fire to the school.
set alight, set on fire, ignite, kindle

► The crime of deliberately setting fire
to a building is **arson**.

fire VERB

1 *firing pots in a kiln*
bake, harden, heat

2 *firing a rifle*
shoot, discharge, let off, set off

► To fire a missile is to **launch** it.

3 *(informal) He was fired for being late
for work.*
dismiss, discharge
(informal) sack

4 *The story fired our imagination.*
excite, stimulate, stir up, rouse,
animate, inflame

fireworks PLURAL NOUN

a display of fireworks
pyrotechnics

► A person who designs fireworks
is a **pyrotechnician**.

firm❶ NOUN

a family-run firm
company, business, corporation,
organization, enterprise

firm❷ ADJECTIVE

1 *The ground was firm underfoot.*
hard, solid, dense, compact, rigid,

inflexible, unyielding, set
OPPOSITE soft

2 *a firm grip*
secure, tight, strong, stable, fixed, rooted, sturdy, steady, immovable

3 *a firm belief in yourself*
definite, certain, sure, decided, determined, resolute, unshakeable, unwavering, unswerving
OPPOSITE unsure

4 *firm friends*
close, devoted, faithful, loyal, constant, steadfast, long-standing

first ADJECTIVE

1 *the first chapter of a book*
earliest, opening, introductory, preliminary
▶ The first meeting of a group, or first issue of a magazine, is its **inaugural** meeting or issue.
▶ The first voyage of a ship is its **maiden** voyage.

2 *starting from first principles*
basic, fundamental, essential, rudimentary

3 *Safety is our first priority.*
foremost, principal, key, main, chief, primary, central

▷ **at first**
At first, no one spoke.
at the beginning, to start with, initially, originally

first-class ADJECTIVE

a first-class game of cricket
excellent, first-rate, outstanding, superb, exceptional, superior, superlative, top-notch
OPPOSITES second-rate, mediocre

fish NOUN

 WORD WEB

some common fish
bream, catfish, cod, dogfish, eel, flounder, haddock, hake, halibut, herring, mackerel, marlin, minnow, monkfish, mullet, pike, pilchard, roach, salmon, sardine, shark, sole, sprat, stickleback, stingray, sturgeon, swordfish, trout, tuna, turbot, whiting

▶ Fish with skeletons made of bone are **bony fish**. Fish such as sharks, with skeletons made of cartilage, are **cartilaginous fish**.
▶ Fish that live mainly in the sea are **marine fish** and fish that live mainly in rivers are **freshwater fish**. A tiny freshwater fish is a **minnow**. Most fish reproduce by **spawning** (laying and fertilizing eggs).
▶ The scientific study of fish is **ichthyology**.

parts of a fish
backbone, belly, fins, gills, lateral line, scales, swim bladder, tail
▶ The fin on the back of a fish is its **dorsal fin**. A fish's tail is also called a **caudal fin**.
Some fish have whiskers known as **barbels**.
FOR SHELLFISH SEE crustacean

fish VERB

fishing in my pocket for the keys
rummage, search, delve, ferret

fishing NOUN

a fishing trip
angling, trawling

fit ADJECTIVE

1 *a meal fit for a king*
suitable, appropriate, fitting, right, good enough, worthy (of)
OPPOSITE unsuitable

2 *going to the gym to keep fit*
healthy, well, strong, robust, in good shape, in trim
(old use) hale and hearty
OPPOSITES unfit, unhealthy

3 *feeling fit to collapse*
ready, liable, likely, about

fit VERB

1 *fitting a new lock on the door*

a b c d e f g h i j k l m n o p q r s t u v w x y z

install, put in place, position, fix

2 *He fits the description in the paper.*
match, correspond to, conform to, go together with, tally with

▌**IDIOM** fit the bill

3 *I chose a dress to fit the occasion*
be suitable for, be appropriate to, suit

fit NOUN

1 *an epileptic fit*
seizure, spasm, convulsion, attack

2 *a fit of anger*
outburst, outbreak, bout, spell, attack

fitful ADJECTIVE

periods of fitful sleep
sporadic, intermittent, irregular, spasmodic

▌**OPPOSITES** regular, steady

fitness NOUN

1 *Swimming will increase your overall fitness.*
health, healthiness, strength, vigour, condition, shape

2 *Do you doubt my fitness for the job?*
suitability, aptitude, capability, ability, competence

fitting ADJECTIVE

a fitting end to the evening
suitable, appropriate, apt, proper, seemly

▌**OPPOSITE** inappropriate

fix VERB

1 *fixing a satellite dish to the roof*
fasten, attach, secure, make firm, connect, join, link, install

2 *Let's fix a time to meet.*
decide on, agree on, set, arrange, settle, determine, specify, finalize

3 *(informal) Can you fix my laptop?*
repair, mend, sort, put right, restore

fix NOUN

(informal) You've got yourself into a real fix.
difficulty, mess, predicament, plight, corner
(informal) jam, hole,

pickle, tight spot

fixation NOUN

a fixation about horses
obsession, preoccupation, infatuation, compulsion
(informal) thing, hang-up

fixed ADJECTIVE

The date is fixed for next Tuesday.
set, arranged, decided, agreed, confirmed, definite, established, predetermined

▌**OPPOSITES** undecided, unconfirmed

fizz VERB

Shake the bottle to make it fizz.
bubble, sparkle, effervesce, froth, foam, fizzle, hiss

fizzy ADJECTIVE

a bottle of fizzy water
sparkling, bubbly, effervescent, gassy, frothy, carbonated

▌**OPPOSITE** still

flabbergasted ADJECTIVE

Julia was flabbergasted by the news.
astonished, amazed, astounded, staggered, stunned, taken aback
(British informal) gobsmacked

flabby ADJECTIVE

an exercise for flabby thighs
fat, fleshy, sagging, slack, loose, lax, floppy, limp, flaccid

▌**OPPOSITE** firm

flag NOUN

hoisting the Olympic flag
banner, pennant, streamer, standard, colours, ensign

flag VERB

1 *The runners were flagging towards the finish.*
tire, weaken, wilt, droop

2 *By afternoon, my energy began to flag.*
diminish, decrease, decline, lessen, fade, dwindle, wane, abate, subside, slump

▌**OPPOSITE** revive

flagrant ADJECTIVE

a flagrant violation of the rules
blatant, glaring, obvious,
conspicuous, undisguised, brazen

flair NOUN

a flair for drawing cartoons
talent, aptitude, skill, facility, gift,
knack

flake NOUN

a flake of plaster from the ceiling
sliver, shaving, paring, wafer,
fragment, chip

flamboyant ADJECTIVE

a flamboyant style of dress
ostentatious, exuberant, showy,
flashy
| OPPOSITES restrained, modest

flammable ADJECTIVE

made of flammable material
inflammable
| OPPOSITES non-flammable,
fireproof, fire-resistant,
fire-retardant

Usage Note

The words **flammable** and
inflammable mean the same
thing. They are not opposites of
each other.

flank NOUN

1 *the horse's flanks*
side, haunch, thigh
2 *the left flank of the battalion*
side, wing, sector, section, part

flank VERB

an avenue flanked by poplar trees
edge, border, fringe, line

flap VERB

1 *clothes flapping in the wind*
flutter, sway, swing, wave about,
thrash about
2 *a bat flapping its wings*
beat, flutter, wag, thrash, flail

flare VERB

1 *A match flared suddenly*

in the darkness.
blaze, burn, flash
2 *a bull flaring its nostrils*
spread, splay, widen, broaden, dilate
▷ **flare up**
The rash tends to flare up at night.
break out, erupt, reappear, worsen

flash NOUN

1 *the flash of a torch light*
blaze, flare, beam, ray, shaft, burst,
gleam, glint, flicker, glimmer,
sparkle
| SEE ALSO light❶

2 *an occasional flash of genius*
burst, outburst, show, display

flash VERB

1 *Two searchlights flashed across the*
sky.
shine, beam, blaze, flare, glare,
gleam, glint, flicker, glimmer,
sparkle
2 *The ball flashed past the keeper into*
the net.
speed, fly, rush, hurtle

flashy ADJECTIVE

Fraser was wearing a flashy tie.
elaborate, decorative, ornate,
ornamented, showy, flamboyant
(informal) snazzy, jazzy
| OPPOSITE plain

flat ADJECTIVE

1 *a flat surface to write on*
level, even, smooth, plane
| OPPOSITE uneven
2 *lying flat on the ground*
horizontal, outstretched, spread out,
spreadeagled
▶ To lie flat, face downwards is to be
prone or **prostrate**, and to lie flat,
face upwards is to be **supine**.
| OPPOSITE upright
3 *a flat tyre*
deflated, punctured, burst
| OPPOSITE inflated
4 *a flat refusal*
outright, straight, positive, absolute,
definite, point-blank *speaking in a*
≫

a b c d e f g h i j k l m n o p q r s t u v w x y z

flat tone
monotonous, toneless, featureless, droning, lifeless, dull, tedious
OPPOSITE lively

flat *NOUN*

a two-bedroom flat in the city
apartment, rooms
▶ A luxurious flat at the top of a building is a **penthouse**.
SEE ALSO building

flatten *VERB*

1 *Flatten the dough with your hands.*
smooth, press, roll out, iron out
2 *The bombing flattened most of the city.*
demolish, destroy, knock down, pull down, level
3 *a track where feet had flattened the grass*
squash, press down, compress, crush, trample

flatter *VERB*

1 *He was only trying to flatter you.*
compliment, praise, fawn on, toady
(informal) butter up
IDIOM curry favour with
2 *I was flattered to be invited.*
honour, gratify, please
(informal) tickle pink

flattery *NOUN*

Flattery never works on her.
compliments, praise, fawning, toadying
(informal) sweet talk, soft soap

flaunt *VERB*

celebrities flaunting their wealth
show off, display, parade, exhibit

flavour *NOUN*

1 *a strong flavour of garlic*
taste, tang, savour, smack, relish
SEE ALSO taste
2 *a city with an East European flavour*
quality, style, character, feeling, atmosphere, air, mood, ambience

flavour *VERB*

rice flavoured with saffron
season, spice, infuse, imbue

flaw *NOUN*

1 *a single flaw in his character*
weakness, fault, shortcoming, deficiency, failing, weak point
IDIOM Achilles' heel
OPPOSITES strength, strong point
2 *I can see a flaw in your argument.*
error, inaccuracy, mistake, fallacy, lapse, slip
3 *a tiny flaw in the glass*
imperfection, defect, blemish, break, chip, crack, fracture

flawless *ADJECTIVE*

a flawless performance
perfect, faultless, immaculate, impeccable, spotless
OPPOSITES imperfect, flawed

fleck *NOUN*

a few flecks of paint
spot, speck, mark, dot, dab
SEE ALSO bit

flee *VERB*

The crowd fled in panic.
run away, bolt, fly, escape, get away, take off, hurry off
(informal) clear off, scram, scarper
IDIOMS take to your heels, beat a hasty retreat

fleet *NOUN*

a fleet of warships
navy, flotilla, convoy, armada

fleeting *ADJECTIVE*

a fleeting glimpse of a deer
brief, momentary, quick, short-lived, cursory, passing, transient
OPPOSITES lengthy, lasting

flesh *NOUN*

1 *The knife slipped and cut into his flesh.*
skin, tissue, muscle, meat, brawn, body
2 *Scoop out the flesh of the pumpkin.*
pulp, marrow, meat

flex *VERB*

a weightlifter flexing his muscles
bend, contract, tighten
OPPOSITE straighten

flex NOUN

a long flex for the computer
cable, lead, wire, cord

flexible ADJECTIVE

1 *shoes with flexible soles*
bendable, supple, pliable, bendy,
elastic, springy
OPPOSITES rigid, inflexible
2 *flexible working hours*
adjustable, adaptable, variable, open
OPPOSITE fixed

flick NOUN

a quick flick of the wrist
swish, twitch, jerk, snap, flip

flick VERB

1 *a horse flicking its tail*
swish, twitch, jerk, whip
2 *flicking a light switch*
press, flip, throw, activate
▷ **flick through**
flicking through a magazine
leaf through, thumb through,
browse through, skim, scan

flicker VERB

1 *candles flickering in the draught*
glimmer, waver, flutter, blink, wink,
sparkle, twinkle, dance
SEE ALSO light❶
2 *I thought I saw her eyelids flicker.*
flutter, quiver, tremble, twitch,
shudder

flight NOUN

1 *a book about the history of flight*
flying, aviation, aeronautics,
air travel
2 *a ten-hour flight to Tokyo*
journey, voyage, trip
3 *the refugees' flight to safety*
escape, getaway, retreat, exit,
exodus

flimsy ADJECTIVE

1 *a flimsy ladder made of rotting wood*
fragile, delicate, frail, brittle, weak,
wobbly, shaky, rickety,
OPPOSITES sturdy, robust
2 *based on flimsy evidence*
weak, insubstantial, unconvincing,
implausible
OPPOSITES sound, substantial

flinch VERB

*I flinched as a stone flew past my
head.*
back off, draw back, falter, recoil,
shrink back, start, wince

fling VERB

flinging pebbles into the sea
throw, cast, sling, toss, hurl, heave,
pitch, lob, launch, propel, let fly
(informal) chuck

flip VERB

*Flip the pancake to cook the other
side.*
toss, turn, flick, spin

flippant ADJECTIVE

a flippant remark about the war
frivolous, facetious, disrespectful,
irreverent, cheeky
OPPOSITE serious

flirt VERB

▷ **flirt with**
1 *She always flirts with boys at parties.*
make advances to, lead on
(informal) chat up
2 *He flirted with the idea of being
a writer.*
toy with, consider, entertain,
trifle with

float VERB

1 *The raft floated gently down the
river.*
sail, drift, glide, slip, slide, waft
2 *The ball appeared to floating in
mid-air.*
hover, hang, be suspended, levitate

flock NOUN

1 *a flock of geese*
SEE **bird**
2 *a flock of sheep*
SEE **animal**

flock VERB

Fans flocked round the stage door.
crowd, gather, collect, congregate,

assemble, mass, throng, swarm, herd, cluster, converge

flog *VERB*
Slaves used to be flogged for running away.
whip, thrash, beat, lash, scourge, flay

flood *NOUN*
1 *The flood swept away several cars.*
deluge, inundation, torrent, spate
2 *We received a flood of emails.*
succession, barrage, storm, volley, rush, profusion, outpouring

flood *VERB*
1 *The river burst its banks and flooded the village.*
inundate, swamp, drown, submerge, immerse, engulf, drench
2 *Shops have been flooded with cheap imports.*
saturate, swamp, overwhelm, glut

floor *NOUN*
1 *a rug on the floor*
ground, flooring, base
2 *the top floor of the building*
storey, level, tier, deck, stage

flop *VERB*
1 *Fiona came in and flopped onto the sofa.*
collapse, drop, fall, slump
2 *His legs flopped over the edge of the bed.*
dangle, droop, hang down, sag, wilt
3 *(informal) Their first CD flopped in the charts.*
be unsuccessful, fail, founder, fall flat

floppy *ADJECTIVE*
a rabbit with long, floppy ears
drooping, droopy, hanging, dangling, limp, saggy, flaccid
▌**OPPOSITES** stiff, erect

flora *NOUN*
SEE **plant**

flounder *VERB*
1 *horses floundering in the mud*
struggle, stumble, stagger, fumble, wallow

2 *I found myself floundering to answer the question.*
struggle, falter, hesitate, blunder
▌**IDIOM** be out of your depth

flourish *VERB*
1 *Our garden is flourishing this year.*
grow well, thrive, bloom, blossom, flower
▌**OPPOSITE** die
2 *Sales have continued to flourish.*
be successful, do well, prosper, thrive, boom, succeed, progress, develop, increase
▌**OPPOSITE** fail
3 *a man flourishing an umbrella*
brandish, wield, wave, shake, display

flout *VERB*
Players were accused of flouting the rules.
disobey, disregard, defy, ignore, breach, contravene, infringe, violate
▌**IDIOM** fly in the face of

flow *VERB*
1 *a river flowing through the forest*
run, pour, stream, roll, course, circulate, sweep, swirl, cascade, teem, gush, surge, spurt
▶ When the tide flows out, it **ebbs**.
2 *traffic flowing in both directions*
move, go, run, rush
3 *words flowing fast from her pen*
come out, emanate, pour, rush

flow *NOUN*
1 *a steady flow of water*
stream, course, current, tide, drift, circulation, flood, gush, spate, flux, outpouring
2 *the constant flow of traffic*
movement, motion, circulation, rush

flower *NOUN*
a bunch of wild flowers
bloom, blossom, bud
▶ A bunch of cut flowers is also called a **bouquet** or **posy**.

WORD WEB

some common flowers

African violet, anemone, aster, bluebell, carnation, chrysanthemum, cornflower, crocus, daffodil, dahlia, daisy, delphinium, forget-me-not, foxglove, freesia, fuchsia, geranium, gladiolus, hyacinth, iris, lilac, lily, lupin, marigold, narcissus, orchid, pansy, petunia, phlox, poinsettia, primrose, rose, snapdragon, snowdrop, sunflower, sweet pea, tulip, violet

► The scientific study of plants and flowers is **botany**.

► A person who sells or arranges cut flowers is a **florist**.

parts of a flower

anthers, filaments, ovary, ovules, petals, pistil, sepals, stamen, stigma, style

► The parts of the **stamen** are: **anthers** (containing **pollen**) and **filaments**.

► The parts of the **pistil** are: **stigma**, **style**, and **ovary** (containing **ovules**).

SEE ALSO plant

flower *VERB*

Our snowdrops started to flower in January.
bloom, blossom, bud

flowery *ADJECTIVE*

a flowery passage from the novel
ornate, elaborate, florid, purple

fluctuate *VERB*

Prices have fluctuated in the past year.
vary, change, alter, shift, waver, oscillate, rise and fall
OPPOSITE stabilize

fluent *ADJECTIVE*

She is a fluent speaker on almost any topic.

articulate, eloquent, communicative
OPPOSITES inarticulate, uncommunicative

fluffy *ADJECTIVE*

a fluffy scarf
feathery, downy, furry, fuzzy, hairy, shaggy

fluid *NOUN*

Fluid was leaking from the engine.
liquid, solution, juice, liquor, gas, vapour
OPPOSITE solid

fluid *ADJECTIVE*

1 *Try to keep the mixture fluid.*
liquid, free-flowing, runny, watery, molten, melted, liquefied
OPPOSITE solid

2 *Our holiday plans are still fluid.*
changeable, variable, flexible, open
OPPOSITE fixed

flurry *NOUN*

1 *a flurry of snow*
swirl, whirl, eddy, gust

2 *a flurry of activity*
burst, outbreak, spurt, fit, bout, spell

flush *VERB*

1 *Amanda flushed with embarrassment.*
blush, go red, colour, redden, burn

2 *The rain flushed away all the dirt.*
wash, rinse, sluice, swill

flustered *ADJECTIVE*

Some passengers were flustered by the noise.
confused, upset, bothered, agitated, unsettled, unnerved, ruffled
(informal) rattled
OPPOSITE calm

flutter *VERB*

1 *a moth fluttering its wings*
flap, beat, flicker, quiver, tremble, vibrate

2 *flags fluttering in the breeze*
waver, flap, ripple, ruffle, undulate

fly *NOUN*

SEE **insect**

fly VERB

1 *Two eagles flew high above our heads.*
glide, soar, swoop, wheel, wing, flit, hover, float

2 *Everyone was flying past us in a hurry.*
run, speed, rush, hurry, tear, zoom

3 *a ship flying a British flag*
display, show, hoist, raise

4 *The morning just seemed to fly.*
go quickly, pass quickly, rush by

foam NOUN

a layer of white foam
bubbles, froth, suds, lather, surf, spume, effervescence

foam VERB

The yeast started to foam.
froth, bubble, seethe, boil, lather, fizz, ferment, effervesce

focus NOUN

1 *the focus of the world's attention*
centre, focal point, target, gist, core, heart, nucleus, pivot, hub

2 *a magazine with a focus on music*
emphasis, spotlight, highlight, concentration, attention, stress, accent

focus VERB

▷ **focus on**
I'm trying to focus on my work.
concentrate on, pay attention to, centre on, zero in on, spotlight, pinpoint

fog NOUN

fog rolling in from the sea
mist, haze, murk, smog
(informal) pea-souper
(Scottish) haar

foggy ADJECTIVE

1 *a cold and foggy morning*
misty, hazy, murky, cloudy, smoggy

2 *a foggy memory of events*
blurred, dim, indistinct, shadowy, obscure

foil❶ NOUN

Watson is the perfect foil to Sherlock Holmes.
contrast, complement, balance, antithesis

foil❷ VERB

The robbery was foiled by French police.
thwart, frustrate, prevent, obstruct, stop, block, check, circumvent, scotch
(informal) scupper

fold❶ VERB

1 *Fold the paper along the dotted line.*
bend, double over, crease, pleat

2 *(informal) Their business folded last year.*
fail, collapse, crash, go under
(informal) go bust
IDIOM go to the wall

fold NOUN

a fold in the centre of the map
crease, pleat, furrow, tuck, overlap, wrinkle

fold❷ NOUN

a sheep fold
enclosure, pen

folder NOUN

a folder full of sketches
file, binder, wallet, envelope, portfolio

follow VERB

1 *A line of cars followed the limousine.*
go after, chase, pursue, track, trail, tail, stalk, hunt, shadow

2 *Iona follows her sister as team captain.*
come after, succeed, replace, supersede, supplant
OPPOSITE precede

3 *Follow the directions on the map.*
carry out, comply with, heed, obey, observe, keep to, adhere to

4 *I like to follow current events.*
take an interest in, pay attention to, keep up with, support

5 *We couldn't follow what she said.*

understand, comprehend, grasp, take in, catch, fathom

6 *If I'm right, then it follows that you're lying.*
mean, happen, result, ensue, arise, come about

follower NOUN

1 *a loyal follower of the president*
supporter, admirer, fan, attendant, retainer
(informal) sidekick

2 *a follower of cubism*
disciple, pupil, believer, adherent, imitator, emulator

following ADJECTIVE
the following day
next, succeeding, subsequent, ensuing

folly NOUN
an act of sheer folly
foolishness, senselessness, stupidity, foolhardiness

fond ADJECTIVE

1 *a fond farewell*
loving, tender, affectionate, warm, caring

2 *a fond hope*
foolish, unrealistic, fanciful, vain, naive

▷ **be fond of**
I'm very fond of blueberry muffins.
be keen on, be partial to, have a liking for
❙ IDIOM have a soft spot for

fondle VERB
a lioness gently fondling her cubs
caress, stroke, nudge, pet, finger, play with

food NOUN
What kind of food do you like?
foodstuffs, refreshments, eatables, nourishment, nutrition, nutriment, sustenance, rations, provisions, victuals, fare, meals, board
(informal) grub, nosh
▶ Food for farm animals is **feed** or **fodder**.

 WORD WEB

terms relating to food and nutrition
calorie, calorific, carbohydrate, dairy, deficiency, deficient, diet, energy, fat, fibre, food chain, food group, high-fat, low-fat, mineral, non-dairy, nutrient, protein, salt, starch, trace element, vegan, vegetarian, vitamin

❙ SEE ALSO **diet**, **digestion**

FOR WAYS TO PREPARE FOOD SEE **cook**

FOR TIPS ON DESCRIBING TASTE SEE **taste**

fool NOUN

1 *Only a fool would believe that story.*
idiot, ass, clown, halfwit, dunce, simpleton, blockhead, buffoon, dunderhead, imbecile, moron
(informal) chump, dope, dummy, dimwit, nitwit, nincompoop, ninny
(British informal) twit, clot, wally

2 *a medieval fool with cap and bells*
jester, clown, buffoon

fool VERB
Don't be fooled by her friendly smile.
deceive, trick, mislead, delude, dupe, gull, hoodwink, hoax
(informal) con, kid, have on, take in
❙ IDIOMS pull the wool over your eyes, take you for a ride

▷ **fool about** or **around**
Stop fooling around and listen!
play about, mess about, misbehave

foolish ADJECTIVE
a foolish idea
stupid, silly, idiotic, senseless, ridiculous, nonsensical, unwise, ill-advised, half-witted, unintelligent, absurd, crazy, mad, hare-brained, foolhardy
(informal) dim-witted, dumb
(British informal) daft, barmy
❙ OPPOSITE sensible

a
b
c
d
e
f
g
h
i
j
k
l
m
n
o
p
q
r
s
t
u
v
w
x
y
z

foot NOUN

1 *one foot in front of the other*
   SEE **word web** BELOW
2 *the foot of the page*
   bottom, base, foundation
   OPPOSITES top, head, summit

WORD WEB

parts of a foot
ankle, arch, ball, heel, instep,
sole, toes

▶ The branch of medicine which
treats foot disorders is **chiropody**
or **podiatry**.

types of animal and bird feet
claw, hoof, pad, paw, talon,
trotter

football NOUN

a friendly game of football
(North American & Australian) soccer

WORD WEB

terms used in football
back of the net, booking,
captain, corner flag, corner kick,
crossbar, defender, deflection,
dugout, far post, forward, foul,
free kick, fullback, goalkeeper,
goal kick, goal line, goalpost,
halftime, hat-trick, header, injury
time, kick-off, linesman, midfield,
near post, offside, penalty kick,
penalty shoot-out, penalty spot,
pitch, possession, red card,
referee, relegation, sending
off, set play, sideline, stadium,
striker, substitution, suspension,
tackle, throw-in, yellow card

FOR TIPS ON WRITING ABOUT SPORT
SEE **sport**

footing NOUN

1 *He lost his footing on the rocks.*
   foothold, base, foundation, ground,
   balance, purchase
2 *on an equal footing with*

the neighbours
status, standing, position,
relationship, terms, basis

footstep NOUN

the sound of footsteps
step, tread, footfall

forage VERB

animals foraging for food
search, hunt, scour, rummage, ferret

forbid VERB

I forbid you to see her again.
prohibit, ban, bar, rule out,
proscribe, veto, debar
OPPOSITES permit, allow

Usage Note

The words **bar** and **debar** mean
the same thing. They are not
opposites of each other.

forbidden ADJECTIVE

*Taking photographs is strictly
forbidden.*
prohibited, banned, barred,
outlawed, vetoed
OPPOSITES permitted, allowed

forbidding ADJECTIVE

*The prison had a grim, forbidding
look.*
threatening, menacing, sinister,
ominous, uninviting, daunting
OPPOSITE inviting

force NOUN

1 *They had to use force to open the
door.*
strength, power, might, muscle,
vigour, effort, energy
2 *The force of the explosion shattered
the glass.*
impact, shock, intensity
3 *an international peace-keeping force*
group, unit, team, corps, body,
detachment, squad

force VERB

1 *They were forced to work for low
wages.*

Left margin: a b c d e f g h i j k l m n o p q r s t u v w x y z

compel, coerce, constrain, drive,
impel, order, make, pressure into,
bully into

2 *I had to force my way through the
crowd.*
push, shove, drive, propel, press,
thrust

3 *Firefighters had to force the door.*
break open, burst open, break down,
kick in

forced *ADJECTIVE*

Zara waved and gave a forced smile.
unnatural, strained, stiff, stilted,
contrived, affected, feigned
(informal) put on
❚ OPPOSITES natural, spontaneous

forceful *ADJECTIVE*

1 *a forceful personality*
strong, powerful, dynamic, vigorous,
assertive, pushy
(informal) in-your-face
❚ OPPOSITES weak, submissive

2 *a forceful argument*
convincing, compelling, strong,
powerful, persuasive, weighty
❚ OPPOSITES weak, unconvincing

forecast *VERB*

Gales have been forecast for Tuesday.
predict, foresee, foretell, prophesy

forecast *NOUN*

the weather forecast for tomorrow
outlook, prediction, prognosis,
prophecy

foreign *ADJECTIVE*

1 *a party of foreign visitors*
overseas, international, non-native
❚ OPPOSITES native, domestic

2 *travelling to foreign countries*
overseas, distant, faraway, exotic,
remote, far-flung

3 *The idea of cooking is foreign to him.*
unnatural, unfamiliar, strange, alien

✴ WORD WEB

French phrases used in English
au fait, au pair, bête noire,
bon voyage, déjà vu, de rigueur,
de trop, double entendre, en
bloc, en passant, en route,
esprit de corps, fait accompli,
joie de vivre, laissez-faire, nom
de plume, nouveau riche, objet
d'art, raison d'être, à la carte,
tête-à-tête

Latin phrases used in English
ad hoc, ad lib, ad nauseam, bona
fide, de facto, in memoriam, in
situ, per annum, per capita, rigor
mortis, status quo, terra firma,
vice versa

foreigner *NOUN*

*Many foreigners have come to live
here.*
overseas visitor, stranger, outsider,
newcomer, incomer, settler
(formal) alien

▶ A foreigner who comes to live in a
country is an **immigrant**.

foremost *ADJECTIVE*

the foremost actor of his generation
leading, greatest, best, pre-eminent,
principal, premier, supreme, chief,
top, prime
(informal) number-one

forensic *ADJECTIVE*

SEE **crime**

foresee *VERB*

Few people foresaw the crisis ahead.
anticipate, expect, predict, forecast,
prophesy, foretell

forest *NOUN*

SEE **tree**

foretell *VERB*

1 *The witches foretold that Macbeth
would be king.*
predict, prophesy, forecast, foresee

2 *The clouds foretold a change in the
weather.*
warn of, herald, signify

forever *ADVERB*

1 *Will you love me forever?*

a
b
c
d
e
f
g
h
i
j
k
l
m
n
o
p
q
r
s
t
u
v
w
x
y
z

for all time, for ever and ever, for good, for eternity, until the end of time, evermore

2 *Cal is forever complaining about something.*
constantly, continually, always, perpetually, incessantly, repeatedly, regularly

forge VERB

1 *Modern horseshoes are forged from steel.*
fashion, hammer out, beat out

2 *That signature has been forged.*
fake, copy, counterfeit, falsify

▷ **forge ahead**
The race favourites were soon forging ahead.
advance, make progress, make headway

forgery NOUN

One of these paintings is a forgery.
fake, copy, counterfeit, fraud, imitation, replica
(informal) phoney

forget VERB

1 *Did you forget your mobile phone?*
leave behind, leave out, overlook

2 *I forgot to switch off the computer.*
omit, neglect, fail
❙ OPPOSITE remember

forgetful ADJECTIVE

He's getting forgetful in his old age.
absent-minded, dreamy, inattentive, heedless, oblivious

forgive VERB

1 *She never forgave him for what he did.*
pardon, excuse, let off, absolve, exonerate

2 *Please forgive my rudeness.*
excuse, pardon, overlook, disregard, indulge, make allowances for
❙ IDIOM turn a blind eye to

fork VERB

The path ahead forks into two.
split, branch, divide, separate, part, diverge

form NOUN

1 *the intricate form of a snowflake*
shape, structure, design, outline, format, layout, formation, configuration, arrangement

2 *drawing the human form*
body, figure, shape, frame, physique, anatomy

3 *Haiku is a form of poetry.*
kind, sort, type, variety, category, class, genre

4 *The team is in top form this season*
performance, ability, condition, shape

5 *Please fill in this form.*
questionnaire, document, sheet, slip

6 *Which form is your sister in?*
class, year
(North American) grade

form VERB

1 *The bat is formed from a single piece of wood.*
shape, mould, model, fashion, build, fabricate, construct

2 *We decided to form a book club.*
set up, establish, found, create, start, institute, launch

3 *Icicles were forming on the window.*
appear, develop, grow, emerge, materialize, take shape

formal ADJECTIVE

1 *Dinner was to be a formal occasion.*
ceremonious, ceremonial, official, stately, grand, solemn
❙ OPPOSITES informal, casual, unofficial

2 *Her manner was always very formal.*
correct, proper, dignified, reserved, stiff, cold, aloof
(informal) stand-offish
❙ OPPOSITES informal, friendly, warm

format NOUN

The book is being reissued in a new format.
design, style, form, appearance, look, layout, arrangement

formation *NOUN*

  1 *an unusual rock formation*
structure, construction,
configuration, arrangement,
grouping, pattern

  2 *the formation of a new team*
creation, establishment, setting up,
foundation, institution

former *ADJECTIVE*

  1 *the former head of the FBI*
previous, preceding, past, ex-,
one-time
(formal) erstwhile

  2 *a photograph of the house in former
times*
earlier, past, previous, prior, bygone,
olden, of old

formerly *ADVERB*

*The painting was formerly done
by hand.*
previously, earlier, before, in the
past, once, at one time, until now

formidable *ADJECTIVE*

*The young crew faces a formidable
challenge.*
daunting, intimidating, forbidding,
difficult, tough, stiff

formula *NOUN*

a formula for making invisible ink
recipe, prescription, procedure

formulate *VERB*

formulating a new plan
devise, think up, come up with,
conceive, concoct, work out,
draw up, forge, hatch

fort *NOUN*

the remains of a Roman fort
fortress, fortification, stronghold,
castle, citadel, tower
❙ SEE ALSO castle

forthcoming *ADJECTIVE*

a list of forthcoming events
upcoming, future, approaching,
impending, imminent

fortify *VERB*

  1 *The wall was built to fortify*
the old city.
defend, protect, secure, strengthen,
reinforce

  2 *I felt fortified after breakfast.*
invigorate, energize, enliven,
strengthen, bolster, boost
❙ OPPOSITE weaken

fortress *NOUN*

SEE **fort**

fortunate *ADJECTIVE*

*We were fortunate to have good
weather.*
lucky, in luck, favoured, blessed
❙ OPPOSITES unfortunate, unlucky

fortunately *ADVERB*

Fortunately, no one was injured.
luckily, happily, thankfully,
mercifully, by good fortune
❙ IDIOM as luck would have it

fortune *NOUN*

  1 *hoping for a change in fortune*
luck, chance, accident, fate, destiny,
predestination

  2 *He left home at a young age to seek
his fortune.*
success, prosperity

  3 *a family that built up a vast fortune*
wealth, riches, assets, possessions,
property, estate
(informal) millions

fortune-teller *NOUN*

*A fortune-teller offered to read my
palm.*
soothsayer, clairvoyant, psychic,
seer, augur, card-reader, astrologer

fortune telling *NOUN*

a crystal ball used for fortune telling
divination, divining, soothsaying,
augury, clairvoyance

 WORD WEB

methods of fortune telling
astrology, cartomancy (card
reading), crystal-ball gazing,
necromancy (communicating
with the dead),   »

a
b
c
d
e
f
g
h
i
j
k
l
m
n
o
p
q
r
s
t
u
v
w
x
y
z

oneiromancy (dream interpretation), palmistry (palm reading), rune-casting, scrying (gazing in a mirror or bowl), sortilege (casting lots), tarot reading, tasseography (reading tea leaves)

SEE ALSO zodiac

forward or **forwards** *ADJECTIVE*

1 *a forward dive from a springboard*
front-facing, front, frontal, onward
OPPOSITES backward, rear

2 *doing some forward planning*
advance, early, future
OPPOSITE retrospective

3 *Would it be too forward to ask him out?*
bold, cheeky, brash, familiar, impudent, presumptuous
OPPOSITE shy

forward *ADVERB*

1 *The queue moved forward very slowly.*
on, onwards, along, ahead

2 *They asked volunteers to step forward.*
out, into view, forth

3 *a seat facing forwards*
to the front, towards the front, ahead
OPPOSITES backwards, back

fossil *NOUN*

WORD WEB

some types of fossil
amber (resin), ammonite, belemnite, bivalve, blastoid, brachiopod, crinoid, dinosaur bone, echinoid (sea urchin), orthoceras, trilobite

▶ To turn a plant or animal into a fossil is to **fossilize** it.
▶ Wood that has been fossilized is **fossil wood** or **petrified wood**.

▶ Coal, natural gas, and petroleum are called **fossil fuels**.
▶ The scientific study of fossils is **palaeontology**.

foster *VERB*

1 *fostering a child*
bring up, rear, raise, care for, look after, take care of
▶ To **adopt** a child is to make them legally a full member of your family.

2 *fostering a love of literature*
encourage, promote, nurture, stimulate, cultivate, develop, further

fought *PAST TENSE*
SEE **fight**

foul *ADJECTIVE*

1 *the foul smell of rotting food*
disgusting, revolting, repulsive, repugnant, offensive, loathsome, nasty, horrible, vile, stinking, sickening, nauseating
(informal) gross
OPPOSITE pleasant

2 *the foul state of the kitchen*
dirty, unclean, filthy, mucky, messy, contaminated
OPPOSITES clean, pure

3 *using foul language*
rude, offensive, improper, indecent, coarse, crude, vulgar, obscene

4 *a foul tackle*
illegal, prohibited, unfair
OPPOSITE fair

found *VERB*

The society was founded a hundred years ago.
establish, set up, start, begin, create, initiate, institute, inaugurate
OPPOSITE dissolve

foundation *NOUN*

1 *There is no foundation for that rumour.*
basis, grounds, evidence, justification

2 *the foundation of the United Nations*
founding, beginning, establishment,

setting up, creation, institution, inception

founder① NOUN

James Hutton was the founder of modern geology.
originator, creator, inventor, father, author, architect

founder② VERB

1 The ship had foundered on the rocks.
go under, sink, submerge
2 The plan foundered after the first few months.
fail, fall through, collapse, come to nothing
(informal) fold, flop, bomb

fountain NOUN

a fountain of water
jet, spout, spray, spring, cascade

fox NOUN

the rare sight of an Arctic fox
► A female fox is a **vixen**.
► A young fox is a **cub**.
► The burrow of a fox is an **earth**.
FOR TIPS ON DESCRIBING ANIMALS SEE **animal**

fox VERB

The last question foxed everyone.
puzzle, baffle, bewilder, mystify, perplex, stump
(informal) flummox, floor

fraction NOUN

I only paid a fraction of the full price.
tiny part, fragment, scrap, snippet
▐ SEE ALSO **bit**

 WORD WEB

types of mathematical fraction
decimal fraction, equivalent fraction, improper fraction, proper fraction

parts of a mathematical fraction
denominator (bottom), numerator (top)
► A whole number plus a fraction is a **mixed number**.

fracture VERB

Ellen fell on the ice and fractured her wrist.
break, crack, split, splinter, snap

fracture NOUN

The X-ray showed a bone fracture.
break, breakage, crack, split, fissure

fragile ADJECTIVE

Reptile eggs are very fragile.
breakable, delicate, frail, brittle, flimsy, weak
▐ OPPOSITES sturdy, robust

fragment NOUN

1 a fragment of broken pottery
bit, piece, chip, sliver, shard, splinter
2 overhearing fragments of a conversation
part, portion, scrap, snippet, snatch

fragment VERB

The comet fragmented into several pieces.
break up, disintegrate, fall apart, fracture, shatter, splinter

fragrance NOUN

the heady fragrance of jasmine
scent, smell, aroma, perfume, bouquet
FOR TIPS ON DESCRIBING SMELLS SEE **smell** NOUN

fragrant ADJECTIVE

The air was fragrant with spices.
sweet-smelling, perfumed, scented, aromatic
▐ OPPOSITES foul-smelling, smelly

frail ADJECTIVE

1 feeling frail after an illness
weak, infirm, feeble
2 That footbridge looks a bit frail.
flimsy, fragile, delicate, rickety, unsound
▐ OPPOSITES strong, robust

frame NOUN

1 a picture frame
mount, mounting, surround, border, setting, edging

》

2 *the frame of an old bicycle*
framework, structure, shell,
skeleton, casing
▶ The framework under a car is the
chassis.

3 *the muscular frame of a bodybuilder*
body, build, physique, anatomy

frame VERB
a face framed by masses of curls
surround, border, edge, set (in)

framework NOUN
1 *the wooden framework of the roof*
frame, structure, shell, skeleton,
scaffolding, support

2 *a new framework for teaching*
plan, system, scheme, strategy,
programme, proposal, blueprint

frank ADJECTIVE
May I be frank with you?
direct, candid, plain, straight,
straightforward, open, honest,
sincere, genuine, forthright, blunt,
matter-of-fact
(informal) upfront
❙ OPPOSITES insincere, evasive

frankly ADVERB
1 *Can we talk frankly?*
candidly, plainly, straightforwardly,
openly, honestly
❙ IDIOM without beating about the
bush

2 *Frankly, I don't believe her.*
to be frank, to be honest,
in all honesty

frantic ADJECTIVE
1 *going frantic with worry*
beside yourself, fraught, desperate,
distraught, overwrought, hysterical,
worked up, berserk
❙ IDIOMS at your wits' end, in a state

2 *a scene of frantic activity*
excited, hectic, frenzied, frenetic,
feverish, wild, mad
❙ OPPOSITE calm

fraud NOUN
1 *being found guilty of fraud*

deceit, deception, dishonesty,
cheating, swindling, chicanery,
sharp practice

2 *The phone-in competition was a
fraud.*
swindle, trick, hoax, pretence, sham
(informal) con, scam

3 *The author was later exposed as a
fraud.*
cheat, swindler, fraudster, trickster,
charlatan
(informal) con man, phoney

fraudulent ADJECTIVE
*Beware of fraudulent email
messages.*
dishonest, bogus, sham, criminal,
corrupt, cheating, swindling
(informal) crooked, phoney, dodgy
❙ OPPOSITE honest

frayed ADJECTIVE
a frayed woollen carpet
tattered, ragged, worn, threadbare
(informal) tatty
(North American informal) raggedy
❙ IDIOM the worse for wear

freak NOUN
1 *a freak of nature*
aberration, abnormality, oddity,
anomaly, fluke

2 *(informal) a health-food freak*
enthusiast, fan, fanatic, devotee
(informal) fiend, nut

free ADJECTIVE
1 *You are free to do as you wish.*
able, allowed, permitted, at liberty
❙ OPPOSITE restricted

2 *All the hostages are now free.*
freed, liberated, released,
emancipated, at large
❙ IDIOM on the loose
❙ OPPOSITES imprisoned, fined,
captive

3 *I got a free drink with my sandwich.*
complimentary, free of charge,
gratis
❙ IDIOM on the house

4 *The bathroom is free now.*

available, unoccupied, vacant, empty, not in use

OPPOSITES engaged, in use

5 *Are you free this weekend?*
available, unoccupied, not busy, at leisure

OPPOSITES busy, occupied

6 *He is very free with his money.*
generous, lavish, liberal, unstinting

OPPOSITE mean

▷ **free from** or **free of**
food which is free of additives
without, clear of, rid of, excused from, exempt from, unaffected by

free VERB

1 *The hostages were eventually freed.*
release, liberate, set free, let go, set loose, untie

▶ To free slaves is to **emancipate** them.

▶ To free hostages by paying money to the captors is to **ransom** them.

OPPOSITES imprison, confine

2 *The hero seeks to free his family of an ancient curse.*
clear, rid, purge

OPPOSITES afflict (with), burden (with)

3 *Rescuers freed the driver from the wreckage.*
extricate, undo, untangle, work loose

freedom NOUN

1 *Colonists fought for freedom in the Revolutionary Wars.*
liberty, independence, liberation, emancipation

2 *the freedom to decide for yourself*
right, entitlement, privilege, licence, prerogative

freely ADVERB

1 *Elephants roam freely in the national park.*
unrestricted, unrestrained, free, at large

2 *He freely admits to taking bribes.*
readily, willingly, voluntarily, openly, frankly, candidly

freeze VERB

1 *Pure water begins to freeze at 0°C.*
become ice, ice over, harden, solidify

OPPOSITE thaw

2 *Vince froze when he heard the scream.*
stand still, remain stationary

IDIOM stop dead in your tracks

3 *Prices have been frozen for another year.*
fix, hold, peg, cap

freezing ADJECTIVE

1 *a freezing winter's day*
chilly, frosty, icy, wintry, raw, bitter, arctic

FOR TIPS ON DESCRIBING WEATHER SEE **weather**

2 *Your hands are freezing!*
frozen, chilled, numb with cold

IDIOMS chilled to the bone, frozen solid

frenzy NOUN

a frenzy of last-minute preparations
excitement, fever, madness, mania, hysteria, panic, fury

frequent ADJECTIVE

1 *sending frequent text messages*
numerous, continual, recurring, recurrent, repeated, periodic, successive

OPPOSITE infrequent

2 *a frequent visitor to our house*
regular, habitual, common, familiar, persistent

OPPOSITE rare

frequent VERB

We frequent the same bookshops.
visit, attend, spend time in, patronize, haunt

frequently ADVERB

These two words are frequently confused
often, continually, repeatedly, regularly, routinely, again and again

fresh ADJECTIVE

1 *a fresh loaf of bread*
new

a
b
c
d
e
f
g
h
i
j
k
l
m
n
o
p
q
r
s
t
u
v
w
x
y
z

»

259

OPPOSITES old, stale

2 *looking for fresh ideas*
original, novel, new, different, innovative
OPPOSITES tired, stale

3 *a bowl of fresh fruit*
natural, raw, unprocessed, unpreserved
OPPOSITES preserved, tinned

4 *Use a fresh sheet of paper.*
clean, unused
OPPOSITE used

5 *getting some fresh air*
cool, crisp, refreshing, brisk, bracing
OPPOSITE stuffy

6 *You'll feel fresh in the morning.*
refreshed, revived, restored, invigorated
OPPOSITES tired, weary

fret *VERB*
Don't fret on my account.
worry, be anxious, concern yourself, distress yourself, agonize, lose sleep

friction *NOUN*
1 *Engine oil reduces friction.*
rubbing, chafing, abrasion, resistance, drag

2 *There was friction between the two teams.*
conflict, disagreement, discord, hostility, antagonism, animosity, acrimony, bad feeling

friend *NOUN*
Helen is an old friend of mine.
companion, comrade, ally, associate, acquaintance
(informal) pal, buddy, chum
(British informal) mate

▶ A friend you confide in is a **confidant** or (for a female friend) a **confidante**.
OPPOSITE enemy

friendly *ADJECTIVE*
1 *Everyone in our street is very friendly.*
amiable, amicable, neighbourly, genial, sociable, convivial, affable, likeable, good-natured, warm, kind-hearted, approachable, cordial, kindly
(informal) pally, chummy

2 *a cafe with a friendly atmosphere*
warm, welcoming, hospitable, cordial, informal, familiar
OPPOSITES unfriendly, hostile

friendship *NOUN*
a friendship which lasted for many years
relationship, attachment, closeness, affection, fondness, familiarity, intimacy, affinity, bond, tie, fellowship, comradeship
OPPOSITE hostility

fright *NOUN*
1 *Miriam was paralysed with fright.*
fear, terror, alarm, horror, panic, dread, trepidation

2 *The explosion gave us all a fright.*
scare, shock, surprise, start, turn, jolt

frighten *VERB*
I didn't mean to frighten you.
scare, terrify, petrify, alarm, startle, shock, panic, unnerve
(North American informal) spook
IDIOM *(informal)* give you the creeps

frightened *ADJECTIVE*
Were you frightened when the lights went out?
afraid, scared, terrified, alarmed, fearful, panicky, petrified
(North American informal) spooked
IDIOMS scared to death, scared stiff

frightening *ADJECTIVE*
The weird music made the film more frightening.
terrifying, horrifying, alarming, shocking, nightmarish, chilling, spine-chilling, hair-raising, blood-curdling, fearsome, eerie, sinister, ghastly
(informal) scary, creepy, spooky

frill *NOUN*
1 *a dress with a lace frill*

ruffle, ruff, flounce, fringe

2 *Our hotel was basic with no frills.*
extra, luxury

ringe NOUN

1 *a scarf with a beaded fringe*
border, edging, frill, trimming

2 *a region on the fringe of the solar
system*
edge, border, margin, rim,
perimeter, periphery, outskirts

frisky ADJECTIVE

Lyndsay's new kittens are very frisky.
playful, lively, high-spirited, sprightly

frivolous ADJECTIVE

wasting time on frivolous matters
light, lightweight, trifling, petty,
paltry, shallow, superficial, trivial
▎**OPPOSITES** serious, weighty

frock NOUN
SEE **clothes**

frog NOUN

WORD WEB

the life cycle of a frog
frogspawn, tadpole
▶ The process whereby a
tadpole develops into a frog is
metamorphosis.
▶ The scientific study of frogs and
other amphibians is **herpetology**.
▶ A related adjective is **ranine**.
▎SEE ALSO **amphibian**

front NOUN

1 *standing at the front of the queue*
head, start, beginning, lead, top

2 *a photo of the front of the building*
face, facing, frontage, facade
▶ The front of a ship is the **bow** or
prow.
▶ The front of a picture is the
foreground.
▎**OPPOSITES** back, rear

3 *putting on a brave front*
appearance, act, show, exterior,
face, facade

4 *The shop was a front for a smuggling
ring.*
cover, disguise, mask, screen

▷ **in front**
*the team in front at the half-way
stage*
ahead, in the lead, leading, at the
fore
(informal) up front

front ADJECTIVE

the front page of the newspaper
first, leading, lead, foremost
▶ The front legs of an animal are its
forelegs (opposite **hind legs**).
▎**OPPOSITES** back, rear

frontier NOUN

*the frontier between France and
Belgium*
border, boundary, borderline,
dividing line

frosty ADJECTIVE

1 *a clear and frosty morning*
cold, crisp, icy, freezing, wintry,
arctic

2 *The assistant gave us a frosty stare.*
unfriendly, unwelcoming, cold, cool,
frigid, stony
▎**OPPOSITES** warm, friendly

froth NOUN

*Would you like froth on your hot
chocolate?*
foam, bubbles, head
▶ The froth on top of soapy water is
lather or **suds**.
▶ Dirty froth is **scum**.

frown VERB

*Mr Hardy frowned as he read the
note.*
scowl, grimace, glower, glare
▎**IDIOMS** knit your brow,
look daggers

▷ **frown on** or **upon**
*Reading novels used to be frowned
upon.*
disapprove of, object to, take
exception to, look askance at
▎**IDIOM** take a dim view of

frown NOUN

*A sulky frown settled on W
ilma's face.*
scowl, grimace, glower, glare,
black look
FOR TIPS ON DESCRIBING FACES SEE face

frozen ADJECTIVE

My feet are frozen!
freezing, chilled, numb with cold
IDIOMS chilled to the bone,
frozen solid

frugal ADJECTIVE

1 *People had to be frugal during
the war.*
thrifty, sparing, economical,
prudent
OPPOSITES wasteful, spendthrift
2 *a frugal meal of bread and
porridge*
meagre, paltry, plain, simple
OPPOSITE lavish

fruit NOUN

 WORD WEB

some varieties of fruit
apple, apricot, avocado,
banana, blackberry or bramble,
blackcurrant, blueberry, cherry,
clementine, cranberry, grape,
grapefruit, guava, kiwi fruit,
kumquat, lemon, lime, lychee,
mandarin, mango, melon,
nectarine, orange, papaya,
peach, pear, persimmon,
pineapple, plantain, plum,
pomegranate, quince, raspberry,
redcurrant, rosehip, satsuma,
sloe, strawberry, tangerine,
tomato
► Lemons, limes, oranges, and
grapefruit are **citrus fruits**.
► Edible fruits are also known as
culinary fruits.

dried fruits
currant, date, prune, raisin,
sultana

fruitful ADJECTIVE

Did you have a fruitful trip?
successful, productive, useful,
worthwhile, profitable, rewarding
OPPOSITE fruitless

fruitless ADJECTIVE

a fruitless search for clues
unsuccessful, unprofitable,
unproductive, futile, pointless,
useless, vain
OPPOSITES fruitful, successful

frustrate VERB

1 *People were frustrated by the long
wait.*
exasperate, discourage, dishearten,
dispirit, irritate, infuriate
2 *Our plans were frustrated by the
weather.*
block, foil, thwart, defeat, check,
hinder, prevent

frustration NOUN

*I could hear the frustration in her
voice.*
exasperation, annoyance, irritation,
vexation, dissatisfaction

fry VERB

SEE **cook**

fuel NOUN

 WORD WEB

some types of fuel
biofuel, charcoal, coal, coke,
diesel, electricity, ethanol,
hydrogen, kerosene, natural gas,
uranium, methane, petrol
(North American gasoline),
petroleum or crude oil, propane,
wood
► Coal, natural gas, and petroleum
are called **fossil fuels**.
SEE ALSO energy

fuel VERB

1 *a car fuelled by electricity and petrol*
power, drive, fire, run
2 *The cinema fuelled his imagination.*

feed, stimulate, incite, provoke,
intensify, fire, stoke, fan

fugitive NOUN

*Police are still searching for the
fugitives.*
runaway, escapee, outlaw, deserter
▶ Someone who is a fugitive from war
or persecution is a **refugee**.

fulfil VERB

1 *All contestants must fulfil these
conditions.*
meet, satisfy, conform to,
comply with

2 *fulfilling a lifelong ambition*
achieve, realize, accomplish, attain,
carry out, complete, succeed in

full ADJECTIVE

1 *My glass is already full.*
filled, loaded, packed, topped up,
brimming
OPPOSITE empty

2 *The cinema is usually full on
Saturdays.*
busy, crowded, jammed, packed,
crammed, congested
(informal) jam-packed, chock-full
OPPOSITE empty

3 *I can't eat any more—I'm full.*
replete, full up, sated, satiated
(informal) stuffed
OPPOSITE hungry

4 *a full account of what happened*
complete, detailed, comprehensive,
thorough, exhaustive, in-depth,
all-encompassing, unabridged
OPPOSITES incomplete, partial,
selective

5 *working at full speed*
top, maximum, greatest, highest
OPPOSITE minimum

6 *a dress with a full skirt*
wide, broad, loose-fitting,
voluminous, capacious
OPPOSITE tight

fully ADVERB

They were fully aware of the risks.
completely, totally, entirely, wholly,
perfectly, quite

fume VERB

Miranda sat silently fuming.
be angry, be furious, be livid, seethe
IDIOMS see red, foam at the mouth

fumes PLURAL NOUN

Lead produces toxic fumes.
gas, smoke, vapour

fun NOUN

*We're planning to have some fun this
weekend.*
amusement, enjoyment, pleasure,
entertainment, recreation,
diversion, merriment, sport, play, a
good time

▷ **make fun of**
*Why do you always make fun of
him?*
jeer at, laugh at, mock, ridicule,
taunt, tease
IDIOM (informal) pull someone's leg

function NOUN

1 *the main function of the program*
purpose, role, use, task, job, duty,
responsibility, mission

2 *The room is being used for a private
function.*
event, occasion, party, reception

function VERB

*The program isn't functioning
properly.*
work, go, operate, run, perform

fund NOUN

a special emergency fund
collection, reserve, savings, pool,
kitty

▷ **funds**
running short of funds
money, cash, savings, capital,
reserves

fund VERB

*The website is funded entirely by
donations.*
finance, pay for, sponsor, subsidize,
back

fundamental ADJECTIVE

the fundamental rules of chess

basic, elementary, essential,
important, main, necessary,
principal

fundamentally ADVERB

*The two texts are fundamentally
the same.*
basically, essentially, primarily,
in essence, at heart, at root

funeral NOUN

*The service was followed by a private
funeral.*
burial, interment, entombment,
cremation

fungus NOUN

fungus growing on the walls
mould

WORD WEB

some types of fungi
mildew, morel, mould,
mushroom, puffball, rust, smut,
toadstool, truffle, yeast

parts of fungi
cap, gills or pores, mycelium
(underground), spores, stem

▶ The scientific study of fungi is
mycology.

funny ADJECTIVE

OVERUSED WORD

a funny joke, situation
amusing, humorous, comic,
comical, hilarious, uproarious,
farcical, witty, entertaining,
diverting, droll
(informal) hysterical, priceless,
side-splitting, rib-tickling

*The best part of the film is the
hilarious car chase.*

▶ A funny situation can be described
as a **scream** or a **hoot**.

❘ OPPOSITES serious, unfunny

a funny feeling, look
strange, odd, peculiar, unusual,

curious, puzzling, perplexing,
weird, queer, bizarre

*Being alone in the graveyard
gave me a **peculiar** feeling.*

a funny taste, smell
strange, odd, peculiar, unusual,
curious, puzzling, perplexing,
weird, queer, bizarre

*The rattlesnake stew had a
curious flavour.*

fur NOUN

the fur of an arctic fox
hair, coat, hide, pelt

furious ADJECTIVE

1 *Tony was furious when he heard the
news.*
angry, irate, enraged, infuriated,
incensed, fuming, raging, seething
(informal) mad, livid

2 *working at a furious rate*
frantic, hectic, frenzied, extreme,
intense
❘ OPPOSITE calm

furnish VERB

1 *furnishing a room*
fit out, decorate, appoint, stock

2 *We were furnished with safety
helmets.*
supply, provide, equip, issue, kit out,
rig out

furrow NOUN

ploughing furrows in a field
groove, rut, ditch, channel, trench

furry ADJECTIVE

a small, furry creature
hairy, woolly, fleecy, fuzzy, fluffy,
downy

further ADJECTIVE

*See our website for further
information.*
more, extra, additional,
supplementary

further VERB

*furthering the campaign for civil
rights*

advance, promote, forward, boost,
aid, help, assist, facilitate
OPPOSITE impede

urthermore ADVERB

Furthermore, I can prove the theory.
moreover, in addition, further,
besides, also, what's more

urthest ADJECTIVE

the furthest star in our galaxy
most distant, remotest,
furthermost, outermost, utmost,
extreme

furtive ADJECTIVE

a furtive glance backwards
secretive, stealthy, surreptitious,
clandestine, covert, conspiratorial,
sneaky, underhand
IDIOM cloak-and-dagger
OPPOSITES open, overt

fury NOUN

1 *The eyes of the creature blazed
with fury.*
anger, rage, wrath, indignation
2 *There was no shelter from the fury of
the storm.*
ferocity, fierceness, intensity,
severity, violence, vehemence,
turbulence, savagery

fuse VERB

*Two or more cells can be fused
together.*
merge, unite, join, combine,
blend, melt
▶ To fuse metals together when
making or mending something is to
solder or weld them.

fuss NOUN

making a fuss about nothing
bother, commotion, excitement,
trouble, palaver, hullabaloo,
furore, stir
(informal) to-do
IDIOM song and dance

fuss VERB

I wish you'd stop fussing.
worry, fret, bother, get worked up
IDIOMS *(informal)* get in a flap,
get in a tizzy

fussy ADJECTIVE

1 *Our cat is fussy about her food.*
finicky, hard to please, particular,
fastidious
(informal) choosy, picky, pernickety
2 *a carpet with a fussy design*
fancy, elaborate, busy, ornate, florid

futile ADJECTIVE

a futile attempt to escape
fruitless, pointless, unsuccessful,
useless, ineffectual, vain, wasted
OPPOSITES successful, fruitful

future NOUN

1 *He has a bright future as an actor.*
outlook, prospects
OPPOSITE past
2 *The old woman offered to tell my
future.*
fortune, destiny, fate, stars
SEE ALSO fortune telling

future ADJECTIVE

1 *at a future date*
later, following, ensuing, to come
OPPOSITES past, previous, earlier
2 *a future president*
to be, prospective, intended,
aspiring, potential, would-be
OPPOSITES former, past

fuzzy ADJECTIVE

1 *a fuzzy image*
blurred, bleary, unfocused, unclear,
indistinct, hazy, cloudy
OPPOSITE clear
2 *a fuzzy ball of wool*
fluffy, frizzy, furry, woolly, fleecy

a
b
c
d
e
f
g
h
i
j
k
l
m
n
o
p
q
r
s
t
u
v
w
x
y
z

Gg

gadget NOUN

a handy kitchen gadget
tool, instrument, implement,
utensil, device, contraption
(*informal*) gizmo

gain VERB

1 *Nila gained a place at art college.*
get, acquire, obtain, achieve, attain,
earn, win
(*informal*) land
OPPOSITE lose

2 *I'm trying not to gain weight.*
put on, increase in, build up

▷ **gain on someone**
The other car was gaining on us fast.
catch up with, reduce the lead of
OPPOSITE fall behind

gale NOUN

a ship caught in a howling gale
SEE **weather**

gamble VERB

1 *He gambled away all their savings.*
bet, wager

2 *I decided to gamble on a new idea.*
take a risk, take a chance, venture

gamble NOUN

*Using an inexperienced team was a
gamble.*
risk, chance, speculation
(*informal*) punt

▶ A gamble that is unlikely to succeed
is a **long shot**.

game NOUN

1 *an old-fashioned party game*
amusement, pastime, sport, activity,
recreation

2 *Are you going to the game this
Saturday?*
match, contest, competition,
tournament, fixture, tie

gang NOUN

1 *a gang of bullies*
group, band, crowd, pack, set, mob
(*informal*) bunch

2 *a gang of builders*
team, unit, crew, squad,
detachment, shift

gaol NOUN

SEE **jail**

gap NOUN

1 *a gap between the trees*
opening, space, hole, aperture,
break, breach, rift, crack, crevice,
chink

2 *returning after a gap of two years*
break, interval, interruption, pause,
lull

3 *the widening gap between rich and
poor*
difference, disparity, separation,
contrast, gulf, chasm

gape VERB

1 *Anne could only gape in surprise.*
stare, be open-mouthed, gaze
(*informal*) gawp

2 *A huge canyon gaped in front of us.*
stretch, open, part, yawn

gaping ADJECTIVE

a gaping hole in the ground
wide, broad, yawning, vast,
cavernous

garden NOUN

a vegetable garden
plot, patch

▶ A rented garden for growing
vegetables is an **allotment**.

▶ A garden planted with trees is an
orchard.

▶ A formal word for gardening
is **horticulture**, and a related
adjective is **horticultural**.

garish *ADJECTIVE*
a room painted in garish colours
lurid, loud, glaring, gaudy, showy
OPPOSITES subtle, subdued

garment *NOUN*
SEE **clothes**

garnish *VERB*
a table garnished with flowers
decorate, ornament, trim, dress,
adorn, embellish

gas *NOUN*
The air we breathe is a mixture
of gases.
vapour, fumes
SEE ALSO fuel

gash *NOUN*
a deep gash on my knee
cut, slash, slit, wound, laceration

gasp *VERB*
Gordon ran up to me, gasping for
breath.
gulp, pant, puff, wheeze

gate *NOUN*
Please enter by the main gate.
gateway, doorway, entrance, portal

gather *VERB*
1 A crowd gathered to watch the
fireworks.
assemble, collect, come together,
congregate, converge, rally
OPPOSITE disperse
2 gathering a search party
bring together, round up, assemble,
muster, marshal, summon
3 gathering sticks of wood
pick, pluck, collect, harvest, reap
4 I gather that you've been ill.
understand, hear, learn, believe

gathering *NOUN*
an annual family gathering
assembly, meeting, get-together,
party, rally, convention, congress,
audience, crowd

gaudy *ADJECTIVE*
a man wearing a gaudy tie

flashy, showy, loud, glaring, garish,
lurid, ostentatious
OPPOSITE subdued

gauge *VERB*
1 gauging the temperature of the
water
measure, calculate, work out,
compute, determine, ascertain
2 gauging the mood of the crowd
judge, estimate, assess, reckon

gaunt *ADJECTIVE*
an old woman with gaunt features
haggard, drawn, thin, skinny,
scraggy, scrawny, wasted, skeletal,
cadaverous

gaze *VERB*
Norman gazed blankly into the
distance.
stare, look, gape
(informal) gawp

gear *NOUN*
1 (informal) a car stuffed with camping
gear
equipment, apparatus, materials,
paraphernalia, tackle, kit
2 (informal) a new line in sports gear
clothing, clothes, garments, outfits,
garb, attire

gem *NOUN*
a silver casket studded with gems
jewel, gemstone, precious stone

 WORD WEB

some common gemstones
agate, amber, amethyst,
aquamarine, carnelian, diamond,
emerald, garnet, jade, jasper,
jet, lapis lazuli, malachite,
moonstone, onyx, opal, pearl,
rose quartz, ruby, sapphire,
tiger's eye, topaz, tourmaline,
turquoise
► The scientific study of gemstones
is **gemology**.
► The art of cutting and polishing
gemstones is **lapidary**.

a
b
c
d
e
f
g
h
i
j
k
l
m
n
o
p
q
r
s
t
u
v
w
x
y
z

general ADJECTIVE

1 *There was a general feeling of relief.*
widespread, extensive, broad,
sweeping, overall, prevalent
IDIOM across the board
OPPOSITES localized, restricted

2 *I've got a general idea of where we are.*
rough, approximate, vague, broad,
loose, indefinite, imprecise
OPPOSITES specific, detailed

generally ADVERB

1 *I generally travel by bus.*
usually, normally, as a rule, chiefly,
mostly, mainly, predominantly,
on the whole

2 *a view that is generally held*
widely, commonly, popularly,
extensively, universally

generate VERB

The website has generated a lot of interest.
create, produce, bring about, give
rise to, prompt, stimulate, trigger,
spark

generous ADJECTIVE

1 *He is always generous to his friends.*
unselfish, charitable, kind-hearted,
magnanimous, giving, bountiful
OPPOSITES selfish, mean

2 *a generous portion of chips*
ample, large, lavish, plentiful,
abundant, copious
OPPOSITE meagre

genial ADJECTIVE

a genial atmosphere
friendly, kind, warm, warm-hearted,
kindly, good-natured, pleasant,
agreeable, cordial, amiable, affable
OPPOSITES unfriendly, cold

genius NOUN

1 *Luke is a genius at maths.*
expert, master, mastermind, wizard,
ace, virtuoso, maestro
(*informal*) egghead

2 *a genius for telling jokes*
talent, aptitude, expertise, ability,
flair, gift, knack

gentle ADJECTIVE

1 *Mattie was shy and gentle by nature*
kind, tender, good-tempered,
humane, mild, placid
OPPOSITES rough, harsh

2 *a gentle breeze*
light, slight, mild, soft, faint
OPPOSITES strong, severe

3 *a gentle slope downwards*
gradual, slight, easy
OPPOSITE steep

genuine ADJECTIVE

1 *a genuine diamond*
real, actual, true, authentic,
bona fide
OPPOSITES fake, imitation

2 *She seems like a very genuine person.*
honest, sincere, frank, earnest,
straightforward, natural, candid
OPPOSITES false, insincere

geometric ADJECTIVE

FOR GEOMETRIC SHAPES SEE shape

gesture NOUN

a gesture of farewell
sign, signal, motion, movement,
indication

gesture VERB

She gestured to us to keep quiet.
signal, indicate, motion, give a sign

get VERB

1 *Where did you get those trainers?*
acquire, obtain, come by, get hold
of, buy, purchase

2 *She got an award for gymnastics.*
receive, be given, gain, earn, win,
achieve

3 *It's starting to get dark outside.*
become, grow, turn, go

4 *What time did you get home?*
reach, arrive at, come to
OPPOSITE leave

5 *Could you get me a fork, please?*
bring, fetch, collect, pick up, retrieve

6 *You'll never get her to agree.*
persuade, urge, influence, coax

7 *We all got a stomach bug on holiday.*
catch, develop, contract, pick up
(*informal*) go down with, come down
with

8 (*informal*) *I don't get your point.*
understand, comprehend, follow,
grasp, see, fathom

▷ **get on** or **along**

1 *How are you getting on with the painting?*
manage, fare, cope, prosper,
succeed

2 *We didn't get along at first.*
harmonize, gel, connect
(*informal*) hit it off

▷ **get out of**

I can't get out of going to the party.
avoid, evade, escape, dodge, shirk
(*informal*) wriggle out of

▷ **get over**

He never got over his disappointment.
recover from, get better from,
shake off, survive

▷ **have got to**

You've got to tell her the truth.
must, need to, should, ought to,
be obliged to

ghastly *ADJECTIVE*

a ghastly scream in the night
appalling, awful, dreadful, frightful,
grim, grisly, horrible, horrifying,
shocking, monstrous, terrible

ghost *NOUN*

They say the house is haunted by ghosts.
spirit, spectre, phantom, ghoul,
apparition, shade, wraith
(*informal*) spook

▶ A ghost or spirit that throws things
about noisily is a **poltergeist**.
FOR TIPS ON WRITING HORROR FICTION
SEE **horror**

ghostly *ADJECTIVE*

the icy touch of a ghostly hand
spectral, phantom, ghoulish,
unearthly, eerie, sinister, uncanny
(*informal*) creepy, spooky

giant *NOUN*

Argus was a giant with a hundred eyes.
SEE **fantasy**

giant *ADJECTIVE*

the trunk of a giant redwood tree
gigantic, huge, enormous, massive,
immense, mammoth, colossal,
mighty

| **OPPOSITES** tiny, miniature
| **SEE ALSO big**

giddy *ADJECTIVE*

I felt giddy when I looked down.
dizzy, light-headed, faint, unsteady
(*informal*) woozy

gift *NOUN*

1 *a birthday gift*
present, offering
(*British informal*) prezzie

2 *You have a real gift for drawing.*
talent, ability, flair, knack, genius,
aptitude, bent

gifted *ADJECTIVE*

a gifted pianist
talented, skilled, accomplished,
capable, able, proficient, expert

gigantic *ADJECTIVE*

A gigantic wall surrounded the city.
huge, giant, enormous, massive,
colossal, immense, vast, mammoth,
monumental, mountainous
(*informal*) whopping, humongous
(*literary*) gargantuan

| **OPPOSITES** tiny, minuscule
| **SEE ALSO big**

giggle *VERB*

I saw them whispering and giggling together.
snigger, titter, chuckle, chortle,
laugh

girl *NOUN*

a girl of thirteen or fourteen
young woman, young lady, miss, lass
(*old use*) damsel, maid, maiden

give *VERB*

1 *I gave her a brooch for her birthday.*

a
b
c
d
e
f
g
h
i
j
k
l
m
n
o
p
q
r
s
t
u
v
w
x
y
z

present with, offer, supply with, issue with, hand over to, deliver to

2 *giving money to charity*
contribute, donate, grant, award, bestow

3 *giving a loud yawn*
utter, emit, let out, produce, make, execute

4 *giving a free performance*
present, put on, lay on, organize, arrange, host, throw

5 *The branch gave under their weight.*
collapse, give way, bend, break, buckle

▷ **give in**
I'm not going to give in now!
surrender, yield, submit, capitulate, concede defeat

▷ **give up**
We gave up waiting for the bus.
abandon, stop, cease, discontinue, renounce, forgo
(*informal*) quit

glad *ADJECTIVE*
I'm glad that you like your present.
pleased, happy, delighted, thrilled
IDIOMS (*informal*) over the moon, tickled pink
OPPOSITES sad, sorry

▷ **be glad of**
We'd be glad of your help.
appreciate, be grateful for, value

gladly *ADVERB*
I would gladly change places with her.
willingly, happily, readily
OPPOSITES unwillingly, reluctantly

glamorous *ADJECTIVE*
the glamorous life of a film star
attractive, elegant, stylish, fashionable, chic, exotic, glittering
(*informal*) glitzy

glance *VERB*
1 *Ed glanced quickly at his watch.*
look, peek, peep, glimpse
2 *I glanced briefly through the papers.*
browse, skim, scan, flick, leaf, thumb

glance *NOUN*
a quick glance backwards
look, peek, peep, glimpse

glare *VERB*
1 *Sophie glared at him without speaking.*
stare, frown, scowl, glower
IDIOM look daggers
2 *A bright light glared in my face.*
dazzle, blaze, shine, flash

glare *NOUN*
1 *the glare of the headlights*
dazzle, blaze, brightness, brilliance
2 *The manager gave us an angry glare.*
stare, scowl, glower, frown, black look

glaring *ADJECTIVE*
a glaring omission in the text
obvious, conspicuous, noticeable, unmistakable, unmissable, striking, blatant

glasses *PLURAL NOUN*
a pair of glasses with designer frames
spectacles
(*North American*) eyeglasses

 WORD WEB

some types of glasses
bifocals, contact lenses, pince-nez, reading glasses, sunglasses

► A glass lens worn over one eye is a **monocle**.

► A pair of glasses on a long handle is a **lorgnette**.
SEE ALSO eye, lens

gleam *NOUN*
a gleam of moonlight
glimmer, glint, flash, ray, shaft

gleam *VERB*
lights gleaming on the water
glimmer, glint, glisten, shimmer, shine

a b c d e f g h i j k l m n o p q r s t u v w x y z

glide VERB

The balloon glided gently over the treetops.

slide, slip, drift, float, coast

glimmer VERB

The city lights glimmered in the distance.

gleam, glint, glow, glisten, shimmer, flicker, blink

glimpse NOUN

We caught a glimpse of a whale in the distance.

peek, peep, glance, sighting, view

glimpse VERB

I glimpsed a deer running through the forest.

catch sight of, spot, spy, sight

glint VERB

Sunlight glinted off the windows.

flash, glitter, sparkle, twinkle

glisten VERB

The pavement glistened with frost.

gleam, shine, glint, shimmer, glimmer

glitter VERB

The sequins glittered under the lights.

sparkle, twinkle, shimmer, glimmer, glint, glisten, flash, shine

gloat VERB

They were still gloating about the score.

boast, brag, crow, show off

global ADJECTIVE

The Internet is a global network of computers.

worldwide, international, universal

ⅠOPPOSITE local

globe NOUN

1 *The alchemist stared into a crystal globe.*

ball, sphere, orb

2 *travelling around the globe*

world, planet, earth

gloom NOUN

1 *in the gloom of the cave*

darkness, dimness, shade, shadow, murk

▶ The dim light of the evening is **dusk** or **twilight**.

2 *A feeling of gloom descended on me.*

depression, sadness, unhappiness, melancholy, misery, despair, dejection, woe

gloomy ADJECTIVE

1 *a cold and gloomy cellar*

dark, dingy, dim, shadowy, murky, dismal, dreary, sombre, cheerless

ⅠOPPOSITE bright

2 *I stayed in bed feeling gloomy.*

depressed, sad, unhappy, glum, miserable, melancholy, low, down, downcast, dejected, despondent, crestfallen

(*informal*) fed up

ⅠIDIOMS (*informal*) down in the dumps, down in the mouth

ⅠOPPOSITE cheerful

glorious ADJECTIVE

the sight of a glorious sunset

magnificent, splendid, stunning, spectacular, superb, magnificent, wonderful, marvellous, fine

glossy ADJECTIVE

a cat with a glossy coat

shiny, shining, gleaming, lustrous, sleek, silky, polished

ⅠOPPOSITE dull

glove NOUN

a pair of sheepskin gloves

▶ Gloves without separate parts for the fingers are **mittens**.

▶ A glove with a wide cuff covering the wrist is a **gauntlet**.

ⅠSEE ALSO clothes

glow NOUN

the soft glow of candlelight

shine, gleam, radiance, glimmer

glow VERB

A flying saucer glowed in the night sky.

a
b
c
d
e
f
g
h
i
j
k
l
m
n
o
p
q
r
s
t
u
v
w
x
y
z

shine, gleam, glimmer, beam, burn, flare

▶ Something that glows in the dark is **luminous** or **phosphorescent**.

glower VERB

Hawkins glowered at his captors.
glare, scowl, frown, stare angrily
❙ IDIOM look daggers

glue NOUN

a tube of glue
adhesive, paste, gum

glue VERB

Glue the edges together.
stick, paste, bond, seal

glum ADJECTIVE

Why are you looking so glum?
depressed, sad, unhappy, gloomy, miserable, melancholy, low, down, downcast, dejected, despondent, crestfallen
(informal) fed up
❙ IDIOM (informal) down in the dumps
❙ OPPOSITE cheerful

gnarled ADJECTIVE

a gnarled tree trunk
bent, twisted, crooked, distorted, knobbly, knotty

gnaw VERB

a dog gnawing at a bone
chew, bite, nibble, munch

go VERB

1 *Our bus went slowly up the hill.*
move, progress, proceed, advance, make your way
❙ SEE ALSO move

2 *Are you going into town today?*
travel, journey

3 *Some of the guests had already gone.*
leave, depart, set off, withdraw, absent yourself

4 *A path goes all the way to the summit.*
extend, lead, reach, stretch, run

5 *My fingers went blue with cold.*
become, turn, grow

6 *The cups go on the top shelf.*
belong, be kept, be placed

7 *Soon, all the money had gone.*
be used up, be spent, disappear, vanish

8 *Is that old clock still going?*
function, operate, work, run

9 *The morning went quickly.*
pass, go by, elapse

▷ **go back**
Let's go back to the house.
return, retreat, retrace your steps

▷ **go in for**
Are you going in for the race this year?
enter, take part in, participate in

▷ **go off**

1 *A firework went off by mistake.*
explode, blow up, detonate

2 *This milk has gone off.*
go bad, turn sour, spoil, rot

▷ **go on**

1 *What's going on over there?*
happen, occur, take place

2 *Please go on with your story.*
carry on, continue, keep going, proceed

▷ **go through**
The family went through a crisis.
experience, undergo, face, suffer, endure

▷ **go with**
Do these shoes go with my dress?
match, suit, blend with, coordinate with, harmonize with

go NOUN

Can I have a go on your laptop?
turn, try, chance, opportunity, spell, stint
(informal) shot, bash, stab

goal NOUN

1 *scoring a late goal*
▶ Three goals scored by the same player is a **hat-trick**.
FOR TIPS ON WRITING ABOUT SPORT SEE **sport**

2 *The goal of the society is to protect wildlife.*

aim, objective, purpose, object, end, target, ambition, intention

god, goddess NOUN

the gods of ancient Greece
deity, divine being, immortal

golden ADJECTIVE

1 *a golden helmet*
gold
► Something that is covered with a thin layer of gold is **gilded** or **gilt**.

2 *golden hair*
fair, blonde, flaxen

good ADJECTIVE

That's a really good idea!
excellent, fine, lovely, nice, wonderful
(*informal*) fantastic, great, super, cool
┌ **OPPOSITES** bad, poor, awful

OVERUSED WORD

a good person, good deed
honest, worthy, honourable, moral, decent, virtuous, noble, kind, humane, charitable, merciful
Lancelot is portrayed as an ***honourable*** *knight.*
┌ **OPPOSITES** wicked, evil

good behaviour
well behaved, obedient, exemplary, angelic
The kittens are surprisingly ***well behaved***.
┌ **OPPOSITES** naughty, disobedient

a good friend
true, loyal, loving, reliable, trusty, trustworthy
You have always been a ***true*** *friend to me.*

a good experience, good news
pleasant, enjoyable, delightful, agreeable, pleasing
I found the book more ***enjoyable*** *than the film.*

┌ **OPPOSITES** unpleasant, disagreeable

good food, a good meal
delicious, healthy, nourishing, nutritious, tasty, appetizing, well-cooked, wholesome, substantial, hearty
Start the day with a ***nutritious*** *breakfast.*

good weather
fine, fair, favourable
We are hoping for ***fine*** *weather tomorrow.*
┌ **OPPOSITES** harsh, adverse

a good feeling, good mood
happy, cheerful, light-hearted, positive, contented, good-humoured, buoyant
(*informal*) chirpy
Gwen began the day in a ***buoyant*** *mood.*

a good performer, good work
capable, skilled, talented, able, competent, commendable, sound
Cézanne was a ***talented*** *painter.*
┌ **OPPOSITES** poor, awful

good grammar, good spelling
accurate, correct, exact, proper
Can you translate this into ***correct*** *French?*
┌ **OPPOSITES** poor, awful

good timing, a good moment
convenient, suitable, fortunate, appropriate, opportune
Is this a ***convenient*** *time for a chat?*
┌ **OPPOSITES** inconvenient, unsuitable

a good excuse, good reason
acceptable, valid, satisfactory, proper, legitimate, substantial,
»

a
b
c
d
e
f
g
h
i
j
k
l
m
n
o
p
q
r
s
t
u
v
w
x
y
z

strong, convincing

*That is not a **valid** excuse for being late.*

OPPOSITES poor, unacceptable

a good look, good clean
thorough, comprehensive, rigorous, careful, complete, full

*My locker needs a **thorough** clean-out!*

OPPOSITES rough, superficial

a good distance from something
large, long, considerable, substantial

*The Sun is a **considerable** distance from the Earth.*

OPPOSITE short

something that is good for you
beneficial, advantageous, helpful, valuable, rewarding, health-giving

*Eating garlic is **beneficial** for your heart.*

OPPOSITES harmful, detrimental

goodbye NOUN
saying goodbye to your friends
farewell
(*informal*) cheerio, bye

good-looking ADJECTIVE
I think your cousin is quite good-looking.
attractive, handsome, pretty

OPPOSITE ugly

goods PLURAL NOUN
a cache of stolen goods
property, merchandise, wares, articles, produce, cargo

gorgeous ADJECTIVE
a gorgeous sunset
beautiful, glorious, dazzling, stunning, splendid, superb, attractive, glamorous, handsome

SEE ALSO beautiful

gossip VERB
Those two are always gossiping.
chatter, tell tales
(*British informal*) natter

gossip NOUN
1 *I want to hear all the gossip.*
chatter, rumour, hearsay, scandal
(*informal*) tittle-tattle
2 *She is a dreadful gossip.*
busybody, chatterbox, telltale, scandalmonger

gouge VERB
gouging a hole in the wall
dig, hollow out, scoop out, excavate

govern VERB
The ancient Romans governed a vast empire.
rule, run, administer, direct, command, manage, oversee, be in charge of, preside over

gown NOUN
a silk evening gown
dress, frock, robe

grab VERB
Tessa reached out and grabbed my hand.
seize, grasp, catch, clutch, grip, get hold of, snatch

graceful ADJECTIVE
the graceful stride of a gazelle
elegant, flowing, stylish, smooth, agile, nimble, fluid

OPPOSITES clumsy, graceless

gracious ADJECTIVE
Thank you for being such a gracious host.
polite, courteous, good-natured, pleasant, agreeable, civil

grade NOUN
A black belt is the highest grade in judo.
class, standard, level, stage, rank, degree

grade VERB
Eggs are graded according to size.
classify, class, categorize, arrange,

group, sort, bracket, rank

gradient *NOUN*
climbing a steep gradient
slope, incline, rise, ramp

gradual *ADJECTIVE*
a gradual change in the weather
steady, slow, gentle, moderate,
unhurried, regular, even
OPPOSITES sudden, abrupt

gradually *ADVERB*
*Add the water gradually to the
mixture.*
steadily, slowly, gently, gingerly,
bit by bit
OPPOSITES suddenly, all at once

grain *NOUN*
1 *a field of grain*
cereal, corn
2 *a few grains of sand*
bit, particle, speck, granule

grand *ADJECTIVE*
1 *The wedding was a grand occasion.*
magnificent, splendid, stately,
impressive, big, great, important,
imposing
2 (*informal*) *You're doing a grand job!*
excellent, fine, good, splendid,
first-class

grant *VERB*
1 *They were granted permission to
film.*
give, allow, permit, award
(*formal*) accord
2 *I grant that I'm no expert.*
admit, accept, acknowledge,
confess, recognize

graphic *ADJECTIVE*
1 *the graphic arts*
pictorial, illustrative
2 *a graphic description of war*
detailed, explicit, vivid, realistic

grapple *VERB*
*The guards grappled the man to the
ground.*
wrestle, struggle, tussle, scuffle
▷ **grapple with**
a country still grappling with poverty

tackle, deal with, confront, face
IDIOM get to grips with

grasp *VERB*
1 *Dean managed to grasp the end of
the rope.*
clutch, grab, grip, seize, catch,
snatch, take hold of, hang on to
2 *The idea of infinity is difficult to
grasp.*
understand, comprehend, follow,
take in, fathom
IDIOM take on board

grasp *NOUN*
1 *Keep a firm grasp on the leash.*
hold, grip, clutch
2 *You will need a good grasp of
German.*
understanding, comprehension,
knowledge, mastery, command, grip

grass *NOUN*
Please keep off the grass.
lawn, turf, green

grate *VERB*
1 *grating some cheese*
shred, grind, mince
2 *The keel of the boat grated on the
sand.*
scrape, scratch, rasp
▷ **grate on**
His voice grates on my nerves.
annoy, irritate, jar on

grateful *ADJECTIVE*
I was grateful for their help.
thankful, appreciative, obliged,
indebted, beholden
OPPOSITE ungrateful

gratitude *NOUN*
a way of showing our gratitude
thanks, appreciation

grave❶ *NOUN*
SEE **tomb**

grave❷ *ADJECTIVE*
1 *Jim turned to me with a grave
expression.*
solemn, serious, grim, sombre, dour,
heavy-hearted

》   275

OPPOSITE cheerful

2 *You are in grave danger.*
serious, important, profound, weighty, significant, terrible, dire
OPPOSITE trivial

graveyard NOUN
Some famous people are buried in the graveyard.
burial ground, cemetery, churchyard

graze VERB
Dirk grazed his knee on the pavement.
scrape, scratch, skin, scuff, chafe, cut

grease NOUN
a thick layer of grease
oil, fat, lubricant

greasy ADJECTIVE
a plate of greasy food
fatty, oily

great ADJECTIVE
1 *A great canyon stretched before us.*
large, huge, big, enormous, immense, gigantic, colossal, mighty, vast, extensive
OPPOSITE small

2 *Theirs is a story of great courage.*
considerable, exceptional, outstanding, extraordinary, superlative, prodigious, tremendous, extreme
OPPOSITE little

3 *Mozart was a great composer.*
famous, notable, celebrated, eminent, distinguished, important, outstanding, major, leading, prominent
OPPOSITES insignificant, minor

4 (*informal*) *The food was great!*
excellent, marvellous, outstanding, superb, tremendous, wonderful, enjoyable
(*informal*) brilliant, fantastic, super, smashing, terrific, fabulous
OPPOSITES bad, awful

greed NOUN
Midas was driven by his greed for gold.
avarice, covetousness, acquisitiveness, hunger, craving, gluttony

greedy ADJECTIVE
1 *Don't be greedy—leave some food for me!*
gluttonous
(*informal*) piggish

2 *a story about a greedy landowner*
grasping, covetous, avaricious
(*informal*) money-grubbing

green ADJECTIVE
an awareness of green issues
environmental, ecological, conservation, eco-
SEE ALSO environment

green ADJECTIVE, NOUN

WORD WEB

some shades of green
emerald, jade, khaki, lime, mint, olive, pea green, sea green, teal
FOR TIPS ON DESCRIBING COLOURS
SEE **colour**

greet VERB
She greeted us with a friendly wave.
welcome, hail, receive, salute

grey ADJECTIVE
1 *straggly wisps of grey hair*
silver, silvery, grizzly, hoary, whitish

2 *Nora's face looked grey and drawn.*
pale, pallid, pasty, ashen, wan

3 *The day began cold and grey.*
dull, cloudy, overcast, sunless, murky

grey ADJECTIVE, NOUN

WORD WEB

some shades of grey
ash, charcoal, gunmetal, silver, slate, smoke
FOR TIPS ON DESCRIBING COLOURS
SEE **colour**

a
b
c
d
e
f
g
h
i
j
k
l
m
n
o
p
q
r
s
t
u
v
w
x
y
z

grief NOUN

> *Juliet is overcome with grief at Romeo's death.*
> sorrow, mourning, sadness, unhappiness, distress, anguish, heartache, heartbreak, woe
> **OPPOSITE** joy

grieve VERB

> **1** *The family is still grieving over their loss.*
> mourn, lament, sorrow, weep
> **OPPOSITE** rejoice
>
> **2** *It grieves me to tell you this.*
> sadden, upset, distress, hurt, pain, wound
> **OPPOSITE** please

grim ADJECTIVE

> **1** *wearing a grim expression*
> stern, severe, harsh, bad-tempered, sullen
> **OPPOSITE** cheerful
>
> **2** *the grim details of the murder*
> unpleasant, horrible, dreadful, terrible, hideous, shocking, gruesome, grisly
> **OPPOSITE** pleasant

grime NOUN

> *a floor covered with grime*
> dirt, filth, muck, mire, mess

grimy ADJECTIVE

> *a grimy pair of overalls*
> dirty, filthy, grubby, mucky, soiled
> **OPPOSITE** clean

grin NOUN, VERB

> *Everyone is grinning in the photograph.*
> smile, beam, smirk
> ▶ A large grin is a **broad**, **wide**, or **cheesy** grin.

grind VERB

> **1** *Grind the spices into a fine powder.*
> crush, pound, powder, pulverize, mill
>
> **2** *a tool for grinding knives*
> sharpen, file, hone, whet
>
> **3** *The gears ground against each other.*
> rub, grate, scrape, chafe

grip VERB

> **1** *Grip the handle tightly.*
> grasp, seize, clutch, clasp, hold
>
> **2** *I was gripped by the last chapter.*
> fascinate, engross, enthral, absorb, captivate, rivet, entrance, mesmerize

grip NOUN

> **1** *keeping a tight grip*
> hold, grasp, clasp, clutch
>
> **2** *in the grip of panic*
> power, control, influence, clutches

gripping ADJECTIVE

> *a gripping final chapter*
> engrossing, enthralling, absorbing, riveting, spellbinding, mesmerizing, compelling, thrilling, action-packed
> (*informal*) unputdownable

grisly ADJECTIVE

> *the grisly discovery of a human skull*
> gruesome, gory, ghastly, hideous, nasty, revolting, sickening

grit NOUN

> **1** *a piece of grit in my shoe*
> gravel, dust, sand
>
> **2** *The contestants showed grit and stamina.*
> bravery, courage, toughness, spirit, pluck
> (*informal*) guts

groan VERB

> **1** *groaning with pain*
> cry, moan, sigh, wail
>
> **2** *groaning under the weight*
> creak

groove NOUN

> *The skates cut grooves in the ice.*
> channel, furrow, trench, rut, scratch

grope VERB

> *I groped in the dark for the light switch.*
> fumble, feel about, flounder, scrabble

gross ADJECTIVE

> **1** *a gross exaggeration*
> extreme, glaring, obvious, sheer,

a
b
c
d
e
f
g
h
i
j
k
l
m
n
o
p
q
r
s
t
u
v
w
x
y
z

blatant, outright

2 *I was shocked by their gross behaviour.*
offensive, rude, coarse, vulgar

3 *(informal) Sweaty feet smell gross!*
disgusting, repulsive, revolting, foul, obnoxious, sickening

ground NOUN

1 *planting seeds in the ground*
earth, soil, land

2 *a football ground*
field, pitch, park, stadium, arena

3 *Both books cover the same ground.*
subject, topic, material, matter

grounds PLURAL NOUN

1 *a country house with extensive grounds*
gardens, estate, park, land

2 *the grounds for divorce*
reason, basis, justification, cause, argument, rationale, excuse, pretext

group NOUN

1 *Japan consists of a group of islands.*
collection, set, batch, cluster, clump

2 *a group of onlookers*
crowd, gathering, band, body, gang
(*informal*) bunch

3 *The book group meets once a month.*
club, society, association, circle

4 *sorting fossils into groups*
category, class, type, kind, sort
FOR COLLECTIVE NOUNS SEE
collective noun

group VERB

Entries are grouped according to age.
categorize, classify, class, organize, arrange, sort, bracket, range

grow VERB

1 *Mangrove trees can grow in salt water.*
get bigger, put on growth, spring up, sprout, flourish, thrive

2 *Our website has grown over the past year.*
increase, develop, enlarge, expand, build up, swell, mushroom

▌ OPPOSITE decrease

3 *a farm which grows organic vegetables*
cultivate, produce, raise, farm, propagate

4 *It is growing dark outside.*
become, get, turn, begin to be

grown-up ADJECTIVE

a leopard with two grown-up cubs
adult, mature, fully grown
▌ OPPOSITES young, under age

growth NOUN

1 *a growth of interest in tennis*
increase, rise, spread, expansion, development, enlargement, escalation, build-up, mushrooming

2 *an unusual growth on the skin*
lump, swelling, tumour
► An abnormal growth on a tree trunk is a **burr**.

grub NOUN

1 *Moles feed on grubs and earthworms.*
larva, maggot, caterpillar

2 *(informal) cooking tasty grub*
SEE **food**

grubby ADJECTIVE

a set of grubby fingers
dirty, filthy, grimy, messy, mucky, soiled, stained
(*British informal*) manky
▌ OPPOSITE clean

grudge NOUN

harbouring a grudge against the world
grievance, bitterness, resentment, hard feelings, ill-will, spite, rancour
▌ IDIOM a chip on your shoulder

gruelling ADJECTIVE

a gruelling uphill climb
hard, tough, demanding, exhausting, challenging, difficult, laborious, strenuous, taxing, exacting, back-breaking, punishing
▌ OPPOSITE easy

gruesome ADJECTIVE

the gruesome sight of dead bodies

grisly, gory, ghastly, hideous, monstrous, revolting, sickening, appalling, dreadful, shocking, horrifying, frightful, abominable

gruff ADJECTIVE

speaking in a gruff voice
harsh, rough, hoarse, husky, throaty
FOR TIPS ON DESCRIBING VOICES SEE **sound❶**

grumble VERB

What are you grumbling about now?
complain, protest, whine, grouse, carp, make a fuss
(*informal*) gripe, moan
(*British informal*) whinge

grumpy ADJECTIVE

Mark is always grumpy in the morning.
bad-tempered, cross, irritable, testy, tetchy, grouchy, cantankerous, crotchety
(*North American*) cranky, ornery
OPPOSITES good-humoured, cheerful

guarantee NOUN

You have my personal guarantee.
promise, assurance, pledge, vow, word

guarantee VERB

I guarantee that you will like this book.
promise, assure, pledge, vow, give your word

guard VERB

Cerberus guarded the gate to Hades.
protect, defend, stand guard over, patrol, safeguard, shield, watch over

guard NOUN

a team of security guards
sentry, sentinel, warder, lookout, watchman

guardian NOUN

a guardian of human rights
defender, protector, keeper, minder, custodian

guess NOUN

My guess is that they have got lost.
theory, surmise, conjecture, opinion, belief, feeling, suspicion, supposition, speculation, estimate, hunch

guess VERB

1 *Can you guess how old the tree is?*
estimate, judge, work out, gauge, reckon, predict, speculate, conjecture, surmise

2 (*informal*) *I guess you must be feeling hungry.*
suppose, imagine, expect, assume, think, suspect
(*informal*) reckon
IDIOMS I take it, I dare say

guest NOUN

1 *We are expecting guests this weekend.*
visitor, caller, company

2 *The pool is for hotel guests only.*
client, customer, resident

guide NOUN

1 *Our guide met us outside the hotel.*
courier, escort, leader, chaperone

2 *a pocket guide for tourists*
guidebook, handbook, manual, companion

guide VERB

being guided by the stars at night
direct, lead, conduct, steer, pilot, escort, usher, shepherd, show the way

guilt NOUN

1 *She tearfully admitted her guilt.*
culpability, responsibility, liability, blame, wrongdoing
OPPOSITE innocence

2 *a nagging feeling of guilt*
shame, remorse, regret, contrition, shamefacedness, sheepishness

guilty ADJECTIVE

1 *Simpson was found guilty of kidnapping.*
culpable, responsible, to blame, at fault, in the wrong, liable

a
b
c
d
e
f
g
h
i
j
k
l
m
n
o
p
q
r
s
t
u
v
w
x
y
z

》

OPPOSITE innocent

2 *I felt guilty about not inviting her.*
ashamed, guilt-ridden, remorseful,
sorry, repentant, conscience-
stricken, contrite, shamefaced,
sheepish

OPPOSITE unrepentant

guitar NOUN

WORD WEB

some types of guitar
acoustic guitar, bass guitar,
classical guitar, electric guitar,
pedal steel guitar

► A musician who plays the guitar is
a **guitarist**.

parts of a guitar and related terms
bridge, fretboard, frets, neck,
nut, pickup, plectrum
(*North American* pick), soundhole,
strings, tuning pegs, whammy
bar

FOR OTHER MUSICAL INSTRUMENTS
SEE **music**

gulp VERB
*He gulped down the sandwich in
one go.*
swallow, bolt, gobble, guzzle,
devour

SEE ALSO eat

gulp NOUN
taking long gulps of water
swallow, mouthful
(*informal*) swig

gun NOUN
SEE **weapon**

gush VERB
Water gushed from the broken pipe.
rush, stream, flow, pour, flood,
spout, spurt, squirt

gush NOUN
a gush of water from the pipe
rush, stream, torrent, cascade,
flood, jet, spout, spurt

gust NOUN
a sudden gust of wind
blast, rush, puff, squall, flurry

guzzle VERB
The seagulls guzzled all the bread.
gobble, gulp, bolt, devour

SEE ALSO eat

Hh

habit *NOUN*

1 *developing a habit of regular exercise*
custom, practice, routine, rule

2 *Mr Gomez had an odd habit of talking to himself.*
mannerism, way, tendency, inclination, quirk

hack *VERB*
hacking through the dense undergrowth
chop, cut, hew, slash, lop

haggard *ADJECTIVE*
The survivors looked tired and haggard.
drawn, gaunt, thin, pinched, wasted, shrunken, wan

haggle *VERB*
They haggled over the price for several minutes.
bargain, negotiate, argue, wrangle

hair *NOUN*

1 *a girl with wavy auburn hair*
locks, tresses, curls
(*informal*) mop
▶ A mass of hair is a **head of hair** or **shock of hair**.
▶ A single thread of hair is a **strand**.

2 *a poodle with short hair*
fur, coat, wool, fleece, mane

 WRITING TIPS

describing hair

It was the same with his hair, sparse and irregular of growth, muddy-yellow and dirty-yellow, rising on his head and sprouting out of his face in unexpected tufts and bunches, in appearance like clumped and wind-blown grain.
— *Jack London, White Fang*

adjectives
bushy, close-cropped, curly, dishevelled, fine, frizzy, glossy, greasy, lank, luxuriant, shaggy, shaven, shock-headed, silky, silken, sleek, spiky, straggly, straight, stringy, stubby, tangled, thick, thinning, tousled, unkempt, wavy, windswept, wispy

colour
auburn, blond (male) or blonde (female), brown, brunette, dark, dyed, fair, flaxen, ginger, grizzled, hoary, mousy, platinum blonde, raven, red, silver, strawberry blonde, streaked, white

hairstyles
Afro, beehive, bob, braid, bun, bunches, chignon, cornrows, crew cut, curls, dreadlocks, French braid, fringe (*North American* bangs), highlights, Mohican, parting, perm, pigtail, plait, ponytail, queue, quiff, ringlets, skinhead, spikes, topknot

facial hair
beard, bristle, goatee beard, handlebar moustache, moustache, sideburns, stubble, whiskers
▶ Someone with a lot of hair is **hairy** or (*formal*) **hirsute**.   »

> **artificial hair**
> false beard or moustache,
> hairpiece, toupee, wig
> **SEE ALSO colour, texture**

hairy ADJECTIVE

1 *the hairy coat of a mammoth*
shaggy, bushy, woolly, fleecy, furry,
fuzzy, long-haired

2 *a man with a hairy chin*
bristly, stubbled, stubbly, bearded,
unshaven, hirsute

3 (*informal*) *The journey home was a bit hairy.*
dangerous, hazardous, perilous,
risky, tricky
(*informal*) dodgy, dicey

half NOUN

Only half of the Earth is exposed to the sun at any time.
fifty per cent

▶ A half of a circle is a **semicircle** and a half of a sphere is a **hemisphere**.

OPPOSITE whole

half-hearted ADJECTIVE

a half-hearted attempt to smile
unenthusiastic, feeble, weak,
indifferent, apathetic, lukewarm

OPPOSITE enthusiastic

halfway ADJECTIVE

the halfway point in the race
midway, middle, mid, intermediate,
centre

hall NOUN

1 *Leave your umbrella in the hall.*
entrance hall, hallway, lobby, foyer,
vestibule

2 *The hall was full for the concert.*
assembly room, auditorium, concert
hall, theatre

halt VERB

1 *The bus halted at the red light.*
stop, come to a halt, come to a
standstill, draw up, pull up

OPPOSITES start, go

2 *A sudden noise halted us in our tracks.*

stop, check, stall, block, arrest, curb,
stem

hammer VERB

a fist hammering on the door
strike, beat, knock, batter, thump,
pummel, pound

hamper VERB

Bad weather hampered the rescuers.
hinder, obstruct, impede, restrict,
handicap, frustrate, hold up, slow
down, delay

OPPOSITE help

hand NOUN

1 *a cold and clammy hand*
fist, palm
(*informal*) paw, mitt

▶ Work that you do with your hands is **manual** work.

▶ Someone who is able to use their left and right hands equally well is **ambidextrous**.

2 *written in a distinct hand*
handwriting, script

3 *a farm hand*
labourer, worker, employee

hand VERB

The postman handed me several letters.
give, pass, present, let someone
have, offer

▷ **hand something down**
This ring has been handed down in our family.
pass down, pass on, bequeath

handicap NOUN

1 *Lack of experience may be a handicap.*
disadvantage, drawback, hindrance,
obstacle, problem, difficulty, barrier,
limitation

IDIOM stumbling block
OPPOSITE advantage

2 *a visual handicap*
disability, impairment, infirmity

handicap VERB

The search was handicapped by bad weather.

a
b
c
d
e
f
g
h
i
j
k
l
m
n
o
p
q
r
s
t
u
v
w
x
y
z

hamper, hinder, impede, hold up,
slow down, restrict, constrain
❚ **OPPOSITE** help

handle NOUN

turning the door handle
grip, handgrip, knob, shaft
▶ The handle of a sword is the **hilt**.

handle VERB

1 *Please don't handle the exhibits.*
touch, feel, hold, stroke, fondle,
finger, pick up, grasp
2 *I thought you handled the situation
well.*
manage, tackle, deal with, cope
with, attend to, see to

handsome ADJECTIVE

1 *a handsome young man*
attractive, good-looking, gorgeous,
beautiful, striking
(*informal*) dishy
❚ **OPPOSITES** ugly, unattractive
2 *making a handsome profit*
big, large, substantial, sizeable,
considerable, ample
(*informal*) tidy
❚ **OPPOSITE** slight

handy ADJECTIVE

1 *a handy kitchen tool*
useful, helpful, convenient, practical,
easy to use, user-friendly
❚ **OPPOSITES** awkward, useless
2 *Always keep an umbrella handy.*
ready, available, accessible,
close at hand, nearby, within reach,
at the ready
❚ **OPPOSITE** inaccessible
3 *I'm not very handy with chopsticks.*
skilled, adept, proficient, dexterous,
deft
❚ **OPPOSITES** clumsy, inept

hang VERB

1 *a chandelier hanging from the ceiling*
be suspended, dangle, swing, sway
2 *a jacket hanging over a chair*
droop, drape, flop, trail, cascade
3 *a tree hung with fairy lights*
decorate, adorn, festoon,

string, drape
4 *Our breath hung in the icy air.*
float, hover, drift, linger, cling
5 *sentenced to be hanged*
execute, send to the gallows
(*informal*) string up
▷ **hang about** or **around**
*We had to hang about in the cold for
hours.*
wait around, linger, loiter, dawdle
▷ **hang on**
(*informal*) *Could you hang on for a
second?*
wait, stay, remain
▷ **hang on to something**
1 *Ray hung on to the side of the boat.*
hold, grip, grasp, clutch, clasp
2 *Hang on to your entrance ticket.*
keep, retain, save, keep a hold of

hanker VERB

*Ted is still hankering after a
motorbike.*
long for, yearn for, hunger for, fancy,
feel like
(*informal*) itch for

haphazard ADJECTIVE

*The books were shelved in a
haphazard way.*
random, unplanned, arbitrary,
disorderly, chaotic,
higgledy-piggledy
❚ **OPPOSITE** orderly

happen VERB

1 *What happened on the night of the
murder?*
take place, occur, arise, come about,
crop up, emerge, result
2 *I happened to be off school that day.*
chance, have the fortune

happening NOUN

a strange happening in the night
event, occurrence, incident, episode,
affair

happily ADVERB

1 *living happily ever after*
cheerfully, joyfully, cheerily, merrily
❚ **OPPOSITE** unhappily

《

2 *I will happily answer any questions.*
gladly, willingly, readily
❙ **OPPOSITES** unwillingly,
reluctantly

happiness NOUN

a face glowing with happiness
joy, joyfulness, pleasure, delight,
jubilation, contentment, gladness,
cheerfulness, merriment, ecstasy,
bliss
❙ **OPPOSITE** sorrow

happy ADJECTIVE

OVERUSED WORD

a happy mood, happy person
cheerful, joyful, jolly, merry,
jovial, gleeful, light-hearted,
contented, carefree, upbeat
*There was a **carefree**
atmosphere on the last day of
term.*
❙ **OPPOSITES** unhappy, sad

a very happy feeling
thrilled, ecstatic, elated,
overjoyed
(*informal*) over the moon, thrilled
to bits, tickled pink
*Bella was **ecstatic** when she
heard the news.*

a happy time, happy experience
enjoyable, pleasant, delightful,
joyous, glorious, blissful,
heavenly, idyllic
*They spent a **glorious** summer
on the island.*

being happy to do something
glad, pleased, delighted, willing,
keen
*Would you be **willing** to sign our
petition?*
❙ **OPPOSITE** unwilling

a happy coincidence
lucky, fortunate, favourable,
timely

*By a **lucky** coincidence, we took
the same train.*
❙ **OPPOSITE** unfortunate

harass VERB

being harassed with junk email
pester, trouble, bother, annoy,
disturb, plague, torment, badger,
hound
(*informal*) hassle, bug

harbour NOUN

an old fishing harbour
port, dock, mooring, quay, pier,
wharf
▶ A harbour for yachts is a **marina**.

harbour VERB

1 *harbouring a grudge against his
brother*
bear, hold, feel, nurse
2 *harbouring a fugitive*
shelter, protect, shield, hide, conceal

hard ADJECTIVE

OVERUSED WORD

hard ground, a hard surface
solid, firm, dense, compact,
rigid, stiff
*The core of the Moon is **solid**
rock.*
❙ **OPPOSITE** soft

a hard blow, hard thrust
strong, forceful, heavy, hefty,
powerful, violent, mighty
*The injury was caused by a
heavy blow to the head.*
❙ **OPPOSITE** light

a hard task, hard work
strenuous, arduous, tough,
difficult, gruelling, tiring,
exhausting, laborious,
back-breaking
*Picking cotton in the fields was
strenuous work.*
❙ **OPPOSITES** easy, light

a hard worker
industrious, diligent, keen,
assiduous, conscientious,
energetic
*At first, Freda was a **diligent**
student.*

OPPOSITE lazy

*hard evidence, hard
information*
real, reliable, concrete, specific
*Can you provide **concrete** proof
of your whereabouts?*

OPPOSITE lazy

a hard person, hard treatment
harsh, stern, strict, severe,
cruel, hard-hearted,
heartless, unfeeling, unkind,
unsympathetic
*In the film, he plays a
hard-hearted gangster.*

OPPOSITE mild

a hard problem, hard question
difficult, complicated, complex,
intricate, perplexing, puzzling,
baffling, knotty, thorny
*No one has deciphered the
intricate code.*

OPPOSITE simple

hard ADVERB
1 *I've been working hard all morning.*
diligently, industriously,
energetically, keenly, assiduously,
conscientiously, intently
(*informal*) like mad
2 *It's been raining hard all afternoon.*
heavily, steadily
(*informal*) cats and dogs
3 *Louise stared hard at the screen.*
intently, closely, carefully,
searchingly

harden VERB
*Leave the mixture to harden
overnight.*

set, solidify, stiffen, thicken
OPPOSITE soften

hardly ADVERB
I could hardly hear the lead singer.
barely, scarcely, only just,
with difficulty
OPPOSITE easily

hardship NOUN
a childhood full of hardship
suffering, trouble, distress, misery,
misfortune, adversity, need, want,
privation, poverty
OPPOSITES prosperity, comfort

hardy ADJECTIVE
Highland cattle are hardy animals.
tough, strong, robust, sturdy,
hearty, rugged
OPPOSITES delicate, tender

harm VERB
1 *No animals were harmed in making
this film.*
hurt, injure, ill-treat, mistreat,
wound
IDIOM lay a finger on
2 *chemicals which harm the
environment*
damage, spoil, ruin, wreck, impair

harm NOUN
You've done enough harm already.
damage, injury, hurt, pain
OPPOSITES good, benefit

harmful ADJECTIVE
*Ultraviolet rays are harmful to your
skin.*
damaging, detrimental, dangerous,
hazardous, destructive, injurious,
unhealthy
OPPOSITES harmless, beneficial

harmless ADJECTIVE
1 *The bite of a grass snake is harmless.*
safe, innocuous, non-poisonous,
non-toxic
OPPOSITES harmful, dangerous,
poisonous
2 *It was just a bit of harmless fun.*
innocent, inoffensive

a
b
c
d
e
f
g
h
i
j
k
l
m
n
o
p
q
r
s
t
u
v
w
x
y
z

harsh *ADJECTIVE*

1 *a harsh cry of a seagull*
rough, rasping, grating, jarring, discordant, shrill, strident, raucous
OPPOSITES soft, gentle

2 *the harsh light of a bare bulb*
bright, brilliant, dazzling, glaring
OPPOSITES soft, subdued

3 *harsh weather conditions*
severe, adverse, tough, bleak, inhospitable
OPPOSITE mild

4 *harsh treatment of the prisoners*
cruel, inhumane, brutal, ruthless, heartless

5 *saying some harsh words*
sharp, stern, unkind, unfriendly, critical, scathing
OPPOSITE kind

harvest *NOUN*
this year's harvest of rice
crop, yield, return, produce
▶ A plentiful harvest is a **bumper harvest**.

hassle *NOUN*
(*informal*) *It was such a hassle getting here!*
inconvenience, bother, nuisance, trouble, annoyance
(*informal*) headache
IDIOM (*informal*) pain in the neck

haste *NOUN*
In her haste, she forgot to lock the door.
hurry, rush, speed, urgency

hasten *VERB*
Eric hastened to correct his mistake.
hurry, rush, be quick, race, dash

hasty *ADJECTIVE*
Don't make any hasty decisions.
hurried, rash, reckless, impulsive, impetuous, precipitate
IDIOM spur-of-the-moment
OPPOSITES careful, considered

hat *NOUN*

 WORD WEB

some types of hat
balaclava, baseball cap, bearskin, beret, boater, bonnet, bowler, cap, cloche, deerstalker, fedora, fez, helmet, mitre, mortarboard, panama hat, skullcap, sombrero, sou'wester, stetson, sun hat, tam-o'shanter, top hat, trilby, turban

hatch *VERB*
hatching a scheme to make money
plan, develop, conceive, think up, devise
(*informal*) cook up, dream up

hate *VERB*

1 *The Montagues and Capulets hate each other.*
dislike, detest, despise, loathe, be unable to bear, be unable to stand
(*formal*) abhor
OPPOSITES like, love

2 *I hate to disturb you.*
be sorry, be reluctant, be loath, regret

hate *NOUN*

1 *an instinctive hate of anything new*
SEE **hatred**

2 *Name one of your pet hates.*
dislike, bugbear

hatred *NOUN*
a heart filled with hatred and rage
hate, loathing, dislike, hostility, enmity, contempt, detestation, abhorrence, odium
OPPOSITE love

haughty *ADJECTIVE*
The butler replied with a haughty look.
proud, arrogant, conceited, lofty, superior, pompous, disdainful
(*informal*) stuck-up
OPPOSITE modest

haul VERB

Grant hauled his bike out of the shed.
drag, pull, tow, heave, lug

haunt VERB

The heroine is haunted by visions of evil.
torment, trouble, disturb, plague, prey on

have VERB

1 Do you have your own computer?
own, possess

2 Our house has two bedrooms.
contain, include, incorporate, comprise, consist of

3 We're having a barbecue at the weekend.
hold, organize, provide, host, throw

4 I'm having some trouble with my computer.
experience, go through, meet with, run into, face, suffer

5 We've had lots of email messages.
receive, get, be given, be sent

6 Will you have some coffee?
take, accept, receive

7 One of the giraffes has had a baby.
give birth to, bear, produce

8 I have to be home by nine o'clock.
must, need to, ought to, be obliged to, should

haven NOUN

The Galapagos Islands are a haven for wildlife.
refuge, shelter, retreat, sanctuary

havoc NOUN

A virus can cause havoc to your computer.
chaos, mayhem, disorder, disruption, pandemonium

hazard NOUN

Their journey was fraught with hazards.
danger, risk, threat, peril, trap, pitfall, snag

hazardous ADJECTIVE

the hazardous trip to the South Pole
dangerous, risky, unsafe, perilous, precarious, high-risk
OPPOSITE safe

haze NOUN

the haze of smoke from forest fires
mist, cloud, fog, steam, vapour

hazy ADJECTIVE

1 The city looked hazy in the distance.
blurred, misty, unclear, dim, faint
OPPOSITES clear, sharp

2 a hazy memory of events
uncertain, vague

head NOUN

1 Gene hit his head on the car door.
skull, crown
(informal) nut

2 All the details are in my head.
brain, mind, intellect, intelligence

3 standing at the head of the queue
front, start, lead, top
OPPOSITES back, rear

4 the head of the music department
chief, leader, manager, director, controller
(informal) boss

head VERB

Professor Rees headed the inquiry.
lead, direct, command, manage, oversee, be in charge of, preside over

▷ **head for**

As night fell, we headed for home.
go towards, make for, aim for

heading NOUN

Each chapter has a different heading.
title, caption, headline, rubric

headlong ADJECTIVE

a headlong dash for shelter
quick, hurried, hasty, breakneck

heady ADJECTIVE

1 the heady scent of jasmine
potent, strong, intoxicating

2 the heady years of the 1960s
exciting, thrilling, exhilarating, stimulating

a
b
c
d
e
f
g
h
i
j
k
l
m
n
o
p
q
r
s
t
u
v
w
x
y
z

heal *VERB*
> *It took a month for the wound to heal.*
> get better, recover, mend, be cured

health *NOUN*
> **1** *How is your health these days?*
> condition, constitution
> **2** *I am slowly returning to health.*
> well-being, fitness, strength, vigour, good shape

healthy *ADJECTIVE*
> **1** *She was always healthy as a child.*
> well, fit, strong, sturdy, vigorous, robust
> (*informal*) in good shape
> **IDIOMS** in fine fettle, fighting fit
> **OPPOSITE** ill
> **2** *Porridge makes a healthy breakfast.*
> health-giving, wholesome, invigorating, nourishing, nutritious, good for you
> **OPPOSITE** unhealthy

heap *NOUN*
> *an untidy heap of clothes*
> pile, stack, mound, mountain, collection, mass

heap *VERB*
> *We heaped up all the rubbish in the corner.*
> pile, stack, collect, bank, mass

hear *VERB*
> **1** *Did you hear what she said?*
> catch, listen to, make out, pick up, overhear, pay attention to
> ▶ A sound that you can hear is **audible**.
> ▶ A sound that you cannot hear is **inaudible**.
> **2** *Have you heard the news?*
> be told, discover, find out, learn, gather, glean

heart *NOUN*
> **1** *Have you no heart?*
> compassion, feeling, sympathy, tenderness, affection, humanity, kindness, love
> **2** *We wandered deep into the*

heart of the forest.
> centre, middle, core, nucleus, hub

heartless *ADJECTIVE*
> *How could she be so heartless?*
> hard-hearted, callous, cruel, inhuman, unfeeling, unkind, pitiless, ruthless
> **OPPOSITES** kind, compassionate

hearty *ADJECTIVE*
> **1** *Mr Gaskell gave a hearty laugh.*
> strong, forceful, vigorous, loud, spirited
> **OPPOSITE** feeble
> **2** *They gave us a hearty welcome.*
> enthusiastic, wholehearted, sincere, genuine, warm, heartfelt
> **OPPOSITES** unenthusiastic, half-hearted
> **3** *eating a hearty breakfast*
> large, substantial, ample, satisfying, filling
> **OPPOSITE** light

heat *NOUN*
> **1** *the heat of the midday sun*
> warmth, hotness, high temperature
> ▶ A long period of hot weather is a **heatwave**.
> **OPPOSITE** cold
> **2** *in the heat of the debate*
> passion, intensity, fervour, vehemence

heat *VERB*
> *The fire will gradually heat the room.*
> warm, heat up
> **OPPOSITES** cool, cool down

heave *VERB*
> *The men heaved the piano into position.*
> haul, drag, pull, draw, tow, tug, hoist, lug

heavy *ADJECTIVE*
> **1** *The box was too heavy to lift.*
> weighty, massive, bulky, hefty, ponderous
> **OPPOSITE** light
> **2** *A heavy mist hung over the valley.*
> dense, thick, solid

| **OPPOSITE** thin

3 *The rain has caused heavy flooding.*
severe, extreme, torrential

4 *Both sides suffered heavy losses in the battle.*
large, substantial, considerable

5 *Digging the garden is heavy work.*
hard, tough, gruelling,
back-breaking, strenuous, arduous

6 *This book makes heavy reading.*
serious, intense, demanding

7 *lying down after a heavy meal*
filling, stodgy, rich

hectic *ADJECTIVE*
the hectic preparations for the big day
frantic, feverish, frenzied, frenetic,
chaotic, busy
(*informal*) manic
| **OPPOSITES** quiet, leisurely

heed *VERB*
They refused to heed our advice.
listen to, pay attention to, take
notice of, attend to, regard, obey,
follow, mark, mind, note
| **OPPOSITE** ignore

hefty *ADJECTIVE*
1 *an actor with a hefty physique*
strong, sturdy, muscular, powerful,
brawny, burly, beefy, hulking,
strapping
| **OPPOSITE** slight

2 *The alchemist lifted down a hefty tome.*
weighty, large, massive, bulky,
ponderous

3 *They had to pay a hefty fine.*
substantial, considerable, sizeable,
large

height *NOUN*
1 *measuring the height of a building*
altitude, elevation
▶ The natural height of your body is
your **stature**.

2 *the dizzying heights of the Himalayas*
summit, peak, crest, crown, cap,
pinnacle

3 *at the height of her career*
peak, high point, pinnacle, zenith,
climax

heighten *VERB*
The music heightens the tension in the film.
intensify, increase, enhance, add
to, strengthen, magnify, boost,
reinforce

help *VERB*
1 *Could you please help me with my luggage?*
aid, assist, give assistance to
| **IDIOMS** give a hand to,
lend a hand to
▶ To help someone to commit a crime
is to **abet** them.

2 *The money will help victims of the earthquake.*
be helpful to, benefit, support,
serve, be of service to

3 *This medicine will help your cough.*
make better, cure, ease, relieve,
soothe, alleviate, improve
| **OPPOSITES** aggravate, worsen

4 *I couldn't help smiling.*
avoid, resist, refrain from, keep
from, stop

help *NOUN*
1 *Thank you for your help.*
aid, assistance, support, guidance,
cooperation, advice
| **OPPOSITE** hindrance

2 *The money will be of great help to us.*
use, benefit

helpful *ADJECTIVE*
1 *The staff were friendly and helpful.*
obliging, accommodating,
considerate, thoughtful,
sympathetic, kind,
cooperative
| **OPPOSITE** unhelpful

2 *The website offers some helpful advice.*
useful, valuable, worthwhile,
beneficial, profitable
| **OPPOSITE** worthless

helping *NOUN*
a second helping of trifle
serving, portion, plateful, amount, share, ration

helpless *ADJECTIVE*
The cubs are born blind and helpless.
powerless, weak, feeble, dependent, defenceless, vulnerable
▮ **OPPOSITES** independent, strong

hem *VERB*
▷ **hem someone in**
The bus was hemmed in by the traffic.
shut in, box in, encircle, enclose, surround

herb *NOUN*

 WORD WEB

some common herbs
basil, camomile, caraway, chervil, chicory, chives, coriander, cumin, dill, fennel, fenugreek, hyssop, lemon balm, liquorice, lovage, marjoram, mint, oregano, parsley, peppermint, rosemary, sage, tarragon, thyme
► The use of herbs to treat illness is **herbal medicine** or **herbalism**, and someone who practises this is a **herbalist**.

herd *NOUN*
FOR GROUPS OF ANIMALS SEE collective noun

hereditary *ADJECTIVE*
1 *a hereditary disease*
genetic, inherited, innate, inborn
2 *hereditary wealth*
inherited, passed down, bequeathed, ancestral

heritage *NOUN*
exploring her African heritage
ancestry, lineage, background, descent, history, roots, tradition, culture

hero *NOUN*
1 *one of my sporting heroes*
idol, role model, star, celebrity, legend, giant
2 *the hero of the film*
protagonist, main character, lead

heroic *ADJECTIVE*
a heroic rescue attempt
bold, brave, courageous, daring, audacious, fearless, intrepid, valiant
(*informal*) gutsy
▮ **OPPOSITE** cowardly

hesitant *ADJECTIVE*
1 *I'm still hesitant about asking her.*
uncertain, unsure, doubtful, dubious, undecided, ambivalent
▮ **IDIOM** in two minds
▮ **OPPOSITE** certain
2 *taking a hesitant step forward*
tentative, cautious, timid, wary, diffident
▮ **OPPOSITE** confident

hesitate *VERB*
I hesitated before picking up the phone.
pause, delay, wait, hold back, falter, stall, dither, waver, vacillate
(*informal*) dilly-dally
▮ **IDIOM** think twice

hidden *ADJECTIVE*
1 *a hidden camera*
concealed, secret, unseen, out of sight, invisible, camouflaged
▮ **OPPOSITE** visible
2 *The poem has a hidden meaning.*
obscure, mysterious, secret, covert, coded, cryptic
▮ **OPPOSITE** obvious

hide *VERB*
1 *We hid in the bushes until they had gone.*
go into hiding, take cover, take refuge, keep out of sight
▮ **IDIOMS** lie low, go to ground
2 *She hid the letters in a secret drawer.*
conceal, secrete, bury, put out of sight

(*informal*) stash
┃ **OPPOSITE** expose

3 *The mist hid our view of the hills.*
cover, obscure, screen, mask,
shroud, veil, blot out, eclipse
┃ **OPPOSITE** uncover

4 *I tried to hide my true feelings.*
disguise, conceal, keep secret,
suppress, bottle up, camouflage,
cloak
┃ **IDIOM** keep a lid on
┃ **OPPOSITES** show, reveal

hideous *ADJECTIVE*
The legend tells of a hideous beast.
ugly, grotesque, monstrous,
revolting, repulsive, ghastly,
gruesome, horrible, appalling,
dreadful, frightful
┃ **OPPOSITE** beautiful

high *ADJECTIVE*
1 *a castle surrounded by a high wall*
tall, towering, elevated, giant, lofty
┃ **OPPOSITE** low

2 *an officer of high rank*
senior, top, leading, important,
prominent, powerful, exalted
┃ **OPPOSITES** low, junior

3 *the high cost of living*
expensive, dear, costly, excessive,
exorbitant, inflated
(*informal*) steep
┃ **OPPOSITE** low

4 *a warning of high winds*
strong, powerful, forceful, extreme
┃ **OPPOSITES** light, gentle

5 *a high voice*
high-pitched, squeaky, shrill,
piercing
▶ A high singing voice is **soprano** or
treble.
┃ **OPPOSITE** deep

highlight *NOUN*
What was the highlight of your trip?
high point, high spot, best moment,
climax
┃ **OPPOSITES** low point, nadir

highly *ADVERB*
1 *a highly experienced doctor*
very, extremely, exceptionally,
considerably, decidedly

2 *People think very highly of her work.*
well, favourably, approvingly,
admiringly, enthusiastically

hike *VERB*
We often go hiking across the moors.
walk, trek, ramble, tramp, backpack

hilarious *ADJECTIVE*
a hilarious joke
funny, amusing, comical, uproarious
(*informal*) hysterical, priceless
┃ **SEE ALSO funny**

hill *NOUN*
1 *a valley between two hills*
mount, peak, ridge, fell
▶ A small hill is a **hillock**, **knoll**, or
mound.
FOR TIPS ON DESCRIBING LANDSCAPE SEE
landscape

2 *Their house is at the top of the hill.*
slope, rise, incline, ascent, gradient
(*Scottish*) brae

hinder *VERB*
*A sandstorm hindered the rescue
attempt.*
hamper, obstruct, impede,
handicap, restrict, hold up, slow
down, get in the way of, interfere
with
┃ **OPPOSITE** help

hindrance *NOUN*
*Parked cars can be a hindrance to
cyclists.*
obstacle, obstruction,
inconvenience, handicap,
disadvantage, drawback
┃ **OPPOSITE** help

hint *NOUN*
1 *Can you give me a hint?*
clue, indication, sign, suggestion,
inkling, intimation

2 *some handy hints on sewing*
tip, pointer, suggestion, guideline

a
b
c
d
e
f
g
h
i
j
k
l
m
n
o
p
q
r
s
t
u
v
w
x
y
z

hint *VERB*

He hinted that he might be retiring soon.

give a hint, suggest, imply, intimate

▶ To hint at something unpleasant is to **insinuate**.

hire *VERB*

1 *hiring a car*
rent, lease, charter

2 *hiring extra staff for Christmas*
employ, engage, recruit, take on
❙ OPPOSITE dismiss

historic *ADJECTIVE*

The Moon landing was a historic event.

famous, important, notable, celebrated, renowned, momentous, significant, major, ground-breaking
❙ OPPOSITES unimportant, minor

Usage Note

The words **historic** and **historical** are not synonyms. A **historical** event took place in the past, but a **historic** event is important in history, and may refer to the past or present: *Today is a historic day for the people of Beijing.*

historical *ADJECTIVE*

1 *reading historical documents*
past, former, old, ancient, bygone, olden
❙ OPPOSITES contemporary, recent

2 *Was King Arthur a historical figure?*
real, real-life, true, actual, authentic, documented
❙ OPPOSITES fictitious, legendary

WRITING TIPS

writing historical fiction

Master Shakespeare must have heard the commotion already, because he was standing at the top of the stairs, with his doublet and shirt both unbuttoned and a quill pen still in his hand.
— *Susan Cooper, King of Shadows*

clothes

bodice, bonnet, breeches, bustle, cape, cloak, corset, cravat, crinoline, doublet, drawers, farthingale, frock coat, gauntlet, gown, hose, petticoat, raiment, robe, ruff, shawl, toga, top hat, tricorn hat, tunic

occupations

apothecary, barrow boy, blacksmith, chimney sweep, clerk, cobbler, costermonger, draper, dressmaker, executioner, governess, housemaid, innkeeper, kitchen maid, laundress, merchant, pedlar, seamstress, spinner, stable-hand, tanner, weaver, wheelwright, wigmaker

setting

battlefield, frontier, imperial court, industrial town, inn, market, monastery, orphanage, outpost, tavern, workhouse

transport

airship, chariot, galleon, hansom cab, horse-drawn carriage, penny-farthing, sedan chair, stagecoach, steamboat, steam train

weapons

ballista, blunderbuss, bow and arrow, broadsword, cannon, catapult, claymore, cutlass, dagger, gunpowder, lance, longbow, mace, sabre, samurai sword, siege tower, shield, spear, trebuchet

other details

candlelight, farthing, flagon, gallows, gaslight, goblet, groat, guinea, lantern, oil lamp, parasol, parchment, plague, powdered wig, quill pen, shilling, telegraph

FOR WORDS IN OLD AND POETIC USE SEE old

history NOUN

1 *Dr Sachs is an expert on American history.*
heritage, past, antiquity, past times, olden days

► The arrangement of events in the order in which they happened is **chronology**.

2 *writing a history of the Civil War*
account, chronicle, record

► The history of a person's life is their **biography**.

► The history of your own life is your **autobiography** or **memoirs**.

► A chronological list of key events is a **timeline**.

hit VERB

OVERUSED WORD

hit a person, animal
strike, beat, thump, punch, slap, smack, swipe, slog, cuff
(*informal*) whack, thump, wallop, clout, clobber, sock, belt, biff
(*North American informal*) slug
(*old use*) smite

► To hit someone with a stick is to **club** them.

*In judo, you are not allowed to **strike** your opponent.*

hit an object, surface
knock, bang, bump, bash, strike, thump, rap, crack, slam
(*informal*) whack

► To hit your toe on something is to **stub** it.

*Mind you don't **bump** your head on the ceiling.*

hit something in an accident
crash into, smash into, collide with, run into, plough into, meet head on

*A lorry had **ploughed into** the side of their house.*

hit gently, lightly
tap, pat, patter, rap

***Pat** the dough with your hands on a floured surface.*

hit repeatedly
batter, buffet, pound, pummel, drum

*Betty **drummed** her fingers impatiently on the desk.*

hit a note, target
reach, attain

*Can you **reach** the high notes in this aria?*

OPPOSITES miss, fall short of

hit a problem, difficulty
run into, come across, encounter, face, confront

*I **encountered** a snag while installing the program.*

hit NOUN

1 *a nasty hit on the head*
bump, blow, bang, strike, knock, whack, punch, slap, smack, swipe

2 *The book was an instant hit.*
success, triumph
(*informal*) winner
OPPOSITES failure, flop

hitch VERB

1 *She hitched the baby higher on her hip.*
pull, lift, raise, draw

2 *hitching a trailer to a tractor*
attach, connect, hook up, harness, yoke, couple

hitch NOUN

The evening went without a hitch.
problem, difficulty, snag, complication, obstacle, setback
(*informal*) hiccup, glitch

hoard NOUN

a hoard of old magazines
cache, store, stock, supply, pile,
stockpile, reserve
(*informal*) stash

▶ A hoard of treasure is a **treasure
trove**.

hoard VERB

Squirrels hoard nuts for the winter.
store, collect, gather, save, pile up,
stockpile, put aside, put by
(*informal*) stash away

hoarse ADJECTIVE

Her voice was hoarse from shouting.
rough, harsh, husky, croaky, throaty,
gruff, rasping, gravelly
**FOR TIPS ON DESCRIBING VOICES SEE
sound❶**

hoax NOUN

The email was just a hoax.
joke, practical joke, prank, trick,
spoof, fraud
(*informal*) con, scam

hobby NOUN

My favourite hobby is knitting.
pastime, pursuit, interest, activity,
recreation, amusement

hoist VERB

*The women hoisted the bundles onto
their heads.*
lift, raise, heave, elevate, pull up,
haul up, winch up

hold VERB

1 *Hold the reins loosely in your left
hand.*
clasp, grasp, grip, cling to, hang on
to, clutch, seize, squeeze
2 *a woman holding a baby*
embrace, hug, cradle
3 *The tank should hold ten litres.*
contain, take, have space for,
accommodate
4 *Will the ladder hold my weight?*
bear, support, carry, take
5 *If our luck holds, we could reach the
final.*
continue, last, carry on, persist, stay

6 *She has always held strong opinions.*
believe in, maintain, stick to
7 *We will be holding a public meeting.*
host, put on, organize, arrange,
convene, call
8 *Three suspects are being held in
prison.*
confine, detain, keep

▷ **hold out**
1 *The stranger held out his hand in
greeting.*
extend, reach out, stick out,
stretch out
2 *Our supplies won't hold out much
longer.*
keep going, last, carry on, continue,
endure

▷ **hold up**
1 *Hold up your hand if you know the
answer.*
lift, put up, raise, elevate, hoist
2 *Roadworks were holding up the
traffic.*
delay, hinder, impede, slow down

hold NOUN

1 *Keep a firm hold on the leash.*
grip, grasp, clutch, clasp
2 *The myth had a strange hold on my
imagination.*
influence, power, dominance, pull,
sway

hole NOUN

1 *The meteor left a hole in the ground.*
pit, hollow, crater, dent, depression,
cavity, chasm, abyss
2 *mending a hole in the roof*
gap, opening, breach, break, cut,
slit, gash, split, tear, rift, vent
3 *a rabbit hole*
burrow, lair, den, earth, sett

holiday NOUN

*We spent our summer holiday in
France.*
vacation, break, leave, time off

hollow ADJECTIVE

1 *a hollow tube*
empty, unfilled, void

OPPOSITE solid

2 *a hollow promise*
insincere, empty, meaningless
OPPOSITE sincere

3 *hollow cheeks*
sunken, wasted, deep-set, concave
OPPOSITES plump, chubby

hollow NOUN
digging a hollow in the sand
hole, pit, crater, cavity, depression, dent, dip

hollow VERB
a cave hollowed out of the rock
dig, excavate, gouge, scoop

holy ADJECTIVE
1 *a pilgrimage to a holy shrine*
sacred, blessed, revered, venerated, sanctified, hallowed

2 *The pilgrims were holy people.*
religious, spiritual, devout, pious, godly, saintly

home NOUN
The cottage was their home for ten years.
residence, house, dwelling, abode, lodging
▶ A home for the sick is a **convalescent home** or **nursing home**.
▶ A place where a bird or animal lives is its **habitat**.

homely ADJECTIVE
a small hotel with a homely atmosphere
friendly, informal, cosy, familiar, relaxed, easy-going, comfortable, snug

honest ADJECTIVE
1 *an honest citizen*
good, honourable, upright, virtuous, moral, decent, law-abiding, scrupulous, trustworthy
OPPOSITE dishonest

2 *Please give me your honest opinion.*
sincere, genuine, truthful, direct, frank, candid, plain, straightforward, unbiased

OPPOSITE insincere

honour NOUN
1 *Claudio feels that his honour is at stake.*
reputation, good name, repute, standing

2 *I believe he is a man of honour.*
integrity, honesty, fairness, morality, decency, principles

3 *the honour of playing for your country*
privilege, distinction, glory, prestige, kudos

honour VERB
a service to honour the dead
pay tribute to, salute, recognize, celebrate, praise, acclaim

honourable ADJECTIVE
1 *an honourable man*
honest, virtuous, good, upright, moral, principled, decent, fair, noble, worthy, righteous

2 *an honourable thing to do*
noble, admirable, praiseworthy, decent
OPPOSITE unworthy

hook NOUN
1 *hanging your coat on a hook*
peg, nail

2 *a cloak fastened with a hook*
clasp, clip, fastener

hook VERB
1 *Hook the curtains onto the track.*
attach, fasten, hitch, connect, couple

2 *I managed to hook a small fish.*
catch, land, take

hoop NOUN
throwing a ball through a hoop
ring, circle, band, loop, circlet

hop VERB
hopping about in excitement
jump, leap, skip, spring, bound, caper, prance, dance

hope NOUN
1 *The team has high hopes for the future.*

a
b
c
d
e
f
g
h
i
j
k
l
m
n
o
p
q
r
s
t
u
v
w
x
y
z

ambition, aspiration, dream, desire, wish, plan

2 *There was little hope of escape.*
prospect, expectation, likelihood

hope VERB

I hope to see you again soon.
wish, trust, expect, look forward

hopeful ADJECTIVE

1 *feeling hopeful about the future*
optimistic, confident, positive, buoyant, expectant

❙ **OPPOSITE** pessimistic

2 *Our chances are looking more hopeful.*
promising, encouraging, favourable, reassuring

❙ **OPPOSITE** discouraging

hopeless ADJECTIVE

1 *The plight of the crew was hopeless.*
desperate, wretched, impossible, futile, beyond hope

❙ **OPPOSITE** hopeful

2 *I'm hopeless at algebra.*
bad, poor, incompetent, awful (*informal*) useless, rubbish, lousy, pathetic

❙ **OPPOSITES** good, competent

hopelessly ADVERB

Silvius is hopelessly in love with Phoebe.
utterly, completely, totally, deeply

horde NOUN

Hordes of people thronged the streets.
crowd, mob, throng, mass, swarm, gang, pack

horizontal ADJECTIVE

Draw a horizontal line.
flat, level

❙ **OPPOSITES** vertical, upright

horoscope NOUN

SEE **zodiac**

horrible ADJECTIVE

the horrible stench of rotten eggs
awful, terrible, dreadful, appalling, unpleasant, disagreeable, offensive, objectionable, disgusting, repulsive, revolting, horrendous, horrid, nasty, hateful, odious, loathsome, ghastly

❙ **OPPOSITE** pleasant

horrific ADJECTIVE

The film starts with a horrific battle scene.
horrifying, terrifying, shocking, gruesome, dreadful, appalling, ghastly, hideous, atrocious, grisly, sickening

horrify VERB

1 *The scene may horrify some viewers.*
frighten, scare, alarm, terrify, disgust, offend, sicken

2 *We were horrified by all the waste.*
appal, shock, outrage, scandalize

horror NOUN

1 *Rowan's eyes filled with horror.*
terror, fear, fright, alarm, panic, dread

2 *The film depicts the full horror of war.*
awfulness, hideousness, gruesomeness, ghastliness, grimness

 WRITING TIPS

writing horror fiction

I trembled and my heart failed within me, when, on looking up, I saw by the light of the moon the daemon at the casement. A ghastly grin wrinkled his lips as he gazed on me.
— *Mary Shelley, Frankenstein*

characters

ghost, ghost-hunter, ghoul, mummy, necromancer, phantom, poltergeist, spectre, spirit, vampire, vampire-slayer, werewolf, wraith, zombie

setting

catacombs, cemetery, crypt, dungeon, graveyard, haunted mansion, mausoleum,

necropolis, tomb

useful words & phrases
accursed, afterlife, apparition,
beyond the grave, coffin, corpse,
curse, dark side, eerie, exorcism,
ghostly, ghoulish, gore,
Halloween, haunting, hex, living
dead, lycanthropy, macabre,
malediction, mortal remains,
necromancy, nightmare, occult,
other-worldly, paranormal,
possession, reanimation,
sarcophagus, seance, shroud,
soul, spectral, supernatural,
trance, uncanny, undead,
unearthly, vampirism, voodoo

horse NOUN
a horse pulling a carriage
mount, charger, nag
(*poetic*) steed

 WORD WEB

some types of horse
bronco, carthorse, Clydesdale,
mustang, pony, racehorse,
Shetland pony, shire horse,
warhorse

▶ A male horse is a **stallion** and a
female is a **mare**.

▶ A young horse is a **foal**, **colt**
(male), or **filly** (female).

▶ A cross between a donkey and a
horse is a **mule**.

parts of a horse's body
coat, fetlock, flank, hoof, mane,
withers

colours of a horse's coat
bay, chestnut, dappled, dun,
grey, palomino, piebald, pinto,
roan

noises made by a horse
neigh, snicker, snort, whinny

ways a horse can move
canter, gallop, trot, walk

▶ An **equine** activity involves
horses and an **equestrian** activity
involves horse-riding.

▶ A person who rides a horse in a
race is a **jockey**.

▶ Soldiers who fight on horseback
are **cavalry**.

hospital NOUN
a small community hospital
clinic, infirmary, sanatorium
❚ SEE ALSO **medicine**

hostile ADJECTIVE
1 *The men glared at us in a hostile
manner.*
aggressive, antagonistic,
confrontational, unfriendly,
unwelcoming, warlike, belligerent
❚ OPPOSITE friendly
2 *The North Pole has a hostile climate.*
harsh, adverse, unfavourable,
inhospitable
❚ OPPOSITE favourable

hostility NOUN
*There is still hostility between our
countries.*
dislike, enmity, unfriendliness,
aggression, antagonism, hate,
hatred, bad feeling, ill-will, malice,
venom
❚ OPPOSITE friendship

hot ADJECTIVE
1 *a hot summer's day*
warm, balmy, blazing, scorching,
blistering, roasting, baking,
sweltering, stifling
❚ OPPOSITES cold, cool
2 *a bowl of hot soup*
burning, boiling, scalding, searing,
sizzling, steaming, red-hot,
piping hot
❚ OPPOSITES cold, cool
3 *a hot curry sauce*
spicy, peppery, fiery
❚ OPPOSITE mild
4 *a hot temper*
fierce, fiery, violent, passionate,

a
b
c
d
e
f
g
h
i
j
k
l
m
n
o
p
q
r
s
t
u
v
w
x
y
z

raging, volatile, intense
❙ OPPOSITES calm, mild

house NOUN

1 *She still lives in the family house.*
residence, home, dwelling, abode, lodging
▶ A small shabby house is a **hovel**.
❙ SEE ALSO **accommodation**

2 *He was related to the House of Stuart.*
family, dynasty, clan, line

house VERB

The building can house 200 students.
accommodate, lodge, shelter, take in, quarter, board

hover VERB

1 *A helicopter hovered overhead.*
hang, float, drift, be suspended, be poised

2 *I hovered just outside the door.*
linger, pause, wait about, dally, loiter
(*informal*) hang about

however ADVERB

1 *I can't remember, however hard I try.*
no matter how

2 *The film is enjoyable; however, it is rather long.*
nevertheless, nonetheless, yet, still, even so, for all that

howl VERB

1 *a baby howling in its pram*
cry, wail, bawl, scream, yell, shriek
(*informal*) holler

2 *wolves howling in the night*
bay, yowl, yelp

huddle VERB

1 *We huddled around the fire to get warm.*
crowd, gather, congregate, flock, cluster, pack

2 *I huddled under the blankets and tried to sleep.*
curl up, nestle, cuddle, snuggle, squeeze

hue NOUN

an unnatural hue of green
colour, shade, tint, tone, tinge
FOR TIPS ON DESCRIBING COLOURS SEE
colour

hug VERB

The two friends laughed and hugged each other.
embrace, clasp, cuddle, squeeze, cling to, hold tight

hug NOUN

Izzie gave her dad a huge hug.
embrace, clasp, cuddle, squeeze

huge ADJECTIVE

Woolly mammoths were huge creatures.
enormous, gigantic, massive, colossal, giant, immense, vast, mighty, mammoth, monumental, hulking, great, big, large
(*informal*) whopping, humongous
(*literary*) gargantuan
❙ OPPOSITES small, tiny
❙ SEE ALSO **big**

hum VERB

the sound of insects humming
drone, buzz, murmur, purr, whirr

hum NOUN

the hum of an engine
drone, whirr, throb, murmur, purr

humane ADJECTIVE

A humane society should treat animals well.
kind, compassionate, sympathetic, civilized, benevolent, kind-hearted, charitable, loving, merciful
❙ OPPOSITE cruel

humanity NOUN

1 *the future of humanity*
the human race, human beings, humans, people, humankind, mankind, Homo sapiens

2 *appealing to our sense of humanity*
compassion, kindness, sympathy, humaneness, benevolence, charity, mercy, brotherly love, fellow feeling
❙ OPPOSITE cruelty

umans *PLURAL NOUN*

Humans have smaller brains than whales.

human beings, the human race, people, humanity, humankind, mankind, Homo sapiens

umble *ADJECTIVE*

1 *The book is about a humble watchmaker.*

modest, meek, unassuming, self-effacing, unassertive, submissive

OPPOSITE proud

2 *a painting of a humble domestic scene*

simple, modest, plain, ordinary, commonplace, lowly

OPPOSITE grand

humid *ADJECTIVE*

the humid climate of tropical forests

muggy, clammy, close, sultry, sticky, moist, steamy

OPPOSITE fresh

humiliate *VERB*

Nat felt humiliated by his failure.

embarrass, disgrace, shame, make ashamed, humble, crush, degrade, demean, mortify (*informal*) put someone in their place, take someone down a peg

humiliating *ADJECTIVE*

The team suffered a humiliating defeat.

embarrassing, crushing, degrading, demeaning, humbling, undignified, ignominious, mortifying

OPPOSITE glorious

humorous *ADJECTIVE*

a humorous anecdote

amusing, funny, comic, comical, witty, entertaining, droll

OPPOSITE serious

SEE ALSO **funny**

humour *NOUN*

1 *I liked the humour in the film.*

comedy, wit, hilarity, satire, irony, jokes, witticisms

OPPOSITE seriousness

2 *Oleg awoke in a bad humour.*

mood, temper, disposition, frame of mind, spirits

hump *NOUN*

The grey whale has a low hump on its back.

bump, lump, bulge, swelling

hunch *NOUN*

following a hunch about the murder case

feeling, intuition, inkling, guess, impression, suspicion, idea, notion, fancy

IDIOM gut feeling

hunger *NOUN*

feeling faint with hunger

lack of food, starvation, undernourishment

▶ A severe shortage of food in an area is **famine**.

▶ Bad health caused by not having enough food is **malnutrition**.

hungry *ADJECTIVE*

1 *feeling hungry between meals*

starving, starved, famished, ravenous, undernourished, underfed (*informal*) peckish

2 *hungry for success*

eager, keen, longing, yearning, craving, greedy (*informal*) itching

hunt *VERB*

1 *Some Native American tribes used to hunt buffalo.*

chase, pursue, track, trail, hound, stalk

▶ An animal which hunts other animals for food is **predator**.

2 *hunting in the attic for old photos*

search, seek, look, rummage, ferret, root around, scour around

IDIOM look high and low

hunt NOUN

Police have begun the hunt for clues.
search, quest, chase, pursuit (of),
forage

hurdle NOUN

1 The runners cleared the
first hurdle.
fence, barrier, jump,
barricade, obstacle

2 Our biggest hurdle is our lack of
confidence.
difficulty, problem, handicap,
hindrance, impediment, snag
IDIOM stumbling block

hurl VERB

I hurled the ball as far as I could.
throw, fling, pitch, toss, cast, sling,
launch
(informal) chuck

hurried ADJECTIVE

a hurried glance at the clock
quick, hasty, speedy, swift, rapid,
rushed, brisk, cursory

hurry VERB

1 We'd better hurry or we'll miss the
bus.
be quick, hasten, make speed
(informal) get a move on, step on it
IDIOM (informal) get your skates on
OPPOSITE dawdle

2 An ambulance crew hurried to the
scene.
rush, dash, race, fly, speed, sprint,
hurtle, scurry
OPPOSITES amble, stroll

3 I don't mean to hurry you.
hasten, hustle, speed up, urge on
OPPOSITE slow down

hurry NOUN

In my hurry, I left my purse behind.
rush, haste, speed, urgency

hurt VERB

1 Jennie hurt her wrist playing hockey.
injure, wound, damage, harm,
maim, bruise, cut
▶ To hurt someone deliberately is to
torment or **torture** them.

2 My left knee hurts.
be sore, be painful, ache, throb,
sting, smart

3 Your letter hurt me deeply.
upset, distress, offend, grieve,
sadden, pain, wound, sting

hurtful ADJECTIVE

That was a very hurtful remark.
upsetting, distressing, unkind, cruel,
mean, spiteful, wounding, nasty,
malicious

hurtle VERB

The train hurtled along at
top speed.
rush, speed, race, dash, fly, charge,
tear, shoot, zoom

husband NOUN

She lives with her husband and
two sons.
spouse, partner, consort
IDIOM (informal) other half

hush VERB

The speaker tried to hush
the crowd.
silence, quieten, settle, still, calm
(informal) shut up

▷ **hush something up**
They tried to hush up the scandal.
cover up, hide, conceal, keep quiet,
keep secret, suppress
IDIOM sweep under the carpet

hush NOUN

There was a sudden hush in the
room.
silence, quiet, stillness, calm,
tranquillity

husky ADJECTIVE

a husky voice
hoarse, throaty, gruff, rasping,
gravelly, rough, croaky
FOR TIPS ON DESCRIBING VOICES SEE
sound❶

hut NOUN

a hut in the garden
shed, shack, cabin, den, shelter,
shanty, hovel

hygienic *ADJECTIVE*
   a hygienic surface for preparing food
   sanitary, clean, disinfected,
   sterilized, sterile, germ-free
   OPPOSITES unhygienic, insanitary

hysteria *NOUN*
   *The crowd was on the
   verge of hysteria.*
   frenzy, mania, madness, craziness,
   hysterics

hysterical *ADJECTIVE*
   1 *Some of the mob became hysterical.*
      crazy, frenzied, mad, delirious,
      raving, wild, uncontrollable
   2 (*informal*) *a hysterical joke*
      hilarious, funny, amusing, comical,
      uproarious
      (*informal*) priceless, side-splitting
      SEE ALSO funny

a
b
c
d
e
f
g
h
i
j
k
l
m
n
o
p
q
r
s
t
u
v
w
x
y
z

ice NOUN

WORD WEB

various forms of ice
black ice, floe, frost, glacier,
iceberg, ice cap, ice field, icicle,
pack ice, sheet ice

▶ A permanently frozen layer of soil
is **permafrost**.

▶ The scientific study of ice and
glaciers is **glaciology**.

ICT NOUN
SEE **computer**

icy ADJECTIVE

1 *an icy wind*
cold, freezing, frosty, wintry, arctic,
bitter, biting, raw

2 *an icy pavement*
frozen, slippery, glacial, glassy, rimy

idea NOUN

1 *I've got a great idea!*
plan, scheme, proposal, suggestion,
proposition, inspiration

2 *He has some odd ideas about life.*
belief, opinion, view, theory,
notion, concept, conception,
hypothesis

3 *the central idea of the poem*
point, meaning, intention, thought

4 *Have you any idea what will
happen?*
clue, hint, inkling, impression, sense,
suspicion, hunch

ideal ADJECTIVE
ideal conditions for sailing
perfect, excellent, suitable, faultless,
the best

ideal NOUN

1 *an ideal of perfect beauty*
model, icon, epitome, pattern,
example, standard, exemplar

2 *the ideals of the French revolution*
principle, belief, conviction

identical ADJECTIVE
wearing identical outfits
matching, alike, indistinguishable,
interchangeable, twin, the same
┃ OPPOSITE different

identify VERB

1 *identifying a face in the crowd*
recognize, name, distinguish,
pick out, single out

2 *identifying the nature of the problem*
diagnose, discover, spot
(*informal*) put a name to

▷ **identify with**
*Can you identify with the hero of the
film?*
sympathize with, empathize with,
feel for, relate to, understand
(*informal*) put yourself in someone's
shoes

idiot NOUN
I felt like such an idiot.
fool, ass, clown, halfwit, dunce,
simpleton, blockhead, buffoon,
dunderhead, imbecile, moron
(*informal*) chump, dope, dummy,
dimwit, nitwit, nincompoop, ninny
(*British informal*) twit, clot, wally

idiotic ADJECTIVE
an idiotic scheme
stupid, foolish, senseless, silly,
ridiculous, nonsensical, unwise,
ill-advised, half-witted, unintelligent,
absurd, crazy, mad, hare-brained,
foolhardy
(*informal*) dim-witted, dumb
(*British informal*) daft, barmy
┃ OPPOSITE sensible

idle *ADJECTIVE*

1 *an idle fellow*
lazy, indolent, slothful, work-shy
⎮ **OPPOSITES** hard-working, industrious

2 *The computers lay idle all week.*
inactive, unused, inoperative
⎮ **OPPOSITES** active, in use

3 *spending an idle moment*
unoccupied, spare, free
⎮ **OPPOSITE** busy

4 *making an idle comment*
frivolous, trivial, trifling, unimportant, empty, meaningless
⎮ **OPPOSITE** serious

idol *NOUN*

1 *an ancient clay idol*
god, deity, icon, effigy, statue, figurine

2 *a former pop idol*
star, superstar, celebrity, icon
(*informal*) pin-up

idolize *VERB*

Greg idolizes his big brother.
adore, love, worship, be devoted to, look up to

ignite *VERB*

1 *igniting a match*
light, set fire to, set alight

2 *The oven would not ignite.*
catch fire, light, burn, kindle, spark

ignorant *ADJECTIVE*

What an ignorant lot you are!
uneducated, uninformed, illiterate

▷ **ignorant of**
ignorant of the facts in the case
unaware of, unfamiliar with, unacquainted with
⎮ **OPPOSITE** aware of

ignore *VERB*

1 *Why are you ignoring me?*
take no notice of, pay no attention to, neglect, spurn, snub
⎮ **IDIOM** give you the cold shoulder

2 *I'll ignore that remark.*
disregard, overlook, brush aside
⎮ **IDIOM** turn a blind eye to

ill *ADJECTIVE*

1 *She was ill with flu for three weeks.*
unwell, sick, poorly, sickly, ailing, infirm, unfit, indisposed
⎮ **IDIOM** under the weather

▶ Someone who feels ill may be **nauseous** or **queasy**.

▶ Someone who looks ill may be **peaky** or **off colour**.
⎮ **OPPOSITES** healthy, well
⎮ **SEE ALSO illness**

2 *the ill effects of a poor diet*
bad, harmful, adverse, damaging, detrimental, deleterious
⎮ **OPPOSITES** good, beneficial

ill *ADVERB*

1 *ill prepared for the rainy season*
badly, poorly, inadequately
⎮ **OPPOSITE** well

2 *an expense they could ill afford*
barely, scarcely, hardly
⎮ **OPPOSITE** easily

illegal *ADJECTIVE*

an illegal copy of a DVD
unlawful, illicit, criminal, banned, prohibited, forbidden, outlawed, against the law, unlicensed
(*informal*) crooked
⎮ **OPPOSITE** legal

illegible *ADJECTIVE*

an illegible signature
unreadable, indecipherable, unintelligible, unclear, indistinct
⎮ **OPPOSITES** legible, readable

illness *NOUN*

suffering from a mysterious illness
sickness, ailment, disease, disorder, complaint, condition, affliction, malady, infirmity, infection, virus
(*informal*) bug

▶ A sudden illness is an **attack** or **fit**.

▶ A period of illness is a **bout**.

▶ A general outbreak of illness in a particular area is an **epidemic**.

》

WORD WEB

some common illnesses

allergy, anaemia, appendicitis, asthma, bronchitis, chickenpox, chill, cold, cough, diarrhoea, eczema, fever, flu, glandular fever, hay fever, headache, indigestion, influenza, jaundice, laryngitis, measles, migraine, mumps, pneumonia, stomach ache, tonsillitis, ulcer, whooping cough

ills PLURAL NOUN
the ills of modern life
problem, trouble, drawback, trial, tribulation
(informal) headache

illusion NOUN
1 Was it a real UFO, or just an illusion?
mirage, apparition, dream, fantasy
IDIOM figment of your imagination
2 Perspective gives a drawing the illusion of depth.
appearance, impression, semblance

illustrate VERB
1 a painting which illustrates a scene from 'Macbeth'
depict, picture, portray
2 a talk illustrating the importance of road safety
show, demonstrate, explain, make clear, get across
IDIOM bring home

illustration NOUN
1 a book with colour illustrations
picture, photograph, print, plate, figure, drawing, sketch, diagram
2 Let me give you an illustration.
example, instance, demonstration, specimen, case

image NOUN
1 The film contains graphic images of war.
picture, portrayal, depiction, representation
2 Amy frowned at her image in the mirror.
reflection, likeness
3 Martin is the image of his father.
double, twin
4 trying to improve his image
reputation, profile, persona

imaginary ADJECTIVE
The story is set in an imaginary world.
imagined, non-existent, unreal, made-up, invented, fanciful, fictitious, fictional, make-believe, pretend
OPPOSITE real

imagination NOUN
1 It's all in your imagination.
mind, fancy, dreams
2 writing which lacks imagination
creativity, inventiveness, ingenuity, inspiration, originality, vision

imaginative ADJECTIVE
Edgar Allan Poe wrote highly imaginative stories.
creative, inventive, inspired, original, innovative, fanciful, visionary
OPPOSITES unimaginative, dull

imagine VERB
1 Can you imagine life without computers?
picture, visualize, envisage, conceive of
IDIOM see in your mind's eye
2 I imagine you'd like something to eat.
suppose, assume, presume, expect, take it

imitate VERB
1 At first, he imitated the style of other authors.
copy, reproduce, echo, ape, simulate, follow, mirror, match
2 a comedian who imitates famous people
mimic, impersonate, do an impression of
(informal) send up, take off

imitation ADJECTIVE

a rug made from imitation fur
artificial, synthetic, fake, sham,
mock, man-made

OPPOSITES real, genuine

imitation NOUN

an imitation of a Roman coin
copy, replica, reproduction,
duplicate

▶ An imitation made to deceive
someone is a **fake** or a **forgery**.

immature ADJECTIVE

He is quite immature for his age.
childish, babyish, infantile, juvenile

OPPOSITE mature

immediate ADJECTIVE

1 They sent an immediate response.
instant, instantaneous, prompt,
speedy, swift, urgent, quick,
direct
(informal) snappy

OPPOSITE slow

2 our immediate neighbours
closest, nearest, adjacent, next

OPPOSITE distant

immediately ADVERB

1 Call an ambulance immediately!
at once, now, straight away, right
away, without delay, instantly,
promptly

2 I was sitting immediately behind
you.
right, exactly, directly, just

immense ADJECTIVE

the immense size of the solar system
huge, enormous, gigantic,
massive, colossal, giant, vast,
mighty, mammoth, monumental,
hulking, great, big, large
(informal) whopping,
humongous

OPPOSITES small, tiny

SEE ALSO big

immerse VERB

Immerse the cloth in soapy water.
submerge, dip, dunk

▷ **be immersed in**

I found Ellen immersed in her book.
be absorbed in, be engrossed in,
be interested in, be preoccupied
with, concentrate on, focus on

imminent ADJECTIVE

By now, war was imminent.
near, close, approaching, impending,
forthcoming, expected, looming

immobile ADJECTIVE

A figure stood immobile at the
window.
unmoving, motionless, stationary,
still

OPPOSITE mobile

immoral ADJECTIVE

Do you believe animal testing is
immoral?
wrong, unethical, bad, wicked,
sinful, dishonest, corrupt,
unprincipled

OPPOSITES moral, right

immortal ADJECTIVE

1 the immortal gods of Mount Olympus
undying, deathless, ageless, eternal

OPPOSITE mortal

2 the immortal words of Shakespeare
everlasting, enduring, timeless,
perennial

OPPOSITE ephemeral

immune ADJECTIVE

▷ **immune from**

No one is immune from the law.
exempt from, not subject to,
not liable to

OPPOSITE liable to

▷ **immune to**

Make your computer immune to
viruses.
resistant to, protected from, safe
from, secure against

OPPOSITE susceptible to

impact NOUN

1 a crater caused by the impact of a
meteor
crash, collision, smash, bump, blow,
knock, bang, jolt

》

2 *the impact of the Internet on our lives*
effect, influence

impair VERB
Very loud noise can impair your hearing.
damage, harm, injure, weaken, diminish

impartial ADJECTIVE
offering impartial advice
unbiased, neutral, unprejudiced, disinterested, detached, objective, independent, non-partisan, even-handed
❙ OPPOSITES biased, partisan

impatient ADJECTIVE
1 *As time went on, I grew more and more impatient.*
restless, agitated, anxious, edgy, fidgety
❙ OPPOSITE patient
2 *Mr Crockett gave an impatient sigh.*
irritated, cross, snappy, tetchy, curt, brusque
3 *We were impatient for the show to begin.*
anxious, eager, keen, in a hurry (*informal*) itching
❙ OPPOSITE reluctant

impede VERB
impeding the flow of traffic
hinder, obstruct, hamper, delay, disrupt, hold back, interfere with, get in the way of

imperfect ADJECTIVE
The items on this shelf are imperfect.
damaged, faulty, defective, flawed, substandard, incomplete
❙ OPPOSITE perfect

impertinent ADJECTIVE
an impertinent remark
rude, cheeky, impolite, impudent, insolent, disrespectful
❙ OPPOSITES respectful, polite

implement NOUN
garden implements

tool, appliance, device, utensil, gadget, instrument, contraption (*informal*) gizmo

implore VERB
I implore you to reconsider.
beg, entreat, plead with, appeal to, urge

imply VERB
Are you implying that I am a liar?
suggest, hint, indicate, insinuate, make out

Usage Note

The words **imply** and **infer** are not synonyms.

impolite ADJECTIVE
It would be impolite to refuse the invitation.
rude, bad-mannered, discourteous, uncivil, disrespectful, insulting
❙ OPPOSITE polite

import VERB
importing goods from China
bring in, ship in
❙ OPPOSITE export

importance NOUN
a decision of real importance
significance, momentousness, seriousness, consequence, weight, import, moment, note

important ADJECTIVE
1 *an important moment for our country*
major, significant, momentous, big, central, historic, pivotal
2 *I have some important business to attend to.*
serious, urgent, pressing, weighty, vital, essential, crucial
3 *an important figure in American history*
prominent, influential, powerful, high-ranking, notable, eminent, distinguished
❙ OPPOSITES unimportant, minor

mpose *VERB*

The British parliament imposed a
tax on tea.
introduce, enforce, fix, inflict,
prescribe, set

▷ **impose on**

Are you sure I'm not imposing on
you?
inconvenience, intrude on, take
advantage of, put out

mposing *ADJECTIVE*

the imposing facade of the cathedral
grand, great, impressive, stately,
magnificent, splendid, majestic,
dignified, striking, commanding,
awesome

OPPOSITE insignificant

mpossible *ADJECTIVE*

1 It's impossible to get there and back
in a day.
impractical, unrealistic, unworkable,
unthinkable, unachievable,
unattainable, not viable, out of the
question

OPPOSITES possible, realistic

2 (informal) Really, you are impossible
at times!
unreasonable, difficult, awkward,
infuriating, exasperating,
maddening, unbearable

OPPOSITE reasonable

mpress *VERB*

1 Beth tried hard to impress the
judges.
make an impression on, influence,
leave your mark on, stick in
someone's mind

2 impressing the need for change
emphasize, stress, highlight,
underline, bring home to you

mpression *NOUN*

1 The book made a big impression on
me.
impact, influence, effect, mark

2 I had the impression that something
was wrong.
feeling, sense, idea, notion,
suspicion, hunch, fancy

3 My sister does a good impression of
the Queen.
imitation, impersonation, caricature
(informal) send-up, take-off

impressive *ADJECTIVE*

The film includes some impressive
special effects.
striking, effective, powerful,
spectacular, stunning, breathtaking,
awesome, grand, imposing,
prodigious

OPPOSITES unimpressive,
uninspiring

imprison *VERB*

Galileo was arrested and imprisoned
for his ideas.
send to prison, jail, lock up,
incarcerate, confine, detain
(informal) put away, send down

IDIOM put under lock and key

OPPOSITE release

improbable *ADJECTIVE*

a story with an improbable ending
unlikely, unrealistic, unbelievable,
implausible, incredible,
unconvincing

OPPOSITES believable, realistic

improve *VERB*

1 trying to improve your writing
make better, refine, enhance,
amend, revise, correct, upgrade

2 My playing has improved this year.
get better, advance, progress,
develop, move on

OPPOSITE deteriorate

3 Her health is slowly improving.
get better, recover, recuperate,
pick up, rally, revive

IDIOM be on the mend

OPPOSITE get worse

improvement *NOUN*

1 showing signs of improvement
getting better, advance, progress,
development, recovery, upturn

2 making improvements to the text
amendment, correction, revision,
modification, enhancement

a
b
c
d
e
f
g
h
i
j
k
l
m
n
o
p
q
r
s
t
u
v
w
x
y
z

impudent ADJECTIVE
>an impudent grin on his face
>cheeky, insolent, rude, impolite,
>impertinent, disrespectful
>| OPPOSITES respectful, polite

impulse NOUN
>a sudden impulse to laugh out loud
>desire, instinct, urge, compulsion,
>drive, whim, notion, fancy

impulsive ADJECTIVE
>an impulsive decision to dye her hair
>hasty, rash, reckless, sudden,
>spontaneous, unplanned,
>unpremeditated, thoughtless,
>unthinking, impetuous, impromptu,
>spur-of-the-moment
>| OPPOSITES deliberate, premeditated

inaccessible ADJECTIVE
>an inaccessible part of the island
>unreachable, isolated, remote,
>out-of-the-way, hard to find
>| OPPOSITE accessible

inaccurate ADJECTIVE
>The information you gave is
>inaccurate.
>wrong, incorrect, inexact, imprecise,
>mistaken, false, erroneous, untrue
>| OPPOSITES accurate, correct

inadequate ADJECTIVE
>an inadequate supply of water
>insufficient, deficient, not enough,
>poor, limited, scarce, scanty,
>meagre, paltry
>| OPPOSITE adequate

inappropriate ADJECTIVE
>Some scenes are inappropriate for
>children.
>unsuitable, unfitting, out of place,
>improper, unbecoming, unseemly
>| OPPOSITE appropriate

inaudible ADJECTIVE
>an inaudible sigh
>indistinct, muffled, muted, faint
>| OPPOSITE audible

incapable ADJECTIVE
>▷ **incapable of**
>incapable of making a decision
>unable to, incompetent at, unfit to,
>unsuited to, ineffective at
>(informal) not up to
>| OPPOSITE capable of

incensed ADJECTIVE
>SEE **angry**

incentive NOUN
>an incentive to try harder
>inducement, motivation, stimulus,
>spur

incident NOUN
>an amusing incident at school
>event, happening, occurrence,
>episode, affair

incidental ADJECTIVE
>details which are incidental to the
>plot
>unimportant, inessential, secondary,
>minor, subordinate, subsidiary,
>peripheral, tangential
>| OPPOSITES essential, key

incite VERB
>accused of inciting rebellion
>provoke, instigate, arouse, stir up,
>whip up, kindle, inflame

inclination NOUN
>**1** The child shows a strong inclination
>towards music.
>tendency, leaning, propensity,
>predisposition, penchant, bent
>**2** That night, I felt no inclination for
>sleep.
>desire, taste, liking, preference, urge

incline NOUN
>at the top of a steep incline
>slope, hill, rise, gradient, ascent,
>ramp

inclined ADJECTIVE
>▷ **be inclined to**
>**1** I'm inclined to agree with her.
>be disposed to, be of a mind to
>**2** Angus is inclined to say the wrong
>thing.

tend to, be in the habit of,
be liable to, be prone to, be given to,
be apt to

include VERB
*The cost includes postage and
packing.*
contain, incorporate, cover,
comprise, encompass, involve, take
in, allow for, take into account
OPPOSITE exclude

income NOUN
the average income per household
earnings, pay, salary, wages, takings,
revenue
OPPOSITE expenditure

incoming ADJECTIVE
1 *an incoming wave*
approaching, arriving, inbound,
inward
OPPOSITES outgoing, outward
2 *the incoming president*
next, future, elect, designate
OPPOSITE outgoing

> **Usage Note**
>
> The adjectives **elect** and
> **designate** come after a noun: *the
> president elect.*

incompetent ADJECTIVE
He is an incompetent buffoon!
inept, unskilful, inexpert,
amateurish, bungling
(*informal*) useless
OPPOSITE competent

incomplete ADJECTIVE
1 *The new stadium is still incomplete.*
unfinished, uncompleted, not ready
OPPOSITE complete
2 *an incomplete summary*
partial, fragmentary, bitty, limited,
imperfect
OPPOSITE full

incomprehensible ADJECTIVE
He left an incomprehensible message.
unintelligible, unclear, abstruse

indecipherable, unfathomable,
OPPOSITES comprehensible,
intelligible

inconsiderate ADJECTIVE
*Some drivers are inconsiderate to
cyclists.*
selfish, unthinking, thoughtless,
insensitive, uncaring, tactless
OPPOSITE considerate

inconsistent ADJECTIVE
1 *Their performance has been
inconsistent this season.*
changeable, variable, unreliable,
unpredictable, erratic, fickle
2 *The two accounts are inconsistent.*
contradictory, conflicting,
irreconcilable, at odds, at variance
OPPOSITE consistent

inconspicuous ADJECTIVE
trying to remain inconspicuous
unnoticed, unobtrusive,
camouflaged, out of sight
OPPOSITE conspicuous

inconvenient ADJECTIVE
arriving at an inconvenient moment
awkward, difficult, bad, unsuitable,
unfortunate, untimely, inopportune
OPPOSITE convenient

incorporate VERB
1 *The show incorporates some
well-known tunes.*
include, contain, embrace
OPPOSITE exclude
2 *Incorporate the egg into the mixture.*
integrate, combine, blend, absorb,
take in

incorrect ADJECTIVE
an incorrect answer
wrong, mistaken, inaccurate, false,
untrue
OPPOSITE correct

increase VERB
1 *increasing the size of the page*
make bigger, enlarge, expand,
widen, broaden
2 *increasing our efforts to reduce waste*

>>

a b c d e f g h i j k l m n o p q r s t u v w x y z

intensify, strengthen, develop, enhance, augment, add to, step up

3 *increasing prices*
put up, raise

4 *increasing the volume*
turn up, amplify, boost

5 *The population continues to increase.*
grow, mount, go up, build up, rise, soar, escalate, multiply
FOR OPPOSITES SEE **decrease**

increase NOUN
an increase in Internet sales
rise, growth, expansion, enlargement, leap, surge
(*informal*) hike
❙ **OPPOSITE** decrease

incredible ADJECTIVE
1 *I find her story incredible.*
unbelievable, unlikely, improbable, implausible, unconvincing, far-fetched
❙ **OPPOSITE** credible

2 *an incredible feat of engineering*
extraordinary, marvellous, amazing, astounding, phenomenal, spectacular, magnificent, breathtaking, prodigious

independence NOUN
The islanders value their independence.
freedom, liberty, autonomy, self-rule
❙ **OPPOSITE** dependence

independent ADJECTIVE
1 *a very independent person*
self-sufficient, self-reliant
❙ **OPPOSITE** dependent

2 *Luxembourg is an independent country.*
autonomous, self-governing

3 *We need an independent opinion.*
impartial, unbiased, neutral, objective, disinterested, non-partisan
❙ **OPPOSITE** biased

indicate VERB
1 *Please indicate your preference.*
specify, point out, show,

reveal, make known

2 *A red light indicates danger.*
mean, stand for, denote, express, signal, signify, communicate, convey

indication NOUN
He gave no indication of his feelings.
sign, signal, hint, clue, inkling, evidence, token, warning, symptom, pointer

indifferent ADJECTIVE
1 *Her eyes had grown cold and indifferent.*
uninterested, unconcerned, detached, impassive, uncaring, unmoved, unenthusiastic
❙ **OPPOSITE** enthusiastic

2 *The food in the restaurant was indifferent.*
mediocre, ordinary, average, unexciting, uninspired, middle-of-the-road
❙ **OPPOSITE** excellent

indignant ADJECTIVE
an indignant voice at the end of the phone
annoyed, displeased, angry, resentful, affronted, offended, outraged, aggrieved, piqued
(*informal*) peeved

indirect ADJECTIVE
an indirect route into town
roundabout, circuitous, winding, meandering, tortuous
❙ **OPPOSITE** direct

indistinct ADJECTIVE
1 *an indistinct figure in the distance*
unclear, indefinite, vague, shadowy, obscure, hazy, blurred, blurry
❙ **OPPOSITE** clear

2 *indistinct sounds of people talking*
muffled, mumbled, muted, faint, weak, inaudible, unintelligible, incoherent
❙ **OPPOSITES** distinct, clear

individual ADJECTIVE
1 *an individual portion*
single, separate, discrete, lone, solo

2 *Her artwork has an individual style.*
characteristic, distinct, distinctive, special, unique, personal, singular

individual NOUN
a rather odd individual
person, character, man, woman
(*informal*) sort, type

induce VERB
1 *Nothing would induce me to live there.*
persuade, convince, prompt, coax, tempt, prevail upon
2 *Some headaches are induced by stress.*
cause, produce, generate, provoke, bring on, lead to, give rise to

indulge VERB
1 *Miss Ramsay did not believe in indulging children.*
spoil, pamper, pander to, mollycoddle, cosset
2 *Her husband indulged her every wish*
satisfy, gratify, fulfil, meet, yield to, give in to
▷ **indulge in**
indulging in a slice of cake
enjoy, treat yourself to, revel in, luxuriate in

indulgent ADJECTIVE
an indulgent attitude towards his pupils
tolerant, patient, permissive, lenient, easy-going, generous, liberal
OPPOSITE strict

industry NOUN
1 *the computer industry*
business, trade, commerce, manufacturing, production
2 *The city grew through the industry of its inhabitants.*
hard work, effort, energy, endeavour, industriousness, diligence, application
OPPOSITE laziness

ineffective ADJECTIVE
1 *an ineffective treatment for colds*
unsuccessful, ineffectual, unproductive
OPPOSITES effective, successful
2 *an ineffective leader*
incompetent, inept, incapable, unfit, inadequate
(*informal*) useless

inefficient ADJECTIVE
1 *an inefficient way of doing things*
ineffective, unproductive, unsystematic, disorganized, inept, slow, sloppy
2 *inefficient use of fuel*
wasteful, uneconomical, extravagant
OPPOSITE efficient

inequality NOUN
Is there still inequality between men and women?
imbalance, inequity, disparity, discrepancy, unfairness, bias
OPPOSITE equality

inevitable ADJECTIVE
It was inevitable that they would meet.
unavoidable, inescapable, certain, sure, definite

inexpensive ADJECTIVE
an inexpensive holiday
cheap, low-priced, low-cost, cut-price, affordable, economical, bargain, budget
OPPOSITE expensive

infamous ADJECTIVE
Jessie James was an infamous outlaw.
notorious, villainous, disreputable, scandalous

infant NOUN
a picture of me as an infant
baby, newborn, small child, tot, toddler

infect VERB
A virus had infected the water supply.
contaminate, pollute, poison

infection NOUN
The infection spread rapidly.
disease, virus,

contagion, contamination

infectious *ADJECTIVE*

Chickenpox is highly infectious.
contagious, communicable
(*informal*) catching
OPPOSITE non-infectious

infer *VERB*

What can we infer from this letter?
conclude, deduce, gather,
work out

Usage Note

The words **infer** and **imply** are not
synonyms.

inferior *ADJECTIVE*

1 *goods of inferior quality*
poor, bad, second-rate, low-grade,
substandard, cheap, shoddy
2 *soldiers of inferior rank*
lesser, lower, junior, subordinate
OPPOSITE superior

infertile *ADJECTIVE*

an infertile landscape
barren, unproductive, sterile
OPPOSITE fertile

infested *ADJECTIVE*

The cellar was infested with mice.
swarming, teeming, crawling,
overrun, plagued

infinite *ADJECTIVE*

1 *the theory that the universe is infinite*
boundless, unbounded, limitless,
never-ending, unending
OPPOSITE finite
2 *a job requiring infinite patience*
unlimited, endless, inexhaustible,
immeasurable
OPPOSITE limited

infirm *ADJECTIVE*

*Most of the patients are elderly
and infirm.*
frail, weak, feeble, poorly, ill,
unwell
► People who have to stay in bed are
bedridden.
OPPOSITE healthy

inflammable *ADJECTIVE*

SEE **flammable**

Usage Note

The words **inflammable** and
flammable mean the same thing.
They are not opposites of each
other.

inflammation *NOUN*

an inflammation on your skin
swelling, redness, soreness,
infection

inflate *VERB*

1 *a pump for inflating balloons*
blow up, pump up
OPPOSITE deflate
2 *inflating the price of oil*
increase, raise, escalate, put up
(*informal*) hike up, jack up
OPPOSITE lower

inflict *VERB*

*a leader who inflicted suffering on
his people*
administer, deal out, mete out,
exact, impose, force

influence *NOUN*

1 *Jazz had a major influence on his
music.*
effect, impact, hold, pull, sway
2 *Europe had no influence in the
region.*
power, authority, dominance,
control, leverage, weight
(*informal*) clout

influence *VERB*

*Did anything influence your
decision?*
affect, have an impact on, guide,
shape, direct, control, govern,
determine

influential *ADJECTIVE*

*She knows some very influential
people.*
important, leading, powerful,
significant
OPPOSITE unimportant

inform *VERB*

Please inform us if you move house.
tell, let someone know, notify, advise, send word to

informal *ADJECTIVE*

1 *The dinner will be very informal.*
casual, relaxed, easy-going, friendly, homely
(*informal*) laid-back

2 *written in an informal style*
colloquial, vernacular, familiar, everyday, popular, chatty
❙ OPPOSITE formal

information *NOUN*

There is more information on our website.
details, particulars, facts, data, advice, guidance, knowledge
(*informal*) info

informative *ADJECTIVE*

a very informative website
helpful, useful, instructive, illuminating, revealing
❙ OPPOSITE unhelpful

infuriate *VERB*

My answer just infuriated her.
anger, enrage, incense, madden, exasperate

ingenious *ADJECTIVE*

It seemed like an ingenious plan.
clever, brilliant, inspired, inventive, imaginative, original, crafty, cunning, shrewd

inhabit *VERB*

People once inhabited these caves.
live in, occupy, dwell in, reside in, populate, settle in

inhabitant *NOUN*

The island has fewer than a hundred inhabitants.
resident, dweller, native, occupier, occupant
▶ An inhabitant of a particular city or country is a **citizen**.
▶ The inhabitants of a place are its **population**.

inhabited *ADJECTIVE*

Is the island inhabited?
occupied, lived-in
❙ OPPOSITE uninhabited

inhale *VERB*

inhaling toxic fumes
breathe in, draw in, suck in
❙ OPPOSITE exhale

inherit *VERB*

She inherited the farm from her uncle.
succeed to, be left, come into

inherited *ADJECTIVE*

Eye colour is an inherited characteristic.
hereditary, passed down, genetic

inhuman *ADJECTIVE*

an act of inhuman cruelty
barbaric, inhumane, savage, cruel, merciless, heartless
❙ OPPOSITE humane

initial *ADJECTIVE*

1 *My initial reaction was to say no.*
first, earliest, primary, immediate
❙ OPPOSITES final, eventual

2 *the initial part of the poem*
opening, preliminary, introductory, preparatory
❙ OPPOSITES final, closing

initially *ADVERB*

Initially, I thought the book was boring.
at first, in the beginning, to begin with, to start with, at the outset

initiative *NOUN*

They had to use their initiative to survive.
resourcefulness, inventiveness, originality, ingenuity, enterprise

inject *VERB*

1 *injecting air into a tube*
insert, push, force, shoot

2 *injecting confidence into the team*
introduce, instil, infuse

injection NOUN
> *an injection against polio*
> inoculation, vaccination,
> immunization
> (*informal*) jab, shot

injure VERB
> *Some passengers were seriously
> injured.*
> hurt, wound, harm
> ► To injure someone causing
>   permanent damage is to **maim**
>   them.

injured ADJECTIVE
> **1** *Which is your injured arm?*
> wounded, hurt, damaged, sore,
> broken, fractured, bruised
> ┃ **OPPOSITE** uninjured
> **2** *an injured tone of voice*
> hurt, offended, upset, wounded,
> pained, aggrieved

injury NOUN
> *They escaped without any serious
> injury.*
> wound, harm, hurt

 WORD WEB

some types of injury
bite, bruise, burn, cut, fracture,
gash, graze, scald, scratch,
sprain, sting, strain

inner ADJECTIVE
> **1** *A passageway leads to the inner
> chamber.*
> central, inside, interior, internal,
> inward, middle
> **2** *hiding your inner feelings*
> innermost, personal, private,
> intimate, secret, hidden, concealed,
> underlying
> ┃ **OPPOSITE** outer

innocent ADJECTIVE
> **1** *He was found innocent of murder.*
> guiltless, blameless, faultless, free
> from blame
> ┃ **OPPOSITE** guilty

2 *She looks so sweet and innocent.*
> angelic, virtuous, pure,
> inexperienced, naive, ingenuous,
> artless
> ┃ **OPPOSITES** wicked, cunning
> **3** *a bit of innocent fun*
> harmless, inoffensive, innocuous

innovative ADJECTIVE
> *an innovative design*
> original, new, novel, fresh, creative,
> inventive, ingenious, pioneering,
> groundbreaking, revolutionary,
> radical, experimental

innumerable ADJECTIVE
> *The Sun is just one of innumerable
> stars.*
> countless, numberless, uncountable,
> untold

inquire VERB
> ▷ **inquire into**
> *The police are inquiring into the case.*
> look into, investigate, examine,
> explore
> ┃ **SEE ALSO** enquire

inquiry NOUN
> *an official inquiry about the accident*
> investigation, inspection,
> examination

inquisitive ADJECTIVE
> *Chimpanzees are naturally
> inquisitive.*
> curious, questioning, inquiring,
> probing
> ► An uncomplimentary word is **nosy**.

insane ADJECTIVE
> **1** *The patient believed he was going
> insane.*
> mentally ill, mad, crazy, deranged,
> demented, unhinged
> (*informal*) nuts, bonkers, loopy
> (*British informal*) crackers, potty
> ┃ **IDIOMS** off your head,
> stark raving mad
> (*informal*) off your rocker,
> off your trolley
> ┃ **OPPOSITE** sane
> **2** *The whole idea seems insane now.*

crazy, mad, senseless, stupid, foolish, idiotic, foolhardy, absurd, ludicrous, preposterous, hare-brained
(*informal*) nutty
(*British informal*) daft, barmy
| OPPOSITES sensible, wise

inscription NOUN
the inscription on the tomb
engraving, carving, writing

insect NOUN
night-flying insects
bug
(*informal*) creepy-crawly, minibeast

WORD WEB

some types of insect
ant, aphid, bee, beetle, bluebottle, bumblebee, butterfly, cicada, cockroach (*North American* roach), crane fly (*informal* daddy-long-legs), cricket, dragonfly, earwig, firefly, flea, fly, glow-worm, gnat, grasshopper, greenfly, hornet, horsefly, lacewing, ladybird (*North American* ladybug), locust, louse, mantis, mayfly, midge, mosquito, moth, stick insect, termite, tsetse fly, wasp, weevil

life stages of insects
caterpillar, chrysalis, grub, larva, maggot, pupa

parts of an insect's body
head, thorax, abdomen; antennae, legs, mandibles, wings

▶ The scientific study of insects is **entomology**.

insecure ADJECTIVE
1 *an insecure ladder*
unsafe, unsteady, unstable, loose, shaky, wobbly, dangerous, hazardous, precarious
2 *feeling insecure*
unconfident, uncertain, self-conscious, diffident, hesitant, anxious, nervous, apprehensive, uneasy
| OPPOSITES secure, self-confident

insensitive ADJECTIVE
an insensitive comment
thoughtless, tactless, unfeeling, uncaring, unsympathetic, callous
| OPPOSITE sensitive

insert VERB
Please insert a coin in the slot.
put in, place, push in, slide in, slot in, install, implant, load
(*informal*) pop in, stick in

inside NOUN
1 *the inside of a bird's nest*
interior, inner surface, centre, core, heart, middle
| OPPOSITE outside
2 (*informal*) *a pain in your insides*
stomach, belly, gut, bowels, intestines
(*informal*) innards

inside ADJECTIVE
an inside door
interior, inner, internal, innermost, indoor
| OPPOSITES outside, outer

insignificant ADJECTIVE
making some insignificant changes
unimportant, minor, trivial, trifling, negligible, slight, insubstantial, paltry, petty
| OPPOSITES significant, major

insincere ADJECTIVE
an insincere smile
false, pretended, feigned, hollow, hypocritical, disingenuous
(*informal*) two-faced, phoney, put-on
| OPPOSITE sincere

insist VERB
He insisted that no one else was to blame.
declare, state, assert, maintain, protest, stress, emphasize, swear, vow, claim

»

▷ **insist on**
The organization insists on secrecy.
demand, require

insistent *ADJECTIVE*
hours of insistent questioning
persistent, unrelenting, unremitting, dogged, tenacious

insolent *ADJECTIVE*
an insolent stare
rude, impudent, disrespectful, impolite, impertinent, arrogant, brazen
(*informal*) cheeky
❙ **OPPOSITES** polite, respectful

inspect *VERB*
inspecting the damage
examine, investigate, check, look over, study, survey, scrutinize, monitor, vet
(*informal*) check out
❙ **IDIOM** (*informal*) give the once-over

inspection *NOUN*
a safety inspection
check, check-up, examination, review, survey, scrutiny, investigation

inspiration *NOUN*
1 *I had a sudden inspiration.*
idea, bright idea, thought, revelation
(*informal*) brainwave
2 *What was the inspiration behind your story?*
impulse, motivation, stimulus, influence, spur

inspire *VERB*
1 *I felt inspired to write a poem.*
motivate, stimulate, prompt, encourage, stir, rouse, galvanize, spur on
2 *a manager who inspired loyalty in his players*
arouse, induce, awaken, kindle, trigger, bring out

install *VERB*
installing a new cooker
put in, set up, fix, place, position, establish

❙ **OPPOSITE** remove

instalment *NOUN*
the first instalment of the new series
episode, part, programme, issue, section

instance *NOUN*
Give me an instance of what you mean.
example, illustration, case, sample

instant *ADJECTIVE*
an instant reaction
immediate, instantaneous, quick, rapid, fast, prompt, snappy, speedy, swift, direct

instant *NOUN*
I only saw the figure for an instant.
moment, second, flash
(*informal*) tick, jiffy
❙ **IDIOMS** split second, twinkling of an eye

instead *ADVERB*
▷ **instead of**
Try using yogurt instead of cream.
in place of, in lieu of, rather than

instinct *NOUN*
following your own instincts
impulse, inclination, intuition, hunch, feeling, urge, compulsion

instinctive *ADJECTIVE*
an instinctive fear of snakes
intuitive, natural, innate, inherent, automatic, involuntary, reflex, spontaneous, impulsive, unconscious, unthinking
❙ **OPPOSITES** deliberate, conscious

instruct *VERB*
1 *All the staff are instructed in first aid.*
teach, train, coach, tutor, educate, school
2 *The guide instructed us to wait.*
tell, order, direct, command

instructions *PLURAL NOUN*
1 *an hour of swimming instruction*
teaching, training, coaching, tutoring, education, schooling

2 *Please follow the instructions carefully.*
direction, guideline, order, command, directive

instructor NOUN
a qualified skiing instructor
teacher, trainer, tutor, coach

instrument NOUN
an instrument for measuring wind speed
tool, implement, utensil, appliance, device, gadget, contraption
(*informal*) gizmo
FOR MUSICAL INSTRUMENTS SEE music

insufficient ADJECTIVE
an insufficient amount of water
inadequate, deficient, not enough, too little, scant, scanty
OPPOSITES enough, excessive

insult VERB
I apologize if I have insulted you.
offend, outrage, be rude to, hurt, injure, slight, snub

insult NOUN
Would it be an insult to refuse her offer?
affront, slight, slur, snub
(*informal*) put-down

insulting ADJECTIVE
an insulting comment about my hair
offensive, rude, impolite, derogatory, disparaging, belittling, scornful, uncomplimentary
OPPOSITE complimentary

intact ADJECTIVE
The skeleton was largely intact.
unbroken, whole, undamaged, unharmed, complete, perfect
(*informal*) in one piece

integral ADJECTIVE
This scene is an integral part of the film.
essential, vital, key, fundamental, basic, intrinsic, necessary
OPPOSITE peripheral

integrate VERB
They decided to integrate the two classes.
combine, join, merge, unite, unify, amalgamate, bring together
OPPOSITE separate

integrity NOUN
Is there any reason to doubt his integrity?
honesty, honour, loyalty, trustworthiness, reliability, sincerity, fidelity, virtue, rectitude
(*formal*) probity
OPPOSITE dishonesty

intelligence NOUN
1 *The robot shows signs of intelligence.*
cleverness, understanding, comprehension, reason, sense, wisdom, insight, intellect, brainpower, wits
(*informal*) brains
2 *a mission to gather secret intelligence*
information, knowledge, data, facts, reports

intelligent ADJECTIVE
an intelligent alien life-form
clever, bright, smart, quick-witted, sharp, perceptive, shrewd, able, brilliant, rational, thinking
(*informal*) brainy
OPPOSITES unintelligent, stupid

intelligible ADJECTIVE
The message was scarcely intelligible.
understandable, comprehensible, clear, plain, unambiguous, coherent, lucid
OPPOSITE incomprehensible

intend VERB
What do you intend to do?
plan, aim, mean, have in mind, plot, propose, envisage
▷ **be intended for**
The class is intended for beginners.
be aimed at, be designed for, be meant for, be set up for

intense ADJECTIVE
1 *a sudden, intense pain*

extreme, acute, severe, sharp, great, strong, violent

OPPOSITES slight, mild

2 *The debate aroused intense feelings.*
deep, passionate, powerful, strong, profound

OPPOSITE mild

intensity NOUN
the intensity of the midday sun
strength, power, force, ferocity, fierceness, severity

intensive ADJECTIVE
an intensive search of the area
detailed, thorough, rigorous, exhaustive, concentrated, in-depth, meticulous, methodical, painstaking, minute

OPPOSITE superficial

intent ADJECTIVE
an intent look of concentration
attentive, focused, absorbed, engrossed, preoccupied, rapt

▷ **intent on**
Why are you intent on leaving?
determined to, resolved to, committed to, set on, fixed on, bent on

intention NOUN
Our intention is to raise a thousand dollars.
aim, objective, target, goal, ambition, plan, intent

intentional ADJECTIVE
an intentional foul
deliberate, conscious, calculated, planned, intended, meant, wilful, done on purpose

OPPOSITE accidental

intercept VERB
A defender intercepted the pass.
check, stop, block, catch, cut off, head off, deflect

interest NOUN

1 *Craig listened with increasing interest.*
curiosity, attention, involvement, attentiveness, regard, notice

2 *The information is of no interest to anyone.*
importance, significance, import, concern, consequence, relevance, note, value

3 *My interests include painting and photography.*
hobby, pastime, pursuit, activity, diversion, amusement

interest VERB
Science fiction has always interested me.
appeal to, be of interest to, attract, excite, fascinate, absorb, capture someone's imagination

IDIOMS (*informal*) tickle your fancy, float your boat

OPPOSITE bore

▷ **be interested in**
Are you interested in fashion?
be keen on, care about, follow

interesting ADJECTIVE
Tell us about your interesting adventures.
fascinating, absorbing, enthralling, captivating, engrossing, riveting, gripping, entertaining, intriguing, diverting, engaging, stimulating

OPPOSITES boring, dull

interfere VERB

▷ **interfere in**
Please stop interfering in my affairs!
intervene in, intrude in, meddle in, pry into, encroach on, butt in on

IDIOMS (*informal*) poke your nose into, stick your oar into

▷ **interfere with**
The weather interfered with our plans.
hamper, hinder, get in the way of, obstruct

interior ADJECTIVE, NOUN
SEE **inside** ADJECTIVE, NOUN

intermediate ADJECTIVE
an intermediate stage of development

middle, midway, halfway,
in-between, transitional

internal *ADJECTIVE*
the internal parts of the engine
inner, inside, interior
OPPOSITE external

international *ADJECTIVE*
an international rescue team
global, worldwide, multinational,
intercontinental

Internet *NOUN*
downloading music from the Internet
the Web, the World Wide Web
(*informal*) the Net
► To view information on the Internet
is to view it **online**.
FOR TERMS RELATED TO THE INTERNET
SEE **computer**

interpret *VERB*
Can you interpret this old writing?
explain, elucidate, make sense of,
clarify, translate, decipher, decode

interpretation *NOUN*
a new interpretation of the poem
explanation, elucidation,
clarification, exposition, analysis

interrogate *VERB*
interrogating a suspect
question, interview, examine,
cross-examine, quiz
(*informal*) grill

interrupt *VERB*
1 *Please don't interrupt while I am
speaking.*
intervene, interject, break in, butt
in, cut in
2 *Heavy rain interrupted the tennis
match.*
stop, suspend, disrupt, break off,
cut short
3 *The new houses will interrupt the
view.*
get in the way of, obstruct, obscure

interruption *NOUN*
*I worked for an hour without any
interruption.*

break, pause, stop, gap, halt,
disruption, suspension

interval *NOUN*
1 *There will be a short interval after
the first act.*
intermission, interlude, recess,
break, pause, time-out
(*informal*) breather
2 *There are signs at regular intervals
along the road.*
space, gap, distance

intervene *VERB*
A man intervened to stop the fight.
intercede, step in, interfere,
interrupt, butt in

interview *VERB*
*interviewing the author about her
work*
question, talk to, interrogate,
examine, quiz, sound out
(*informal*) grill

intimate *ADJECTIVE*
1 *They have been intimate friends for
years.*
close, cherished, dear, bosom
OPPOSITE distant
2 *an intimate atmosphere*
friendly, warm, welcoming, informal,
cosy
3 *They printed intimate details about
her life.*
personal, private, confidential,
secret
4 *an intimate knowledge of
Shakespeare's work*
detailed, thorough, deep, profound,
exhaustive, in-depth

intimidate *VERB*
trying to intimidate a witness
bully, threaten, frighten, menace,
scare, terrify, terrorize, persecute

intrepid *ADJECTIVE*
an intrepid female explorer
daring, bold, fearless, courageous,
brave, valiant, heroic, plucky

a
b
c
d
e
f
g
h
i
j
k
l
m
n
o
p
q
r
s
t
u
v
w
x
y
z

intricate ADJECTIVE

an intricate network of cables
complex, complicated, elaborate,
sophisticated, involved, convoluted
OPPOSITE simple

intriguing ADJECTIVE

The results of the experiment are
intriguing.
interesting, fascinating, absorbing,
captivating, beguiling

introduce VERB

1 When was printing introduced in
Europe?
establish, institute, bring in, set up,
create, start, begin, initiate, launch,
inaugurate

2 Let me introduce you to my friend.
present, make known, acquaint
(with)

3 I was asked to introduce the speaker.
announce, give an introduction to,
lead into

introduction NOUN

1 the introduction of the metric system
establishment, institution, founding,
inauguration, launch

2 The plot is outlined in the
introduction.
preface, foreword, preamble,
prelude
(informal) intro

▶ An introduction to a play is a
prologue.

▶ An introduction to an opera or ballet
is an **overture**.

intrude VERB

I didn't mean to intrude.
interrupt, intervene, break in, butt in

▷ **intrude on**
intruding on your space
encroach on, infringe on, trespass
on, violate, invade

intruder NOUN

Some intruders broke into the
building.
trespasser, interloper, prowler,
burglar

invade VERB

1 The Vikings invaded many parts of
Europe.
attack, raid, occupy, overrun,
conquer, capture, seize

2 invading your privacy
intrude on, encroach on, infringe on,
trespass on, violate

invalid ADJECTIVE

1 an invalid passport
unacceptable, illegitimate, void

2 an invalid argument
false, unsound, untenable,
unjustifiable, indefensible, spurious,
fallacious
OPPOSITE valid

invaluable ADJECTIVE

an invaluable member of the squad
indispensable, irreplaceable, crucial,
essential, vital, all-important
OPPOSITES dispensable, worthless

invasion NOUN

the Viking invasion of Ireland
attack, raid, occupation, capture,
seizure, conquest

invent VERB

1 Who invented the telescope?
create, design, devise, originate,
think up, conceive

2 inventing an excuse
make up, fabricate, concoct,
dream up

invention NOUN

1 The recipe is my own invention.
creation, design, discovery,
innovation
(informal) brainchild

2 The newspaper article was mostly
invention.
fantasy, fiction, fabrication, lies,
deceit, falsehood

inventive ADJECTIVE

a book full of inventive characters
creative, original, imaginative,
ingenious, inspired, innovative,
novel

inventor *NOUN*

the inventor of the steam engine
creator, designer, originator,
discoverer, deviser, author, architect

investigate *VERB*

investigating the cause of the accident
examine, explore, inquire into, look into, study, scrutinize, consider, follow up, probe, research
(*informal*) go into

investigation *NOUN*

an investigation into the accident
examination, inquiry, inspection, study, review, survey

invigorating *ADJECTIVE*

an invigorating walk before breakfast
refreshing, stimulating, reviving, bracing

invisible *ADJECTIVE*

Neptune is invisible to the naked eye.
out of sight, unseen, undetectable, unnoticeable, unnoticed, unobserved, inconspicuous, hidden, concealed, covered, obscured
OPPOSITE visible

invitation *NOUN*

an invitation to attend the ceremony
request, call, summons
(*informal*) invite

invite *VERB*

1 *Who are you inviting to your party?*
ask, summon, have someone round
(*formal*) request someone's company
2 *That sort of thing just invites trouble.*
ask for, lead to, bring about, encourage, induce, provoke

inviting *ADJECTIVE*

An inviting smell came from the kitchen.
attractive, appealing, pleasant, welcoming, agreeable, appetizing, tempting, enticing, alluring
OPPOSITE repulsive

involve *VERB*

1 *Her job involves a lot of travel.*
include, comprise, require, demand, necessitate, mean
2 *a decision which involves our family*
affect, concern, interest, touch

involved *ADJECTIVE*

The plot is too involved to summarize.
complex, complicated, elaborate, intricate, convoluted
OPPOSITE simple
▷ **involved in**
Are you involved in the theatre?
associated with, connected with, concerned with, caught up in, mixed up in

involvement *NOUN*

He denied any involvement in the murder.
participation, part, collaboration, complicity, connection, association, entanglement

irrational *ADJECTIVE*

an irrational fear of dentists
unreasonable, illogical, senseless, groundless, unfounded, nonsensical, absurd
OPPOSITE rational

irregular *ADJECTIVE*

1 *a planet with an irregular orbit*
varying, variable, erratic, changeable, unpredictable, uneven, random, fitful, patchy
OPPOSITES regular, orderly
2 *The suggestion is highly irregular!*
abnormal, unusual, exceptional, unconventional, improper
OPPOSITES normal, usual

irrelevant *ADJECTIVE*

a lot of irrelevant detail
inappropriate, unnecessary, inessential, pointless, immaterial, unrelated, unconnected, extraneous
IDIOM beside the point
OPPOSITE relevant

irresistible *ADJECTIVE*

an irresistible urge to giggle
overwhelming, overpowering, uncontrollable, unavoidable, powerful, compelling

irresponsible *ADJECTIVE*

Was it irresponsible to publish the article?
reckless, rash, thoughtless, inconsiderate, uncaring, unthinking, negligent, imprudent, injudicious, ill-advised
OPPOSITE responsible

irritable *ADJECTIVE*

Mr Hodges arrived in an irritable mood.
bad-tempered, grumpy, short-tempered, cross, impatient, irascible, snappy, touchy, testy, grouchy, prickly, peevish, quarrelsome
(*British informal*) stroppy, shirty
OPPOSITES good-humoured, cheerful
SEE ALSO bad-tempered

irritate *VERB*

1 *The noise began to irritate me.*
annoy, bother, exasperate, anger, provoke, madden, vex
(*informal*) bug, rile, get to
IDIOM get on your nerves

2 *Soap may irritate your skin.*
inflame, itch, burn

island *NOUN*

an island in the South Pacific
(*literary*) isle
► A small island is an **islet**.
► A coral island is an **atoll**.
► A group of islands is an **archipelago**.
► An uninhabited island is a **desert island**.

isolated *ADJECTIVE*

1 *an isolated cave in the mountains*
remote, secluded, out-of-the-way, outlying, inaccessible, cut off
OPPOSITE accessible

2 *an isolated sighting of a UFO*
single, solitary, lone, unique, uncommon, unusual, exceptional
(*informal*) one-off
OPPOSITE common

issue *VERB*

1 *They issued blankets to the refugees.*
give out, distribute, supply, furnish, equip

2 *issuing a new set of stamps*
bring out, put out, produce, publish, release, circulate, print, broadcast

3 *We saw smoke issuing from the chimney.*
come out, emerge, appear, flow out, gush, erupt

issue *NOUN*

1 *a newspaper which covers local issues*
matter, subject, topic, affair, concern, question, problem, situation

2 *a special issue of the magazine*
edition, number, instalment, copy

itch *NOUN*

1 *an annoying itch on my foot*
tickle, tingling, prickle

2 *You've always had an itch to travel.*
desire, longing, yearning, craving, hankering, urge, wish, ache, thirst, hunger

item *NOUN*

1 *I bought a few items in the sale.*
thing, object, article

2 *an interesting item in the paper*
article, piece, report, feature, bulletin, write-up

Jj

jab *VERB*

A passer-by jabbed me in the ribs.
poke, prod, elbow, nudge, stab, dig

jacket *NOUN*

1 *a book jacket*
cover, sleeve, wrapper
2 *a leather jacket*
FOR ITEMS OF CLOTHING SEE clothes

jagged *ADJECTIVE*

Holly leaves have jagged edges.
spiky, toothed, serrated, prickly,
thorny, barbed, ragged
OPPOSITE smooth

jail *NOUN*
SEE prison

jam *NOUN*

1 *a jam on the motorway*
traffic jam, hold-up, tailback,
blockage, congestion, bottleneck
2 *(informal) I'm in a bit of a jam.*
difficulty, mess, predicament, plight
(informal) fix
IDIOM tight corner

jam *VERB*

1 *Someone had jammed the door open.*
prop, wedge, stick
2 *The paper has jammed in the printer.*
become stuck, stick, catch
3 *I jammed my things into a suitcase.*
cram, pack, stuff, squeeze, squash,
crush, ram, crowd
4 *The roads are jammed at rush hour.*
block, clog, obstruct, congest
(informal) bung up

jangle *NOUN, VERB*
SEE jingle

jar❶ *NOUN*

an earthenware jar
pot, container, vase, crock

jar❷ *VERB*

1 *I jarred my wrist when I fell.*
jolt, jerk, shake, vibrate
2 *Those colours jar with each other.*
clash, conflict, be incompatible,
be at odds
OPPOSITES harmonize, go together

jargon *NOUN*

Try to avoid using technical jargon.
slang, idiom, argot
(informal) lingo, gobbledegook

jaws *PLURAL NOUN*

the massive jaws of a sperm whale
mouth, muzzle, maw
(informal) chops

jealous *ADJECTIVE*

*Some people were jealous of her
popularity.*
envious, resentful, grudging
IDIOM green with envy (at)

jealousy *NOUN*

*I couldn't help feeling a twinge of
jealousy.*
envy, resentment, bitterness

jeer *VERB*

*Some of the audience whistled and
jeered.*
boo, hiss, sneer, taunt, mock, scoff,
ridicule
OPPOSITE cheer

jeopardize *VERB*

*an injury that could jeopardize her
career*
endanger, threaten, undermine,
compromise, imperil

jerk *VERB*

1 *The train suddenly jerked to a halt.*
jolt, lurch, judder, shudder, bump,
bounce
2 *I just managed to jerk my arm free.*

»

a
b
c
d
e
f
g
h
i
j
k
l
m
n
o
p
q
r
s
t
u
v
w
x
y
z

pull, tug, yank, pluck, wrench

jet *NOUN*
a high jet of water
spout, spurt, spray, squirt, gush, stream, fountain

jewel *NOUN*
SEE **gem**

jewellery *NOUN*

 WORD WEB

some items of jewellery
anklet, bangle, beads, bindi, body jewel, bracelet, brooch, cameo, chain, charm, choker, clasp, crown, cufflinks, diadem, earring, engagement ring, lapel pin, locket, nail jewel, necklace, necklet, pendant, pin, ring, tiara, tiepin, toe ring, wedding ring

► A person who sells or makes jewellery is a **jeweller**.
► A person who makes gold or silver jewellery is a **goldsmith** or **silversmith**.

I SEE ALSO **gem**

jingle *NOUN, VERB*
the noise of sleigh bells jingling
tinkle, jangle, ring, chink, clink
FOR TIPS ON DESCRIBING SOUNDS SEE **sound❶**

job *NOUN*
1 *applying for a job as a model*
post, position, profession, occupation, employment, trade, work, career, vocation, calling
► A person who has no job is **jobless** or **unemployed**.
FOR TYPES OF JOB SEE **occupation**
2 *Whose job is it to do the washing-up?*
duty, task, assignment, chore, errand

jog *VERB*
1 *a man jogging round the park*
run, trot, lope
2 *I jogged his elbow by accident.*
nudge, prod, jolt, jostle, jar, knock, bump
3 *The photograph may jog your memory.*
prompt, stir, arouse, stimulate, spark, set off

join *VERB*
1 *The two roads join here.*
come together, meet, converge, merge, unite, combine, amalgamate
I OPPOSITES divide, separate
2 *Join the threads together.*
put together, connect, fasten, attach, fix, link, couple, bond
I OPPOSITES detach, separate
3 *I joined the crowd going into the cinema.*
follow, go with, team up with (*informal*) tag along with
4 *joining a local sports club*
become a member of, enrol in, sign up for
► To join the army is to **enlist**.
I OPPOSITES leave, resign from

join *NOUN*
If you look hard, you can see the join.
joint, connection, link, mend, seam

joint *ADJECTIVE*
a joint effort between several writers
combined, shared, common, communal, cooperative, united, collective, mutual, concerted
I OPPOSITE individual

joke *NOUN*
1 *Do you know any good jokes?*
jest, quip, witticism (*informal*) gag, crack, wisecrack
2 *The whole thing has become a joke.*
farce, fiasco, travesty (*informal*) shambles

joke *VERB*
Those two are always laughing and joking.
jest, clown, have a laugh, make jokes, tease

a b c d e f g h i j k l m n o p q r s t u v w x y z

olly *ADJECTIVE*

Glenn was in his usual, jolly mood.
cheerful, good-humoured, happy,
merry, joyful, cheery, bright, sunny,
chirpy
(*informal*) upbeat
❙ **OPPOSITE** gloomy

olt *VERB*

The car jolted over the speed bumps.
jerk, lurch, judder, shudder, bump,
bounce

ostle *VERB*

*Some people jostled their way to the
front.*
push, shove, elbow, barge, press,
scramble, jockey

ot *VERB*

▷ **jot down**
I quickly jotted down a few ideas.
make a note of, write down, take
down, note, scribble

ournal *NOUN*

1 *an article in a journal*
magazine, periodical, newspaper,
review, bulletin, gazette
2 *keeping a journal of the voyage*
diary, log, logbook, record, account,
chronicle

ournalist *NOUN*

a journalist on the local paper
reporter, correspondent, columnist,
writer

ourney *NOUN*

a journey to the South Pole
voyage, trip, expedition, passage,
tour, route, travels
▶ A long adventurous journey is an
odyssey.
▶ A journey to a holy place is a
pilgrimage.

ovial *ADJECTIVE*

Our guests were in a jovial mood.
cheerful, happy, jolly, merry,
good-humoured, joyful, sunny,
convivial
❙ **OPPOSITE** sad

joy *NOUN*

My heart almost leaped with joy.
happiness, joyfulness, delight,
cheerfulness, gladness, mirth,
glee, jubilation, rejoicing, bliss,
ecstasy, elation, exultation,
euphoria, rapture
❙ **OPPOSITE** sorrow

joyful *ADJECTIVE*

The wedding was a joyful occasion.
happy, cheerful, merry,
joyous, jolly, jovial,
good-humoured
❙ **OPPOSITE** sad

judge *NOUN*

1 *a panel of international judges*
adjudicator, referee,
umpire
2 *appearing before a judge*
magistrate, sheriff, justice

judge *VERB*

1 *The umpire judged that the ball
was out.*
rule, decide, decree, pronounce,
adjudicate
(*formal*) deem
2 *Entries will be judged by a panel
of experts.*
assess, evaluate, appraise, rate,
examine
3 *You can judge the age of the amber
from its colour.*
gauge, estimate, reckon, deduce,
guess, surmise

judgement *NOUN*

1 *the judgement of the court*
decision, verdict, finding, ruling,
pronouncement, decree
2 *In your judgement, which is the
better poem?*
opinion, view, belief, assessment,
appraisal, estimate
3 *showing a lack of judgement*
wisdom, sense, understanding,
perception, discrimination,
discernment

a
b
c
d
e
f
g
h
i
j
k
l
m
n
o
p
q
r
s
t
u
v
w
x
y
z

325

jug NOUN
a jug of milk
pitcher, ewer

juice NOUN
the juice of a lemon
liquid, fluid, sap, milk, extract

jumble VERB
Please don't jumble the pages.
muddle, mix up, mess up,
disorganize, disorder,
shuffle, tangle
❙ OPPOSITES arrange, order

jumble NOUN
*His clothes were in a jumble on the
floor.*
mess, muddle, clutter, chaos,
confusion, disarray, disorder
(*informal*) hotchpotch
(*North American*) hodgepodge

jump VERB
1 *Suddenly a deer jumped in
front of us.*
leap, spring, bound, hop, skip,
prance, pounce
2 *All the horses jumped the first
hurdle.*
leap over, vault, clear
3 *The loud bang made
everyone jump.*
start, flinch, jolt

jump NOUN
1 *Rebecca cleared the stairs in a single
jump.*
leap, spring, bound, vault,
hop, skip
2 *I awoke with a jump.*
start, jolt, jerk, spasm, judder
3 *a sharp jump in prices*
increase, rise, leap, surge
(*informal*) hike

junction NOUN
Turn left at the junction.
intersection, crossroads,
interchange

jungle NOUN
SEE **rainforest**

junior ADJECTIVE
1 *the junior hockey team*
younger
2 *a junior officer*
low-ranking, minor, lesser,
subordinate
❙ OPPOSITE senior

junk NOUN
The garage is full of old junk.
rubbish, clutter, jumble, trash,
garbage, waste, refuse, scrap,
odds and ends, bric-a-brac

just ADJECTIVE
1 *a just decision*
fair, impartial, unbiased,
even-handed, honourable, upright,
principled
❙ OPPOSITES unjust, unfair
2 *a just reward*
deserved, merited, rightful, due,
proper, fitting, appropriate
❙ OPPOSITE undeserved

just ADVERB
1 *The colour is just right.*
exactly, precisely, absolutely
2 *She was just a child then.*
only, simply, merely
3 *It's just after nine o'clock.*
slightly, barely, scarcely

justice NOUN
1 *demanding to be treated
with justice*
fairness, justness, right, honesty,
impartiality, even-handedness,
equity, fair play
❙ OPPOSITE injustice
2 *a court of justice*
law

justifiable ADJECTIVE
Is it ever justifiable to lie?
defensible, warranted, well-founded
valid, legitimate, reasonable
❙ OPPOSITE unjustifiable

justify VERB
How can you justify the cost?
defend, excuse, account for, explain,
vindicate

jut VERB

▷ **jut out**

a nail jutting out from the wall

stick out, project, protrude, extend, overhang

juvenile ADJECTIVE

1 a range of juvenile fiction

children's, young people's

OPPOSITE adult

2 His jokes are really juvenile.

childish, babyish, immature

OPPOSITE mature

Kk

keen *ADJECTIVE*

1 *Karen is a keen photographer.*
enthusiastic, eager, fervent, avid, devoted, committed, motivated
OPPOSITE unenthusiastic

2 *a knife with a keen edge*
sharp, razor-sharp, honed
OPPOSITE blunt

3 *keen eyesight*
sharp, acute, piercing
OPPOSITE poor

4 *a keen autumn wind*
bitter, cold, icy, biting, penetrating
OPPOSITE mild

▷ **be keen on**
I'm not very keen on flying.
be fond of, like, enjoy, be partial to
(*informal*) be mad on, be into
IDIOM have a soft spot for

keep *VERB*

1 *I've kept all of her letters.*
save, conserve, preserve, retain, hang on to, hold on to, guard, store

2 *It costs money to keep a pet.*
support, maintain, provide for, pay for

3 *Doreen tried to keep calm.*
stay, remain

4 *I won't keep you long.*
delay, detain, hold up, keep waiting

5 *Why do you keep asking me questions?*
persist in, go on, carry on, continue, insist on

6 *The milk will keep until tomorrow.*
last, be usable, stay good

7 *Where do you keep the cutlery?*
store, house, put, stow

▷ **keep off**

1 *Lets hope the rain keeps off.*
stay away

2 *Please keep off the grass.*
avoid, stay away from, steer clear of

▷ **keep to**

1 *keeping to the cycle path*
stay on, stay within

2 *keeping to your promise*
abide by, adhere to, hold to, carry out, make good, honour

▷ **keep something up**
Keep up the good work!
carry on, continue, maintain

keeper *NOUN*
the keeper of the lighthouse
guardian, curator, custodian, caretaker, steward

keeping *NOUN*

▷ **in keeping with**
a hairstyle in keeping with the period
consistent with, in harmony with, compatible with, in line with, appropriate to, suitable to, befitting

key *NOUN*
the key to the riddle
answer, solution, explanation, clue

keyboard *NOUN*
FOR MUSICAL INSTRUMENTS SEE **music**

kick *VERB*

1 *kicking the ball into the back of the net*
strike, boot, drive, send, propel, punt, tap, nudge, flick

2 *a beetle kicking its legs in the air*
wave, flail, swing, shake

kick *NOUN*

1 *a long kick from the goalkeeper*
strike, boot, punt, blow, tap, nudge, flick

2 (*informal*) *I still get a kick out of watching this film.*
thrill, excitement, tingle, frisson
(*informal*) buzz

kid *NOUN*
  SEE **child**

kidnap *VERB*
  a story about a boy who is kidnapped by aliens
  abduct, capture, seize, carry off, snatch, take hostage

kill *VERB*
  The victim was killed by an unknown poison.
  (*informal*) bump off, do away with (*old use*) slay
► To kill someone deliberately is to **murder** them.
► To kill someone brutally is to **butcher** them.
► To kill large numbers of people is to **massacre** or **slaughter** them.
► To kill someone as a punishment is to **execute** them or **put them to death**.
► To kill someone for political reasons is to **assassinate** them.

killing *NOUN*
  the killing of innocent people
  murder, homicide, assassination, execution, massacre, slaughter, butchery

kind¹ *NOUN*
  What kind of music do you like?
  sort, type, variety, style, category, class, genre

kind² *ADJECTIVE*
  It was very kind of you to help me.
  kind-hearted, caring, good-natured, kindly, affectionate, warm, genial, loving, sweet, gentle, amiable, friendly, generous, sympathetic, thoughtful, obliging, considerate, understanding, compassionate, unselfish, giving, gracious, merciful, benevolent, charitable, humane, neighbourly
  OPPOSITES unkind, cruel

kindly *ADJECTIVE*
  a kindly old gentleman
  kind-hearted, good-natured, kind, caring, compassionate, generous, warm, friendly, genial, amiable, sympathetic, considerate, benevolent, well-meaning

kindness *NOUN*
  The family treated me with great kindness.
  kind-heartedness, benevolence, compassion, generosity, warmth, affection, sympathy, good nature
  OPPOSITE cruelty

king *NOUN*
  Darius was the king of the Persian Empire.
  monarch, sovereign, ruler

kingdom *NOUN*
  ruling over a vast kingdom
  realm, monarchy, empire, dominion, domain

kiss *NOUN*
  a kiss on the cheek
  (*informal*) peck

kit *NOUN*
  1 *an emergency repair kit*
  equipment, apparatus, materials, paraphernalia, tools, tackle
  2 *a spare football kit*
  clothing, clothes, outfit, strip (*informal*) gear, get-up

kitchen *NOUN*
  the kitchen of a grand hotel
► A small kitchen is a **kitchenette**.
► The kitchen on a ship or aircraft is the **galley**.

kitten *NOUN*
  SEE **cat**

knack *NOUN*
  Phil has a knack for taking photographs.
  skill, talent, gift, flair, bent, genius

knead *VERB*
  Knead the dough until it is smooth.
  work, press, squeeze, pummel

knife *NOUN*
  a sharp kitchen knife
  blade, cutter

▶ A large heavy knife used by a butcher is a **cleaver**.

▶ A sharp thin knife used by a surgeon is a **scalpel**.

SEE ALSO weapon

knight NOUN

a medieval knight

▶ A boy training to be a knight was first a **page** and then a **squire**.

FOR TIPS ON WRITING HISTORICAL FICTION SEE historical

knit VERB

1 *The broken bones will eventually knit together.*
join, fuse, bond, merge, coalesce

2 *Mrs Oliphant knitted her brows.*
furrow, wrinkle, gather

knob NOUN

1 *a old wooden door knob*
handle

2 *a hard knob of skin*
lump, bump, bulge, protrusion, knot, boss

3 *a small knob of butter*
piece, bit, pat, lump, chunk

knobbly ADJECTIVE

a knobbly piece of wood
lumpy, bumpy, gnarled

knock VERB

1 *Someone is knocking at the door.*
rap, tap, pound, pummel, hammer, bang, thump

2 *Don't knock your head on the way out.*
bump, bang, bash, hit, strike, crack
(*informal*) whack

SEE ALSO hit

knock NOUN

1 *We heard a knock at the door.*
rap, tap, pounding, pummelling, hammering, banging

2 *The bike has had a few knocks over the years.*
bump, bang, bash, hit, strike, blow, crash, collision

knot NOUN

1 *combing the knots out of your hair*

tangle, snarl, lump, mass

2 *surrounded by a knot of people*
cluster, group, huddle, circle, ring, band, bunch

knot VERB

Knot the two threads together.
tie, bind, fasten, join, lash, entwine
OPPOSITE untie

know VERB

1 *None of us knew how to speak Russian.*
understand, comprehend, have knowledge of, be conversant with, be versed in
OPPOSITE be ignorant of

2 *Do you know where we are?*
recognize, realize, appreciate, be aware of
OPPOSITE be unaware of

3 *I know her sister quite well.*
be acquainted with, be familiar with, be a friend of
OPPOSITE be unfamiliar with

knowledge NOUN

1 *a good knowledge of Italian*
understanding, grasp, command, mastery, familiarity (with), grounding (in)

▶ A slight knowledge of a subject is a **smattering** of it.

2 *a book containing ancient knowledge*
learning, wisdom, scholarship, erudition
(*informal*) know-how

knowledgeable ADJECTIVE

We were shown around by a knowledgeable guide.
well-informed, learned, erudite, scholarly, educated, cultured
OPPOSITE ignorant

▷ **be knowledgeable about**
Lou is very knowledgeable about jazz.
be well informed about, know a lot about, be familiar with, be conversant with, be au fait with
(*informal*) be up on

L

abel *NOUN*

an address label

tag, ticket, sticker, tab, docket

abel *VERB*

1 *Please label your belongings.*

tag, mark, name, identify

2 *People usually labelled him as a loner.*

categorize, classify, mark out, stamp, brand, dub

aborious *ADJECTIVE*

1 *a laborious climb to the top*

strenuous, arduous, hard, tough, difficult, stiff, tiring, exhausting, gruelling, exacting, punishing, back-breaking

OPPOSITES easy, effortless

2 *a style which is laborious to read*

heavy, ponderous, strained, overwrought, unnatural, stilted, stiff

OPPOSITES natural, flowing

labour *NOUN*

1 *It took hours of painstaking labour to restore the painting.*

work, effort, industry, exertion, toil, drudgery

(*informal*) slog

2 *a severe shortage of labour*

workers, employees

labour *VERB*

Rescuers laboured through the night to reach survivors.

work hard, exert yourself, toil

(*informal*) slave away

lack *NOUN*

My nerves were frayed from lack of sleep.

absence, shortage, scarcity, want, dearth, deficiency, shortfall

(*formal*) paucity

▶ A general lack of food is a **famine**.

▶ A general lack of water is a **drought**.

OPPOSITE abundance

lack *VERB*

I find his writing lacks emotion.

be without, be short of, be deficient in, be low on, want, miss

OPPOSITE possess

laden *ADJECTIVE*

shelves laden with jars of fruit

filled, packed, crammed, stuffed, chock-full, groaning

lady *NOUN*

SEE **woman**

lag *VERB*

One runner lagged behind the others.

straggle, trail, fall behind, drop behind

lair *NOUN*

the lair of the cyclops

den, refuge, shelter, hideout, hiding place

lake *NOUN*

a cabin on the shores of a lake

pond, pool

▶ A lake in Scotland is a **loch**.

▶ A salt-water lake is a **lagoon**.

▶ A lake used to supply water is a **reservoir**.

lame *ADJECTIVE*

1 *a lame horse*

disabled, crippled, limping, hobbling

2 *What a lame excuse!*

feeble, flimsy, poor, unconvincing, inadequate, weak, tame

lamp *NOUN*

SEE **light❶**

land *NOUN*

1 *a villa set in acres of land*

grounds, estate, property

a
b
c
d
e
f
g
h
i
j
k
l
m
n
o
p
q
r
s
t
u
v
w
x
y
z

》

2 *the arid land of the Indus valley*
ground, soil, earth

3 *China is a land with an ancient history.*
country, nation, state, region, territory, province, realm

land *VERB*

1 *The plane landed exactly on time.*
touch down, arrive
❙ OPPOSITE take off

2 *Six hundred Viking ships landed at Hamburg.*
dock, berth, come ashore, put in

3 *How did these papers land on my desk?*
arrive, turn up, end up, wind up, settle

landmark *NOUN*

1 *a landmark that can be seen for miles around*
feature, sight, monument

2 *a landmark in the history of science*
milestone, turning point, watershed

landscape *NOUN*

The best way to see the landscape is by foot or bike.
countryside, scenery, terrain, view, scene, outlook, prospect, panorama

▶ The landscape of a city is a **cityscape**.

▶ The study of features of the landscape is **topography**.

WRITING TIPS

describing landscape

For a mile from Hugh's home the path sloped gradually to the river, twisting through knolls, edging ploughed fields, running by greystone dykes, and skirting a birch wood.
— *Neil Gunn, Morning Tide*

areas of landscape

bush, desert, grassland, island, marsh, moor, peninsula, plain, plateau, prairie, rainforest, savannah, steppe, swamp, tundra, wasteland, wetland

landscape features

beach, bog, brae, cave, cavern, copse, crag, crevasse, crevice, dell, dune, escarpment, fell, fen, forest, glen, gorge, gully, hill, hillock, hillside, hummock, knoll, ledge, meadow (*poetic* lea), mountain, pass, precipice, range, ridge, rise, riverbank, slope, wood, valley

areas of water

bay, bayou, billabong, cove, creek, estuary (*Scottish* firth), fjord, geyser, glacier, ice floe, inlet, lagoon, lake, loch, oasis, pond, pool, ravine, river, rivulet, sound, spring, stream, waterhole

man-made features

bridge, canal, dam, dyke, field, furrow, path, track

adjectives

arid, bare, barren, bleak, craggy, enclosed, exposed, fallow, farmed, fenced, fertile, furrowed, hilly, inhospitable, irrigated, jagged, lunar, lush, mountainous, open, patchwork, pitted, ploughed, rocky, rugged, shady, sheltered, steep, sun-drenched, wooded

lane *NOUN*

a narrow country lane
track, path, trail, walk, passageway, alley

language *NOUN*

1 *Sanskrit is an ancient language.*
tongue, speech, dialect (*informal*) lingo

2 *The author uses very poetic language.*
wording, phrasing, vocabulary, expression, style, turn of phrase, terminology

lap NOUN

1 *Rachael sat the baby on her lap.*
knees, thighs

2 *the last lap of the race*
circuit, round, leg

lapse NOUN

1 *a short lapse in concentration*
failure, error, fault, slip, flaw,
weakness, shortcoming

2 *We resumed training after a lapse of
six weeks.*
interval, gap, break, interlude, lull,
pause, hiatus

lapse VERB

1 *Your membership has lapsed.*
expire, become void, run out

2 *lapsing in and out of consciousness*
drift, slip, slide, sink

large ADJECTIVE

1 *the large skull of a prehistoric
mammal*
big, huge, enormous, gigantic,
great, immense, giant, colossal,
massive, mammoth, bulky, hefty,
weighty, mighty
(*informal*) whopping, humongous

2 *a large helping of pudding*
ample, generous, plentiful,
abundant, lavish

3 *the largest room in the house*
spacious, extensive, sizeable, roomy

4 *flying over a large area of desert*
wide, broad, extensive, widespread,
vast

5 *a large number of complaints*
considerable, substantial, high

▶ An extremely large number or figure
is **astronomical**.
┃ OPPOSITES small, tiny
┃ SEE ALSO big

largely ADVERB

*The abbey was largely destroyed by
fire.*
mainly, chiefly, mostly, principally,
to a large extent

lash VERB

1 *rain lashing against the window*

beat, pound, pelt, batter

2 *a crocodile lashing its tail*
swish, flick, whip

3 *pieces of wood loosely lashed together*
tie, fasten, bind, tether, knot, hitch

last ADJECTIVE

1 *the last chapter of 'Moby Dick'*
final, closing, concluding,
terminating, ultimate
┃ OPPOSITE first

2 *Did you see the last James Bond film?*
latest, most recent
┃ OPPOSITE next

last NOUN

▷ **at last**
At last someone was listening to me.
finally, eventually, in the end

last VERB

1 *Let's hope our luck will last.*
carry on, continue, keep on, stay,
remain, persist, endure, hold
┃ OPPOSITES end, wear out

2 *How many days can you last without
water?*
hold out, keep going, live, survive

lasting ADJECTIVE

a lasting memory of our trip
enduring, abiding, long-lasting,
long-lived, undying, everlasting,
permanent, durable

lastly ADVERB

Lastly, I would like to say thanks.
finally, in the last place, in conclusion

late ADJECTIVE

1 *My bus was late again.*
delayed, overdue
┃ OPPOSITES early, punctual, on time

2 *the late craze for sudoku*
recent, latter-day

3 *a portrait of his late wife*
dead, deceased, departed, former

lately ADVERB

It has been a lot warmer lately.
recently, latterly, of late

later ADJECTIVE

The mystery is revealed in

a
b
c
d
e
f
g
h
i
j
k
l
m
n
o
p
q
r
s
t
u
v
w
x
y
z

a later chapter.
subsequent, future, following,
succeeding, upcoming, ensuing,
to come

later *ADVERB*

1 *The letter arrived a week later.*
afterwards, after that, subsequently
2 *I'll phone you later.*
in a while, at a later date, in the
future, in due course

latter *ADJECTIVE*

in the latter part of the year
later, more recent, second, last, final

laugh *VERB*

That story always makes me laugh.
chuckle, chortle, guffaw, giggle,
titter, burst out laughing, roar with
laughter, fall about laughing
(*informal*) crack up

❙ **IDIOMS** be in stitches, have
hysterics, be rolling in the aisles

▷ **laugh at**
*Many people laughed at Newton's
ideas.*
make fun of, mock, ridicule, scoff at,
jeer at, deride, poke fun at

❙ **IDIOM** (*informal*) take the mickey
out of

laughter *NOUN*

sounds of laughter from the audience
laughing, amusement, humour,
hilarity, mirth, merriment

launch *VERB*

1 *The space shuttle will be launched
next month.*
send off, set off, blast off
2 *launching a javelin into the air*
throw, propel, hurl, pitch, fling, let
fly, fire, shoot
3 *Their website was launched last year.*
begin, start, set up, open, establish,
found, initiate, inaugurate, introduce

lavatory *NOUN*

a public lavatory
toilet, bathroom, WC, convenience,
cloakroom, washroom
(*British informal*) loo

(*North American*) restroom

lavish *ADJECTIVE*

1 *a lavish wedding breakfast*
sumptuous, luxurious, extravagant,
opulent, rich, grand, splendid
❙ **OPPOSITES** meagre, paltry
2 *spending lavish amounts of money*
abundant, copious, generous,
plentiful, extravagant
3 *One review was lavish in its praise
for the film.*
generous, bountiful, liberal,
unsparing, unstinting
❙ **OPPOSITES** mean, sparing

law *NOUN*

a law against child labour
regulation, statute, rule, ruling,
decree, edict, order, commandment,
directive
▶ A law passed by parliament is an **act**.
▶ A proposed law to be discussed by
parliament is a **bill**.

lay *VERB*

1 *Hugh laid the book down carefully
on his desk.*
put down, set down, place, position,
deposit, rest, leave
2 *laying the table for tea*
set out, arrange
3 *laying plans for the future*
devise, prepare, plan, conceive,
concoct, formulate, work out, hatch

▷ **lay something on**
*Our hosts had laid on
entertainment.*
provide, supply, furnish, prepare,
organize, line up

layer *NOUN*

1 *a new layer of paint*
coat, coating, covering, film, skin,
blanket, sheet
2 *a layer of sedimentary rock*
seam, stratum, tier, thickness

laze *VERB*

spending all day lazing in bed
be lazy, idle, loaf, lounge, relax,
take it easy, lie about

a b c d e f g h i j k l m n o p q r s t u v w x y z

lazy *ADJECTIVE*

Dylan was too lazy to walk to the shops.
idle, indolent, slothful, inactive, lethargic, sluggish

lead *VERB*

1 *Finn led us through the underground caves.*
guide, conduct, escort, usher, steer, pilot, shepherd
OPPOSITE follow

2 *Our crew led from the start of the race.*
be in front, be in the lead, head the field

3 *A former judge was chosen to lead the inquiry.*
be in charge of, direct, command, head, manage, supervise, preside over
(*informal*) head up

4 *Does this road lead to the city centre?*
go, run, make its way

5 *I prefer to lead a quiet life.*
live, pass, spend, experience, enjoy

▷ **lead to**
a plan which may lead to disaster
result in, cause, bring about, give rise to, occasion, generate, spark

lead *NOUN*

1 *Our team were in the lead.*
first place, front position
▶ The leading part of an army or fleet is the **vanguard**.

2 *following up a new lead*
clue, pointer, tip-off

3 *providing a lead for others*
example, model, pattern, guidance, leadership, direction

4 *playing the lead in a musical*
principal part, starring role, title role

5 *a dog's lead*
leash, strap, chain, tether, rein

6 *an electrical lead*
cable, flex, wire

leader *NOUN*

1 *the leader of the ruling party*
head, chief, commander, captain, director, principal, ruler
(*informal*) boss
▶ The leader of a group of wrongdoers is the **ringleader**.
OPPOSITE follower

2 *the leader after the first lap*
front runner

leadership *NOUN*

1 *taking over the leadership of the party*
command, control, rule, dominion, captaincy, directorship

2 *a need for strong leadership*
governance, authority, management, guidance, direction

leaf *NOUN*

1 *the leaf of a maple tree*
▶ A mass of leaves is **foliage** or **greenery**.

2 *A single leaf had been torn from the book.*
page, sheet
SEE ALSO plant, tree

league *NOUN*

1 *a league of Baltic states*
alliance, union, confederation, federation, coalition, consortium

2 *His writing is not in the same league as Tolkien.*
class, level, standard, grade, rank

leak *NOUN*

1 *mending a leak in a pipe*
crack, hole, opening, split, rent, fissure, rupture, perforation
▶ A leak in a tyre is a **puncture**.

2 *a gas leak*
escape, discharge, leakage, drip

3 *a leak of secret information*
disclosure, revelation, exposé

leak *VERB*

1 *Gallons of oil leaked from the tanker.*
escape, seep, ooze, drain, drip, dribble, trickle

2 *Details of the plan were leaked to the press.*
reveal, disclose, divulge, pass on, let out, make known, make public

a
b
c
d
e
f
g
h
i
j
k
l
m
n
o
p
q
r
s
t
u
v
w
x
y
z

lean❶ ADJECTIVE

a dancer with a strong, lean figure
slim, slender, thin, svelte, trim, wiry, spindly

OPPOSITES fat, plump
FOR TIPS ON DESCRIBING BODIES SEE **body**

lean❷ VERB

1 *Two boys were leaning against the front wall.*
recline, rest, prop yourself, support yourself

2 *The Tower of Pisa leans to one side.*
slope, tilt, tip, incline, slant, list, bank

▷ **lean on someone**
Jacques had no family or friends to lean on.
rely on, depend on, count on, bank on

leap VERB

1 *a fish leaping out of the water*
jump, spring, bound, vault

2 *Prices have leapt by more than a third.*
rise sharply, jump, soar, rocket, shoot up

leap NOUN

1 *a leap across a puddle*
jump, spring, bound, vault

2 *a leap in the cost of living*
sharp rise, jump, surge
(informal) hike

learn VERB

1 *learning the basics of cookery*
acquire, master, pick up, absorb, digest
(informal) get the hang of

2 *learning the words of a song*
learn by heart, memorize, master

3 *I later learned that we had met before.*
discover, find out, hear, gather, grasp

learner NOUN

a class for language learners
beginner, starter, novice

▶ Someone learning things at school or college is a **pupil** or **student**.

▶ Someone learning a trade is an **apprentice** or **trainee**.

OPPOSITE expert

learning NOUN

The city became a centre of learning.
study, education, knowledge, erudition, scholarship, research

OPPOSITE ignorance

least ADJECTIVE

1 *scoring the least number of points*
fewest, lowest

2 *I found the house without the least difficulty.*
slightest, smallest, tiniest

leave VERB

1 *We'll be leaving tomorrow morning.*
go, go away, depart, withdraw, take your leave, go out, set off, say goodbye
(informal) take off, disappear

OPPOSITE arrive

2 *Bond left the room in a hurry.*
exit, go out of, depart from, quit, vacate

▶ To leave a dangerous place is to **evacuate** it.

OPPOSITE enter

3 *Don't leave me here on my own!*
abandon, desert, forsake

4 *You can leave your coat in here.*
place, position, put down, set down, deposit

5 *He claims he was forced to leave his job.*
give up, quit, resign from, step down from
(informal) jack in

6 *I'll leave all the arrangements to you.*
pass on, hand over, refer, entrust

7 *She left all her money to charity.*
bequeath, hand down, will, endow

▷ **leave someone or something out**
You've left out the best part of the story.
miss out, omit, exclude, overlook, pass over, skip, drop

eave NOUN

1 *applying for leave to stay in the UK*
permission, authorization, consent,
approval, sanction

2 *Dr Dass is on leave for a week.*
holiday, vacation, time off

ecture NOUN

1 *listening to a lecture on evolution*
talk, speech, address, lesson,
presentation

2 *getting a lecture on how to behave*
reprimand, warning, scolding
(*informal*) telling-off, talking-to,
dressing-down

edge NOUN

a narrow ledge of rock
shelf, projection
▶ A ledge under a window is a
windowsill.

eft ADJECTIVE

on the left side of the road
left-hand
▶ The left side of a ship when you face
forwards is the **port** side.
▌OPPOSITE right

eg NOUN

1 *Boris fell and bruised his leg.*
SEE **body**

2 *the final leg of the competition*
part, stage, section, phase, stretch

egal ADJECTIVE

Is it legal to download this file?
lawful, legitimate, within the law,
permissible, permitted, allowed
▌OPPOSITE illegal

legend NOUN

1 *the legend of the Loch Ness Monster*
myth, story, folk tale, fairy tale,
fable, saga, tradition
FOR TIPS ON WRITING FANTASY FICTION
SEE **fantasy**

2 *a sporting legend*
hero, heroine, celebrity, star, icon,
giant, luminary

legendary ADJECTIVE

1 *the legendary city of Camelot*
mythical, mythological, fabulous,
fabled, fairy-tale, traditional
▌OPPOSITE historical

2 *his legendary ability to score goals*
famous, well-known, celebrated,
renowned, acclaimed, esteemed

legible ADJECTIVE

The inscription is now barely legible.
readable, clear, distinct, neat
▌OPPOSITE illegible

legitimate ADJECTIVE

a legitimate claim to the throne
legal, proper, rightful, authorized,
licensed, permitted

leisure NOUN

living a life of leisure
free time, spare time, relaxation,
recreation, rest

leisurely ADJECTIVE

a leisurely stroll in the park
unhurried, relaxed, relaxing, gentle,
easy, restful, slow
▌OPPOSITE fast

lend VERB

1 *Could you lend me some money?*
loan, advance, let someone have
▌OPPOSITE borrow

2 *Moonlight lent an air of mystery to
the scene.*
give, add, impart, bestow, confer,
contribute, supply

length NOUN

1 *measuring the length of a room*
extent, size, distance, expanse,
range, span
▶ To measure the length of something
is to measure it **lengthways** or
lengthwise.

2 *for a short length of time*
period, duration, space, stretch

▷ **at length**

1 *At length, someone broke the silence.*
eventually, in time, in the end,
finally, at long last

2 *The author spoke at length about his
new book.*
for a long time, in detail, in depth

a
b
c
d
e
f
g
h
i
j
k
l
m
n
o
p
q
r
s
t
u
v
w
x
y
z

lengthen VERB

1 *Anna deliberately lengthened her stride.*
extend, make longer, elongate, stretch

OPPOSITE shorten

2 *The afternoon shadows began to lengthen.*
draw out, get longer, stretch out

lengthy ADJECTIVE

Making an animated film is a lengthy process.
long, drawn-out, extended, prolonged, protracted, time-consuming, long-running, long-winded, interminable

OPPOSITES short, brief

lenient ADJECTIVE

I think the referee was too lenient.
easy-going, soft-hearted, tolerant, forgiving, indulgent, charitable, merciful

OPPOSITE strict

lens NOUN

> **WORD WEB**
>
> **instruments which use lenses**
> binoculars, camera, magnifying glass, microscope, spectacles, telescope
>
> ▶ A **concave** lens has a surface which curves inwards, and a **convex** lens has a surface which curves outwards.
>
> **SEE ALSO glasses, photography**

lessen VERB

1 *some medicine to lessen the pain*
minimize, reduce, relieve

2 *The storm lessened during the night.*
diminish, decrease, dwindle, subside, weaken, ease off, tail off, die down, ebb, wane, recede

OPPOSITE increase

lesser ADJECTIVE

1 *Which is the lesser of these two numbers?*
smaller, lower

OPPOSITE greater

2 *committing a lesser offence*
less important, minor, secondary, inferior

lesson NOUN

a weekly music lesson
class, period, session, tutorial, instruction

let VERB

1 *My parents let me go to the party.*
allow, permit, give permission to, consent to, agree to, authorize

OPPOSITE forbid

2 *A microscope lets you see tiny objects*
enable, allow, equip, empower

3 *Our neighbours are letting their garage.*
lease, rent out, hire out

▷ **let someone off**
We were let off classes for the day.
excuse from, exempt from, spare from

▷ **let something off**
Someone had let off a stink bomb.
set off, detonate, explode, discharge

▷ **let something out**

1 *Suddenly Molly let out a scream.*
utter, emit, give, produce, express

2 *Who let out the secret?*
reveal, divulge, disclose, make known, give away, let slip

lethal ADJECTIVE

a lethal dose of poison
deadly, fatal, mortal, life-threatening, poisonous, toxic

letter NOUN

1 *an ancient runic letter*
character, symbol, sign, figure

▶ The letters a, e, i, o, u, and sometimes y are **vowels**.

▶ The other letters are **consonants**.

2 *a handwritten letter*
note, message, missive, communication, dispatch

▶ Letters people send each other are **correspondence**.

evel *ADJECTIVE*

1 *a level piece of ground*
even, flat, horizontal, plane, smooth,
flush
OPPOSITE uneven

2 *At half-time the scores were level.*
equal, even, the same, matching,
tied, drawn
IDIOMS all square, level pegging,
neck and neck

evel *NOUN*

1 *checking the level of the water*
height, position

2 *the top level of the building*
floor, storey, tier

3 *studying at an advanced level*
grade, standard, stage, rank, degree

evel *VERB*

1 *using a roller to level the lawn*
even out, flatten, smooth

2 *A massive earthquake levelled the
village.*
knock down, demolish, destroy,
devastate

3 *A late goal levelled the score.*
equal, equalize, make level, even up

4 *Robin levelled an arrow at the target.*
aim, point, direct, train, line up

ever *VERB*

Slowly, they levered open the coffin.
prise, wrench, force

iable *ADJECTIVE*

1 *Uncle Ned is liable to forget things.*
likely, inclined, disposed, prone, apt,
given
OPPOSITE unlikely

2 *We are not liable for any loss or
damage.*
responsible, answerable,
accountable

iberal *ADJECTIVE*

1 *Apply a liberal amount of hair gel.*
generous, abundant, copious,
ample, plentiful, lavish, unsparing,
unstinting
OPPOSITES meagre, miserly

2 *taking a liberal point of view*

broad-minded, open-minded,
tolerant, permissive, enlightened,
lenient, easy-going
OPPOSITE strict

liberate *VERB*

a plan to liberate the hostages
free, set free, release, emancipate,
discharge, let go, set loose
OPPOSITE imprison

liberty *NOUN*

1 *Many former slaves had purchased
their own liberty.*
liberation, release, emancipation
OPPOSITES imprisonment, slavery

2 *the liberty to come and go as you
please*
freedom, independence
OPPOSITE constraint

licence *NOUN*

a licence to practise as a vet
permit, certificate, authorization,
warrant, pass

license *VERB*

Are you licensed to drive this vehicle?
permit, allow, authorize, entitle,
certify

lid *NOUN*

the lid of a sarcophagus
cover, covering, cap, top

lie^❶ *NOUN*

spreading rumours and lies
untruth, falsehood, fib, fabrication,
deception
(*informal*) whopper
IDIOM tall story
OPPOSITE truth

lie *VERB*

Why would he lie about his past?
tell a lie, fib, dissemble, bluff
▶ To tell a lie while you are under oath
in a law court is to **commit perjury**
or **perjure yourself**.
OPPOSITE tell the truth

lie^❷ *VERB*

1 *lying flat on your back*
recline, stretch out, sprawl,

lounge, rest, repose
- ▶ To lie face downwards is to **be prone** or **be prostrate**.
- ▶ To lie face upwards is to **be supine**.
2 *Tutankhamen's tomb lies in the Valley of the Kings.*
be sited, be situated, be located, be placed, be found

life *NOUN*
1 *I owe you my life.*
existence, being, survival
2 *leading a life of relative ease*
way of life, lifestyle
3 *feeling full of life*
energy, liveliness, vigour, vitality, vivacity, spirit, sprightliness, animation, exuberance, dynamism, zest
4 *I'm reading a life of Dickens.*
life story, biography, autobiography
5 *extending the life of a battery*
duration, lifetime, lifespan

lifeless *ADJECTIVE*
SEE **dead**

lift *VERB*
1 *lifting a statue into position*
raise, pick up, pull up, elevate, hoist
2 *One by one, the balloons lifted into the sky.*
rise, ascend, soar
3 *The ban has finally been lifted.*
remove, withdraw, cancel, revoke, rescind

lift *NOUN*
1 *She signalled with a slight lift of her chin.*
raising, lifting, elevation, push-up, hoist
2 *Would you like a lift into town?*
ride, run

light⁰ *NOUN*

WORD WEB

some kinds of natural light
daylight, moonlight, starlight, sunlight, twilight

sources of artificial light
bulb, candle, chandelier, flambeau, floodlight, fluorescent lamp, headlamp or headlight, lamp, lantern, laser, LED or light-emitting diode, neon light, searchlight, spotlight, street light, torch

WRITING TIPS

describing light

Long orange rays of evening sun stole in through chinks in the blind, striking on the large mirror, and being thence reflected upon the crimson hangings and woodwork of the heavy bedstead, so that the general tone of light was remarkably warm.
— *Thomas Hardy*, *Wessex Tales*

effects of light
beam, blaze, burn, dazzle, flame, flare, flash, flicker, glare, gleam, glimmer, glint, glisten, glitter, glow, halo, lustre, pulse, radiance, ray, reflection, shaft, shimmer, shine, sparkle, twinkle, wink

adjectives
bright, brilliant, dappled, diffused, dim, harsh, luminous, lustrous, muted, pale, pulsating, radiant, scintillating, silhouetted, soft, sparkling, strong, warm, weak

light *ADJECTIVE*
1 *a light and airy studio*
bright, well-lit, illuminated, sunny
❘ OPPOSITES dim, gloomy
2 *a light shade of grey*
pale, faint, delicate, subtle
❘ OPPOSITES dark, deep

light *VERB*
1 *lighting the candles on a cake*

ignite, set alight, set fire to, kindle,
switch on
❙ **OPPOSITE** extinguish

2 *a sky lit by the full moon*
light up, illuminate, brighten, shine
on, shed light on
❙ **OPPOSITE** darken

light² ADJECTIVE

1 *carrying a light load*
lightweight, portable, weightless,
slight
❙ **OPPOSITES** heavy, weighty

2 *a light breeze*
gentle, faint, slight, soft
❙ **OPPOSITES** strong, forceful

3 *eating a light breakfast*
small, modest, simple, insubstantial
❙ **OPPOSITES** heavy, substantial

4 *doing some light housework*
easy, undemanding, effortless
❙ **OPPOSITES** heavy, demanding

5 *I bought a magazine for some light
reading.*
undemanding, entertaining,
lightweight, frivolous, superficial
❙ **OPPOSITES** serious, profound

like¹ VERB

OVERUSED WORD

*to like a person, animal, or
possession*
admire, adore, love, be attached
to, be fond of, care for, cherish,
esteem, hold dear, be attracted
to, be interested in, be taken
with, be infatuated with, be
smitten with
(*informal*) fancy

❙ **IDIOMS** have a soft spot for,
think the world of

*Noel **is very taken with** his new
laptop.*

to like a taste, book, film, etc
be partial to, have a taste for,
have a liking for, have a

preference for, be keen on, enjoy,
appreciate, prefer
(*informal*) be mad on

*Chaffinches **are partial to**
peanuts.*

*I used to **enjoy** fantasy, but now I
prefer science fiction.*

❙ **OPPOSITE** dislike

to like doing something
delight in, take pleasure in, enjoy,
relish, savour, revel in, wallow in,
have a penchant for

*This is a film that **delights in**
shocking the audience.*

like² PREPOSITION

1 *making a noise like a strangled cat*
similar to, the same as, resembling,
identical to, akin to, in the manner of
❙ **OPPOSITE** unlike

2 *fictional detectives, like Holmes and
Poirot*
such as, for example, for instance,
namely

likeable ADJECTIVE

*The main character is a likeable
rogue.*
pleasant, appealing, attractive,
agreeable, amiable, engaging,
charming

likelihood NOUN

*What is the likelihood of being struck
by lightning?*
probability, chance, prospect, odds,
risk, promise

likely ADJECTIVE

1 *forecasting where earthquakes are
likely to occur*
probable, expected, anticipated,
predictable, foreseeable
❙ **OPPOSITE** unlikely

2 *a likely reason for their defeat*
plausible, credible, reasonable,
feasible, believable
❙ **OPPOSITE** implausible

likeness *NOUN*

1 *a strong likeness between the two sisters*
resemblance, similarity, correspondence
❚ **OPPOSITE** difference

2 *This photo is a good likeness of my grandfather.*
image, representation, picture, portrait, depiction, portrayal

liking *NOUN*

Otto has a liking for classical music.
fondness, taste, love, passion, affection, preference, partiality, inclination, penchant
❚ **OPPOSITES** dislike, distaste

limb *NOUN*

SEE **body**

limit *NOUN*

1 *This stone marks the limit of the old city.*
border, boundary, edge, perimeter, frontier

2 *The course has a limit of twenty places.*
maximum, restriction, threshold, ceiling, cut-off point
▶ A limit on time is a **deadline** or **time limit**.

limit *VERB*

trying to limit the costs
put a limit on, restrict, ration, curb, cap, rein in

limited *ADJECTIVE*

1 *a limited supply of fuel*
restricted, short, inadequate, insufficient, rationed, finite, fixed
❚ **OPPOSITE** limitless

2 *squeezing into a limited space*
small, cramped, restricted, narrow, tight, confined

limp❶ *VERB*

limping off the pitch with a twisted ankle
hobble, hop, falter, stumble

limp❷ *ADJECTIVE*

The child's hand was quite limp and cold.
floppy, drooping, droopy, sagging, wilting, soft, flabby, flaccid, slack
❚ **OPPOSITES** rigid, firm

line *NOUN*

1 *a faint line of red ink*
stroke, rule, dash, underline, stripe, strip, streak, band, bar, belt
▶ A line cut into a surface is a **groove**, **score**, or **scratch**.
▶ A line on a person's skin is a **wrinkle**.
▶ A deep groove or wrinkle is a **furrow**.
▶ A line on fabric is a **crease**.

2 *a long line of people at the bus stop*
queue, row, file, column, rank, procession, chain
▶ A line of police officers forming a barrier is a **cordon**.
▶ A line of schoolchildren walking in pairs is a **crocodile**.

3 *clothes hanging on a washing line*
cord, rope, string, thread, wire, cable, flex, lead

linger *VERB*

1 *The smell of burning lingered in the air.*
continue, remain, stay, last, persist, endure
❚ **OPPOSITE** disappear

2 *We mustn't linger any longer.*
hang about, wait about, loiter, dawdle, dally, delay
(old use) tarry
❚ **OPPOSITE** hurry

link *NOUN*

the evolutionary link between birds and dinosaurs
relationship, association, connection, bond, tie

link *VERB*

1 *All our computers are all linked to the Internet.*
connect, attach, fasten, join, couple, hook up, wire up

❙ OPPOSITE separate

2 *Melting ice has been linked with global warming.*
associate, connect, relate, bracket
❙ OPPOSITE disassociate (from)

lion NOUN
Lions usually stalk their prey.
▶ A female lion is a **lioness**.
▶ A young lion is a **cub**.
▶ A group of lions is a **pride**.
▶ The fur collar on a male lion is its **mane**.
▶ A **mountain lion** is another name for a **puma** or **cougar**.
❙ SEE ALSO cat
FOR TIPS ON DESCRIBING ANIMALS SEE **animal**

liquid NOUN
Stir the liquid until it thickens.
fluid, solution, juice, liquor
▶ The liquid inside a plant is **sap**.
❙ OPPOSITE solid

liquid ADJECTIVE
Pour the liquid jelly into a mould.
runny, watery, fluid, flowing, running, sloppy
▶ To make something liquid is to **liquefy** it.
▶ To make food into a liquid or pulp is to **liquidize** it.
▶ To liquefy something by heating is to **melt** it.
▶ Liquid metal or rock is **molten**.
❙ OPPOSITE solid

list❶ NOUN
I'll add your name to the list.
register, roll, rota, catalogue, directory, inventory, checklist
▶ A list of topics mentioned in a book is an **index**.
▶ A list of things to choose from is a **menu**.

list VERB
The books are listed in alphabetical order.
record, register, write down, catalogue, index, itemize

list❷ VERB
The ship listed dangerously to one side.
lean, tilt, tip, pitch, incline, slant, slope

listen VERB
Do you think anyone is listening?
pay attention, attend
❙ IDIOMS keep your ears open, be all ears
▶ To listen secretly to a private conversation is to **eavesdrop**.
▷ **listen to someone**
Nobody ever listens to me.
pay attention to, take notice of, attend to, heed

literature NOUN
1 *a course in American literature*
writing, books
FOR TYPES OF LITERATURE SEE **drama, fiction, poetry**

2 *some advertising literature*
brochures, leaflets, pamphlets, handouts
(*informal*) blurb

litter NOUN
litter lying in the streets
rubbish, refuse, waste, junk, clutter, mess
(*North American*) garbage, trash

litter VERB
The desk was littered with scraps of paper.
scatter, strew, clutter

little ADJECTIVE

OVERUSED WORD

little in size, scale
small, tiny, minute, petite, compact, mini, miniature, minuscule, midget, diminutive
(*informal*) teeny, titchy
(*Scottish*) wee
*Microbes are so **minute** they can only be seen through a microscope.*   **》**

| **OPPOSITES** big, large

little in age
young, small (*Scottish*) wee
*Mozart wrote several small operas when he was **young***.
| **OPPOSITES** old, big

a little brother, little sister
younger, baby (*Scottish*) wee
*I didn't know you had a **younger** brother?*
| **OPPOSITES** elder, older

a little time, a little while
brief, short, fleeting, passing, cursory
*For a **fleeting** moment, Gil felt like a child again.*
| **OPPOSITES** lengthy, long

a little problem
slight, minor, unimportant, insignificant, trivial, trifling
*I have a **slight** problem with my Internet connection.*
| **OPPOSITE** major

little left of something
hardly any, insufficient, meagre, paltry, scarcely any
*There was **scarcely any** food left by the time we arrived.*
| **OPPOSITES** ample, plenty

a little amount of something
some, a bit of, a spot of, a touch of, a dash of, a pinch of
(*informal*) a smidgen of, a tad of
*Would you like **a spot of** milk in your tea?*
| **OPPOSITES** plenty of, lots of

a little
a bit, slightly, rather, somewhat, to some degree
*The opening chapter reminds me **somewhat** of Poe.*

live VERB
1 *Giant tortoises can live for over a hundred years.*
stay alive, survive, exist, subsist
| **OPPOSITE** die
2 *living a life of luxury*
lead, experience, go through, spend, pass
3 *Whereabouts do you live?*
reside, dwell
▷ **live in**
We used to live in a basement flat.
inhabit, occupy, dwell in, reside in
▷ **live on**
Whales live mainly on plankton.
eat, feed on, subsist on

live ADJECTIVE
1 *eating live insects*
alive, living, breathing
| **OPPOSITE** dead
2 *using live ammunition*
active, unexploded, primed

lively ADJECTIVE
1 *feeling in a lively mood*
active, energetic, vigorous, dynamic, animated, spirited, vibrant, vivacious, buoyant, exuberant, sprightly, frisky, chirpy, perky
| **IDIOM** (*informal*) full of beans
| **OPPOSITE** inactive
2 *The city is always lively at fiesta time.*
busy, bustling, crowded, exciting, buzzing, vibrant
| **OPPOSITES** quiet, dead

livid (*informal*) ADJECTIVE
SEE **angry**

living ADJECTIVE
1 *Miss Cooper had no living relatives.*
alive, surviving
| **OPPOSITES** dead, deceased
2 *Basque is a living language.*
current, existing, in use
| **OPPOSITES** dead, extinct

living *NOUN*

1 *a guide to healthier living*
way of life, lifestyle

2 *He makes a living from painting.*
income, livelihood, subsistence
IDIOMS bread and butter,
daily bread

3 *What does she do for a living?*
job, occupation, profession, trade,
career

load *NOUN*

1 *carrying a heavy load*
burden, weight

2 *a lorry picking up a load for delivery*
cargo, consignment, goods, freight

▷ **loads of**
(*informal*) *We had loads of time to
spare.*
plenty of, lots of
(*informal*) tons of, masses of,
oodles of

load *VERB*

1 *loading dishes into the dishwasher*
pack, stack, pile, heap, stow

2 *loading a van with furniture*
fill up, pack, stock

3 *Diane arrived loaded with shopping
bags.*
weigh down, burden, saddle,
encumber

loan *NOUN*

a loan from the bank
advance
► A system which allows you to pay for
something later is **credit**.
► A loan to buy a house is a **mortgage**.

loath *ADJECTIVE*

I'm loath to ask for their help again.
reluctant, unwilling, disinclined
OPPOSITES willing, keen

loathe *VERB*

My brother loathes the colour pink.
hate, detest, despise, be unable to
bear, be unable to stand
(*formal*) abhor
OPPOSITES love, adore

loathsome *ADJECTIVE*

*the most loathsome creature I have
ever seen*
repulsive, repugnant, abhorrent,
revolting, obnoxious, vile,
abominable, horrible, foul, hateful,
detestable
(*formal*) noisome

local *ADJECTIVE*

events at your local library
neighbourhood, community,
nearby, neighbouring

locate *VERB*

1 *I can't locate the book you asked for.*
find, discover, track down, detect,
pinpoint, unearth
IDIOM lay your hands on
OPPOSITE lose

2 *The gallery is located in the city
centre.*
place, position, site, situate, set up,
establish, station, base

location *NOUN*

*Most of the movie was filmed in this
location.*
position, situation, place, site, spot,
setting, whereabouts, locality, locale

lock❶ *NOUN*

a lock on a door
fastening, clasp, catch, padlock,
bolt, latch

lock *VERB*

1 *Remember to lock the door.*
fasten, secure, bolt, latch, padlock,
chain, seal

2 *The back wheels had locked fast.*
stick, become stuck, jam, seize up

lock❷ *NOUN*

a lock of hair
tress, curl, tuft, wisp, coil, hank,
ringlet
FOR TIPS ON DESCRIBING HAIR SEE hair

lodge *VERB*

1 *Where are you lodging at present?*
reside, stay, board, live, dwell
(*North American*) room

»

a
b
c
d
e
f
g
h
i
j
k
l
m
n
o
p
q
r
s
t
u
v
w
x
y
z

2 *The animals are lodged indoors in the winter.*
house, accommodate, board, put up

3 *The bullet had lodged in his chest.*
get caught, become stuck, jam, wedge, fix, embed

log NOUN
keeping a log of your computer time
record, register, account, tally, diary, journal, logbook

logical ADJECTIVE
1 *Holmes used logical methods of deduction.*
rational, analytical, methodical, systematic, sound, valid
❙ **OPPOSITE** illogical

2 *the logical thing to do*
sensible, reasonable, natural, understandable

lone ADJECTIVE
A lone figure appeared on the horizon.
single, solitary, unaccompanied, isolated, solo

lonely ADJECTIVE
1 *I felt lonely in the house by myself.*
alone, friendless, lonesome, abandoned, neglected, forlorn, forsaken

2 *a lonely cottage in the Highlands*
deserted, isolated, remote, secluded, out-of-the-way

long❶ ADJECTIVE
a long and awkward silence
lengthy, prolonged, extended, extensive, long-lasting, drawn-out, interminable
❙ **OPPOSITES** short, brief

long❷ VERB
▷ **long for something**
We were all longing for a rest.
yearn for, crave, wish for, desire, hunger for, pine for, hanker after, itch for, be desperate for
(*informal*) be dying for

look VERB
1 *A woman was looking in our direction.*
gaze, peer, glance, watch, stare

2 *Those shoes look a bit dated now.*
appear, seem, come across as

▷ **look after someone or something**
Would you look after my cat while I'm away?
care for, take care of, tend, mind, watch over, guard, protect
❙ **IDIOM** keep an eye on

▶ To look after sick people is to **nurse** them.

▷ **look for something**
looking for information on the Internet
search for, hunt for, seek

▷ **look into something**
looking into our family history
investigate, inquire into, find out about, examine, explore

▷ **look out for something**
Look out for sharp bends in the road.
beware of, watch out for, be careful of, pay attention to
❙ **IDIOMS** keep an eye open for, keep your eyes peeled

▷ **look something up**
looking up a word in the dictionary
find, search for, track down, research, locate

OVERUSED WORD

to look at something
watch, observe, view, regard, contemplate, inspect, take in, eye, ogle
(*North American*) eyeball
*Lance **inspected** himself in the mirror.*

to look quickly
glance, glimpse, peek, peep, sneak a look
*I thought I **glimpsed** the fin of a shark.*

to look carefully, look intently
stare, peer, squint, study, scrutinize, examine, inspect, take a good look at

*Holmes knelt down and **peered** at the footprints.*

to look over a wide area
scan, survey

*Patrick would **scan** the night sky for hours.*

to look angrily
glare, glower, grimace, frown, scowl

*Mr Davies merely **glowered** at us in silence.*

to look in amazement
gape, stare wide-eyed, stare open-mouthed, goggle
(*informal*) gawk, gawp

▌**IDIOM** have your eyes on stalks
*I found myself **gaping** in genuine surprise.*

look *NOUN*

1 *Take a look at this website.*
glance, gaze, glimpse, peek, peep, sight, view, squint
(*informal*) eyeful
2 *a house with a lived-in look*
appearance, air, aspect, bearing, manner, mien, demeanour
3 *The girl turned to us with a look of horror.*
expression, face, countenance

lookout *NOUN*

Lookouts were posted along the wall.
sentry, guard, sentinel, watchman

loom *VERB*

1 *A figure loomed out of the mist.*
appear, emerge, arise, take shape
2 *A sheer cliff face loomed before us.*
rise, tower, stand out, hang over

loop *NOUN*

Make a loop in the string.
coil, ring, hoop, circle, noose, bend, curl, twist, kink

loop *VERB*

Loop the thread around your finger.
coil, wind, twist, curl, bend, turn, snake

loose *ADJECTIVE*

1 *Some of the roof tiles are loose.*
insecure, unfixed, movable, unsteady, shaky, wobbly
▌**OPPOSITES** firm, secure
2 *wearing your hair loose*
untied, free, down
▌**OPPOSITE** tied
3 *These jeans are loose around the waist.*
slack, baggy, roomy, loose-fitting
▌**OPPOSITE** tight
4 *Chickens roamed loose in the backyard.*
free, at large, at liberty, on the loose, unconfined, unrestricted
▌**OPPOSITE** confined
5 *a loose translation of the poem*
rough, general, vague, inexact
▌**OPPOSITES** exact, literal

loosen *VERB*

1 *Can you loosen this knot?*
undo, unfasten, untie, free, loose, slacken
▌**OPPOSITE** tighten
2 *I loosened my hold on the rope.*
relax, slacken, ease, release, let go
▌**OPPOSITE** tighten

loot *NOUN*

a bag full of stolen loot
spoils, plunder, stolen goods, booty

loot *VERB*

Rioters looted the shops.
raid, ransack, rob, steal from, pillage, plunder

lorry *NOUN*
SEE **vehicle**

lose *VERB*

1 *I've lost one of my earrings.*
mislay, misplace
▌**OPPOSITE** find

a
b
c
d
e
f
g
h
i
j
k
l
m
n
o
p
q
r
s
t
u
v
w
x
y
z

》

2 *By now, we had lost a lot of time.*
waste, squander, let pass

3 *Our team lost by two goals to one.*
be defeated, get beaten, suffer a
defeat
OPPOSITE win

loss NOUN

1 *the loss of key computer files*
losing, mislaying, misplacement,
disappearance, theft

2 *a severe loss of memory*
failure, deprivation, erosion,
depletion

3 *the loss of a dear friend*
death, decease, passing
(*old use*) demise

lost ADJECTIVE

1 *I eventually found my lost keys.*
missing, mislaid, misplaced
OPPOSITE found

2 *The quagga is a lost species of zebra.*
vanished, gone, extinct, wiped out

3 *Giles appeared to be lost in thought.*
absorbed, engrossed, preoccupied,
deep, immersed, rapt

lot NOUN

a second lot of parcels to deliver
group, batch, set, crowd, collection

▷ **a lot of**

patients who need a lot of care
a large amount of, a good deal of,
a great deal of, plenty of

▷ **lots of**

I got lots of emails on my birthday.
a great number of, many, numerous,
plenty, plenty of, a wealth of,
an abundance of, galore
(*informal*) loads of, tons of, masses
of, stacks of, oodles of, hundreds of

Usage Note

The word *galore* comes after a
noun: *a film that offers action and
stunts galore.*

loud ADJECTIVE

1 *That music is too loud!*

noisy, blaring, booming, deafening,
resounding, thunderous,
penetrating, piercing, ear-splitting,
stentorian

▶ A noise which is loud enough to hear
is **audible**.

▶ A technical term for loud in music is
forte.
OPPOSITES quiet, soft

2 *a man wearing a loud tie*
bright, gaudy, garish, showy,
ostentatious
(*informal*) flashy
OPPOSITES muted, subdued

lounge VERB

*Dan lounged in his bedroom all
morning.*
laze, idle, loaf, relax, take it easy,
sprawl, slouch, lie around, loll

lovable ADJECTIVE

a lovable family pet
adorable, dear, sweet, charming,
likeable, lovely, appealing, attractive,
cuddly, enchanting, endearing
OPPOSITE hateful

love NOUN

1 *the love between Romeo and Juliet*
adoration, infatuation, affection,
fondness, attachment, tenderness,
passion, warmth, intimacy

2 *indulging a love of shopping*
liking, fondness, taste, passion,
enthusiasm, keenness, zest, zeal,
partiality

3 *Elsa believed she had met her true
love.*
sweetheart, beloved, loved one,
darling, dearest

love VERB

1 *It's obvious that those two love each
other.*
be in love with, adore, care for,
cherish, hold dear, treasure, worship,
idolize, be infatuated with, be
besotted with, be smitten with
(*informal*) be crazy about
IDIOM carry a torch for

a *b* *c* *d* *e* *f* *g* *h* *i* *j* *k* *l* *m* *n* *o* *p* *q* *r* *s* *t* *u* *v* *w* *x* *y* *z*

▶ A relationship between two people who love each other is a **romance**.

2 *My brother loves anything to do with football.*
like, be fond of, be partial to, have a weakness for, have a passion for, delight in, enjoy

IDIOMS have a soft spot for *(informal)* have a thing about

OPPOSITE hate

Usage Note

You can use the suffix **-phile** to describe a person who loves something. For example, a *bibliophile* is someone who loves books, and a *cinephile* is someone who loves the cinema.

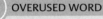

ovely *ADJECTIVE*

OVERUSED WORD

a lovely person
charming, delightful, lovable, likeable, dear, sweet, enchanting, endearing, adorable
*Jemma is a **charming** girl.*

a lovely day, lovely weather
fine, glorious, bright, fair, sunny
*It was **glorious** weather for a bike ride.*

a lovely view
scenic, picturesque, pleasing, glorious, splendid
*You get a **splendid** view from the cable car.*

a lovely experience, a lovely time
pleasant, pleasing, enjoyable, delightful, marvellous, wonderful
(informal) fantastic, terrific, brilliant, smashing
*I had an **enjoyable** time doing absolutely nothing!*

looking lovely
appealing, attractive, pretty, good-looking, beautiful, glamorous, alluring, ravishing
(informal) cute
(Scottish) bonny
*You look particularly **attractive** in that hat.*

lover *NOUN*

1 *Some lovers send each other Valentine cards.*
boyfriend, girlfriend, sweetheart, beloved

2 *Carl is a great lover of musicals.*
admirer, fan, devotee, enthusiast

loving *ADJECTIVE*
growing up in a loving family
affectionate, kind, friendly, warm, tender, fond, devoted, passionate
OPPOSITE unfriendly

low *ADJECTIVE*

1 *a garden surrounded by a low wall*
short, shallow, sunken, squat
OPPOSITES high, tall

2 *soldiers of low rank*
junior, inferior, lowly, modest, humble
OPPOSITES high, senior

3 *producing work of low quality*
poor, inferior, substandard, unsatisfactory
OPPOSITES high, superior

4 *playing low notes on a cello*
bass, deep, sonorous
OPPOSITE high

5 *We spoke in low whispers.*
quiet, soft, muted, subdued, muffled, hushed
OPPOSITE loud

lower *VERB*

1 *Some shops have lowered their prices.*
reduce, cut, drop, decrease, lessen, bring down
(informal) slash

》

a
b
c
d
e
f
g
h
i
j
k
l
m
n
o
p
q
r
s
t
u
v
w
x
y
z

2 *Please lower your voices.*
quieten, soften, turn down, tone down, muffle, hush

3 *lowering a flag*
take down, let down, dip, let fall
❙ OPPOSITE raise

lowly *ADJECTIVE*
He had risen from a lowly background.
humble, ordinary, simple, plain, modest

loyal *ADJECTIVE*
a loyal supporter of the club
faithful, devoted, true, steadfast, constant, staunch, reliable, dependable, trusty
❙ OPPOSITE disloyal

luck *NOUN*
1 *I found the website by pure luck.*
chance, accident, fortune, fate, serendipity

2 *A four-leaf clover is said to bring you luck.*
good fortune, success, prosperity

lucky *ADJECTIVE*
1 *It was just a lucky guess.*
accidental, chance, fortuitous, serendipitous, providential

2 *Are you feeling lucky today?*
fortunate, favoured, charmed, blessed, in luck
❙ OPPOSITE unlucky

ludicrous *ADJECTIVE*
The film is hampered by a ludicrous plot.
ridiculous, absurd, laughable, idiotic, nonsensical, foolish, preposterous, crazy, senseless, asinine
(*British informal*) daft

luggage *NOUN*
Put your luggage on the trolley.
baggage, cases, suitcases, bags

lull *VERB*
lulling a baby to sleep
soothe, calm, hush, quieten, pacify, subdue

lull *NOUN*
during a brief lull in the conversation
pause, break, gap, interval, respite, calm, breathing space
(*informal*) let-up, breather

lumber *VERB*
1 *A rhinoceros lumbered past our jeep.*
trundle, shamble, trudge, tramp, blunder, clump

2 (*informal*) *Why am I lumbered with the washing up?*
burden, encumber, saddle, land

lump *NOUN*
1 *a lump of volcanic rock*
chunk, piece, cluster, clump, wad, mass, hunk, wedge, block
▶ A lump of gold is a **nugget**.
▶ A lump of earth is a **clod**.
▶ A lump of blood is a **clot**.

2 *a lump where I banged my head*
bump, swelling, bulge, protrusion

lump *VERB*
▷ **lump things together**
The text is lumped together in a single file.
put together, combine, merge, bunch up

lunge *VERB*
The creature lunged forward and grabbed my leg.
thrust, charge, rush, dive, spring, pounce, throw yourself, launch yourself

lurch *VERB*
1 *It looked like a zombie lurching towards us.*
stagger, stumble, totter, sway, reel, roll, rock

2 *The bus suddenly lurched to one side.*
veer, swerve, swing, lean, list

lure *VERB*
trying to lure shoppers to spend more
attract, entice, tempt, coax, draw, invite, persuade, seduce, inveigle
▶ Something used to lure an animal into a trap is **bait**.
❙ OPPOSITES deter, put off

urk VERB

> I had the feeling that someone was
> lurking in the shadows.
> skulk, loiter, prowl, crouch, hide,
> lie in wait, lie low

luscious ADJECTIVE

> a luscious coating of chocolate
> rich, thick, full, luxuriant, lush

lush ADJECTIVE

> an area of lush vegetation
> rich, dense, thick, profuse,
> abundant, rampant, luxuriant,
> luscious

luxuriant ADJECTIVE

> SEE **lush**

luxurious ADJECTIVE

> a room with luxurious furnishings
> rich, expensive, costly, lavish, lush,
> sumptuous, opulent, de luxe,

magnificent, splendid, extravagant
(*informal*) plush, swanky
❙ **OPPOSITES** simple, austere

Usage Note
The words **luxurious** and **luxuriant** do not mean the same thing. A *luxurious hair salon* is expensive and comfortable, but *luxuriant hair* is thick and abundant.

luxury NOUN

> 1 Dining out is a luxury these days.
> indulgence, extravagance, treat, frill
> ❙ **OPPOSITE** necessity
> 2 Only the nobility lived in luxury.
> affluence, wealth, richness,
> splendour, opulence,
> sumptuousness
> ❙ **OPPOSITE** poverty

Mm

machine *NOUN*
> *a machine for making ice-cream*
> appliance, device, apparatus, engine, contraption, mechanism

mad *ADJECTIVE*
> **1** *Have you gone completely mad?*
> insane, crazy, deranged, demented, unbalanced, unhinged
> (*informal*) nuts, bonkers, loopy
> (*British informal*) crackers, potty
> **❙ IDIOMS** (*informal*) off your head, round the bend, round the twist
> **❙ OPPOSITE** sane
>
> **2** *a mad idea that might just work*
> foolish, idiotic, senseless, crazy, stupid, silly, absurd, asinine, hare-brained
> (*informal*) crackpot, cockeyed
> (*British informal*) daft
>
> **3** (*informal*) *Nick is mad about football.*
> fanatical, enthusiastic, passionate, fervent, wild
> (*informal*) crazy, nuts
>
> **4** (*informal*) *Please don't get mad when you hear this.*
> angry, furious, infuriated, annoyed, cross, beside yourself, frenzied, hysterical

madness *NOUN*
> **1** *Ophelia is driven into madness.*
> insanity, mental illness, derangement, lunacy, mania
> **❙ OPPOSITE** sanity
>
> **2** *It would be sheer madness to go alone.*
> foolishness, folly, idiocy, stupidity, senselessness
> **❙ OPPOSITE** sense

magazine *NOUN*
> *a cookery magazine*
> journal, periodical, supplement, comic
> (*informal*) mag

magic *ADJECTIVE*
> SEE **magical**

magic *NOUN*
> **1** *Gandalf uses magic to fight his enemies.*
> sorcery, witchcraft, wizardry, enchantment, black magic, the black arts, the supernatural, the occult, necromancy
> **FOR TIPS ON WRITING FANTASY FICTION** SEE **fantasy**
>
> **2** *performing magic with a pack of cards*
> conjuring, illusion, sleight of hand
>
> **3** *discovering the magic of nature*
> charm, allure, fascination, mystery, enchantment, wonder

magical *ADJECTIVE*
> **1** *a crystal with magical powers*
> supernatural, magic, mystical, occult, other-worldly
>
> **2** *a magical performance of 'The Nutcracker'*
> enchanting, entrancing, captivating, spellbinding, bewitching, charming, alluring, enthralling, delightful

magician *NOUN*
> **1** *a magician who performs card tricks*
> conjuror, illusionist
>
> **2** *Merlin, the legendary magician*
> sorcerer, sorceress, witch, wizard, warlock, enchanter, enchantress, necromancer

magnificent *ADJECTIVE*
> **1** *magnificent coastal scenery*
> splendid, spectacular, glorious, superb, impressive, striking, dazzling, breathtaking, awe-inspiring
> **❙ OPPOSITES** uninspiring, ordinary

2 *a magnificent mansion*
grand, imposing, stately, majestic, palatial, luxurious, sumptuous

3 *a magnificent goal*
excellent, first-class, outstanding, wonderful, marvellous, superb (*informal*) fabulous, fantastic, terrific, brilliant

magnify VERB
This picture has been magnified many times.
enlarge, make larger, amplify, boost (*informal*) blow up
❙ **OPPOSITES** reduce, minimize

mail NOUN
a delivery of mail
post, letters, correspondence, email

mail VERB
Can you mail this letter for me?
post, send, dispatch, ship

maim VERB
SEE **injure**

main ADJECTIVE
What is the main theme of the play?
principal, chief, major, central, leading, dominant, key, basic, essential, fundamental, primary, prime, predominant, pre-eminent, foremost
❙ **OPPOSITES** minor, secondary

mainly ADVERB
Vitamin C is found mainly in fruits and vegetables.
mostly, chiefly, principally, primarily, predominantly, largely, on the whole, for the most part

maintain VERB
1 *trying to maintain the peace*
keep, preserve, prolong, perpetuate
2 *A team of gardeners maintain the grounds.*
look after, take care of, keep in order
3 *the cost of maintaining a family*
support, keep, provide for, sustain
4 *He still maintains that he's innocent.*
claim, insist, assert, declare, state, affirm, contend, profess

majestic ADJECTIVE
the ruins of what was once a majestic city
grand, magnificent, splendid, impressive, imposing, stately, noble

major ADJECTIVE
1 *Winning the Oscar was a major achievement.*
big, great, considerable, significant, important, serious, weighty
❙ **OPPOSITES** minor, trivial
2 *the major plays of Tennessee Williams*
chief, principal, primary, leading, foremost, greatest, finest
❙ **OPPOSITES** minor, lesser

majority NOUN
▷ **the majority of**
The majority of Americans live in cities.
the greater number of, the bulk of, most
❙ **IDIOM** the lion's share of
❙ **OPPOSITE** minority

make VERB
1 *making a model aeroplane*
build, construct, assemble, put together, manufacture, fashion
2 *trying not to make a noise*
cause, produce, create, generate
3 *making a huge profit*
gain, get, obtain, acquire, earn, win
4 *They made me do it.*
force to, compel to, drive to, coerce into, press into
5 *We should make the coast before nightfall.*
reach, arrive at, get to, get as far as
6 *I think she'll make a good actress.*
become, grow into, turn into, change into
7 *What time do you make it?*
calculate, estimate, reckon
8 *5 and 8 make 13*
add up to, come to, total
9 *making a clumsy shot at goal*

»

perform, execute, carry out, give, do
10 *making your bed in the morning*
   arrange, tidy
11 *I'll make you an offer.*
   propose, suggest

▷ **make for**
making for the nearest exit
go towards, head for
IDIOM make a beeline for

▷ **make off**
The gang made off in a stolen car.
leave, escape, get away, run away,
disappear
(*informal*) clear off, scarper
IDIOM (*informal*) do a runner

▷ **make something out**
1 *Can you make out a figure in the
   background?*
   see, detect, discern, distinguish,
   recognize, spot
2 *I can't make out what you're saying.*
   understand, follow, grasp, work out,
   comprehend, fathom, make sense of
3 *Miles made out that he was a genius.*
   claim, allege, suggest, imply,
   insinuate, pretend

▷ **make something up**
making up a new recipe
create, invent, think up, concoct,
fabricate

▷ **make up for something**
*The writing makes up for the
far-fetched plot.*
compensate for, cancel out, offset

make *NOUN*
What make of phone do you have?
brand, model, label

male *ADJECTIVE*
a male model
masculine
▶ Something that is suitable for a man
  is **manly**.
  OPPOSITE female
  SEE ALSO man

malicious *ADJECTIVE*
spreading malicious rumours
malevolent, hostile, malign, spiteful,
vindictive, vicious, hurtful

mammal *NOUN*

WORD WEB

*some animals which are
mammals*

aardvark, anteater, antelope,
armadillo, baboon, badger, bat,
bear, beaver, bison, camel, cat,
chimpanzee, chipmunk, cow,
deer, dog, dolphin, dormouse,
echidna, elephant, elk, ferret,
fox, gazelle, gibbon, giraffe,
goat, gorilla, hare, hedgehog,
hippopotamus, horse, hyena,
lemming, lemur, leopard, lion,
lynx, manatee, meerkat, mole,
mongoose, monkey, moose,
mouse, narwhal,
orang-utan, otter, panda, pig,
polar bear, porcupine, porpoise,
rabbit, raccoon, rat, reindeer,
rhinoceros, seal, sea lion, sheep,
shrew, skunk, sloth, squirrel,
tapir, tiger, vole, walrus, weasel,
whale, wildebeest, wolf, yak,
zebra

▶ A related adjective is
  mammalian.
▶ When a female mammal produces
  milk she is **lactating**.
  SEE ALSO cat, **dog**, **horse**,
  marsupial, **rodent**
  FOR TIPS ON DESCRIBING ANIMALS
  SEE **animal**

man *NOUN*
1 *the man at the ticket desk*
   gentleman, male, fellow
   (*informal*) guy, gent
   (*British informal*) bloke, chap
▶ An unmarried man is a **bachelor**.
▶ A man whose wife has died is a
  widower.
2 *the evolution of man*
   mankind, humankind, the human
   race, humanity, Homo sapiens

manage *VERB*
1 *His son manages the business now.*

be in charge of, run, direct, lead, control, govern, rule, supervise, oversee, preside over

2 *I can't manage any more work just now.*

cope with, deal with, take on, carry out

3 *We'll have to manage without the car.*

cope, make do, get along, get by, survive

(*informal*) muddle through

⎮ **IDIOM** make ends meet

manager *NOUN*

the manager of the bookshop
director, head, chief, proprietor
(*informal*) boss

mania *NOUN*

the current mania for blogging
craze, enthusiasm, passion, obsession (with), fixation (with), fad, rage

manipulate *VERB*

1 *The therapist began to manipulate my muscles.*

work, handle, pull, push, turn, twist
(*informal*) twiddle

2 *She uses her charm to manipulate people.*

take advantage of, use, exploit, impose on

manly *ADJECTIVE*

SEE **masculine**

man-made *ADJECTIVE*

a man-made fibre
synthetic, artificial, imitation, mock, fake

⎮ **OPPOSITES** natural, real

manner *NOUN*

1 *Dr Evans had an odd manner of speaking.*

way, style, fashion, method, mode, means, system, technique

2 *I was put off by her frosty manner.*

behaviour, conduct, attitude, air, aspect, demeanour, bearing, mien

▷ **manners**

Some people have no manners at all!
politeness, courtesy, civility, decorum, etiquette, social graces

manoeuvre *NOUN*

1 *Parking a bus is a difficult manoeuvre.*

move, operation

2 *The opposition used a clever manoeuvre.*

strategy, tactic, trick, dodge, plan, plot, scheme

manoeuvre *VERB*

Roz manoeuvred her wheelchair out of the room.

guide, move, pilot, steer, navigate

manufacture *VERB*

a factory which manufactures tyres
make, build, construct, assemble, put together, turn out

many *ADJECTIVE*

Our universe may be one of many universes.

numerous, a lot of, plenty of, countless, innumerable, untold, myriad

(*informal*) umpteen, lots of, masses of

⎮ **OPPOSITE** few

Usage Note

Words which include 'many' in their meaning often begin with **multi-**, for example *multicultural* and *multimedia*.

map *NOUN*

a road map of France
chart, diagram, plan

▶ A book of maps is an **atlas**.

▶ A person who draws maps is a **cartographer**.

mar *VERB*

The film is marred by a terrible soundtrack.

spoil, ruin, wreck, damage, impair, taint, tarnish

》

a
b
c
d
e
f
g
h
i
j
k
l
m
n
o
p
q
r
s
t
u
v
w
x
y
z

❙ **OPPOSITE** enhance

march *VERB*

> *a brass band marching down the street*
> parade, troop, stride, strut, pace, tread, file

margin *NOUN*

> **1** *Leave a wide margin around the text.*
> border, edge, rim, verge, fringe, periphery
> **2** *We won by a narrow margin.*
> gap, amount, distance

marginal *ADJECTIVE*

> *I can see a marginal improvement.*
> slight, small, minimal, minor, unimportant, negligible, borderline
> ❙ **OPPOSITES** great, marked

marine *ADJECTIVE*

> SEE **sea**

mark *NOUN*

> **1** *leaving muddy paw marks on the floor*
> spot, stain, blemish, blotch, blot, smear, smudge, streak, speck
> (*informal*) splodge
> **2** *What mark did you get in the test?*
> score, grade
> **3** *They stood in silence as a mark of respect.*
> sign, token, indication, symbol, emblem

mark *VERB*

> **1** *Please try not to mark the pages.*
> stain, dirty, blot, smudge, smear, streak
> **2** *marking an exam paper*
> correct, grade, assess
> **3** *She'll be back, you mark my words!*
> mind, heed, attend to, listen to, note, take note of

marked *ADJECTIVE*

> *a marked difference in style*
> noticeable, considerable, pronounced, clear, obvious, distinct, decided, striking
> ❙ **OPPOSITES** slight, marginal

market *NOUN*

> SEE **shop**

marriage *NOUN*

> **1** *celebrating twenty years of marriage*
> matrimony, wedlock
> **2** *Today is the anniversary of their marriage.*
> wedding, union
> (*formal*) nuptials

married *ADJECTIVE*

> *a married couple*
> ▶ A couple who have promised to marry are **engaged** to each other.
> ▶ A man who is engaged to be married is a **fiancé** and the woman he is engaged to is his **fiancée**.
> ❙ **OPPOSITES** unmarried, single

marry *VERB*

> *In what year did your grandparents marry?*
> get married, wed
> ❙ **IDIOMS** (*informal*) tie the knot, get hitched

marsh *NOUN*

> *an unspoiled area of salt marshes*
> swamp, bog, wetland, marshland, fen

marsupial *NOUN*

 WORD WEB

> ***some animals which are marsupials***
> bandicoot, kangaroo, koala, opossum, Tasmanian devil, wallaby, wombat
>
> ❙ **SEE ALSO mammal**
> **FOR TIPS ON DESCRIBING ANIMALS** SEE **animal**

martial *ADJECTIVE*

 WORD WEB

> ***some martial arts***
> aikido, capoeira, judo, ju-jitsu, karate, kendo, kick-boxing,

kung fu, tae kwon do, t'ai chi or
t'ai chi ch'uan

marvel *NOUN*
> the marvels of modern science
> wonder, miracle, phenomenon,
> sensation

marvel *VERB*
▷ **marvel at**
> Audiences marvelled at Houdini's
> skill.
> admire, wonder at, be amazed by,
> be astonished by

marvellous *ADJECTIVE*
> a marvellous performance of a
> major classic
> excellent, superb, splendid,
> magnificent, glorious, sublime,
> wonderful, tremendous, amazing,
> remarkable, extraordinary,
> incredible, phenomenal
> (*informal*) brilliant, fantastic, terrific,
> super, smashing
> **OPPOSITES** terrible, awful

masculine *ADJECTIVE*
> a deep, masculine voice
> male, manly, macho, virile
> **OPPOSITE** feminine

mash *VERB*
> Mash the potatoes with a little
> butter.
> crush, pound, pulp, smash, squash
> ► To make something into powder is
> to **grind** or **pulverize** it.

mask *VERB*
> The door was masked by a curtain.
> conceal, hide, cover, obscure, screen,
> veil, shroud, camouflage

mass *NOUN*
> sifting through a mass of papers
> heap, pile, mound, stack, collection,
> quantity, accumulation
> (*informal*) load

massacre *VERB*
> SEE **kill**

massive *ADJECTIVE*
> Near the entrance stood a massive
> bronze statue.
> enormous, huge, gigantic, colossal,
> giant, immense, vast, mighty,
> mammoth, monumental, hulking,
> great, big, large
> (*informal*) whopping, humongous
> (*literary*) gargantuan
> **OPPOSITES** small, tiny
> **SEE ALSO big**

master *NOUN*
> 1 a computer game called Masters of
> the Universe
> lord, ruler, sovereign, governor
> 2 Sherlock Holmes was a master of
> disguises.
> expert, genius, ace, wizard, virtuoso,
> maestro
> (*informal*) whizz
> (*British informal*) dab hand

master *VERB*
> 1 Have you mastered the guitar yet?
> grasp, learn, understand, become
> proficient in, pick up
> (*informal*) get the hang of, get to
> grips with
> 2 mastering my fear of heights
> overcome, conquer, defeat, triumph
> over, get the better of, control, curb,
> subdue, tame
> **OPPOSITES** succumb to, give in to

masterly *ADJECTIVE*
> a masterly header into the net
> expert, skilful, proficient,
> accomplished, deft, adept, adroit
> **OPPOSITES** clumsy, inept

match *NOUN*
> 1 the first match of the season
> game, contest, competition, fixture,
> tournament, tie
> **FOR TIPS ON WRITING ABOUT SPORT** SEE
> **sport**
> 2 Those colours are a good match.
> combination, pairing, marriage
> **OPPOSITE** contrast

match *VERB*

> *Does this tie match my shirt?*
> go with, suit, fit with, blend with, tone in with
>
> **❙ OPPOSITES** contrast with, clash with

matching *ADJECTIVE*

> *a hat with a matching scarf*
> coordinating, corresponding, complementary, equivalent, twin, paired
>
> **❙ OPPOSITES** contrasting, clashing

mate *NOUN*

> **1** (*British informal*) *Gary is one of my best mates.*
> friend
> (*informal*) pal, chum, buddy
> **2** *a bird calling for its mate*
> partner
> **3** *a plumber's mate*
> assistant, helper, apprentice

material *NOUN*

> **1** *collecting material for a book*
> information, facts, data, ideas, notes, details, particulars
> **2** *a range of art materials*
> supplies, stuff, substances, things
> **3** *clothes made of lightweight material*
> cloth, fabric, textile
>
> **❙ SEE ALSO fabric**

mathematics *NOUN*

> *a professor of mathematics*
> (*informal*) maths
> (*North American*) math

 WORD WEB

> ***branches of mathematics***
> algebra, arithmetic, calculus, geometry, set theory, statistics, trigonometry
>
> ***terms used in mathematics***
> acute angle, addition, calculation, calculator, cardinal number, constant, cosine, decimal, diameter, digit, division, equation, exponent, factor, formula, fraction, hypotenuse, index, integer, locus, long division, matrix, median, multiplication, obtuse angle, ordinal number, pi, power, prime number, product, quotient, reciprocal, remainder, sector, sine, square root, subtraction, symbol, symmetry, tangent, vector, whole number

matted *ADJECTIVE*

> *a dog with a matted coat*
> tangled, knotted, uncombed, unkempt, dishevelled

matter *NOUN*

> **1** *Peat consists mainly of plant matter.*
> material, stuff, substance
> **2** *This is a matter of great importance.*
> affair, concern, issue, business, situation, incident, subject, topic, thing
> **3** *What's the matter with the car?*
> problem, difficulty, trouble, worry

matter *VERB*

> *Will it matter if I'm late?*
> be important, count, make a difference

mature *ADJECTIVE*

> **1** *The zoo has two mature gorillas.*
> adult, fully grown, well developed
>
> **❙ OPPOSITE** young
> **2** *He is very mature for his age.*
> grown-up, responsible, sensible
>
> **❙ OPPOSITES** immature, childish

maximum *NOUN*

> *The heat is at its maximum at midday.*
> highest point, peak, top, upper limit, ceiling

maximum *ADJECTIVE*

> *The ship has a maximum speed of 40 knots.*
> greatest, top, highest, biggest, largest, fullest, utmost
>
> **❙ OPPOSITE** minimum

a b c d e f g h i j k l **m** n o p q r s t u v w x y z

maybe *ADVERB*
> *Maybe they've got lost.*
> perhaps, possibly
> (*old use*) perchance, peradventure
> **OPPOSITE** definitely

mayhem *NOUN*
> SEE **chaos**

maze *NOUN*
> *a maze of underground tunnels*
> labyrinth, network, web, tangle,
> warren

meadow *NOUN*
> *cows grazing in a meadow*
> field, pasture
> (*poetic*) lea

meagre *ADJECTIVE*
> *a meagre ration of rice and water*
> scant, sparse, poor, scanty,
> inadequate, insufficient, skimpy,
> paltry
> (*informal*) measly, stingy
> **OPPOSITES** generous, ample

meal *NOUN*
> *a simple meal of bread and cheese*
> (*formal*) repast

WORD WEB

some types of meal
afternoon tea, banquet,
barbecue, breakfast,
brunch, buffet, dinner,
(*informal*) elevenses, feast, high
tea, lunch or luncheon, picnic,
snack, supper, takeaway, tea, tea
break

SEE ALSO food

mean① *VERB*
> **1** *Do you know what this symbol*
> *means?*
> indicate, signify, denote, symbolize,
> represent, stand for, express, convey,
> communicate, suggest, imply
> **2** *I didn't mean to cause any harm.*
> intend, aim, plan, set out, propose,
> want, have in mind

mean② *ADJECTIVE*
> **1** *Scrooge was too mean to buy gifts.*
> selfish, miserly, uncharitable,
> penny-pinching, parsimonious
> (*informal*) stingy, tight, tight-fisted
> **OPPOSITE** generous
> **2** *That was a mean thing to say.*
> unkind, unpleasant, spiteful, vicious,
> cruel, malicious, horrible, nasty
> (*informal*) rotten
> **OPPOSITE** kind

meaning *NOUN*
> *What is the meaning of this word?*
> sense, explanation, interpretation,
> definition, significance, import, gist

meaningful *ADJECTIVE*
> *The two friends exchanged a*
> *meaningful look.*
> pointed, significant, expressive,
> suggestive, revealing, pregnant
> **OPPOSITES** insignificant,
> inconsequential

meaningless *ADJECTIVE*
> **1** *a meaningless promise*
> empty, hollow, insincere, pointless,
> worthless, ineffectual
> **OPPOSITES** serious, worthwhile
> **2** *a meaningless string of numbers and*
> *letters*
> unintelligible, incomprehensible,
> incoherent

means *PLURAL NOUN*
> **1** *Camels are used as a means of*
> *transport.*
> method, mode, medium, channel,
> course, way
> **2** *lacking the means to support*
> *yourself*
> money, resources, assets, funds,
> finance, capital, wherewithal

measure *VERB*
> *measuring the amount of fuel used*
> calculate, gauge, quantify, weigh,
> assess

measure *NOUN*
> **1** *using money as a measure of wealth*
> gauge, standard, scale, indicator,

a
b
c
d
e
f
g
h
i
j
k
l
m
n
o
p
q
r
s
t
u
v
w
x
y
z

yardstick, barometer

2 *At least we know the measure of the problem.*
size, extent, magnitude

3 *taking measures to improve air quality*
step, action, course, procedure, initiative

 WORD WEB

> *metric weights and measures*
> centimetre, gram, hectare, kilo or kilogram, kilolitre, kilometre, litre, metre, milligram, millilitre, millimetre, tonne
>
> *imperial weights and measures*
> acre, foot, gallon, inch, mile, ounce, pint, pound, quart, stone, ton, yard
>
> ► The depth of the sea is measured in **fathoms**.
> ► The speed of a boat or ship is measured in **knots**.
> ► The distance of an object in space is measured in **light years**.
> **FOR MEASUREMENTS USED IN COOKING** SEE **cook**

measurement *NOUN*

What are the measurements of the room?
dimensions, size, extent, proportions
► The measurement around something is its **girth**.

meat *NOUN*

carving the meat from a turkey
flesh

 WORD WEB

> *some kinds of meat*
> bacon, beef, chicken, duck, game, gammon, goose, ham, lamb, mutton, offal, pork, turkey, veal, venison

medal *NOUN*

winning a bronze medal
award, prize, trophy
► A person who wins a medal is a **medallist**.

meddle *VERB*

1 *meddling in other people's affairs*
interfere, intrude, intervene, pry
IDIOMS (*informal*) poke your nose in, stick your oar in

2 *Someone has been meddling with my computer.*
fiddle about, tinker, tamper

media *NOUN*

FOR TERMS USED IN MEDIA STUDIES SEE **film**, **television**

medicine *NOUN*

1 *a spoonful of cough medicine*
drug, medication, treatment, remedy, cure
► Medicine which a doctor gives you is a **prescription**.

2 *a plant used in herbal medicine*
therapy, treatment, healing

 WORD WEB

> *some types of medicine*
> anaesthetic, antibiotic, antidote, antiseptic, expectorant, painkiller, sedative, stimulant, tonic, tranquillizer
>
> *methods of taking medicine*
> capsule, eardrops, eyedrops, gargle, inhaler, injection, lotion, lozenge, ointment, pill, tablet, tincture
>
> ► An amount of medicine taken at one time is a **dose**.
>
> *medical instruments*
> forceps, scalpel, stethoscope, syringe, thermometer, tweezers
>
> *some forms of alternative medicine*
> acupuncture, aromatherapy, Ayurveda, chiropractic,

a b c d e f g h i j k l m n o p q r s t u v w x y z

herbal medicine or herbalism,
homeopathy, naturopathy,
reflexology, shiatsu, traditional
Chinese medicine

*people involved in health and
medicine*
anaesthetist, cardiologist,
chiropodist, chiropractor,
dentist, dermatologist,
doctor, GP, gynaecologist,
herbalist, homeopath, midwife,
neurologist, nurse, obstetrician,
oncologist, ophthalmologist,
optician, orthodontist,
osteopath, paediatrician,
paramedic, pharmacist,
physician, physiotherapist,
podiatrist, psychiatrist,
psychologist, radiologist,
speech therapist, surgeon

mediocre *ADJECTIVE*
I thought the film was rather
mediocre.
ordinary, average, commonplace,
indifferent, second-rate,
run-of-the-mill, undistinguished,
uninspiring, forgettable, lacklustre,
pedestrian
(*informal*) so-so
❙ **OPPOSITES** outstanding, exceptional

medium *ADJECTIVE*
a man of medium height and build
average, middle, middle-sized,
middling, standard, moderate,
normal

medium *NOUN*
a new medium of communication
means, mode, method, way,
channel, vehicle, avenue

meek *ADJECTIVE*
That cat looks meek but she has
sharp claws.
gentle, mild, docile, tame, obedient,
submissive
❙ **OPPOSITE** aggressive

meet *VERB*
1 We're meeting outside the cinema.
assemble, gather, get together,
congregate, convene
2 I met an old friend at the party.
encounter, run into, come across,
stumble across, chance on,
happen on
(*informal*) bump into
3 When did you two first meet?
become acquainted (with), be
introduced (to), get to know
4 The two roads meet here.
come together, converge, connect,
touch, join, cross, intersect, link up
5 My parents met me at the station.
greet, pick up, welcome
6 She meets all the requirements for
the job.
fulfil, satisfy, match, answer,
comply with

meeting *NOUN*
1 a story about the meeting of two
cultures
coming together, convergence,
intersection, confluence, union
2 a meeting of the library committee
gathering, assembly, council, forum,
congress, conference
▶ A large outdoor public meeting is a
rally.
▶ A formal meeting with an important
person is an **audience**.

melancholy *ADJECTIVE*
playing a melancholy tune
sad, sorrowful, mournful, doleful,
unhappy, gloomy, wistful, sombre
❙ **OPPOSITE** cheerful
❙ **SEE ALSO sad**

mellow *ADJECTIVE*
the mellow tones of a saxophone
soft, sweet-sounding, dulcet, warm
❙ **OPPOSITE** harsh

melody *NOUN*
a song with a simple melody
tune, air, theme

a
b
c
d
e
f
g
h
i
j
k
l
m
n
o
p
q
r
s
t
u
v
w
x
y
z

melt VERB

1 *The ice caps have already begun to melt.*
thaw, defrost, soften, liquefy
▶ To melt ore to extract its metal is to **smelt** it.
▶ Rock or metal that has melted through great heat is **molten**.
OPPOSITE freeze

2 *Soon the crowd began to melt away.*
disperse, break up, drift away, disappear, vanish, fade

member NOUN

▷ **be a member of something**
Are you a member of the sports club?
belong to, subscribe to

memoir NOUN

a memoir of her childhood
record, account, history, chronicle, narrative, story

memorable ADJECTIVE

a memorable day in our history
unforgettable, notable, noteworthy, historic, momentous, significant, remarkable, outstanding
OPPOSITE ordinary

memorize VERB

memorizing the words to a song
learn, learn by heart, commit to memory
OPPOSITE forget

memory NOUN

My earliest memory is of watching the sea.
recollection, remembrance, reminiscence, reminder, impression
▷ **in memory of**
a statue in memory of Robert Burns
in honour of, in tribute to, commemorating, in remembrance of, in recognition of

menace NOUN

1 *Sharks can be a menace to divers.*
danger, threat, risk, hazard, peril
2 *That car alarm is an absolute menace!*
nuisance, annoyance, irritation, inconvenience
(*informal*) pest

mend VERB

mending a hole in the road
repair, fix, put right, restore, renovate, patch

mention VERB

1 *Please don't mention this to anyone.*
refer to, allude to, speak about, touch on, hint at
2 *She mentioned that she had been ill.*
say, remark, reveal, disclose, divulge
(*informal*) let out
3 *The programme mentioned all the cast.*
name, acknowledge, list, cite, reference

mercy NOUN

The Mongols showed no mercy to their enemies.
compassion, humanity, sympathy, pity, leniency, clemency, kindness, charity
OPPOSITE cruelty

merely ADVERB

I started a blog merely for my own use.
only, just, simply, purely, solely

merge VERB

1 *a plan to merge the two newspapers*
join together, combine, integrate, unite, amalgamate, conflate, consolidate
2 *Two smaller rivers merge to form the Danube.*
come together, converge, join, meet
OPPOSITE separate

merit NOUN

1 *a musician of great merit*
excellence, quality, calibre, distinction, worth, talent
2 *the merits of regular exercise*
benefit, advantage, virtue, asset, value, good point

merit VERB

a charity which merits our full support
deserve, justify, warrant, be worthy of, be entitled to, earn, rate

merry ADJECTIVE

whistling a merry tune
cheerful, happy, light-hearted, joyful, jolly, bright, sunny, cheery, lively, spirited, chirpy
❚ OPPOSITES sad, gloomy

mess NOUN

1 *Please clear up this mess.*
untidiness, clutter, jumble, muddle, chaos, disorder, disarray, litter
(*informal*) shambles, tip

2 *making a real mess of things*
disaster, botch
(*informal*) hash

3 *How can we get out of this mess?*
difficulty, problem, predicament, plight, trouble
(*informal*) fix, jam
❚ IDIOMS tight spot, tight corner

mess VERB

▷ **mess about** or **around**
I spent the day messing about at home.
potter about, lounge about, play about, fool around
(*informal*) muck about

▷ **mess something up**

1 *I don't want to mess up my hair.*
make a mess of, mix up, muddle, jumble, tangle, dishevel

2 *I think I messed up my audition .*
make a mess of, bungle
(*informal*) botch, make a hash of

message NOUN

1 *Did you get my message?*
note, letter, communication, missive, memo, communiqué, dispatch

2 *What is the main message of the poem?*
meaning, sense, import, idea, point, moral, gist, thrust

messy ADJECTIVE

1 *This kitchen is really messy!*
untidy, disorderly, chaotic, muddled, dirty, filthy, grubby, mucky
(*informal*) higgledy-piggledy
❚ OPPOSITES neat, tidy, clean

2 (*informal*) *His parents went through a messy divorce.*
difficult, unpleasant, nasty, bitter, acrimonious

metal NOUN

 WORD WEB

some common metals
aluminium, brass, bronze, copper, gold, iron, lead, magnesium, mercury, nickel, pewter, platinum, silver, steel, tin, zinc

▶ A metal formed by mixing two or more metals is an **alloy**.

▶ Rock which contains a particular metal is **ore**.
iron ore

▶ The process of melting ore to extract the metal is **smelting**.

▶ Something that looks or sounds like metal is **metallic**.

▶ The study of metals is **metallurgy**.

method NOUN

modern methods of manufacture
technique, way, procedure, process, system, approach, routine

methodical ADJECTIVE

a methodical way of working
orderly, systematic, structured, organized, well-ordered, disciplined, deliberate, efficient, businesslike
❚ OPPOSITES disorderly, haphazard

middle NOUN

1 *an island in the middle of the lake*
centre, midpoint, core, heart, hub

2 *Tie the rope around your middle.*
waist, midriff, stomach, belly
(*informal*) tummy

a
b
c
d
e
f
g
h
i
j
k
l
m
n
o
p
q
r
s
t
u
v
w
x
y
z

middle ADJECTIVE
1 *the middle section of the tunnel*
central, midway, mid
2 *a middle size of egg*
medium, average, moderate

might NOUN
I banged at the door with all my might.
strength, power, force, energy, vigour, brawn

mighty ADJECTIVE
the mighty force of a tsunami
powerful, forceful, vigorous, ferocious, violent, hefty, great
▐ OPPOSITES weak, feeble

mild ADJECTIVE
1 *a mild punishment*
light, lenient, merciful, reasonable
▐ OPPOSITES severe, harsh
2 *a horse with a mild temper*
easy-going, gentle, docile, placid, good-tempered, kind, soft-hearted
3 *a mild flavour of garlic*
slight, faint, subtle, light
▐ OPPOSITES strong, pronounced
4 *a spot of mild weather*
pleasant, warm, balmy, temperate, clement
▐ OPPOSITES harsh, inclement

milky ADJECTIVE
Rubber trees produce a milky sap.
whitish, cloudy, misty, chalky, opaque
▐ OPPOSITE clear

mimic VERB
Graham can mimic any of his teachers.
do impressions of, imitate, impersonate, pretend to be, caricature, parody
(*informal*) take off

mind NOUN
1 *Miss Appleton's mind was as sharp as ever.*
brain, intelligence, intellect, head, sense, understanding, wits, judgement, mental powers, reasoning
▐ IDIOM (*humorous*) grey matter
2 *Are you sure you won't change your mind?*
wishes, intention, fancy, inclination, thoughts, opinion, point of view

mind VERB
1 *Would you mind my bag for a minute?*
guard, look after, watch, care for
▐ IDIOM keep an eye on
2 *Mind the step.*
look out for, watch out for, beware of, pay attention to, heed, note
3 *They won't mind if I'm late.*
bother, care, worry, be upset, take offence, object, disapprove

mine NOUN
an abandoned coal mine
pit, colliery
▶ A place where coal is removed from the surface is an **opencast mine**.
▶ A place where stone or slate is removed is a **quarry**.

mingle VERB
I tried to mingle with the other guests.
mix in, circulate, blend, combine, merge, fuse

miniature ADJECTIVE
a doll with miniature shoes and socks
tiny, minute, diminutive, small-scale, baby, mini, minuscule
▐ SEE ALSO small

minimum ADJECTIVE
Set the oven to the minimum temperature.
least, smallest, lowest, bottom
▐ OPPOSITE maximum

minor ADJECTIVE
I only had a minor part in the play.
small, unimportant, insignificant, inferior, lesser, subordinate, trivial, trifling, petty
▐ OPPOSITE major

minute ADJECTIVE

1 *You can hardly see the minute crack.*
tiny, minuscule, microscopic, negligible
OPPOSITE large

2 *Each flower is drawn in minute detail.*
exhaustive, thorough, meticulous, painstaking
OPPOSITE rough

miraculous ADJECTIVE

The patient made a miraculous recovery.
amazing, astonishing, astounding, extraordinary, incredible, inexplicable, sensational, phenomenal

misbehave VERB

kids caught misbehaving in the playground
behave badly, be naughty, be disobedient, get up to mischief
OPPOSITE behave

miscellaneous ADJECTIVE

a bag containing miscellaneous items
assorted, various, varied, different, mixed, sundry, diverse, heterogeneous

mischief NOUN

The twins are always getting up to mischief.
naughtiness, bad behaviour, misbehaviour, disobedience, playfulness, roguishness

miser NOUN

the story of a miser who hoards his treasure
penny-pincher, Scrooge
(*informal*) skinflint, cheapskate

miserable ADJECTIVE

1 *You look miserable. What's the matter?*
sad, unhappy, sorrowful, gloomy, glum, downhearted, despondent, dejected, depressed, melancholy, mournful, tearful

IDIOMS (*informal*) down in the mouth, down in the dumps
OPPOSITES cheerful, happy

2 *The refugees live in miserable conditions.*
distressing, uncomfortable, wretched, pitiful, pathetic, squalid
OPPOSITE comfortable

3 *The weather was cold and miserable.*
dismal, dreary, bleak, depressing, cheerless, drab
(*Scottish*) dreich
OPPOSITES fine, mild

miserly ADJECTIVE

He was too miserly to donate any money.
mean, selfish, penny-pinching, parsimonious
(*informal*) stingy, tight, tight-fisted
OPPOSITE generous

misery NOUN

overwhelmed by feelings of misery and loneliness
unhappiness, wretchedness, sorrow, sadness, gloom, grief, distress, despair, anguish, suffering, torment, heartache, depression, dejection, despondency
OPPOSITE happiness

misfortune NOUN

I heard about her family's misfortune.
bad luck, trouble, hardship, adversity, affliction, setback, mishap
OPPOSITE good luck

misguided ADJECTIVE

a misguided attempt to make a sequel
unwise, ill-advised, ill-judged, ill-considered, imprudent
OPPOSITES wise, prudent

mishap NOUN

I had a slight mishap with my computer.
accident, problem, difficulty, setback

a
b
c
d
e
f
g
h
i
j
k
l
m
n
o
p
q
r
s
t
u
v
w
x
y
z

a
b
c
d
e
f
g
h
i
j
k
l
m
n
o
p
q
r
s
t
u
v
w
x
y
z

mislay VERB

I seem to have mislaid my watch.
lose, misplace
OPPOSITE find

misleading ADJECTIVE

The directions on the map are
misleading.
confusing, unreliable, deceptive,
ambiguous, unclear

miss VERB

1 I don't want to miss the start of the
film.
be too late for

2 One of the stones just missed a
passer-by.
fall short of, go wide of, overshoot

3 If we leave now, we should miss the
traffic.
avoid, evade, bypass, beat

4 I missed my friends over the holidays.
long for, yearn for, pine for

▷ **miss something out**
Don't miss out the gory details!
leave out, omit, exclude, cut out,
pass over, overlook, ignore, skip

missile NOUN

SEE **weapon**

missing ADJECTIVE

1 She found the missing keys in a
drawer.
lost, mislaid, misplaced, absent,
astray

2 What is missing from this
photograph?
absent, lacking, wanting, left out,
omitted

mission NOUN

1 The mission of the society is to
protect wildlife.
aim, purpose, objective, task, job,
vocation, calling

2 a mission to explore the galaxy
expedition, journey, voyage,
exploration, quest

mist NOUN

1 a landscape enveloped in mist

fog, haze, cloud, drizzle, smog

2 wiping the mist from the window
condensation, steam, vapour

mistake NOUN

This article is full of mistakes.
error, fault, inaccuracy,
miscalculation, misinterpretation,
blunder, lapse, slip, slip-up
(informal) howler
(British informal) clanger

▶ A spelling mistake is a **misspelling**.

▶ A mistake made during printing is a
misprint.

▶ A mistake where something is left
out is an **omission** or **oversight**.

▶ An embarrassing mistake is a **gaffe**
or **faux pas**.

▷ **make a mistake**
You've made a mistake in the
formula.
err, miscalculate, blunder, slip up

mistake VERB

At first, I mistook the meaning of her
letter.
misunderstand, misinterpret,
misconstrue, misread, get wrong

▷ **mistake someone for something**
People often mistake him for his
brother.
confuse someone with, take
someone for, mix someone up with
someone

mistaken ADJECTIVE

1 a mistaken view of the past
inaccurate, erroneous, false,
incorrect, unfounded, misguided,
fallacious
OPPOSITES accurate, well-founded

2 I'm afraid you are mistaken.
wrong, in error, misinformed, under
a false impression
IDIOM (informal) barking up the
wrong tree
OPPOSITES correct, spot-on

mistrust VERB

Do you have any reason to mistrust
him?

distrust, have doubts about, suspect, be wary of, be chary of, have misgivings about, have reservations about

OPPOSITE trust

misty *ADJECTIVE*

1 *a cold and misty morning*
foggy, hazy

2 *looking through a misty window*
steamy, cloudy, smoky, opaque

3 *We saw a misty figure approaching.*
faint, fuzzy, blurred, dim, indistinct, shadowy, vague

OPPOSITE clear

misunderstand *VERB*

People sometimes misunderstand the lyrics.
mistake, misinterpret, misconstrue, misread, get wrong, miss the point of

IDIOM get the wrong end of the stick

OPPOSITE understand

misuse *VERB, NOUN*
SEE **abuse**

mix *VERB*

Mix the ingredients thoroughly.
combine, blend, mingle, incorporate, amalgamate, fuse

▷ **mix something up**
Please don't mix up my CDs.
muddle, jumble, shuffle, confuse

▷ **mix with**
mixing with the wrong sort of people
associate with, socialize with, keep company with, consort with

IDIOM rub shoulders with

mix *NOUN*

The style is a strange mix of antique and modern.
mixture, blend, combination, compound, mingling, amalgamation, fusion, union

mixed *ADJECTIVE*

a teaspoon of mixed herbs
assorted, varied, various, different, miscellaneous, sundry, diverse, heterogeneous

OPPOSITE homogeneous

mixture *NOUN*

1 *a mixture of fear and excitement*
mix, blend, combination, compound, mingling

▶ A mixture of metals is an **alloy**.

▶ A mixture of two different species of plant or animal is a **hybrid**.

2 *The book contains an odd mixture of stories.*
assortment, collection, variety, miscellany, medley, jumble, ragbag

▶ A confused mixture is a **mishmash**.

mix-up *NOUN*

There was a mix-up with our tickets.
confusion, misunderstanding, mistake, error, blunder, muddle

moan *VERB*

1 *an animal moaning in pain*
cry, groan, sigh, wail, howl, whimper

2 (*informal*) *Ted is always moaning about something.*
complain, grumble, grouse, carp, bleat, whine
(*informal*) gripe
(*British informal*) whinge

mob *NOUN*

an angry mob of protesters
crowd, horde, throng, mass, multitude, rabble, gang, pack, herd

mob *VERB*

The stars were mobbed by reporters.
surround, crowd round, besiege, hem in, jostle

mobile *ADJECTIVE*

1 *a mobile x-ray unit*
movable, transportable, portable, travelling

OPPOSITES stationary, fixed

2 *You should be mobile in a day or two.*
moving about, active
(*informal*) up and about

OPPOSITE immobile

a
b
c
d
e
f
g
h
i
j
k
l
m
n
o
p
q
r
s
t
u
v
w
x
y
z

mock VERB

a writer who loves to mock society
ridicule, laugh at, make fun of, jeer at, scoff at, sneer at, scorn, deride
IDIOM (*informal*) take the mickey out of

mock ADJECTIVE

a bag made of mock leather
imitation, artificial, fake, reproduction, man-made, sham, pretend, simulated
OPPOSITES real, genuine

mode NOUN

a new mode of thinking
way, manner, method, system, means, style, approach

model NOUN

1 *a model of the Eiffel Tower*
replica, copy, reproduction, miniature, toy, dummy
2 *the latest model of mobile phone*
design, type, version
3 *a model of success*
example, ideal

model ADJECTIVE

1 *an exhibition of model railways*
miniature, replica, toy, dummy
2 *a model student*
ideal, perfect, exemplary, faultless

model VERB

an animator who models figures in clay
make, mould, shape, construct, fashion

moderate ADJECTIVE

1 *Their first CD was a moderate success.*
average, fair, modest, medium, reasonable, passable, tolerable
OPPOSITES exceptional, great
2 *holding moderate views*
non-extremist, middle-of-the-road
OPPOSITES extremist, radical

moderately ADVERB

I'm moderately happy with my score.
fairly, reasonably, relatively, quite, rather, somewhat
(*informal*) pretty

modern ADJECTIVE

1 *the speed of modern computers*
present-day, current, contemporary, the latest, recent, advanced
OPPOSITE past
2 *a very modern hairstyle*
fashionable, up to date, stylish, modish, trendsetting, newfangled
(*informal*) trendy, hip
OPPOSITES old-fashioned, out of date, retro

modest ADJECTIVE

1 *He's very modest about his work.*
humble, unassuming, self-effacing, diffident, reserved, shy, bashful, coy
OPPOSITES conceited, boastful
2 *a modest increase in sales*
moderate, reasonable, average, medium, limited
OPPOSITE considerable
3 *living in a modest flat*
simple, ordinary, plain, humble
OPPOSITES grand, ostentatious
4 *dressed in a modest style*
demure, decent, decorous, proper, seemly
OPPOSITES immodest, indecent

modify VERB

We've had to modify our travel plans.
adapt, alter, change, adjust, refine, revise, vary
(*informal*) tweak

moist ADJECTIVE

1 *a current of warm, moist air*
damp, dank, wet, humid, muggy, clammy, steamy
2 *a rich and moist fruitcake*
juicy, soft, tender, succulent
OPPOSITE dry

moisture NOUN

a patch of moisture on the wall
wetness, dampness, damp, wet, condensation, humidity, dew

mollusc NOUN

WORD WEB

some animals which are molluscs

abalone, clam, cuttlefish, limpet, mussel, nautilus, octopus, oyster, scallop, sea slug, slug, snail, squid, razor shell, whelk

► Molluscs such as oysters and mussels, which have a shell with two hinged parts, are **bivalves**.

► Molluscs such as slugs and snails, which move by means of a fleshy foot, are **gastropods**.

moment NOUN

1 *The dream only lasted for a moment.*
short while, minute, second, instant, flash
(*informal*) jiffy, tick

2 *a great moment in the history of science*
time, occasion, point, juncture

momentary ADJECTIVE

a momentary flash of genius
brief, short, short-lived, temporary, fleeting, passing
❙ **OPPOSITES** lengthy, long-lived

momentous ADJECTIVE

reaching a momentous decision
very important, significant, historic, major, far-reaching, pivotal
(*informal*) earth-shattering
❙ **OPPOSITES** insignificant, trivial

monarch NOUN

SEE **ruler**

money NOUN

1 *How much money do you have with you?*
cash, currency, change, coins, notes
(*informal*) dough
(*British informal*) dosh

2 *The family lost all their money in the crash.*
funds, finance, capital, wealth, riches, means, wherewithal

monster NOUN

a legendary sea monster that attacks ships
beast, giant, ogre, leviathan, brute, fiend, demon

monstrous ADJECTIVE

1 *The volcano triggered a monstrous tidal wave.*
huge, gigantic, enormous, massive, immense, colossal, great, mighty, towering, vast

2 *Mr Hyde commits a series of monstrous crimes.*
horrifying, shocking, wicked, evil, hideous, vile, atrocious, abominable, dreadful, horrible, gruesome, grisly, outrageous, scandalous

mood NOUN

Mr Leslie arrived in a foul mood.
temper, humour, state of mind, frame of mind, disposition

moody ADJECTIVE

Paula slumped on the chair, looking moody.
sulky, sullen, grumpy, bad-tempered, temperamental, touchy, miserable, gloomy, glum, morose
❙ **OPPOSITE** cheerful

moon NOUN

Saturn has a large number of moons.
satellite

WORD WEB

phases of the Moon

new moon, crescent moon, half moon, gibbous moon, full moon

► The Moon **waxes** when it appears gradually bigger before a full moon.

► The Moon **wanes** when it appears gradually smaller after a full moon.

► The times when the Moon rises and sets each day are **moonrise** and **moonset**.　》

> ▶ A landscape on the Moon is a
> **moonscape**.
> ▶ A related adjective is **lunar**.
> *a lunar eclipse*
> **❙ SEE ALSO planet, space**

moor❶ *NOUN*
> *The monument stands on a*
> *windswept moor.*
> moorland, heath, fell
> **FOR TIPS ON DESCRIBING LANDSCAPE** SEE
> **landscape**

moor❷ *VERB*
> *Several yachts were moored in the*
> *harbour.*
> tie up, secure, fasten, anchor, berth,
> dock

moral *ADJECTIVE*
> *trying to lead a moral life*
> good, virtuous, upright, honourable,
> principled, honest, just, truthful,
> decent, ethical, righteous
> **❙ OPPOSITE immoral**

moral *NOUN*
> *The moral of this story is to be*
> *careful what you wish for.*
> lesson, message, meaning, teaching

morale *NOUN*
> *A win would improve the team's*
> *morale.*
> confidence, self-esteem, spirit,
> attitude, motivation, state of mind

morbid *ADJECTIVE*
> *Jules took a morbid interest in*
> *skeletons.*
> ghoulish, macabre, gruesome,
> unhealthy, unwholesome
> (*informal*) sick

more *ADJECTIVE*
> *We need more light in this room.*
> extra, further, added, additional,
> supplementary
> **❙ OPPOSITES less, fewer**

morning *NOUN*
> *going for a walk in the early morning*
> daybreak, dawn,

first light, sunrise
(*North American*) sunup

morsel *NOUN*
> *You haven't eaten a morsel of food.*
> bite, crumb, mouthful, taste, nibble,
> piece, scrap, fragment

mortal *ADJECTIVE*
> **1** *a goddess who fell in love with a*
> *mortal man*
> **❙ OPPOSITE immortal**
> **2** *I believe you are in mortal danger.*
> deadly, lethal, fatal
> **3** *The brothers became mortal enemies.*
> bitter, irreconcilable

mostly *ADVERB*
> **1** *The account is written mostly from*
> *memory.*
> mainly, largely, chiefly, primarily,
> principally, predominantly, in the
> main, for the most part
> **2** *Floods mostly occur during monsoon*
> *season.*
> generally, usually, normally,
> typically, ordinarily, as a rule

mother *NOUN*
> *My mother uses her maiden name.*
> (*informal*) mum, mummy, ma
> (*North American informal*) mom,
> mommy
> ▶ A related adjective is **maternal**.
> **FOR OTHER MEMBERS OF A FAMILY** SEE
> **family**

motion *NOUN*
> *He silenced the audience with a*
> *motion of his hand.*
> gesture, movement, gesticulation

motivate *VERB*
> *What motivated you to write a*
> *book?*
> prompt, drive, stimulate, influence,
> inspire, urge, induce, impel, provoke,
> spur

motive *NOUN*
> *The police can find no motive for the*
> *crime.*
> cause, motivation, reason, rationale,
> purpose, grounds

motor *NOUN*
SEE **engine**

motto *NOUN*
Her motto has always been 'Keep it simple'.
slogan, proverb, saying, maxim, adage, axiom, golden rule

mould *VERB*
a little figure moulded out of marzipan
shape, form, fashion, model, sculpt, work, cast

mouldy *ADJECTIVE*
a lump of mouldy cheese
rotten, rotting, decaying, musty

mound *NOUN*
1 The letter was buried under a mound of paper.
heap, pile, stack, mountain, mass
2 an observatory built on top of a mound
hill, hillock, rise, hump
► An ancient mound of earth over a grave is a **barrow**.
► A mound on which a castle or camp was built is a **motte**.

mount *VERB*
1 I heard footsteps slowly mounting the stairs.
go up, climb, ascend, scale
OPPOSITE descend
2 Chandra mounted her bicycle and rode off.
get on, climb onto, jump onto, hop onto, bestride
OPPOSITE dismount
3 Tension began to mount in the audience.
grow, increase, rise, escalate, intensify, build up
OPPOSITES fall, lessen
4 The library is mounting a new exhibition.
put on, set up, display, install, stage, present

mountain *NOUN*
1 a pass through the mountains
mount, peak, summit
► A line of mountains is a **range**.
► A long narrow hilltop or mountain range is a **ridge**.
► An area of land with many mountains is said to be **mountainous**.
FOR TIPS ON DESCRIBING LANDSCAPE SEE **landscape**
2 a mountain of laundry to do
heap, pile, mound, stack, mass

mourn *VERB*
mourning the loss of a dear friend
grieve for, lament for

mournful *ADJECTIVE*
SEE **sad**

mouth *NOUN*
1 staring into the mouth of a crocodile
jaws, muzzle, maw (informal) chops, trap
► A related adjective is **oral**.
2 a village at the mouth of the river
outlet, estuary, delta (Scottish) firth
3 the yawning mouth of the cavern
entrance, opening

move *VERB*
1 The robot can move in any direction.
go, walk, step, proceed, travel, change position, budge, stir, shift
2 We need to move the piano to the front of the stage.
shift, lift, carry, push, slide, transport, remove, transfer
3 I heard you were moving to Cardiff.
move house, move away, relocate, transfer, decamp
► To move abroad permanently is to **emigrate**.
4 The story of Anne Frank moved me deeply.
affect, touch, stir, shake, impress, inspire

»

a
b
c
d
e
f
g
h
i
j
k
l
m
n
o
p
q
r
s
t
u
v
w
x
y
z

OVERUSED WORD

to move forwards, move towards a place

advance, approach, proceed, progress, press on, make headway, gain ground

*Everyone started panicking as the tornado **advanced**.*

to move back, move away

retreat, withdraw, reverse, retire, back away, fall back, give way

*The werewolves **fell back** as dawn began to break.*

to move upwards

rise, ascend, climb, mount, soar

*I looked out the window as we **climbed** above the clouds.*

to move downwards

drop, descend, fall, dive, plunge, sink, swoop, nosedive

*The film captures a falcon **swooping** down on its prey.*

to move from side to side

sway, swing, wave, rock, wag, swish, flourish, brandish, undulate

*The samurai stepped forward, **swinging** his sword.*

to move quickly

hurry, dash, race, run, rush, hasten, hurtle, career, fly, speed, sweep, shoot, zoom

*A boy went **careering** past on a skateboard.*

SEE ALSO run

to move slowly, aimlessly

amble, stroll, saunter, dawdle, crawl, drift, wander, meander, (*informal*) mosey

*Carmen the cat yawned and **strolled** over to her basket.*

SEE ALSO walk

to move clumsily

stumble, stagger, shuffle, lurch, lumber, flounder, reel, totter, trundle, trip

*Leo **stumbled** into the room, dressed as Frankenstein's monster.*

to move gracefully

flow, glide, dance, drift, flit, float, slide, slip

*Ghostly figures **glided** silently through my dreams.*

to move restlessly

toss, turn, stir, twist, shake, fidget, twitch, jerk, flap

*One of the children kept **twitching** in his seat.*

to move stealthily

creep, crawl, edge, inch, slink, slither, tiptoe

*Agent 007 **edged** carefully along the window ledge.*

move NOUN

1 *Someone was watching our every move.*

movement, motion, action, gesture, step, deed, manoeuvre

2 *It's your move next.*

turn, go

movement NOUN

1 *The robot made a sudden, jerky movement.*

motion, move, action, gesture

2 *the slow movement of traffic*

progress, advance, moving, shifting

3 *Her mother was involved in the peace movement.*

organization, group, party, faction, campaign, lobby, initiative

movie NOUN

SEE **film**

moving ADJECTIVE

The song was so moving that I started to cry.

emotional, affecting, touching, poignant, heart-rending, stirring, inspiring
(*informal*) tear-jerking

much *ADJECTIVE*
There is still much work to be done.
a lot of, a great deal of, plenty, ample
OPPOSITE little

much *ADVERB*
1 *I find texting much quicker than email.*
a great deal, a lot, considerably, substantially, markedly, greatly, far
2 *The price is much the same as before.*
approximately, more or less, by and large

muck *NOUN*
1 *clearing muck out of the stable*
dung, manure, droppings
2 (*informal*) *scraping muck off the windscreen*
dirt, filth, grime, mud, sludge, mess
(*informal*) gunge, gunk

mucky *ADJECTIVE*
a pair of mucky old hiking boots
dirty, messy, muddy, grimy, grubby, filthy, foul, soiled, squalid
OPPOSITE clean

mud *NOUN*
a trail of mud on the carpet
dirt, muck, mire, sludge, clay, soil, silt

muddle *NOUN*
1 *There was a muddle over the invitations.*
confusion, misunderstanding
(*informal*) mix-up
2 *These files are all in a muddle.*
jumble, mess, tangle, disorder, disarray

muddle *VERB*
1 *The words to the song are all muddled.*
mix up, mess up, disorder, jumble up, shuffle, tangle
OPPOSITE tidy
2 *I got muddled trying to follow the instructions.*
confuse, bewilder, puzzle, perplex, baffle, mystify

muddy *ADJECTIVE*
1 *a pair of muddy trainers*
dirty, messy, mucky, filthy, grimy, caked, soiled
OPPOSITE clean
2 *a muddy football pitch*
boggy, marshy, swampy, waterlogged, wet, sodden, squelchy
OPPOSITES dry, firm

muffle *VERB*
1 *James was well muffled in a hat and scarf.*
wrap up, cover up, swathe, cloak, enfold
2 *I closed the door to muffle the noise.*
deaden, dampen, dull, stifle, smother, soften, mask

muffled *ADJECTIVE*
We heard muffled voices from the next room.
faint, indistinct, unclear, muted, deadened, stifled
OPPOSITE clear

mug *NOUN*
SEE **cup**

muggy *ADJECTIVE*
The weather is often muggy before a storm.
humid, close, clammy, sticky, moist, damp, oppressive
OPPOSITE fresh
FOR TIPS ON DESCRIBING WEATHER SEE **weather**

multiply *VERB*
1 *Multiply the remaining number by ten.*
▶ To multiply a number by two is to **double** it.
▶ To multiply it by three is to **triple** it.
▶ To multiply it by four is to **quadruple** it.
OPPOSITE divide

»

2 *My junk email keeps on multiplying.*
increase, grow, spread, proliferate,
mount up, accumulate, mushroom,
snowball
❙ **OPPOSITE** decrease

mumble *VERB*
Matthew mumbled an apology.
mutter, murmur
❙ **IDIOM** talk under your breath

munch *VERB*
*munching popcorn all through
the film*
chew, chomp, crunch
❙ **SEE ALSO** eat

murder *VERB*
*a woman accused of murdering her
husband*
kill, assassinate
(*informal*) bump off, do away with

murder *NOUN*
*Detectives are treating the case as
murder.*
homicide, killing, assassination
FOR TIPS ON WRITING CRIME FICTION
SEE **crime**

murky *ADJECTIVE*
1 *a cold and murky afternoon*
dark, dull, clouded, overcast, foggy,
misty, grey, leaden, dismal, dreary,
dingy
❙ **OPPOSITES** fine, bright
2 *The water in the well was green and
murky.*
muddy, cloudy, dirty
❙ **OPPOSITE** clear

murmur *VERB*
*The crowd murmured their
approval.*
mutter, mumble, whisper

muscular *ADJECTIVE*
a muscular physique
brawny, beefy, burly, well built,
athletic, sinewy, strapping, strong
❙ **OPPOSITES** puny, weak
**FOR TIPS ON DESCRIBING PEOPLE'S
BODIES** SEE **body**

mushroom *NOUN*
SEE **fungus**

music *NOUN*

 **WORD WEB**

musical styles and genres
bebop, bhangra, blues,
bluegrass, classical music,
country music, dance music,
disco music, early music,
flamenco, folk music, funk,
gospel, heavy metal, hip-hop,
jazz, pop music, punk, ragtime,
rap, reggae, rock, ska, soul,
swing, zydeco

musical forms and compositions
anthem, ballad, carol, concerto,
folk song, fugue, hymn, lullaby,
march, mass, musical, opera,
operetta, oratorio, pibroch,
prelude, raga, requiem, sonata,
song, suit, symphony, tune

families of musical instruments
brass, keyboard, percussion,
strings, woodwind

stringed instruments
acoustic guitar, balalaika, banjo,
bass guitar, bouzouki, cello,
charango, cittern, clarsach,
double bass, dulcimer, electric
guitar, harp, hurdy-gurdy, lute,
lyre, mandolin, oud, pedal
steel guitar, pipa, rebab, sitar,
theorbo, ukulele, vihuela, viol or
viola da gamba, viola,
violin (*informal* fiddle), zither

wind instruments
bagpipes, bassoon, bugle,
clarinet, cor anglais, cornet,
crumhorn, euphonium,
flugelhorn, flute, French horn,
harmonica, oboe, ocarina,
panpipes, piccolo, recorder,
saxophone, shawm, tin whistle,
trombone, trumpet, tuba,
uilleann pipes

keyboard instruments
accordion, clavichord,
harmonium, harpsichord,
keyboard, organ, piano, spinet,
synthesizer

percussion instruments
bass drum, bongo drum,
castanets, cymbals, drum,
gamelan, glockenspiel, gong,
maracas, marimba, mbira or
thumb piano, rattle, snare
drum, steel drum or steelpan,
tabla, tambourine, timpani or
kettledrums, triangle, tubular
bells, vibraphone, xylophone

other terms used in music
chord, clef, counterpoint,
crotchet (*North American* quarter
note), discord, flat, harmony,
key signature, melody,
metronome, minim, natural,
note, octave, pitch, quaver
(*North American* eighth note),
rhythm, scale, semibreve
(*North American* whole
note), semiquaver (*North
American* sixteenth note),
semitone, sharp, stave, tempo,
theme, time signature, tone

musical *ADJECTIVE*
Colette has a very musical voice.
tuneful, melodic, melodious,
harmonious, sweet-sounding
❙ **OPPOSITE** discordant

musician *NOUN*
a musician in an orchestra
performer, instrumentalist

⊛ **WORD WEB**

some types of musician
bassist or bass player, bugler,
cellist, chorister, clarinettist,
composer, conductor, drummer,
fiddler, flautist, guitarist, harpist
or harper, lutenist, oboist,

organist, percussionist, pianist,
piper, singer, timpanist,
trombonist, trumpeter, violinist
(*informal* fiddler), vocalist
▶ A musican who plays music or
sings alone is a **soloist**.
▶ A musician who plays music
to support a singer is an
accompanist.

groups of musicians
band, choir or chorus, duet or
duo, ensemble, group, orchestra,
quartet, quintet, trio
❙ **SEE ALSO** music, song

musty *ADJECTIVE*
a musty smell in the cellar
damp, dank, mouldy, stale, stuffy,
airless
❙ **OPPOSITE** fresh

mute *ADJECTIVE*
*Gwyneth could only stare, mute with
terror.*
silent, speechless, unspeaking,
dumb, tongue-tied

mutilate *VERB*
*His right hand was mutilated by a
firework.*
maim, disfigure, injure, wound,
mangle

mutiny *NOUN*
*the story of a mutiny on board a
battleship*
rebellion, revolt, uprising,
insurrection

mutter *VERB*
*Steve sat muttering to himself in the
corner.*
mumble, murmur, whisper
❙ **IDIOM** talk under your breath

mutual *ADJECTIVE*
*It is in our mutual interest to work
together.*
joint, common, shared, reciprocal

mysterious ADJECTIVE
> The letter contained a mysterious message.
> puzzling, strange, baffling, perplexing, mystifying, bizarre, curious, weird, obscure, unexplained, incomprehensible, inexplicable

mystery NOUN
> The recent UFO sightings remain a mystery.
> puzzle, riddle, secret, enigma, conundrum

mystify VERB
> I was completely mystified by the plot.
> puzzle, baffle, bewilder, perplex

myth NOUN
> the ancient myth of the Minotaur
> legend, fable, saga, folklore

mythical ADJECTIVE
> the mythical world of Narnia
> fabulous, fanciful, imaginary, invented, fictional, legendary, mythological

| **OPPOSITE** real

FOR TIPS ON WRITING FANTASY FICTION SEE fantasy

Nn

nag *VERB*

1 *My mum nagged me to go to the doctor.*
badger, pester, hound, harass, keep on at

2 *a character who is nagged by doubts*
trouble, worry, plague, torment, prey on, niggle

naive *ADJECTIVE*

Tess was still hopelessly naive about life.
innocent, inexperienced, unsophisticated, immature, unworldly, artless, gullible, credulous, green
❙ **IDIOM** wet behind the ears

naked *ADJECTIVE*

a man wearing shorts and naked to the waist
bare, nude, unclothed, undressed, stripped, with nothing on
❙ **IDIOMS** *(humorous)* without a stitch, in the buff, in your birthday suit
❙ **OPPOSITE** clothed

name *NOUN*

What's the name of that song?
title, label, designation
▶ The official names you have are your **first names** or **forenames**, and **surname**.
▶ Names a Christian is given at baptism are **Christian names**.
▶ A false name is an **alias**.
▶ A name people use instead of your real name is a **nickname**.

▶ A false name an author uses is a **pen name** or **pseudonym**.

name *VERB*

1 *They named the new robot Asimo.*
call, label, dub, term, title
▶ To name someone at the ceremony of baptism is to **baptize** or **christen** them.

2 *Name your price.*
specify, designate, nominate, propose, suggest, put forward

nap *NOUN*

taking a nap in the afternoon
rest, sleep, doze, lie-down, siesta
(informal) snooze
❙ **IDIOM** forty winks

narrate *VERB*

The story is narrated by the main character.
tell, recount, relate, report, present
▶ The person who narrates a story is the **narrator**.

narrative *NOUN*

a historical narrative set in Tudor times
account, history, story, tale, chronicle
(informal) yarn
FOR TIPS ON WRITING A BOOK REVIEW SEE **book**

narrow *ADJECTIVE*

1 *crawling through a narrow tunnel*
thin, slender, slight, slim, tight, constricted, confined
❙ **OPPOSITES** wide, broad

2 *a narrow outlook on life*
limited, restricted, close-minded, inadequate, deficient
❙ **OPPOSITES** broad, open-minded

nasty *ADJECTIVE*

1 *a medicine with a nasty taste*
unpleasant, offensive, disgusting, revolting, repulsive, repellent, obnoxious, horrible, horrid, foul, vile, rotten, sickening
(informal) yucky
❙ **OPPOSITES** pleasant, agreeable

a
b
c
d
e
f
g
h
i
j
k
l
m
n
o
p
q
r
s
t
u
v
w
x
y
z

»

2 *Bill Sykes is a thoroughly nasty character.*
unkind, unpleasant, unfriendly, disagreeable, objectionable, odious, malicious, cruel, spiteful, vicious, mean, malevolent
❙ **OPPOSITES** likeable, agreeable

3 *a nasty accident*
serious, dreadful, awful, terrible, severe, painful, ugly
❙ **OPPOSITE** slight
❙ **SEE ALSO bad**

nation NOUN
a treaty between several nations
country, state, land, realm, race, people

national ADJECTIVE
broadcast on national television
nationwide, countrywide, state
❙ **OPPOSITE** local

native ADJECTIVE
1 *the native population of Hawaii*
indigenous, original, local, domestic
❙ **OPPOSITES** immigrant, imported

2 *Is Urdu your native language?*
mother, first, home

natural ADJECTIVE
1 *Is that your natural hair colour?*
real, original, normal
❙ **OPPOSITES** unnatural, fake

2 *a smoothie made with natural ingredients*
unprocessed, unrefined, pure
❙ **OPPOSITES** artificial, processed

3 *It's natural to be nervous before a race.*
normal, common, understandable, reasonable, predictable
❙ **OPPOSITES** abnormal, unnatural

4 *having a natural gift for music*
born, inborn, instinctive, intuitive, native

nature NOUN
1 *a documentary about nature*
the natural world, wildlife, the environment, natural history

2 *Labradors are known for their mild nature.*
character, disposition, temperament, personality, manner, make-up

3 *I like science fiction and things of that nature.*
kind, sort, type, order, description, variety, category, genre

naughty ADJECTIVE
1 *Jake had been the naughtiest kid in his class.*
badly behaved, disobedient, bad, troublesome, mischievous, uncontrollable, unmanageable, wayward, unruly
❙ **OPPOSITE** well behaved

2 *a dictionary with the naughty words left out*
rude, indecent, risqué, dirty, smutty, crude
❙ **OPPOSITE** clean

navigate VERB
navigating a canoe through the rapids
steer, pilot, guide, direct, manoeuvre

navy NOUN
SEE **fleet**

near ADJECTIVE
1 *Mars is a near neighbour of the Earth.*
nearby, next-door, close, adjacent, accessible
❙ **OPPOSITES** far, remote

2 *The message warned us that danger was near.*
imminent, approaching, coming, looming, impending, on its way
(old use) nigh
❙ **IDIOMS** round the corner, in the offing
❙ **OPPOSITE** far off

3 *the death of a near relative*
close, dear, familiar, intimate
❙ **OPPOSITE** distant

nearby ADVERB
A photographer happened to be standing nearby.

close by, not far off, close at hand, within reach

❙ IDIOMS a stone's throw away, within spitting distance

❙ OPPOSITES far away, far off

nearly ADVERB

You're nearly as tall as I am.
almost, practically, virtually, just about, well-nigh

▷ **not nearly**

The sequel is not nearly as good as the first film.
nowhere near, nothing like, not at all, far from

neat ADJECTIVE

1 *Please leave the room as neat as possible.*
clean, tidy, orderly, uncluttered, immaculate, trim, in good order

❙ IDIOM spick and span

❙ OPPOSITES untidy, messy

2 *Craig looked very neat in his kilt.*
smart, elegant, spruce, trim, dapper, well groomed, well turned out
(informal) natty

❙ OPPOSITE scruffy

3 *the neatest handwriting I've ever seen*
clear, precise, well formed, elegant

4 *a neat pass into the penalty area*
skilful, deft, adroit, adept, well executed

❙ OPPOSITE clumsy

necessary ADJECTIVE

Are all these forms strictly necessary?
essential, required, needed, requisite, compulsory, obligatory, mandatory, unavoidable, imperative

❙ OPPOSITE unnecessary

need VERB

1 *I need a pound coin for the locker.*
require, want, be short of, lack

2 *a charity which needs our support*
depend on, rely on

▷ **need to**

We need to leave by 6 o'clock.
have to, must, be required to,
be supposed to, be expected to

need NOUN

1 *a pressing need for more blood donors*
call, demand, requirement, necessity, want

2 *helping people in times of need*
distress, trouble, crisis, emergency, extremity

needless ADJECTIVE

They went to a lot of needless expense.
unnecessary, unwanted, uncalled for, excessive, superfluous, redundant, gratuitous

needlework NOUN

SEE **textiles**

needy ADJECTIVE

a fund to help needy children
poor, deprived, underprivileged, disadvantaged, poverty-stricken, penniless, impoverished, destitute, in need

❙ OPPOSITES wealthy, privileged

negative ADJECTIVE

1 *Why are you being so negative?*
pessimistic, defeatist, fatalistic, unenthusiastic, gloomy, cynical, downbeat

❙ OPPOSITES positive, optimistic, upbeat

2 *Stress can have a negative effect on your health.*
bad, adverse, unfavourable, detrimental, harmful, damaging

❙ OPPOSITES positive, beneficial

neglect VERB

1 *I've been neglecting my email recently.*
ignore, overlook, disregard, pay no attention to, shirk, abandon

2 *You neglected to mention a few things.*
fail, omit, forget

negligible ADJECTIVE

There is a negligible difference in price.

a
b
c
d
e
f
g
h
i
j
k
l
m
n
o
p
q
r
s
t
u
v
w
x
y
z

slight, insignificant, unimportant,
minor, trivial, trifling, minimal
OPPOSITES considerable, significant

negotiate VERB

1 *They refused to negotiate with the kidnappers.*
bargain, haggle, deal, confer,
discuss terms

2 *negotiating a new contract*
work out, agree on, broker
(informal) thrash out

3 *We negotiated our way around the furniture.*
get past, get round, manoeuvre
round

neighbourhood NOUN

1 *living in a run-down neighbourhood*
area, district, community, locality,
vicinity, locale, quarter

2 *a planet in the neighbourhood of Betelgeuse*
vicinity, environs, surrounding area

neighbouring ADJECTIVE

a tour of the neighbouring villages
nearby, bordering, adjacent,
adjoining, surrounding, nearest,
next-door

neighbourly ADJECTIVE

establishing good neighbourly relations
friendly, amicable, cordial, helpful,
obliging, hospitable, sociable
OPPOSITE unfriendly

nerve NOUN

1 *It takes nerve to be a good stunt artist.*
bravery, courage, daring,
fearlessness, pluck, grit
(informal) guts, bottle

2 *He had the nerve to ask me to leave!*
cheek, impudence, audacity,
effrontery, impertinence,
presumption

nervous ADJECTIVE

Do you get nervous before you go on stage?
anxious, worried, apprehensive,

concerned, uneasy, fearful, edgy,
fraught, tense, overwrought,
worked up, keyed up
(informal) uptight, jittery, twitchy
IDIOMS (informal) in a flap,
in a state
OPPOSITES calm, confident

nestle VERB

a baby nestling in its mother's arms
cuddle, curl up, snuggle, huddle,
nuzzle

neutral ADJECTIVE

1 *It's impossible to remain neutral on this issue.*
impartial, detached, uninvolved,
disinterested, objective, unbiased,
non-partisan
OPPOSITES biased, partisan

2 *a room decorated in neutral colours*
dull, drab, colourless, indefinite,
nondescript
OPPOSITES colourful, vibrant

new ADJECTIVE

1 *opening a new jar of mayonnaise*
fresh, unused, pristine, brand new
▶ Something new and unused is **in mint condition**.
OPPOSITES old, used

2 *Have you read the new issue of the magazine?*
latest, current, recent, up-to-date

3 *I've added a new paragraph to my story.*
additional, extra, further,
supplementary

4 *a whole new style of acting*
fresh, original, novel, innovative,
cutting-edge, state-of-the-art,
contemporary

5 *Flying was a new experience for me.*
unfamiliar, unknown, different,
alternative, strange
OPPOSITE familiar

newly ADVERB

The house has been newly refurbished.
recently, lately, not long ago

news NOUN
> *Have you heard the news?*
> information, word, report, bulletin
> *(old use)* tidings

next ADJECTIVE
> **1** *the house next to the corner*
> adjacent, closest, nearest,
> next door
> **OPPOSITE** distant
> **2** *I'm going to miss the next episode.*
> following, succeeding, subsequent,
> upcoming
> **OPPOSITE** previous

next ADVERB
> *I don't know what to do next.*
> from now on, after this, in future
> *(old use)* hereafter
> **OPPOSITE** before

nibble VERB
> SEE **eat**

nice ADJECTIVE
> **1** *That's not a very nice thing to say!*
> pleasant, agreeable
> **OPPOSITES** unpleasant, nasty
> **2** *There's a nice distinction between*
> *copying and plagiarism.*
> fine, subtle, delicate, precise

OVERUSED WORD

a nice person
good, kind, pleasant, friendly,
agreeable, likeable, amiable,
genial, affable, personable,
charming, engaging,
sympathetic, polite, civil,
courteous
The film features a cast of
likeable *characters.*

a nice experience, nice feeling
enjoyable, pleasant, good,
delightful, satisfying, agreeable,
entertaining, amusing,
wonderful, marvellous, splendid
Making my own clothes gives me
a ***satisfying*** *feeling.*

looking nice
beautiful, attractive, pleasing,
lovely, fine, handsome, fetching,
striking
You look particularly ***fetching***
today, Miss Watson.

a nice smell
fragrant, pleasant, sweet,
perfumed, aromatic
I prefer a blend of tea with a
fragrant *aroma.*
OPPOSITES smelly, malodorous

a nice taste, nice food
appetizing, tasty, flavoursome,
delicious, delectable,
mouth-watering
(informal) yummy, scrumptious
Slow cooking will make the dish
more ***flavoursome***.

nice weather, a nice day
fine, sunny, warm, mild,
balmy, dry
If the weather is ***fine***, *I might*
venture outside.
SEE ALSO good, lovely

night NOUN
> *Vampires only come out at night.*
> night-time, dark, the hours of
> darkness
> ▶ The time immediately after sunset
>   when the sky is still light is **twilight**.
> ▶ The time when twilight ends is **dusk**
>   or **nightfall**.
> ▶ A **nightly** event happens every
>   night.
> ▶ A piece of music which conveys the
>   atmosphere of night is a **nocturne**.
> ▶ Animals which are active at night are
>   **nocturnal**.
> **OPPOSITES** day, daytime

nil NOUN
> *The score was nil all at half-time.*
> zero, nought, nothing, none
> ▶ A score of nil in cricket is a **duck**.
> ▶ A score of nil in tennis is **love**.

a
b
c
d
e
f
g
h
i
j
k
l
m
n
o
p
q
r
s
t
u
v
w
x
y
z

nimble *ADJECTIVE*

Tap dancing requires nimble footwork.
agile, skilful, quick, deft, dexterous, adroit, lithe, spry

OPPOSITE clumsy

nip *VERB*

1 *Frost had begun to nip at our toes.*
bite, nibble, peck, pinch, tweak, catch

2 *(informal) I'll just nip along to the post office.*
dash, run, rush
(informal) pop

noble *ADJECTIVE*

1 *an ancient noble family by the name of von Frankenstein*
aristocratic, high-born, upper-class, titled

OPPOSITES low-born, humble, base

2 *Their noble sacrifice will be remembered.*
brave, heroic, courageous, valiant, honourable, worthy, virtuous, gallant

OPPOSITES cowardly, unworthy

3 *a forest of noble redwoods*
grand, stately, magnificent, impressive, imposing, dignified, proud, majestic

noble *NOUN*

a group of nobles loyal to the crown
aristocrat, nobleman, noblewoman, lord, lady, peer

OPPOSITE commoner

nod *VERB*

The others nodded their heads in agreement.
bob, bow, dip, lower, incline

▷ **nod off**
nodding off in front of the fire
fall asleep, doze off, drop off, have a nap

noise *NOUN*

My computer is making a peculiar noise.
sound, racket, din, row, rumpus, uproar, clangour, commotion, hullabaloo, cacophony

FOR TIPS ON DESCRIBING SOUNDS SEE **sound❶**

noisy *ADJECTIVE*

1 *playing noisy music*
loud, blaring, booming, deafening, ear-splitting, thunderous, cacophonous

OPPOSITES quiet, soft

2 *It was crowded and noisy in the dining hall.*
rowdy, raucous, clamorous, uproarious

OPPOSITES quiet, silent

nominate *VERB*

The show has been nominated for a top award.
propose, put forward, recommend, select, choose, name, elect

nonsense *NOUN*

His whole argument is utter nonsense.
rubbish, drivel, gibberish, claptrap, garbage
(informal) gobbledegook, baloney, rot, tripe, twaddle, piffle
(British informal) cobblers, codswallop
(North American informal) flapdoodle
(old use) balderdash, poppycock

OPPOSITES sense, reason

nonsensical *ADJECTIVE*

a head filled with nonsensical notions
absurd, ridiculous, ludicrous, senseless, irrational, illogical, preposterous, crazy, laughable, silly, stupid, foolish, idiotic
(British informal) daft

OPPOSITES sensible, reasonable

non-stop *ADJECTIVE*

1 *the sound of non-stop traffic*
constant, continual, continuous, endless, ceaseless, incessant, never-ending, unending, perpetual, round-the-clock

2 *a non-stop train from Paris to Nice*
direct, express

normal *ADJECTIVE*

1 *It began as just a normal day.*
ordinary, average, typical, usual,
common, standard, regular,
routine, familiar, habitual,
customary, conventional
❙ **IDIOM** run-of-the-mill
❙ **OPPOSITES** abnormal, atypical

2 *It can't be normal to feel this way.*
healthy, natural, rational,
reasonable, sane
❙ **OPPOSITES** unhealthy, unnatural

normally *ADVERB*
She's not normally like this.
usually, ordinarily, as a rule, most of
the time, on the whole, by and large,
typically

north *NOUN, ADJECTIVE, ADVERB*
The Sahara is in the north of Africa.
▶ The parts of a country or continent
in the north are the **northern** parts.
▶ To travel towards the north is to
travel **northward** or **northwards**.
▶ A wind from the north is a **northerly**
wind.
▶ A person who lives in the north of a
country is a **northerner**.

nose *NOUN*

1 *Cyrano is self-conscious about his
enormous nose.*
(British informal) hooter
▶ The openings in your nose are your
nostrils.
▶ An animal's nose is its **muzzle** or
snout.
▶ A long flexible snout is a **trunk** or
proboscis.
▶ A related adjective is **nasal**.
FOR TIPS ON DESCRIBING FACES SEE face

2 *sitting in the nose of the boat*
front, bow, prow

nosy *(informal) ADJECTIVE*
*a nosy reporter who asked a lot of
questions*
inquisitive, curious, prying,
snooping, intrusive

notable *ADJECTIVE*

1 *a notable date in history*
memorable, noteworthy,
significant, major, important,
well known, famous, celebrated,
renowned, noted, prominent
❙ **OPPOSITES** insignificant, minor

2 *a notable lack of enthusiasm*
distinct, definite, obvious,
conspicuous, marked, pronounced,
striking, remarkable

notch *NOUN*
cutting a notch in a tree trunk
cut, nick, groove, score, scratch,
incision

note *NOUN*

1 *a note written in the margin*
comment, annotation, jotting,
entry, record, memo

2 *sending a thank-you note*
message, letter, line, communication

3 *There was a note of anger in her
voice.*
tone, feeling, quality, sense, hint,
suggestion
FOR MUSICAL NOTES SEE music

note *VERB*

1 *I noted the address on a
scrap of paper.*
jot down, make a note of, write
down, take down, scribble, record,
list, enter, pencil in

2 *Did you note what time you
left the house?*
notice, take note of,
pay attention to, heed, mark,
register, observe

nothing *NOUN*

1 *There's nothing more we can do.*
not a thing
(informal) zilch
❙ **IDIOM** *(humorous)* not a sausage

2 *They scored nothing in the first
round.*
nought, zero, nil
❙ **SEE ALSO nil**

notice NOUN

1 *a notice pinned to the wall*
sign, advertisement, poster, placard

2 *Some islands received no notice of the tsunami.*
warning, notification, announcement

▷ **take notice of something**
They took no notice of the warning.
pay attention to, heed, mark

notice VERB

1 *Did you notice what he was wearing?*
note, take note of, heed, mark, register, observe, spot

2 *I noticed a funny smell in the room.*
become aware of, detect, discern

noticeable ADJECTIVE

1 *a noticeable improvement in the weather*
notable, distinct, definite, measurable, perceptible, appreciable, significant, marked, pronounced, salient, unmistakable, striking

2 *At first, the patient had no noticeable symptoms.*
obvious, conspicuous, visible, detectable, discernible, evident, apparent
OPPOSITE imperceptible

notion NOUN

some old-fashioned notions about women
belief, idea, view, thought, opinion, theory, concept

notorious ADJECTIVE

one of the most notorious criminals in the country
infamous, disreputable, scandalous, disgraceful

nought NOUN

SEE **nil**

nourish VERB

1 *The growing embryo is nourished by the egg yolk.*
feed, sustain, support, nurture

2 *nourishing the talent of young artists*
support, encourage, promote, nurture, foster, cultivate

nourishing ADJECTIVE

a bowl of hot, nourishing soup
nutritious, wholesome, healthy, health-giving

novel NOUN

reading a detective novel
► The author of a novel is a **novelist**.
SEE ALSO fiction

novel ADJECTIVE

a novel method of filming underwater
original, new, innovative, fresh, different, imaginative, creative, unusual, unconventional, unorthodox
OPPOSITES traditional, familiar

now ADVERB

1 *My sister is now living in Melbourne.*
at present, at the moment, at this time, currently, nowadays

2 *I'll send them an email now.*
immediately, at once, straight away, right away, without delay, instantly, directly, this instant
(informal) asap

nude ADJECTIVE

a painting of a nude figure
naked, bare, unclothed, undressed
OPPOSITE clothed

nudge VERB

1 *Val nudged me in the ribs and whispered.*
poke, prod, dig, elbow, jab, jolt, bump

2 *We nudged the piano into position.*
ease, inch, manoeuvre

nuisance NOUN

Mosquitoes can be a nuisance in the summer.
annoyance, irritation, inconvenience, bother, menace, pest, drawback
(informal) bind, hassle, pain, headache, drag

numb *ADJECTIVE*
> *My toes were numb with cold.*
> unfeeling, deadened, frozen,
> insensitive, paralysed
> **OPPOSITE** sensitive

number *NOUN*
> **1** *a number greater than zero*
> figure, numeral
> ▶ Any of the numbers from 0 to 9 is a
> **digit**.
> ▶ A negative or positive whole number
> is an **integer**.
> ▶ An amount used in measuring or
> counting is a **unit**.
> **SEE ALSO mathematics**
>
> **2** *a large number of emails*
> amount, quantity, collection, quota,
> total, tally
>
> **3** *the latest number of the magazine*
> edition, issue
>
> **4** *The musical features some well-
> known numbers.*
> song, piece, tune

numerous *ADJECTIVE*
> *The book contains numerous errors.*
> many, a lot of, plenty of, abundant,
> copious, countless, innumerable,
> untold, myriad
> *(informal)* umpteen, lots of,
> masses of
> **OPPOSITE** few

nurse *NOUN*
> SEE **medicine**

nurse *VERB*
> *nursing a sick relative*
> look after, care for, take care of,
> tend, treat

nut *NOUN*

 WORD WEB

> **some edible nuts**
> almond, Brazil, cashew, chestnut,
> coconut, hazelnut, macadamia,
> peanut, pecan, pine nut,
> pistachio, walnut
> ▶ The part inside the shell of a nut is
> the **kernel**.

a
b
c
d
e
f
g
h
i
j
k
l
m
n
o
p
q
r
s
t
u
v
w
x
y
z

385

Oo

a
b
c
d
e
f
g
h
i
j
k
l
m
n
o
p
q
r
s
t
u
v
w
x
y
z

oath *NOUN*
1 *swearing an oath of allegiance*
pledge, promise, vow, word of honour
2 *uttering a stream of oaths*
swear word, curse, expletive, profanity

obedient *ADJECTIVE*
Your dog seems very obedient.
well-behaved, disciplined, manageable, dutiful, docile, biddable, compliant
OPPOSITE disobedient

obese *ADJECTIVE*
SEE **fat**

obey *VERB*
1 *The robot will obey any command.*
follow, carry out, execute, implement, observe, heed, comply with, adhere to, submit to
2 *Do you always obey without question?*
do what you are told, take orders, be obedient, conform
OPPOSITE disobey

object *NOUN*
1 *reports of a strange object in the sky*
article, item, thing, entity
2 *What is the object of this experiment?*
point, purpose, aim, goal, intention, objective
3 *Joe fears becoming an object of ridicule.*
target, focus, butt

object *VERB*
▷ **object to something**
Only one person objected to the plan.
oppose, be opposed to, disapprove of, take exception to, take issue with, protest against, complain about
OPPOSITES accept, agree to

objection *NOUN*
Has anybody got any objections?
protest, complaint, opposition, disapproval, disagreement, dissent

objectionable *ADJECTIVE*
a thoroughly objectionable character
unpleasant, disagreeable, disgusting, foul, offensive, repellent, revolting, obnoxious, nasty
OPPOSITE acceptable

objective *NOUN*
The team's objective is to win a medal.
aim, goal, intention, target, ambition, object, purpose, plan

objective *ADJECTIVE*
an objective account of what happened
impartial, neutral, unbiased, unprejudiced, even-handed, disinterested, uninvolved, dispassionate, detached
OPPOSITE subjective

obligatory *ADJECTIVE*
The wearing of seat belts is obligatory.
compulsory, mandatory, required, prescribed, necessary
OPPOSITE optional

oblige *VERB*
Would you oblige me by delivering this letter?
do someone a favour, help, assist, indulge, humour

obliged *ADJECTIVE*
1 *I felt obliged to accept the invitation.*
bound, compelled, expected, required, constrained
2 *I'm much obliged to you for your help.*

thankful, grateful, appreciative,
indebted, beholden

obliging ADJECTIVE
Thank you for your obliging offer.
helpful, kind, considerate,
thoughtful, generous, agreeable,
cooperative, amenable
❙ OPPOSITE unhelpful

oblong NOUN
an oblong of grass
rectangle
❙ SEE ALSO **shape**

obscene ADJECTIVE
*The film contains some obscene
language.*
indecent, offensive, explicit, rude,
vulgar, coarse, lewd
❙ OPPOSITES clean, decent

obscure ADJECTIVE
1 *The origins of the stone circle
remain obscure.*
uncertain, unclear, mysterious,
vague, hazy, shadowy, murky, dim
❙ OPPOSITE clear
2 *The poem is full of obscure references.*
oblique, enigmatic, cryptic, puzzling,
perplexing, abstruse
❙ OPPOSITE obvious
3 *an obscure Russian composer*
unknown, unheard of, little known,
minor, unrecognized, forgotten,
unsung
❙ OPPOSITES famous,
well known

obscure VERB
A tall hedge obscured the view.
block out, cover, hide, conceal,
mask, screen, veil, shroud, cloak,
obliterate
❙ OPPOSITE reveal

observant ADJECTIVE
*under the observant eyes of the
judges*
alert, attentive, sharp-eyed, vigilant,
watchful
❙ OPPOSITE inattentive

observation NOUN
1 *using a telescope for observation of
the Moon*
study, watching, scrutiny,
surveillance, survey, monitoring
2 *The author makes some interesting
observations.*
comment, remark, statement,
reflection

observe VERB
1 *observing elephants in the wild*
watch, look at, view, study, survey,
monitor, scrutinize, regard,
contemplate
❙ IDIOMS keep an eye on,
keep tabs on
2 *Did you observe anything unusual in
his behaviour?*
notice, note, see, detect, spot,
discern, perceive, witness
3 *observing the rules of the game*
comply with, abide by, keep to,
adhere to, obey, honour, respect,
follow, heed
4 *preparing to observe Hanukkah*
celebrate, honour, keep
5 *'This is a most curious case,' observed
Holmes.*
remark, comment, mention, say,
state, declare
❙ SEE ALSO **say**

obsessed ADJECTIVE
*Jeremy is completely obsessed with
cars.*
infatuated, fixated, preoccupied,
besotted, smitten
❙ IDIOM (informal) have a thing about

obsession NOUN
a childhood obsession with horses
passion, fixation, infatuation,
preoccupation, mania, compulsion
❙ IDIOMS a bee in your bonnet
(informal) a thing about

obsolete ADJECTIVE
*That piece of software is now
obsolete.*
out of date, outdated, outmoded,

a
b
c
d
e
f
g
h
i
j
k
l
m
n
o
p
q
r
s
t
u
v
w
x
y
z

passé, antiquated, dated, archaic, defunct, extinct
IDIOM past its sell-by date
OPPOSITES current, modern

obstacle NOUN

1 *an obstacle in the road*
obstruction, barrier, barricade, block

2 *Your age should not be an obstacle.*
problem, difficulty, hindrance, hurdle, snag, catch, disadvantage, drawback, stumbling block, impediment
IDIOMS a fly in the ointment, a spanner in the works
OPPOSITES aid, advantage

obstinate ADJECTIVE

He's too obstinate to admit that he's wrong.
stubborn, uncooperative, wilful, self-willed, headstrong, pig-headed, inflexible, unyielding, intransigent
OPPOSITES cooperative, compliant

obstruct VERB

1 *The path was obstructed by a fallen tree.*
block, jam, make impassable, clog, choke
(informal) bung up

2 *Charged with obstructing the course of justice*
hinder, hamper, impede, interfere with, hold up, delay, stand in the way of

obstruction NOUN

A fallen tree was causing an obstruction.
blockage, barrier, obstacle, hindrance, impediment, stoppage, hold-up, check

obtain VERB

You must obtain a permit to park here.
get, get hold of, acquire, pick up, procure, come by
IDIOM lay your hands on

obvious ADJECTIVE

1 *There were no obvious marks on the body.*
noticeable, conspicuous, visible, prominent, pronounced, distinct, glaring
OPPOSITES inconspicuous, imperceptible, hidden

2 *It was obvious that the woman was lying.*
clear, evident, apparent, plain, manifest, patent, undeniable, unmistakable
OPPOSITE unclear

obviously ADVERB

There has obviously been some mistake.
clearly, plainly, evidently, apparently, patently, of course, needless to say
OPPOSITES perhaps, arguably

occasion NOUN

1 *We met on a number of occasions.*
time, moment, instance, juncture

2 *Is the dress for a special occasion?*
event, affair, function, happening, incident, occurrence

3 *I've had no occasion to use my new camera.*
opportunity, chance, possibility, need

occasional ADJECTIVE

The forecast is for occasional showers.
intermittent, infrequent, irregular, periodic, sporadic, odd, scattered
OPPOSITES frequent, regular

occasionally ADVERB

Ethan nodded occasionally to show he was listening.
sometimes, every so often, once in a while, now and again, from time to time, on occasion, periodically
OPPOSITES frequently, often

occupant NOUN

the last remaining occupants of the island

resident, inhabitant, occupier, householder, tenant

occupation *NOUN*
  1 *The birth certificate lists his father's occupation.*
  job, employment, profession, post, position, trade, work, line of work, calling
  2 *My favourite occupation is reading.*
  activity, pastime, hobby, pursuit, recreation
  3 *the Roman occupation of Gaul*
  capture, seizure, conquest, invasion, colonization, subjugation

 WORD WEB

some occupations

actor or actress, architect, artist, astronaut, banker, barber, bookseller, builder, bus driver, chef, cleaner, coach, cook, curator, dancer, dentist, detective, diver, doctor, editor, electrician, engineer, farmer, film-maker, firefighter, fisherman, flight attendant, florist, footballer, gardener, hairdresser, imam, janitor, joiner, journalist, lawyer, lecturer, lexicographer, librarian, mechanic, midwife, miner, minister, model, musician, nurse, office worker, optician, painter, paramedic, pharmacist, photographer, pilot, plumber, police officer, politician, postal worker, priest, professor, programmer, psychiatrist, psychologist, rabbi, receptionist, reporter, sailor, scientist, secretary, security guard, shepherd, shopkeeper, singer, soldier, solicitor, stockbroker, surgeon, tailor, teacher, traffic warden, train driver, TV presenter, undertaker, vet, waiter or waitress, web designer, writer, zookeeper

> **FOR OCCUPATIONS IN THE PAST** SEE **historical**
>
> **FOR MEDICAL OCCUPATIONS** SEE **medicine**

occupied *ADJECTIVE*
  1 *This game will keep you occupied for hours.*
  busy, engaged, absorbed, engrossed, involved, active, tied up
  OPPOSITE idle
  2 *Is this seat occupied?*
  in use, taken, engaged, full
  OPPOSITES free, vacant

occupy *VERB*
  1 *A young couple occupy the flat upstairs.*
  live in, reside in, dwell in, inhabit
  2 *The piano occupies most of the room.*
  fill, take up, use up
  3 *That should occupy you for a while.*
  keep you busy, engage your attention, divert, amuse, absorb, engross
  4 *The Romans occupied Britain for nearly 400 years.*
  capture, seize, take over, conquer, colonize, subjugate

occur *VERB*
  1 *Lucy told them what had occurred.*
  happen, take place, come about, arise
  2 *a disease which occurs mainly in childhood*
  appear, develop, be found, crop up, turn up

occurrence *NOUN*
  Highway robbery was once a common occurrence.
  event, happening, incident, phenomenon

a
b
c
d
e
f
g
h
i
j
k
l
m
n
o
p
q
r
s
t
u
v
w
x
y
z

ocean NOUN

WORD WEB

the oceans of the world
Antarctic, Arctic, Atlantic, Indian, Pacific

❙ SEE ALSO **sea**

odd ADJECTIVE

1 *Her behaviour seems rather odd.*
strange, unusual, abnormal, peculiar, curious, puzzling, extraordinary, funny, weird, bizarre, eccentric, quirky, outlandish
❙ IDIOM *(informal)* off the wall
❙ OPPOSITES normal, ordinary

2 *I could only find one odd sock.*
unmatched, unpaired, single, lone, leftover, spare

3 *doing odd jobs around the house*
occasional, casual, irregular, various, sundry

odour NOUN

The odour of burnt toast wafted from the kitchen.
smell, aroma, scent, perfume, fragrance, bouquet
(informal) whiff

▶ An unpleasant odour is a **reek**, **stench**, **stink**, or *(British informal)* **pong**.
FOR TIPS ON DESCRIBING SMELLS SEE **smell** NOUN

offence NOUN

1 *convicted of a minor offence*
crime, wrongdoing, misdeed, misdemeanour, felony, violation, sin
▶ In sports, an offence is a **foul** or an **infringement**.

2 *I didn't mean to cause any offence.*
annoyance, anger, displeasure, resentment, hard feelings, animosity

offend VERB

1 *I hope my email didn't offend you.*
upset, hurt your feelings, annoy, anger, displease, insult, affront

2 *criminals who may offend again*
break the law, commit a crime, do wrong

offensive ADJECTIVE

1 *making offensive remarks*
insulting, rude, impolite, disrespectful, abusive, upsetting, hurtful
❙ OPPOSITE complimentary

2 *Some people find the smell of garlic offensive.*
unpleasant, disagreeable, distasteful, objectionable, off-putting, repellent, repulsive, disgusting, obnoxious, revolting, nasty
❙ OPPOSITES pleasant, agreeable

3 *an offensive weapon*
hostile, attacking, aggressive
❙ OPPOSITE defensive

offer VERB

1 *May I offer a suggestion?*
propose, put forward, suggest, submit, present, proffer
❙ OPPOSITES withdraw, retract

2 *A few people offered to help me clear up.*
volunteer, come forward
❙ OPPOSITE refuse

offer NOUN

Thank you for your offer of help.
proposal, suggestion, proposition

office NOUN

1 *a newspaper office*
workplace, bureau, department

2 *the office of vice president*
post, position, appointment, job, role, function

officer NOUN

an officer of the law
official, office-holder, executive

official ADJECTIVE

The official opening of the museum is next month.
formal, authorized, legitimate, approved, recognized, proper, valid, bona fide
❙ OPPOSITES unofficial, unauthorized

official NOUN

a high-ranking official in the ministry
officer, office-holder, executive, representative, agent

often ADVERB

a word that is often misspelled
frequently, regularly, commonly, constantly, repeatedly, again and again, time after time, many times
(old use) oft

oil VERB

oiling a bicycle chain
lubricate, grease

oily ADJECTIVE

cutting down on oily foods
greasy, fatty, buttery

ointment NOUN

some ointment for a rash
cream, lotion, salve, liniment, balm

OK or okay *(informal)* ADJECTIVE
SEE **all right**

old ADJECTIVE

OVERUSED WORD

an old person
elderly, aged, senior
*Concessions are available for children and **elderly** people.*
❙ OPPOSITE young

an old building, old document
historical, early, ancient, archaic, antiquarian
▶ Something that you respect because it is old is **venerable**.
*The church stands on the site of an **ancient** Celtic monastery.*
❙ OPPOSITE modern

an old machine, old vehicle
old-fashioned, out of date, antiquated, antique, vintage, veteran, early, obsolete
(humorous) antediluvian

*My uncle collects and restores **vintage** motorcycles.*
❙ OPPOSITES up to date, current

old clothes, old furnishings
worn, scruffy, shabby, frayed, threadbare, tatty
❙ IDIOMS falling to pieces
(humorous) having seen better days
*Brian turned up wearing a pair of **scruffy** jeans and a t-shirt.*
❙ OPPOSITES new, pristine

the old days, old times
past, former, earlier, previous, bygone, olden
▶ Times before written records were kept are **prehistoric** times.
*The film is set in the **bygone** era of colonial India.*
❙ OPPOSITES modern, recent

WRITING TIPS

words in old and poetic use

'Though thy crest be shorn and shaven, thou,' I said, 'art sure no craven. / Ghastly grim and ancient raven wandering from the nightly shore — / Tell me what thy lordly name is on the Night's Plutonian shore!' / Quoth the raven, 'Nevermore'.
— *Edgar Allan Poe, The Raven*

parts of thou
thou (you), thee (you), thy (your), thine (yours), thyself (yourself)

verb parts (with thou)
art (are), wert (were), canst (can), couldst (could), dost (do), didst (did), hast (have), hadst (had), mayst (may), shalt (shall), shouldst (should), wilt (will), wouldst (would) ≫

a
b
c
d
e
f
g
h
i
j
k
l
m
n
o
p
q
r
s
t
u
v
w
x
y
z

other old words
hence (from here),
hither (to here),
thence (from there),
thither (to there),
whence (from where),
whither (to where), ere (before),
nay (no), ne'er (never),
o'er (over), oft (often),
quoth (said), twain (two),
thrice (three times)

old-fashioned ADJECTIVE
The illustrations look old-fashioned
now.
out of date, dated, outdated,
outmoded, unfashionable,
antiquated, passé
(informal) old hat

IDIOMS behind the times,
past its sell-by date

OPPOSITES modern, up to date

omit VERB
1 These scenes were omitted from the
final film.
exclude, leave out, cut, drop,
eliminate, miss out, skip
OPPOSITE include
2 You omitted to mention the author's
name.
forget, fail, neglect
OPPOSITE remember

once ADVERB
1 We spoke only once on the phone.
one time, on one occasion
2 California was once part of Mexico.
formerly, at one time, previously,
in the past

once CONJUNCTION
The show will begin once everyone is
seated.
as soon as, when, after

one NOUN
one of only two species of venomous
lizard
▶ Something which is the only one of
its kind is said to be **unique**.

Usage Note
Words which include 'one' in
their meaning often begin with
either **mono-** or **uni-**, for example
monochrome, monologue, unicorn,
and unicycle.

one-sided ADJECTIVE
1 The game has been one-sided so far.
uneven, unequal, unbalanced
2 taking a one-sided view of history
biased, prejudiced, partisan, partial,
slanted, distorted

only ADVERB
1 There is only room for one passenger.
just, no more than, at most, at best
2 This email is for your eyes only.
solely, purely, exclusively

onset NOUN
the onset of the monsoon season
start, beginning, arrival, appearance,
outbreak
OPPOSITE end

ooze VERB
1 jam oozing from a doughnut
seep, leak, escape, dribble, drip
2 a young woman who oozes
confidence
exude, radiate, emanate, gush

opaque ADJECTIVE
1 a window fitted with opaque glass
cloudy, dull
OPPOSITES transparent, translucent
2 using words whose meaning is
opaque
unclear, obscure, incomprehensible,
unintelligible, impenetrable
OPPOSITES clear, plain

open ADJECTIVE
1 Just leave the door open.
unlocked, unfastened, ajar, gaping
OPPOSITES closed, shut
2 an open packet of crisps
opened, unsealed, uncovered,
unwrapped
OPPOSITES closed, sealed

a
b
c
d
e
f
g
h
i
j
k
l
m
n
o
p
q
r
s
t
u
v
w
x
y
z

3 *Several maps were open on the desk.*
unfolded, spread out, unrolled,
unfurled

4 *a view of open countryside*
clear, unrestricted, unenclosed,
extensive, rolling, sweeping
OPPOSITE enclosed

5 *The following choices are open to
you.*
available, accessible, feasible,
possible

6 *being open about your mistakes*
frank, honest, candid, direct,
forthcoming, unreserved, outspoken
(informal) upfront
OPPOSITES secretive, evasive

7 *The idea was met with open hostility.*
plain, undisguised, unconcealed,
overt, manifest, blatant, public
OPPOSITES hidden, suppressed

▷ **be open to**
1 *I am always open to suggestions.*
receptive to, willing to listen to,
responsive to

2 *Computers are open to attack online.*
vulnerable to, susceptible to,
exposed to, liable to, subject to

open *VERB*

1 *opening a window*
unfasten, unlock, unbolt

2 *opening a birthday present*
undo, unwrap, untie, unseal, unfold,
unroll

▶ To open an umbrella is to **unfurl** it.

▶ To open a wine bottle is to **uncork** it.

3 *The exhibition opens next Friday.*
begin, start, commence, get under
way
(informal) kick off
OPPOSITE close

opening *NOUN*

1 *an opening in the fabric of space and
time*
gap, hole, breach, break, split,
rupture, rift

2 *The film has a very dramatic
opening.*
beginning, start, commencement

(informal) kick-off

3 *the opening of the new sports centre*
launch, inauguration

▶ The opening of a new play or film is
the **first night** or **premiere**.

4 *a good opening for an aspiring
musician*
chance, opportunity

opening *ADJECTIVE*
the opening lines of the poem
first, initial, introductory,
preliminary
OPPOSITES final, closing

operate *VERB*

1 *Do you know how to operate this
camera?*
use, work, run, drive, handle,
control, manage

2 *This watch operates even under
water.*
work, function, go, run, perform

3 *They had to operate to save his life.*
carry out an operation, perform
surgery

operation *NOUN*

1 *This lever controls the operation of
the robot.*
performance, working, functioning,
running, action

2 *Defusing a bomb is a dangerous
operation.*
task, activity, action, exercise,
manoeuvre, process, procedure

3 *an operation to remove your
appendix*
surgery

opinion *NOUN*
*What was your honest opinion of
the film?*
view, judgement, impression,
assessment, estimation, point
of view, thought, belief, feeling,
attitude, idea, notion

opponent *NOUN*
*one of the principal opponents of
slavery*
critic, objector, challenger, rival,

adversary, enemy, foe
▶ Your opponents in a game are the **opposition**.

❚ OPPOSITES supporter, ally

opportunity NOUN

1 *There were few opportunities to relax.*
chance, possibility, occasion, moment, time, window

2 *This is an excellent opportunity for me.*
opening, chance
(informal) break

oppose VERB

Pacifists oppose war of any kind.
object to, be against, disapprove of, disagree with, argue against, take a stand against, be hostile towards, fight against, resist, counter, challenge

❚ OPPOSITES support, defend

opposite ADJECTIVE

1 *the opposite side of the street*
facing

2 *holding opposite opinions*
contrasting, conflicting, contradictory, opposed, opposing, different, contrary

❚ OPPOSITES the same, similar

opposite NOUN

In fact, the opposite is true.
reverse, converse, contrary, antithesis

opposition NOUN

1 *despite strong opposition to the scheme*
resistance, objection, disapproval, hostility, antagonism, dissent

❚ OPPOSITE support

2 *Our team easily beat the opposition.*
opponents, rivals

oppressive ADJECTIVE

1 *an oppressive regime*
harsh, brutal, tyrannical, repressive, ruthless

2 *the oppressive midday heat*
stifling, suffocating, sultry,

humid, muggy, close, heavy

opt VERB

Andrew opted to go first.
choose, decide, elect

▷ **opt for**
opting for a healthier lifestyle
choose, select, pick, go for
(informal) plump for

optimistic ADJECTIVE

feeling optimistic about the future
positive, confident, cheerful, buoyant, hopeful, expectant, sanguine
(informal) upbeat

❚ OPPOSITE pessimistic

option NOUN

We had the option to walk or take the bus.
choice, alternative, selection, possibility

optional ADJECTIVE

Tipping is optional in this country.
voluntary, non-compulsory, discretionary

❚ OPPOSITE compulsory

oral ADJECTIVE

Students take an oral exam in each language.
spoken, verbal, unwritten

❚ OPPOSITE written

orange ADJECTIVE

a bright orange colour

FOR TIPS ON DESCRIBING COLOURS SEE **colour**

orbit NOUN

an elliptical orbit around the Sun
circuit, course, path, track

❚ SEE ALSO **planet**

orbit VERB

More than 50 moons orbit Saturn.
circle, travel round, go round

ordeal NOUN

One of the survivors gave an account of their ordeal.
suffering, hardship, trial, trauma,

torment, anguish, torture,
nightmare

order NOUN

1 *Who gave the order to abandon
ship?*
command, instruction, direction,
decree, edict

2 *You can put in an advance order for
the DVD.*
request, demand, reservation,
booking

3 *The CDs are arranged in
alphabetical order.*
arrangement, sequence, series,
succession

4 *keeping your bike in good order*
condition, state, shape, repair
(British informal) nick

5 *restoring order to the streets*
peace, calm, control, quiet,
harmony, law and order
❚ **OPPOSITE** chaos

order VERB

1 *The crew were ordered to return.*
command, instruct, direct, tell,
require, charge

2 *I ordered the tickets over the
Internet.*
request, reserve, apply for, book

3 *These books are ordered by size.*
arrange, organize, sort, classify,
categorize, lay out

orderly ADJECTIVE

1 *Plants are named according to an
orderly system.*
organized, well ordered, systematic,
methodical, neat, tidy
❚ **OPPOSITES** untidy, haphazard

2 *Please form an orderly queue.*
well behaved, controlled, disciplined
❚ **OPPOSITE** disorderly

ordinary ADJECTIVE

1 *It began as just an ordinary day.*
normal, typical, usual, customary,
habitual, regular, routine

2 *The image was taken with an
ordinary camera.*
standard, average, common,
conventional, run-of-the-mill,
everyday
❚ **IDIOM** common or garden
❚ **OPPOSITES** special, unusual

organic ADJECTIVE

1 *organic matter*
living, live, animate, biological

2 *organic farming*
chemical-free, additive-free,
natural, bio-

organism NOUN

an organism from another planet
being, creature, life form,
living thing

organization NOUN

1 *The UN is an international
organization.*
institution, operation, enterprise,
company
(informal) outfit, set-up

2 *the organization of this year's
festival*
coordination, planning,
arrangement, running

organize VERB

1 *Elaine offered to organize the raffle.*
coordinate, plan, see to, set up, put
together, orchestrate

2 *organizing your old emails*
arrange, put in order, sort out, tidy
up, classify, collate

origin NOUN

1 *the origin of life on Earth*
beginning, start, creation, birth,
dawn, emergence, source, cause,
root
❚ **OPPOSITE** end

2 *a man who was proud of his humble
origins*
background, ancestry, descent,
parentage, pedigree, lineage, roots,
stock, birth, family, extraction

original ADJECTIVE

1 *the original inhabitants of Peru*
earliest, first, initial, native,
indigenous

a
b
c
d
e
f
g
h
i
j
k
l
m
n
o
p
q
r
s
t
u
v
w
x
y
z

》

2 *Is that an original painting or a copy?*
genuine, real, authentic, true, bona fide

3 *a film with an original storyline*
inventive, innovative, new, novel, fresh, creative, imaginative, unusual, unconventional, unorthodox, groundbreaking, pioneering

originate VERB

1 *a guitarist who originated his own style of playing*
invent, create, design, conceive, dream up, devise, formulate, develop, pioneer

2 *Rock music originated in the 1950s.*
begin, start, arise, emerge, emanate, spring up, crop up, stem

ornament NOUN
a hanging glass ornament
decoration, bauble, trinket, knick-knack

ornamental ADJECTIVE
ornamental garden furniture
decorative, fancy, ornate, ornamented

ornate ADJECTIVE
a mirror with an ornate frame
elaborate, decorative, ornamented, fancy, showy, fussy
┃ **OPPOSITE** plain

orthodox ADJECTIVE
the orthodox method of baking a cake
conventional, accepted, customary, usual, standard, traditional, regular, established, approved, recognized, official
┃ **OPPOSITES** unorthodox, unconventional

other ADJECTIVE

1 *more expensive than other brands*
alternative, different, separate, distinct

2 *I have some other questions.*
more, further, additional, supplementary, extra

outbreak NOUN

1 *a sudden outbreak of violence*
outburst, eruption, flare-up, upsurge (in), spate, wave, rash, flurry
▶ An outbreak of disease that spreads quickly is an **epidemic**.

2 *since the outbreak of the war*
beginning, start, onset, commencement

outburst NOUN
an outburst of grief and anger
explosion, eruption, outbreak, fit, storm, surge, outpouring

outcome NOUN
What was the outcome of your experiment?
result, consequence, effect, upshot, end result

outcry NOUN
a massive public outcry
protest, protestation, complaints, objections, uproar, fuss, furore, dissent
(informal) ructions, hullabaloo

outdated ADJECTIVE
SEE **out of date**

outdoor ADJECTIVE
an outdoor swimming pool
open-air, out of doors, outside, al fresco
┃ **OPPOSITE** indoor

outer ADJECTIVE
the Earth's outer crust
external, exterior, outside, outermost, outward
┃ **OPPOSITE** inner

outfit NOUN

1 *wearing a new outfit*
clothes, costume, suit, ensemble
(informal) get-up

2 *a video recording outfit*
equipment, apparatus, kit, suite
(informal) set-up, gear

outgoing ADJECTIVE

1 *the outgoing president*

a b c d e f g h i j k l m n o p q r s t u v w x y z

departing, retiring, leaving
┃OPPOSITE incoming

2 *an outgoing personality*
sociable, friendly, unreserved,
extrovert, convivial, gregarious
┃OPPOSITES shy, introverted

outing NOUN

a weekend outing to the zoo
trip, excursion, expedition, jaunt,
day out

outlaw NOUN

a band of outlaws
bandit, fugitive, wanted criminal,
highwayman, brigand

outlet NOUN

1 *The basin has an outlet for excess
water.*
opening, way out, exit, vent,
channel, conduit, duct
┃OPPOSITE inlet

2 *seeking an outlet for your talents*
avenue, channel, means of
expression

3 *a company with outlets throughout
Europe*
shop, store, branch, market

outline NOUN

1 *drawing the outline of a face*
profile, silhouette, shape, form,
contour

2 *giving a brief outline of the plot*
summary, sketch, synopsis, precis,
résumé, rough idea, rundown,
gist
┃IDIOM bare bones

outline VERB

*Storyboards are used to outline the
action of a film.*
summarize, sketch out,
rough out

outlook NOUN

1 *a clear outlook over the surrounding
countryside*
view, vista, prospect, panorama

2 *a positive outlook on life*
point of view, view, attitude, frame
of mind, standpoint, stance

3 *The outlook for tomorrow is bright
and sunny.*
forecast, prediction, prospect,
prognosis

out of date ADJECTIVE

1 *a design which now looks
out of date*
outdated, dated, old-fashioned,
outmoded, unfashionable,
antiquated, passé
(informal) old hat
┃IDIOMS *(informal)* behind the times,
past its sell-by date
┃OPPOSITES modern, up to date

2 *Your library card is out of date.*
expired, invalid, void, lapsed
┃OPPOSITES valid, current

outrage NOUN

1 *Such a waste of public money is
an outrage.*
disgrace, scandal, crime,
atrocity

2 *expressing outrage over the
newspaper article*
anger, fury, indignation, rage,
disgust, horror

outrage VERB

*Viewers were outraged by the
graphic images.*
shock, anger, enrage, infuriate,
scandalize, affront

outrageous ADJECTIVE

1 *an outrageous way to behave*
disgraceful, scandalous, shocking,
atrocious, appalling, monstrous,
shameful
┃OPPOSITES acceptable,
reasonable

2 *making outrageous claims*
exaggerated, inflated, excessive,
improbable, unreasonable,
ridiculous, preposterous

outset NOUN

*The plan was doomed from the
outset.*
start, beginning, starting point
┃IDIOM the word go

a
b
c
d
e
f
g
h
i
j
k
l
m
n
o
p
q
r
s
t
u
v
w
x
y
z

outside *NOUN*

> *The locket is engraved on the outside.*
> exterior, shell, surface, case, skin, facade
>
> **OPPOSITE** inside

outside *ADJECTIVE*

> *the outside wall of the castle*
> exterior, external, outer
>
> **OPPOSITE** inside

outsider *NOUN*

> *Jud still felt like an outsider who didn't belong.*
> newcomer, stranger, alien, foreigner, immigrant, incomer

outskirts *PLURAL NOUN*

> *living on the outskirts of town*
> edges, fringes, periphery, outer areas
>
> ▶ The outskirts of a large town or city are the **suburbs**.
>
> **OPPOSITE** centre

outspoken *ADJECTIVE*

> *an outspoken attack on the prime minister*
> frank, open, forthright, direct, candid, plain-spoken, blunt, straightforward

outstanding *ADJECTIVE*

> 1 *an outstanding performance*
> excellent, exceptional, first-rate, first-class, tremendous, marvellous, wonderful, superb, great, fine, superior, superlative, top-notch *(informal)* brilliant, fantastic, terrific, fabulous, sensational, super
>
> **OPPOSITES** ordinary, second-rate, unexceptional
>
> 2 *an outstanding bill*
> unpaid, unsettled, overdue, owing

outward or **outwards** *ADJECTIVE*

> *In outward appearance, Frankenstein's monster is grotesque.*
> external, exterior, outside, outer, surface, superficial
>
> **OPPOSITE** inward

oval *ADJECTIVE*

> *an oval orbit around the Sun*
> elliptical, egg-shaped

oven *NOUN*

> *a fan-assisted oven*
> cooker, stove
>
> ▶ A special oven for firing pottery is a **kiln**.

over *PREPOSITION*

> 1 *hovering over the ground*
> above, higher than, on top of
>
> 2 *The bus stop is just over the road.*
> across, on the other side of
>
> 3 *costing over a million pounds*
> more than, above, in excess of, upwards of
>
> 4 *an argument over money*
> about, concerning, regarding, relating to

overcast *ADJECTIVE*

> *The sky has been overcast all day.*
> cloudy, dull, grey, sunless, dark, leaden
>
> **FOR TIPS ON DESCRIBING THE WEATHER** SEE **weather**

overcome *VERB*

> 1 *overcoming a fear of heights*
> conquer, defeat, master, get the better of, prevail over *(informal)* lick
>
> 2 *Rescuers were overcome by the fumes.*
> overpower, overwhelm

overflow *VERB*

> *letting the bath water overflow*
> spill over, pour over, brim over, run over, flood

overgrown *ADJECTIVE*

> *The back garden was completely overgrown.*
> unkempt, untidy, tangled, weedy, wild

overhaul *VERB*

> *The engine has been completely overhauled.*
> service, repair, restore, recondition,

renovate, refit, refurbish

overhead ADVERB

A flock of geese flew overhead.
above, high up, in the sky,
above your head

overlook VERB

1 *You have overlooked one
important fact.*
miss, fail to see, fail to notice

2 *I am willing to overlook the error.*
disregard, ignore, pay no attention
to, forget about, pass over
▌ IDIOM turn a blind eye to

3 *The villa overlooks an olive grove.*
have a view of, look on to, look out
on, face

overpowering ADJECTIVE

*The smell of ammonia was
overpowering.*
overwhelming, powerful, strong,
intense, pungent, oppressive,
suffocating, unbearable

overrate VERB

*Do you think the film has been
overrated?*
overvalue, over praise, overestimate,
think too much of
▌ OPPOSITE underestimate

overrun VERB

Giant weeds had overrun the garden.
invade, take over, spread over,
swarm over, inundate, overwhelm

overt ADJECTIVE

*an overt hostility towards
each other*
open, undisguised, clear,
conspicuous, obvious, blatant
▌ OPPOSITE covert

overtake VERB

1 *We overtook the car in front.*
pass, go past, pull ahead of, leave
behind

2 *Texting has overtaken talking on
the phone.*
take over from, surpass, exceed, top,
outstrip, outshine, overshadow

overthrow VERB

*planning to overthrow the
government*
depose, bring down, topple,
defeat, remove, oust, drive out,
unseat

overturn VERB

1 *Our canoe overturned.*
capsize, turn over, keel over,
turn turtle

2 *I accidentally overturned a
milk jug.*
knock over, tip over, topple, upset,
upend

3 *The court overturned the judge's
decision.*
cancel, reverse, repeal, rescind,
revoke, overrule, veto

overwhelm VERB

1 *A tidal wave overwhelmed the
village.*
engulf, flood, inundate, submerge,
swallow up, bury

2 *The attackers overwhelmed us with
sheer numbers.*
defeat, overcome, overpower, crush,
trounce

3 *We have been overwhelmed by the
response.*
affect deeply, move deeply,
overcome
▌ IDIOMS bowl you over,
leave you speechless

overwhelming ADJECTIVE

1 *an overwhelming defeat*
decisive, devastating, crushing,
massive, monumental
▶ An overwhelming victory at an
election is a **landslide**.

2 *an overwhelming urge to laugh*
strong, powerful, overpowering,
irresistible, compelling

owe VERB

*How much do you owe
the bank?*
be in debt (to),
be in arrears (to)

a
b
c
d
e
f
g
h
i
j
k
l
m
n
o
p
q
r
s
t
u
v
w
x
y
z

owing ADJECTIVE

▷ **owing to**

The port prospered owing to its location.

because of, on account of, as a result of, in view of, thanks to, due to

own VERB

Do you own a video camera?

be the owner of, have, possess

▷ **own up to**

No one owned up to sending the email.

confess to, admit to, tell the truth about

⌐ IDIOM come clean about

Pp

pace NOUN

1 *Take a pace backwards.*
step, stride

2 *setting off at a fast pace*
speed, rate, velocity, tempo

pace VERB

pacing anxiously around the room
walk, step, stride, march, pound
SEE ALSO walk

pacify VERB

trying to pacify the audience
calm, quieten, soothe, humour,
appease
OPPOSITES anger, annoy

pack NOUN

1 *a pack of chewing gum*
packet, box, carton, package, bundle

2 *carrying a pack on your back*
bag, rucksack, backpack, haversack,
knapsack

3 *wild dogs which hunt in packs*
group, herd, troop, band

pack VERB

1 *packing a suitcase*
fill, load up

2 *packing everything away in the
cupboard*
stow, store, put away

3 *Over a hundred people packed into
the hall.*
cram, crowd, squeeze, stuff, jam,
wedge

package NOUN

posting a package overseas
parcel, packet, bundle

pad❶ NOUN

1 *a pad of cotton wool*
wad, dressing, cushion, pillow

2 *a writing pad*
notebook, notepad, jotter

pad VERB

a quilt padded with goose feathers
stuff, fill, pack, wad

▶ To put covers and padding on
furniture is to **upholster** it.

pad❷ VERB

padding along in bare feet
SEE **walk**

padding NOUN

a thick layer of padding
stuffing, filling, wadding, lining

▶ The covers and padding on furniture
is **upholstery**.

paddle VERB

children paddling in rock pools
splash about, dabble

▶ To walk through deep water is to
wade.

page NOUN

1 *The last page had been torn from
the book.*
sheet, leaf, folio

2 *I wrote two whole pages of notes.*
side

pain NOUN

1 *I felt a sharp pain in my ankle.*
soreness, ache, pang, stab,
throbbing, twinge

▶ A slight pain is **discomfort**.

2 *the pain of losing a friend*
anguish, agony, suffering, torment,
torture

pain VERB

It pains me to see you like this.
hurt, distress, upset, sadden, grieve,
perturb, trouble, torment

painful ADJECTIVE

1 *Is your knee still painful?*
sore, aching, tender, hurting,
smarting, stinging, throbbing
OPPOSITES painless, pain-free

》

2 *The photos brought back painful memories.*
unpleasant, upsetting, distressing, disagreeable, traumatic, agonizing, harrowing
❙ OPPOSITE pleasant

painstaking *ADJECTIVE*
painstaking attention to detail
meticulous, thorough, careful, conscientious, rigorous, assiduous, scrupulous, punctilious

paint *NOUN*
applying thick daubs of paint
colouring, pigment, dye, stain, tint

paint *VERB*
1 *Each wall was painted a different colour.*
colour, decorate, dye, stain, tint
2 *Cézanne often painted apples.*
depict, portray, represent

painting *NOUN*
a painting of a vase of sunflowers
picture, portrayal, depiction, representation, illustration, image, artwork, canvas
▶ A painting of a person or animal is a **portrait**.
▶ A painting by a famous artist of the past is an **old master**.
❙ SEE ALSO picture
FOR TERMS USED IN DRAWING AND PAINTING SEE drawing

pair *NOUN*
a pair of chopsticks
couple, duo, brace, set
▶ Two people who sing or play music together are a **duet**.
▶ Two people who work or play together are **partners** or a **partnership**.

palace *NOUN*
a palace which once belonged to the royal family
mansion, stately home, castle, chateau

pale *ADJECTIVE*
1 *Leonard's face suddenly turned pale.*
white, pallid, pasty, wan, ashen, sallow, anaemic, colourless
❙ IDIOM *(informal)* like death warmed up
▶ To go pale with fear is to **blanch**.
❙ OPPOSITES rosy-cheeked, flushed
FOR TIPS ON DESCRIBING FACES SEE face
2 *A pale shade of blue*
light, pastel, faint, subtle, faded, muted, bleached
❙ OPPOSITES bright, dark
FOR TIPS ON DESCRIBING COLOURS SEE colour
3 *The pale light of the stars*
dim, faint, low, weak, feeble
❙ OPPOSITES bright, strong
FOR TIPS ON DESCRIBING LIGHT SEE light❶

pamper *VERB*
Isabel didn't believe in pampering children.
spoil, indulge, cosset, mollycoddle, humour

pamphlet *NOUN*
a pamphlet about Internet safety
leaflet, booklet, brochure, circular

pan *NOUN*
heating milk in a pan
pot, saucepan, frying pan

panel *NOUN*
1 *a control panel*
board, unit, console, array
2 *judged by a panel of experts*
group, team, body, board, committee

pang *NOUN*
SEE **pain**

panic *NOUN*
People fled the streets in panic.
alarm, fear, fright, terror, trepidation, frenzy, hysteria
❙ OPPOSITE calm

panic *VERB*

> *If the alarm goes off, don't panic.*
> be alarmed, take fright, become hysterical, be panic-stricken
> *(informal)* freak out
> ❙ **IDIOMS** lose your head, go into a flat spin

pant *VERB*

> *Walter stood panting at the top of the stairs.*
> gasp, wheeze, puff, breathe heavily
> ❙ **IDIOM** huff and puff

pants *PLURAL NOUN*
> SEE **clothes**

paper *NOUN*

> **1** *a pad of recycled paper*
> ▶ A single piece of paper is a **leaf** or **sheet**.
> ▶ Paper and other writing materials are **stationery**.
> **2** *an article in the local paper*
> newspaper, journal, gazette, bulletin *(informal)* rag
> **3** *some important papers to sign*
> document, deed, certificate, paperwork

🛞 **WORD WEB**

> *some types of paper*
> blotting paper, card, cardboard, cartridge paper, crêpe paper, graph paper, greaseproof paper, papyrus, parchment, recycled paper, rice paper, tissue paper, toilet paper, tracing paper, wallpaper, wrapping paper, vellum

parade *NOUN*

> *a parade of street performers*
> procession, march, spectacle, show, display
> ▶ A parade of vehicles or people on horseback is a **cavalcade**.
> ▶ A parade of people in costume is a **pageant**.
> ▶ A display of military music and marching is a **tattoo**.

parade *VERB*

> **1** *A brass band paraded past our window.*
> march, troop, file
> **2** *Niki paraded round the room in her new dress.*
> strut, stride, swagger

parallel *ADJECTIVE*

> *two characters who have led parallel lives*
> similar, corresponding, comparable, analogous, matching, twin
> ❙ **OPPOSITES** divergent, contrasting

paralyse *VERB*

> **1** *Scorpions paralyse their prey with venom.*
> disable, immobilize, incapacitate, deaden, numb
> **2** *Jamal stood and stared, paralysed with fear.*
> immobilize, freeze, petrify

paramount *ADJECTIVE*

> *Secrecy is of paramount importance here.*
> most important, greatest, foremost, utmost, supreme, pre-eminent, chief, prime, primary, key, central *(informal)* number-one

parcel *NOUN*

> *receiving a parcel in the post*
> package, packet, box

parched *ADJECTIVE*

> **1** *a field of parched earth*
> dry, arid, baked, scorched, barren, sterile, waterless
> **2** *(informal) I need a drink of water — I'm parched!*
> thirsty, dry

pardon *VERB*

> **1** *Pardon me for asking.*
> excuse, forgive
> **2** *One of the conspirators was later pardoned.*
> exonerate, reprieve, let off, spare

parent *NOUN*
> SEE **family**

a
b
c
d
e
f
g
h
i
j
k
l
m
n
o
p
q
r
s
t
u
v
w
x
y
z

park _NOUN_

1 _a public park in central Tokyo_
recreation ground, public garden,
playground

2 _The house and surrounding park are
open to visitors._
parkland, gardens, grounds, estate

park _VERB_

You may park your car outside.
leave, position, station

parliament _NOUN_

_The Isle of Man has its own
parliament._
assembly, legislature, congress,
senate, chamber, house
❙ SEE ALSO **politics**

part _NOUN_

1 _the main parts of a computer_
component, constituent, bit,
element, module

2 _I missed the first part of the film._
section, piece, portion, bit, division,
instalment

3 _Our friends are moving to another
part of town._
area, district, region,
neighbourhood, sector, quarter

4 _acting the part of Gandalf_
character, role

part _VERB_

1 _The clouds parted to reveal a full
moon._
separate, divide, move apart, split
❙ OPPOSITE join

2 _We parted on friendly terms._
part company, say goodbye, take
your leave, go your separate ways
❙ OPPOSITE meet

▷ **part with**
_I couldn't bear to part with any of
my books._
discard, get rid of, give away,
dispense with, throw out, hand over,
surrender

partial _ADJECTIVE_

1 _The meal was only a partial success._
limited, imperfect,

incomplete, qualified
❙ OPPOSITES complete, total

2 _taking a partial view of the matter_
biased, prejudiced, partisan,
one-sided, slanted, skewed
❙ OPPOSITES unbiased, even-handed

▷ **be partial to**
_Claire has always been partial to
chocolate._
like, love, enjoy, be fond of,
be keen on
❙ IDIOMS have a soft spot for,
have a taste for

partially _ADVERB_

_The plan was only partially
successful._
to a certain extent, somewhat,
up to a point
❙ OPPOSITE wholly

participate _VERB_

_Twenty-two choirs will be
participating in the event._
take part, join in, be involved,
contribute, play a part
❙ IDIOM have a hand in

particle _NOUN_

a few particles of dust
speck, grain, fragment, bit, piece,
scrap, shred, sliver
❙ SEE ALSO **bit**

particular _ADJECTIVE_

1 _Do you have a particular date in
mind?_
specific, certain, distinct, definite,
exact, precise

2 _Please take particular care with the
china._
special, exceptional, unusual,
extreme, marked, notable

3 _My cat's very particular about her
food._
fussy, finicky, fastidious, faddy,
hard to please
(informal) choosy, picky, pernickety

particularly _ADVERB_

1 _The view is particularly good from
here._

especially, exceptionally, remarkably,
outstandingly, unusually,
uncommonly, uniquely

2 *I particularly asked for front-row
seats.*
specifically, explicitly, expressly,
specially, in particular

particulars PLURAL NOUN
*Inspector Hayes noted all the
particulars.*
details, facts, information,
circumstances

parting NOUN
a sad and tearful parting
farewell, departure, leave-taking,
goodbye, adieu

partition NOUN
1 *a partition between the two rooms*
room divider, screen, barrier, panel
2 *the partition of Europe after the war*
division, partitioning, dividing up,
breaking up, separation

partly ADVERB
*The accident was partly my own
fault.*
in part, to some extent, up to a
point, in some measure
┃ OPPOSITE entirely

partner NOUN
1 *partners in business*
colleague, associate, collaborator,
ally
2 *your relationship with your partner*
spouse, husband, wife, boyfriend,
girlfriend, lover
┃ IDIOMS other half, significant other
▶ An animal's partner is its **mate**.

partnership NOUN
a business partnership
association, collaboration, alliance,
union, affiliation, connection

party NOUN
1 *a party to celebrate New Year*
celebration, festivity, function,
gathering, reception
(informal) get-together, bash, do

2 *We were stuck behind a party of
tourists.*
group, band, crowd, company
(informal) bunch, gang
3 *forming a new political party*
alliance, association, faction, league

pass VERB
1 *We heard footsteps passing along the
corridor.*
go, advance, proceed, progress,
travel, make your way
2 *A crowd watched as the motorcade
passed.*
go by, move past
3 *We tried to pass the car in front.*
overtake, go past, go ahead of, leave
behind
4 *Three years passed before we met
again.*
go by, elapse, roll by
5 *Could you pass me the sugar, please?*
hand, give, deliver, offer, present
6 *Did you pass your audition?*
be successful in, get through,
succeed in
▶ To pass something easily is to **sail
through**, and to pass it barely is to
scrape through.
┃ OPPOSITE fail
7 *They passed the time playing cards.*
spend, occupy, fill, use, employ,
while away
8 *The pain will soon pass.*
go away, come to an end, disappear,
fade
┃ IDIOMS run its course, blow over
▷ **pass out**
*One of the runners passed out in the
heat.*
faint, lose consciousness, black out

pass NOUN
1 *You'll need a pass to go backstage.*
permit, licence, ticket
2 *a narrow mountain pass*
gap, gorge, ravine, canyon, valley

passage NOUN
1 *A secret passage leads to the inner
chamber.*

a
b
c
d
e
f
g
h
i
j
k
l
m
n
o
p
q
r
s
t
u
v
w
x
y
z

passageway, corridor, hallway, tunnel

2 *forcing a passage through the ice*
path, route, way

3 *after a long sea passage*
journey, voyage, crossing

4 *reading a passage from Shakespeare*
excerpt, extract, quotation, piece, section

5 *the passage of time*
passing, progress, advance

passenger NOUN
The bus has seats for 30 passengers.
traveller

▶ Passengers who travel regularly to work are **commuters**.

passion NOUN

1 *a story about youthful passion*
love, emotion, ardour, desire

2 *Cara has a passion for cooking.*
enthusiasm, eagerness, appetite, craving, urge, zest, thirst, mania, obsession

passionate ADJECTIVE

1 *giving a passionate speech*
emotional, intense, impassioned, heartfelt, vehement, fervent
❙ **OPPOSITE** unemotional

2 *a passionate collector of art*
eager, keen, avid, enthusiastic, fanatical
❙ **OPPOSITE** apathetic

passive ADJECTIVE
They say that Pisceans are passive by nature.
inactive, docile, submissive, compliant
❙ **OPPOSITE** active

past ADJECTIVE

1 *learning about past times*
earlier, former, previous, old, olden, bygone, of old, gone by
❙ **OPPOSITE** future

2 *The road has been closed for the past month.*
last, preceding, recent
❙ **OPPOSITE** next

past NOUN

1 *a historical novel set in the distant past*
past times, old days, olden days, days gone by
❙ **OPPOSITE** future

2 *I knew nothing about her colourful past.*
history, background, past life
❙ **OPPOSITE** future

paste NOUN

1 *Mix the powder with water to make a paste.*
pulp, mash, purée

2 *wallpaper paste*
glue, gum, adhesive

pastime NOUN
Ice skating is a popular winter pastime.
activity, hobby, recreation, pursuit, amusement, interest, diversion, entertainment, relaxation, game, sport

pasture NOUN
sheep grazing on hill pastures
grassland, field, meadow

pat VERB
Ellen reached down and patted the horse's neck.
tap, touch, stroke, pet

▶ To touch something quickly and lightly is to **dab** it.

▶ To stroke someone with an open hand is to **caress** them.

pat NOUN
a reassuring pat on the shoulder
tap, touch, stroke, pet

patch NOUN

1 *a damp patch on the carpet*
mark, area, spot, blotch, stain, blemish

2 *a vegetable patch*
plot, area, piece, strip, parcel, bed, allotment
(North American) lot

3 *(informal) going through a difficult patch*

time, period, spell, phase

patch *VERB*

patching a hole in your jeans
mend, repair, stitch up, darn

patchy *ADJECTIVE*

patchy outbreaks of rain
irregular, uneven, varying,
inconsistent, unpredictable

path *NOUN*

1 *a winding path through the forest*
pathway, track, trail, footpath, walk,
walkway, lane

▶ A path for horse-riding is a
bridleway.

▶ A path along a canal is a **towpath**.

2 *the path of a comet*
course, route, way, trajectory

3 *the best path to follow*
course of action, approach, method,
line, avenue, tack

pathetic *ADJECTIVE*

1 *a pathetic little creature bundled in
rags*
pitiful, wretched, sorry,
heartbreaking, moving, touching,
plaintive

2 *(informal) What a pathetic excuse!*
hopeless, useless, weak, feeble,
inadequate, incompetent

patience *NOUN*

*Bird-watching requires great
patience.*
perseverance, persistence,
endurance, tenacity, staying power,
forbearance, tolerance, restraint

❙ OPPOSITE impatience

patient *ADJECTIVE*

1 *Please be patient while we connect
you.*
calm, composed, uncomplaining,
forbearing, tolerant, understanding,
long-suffering

2 *It took hours of patient work to
restore the painting.*
persevering, persistent, unhurried,
untiring, dogged, determined,
tenacious

❙ OPPOSITE impatient

patrol *VERB*

*A security guard patrols the grounds
at night.*
guard, keep watch over,
stand guard over, do the rounds of,
inspect

patrol *NOUN*

an armed military patrol
guard, force, party, squad, detail,
detachment

patter *NOUN, VERB*

FOR TIPS ON DESCRIBING SOUNDS SEE
sound❶

pattern *NOUN*

1 *a dress with a floral pattern*
design, decoration, motif

2 *a strange pattern of behaviour*
system, structure, scheme, plan,
arrangement

3 *following the pattern set by previous
authors*
example, model, standard, norm

 WORD WEB

some types of pattern
checked, criss-cross, dotted,
floral or flowery, geometric,
gingham, herringbone, mosaic,
paisley, pinstriped, polka dot,
spiral, spotted or spotty, striped
or stripy, swirling, symmetrical,
tartan, wavy, whorled, zigzag

▶ A pattern can be **repeating** or
non-repeating.

pause *NOUN*

*There was a pause while the
computer restarted.*
break, gap, halt, rest, lull, stop, wait,
interruption, stoppage, respite
(informal) let-up

▶ A pause in the middle of a
performance is an **interlude** or
interval.

▶ A pause in the middle of a cinema
film is an **intermission**.

▶ A pause for rest is a **breathing
space** or *(informal)* **breather**.

pause *VERB*

1 *I paused at the door before knocking.*
hesitate, wait, delay, hang back

2 *The speaker paused to sip some water.*
halt, stop, break off, rest,
take a break
(informal) take a breather

paw *NOUN*
SEE **foot**

pay *VERB*

1 *How much did you pay for your new phone?*
spend, give out, hand over
(informal) fork out, shell out,
cough up

2 *Who's going to pay the bill?*
pay off, repay, settle, clear, discharge

3 *Sometimes it pays to complain.*
be worthwhile, be beneficial, be to
your advantage, be profitable

4 *I'll make you pay for this!*
suffer

pay *NOUN*

an annual increase in pay
wages, salary, income, earnings,
revenue, remuneration

► A payment for doing a single job is
a **fee**.

payment *NOUN*

1 *the payment of all their debts*
settlement, clearance, discharge,
remittance

2 *She never received any payment for her work.*
earnings, pay, income, fee, revenue,
remuneration, reimbursement

► A voluntary payment to a charity is a
contribution or **donation**.

► Money that is paid back to you is a
refund.

peace *NOUN*

1 *campaigning for world peace*
agreement, harmony, friendliness,
truce, ceasefire

❙ OPPOSITES war, conflict

2 *enjoying the peace of the countryside*
calmness, peacefulness, quiet,
tranquillity, stillness, serenity,
silence, hush

❙ OPPOSITES noise, bustle

peaceful *ADJECTIVE*

a peaceful spot by the water's edge
calm, quiet, relaxing, tranquil,
restful, serene, undisturbed,
untroubled, gentle, placid, soothing,
still

❙ OPPOSITES noisy, busy

peak *NOUN*

1 *snow-capped mountain peaks*
summit, cap, crest, crown, pinnacle,
top, tip, point

2 *She is at the peak of her career as a gymnast.*
top, height, high point, climax,
pinnacle, culmination, apex, zenith

peculiar *ADJECTIVE*

1 *Does this tea smell peculiar to you?*
strange, unusual, odd, curious,
puzzling, extraordinary, abnormal,
funny, weird, bizarre

❙ OPPOSITES normal, ordinary

2 *The twins had developed their own peculiar language.*
characteristic, distinctive, individual,
particular, personal, special, unique,
identifiable

pedigree *NOUN*

a racehorse with an impressive pedigree
ancestry, lineage, descent,
bloodline, parentage, background

peek *VERB*
SEE **look**

peel *NOUN*

a strip of lemon peel
rind, skin, zest

peel *VERB*

1 *peeling a banana*
pare, skin, shell

2 *You can see the paintwork starting to peel.*
fall off, flake off, be shed, slough off

a b c d e f g h i j k l m n o p q r s t u v w x y z

peep *VERB*
1 *peeping through a keyhole*
peek, glance, squint
2 *The sun was just peeping out from the clouds.*
emerge, appear, issue, come into view

peer *VERB*
SEE **look**

peg *NOUN*
I hung my coat and scarf on the peg.
hook, nail, pin

pelt *VERB*
1 *The MP was jeered and pelted with rotten fruit.*
attack, bombard, shower
SEE ALSO throw
2 *Two lads came pelting down the street.*
SEE **run**
3 *It's still pelting down outside.*
rain hard, pour, teem

pen¹ *NOUN*
a ballpoint pen
SEE **writing**

pen² *NOUN*
a sheep pen
enclosure, fold

penalize *VERB*
penalized for committing a foul
punish, discipline

penalty *NOUN*
The penalty for murder is life imprisonment.
punishment, sanction, sentence, fine
OPPOSITE reward

penetrate *VERB*
1 *The bullet had penetrated the man's chest.*
pierce, puncture, perforate, bore through, enter
2 *Your mission is to penetrate deep into enemy territory.*
get through, enter, infiltrate

penetrating *ADJECTIVE*
1 *a penetrating insight*
perceptive, insightful, sharp, astute, keen
2 *a penetrating gaze*
piercing, searching, probing, intent, keen, sharp

penniless *ADJECTIVE*
The family was left penniless and homeless.
poor, impoverished, poverty-stricken, destitute
(formal) in penury
OPPOSITE rich

people *PLURAL NOUN*
1 *How many people are you inviting?*
persons, individuals, humans, human beings
(informal) folk
2 *the people of the United States*
population, citizens, populace, public, inhabitants, society, nation, race

perceive *VERB*
1 *I perceived a change in her voice.*
notice, become aware of, recognize, detect, discern, make out
2 *Skateboarding is often perceived as dangerous.*
regard, view, consider, look on, think of

perception *NOUN*
1 *Frank displayed his usual lack of perception.*
insight, perceptiveness, understanding, sensitivity
2 *common perceptions about men and women*
view, belief, notion, idea, conception, impression

perceptive *ADJECTIVE*
1 *Not very perceptive today, are you?*
observant, sharp, quick, alert
IDIOM *(informal)* on the ball
OPPOSITES unobservant, obtuse
2 *a perceptive analysis of Shakespeare's plays*

》

a
b
c
d
e
f
g
h
i
j
k
l
m
n
o
p
q
r
s
t
u
v
w
x
y
z

insightful, penetrating, shrewd,
astute, keen, intelligent

perch *VERB*
a robin perching on a fence
sit, settle, rest, balance

percussion *NOUN*
SEE **music**

perfect *ADJECTIVE*
1 *The guitar is in perfect condition.*
faultless, flawless, intact,
undamaged, complete, whole, mint,
pristine, immaculate
(informal) tip-top
▎ **OPPOSITES** imperfect, flawed
2 *a perfect copy of your signature*
exact, faithful, accurate, precise,
correct
3 *That dress is perfect on you.*
ideal, just right
(informal) spot on, just the job
4 *a letter from a perfect stranger*
complete, absolute, total, utter

perfect *VERB*
*Jamie spent years perfecting his
recipe.*
make perfect, improve, refine,
polish, hone, fine-tune

perfectly *ADVERB*
1 *Please stand perfectly still.*
completely, absolutely, totally,
utterly, entirely, wholly, altogether
2 *The dress fits perfectly.*
exactly, superbly, excellently,
flawlessly, immaculately,
to perfection

perform *VERB*
1 *Do you enjoy performing on stage?*
act, appear, play, dance, sing
2 *performing a play about bullying*
present, stage, produce, put on
3 *The robot is programmed to perform
simple tasks.*
do, carry out, execute, fulfil,
accomplish

performance *NOUN*
1 *tickets for the evening performance*
show, production, presentation,

showing, screening, staging,
concert, recital
2 *improving the team's performance*
effort, work, endeavour, exertion,
behaviour, conduct

performer *NOUN*
a group of street performers
actor, actress, musician, singer,
dancer, artist, entertainer, player
▎ SEE ALSO **drama**, **music**

perfume *NOUN*
the heady perfume of lilies
smell, scent, fragrance, aroma,
bouquet
FOR TIPS ON DESCRIBING SMELLS SEE
smell *NOUN*

perhaps *ADVERB*
Perhaps no one will notice.
maybe, possibly, conceivably, for all
you know
▎ **OPPOSITE** definitely

peril *NOUN*
the perils of life in the Old West
danger, hazard, risk, menace, threat,
jeopardy
▎ **OPPOSITE** safety

perimeter *NOUN*
*The dotted line marks the perimeter
of the old city.*
edge, border, boundary, limits,
bounds
▶ The distance round the edge of
something is the **circumference**.

period *NOUN*
1 *a long period of drought*
time, span, interval, spell, stretch,
phase
2 *rocks which date from the Jurassic
Period*
age, era, epoch

perish *VERB*
1 *Without sunlight, the plants will
perish.*
die, be killed, pass away
2 *Most fruit perishes quickly.*
go bad, rot, decay, spoil, decompose

a
b
c
d
e
f
g
h
i
j
k
l
m
n
o
p
q
r
s
t
u
v
w
x
y
z

permanent ADJECTIVE

1 suffering permanent brain damage
lasting, long-lasting, long-term,
irreparable, irreversible, everlasting,
enduring

2 Pollution is a permanent problem in
the city.
never-ending, perpetual, persistent,
chronic, perennial

3 offering stray dogs a permanent
home
fixed, long-term, stable, secure
❙ OPPOSITE temporary

permission NOUN

Do you have permission to download
the file?
authorization, consent, agreement,
approval, leave, licence
(informal) go-ahead, say-so

permit VERB

The gallery doesn't permit
photographs.
allow, consent to, give permission
for, authorize, license, grant,
sanction

permit NOUN

You need a permit to fish in the river.
licence, pass, ticket

perpetual ADJECTIVE

Libby's life was a perpetual round of
parties.
constant, continual, continuous,
never-ending, non-stop, endless,
ceaseless, incessant, persistent,
unceasing, unending
❙ OPPOSITES intermittent, short-lived

perplexing ADJECTIVE

one of the most perplexing problems
in science
puzzling, confusing, bewildering,
baffling, mystifying

persecute VERB

1 Galileo and his followers were
persecuted for their beliefs.
oppress, discriminate against,
victimize

2 an innocent man who was persecuted
by the media
harass, hound, intimidate, bully,
pick on, pester, torment

persevere VERB

The rescuers persevered despite the
conditions.
continue, carry on, keep going,
persist
(informal) keep at it, stick at it
❙ OPPOSITE give up

persist VERB

If the pain persists, you should see a
doctor.
continue, carry on, last, linger,
remain, endure
❙ OPPOSITES stop, cease

▷ **persist in**
Why do you persist in arguing
with me?
keep on, insist on
❙ OPPOSITE give up

persistent ADJECTIVE

1 a persistent drip from the tap
constant, continual, incessant,
never-ending, steady, non-stop
❙ OPPOSITE intermittent

2 The interviewer was very persistent.
determined, persevering,
insistent, tenacious, obstinate,
stubborn, dogged, resolute,
unrelenting, tireless,
indefatigable

person NOUN

Not a single person has replied to my
email.
individual, human being, man,
woman, character, soul

personal ADJECTIVE

1 The book is based on her personal
experience.
own, individual, particular,
characteristic, distinctive, unique

2 The contents of the letter are
personal.
confidential, private, secret,
intimate

a
b
c
d
e
f
g
h
i
j
k
l
m
n
o
p
q
r
s
t
u
v
w
x
y
z

personality NOUN

1 *I don't like her abrasive personality.*
character, nature, disposition, temperament, make-up

2 *a well-known TV personality*
celebrity, star, VIP
(*informal*) celeb

WRITING TIPS

describing personality

His character was decided. He was the proudest, most disagreeable man in the world, and every body hoped that he would never come there again.
— *Jane Austen, Pride and Prejudice*

some personality traits

adaptable, assertive, bouncy, brave, bubbly, cheerful, compassionate, confident, cooperative, determined, diligent, easy-going, fearless, feisty, frank, friendly, generous, good-natured, gregarious, helpful, honest, honourable, imaginative, irrepressible, kind-hearted, kindly, (*informal*) laid-back, likeable, lovable, lively, optimistic, outgoing, outspoken, passionate, personable, phlegmatic, reliable, reserved, resilient, resolute, resourceful, responsible, retiring, self-assured, sensitive, shy, sincere, sociable, straightforward, strong-willed, thoughtful, (*informal*) unflappable, (*informal*) upbeat, vivacious, warm

negative traits

abrasive, aggressive, aloof, argumentative, arrogant, belligerent, brash, cold, complacent, conceited, cowardly, cynical, disagreeable, domineering, (*informal*) downbeat, envious, fearful, gullible, haughty, highly strung, impetuous, irresponsible, jealous, manipulative, moody, nervous, obstinate, overbearing, pessimistic, pompous, priggish, proud, quarrelsome, resentful, rude, secretive, selfish, self-centred, self-righteous, self-satisfied, snobbish, (*informal*) snooty, spiteful, (*informal*) stand-offish, stubborn, (*informal*) stuck-up, sulky, surly, taciturn, thick-skinned, thoughtless, timid, truculent, unreasonable, unsociable, (*informal*) uptight, vain, vengeful, volatile, weak-willed

perspective NOUN

Try seeing things from a different perspective.
viewpoint, point of view, standpoint, position, outlook, angle, stance

persuade VERB

I persuaded my friends to sign the petition.
convince, coax, induce, talk into, prevail on, win over, bring round
OPPOSITE dissuade

persuasion NOUN

Jack needed little persuasion to come with us.
convincing, coaxing, urging, encouragement, inducement, enticement

persuasive ADJECTIVE

She used some very persuasive arguments.
convincing, compelling, effective, telling, strong, powerful, forceful, valid, sound, cogent
OPPOSITE unconvincing

pessimistic ADJECTIVE

Are you pessimistic about the future of the planet?

a b c d e f g h i j k l m n o p q r s t u v w x y z

negative, gloomy, downbeat,
despairing, unhopeful, resigned,
cynical

OPPOSITES optimistic, hopeful

pest *NOUN*

1 *getting rid of garden pests*
▶ Pests in general are **vermin**.
▶ A pest which lives on or in another
creature is a **parasite**.
▶ A chemical used to kill harmful pests
is a **pesticide**.

2 *(informal) My cousin can be a pest at
times.*
nuisance, bother, annoyance

IDIOM *(informal)* pain in the neck

pester *VERB*

*Please stop pestering me with
questions!*
annoy, bother, trouble, harass,
badger, hound, nag, plague
(informal) bug, hassle

pet *ADJECTIVE*

1 *Which US president kept a pet
alligator in the White House?*
tame, domesticated, house-trained

2 *Jeff told us his pet theory about
UFOs.*
favourite, favoured, cherished,
personal

petrified *ADJECTIVE*

*I stood for a moment petrified, then
turned and fled.*
terrified, horrified, terror-struck,
paralysed, frozen

IDIOM rooted to the spot

petty *ADJECTIVE*

1 *a list of petty rules and regulations*
minor, trivial, trifling, unimportant,
insignificant, inconsequential,
footling

OPPOSITE important

2 *a petty act of revenge*
small-minded, mean, mean-spirited,
spiteful, ungracious

phase *NOUN*

the start of a new phase in my life
period, time, stage, step,
spell, episode, chapter

phenomenal *ADJECTIVE*

*Daryl was blessed with a
phenomenal memory.*
exceptional, remarkable,
extraordinary, outstanding,
incredible, miraculous, amazing,
astonishing, astounding,
staggering, stupendous,
awesome

OPPOSITE ordinary

phenomenon *NOUN*

1 *The Northern Lights are a natural
phenomenon.*
happening, occurrence, event, fact

2 *The Beatles became a worldwide
phenomenon.*
sensation, wonder, marvel,
prodigy

phobia *NOUN*

 WORD WEB

some types of phobia
acrophobia (fear of heights)
aerophobia (fear of flying)
agoraphobia (fear of open or
crowded spaces)
ailurophobia (fear of cats)
arachnophobia (fear of spiders)
brontophobia (fear of
thunderstorms)
claustrophobia (fear of enclosed
spaces)
cynophobia (fear of dogs)
glossophobia
(fear of public speaking)
mysophobia (fear of germs
and dirt)
necrophobia (fear of death or
the dead)
ophidiophobia (fear of snakes)
phasmophobia (fear of ghosts)
scotophobia (fear of the dark)
trypanophobia (fear of
injections)
xenophobia (fear or dislike of
foreigners)

phone *VERB*

I'll phone you later this evening.
telephone, call, ring, give someone
a call
(informal) give someone a ring, give
someone a bell

photograph *NOUN*

*an old photograph of my great
grandmother*
photo, picture, snap, snapshot, shot,
print, still

photograph *VERB*

photographing the night sky
take a picture of, shoot, snap, film

photography *NOUN*

 WORD WEB

some types of camera
camcorder, cine, compact,
digital, disposable or single-use,
phonecam, pinhole,
SLR (single lens reflex), video,
webcam, (*historical*) box Brownie

parts of a camera
aperture, body, flash, lens,
shutter, viewfinder

*other terms used in
photography*
camera shake, dark room,
developing, exposure, focus,
megapixel, negative, point and
shoot, slide or transparency,
telephoto, tripod, wide-angle,
zoom

▌SEE ALSO **film**

phrase *NOUN*

*a dictionary of common English
phrases*
expression, saying, construction,
idiom

phrase *VERB*

I tried to phrase my email carefully.
express, put into words, formulate,
couch, frame

physical *ADJECTIVE*

1 *The aliens disliked close physical
contact.*
bodily, corporeal, corporal, fleshly
▌OPPOSITES mental, spiritual

2 *Is there physical proof that dark
matter exists?*
material, concrete, solid, substantial,
tangible, visible

pick *VERB*

1 *picking wild flowers in the woods*
pluck, gather, collect, cut, harvest

2 *picking the players for the squad*
choose, select, decide on, settle on,
opt for, single out, nominate, elect

3 *picking the polish off her fingernails*
pull off, scrape, remove, extract

▷ **pick on**
Why are they always picking on me?
victimize, bully, persecute, torment,
single out

▷ **pick up**
Sales have started to pick up.
improve, recover, rally, bounce back,
perk up

▷ **pick something up**

1 *It took two men to pick up the
wardrobe.*
lift, raise, hoist

2 *I'll pick up some milk on the way
home.*
get, collect, fetch, call for

3 *You'll pick up the language in no
time.*
acquire, learn

4 *picking up a distress signal*
receive, detect, hear

picture *NOUN*

1 *looking at pictures in a magazine*
illustration, image, print, painting,
drawing, sketch

▶ A picture which represents a
particular person is a **portrait**.

▶ A picture which represents the artist
himself or herself is a **self-portrait**.

▶ A picture which represents a group
of objects is a **still life**.

▶ A picture which represents a country

scene is a **landscape**.

▶ Pictures on a computer are **graphics**.

❙ SEE ALSO **painting**

2 *taking pictures of the sights*
photograph, photo, snapshot, snap

3 *the popular picture of scientists as boffins*
impression, image, view, idea, notion, concept

picture VERB

1 *the actress who is pictured on the front cover*
depict, illustrate, represent, show, portray, paint, photograph

2 *Can you picture what's happening in the story?*
imagine, visualize

❙ IDIOM see in your mind's eye

picturesque ADJECTIVE

1 *a picturesque thatched cottage*
attractive, pretty, charming, quaint, scenic

❙ OPPOSITE ugly

2 *a picturesque account of her travels*
colourful, descriptive, imaginative, expressive, lively, poetic, vivid

piece NOUN

1 *collecting pieces of driftwood*
bar, block, length, stick, chunk, lump, hunk, bit, chip, fragment, particle, scrap, shred

2 *Who wants the last piece of chocolate?*
bit, portion, part, section, segment, share, slice

3 *a single piece of clothing*
item, article

4 *There are 1000 pieces in this jigsaw.*
part, element, unit, component, constituent

5 *an interesting piece in today's paper*
article, item, report, feature

pier NOUN

fishing boats tied up at the pier
quay, wharf, jetty, landing stage

pierce VERB

A mosquito pierces the skin of its victim.
penetrate, perforate, puncture, bore through, prick, stab, spear, spike

▶ To pierce someone with a spear or spike is to **impale** them.

piercing ADJECTIVE

1 *the piercing wail of an air raid siren*
high-pitched, shrill, strident, penetrating, ear-splitting, deafening

2 *piercing blue eyes*
penetrating, intense, sharp, keen, searching, probing

pig NOUN

a farm rearing free-range pigs

▶ An old word for pigs is **swine**.

▶ A wild pig is a **wild boar**.

▶ A male pig is a **boar** or **hog**.

▶ A female pig is a **sow**.

▶ A young pig is a **piglet**.

▶ A family of piglets is a **litter**.

▶ The smallest piglet in a litter is the **runt**.

FOR TIPS ON DESCRIBING ANIMALS SEE **animal**

pile NOUN

1 *a pile of old newspapers*
heap, stack, mound, mass, collection, accumulation, stockpile, hoard

2 *(informal) winning a pile of money in the lottery*
plenty, a lot, a great deal
(informal) lots, masses, loads, a stack, a slew, a ton, a shedload

pile VERB

1 *Just pile the dirty dishes in the sink.*
heap, stack

2 *We all piled into the minibus.*
crowd, cram, squeeze, pack

▷ **pile up**
The bills are beginning to pile up.
build up, mount up, accumulate, multiply, grow

a
b
c
d
e
f
g
h
i
j
k
l
m
n
o
p
q
r
s
t
u
v
w
x
y
z

pill NOUN

Take one pill every four hours.
tablet, capsule, pellet, lozenge

pillar NOUN

a dome supported by marble pillars
column, post, support, upright, pier,
prop

pillow NOUN

a herb pillow stuffed with lavender
cushion, pad

▶ A long kind of pillow is a **bolster**.

pilot NOUN

SEE **aircraft**

pilot VERB

a game in which you pilot a
spacecraft
navigate, steer, guide, control,
manoeuvre, captain, fly, sail
(informal) skipper

pimple NOUN

a pimple on your chin
spot, boil, pustule
(informal) zit

pin NOUN

a shawl fastened with a pin
brooch, fastener, tack, staple, nail

pin VERB

1 pinning a list on the noticeboard
attach, fasten, secure, tack, nail

2 pinning the suspect to the ground
hold down, press, pinion

pinch VERB

1 Pinch the dough between your
fingers.
nip, squeeze, press, tweak, grip

2 (British informal) Who pinched my
calculator?
steal, take, snatch, pilfer
(informal) swipe, lift, make off with
(British informal) nick

pinch NOUN

1 I felt a sudden pinch on my leg.
nip, squeeze, tweak

2 Add a pinch of cayenne pepper.
SEE **bit**

pine VERB

We left Adam pining in his bedroom.
mope, languish, sicken, waste away

▷ **pine for**

Are you still pining for your old
girlfriend?
long for, yearn for, miss, crave,
hanker after

[IDIOM] carry a torch for

ping NOUN, VERB

FOR TIPS ON DESCRIBING SOUNDS SEE
sound❶

pink ADJECTIVE, NOUN

 WORD WEB

some shades of pink
coral, fuchsia, peach, puce, rose,
salmon

FOR TIPS ON DESCRIBING COLOURS
SEE **colour**

pip NOUN

Remove the pips from the grapes.
seed

▶ To remove pips from fruit is to
deseed it.

pipe NOUN

a drainage pipe
tube, duct, conduit, channel, hose

▶ A water pipe in the street for
attaching to a fire hose is a **hydrant**.

▶ A pipe for carrying oil or gas over
long distances is a **pipeline**.

▶ The system of water pipes in a house
is the **plumbing**.

pipe VERB

1 The groove in the rock was used to
pipe rain water.
carry, convey, run, channel, funnel,
siphon

2 The radio is piped into every hotel
room.
transmit, relay, feed

3 piping a tune on a tin whistle
play, blow, sound, whistle

pirate *NOUN*

    a film about pirates in the Caribbean
    buccaneer, marauder, freebooter

pit *NOUN*

    1 *a deep pit formed by a meteor*
    hole, crater, cavity, hollow,
    depression, pothole, chasm, abyss

    2 *a disused coal pit*
    mine, colliery, quarry

pitch *NOUN*

    1 *a football pitch*
    ground, field, playing field, park

    2 *Dogs can hear at a higher pitch than
    humans.*
    tone, frequency, modulation

    3 *a roof with a steep pitch*
    slope, slant, gradient, incline, angle,
    tilt

pitch *VERB*

    1 *pitching pebbles into a pond*
    throw, toss, fling, hurl, sling, cast,
    lob
    (informal) chuck

    2 *a perfect place to pitch a tent*
    erect, put up, set up

    3 *pitching headlong into the water*
    plunge, dive, drop, topple, plummet

    4 *Our vehicle pitched about in the high
    winds.*
    lurch, toss, rock, roll, reel

pitfall *NOUN*

    *Time travel may have some serious
    pitfalls.*
    difficulty, problem, hazard, danger,
    snag, catch, trap

pitiful *ADJECTIVE*

    1 *a pitiful cry for help*
    sad, sorrowful, mournful, pathetic,
    plaintive, piteous, heart-rending,
    moving, touching

    2 *a pitiful excuse*
    feeble, weak, pathetic, hopeless,
    useless, inadequate, incompetent

pity *NOUN*

    *showing no pity towards their
    captives*
    mercy, compassion, sympathy,
    humanity, kindness, concern,
    feeling

    ▌**OPPOSITE** cruelty

  ▷ **a pity**

    It's a pity you have to leave so soon.
    a shame, unfortunate, bad luck,
    too bad

pity *VERB*

    I pity anyone who has to live there.
    feel sorry for, feel for, sympathize
    with, take pity on,
    commiserate with

pivot *NOUN*

    *The wheel on the barrow acts as a
    pivot.*

  ▶ The point on which a lever turns is
    the **fulcrum**.

  ▶ The point on which a spinning object
    turns is its **axis**.

  ▶ The point on which a wheel turns is
    the **axle** or **hub**.

place *NOUN*

    1 *Is this a good place to park?*
    site, spot, location, position,
    situation, venue

    2 *looking for a quiet place to live*
    area, district, locality,
    neighbourhood, region, vicinity,
    locale

    3 *Save me a place on the bus.*
    seat, space

    4 *being offered a place as a trainee*
    job, position, post, appointment

    5 *Let's go back to my place.*
    home, house, flat, apartment,
    quarters
    (informal) pad

  ▷ **in place of**

    You can use honey in place of sugar.
    instead of, rather than, in exchange
    for, in lieu of, in someone's stead

place *VERB*

    1 *a table placed next to the window*
    locate, situate, position, station

    2 *Place the test tube carefully
    in a rack.*
    put down, set down, lay, deposit,
    stand, leave

a
b
c
d
e
f
g
h
i
j
k
l
m
n
o
p
q
r
s
t
u
v
w
x
y
z

placid *ADJECTIVE*

  1 *a Shetland pony with a placid nature*
  calm, composed, unexcitable, even-tempered
  OPPOSITE excitable

  2 *The sea was placid at that time of the day.*
  calm, quiet, tranquil, peaceful, undisturbed, unruffled
  OPPOSITE stormy

plague *NOUN*

  1 *Millions of people died of the plague.*
  pestilence, epidemic, pandemic, contagion, outbreak

  2 *a plague of wasps in late summer*
  invasion, infestation, swarm

plague *VERB*

  1 *Stop plaguing me with questions!*
  pester, bother, annoy, badger, harass, hound
  (informal) nag, hassle, bug

  2 *I've been plagued by bad luck recently.*
  afflict, beset, trouble, torment, dog, curse, bedevil

plain *ADJECTIVE*

  1 *a room fitted with plain furnishings*
  simple, modest, basic, unelaborate
  OPPOSITES elaborate, ornate

  2 *Jodie was rather plain compared with her sister.*
  unattractive, ordinary, unprepossessing
  OPPOSITE attractive

  3 *It is plain to me that you are not interested.*
  clear, evident, obvious, apparent, manifest, unmistakable
  OPPOSITE unclear

  4 *speaking in very plain terms*
  direct, frank, candid, blunt, honest, sincere, straightforward, forthright, outspoken, unequivocal
  OPPOSITE obscure

plain *NOUN*

  the wide open plains of Wyoming
  grassland, prairie, pampas, savannah, steppe, veld

plan *NOUN*

  1 *We'd better come up with a plan quickly!*
  scheme, strategy, proposal, idea, suggestion, proposition, stratagem
  ▶ A plan to do something bad is a **plot**.

  2 *the plans for the new annexe*
  design, diagram, chart, map, drawing, blueprint

plan *VERB*

  1 *Some of us are planning a surprise party.*
  organize, arrange, devise, design, scheme, plot, work out, map out, formulate

  2 *What do you plan to do next?*
  aim, intend, propose, mean

plane *NOUN*

  SEE **aircraft**

planet *NOUN*

  a planet beyond our solar system
  world

 WORD WEB

  the planets of our solar system (in order from the Sun)
  Mercury, Venus, Earth, Mars, Jupiter, Saturn, Uranus, Neptune

  ▶ A related adjective is **planetary**.
  planetary exploration

  ▶ The four planets closest to the Sun are the **inner planets**, and those farthest from the Sun are the **outer planets**.

  ▶ The planets Jupiter, Saturn, Uranus, and Neptune are **gaseous** planets or **gas giants**.

  ▶ Pluto is classified as a **dwarf planet**.

  ▶ The path followed by a planet is its **orbit**.

  ▶ Minor planets orbiting the Sun are **asteroids** or **planetoids**.

  ▶ Something which orbits a planet is a **satellite**.

a b c d e f g h i j k l m n o p q r s t u v w x y z

▶ The Earth's large satellite is the
Moon.

❙ SEE ALSO space

plant *NOUN*

plants which are native to Australia
vegetation, greenery, plantlife

▶ The plants of a particular place or
time are its **flora**.

WORD WEB

some types of plant
algae, bush, cactus, cereal,
evergreen, fern, flower, fungus,
grass, herb, house plant, lichen,
moss, pot plant, shrub, tree,
vegetable, vine, weed, wildflower

**❙ SEE ALSO flower, fruit, herb,
tree, vegetable**

parts of a plant
bloom, blossom, branch, bud,
flower, fruit, leaf, petal, pod,
root, shoot, stalk, stem, trunk,
twig

▶ A young plant is a **seedling**.

▶ A piece cut off a plant to form a
new plant is a **cutting**.

▶ The scientific study of plants and
flowers is **botany**.

▶ A related adjective is **botanical**.
an exhibition of botanical art

▶ The study of plants and animals
is **natural history** and a person
who studies them is a **naturalist**.

plant *VERB*

1 *planting seeds for next year's crop*
sow, put in the ground

▶ To move a growing plant to a new
position is to **transplant** it.

2 *Plant your feet firmly on the ground.*
place, set, position
(informal) plonk

plaster *NOUN*

putting a plaster on your finger
dressing, sticking plaster, bandage

plate *NOUN*

1 *a serving plate*
dish, platter, salver

2 *The design is first etched on a metal
plate.*
panel, sheet, slab

3 *a full-page colour plate*
illustration, picture, photograph,
print

platform *NOUN*

making a speech from the platform
dais, podium, stage, stand, rostrum

play *VERB*

1 *children playing in the street*
amuse yourself, have fun, romp
about

2 *Do you like playing basketball?*
take part in, participate in,
compete in

3 *We are playing the defending
champions.*
compete against, oppose, challenge,
take on

4 *Hayley is learning to play the
saxophone.*
perform on

5 *Who is going to play the lead role?*
act, perform, take the part of,
portray, represent

play *NOUN*

1 *studying a play by Shakespeare*
drama, theatrical work, piece,
performance, production
❙ SEE ALSO drama

2 *The weekend was a mixture of work
and play.*
recreation, amusement, leisure, fun,
games, sport

player *NOUN*

1 *You need four players for this game.*
contestant, participant, competitor,
contender

2 *We have some experienced players in
the band.*
performer, musician, artist,
instrumentalist

▶ Someone who plays music on their
own is a **soloist**.

a
b
c
d
e
f
g
h
i
j
k
l
m
n
o
p
q
r
s
t
u
v
w
x
y
z

419

playful ADJECTIVE

1 *The kittens are in a playful mood.*
lively, spirited, frisky, frolicsome,
mischievous, roguish, impish

2 *making a playful remark*
light-hearted, joking, teasing,
frivolous, flippant
OPPOSITE serious

plea NOUN

sending out a plea for help
appeal, request, call, entreaty,
petition, supplication

plead VERB

▷ **plead with**
*They pleaded with us to listen to
them.*
beg, entreat, implore, appeal to, ask,
petition

pleasant ADJECTIVE

1 *I spent a pleasant evening talking
with old friends.*
enjoyable, agreeable, pleasing,
pleasurable, delightful, lovely,
entertaining
OPPOSITES unpleasant, disagreeable

2 *The staff there are always pleasant.*
kind, friendly, likeable, charming,
amiable, amicable, cheerful, genial,
good-natured, good-humoured,
approachable, hospitable,
welcoming

3 *a spell of pleasant weather*
fine, mild, sunny, warm, balmy

please VERB

1 *I wish I knew how to please her.*
make happy, satisfy, gratify, delight,
amuse, entertain, charm

2 *Everyone just does as they please.*
like, want, wish, choose, prefer,
see fit

pleased ADJECTIVE

Are you pleased with the result?
happy, satisfied, content, contented,
gratified, thankful, grateful, glad,
delighted, elated, thrilled
OPPOSITES unhappy, dissatisfied,
discontented

pleasing ADJECTIVE

a design which is pleasing to the eye
pleasant, agreeable, satisfying,
gratifying
OPPOSITES unpleasant, disagreeable

pleasure NOUN

1 *Miss Wade gets a lot of pleasure from
her garden.*
enjoyment, happiness, delight,
satisfaction, gratification, comfort,
contentment, gladness, joy, fun

▶ Very great pleasure is **bliss** or
ecstasy.

2 *He talked of the pleasures of being
single.*
joy, comfort, delight

pleat NOUN

How do you iron the pleats in a kilt?
crease, fold, tuck

pledge NOUN

swearing a pledge of allegiance
oath, vow, promise, word,
commitment, guarantee

plentiful ADJECTIVE

the season when olives are plentiful
abundant, prolific, profuse, copious,
ample, generous, bountiful, lavish
OPPOSITE scarce

plenty NOUN

There should be plenty for everyone.
an ample supply, a sufficiency, quite
enough, more than enough, enough
and to spare
OPPOSITE a shortage

▷ **plenty of**
We've still got plenty of time.
a lot of, lots of, a great deal of, many,
ample, abundant
(informal) loads of, masses of, stacks
of, tons of

plight NOUN

*concerned about the plight of the
homeless*
predicament, trouble, difficulty,
problem, dilemma
(informal) bind
IDIOM dire straits

plod *VERB*
  1 *We plodded down the snowy path.*
    tramp, trudge, lumber, clump
  2 *I'm still plodding through the paperwork.*
    labour, toil, slog, wade, plough, drudge

plot *NOUN*
  1 *a plot against the government*
    conspiracy, scheme, secret plan, intrigue
  2 *It was hard to follow the plot of the film.*
    story, storyline, narrative, thread
  3 *a plot of land for sale*
    area, piece, lot, patch
  ► A plot of ground for growing flowers or vegetables is an **allotment**.
  ► A large plot of land is a **tract** of land.

plot *VERB*
  1 *plotting a daring escape*
    plan, devise, concoct, hatch
    (informal) cook up
  2 *They were accused of plotting against the queen.*
    conspire, intrigue, scheme, connive
  3 *plotting the path of a comet*
    chart, map, mark

plough *VERB*
  1 *ploughing a field for potatoes*
    cultivate, till, turn over
  2 *Are you still ploughing through that book?*
    wade, labour, toil, slog, plod, drudge

ploy *NOUN*
    a clever ploy to attract publicity
    scheme, plan, ruse, tactic, stratagem, manoeuvre, gambit
    (informal) wheeze

pluck *VERB*
  1 *plucking berries off the bush*
    pick, pull off, remove, gather, collect, harvest
  2 *A seagull plucked the sandwich out of her hand.*
    grab, seize, snatch, jerk, pull, tug, yank

  3 *Pluck the first note of the chord.*
  ► To run your finger or plectrum across the strings of a guitar is to **strum**.
  ► To pluck the strings of a violin or cello is to play **pizzicato**.

plug *NOUN*
    The kilns were sealed with clay plugs.
    stopper, cork, bung

plug *VERB*
  1 *plugging the leak in the pipe*
    stop up, block, close, fill, seal, bung up
  2 *(informal) The author was there to plug her new book.*
    advertise, publicize, promote, market, push
    (informal) hype

plump *ADJECTIVE*
    a plump little man with a bald head
    chubby, dumpy, fat, tubby, podgy, round, stout, portly
    ┃ OPPOSITE skinny
    ┃ SEE ALSO fat

plunder *VERB*
    Viking raiders plundered the abbey.
    loot, pillage, raid, ransack, rob, steal from

plunge *VERB*
  1 *We saw cormorants plunging into the water.*
    dive, jump, leap, throw yourself, pitch, swoop
  2 *Temperatures have plunged overnight.*
    drop, fall, tumble, plummet
  3 *I plunged my hand in the cold water.*
    dip, lower, dunk, sink, immerse, submerge
  4 *You must plunge a stake into the vampire's heart.*
    thrust, stab, stick, push, shove, sink, force, drive, ram

plunge *NOUN*
    a plunge in temperature
    dive, fall, drop, dip, slump
    (informal) nosedive

a
b
c
d
e
f
g
h
i
j
k
l
m
n
o
p
q
r
s
t
u
v
w
x
y
z

plural ADJECTIVE
> a plural verb
> ❙ OPPOSITE singular

poem NOUN
> a love poem by Robert Burns
> rhyme, verse, lyric
> ❙ SEE ALSO poetry

poetic ADJECTIVE
> an author who uses a poetic style
> expressive, imaginative, lyrical, poetical
> ▶ An uncomplimentary synonym is **flowery**.
> FOR WORDS IN OLD AND POETIC USE SEE **old**

poetry NOUN
> a book of First World War poetry
> poems, verse, rhyme, lyrics, versification

WORD WEB

some forms of poetry
acrostic, alexandrine, ballad, blank verse, cinquain, clerihew, concrete poetry, elegy, epic, free verse, ghazal, Habbie stanza, haiku, limerick, lyric, narrative poetry, nonsense verse, nursery rhyme, ode, rap, sonnet, tanka
▶ A group of lines forming a section of a poem is a **stanza**.
▶ A pairs of rhyming lines within a poem is a **couplet**.
▶ The rhythm of a poem is its **metre**.
▶ The study of poetic metre and structure is **prosody**.
▶ To analyse the metre of a poem is to **scan** it.

point NOUN
> **1** a knife with a very sharp point
> tip, end, nib, spike, prong, barb
> **2** a tiny point of light in the sky
> dot, spot, speck, pinpoint, fleck

3 A buoy marks the point where the channel divides.
location, place, position, site, spot
4 Just at that point, the doorbell rang.
moment, instant, second, time, juncture
5 His sense of humour is one of his good points.
characteristic, feature, attribute, trait, quality, side, aspect
6 I agree with your last point.
idea, argument, thought
7 I didn't get the point of that film at all.
meaning, essence, core, gist, nub, crux
8 There is no point in phoning at this hour.
purpose, reason, aim, object, use, usefulness, sense, advantage

point VERB
> **1** An arrow points the way to the exit.
> indicate, show, signal
> **2** Can you point me in the right direction?
> direct, aim, guide, lead, steer
> ▷ **point out**
> May I point out that this was your idea.
> make known, mention, indicate, specify, detail, draw someone's attention to

pointed ADJECTIVE
> **1** a pointed tusk
> sharp, spiked, spiky, barbed
> (informal) pointy
> ❙ OPPOSITES rounded, blunt
> **2** a pointed reference to recent events
> deliberate, clear, unmistakable, obvious, conspicuous
> ❙ OPPOSITES oblique, obscure

pointless ADJECTIVE
> It would be pointless to continue the experiment.
> useless, senseless, futile, unavailing, idle, vain
> ❙ OPPOSITE worthwhile

a b c d e f g h i j k l m n o p q r s t u v w x y z

poise NOUN

She shows great poise for her age.
calmness, composure, assurance,
self-confidence, dignity, aplomb

poised ADJECTIVE

1 *Guy hesitated, his fingers poised
above the keyboard.*
balanced, suspended, hanging,
hovering

2 *a young singer who is poised to
become a superstar*
ready, prepared, all set, primed
(informal) geared up

poison NOUN

a lethal dose of poison
toxin, venom

▶ A poison to kill plants is **herbicide** or
weedkiller.

▶ A poison to kill insects is **insecticide**
or **pesticide**.

▶ A substance which counteracts the
effects of a poison is an **antidote**.

▶ The scientific study of poisons is
toxicology.

poisonous ADJECTIVE

*This particular mushroom is
poisonous.*
toxic, noxious, deadly, lethal, fatal

▶ Snakes and other animals which
produce a toxic venom are said to be
venomous.

poke VERB

*Someone poked me in the back with
an umbrella.*
prod, dig, jab, stab, nudge, elbow

▷ **poke out**
*Bits of straw were poking out of the
mattress.*
stick out, jut out, project, protrude

poke NOUN

a poke in the back
prod, dig, jab, stab, nudge, elbow

polar ADJECTIVE

*Sea ice is melting in the polar
regions.*
Arctic or Antarctic
⌐ SEE ALSO **ice**

pole NOUN

*The huts are supported on wooden
poles.*
post, pillar, stick, rod, shaft, stake,
staff, prop, stanchion

▶ A strong pole to support sails on a
ship is a **mast** or **spar**.

police NOUN

I think you'd better call the police.
police force, constabulary
(informal) the law, the cops, the fuzz

police officer NOUN

two police officers in a patrol car
policeman or policewoman, officer,
constable
(informal) cop, copper
(North American) patrolman or
patrolwoman, trooper

▶ Police officers of higher rank
are **sergeant**, **inspector**, and
superintendent.

▶ The head of a police force is the
chief constable.

▶ Someone training for the police
force is a **cadet**.

▶ A person who investigates crimes is
a **detective**.

policy NOUN

*What is the school's policy on
bullying?*
approach, strategy, plan of action,
guidelines, code, line, position,
stance

polish VERB

1 *polishing your shoes*
rub down, shine, buff, burnish, wax

2 *polishing the final draft of the script*
refine, improve, perfect, hone,
revise, edit, touch up

▷ **polish something off**
*We polished off a whole plate of
sandwiches.*
finish, get through, eat up

polish NOUN

1 *Marble can be given a high polish.*
shine, sheen, gloss, lustre, sparkle,
brightness, glaze, finish

»

a
b
c
d
e
f
g
h
i
j
k
l
m
n
o
p
q
r
s
t
u
v
w
x
y
z

2 *Here the author demonstrates her polish as a writer.*
refinement, sophistication, elegance, grace, finesse

polished *ADJECTIVE*

1 *handles made of polished brass*
shining, shiny, bright, gleaming, glossy, lustrous
OPPOSITES dull, tarnished

2 *The cast gave a polished performance.*
accomplished, skilful, masterly, expert, adept, adroit

polite *ADJECTIVE*

Mr Pickering was always polite to visitors.
courteous, well mannered, respectful, civil, well behaved, gracious, gentlemanly or ladylike, chivalrous, gallant
OPPOSITES rude, impolite

politics *NOUN*

 WORD WEB

terms used in UK politics
alliance, AM (Assembly Member), assembly, ballot, bill, cabinet, campaign, coalition, conservative, constituency, constitution, devolution, election, electorate, executive, First Minister, first past the post, general election, government, House of Commons, House of Lords, landslide, legislature, liberal, left-wing, lobby, local election, lower house, majority, manifesto, Member of Parliament or MP, minister, ministry, minority, MLA (Member of the Legislative Assembly), MSP (Member of the Scottish Parliament), opinion poll, parliament, party, policy, politician, postal voting, Prime Minister, proportional representation, radical,

referendum, right-wing, single transferable vote, socialist, speaker, upper house, vote

terms used in other political systems
congress, congressman or congresswoman, House of Representatives, president, senate, senator, vice-president

poll *NOUN*

the results of a nationwide poll
election, vote, ballot

▶ A vote on a particular question by all the people in a country is a **referendum**.

▶ An official survey to find out about the population is a **census**.

▶ A person who conducts an opinion poll is a **pollster**.

pollute *VERB*

polluting the air with chemicals
contaminate, poison, infect, dirty, foul
OPPOSITE purify

pompous *ADJECTIVE*

written in a rather pompous academic style
arrogant, self-important, haughty, conceited, pretentious, supercilious, puffed up
(informal) stuck-up
OPPOSITE modest

pond *NOUN*
SEE **pool**

pool *NOUN*

1 *a hot pool formed by a geyser*
pond

▶ A larger area of water is a **lake** or (in Scotland) a **loch**.

▶ A saltwater lake is a **lagoon**.

▶ A pool of water in the desert is an **oasis**.

▶ A pool among rocks on a seashore is a **rock pool**.

2 *a pool of spilled milk*
puddle, patch

3 *a heated indoor pool*
swimming pool, swimming bath

poor *ADJECTIVE*

1 *the son of a poor farm labourer*
impoverished, poverty-stricken, penniless, impecunious, needy, destitute, badly off
(informal) hard up
❙ OPPOSITES rich, affluent

2 *a very poor quality of sound*
bad, inferior, inadequate, unsatisfactory, substandard, deficient, imperfect, incompetent, crude, shoddy
(informal) crummy, rubbishy
❙ OPPOSITES good, superior

3 *Poor Mr Stevens might lose his job.*
unlucky, unfortunate, pitiful, wretched, hapless
❙ OPPOSITE lucky

poorly *ADVERB*

The script is very poorly written.
badly, inadequately, unsatisfactorily, incompetently, crudely, shoddily
❙ OPPOSITE well

poorly *ADJECTIVE*

I've been feeling poorly for weeks.
ill, unwell, unfit, ailing
❙ IDIOMS off colour,
under the weather, below par
❙ OPPOSITE well

pop *NOUN, VERB*

FOR TIPS ON DESCRIBING SOUNDS SEE
sound❶

popular *ADJECTIVE*

1 *a popular children's author*
well liked, well loved, celebrated, favourite, sought after
❙ OPPOSITES unpopular, little known

2 *Podcasting is becoming more popular.*
fashionable, widespread, current, in demand, in vogue
(informal) trendy, hot, big
❙ IDIOM all the rage
❙ OPPOSITES unpopular, out of fashion

3 *a book written for a popular audience*
non-specialist, non-technical, general, lay, amateur
❙ OPPOSITE specialist

population *NOUN*

China has the largest population in the world.
inhabitants, residents, occupants, citizens, people, populace, community

pore *VERB*

▷ **pore over**
I've pored over the letter a hundred times.
examine, study, inspect, look closely at, scrutinize, peruse

port *NOUN*

a bustling Mediterranean port
harbour, docks, seaport
▶ A harbour for yachts and pleasure boats is a **marina**.

portable *ADJECTIVE*

a portable DVD player
transportable, mobile, compact, lightweight
▶ A portable phone is a **mobile phone** or *(North American)* **cell phone**.
▶ A portable computer is a **laptop**, **notebook**, or **netbook**.

portion *NOUN*

1 *the upper portion of the lung*
part, piece, section, division, segment, tranche

2 *a large portion of chips*
helping, serving, ration, share, allocation, quantity, measure, serving, plateful, slice

portrait *NOUN*

a portrait of the artist's mother
picture, image, likeness, representation, painting, drawing, photograph
▶ A portrait which shows a side view of someone is a **profile**.
▶ A portrait which shows someone in outline is a **silhouette**.

》

a
b
c
d
e
f
g
h
i
j
k
l
m
n
o
p
q
r
s
t
u
v
w
x
y
z

▶ A portrait which exaggerates some aspect of a person is a **caricature**.

portray VERB

1 *The book portrays life in rural Australia.*
depict, represent, show, describe, illustrate, render

2 *In the film, he portrays a notorious gangster.*
play, act the part of, appear as

portrayal NOUN

1 *a vivid portrayal of wartime Holland*
depiction, representation, description, evocation

2 *Bela Lugosi's famous portrayal of Dracula*
performance, interpretation, rendition

pose VERB

1 *posing in front of the camera*
model, posture

2 *Global warming poses a serious threat.*
present, put forward, offer, constitute

▷ **pose as someone**
posing as a newspaper reporter
impersonate, pretend to be, pass yourself off as, masquerade as

posh (informal) ADJECTIVE

1 *a posh restaurant*
smart, stylish, high-class, upmarket, fancy, elegant, fashionable, chic, exclusive, luxury, de luxe
(informal) classy, swanky, swish, snazzy

2 *a posh accent*
upper-class, aristocratic

position NOUN

1 *marking our position on the map*
location, place, point, spot, site, situation, whereabouts, locality

2 *a basic yoga position*
pose, posture, stance

3 *You put me in a difficult position.*
situation, state, condition, circumstances, predicament

4 *What's your position on nuclear energy?*
opinion, attitude, outlook, view, viewpoint, thinking, stand

5 *a senior position in the government*
job, post, appointment, situation, rank, status, standing

positive ADJECTIVE

1 *Are you positive this is the man you saw?*
certain, sure, convinced, assured, confident, satisfied
❙ OPPOSITES uncertain, doubtful

2 *a positive reply to the question*
favourable, affirmative
❙ OPPOSITE negative

3 *Don't you have anything positive to say?*
constructive, supportive, encouraging, helpful, useful, productive
❙ OPPOSITE negative

possess VERB

1 *The library possesses the original manuscript.*
own, have

2 *Roy did not possess a sense of humour.*
have, be blessed with, be endowed with, enjoy, boast

3 *What possessed you to take up snorkelling?*
make you think of, come over you

possession NOUN
The photograph is no longer in my possession.
ownership, keeping, care, custody, charge, hands

▷ **possessions**
The refugees had lost all of their possessions.
belongings, property, things, worldly goods, personal effects

possibility NOUN
There's a possibility of snow tomorrow.
chance, likelihood, hope, danger, risk

possible ADJECTIVE

1 *Is it possible that life exists on other planets?*
likely, probable, conceivable, credible, plausible, imaginable
❙ OPPOSITES impossible, unlikely

2 *It's not possible to get there before nightfall.*
feasible, practicable, viable, attainable, workable
(informal) doable
❙ OPPOSITES impossible, out of the question

possibly ADVERB

1 *I couldn't possibly accept the money.*
in any way, under any circumstances, conceivably, at all, ever

2 *This is possibly the best film ever made.*
maybe, perhaps, arguably
❙ OPPOSITES definitely, without a doubt

post❶ NOUN

a wooden post
pole, pillar, shaft, stake, support, prop, strut

post VERB

The timetable will be posted on the board.
display, put up, pin up, announce, advertise

post❷ NOUN

expecting a package in the post
mail, letters, delivery

post VERB

Did you post those letters?
mail, send, dispatch

post❸ NOUN

1 *Are you thinking of applying for the post?*
job, position, situation, appointment, vacancy, opening

2 *We were told to stay at our posts.*
station, position, place, base

post VERB

Guards were posted along the wall.
station, position, place, mount

poster NOUN

a poster for the new film
advertisement, notice, bill, sign, placard

postpone VERB

They've decided to postpone the wedding.
put off, defer, delay, put back, hold over, reschedule
❙ IDIOMS put on ice, put on hold, put on the back burner

▶ To stop a game or meeting that you intend to resume later is to **adjourn** or **suspend** it.
❙ OPPOSITE bring forward

posture NOUN

1 *sitting in an awkward posture*
pose, position, stance

2 *the importance of good posture*
deportment, bearing, carriage, gait

pot NOUN

an earthenware pot
vessel, dish, bowl, jar, pan

potent ADJECTIVE

1 *the most potent form of garlic*
strong, powerful, pungent, heady, intoxicating

2 *a potent argument*
effective, forceful, strong, cogent, compelling, persuasive, convincing
❙ OPPOSITE weak

potential ADJECTIVE

1 *a potential Wimbledon champion*
prospective, budding, future, likely, possible, probable, promising

2 *a potential disaster for mankind*
looming, threatening

potential NOUN

1 *a young actress with great potential*
prospects, promise, capability, future

2 *the potential for disaster*
possibility, risk, threat

potion NOUN

Dr Jekyll drank the potion in one go.

concoction, brew, compound,
medicine, drug, draught

pottery NOUN

WORD WEB

some types of pottery
bone china, china, earthenware,
porcelain, raku, slipware,
stoneware, terracotta

▶ Pottery used to serve food and
drink is **crockery**.

▶ A formal word for pottery is
ceramics.

▶ A person who creates pottery is a
potter or **ceramic artist**.

pouch NOUN
    a leather coin pouch
    bag, purse, sack

poultry NOUN
    SEE **bird**

pounce VERB
    A tiger will stalk its prey before
    pouncing.
    jump, leap, spring, swoop down,
    lunge, attack, ambush

pound VERB
  1 *Huge waves pounded against the*
    sea wall.
    batter, buffet, beat, hit, smash, dash,
    lash
  2 *heavy footsteps pounding up the*
    stairs
    stamp, stomp, tramp, thud, thump,
    clump, clomp
  3 *Stephie felt her heart pounding*
    faster.
    beat, thump, hammer, pulse, race

pour VERB
  1 *Sunlight poured through the front*
    window.
    flow, stream, run, gush, spill, flood
  2 *Linda poured some milk into a*
    saucer.
    tip, splash, spill
    (informal) slosh

▶ To pour wine or other liquid from
one container to another is to
decant it.
  3 *It's absolutely pouring outside!*
    rain heavily, teem, lash down, tip
    down, pelt down
    (informal) bucket
  4 *Crowds poured through the gate.*
    surge, stream, crowd, swarm,
    throng

poverty NOUN
  1 *Bad harvests have caused*
    widespread poverty and famine.
    pennilessness, hardship, need, want,
    destitution, penury
▶ Extreme poverty is known as **abject**
poverty.
    OPPOSITES wealth, affluence
  2 *a noticeable poverty of talent*
    scarcity, shortage, deficiency,
    paucity, dearth, absence, lack
    OPPOSITE abundance

powder NOUN
    Ginger root is dried and then ground
    to powder.
    dust, particles, flour, chalk

powdery ADJECTIVE
    a covering of new-fallen, powdery
    snow
    powder-like, fine, light, loose, dusty,
    floury, sandy, chalky

power NOUN
  1 *the immense power of a tsunami*
    strength, force, might, energy,
    vigour
  2 *the power to move an audience to*
    tears
    skill, talent, ability, capacity,
    capability, potential
  3 *Roman slave-owners had absolute*
    power over their slaves.
    authority, command, control,
    dominance, domination, sway

powerful ADJECTIVE
  1 *a powerful tennis serve*
    strong, forceful, hard, mighty,
    vigorous, formidable, potent

a
b
c
d
e
f
g
h
i
j
k
l
m
n
o
p
q
r
s
t
u
v
w
x
y
z

OPPOSITES weak, ineffective

2 *Persia was once a powerful empire.*
influential, leading, commanding,
dominant, high-powered,
formidable

OPPOSITES powerless, weak

3 *making a powerful argument*
strong, convincing, compelling,
cogent, effective, persuasive,
impressive

4 *a powerful urge to turn and run*
intense, strong, overwhelming,
overpowering, fierce, keen

powerless *ADJECTIVE*

1 *A normal bullet is powerless against
a werewolf.*
ineffective, impotent, useless, weak,
feeble

2 *The citizens were powerless to defend
themselves.*
helpless, defenceless, vulnerable

practical *ADJECTIVE*

1 *We need a practical person to lead
the team.*
down-to-earth, matter-of-fact,
sensible, pragmatic, level-headed,
commonsensical, no-nonsense

OPPOSITE impractical

2 *The idea was not practical from the
start.*
workable, realistic, sensible, feasible,
viable, achievable
(informal) doable

OPPOSITE impractical

3 *Do you have any practical experience
of sailing?*
real, actual, hands-on, empirical

OPPOSITE theoretical

practically *ADVERB*

It's practically midnight already.
almost, just about, nearly, virtually,
as good as

practice *NOUN*

1 *We have extra football practice
this week.*
training, exercises, drill, preparation,
rehearsal, run-through

2 *registering with a dental practice*
business, office, firm
(informal) outfit

3 *My usual practice is to shower before
breakfast.*
custom, habit, convention, routine,
procedure

▷ **in practice**
*What will the plan involve in
practice?*
in effect, in reality, actually, really

practise *VERB*

1 *practising for a music exam*
do exercises, rehearse, train, drill,
prepare

IDIOM go through your paces

► To practise just before the start of a
performance is to **warm up**.

2 *Let's practise that scene again.*
rehearse, go over, go through, run
through, work at

3 *accused of practising witchcraft*
do, perform, carry out, observe,
follow, pursue

pragmatic *ADJECTIVE*

taking a pragmatic approach
practical, down-to-earth,
matter-of-fact, sensible,
commonsensical, level-headed,
no-nonsense

OPPOSITE impractical

praise *VERB*

*Critics have praised the film as
groundbreaking.*
commend, applaud, compliment,
congratulate, pay tribute to,
speak highly of
(informal) rave about

IDIOM sing the praises of

► A piece of writing which praises a
person or thing is
a **panegyric**.

OPPOSITES criticize, condemn

praise *NOUN*

*a performance which received critical
praise*
approval, acclaim, admiration,
commendation, compliments,

a
b
c
d
e
f
g
h
i
j
k
l
m
n
o
p
q
r
s
t
u
v
w
x
y
z

congratulations, plaudits

IDIOM a pat on the back

prance *VERB*

The lead guitarist was prancing about on stage.

leap, skip, romp, cavort, caper, frolic

precarious *ADJECTIVE*

1 *a precarious stretch of narrow road*

dangerous, perilous, risky, hazardous

OPPOSITE safe

2 *That chimney looks a bit precarious.*

unsafe, unstable, unsteady, insecure, shaky, wobbly, rickety

OPPOSITE secure

precaution *NOUN*

wearing a helmet as a precaution

safeguard, safety measure, preventative measure

precede *VERB*

A firework display preceded the concert.

come before, go before, lead into, lead up to

IDIOM pave the way for

OPPOSITES follow, succeed

precedent *NOUN*

setting a useful precedent

example, model, pattern, standard, yardstick, benchmark

precious *ADJECTIVE*

1 *trading ships laden with precious silks and spices*

valuable, costly, expensive, priceless

OPPOSITE worthless

FOR PRECIOUS STONES SEE gem

2 *Her most precious possession was a faded letter.*

treasured, cherished, valued, prized, dearest, beloved

precise *ADJECTIVE*

1 *Can you tell me the precise time?*

exact, accurate, correct, true, right

OPPOSITE rough

2 *We were given precise instructions.*

careful, detailed, specific, particular,

definite, explicit

OPPOSITES vague, imprecise

precision *NOUN*

The figures are carved with great precision.

accuracy, exactness, correctness, care, meticulousness, exactitude

predict *VERB*

My horoscope predicts a new romance.

forecast, foretell, prophesy, foresee

predictable *ADJECTIVE*

The outcome of the match was predictable.

foreseeable, to be expected, likely, unsurprising, inevitable

OPPOSITE unpredictable

prediction *NOUN*

What is your prediction for next year?

forecast, prophecy, prognosis

preface *NOUN*

The title of the book is explained in the preface.

introduction, prologue

FOR TIPS ON WRITING A BOOK REVIEW SEE book

prefer *VERB*

Would you prefer tea or coffee?

rather have, sooner have, go for, opt for, plump for, choose, fancy

preferable *ADJECTIVE*

▷ **preferable to**

I find a face wash preferable to soap.

better than, superior to, more suitable than, more desirable than

OPPOSITE inferior to

preference *NOUN*

1 *Heather has a preference for sweet things.*

liking, fondness, taste, fancy, partiality, inclination, penchant

2 *Preference will be given to overseas students.*

priority, precedence, favour

prefix *NOUN*
> *Some opposites are formed by adding a prefix.*
> **OPPOSITE** suffix

pregnant *ADJECTIVE*
> *a woman who is six-months pregnant*
> expectant, carrying a baby
> *(informal)* expecting
> ▶ Clothing designed for pregnant women is **maternity** clothing.
> ▶ A medical appointment during pregnancy is an **antenatal** appointment.
> ▶ A doctor who specializes in pregnancy and childbirth is an **obstetrician**.

prehistoric *ADJECTIVE*

 WORD WEB

> *prehistoric remains*
> barrow or tumulus, cromlech or stone circle, dolmen, hill fort, menhir or standing stone
> ▶ A person who studies prehistory by examining remains is an **archaeologist**.

> *prehistoric periods*
> Stone Age, Bronze Age, Iron Age, Ice Age
> ▶ Formal names for the Old, Middle, and New Stone Ages are **Palaeolithic**, **Mesolithic**, and **Neolithic** periods.
> ▶ Prehistoric people who lived during the Stone Age were **Neanderthals**.

> *some prehistoric animals*
> cave bear, dinosaur, glyptodon, ground sloth, macrauchenia, sabre-toothed cat or smilodon, sabre-toothed squirrel, woolly mammoth, woolly rhino

> ▶ A person who studies fossils of prehistoric life is a **palaeontologist**.
> **SEE ALSO** fossil

prejudice *NOUN*
> *trying to stamp out racial prejudice*
> discrimination, intolerance, bigotry, narrow-mindedness, bias, partiality
> ▶ Prejudice against other races is **racism**.
> ▶ Prejudice against other nations is **xenophobia**.
> ▶ Prejudice against the other sex is **sexism**.
> ▶ Prejudice against older or younger people is **ageism**.
> **OPPOSITES** impartiality, tolerance

prejudiced *ADJECTIVE*
> *a prejudiced attitude toward native culture*
> discriminatory, biased, partial, partisan, bigoted, narrow-minded, intolerant
> **OPPOSITES** impartial, tolerant

preliminary *ADJECTIVE*
> *knocked out in the preliminary round*
> first, initial, introductory, early, opening, preparatory

prelude *NOUN*
> *The award was a prelude to a glittering career.*
> introduction, precursor, preamble, lead-in, opening
> **OPPOSITE** swansong

premature *ADJECTIVE*
> *her premature death at the age of 40*
> early, untimely, unseasonable, before your time

premises *PLURAL NOUN*
> *No one is allowed on the premises after dark.*
> property, grounds, site, buildings

a
b
c
d
e
f
g
h
i
j
k
l
m
n
o
p
q
r
s
t
u
v
w
x
y
z

preoccupied ADJECTIVE

▷ **preoccupied with something**
Danielle is always preoccupied with her looks.
obsessed with, concerned with, fixated with, absorbed in, engrossed in, wrapped up in

preparation NOUN

1 *An event like this requires months of preparation.*
planning, organization, arrangement, setting-up, development, groundwork

2 *a preparation of healing herbs*
mixture, compound, concoction, potion, medicine, brew

prepare VERB

1 *The city is preparing to host the Olympics.*
get ready, plan, make preparations, make arrangements, make provisions

▶ To prepare for a play is to **rehearse**.
▶ To prepare to take part in a sport is to **train**.

2 *preparing a surprise party*
arrange, organize, make arrangements for, plan, set up

3 *preparing a new menu*
produce, put together, draw up, compile, compose, assemble

prepared ADJECTIVE

1 *I don't feel prepared for this exam at all.*
ready, all set, primed

2 *Are you prepared to take the risk?*
willing, disposed, inclined, of a mind, minded

presence NOUN

Lori swore she felt the presence of a ghost.
existence, attendance, appearance

present ADJECTIVE

1 *Is there a doctor present?*
here, in attendance, at hand

2 *the present world record holder*
current, existing
OPPOSITES past, former

present NOUN

The opening chapter takes place in the present.
now, today, the here and now, the present time, nowadays
OPPOSITES past, future

present NOUN

a birthday present
gift, offering, donation
(British informal) prezzie

present VERB

1 *A celebrity was asked to present the prizes.*
hand over, award, bestow, confer

2 *I'd like to present my latest invention.*
introduce, put forward, show, display, exhibit, make known

3 *presenting a series of one-act plays*
put on, perform, stage, mount

4 *How does Shakespeare present women?*
represent, depict, portray, show, describe

5 *Climate change presents a major challenge.*
offer, provide, set out, open up

presentation NOUN

1 *the presentation of the medals*
awarding, handing over, bestowal

2 *the presentation of women in Shakespeare*
representation, depiction, portrayal, description

3 *Each dish was awarded marks for presentation.*
appearance, arrangement, layout, display

preserve VERB

1 *Salt was used to preserve meat and fish.*
keep, save, store

2 *campaigning to preserve the rainforest*
look after, protect, conserve, defend, safeguard, maintain
OPPOSITE destroy

preserve NOUN
> *Writing was once was the preserve of scribes.*
> domain, territory, field, sphere, realm

press VERB
> **1** *The olives are then pressed to extract their oil.*
> push, squeeze, squash, crush, cram, compress, hold down, force down
> **2** *Press the garment under a damp cloth.*
> iron, flatten, smooth
> **3** *A mob of fans pressed round the singer.*
> gather, crowd, cluster, throng, swarm, flock
> **4** *I must press you for an answer.*
> urge, push, force, pressurize, coerce
> (informal) lean on

press NOUN
> **1** *an article in the local press*
> newspapers, magazines
> **2** *an interview with the press*
> journalists, reporters, the media

pressure NOUN
> **1** *Apply steady pressure to the wound.*
> force, compression, squeezing, weight, load
> **2** *Do you sometimes feel pressure to fit in?*
> influence, persuasion, intimidation, coercion, duress
> **3** *I've been under a lot of pressure lately.*
> stress, strain, tension

pressurize VERB
> *Don't feel pressurized into saying yes.*
> push, press, force, compel, coerce, bully, intimidate, browbeat
> (informal) lean on

prestige NOUN
> *the prestige of winning an Oscar*
> glory, honour, credit, renown, distinction, status, kudos, cachet

prestigious ADJECTIVE
> *winning a prestigious award*
> distinguished, respected, renowned, highly regarded

presumably ADVERB
> *Presumably help will arrive soon.*
> I presume, I expect, I imagine, doubtless, no doubt, I dare say

presume VERB
> **1** *I presume you know how to use a camera.*
> assume, suppose, imagine, expect
> **❙ IDIOM** I take it
> **2** *I wouldn't presume to doubt your word.*
> dare, venture, be so bold as, go so far as, take the liberty of

pretend VERB
> **1** *Edward lay still, pretending to be dead.*
> act like, make as if, make believe, play at, affect
> **2** *Is he dead, or just pretending?*
> bluff, sham, pose, fake it
> (informal) kid on, put it on

pretty ADJECTIVE
> *That's a pretty brooch you're wearing.*
> attractive, beautiful, lovely, nice, appealing, pleasing, charming, fetching, dainty, picturesque
> (informal) cute
> (Scottish) bonny
> **❙ OPPOSITE** ugly

prevent VERB
> **1** *Only sheer luck prevented an accident.*
> avert, avoid, stop, pre-empt, forestall, head off
> **❙ IDIOM** nip in the bud
> **2** *Her illness prevented her from travelling.*
> stop, bar, block, preclude, obstruct, impede, inhibit, thwart
> **3** *Some people say that garlic prevents colds.*
> stave off, ward off, fend off
> **❙ IDIOM** keep at bay

a
b
c
d
e
f
g
h
i
j
k
l
m
n
o
p
q
r
s
t
u
v
w
x
y
z

previous *ADJECTIVE*

  1 *The couple had met on a previous occasion.*
  earlier, former, prior, past

  2 *the previous owners of the house*
  preceding, former, last, most recent
  ❙ OPPOSITE subsequent

prey *NOUN*

  a falcon feasting on its prey
  quarry, kill, victim
  ❙ OPPOSITE predator

prey *VERB*

  ▷ **prey on**
  Crocodiles prey on mammals and fish.
  hunt, kill, feed on

price *NOUN*

  1 *What's the price of a return ticket to Sydney?*
  cost, charge, fee, fare, rate, expense, amount, figure, sum
  (informal) damage
  ▶ The price you pay to send a letter is the **postage**.
  ▶ The price you pay to use a private road, bridge, or tunnel is a **toll**.

  2 *paying the price of failure*
  consequence, result, penalty, cost, downside

priceless *ADJECTIVE*

  1 *The museum boasts many priceless works of art.*
  precious, rare, invaluable, irreplaceable, expensive, costly
  ❙ OPPOSITE worthless

  2 *(informal) Their comedy sketch was priceless.*
  funny, amusing, comic, hilarious, witty

prick *VERB*

  Prick the pastry all over with a fork.
  pierce, puncture, stab, jab, perforate, spike

prickle *NOUN*

  A hedgehog uses its prickles for defence.

spike, spine, needle, barb, thorn
  ▶ The prickles on a hedgehog or porcupine are also called **quills**.

prickly *ADJECTIVE*

  1 *Most cacti have prickly stems.*
  spiky, spiked, thorny, spiny, bristly, barbed

  2 *My instructor can be prickly at times.*
  bad-tempered, irritable, grumpy, tetchy, testy

pride *NOUN*

  1 *Erica takes great pride in her art.*
  satisfaction, pleasure, delight, joy, fulfilment, gratification

  2 *I admit I felt a surge of pride during the speech.*
  self-esteem, self-respect, dignity, honour
  ❙ OPPOSITE shame

  3 *Finally, the hero is forced to swallow his pride.*
  arrogance, conceitedness, vanity, self-importance, big-headedness, egotism, snobbery
  ❙ OPPOSITE humility

priest *NOUN*

  SEE **religion**

prim *ADJECTIVE*

  a rather prim and proper young lady
  prudish, strait-laced, formal, demure

primarily *ADVERB*

  a website aimed primarily at teenagers
  chiefly, especially, mainly, mostly, largely, predominantly, principally, above all, first and foremost

primary *ADJECTIVE*

  The primary aim of a website is to communicate.
  main, chief, principal, foremost, most important, key, central
  ❙ OPPOSITE secondary

prime *ADJECTIVE*

  1 *the prime suspect in a murder case*
  main, chief, top, principal, foremost, leading

(informal) number-one

2 *a dish made from prime cuts of meat*
best, superior, first-class, choice, select, top-quality, finest

primitive ADJECTIVE

1 *the site of a primitive human settlement*
ancient, early, prehistoric, primeval, primordial
▌**OPPOSITES** civilized, advanced

2 *a primitive type of computer*
crude, basic, simple, rudimentary, undeveloped
▌**OPPOSITES** advanced, sophisticated

prince, princess NOUN
SEE **ruler**

principal ADJECTIVE

What is the principal aim of the experiment?
main, chief, primary, foremost, most important, key, central, predominant, pre-eminent, leading, supreme, major, top
▌**OPPOSITES** secondary, minor

principle NOUN

1 *following the principles of Buddhism*
rule, standard, code, ethic, tenet, precept, doctrine, creed

2 *learning the principles of good design*
basics, fundamentals, essentials

print NOUN

1 *The tiny print was difficult to read.*
type, printing, lettering, letters, characters

2 *the print of a foot in the sand*
mark, impression, footprint, fingerprint

3 *a full-size print of the Mona Lisa*
copy, reproduction, duplicate, photograph

priority NOUN

1 *Traffic on the main road has priority.*
precedence, right of way

2 *giving priority to first-time buyers*
preference, precedence, favour, first place

prise VERB

Slowly, we began to prise the lid off the coffin.
lever, force, wrench

prison NOUN

sentenced to six months in prison
jail, imprisonment, confinement
(British informal) nick
(North American) penitentiary
(North American informal) pen
▶ A large prison where prisoners-of-war are held is a **prison camp**.

prisoner NOUN

an escaped prisoner
convict, inmate, captive
(informal) jailbird, con
▶ A person who is held prisoner until some demand is met is a **hostage**.
▶ A person who is captured by the opposite side during a war is a **prisoner-of-war**.

private ADJECTIVE

1 *Always keep your password private.*
secret, confidential, personal, intimate
▶ Secret official documents are **classified** documents.
▌**OPPOSITES** public, known

2 *Can we go somewhere a little more private?*
quiet, secluded, hidden, concealed
▌**OPPOSITES** public, open

3 *a private school*
independent
▌**OPPOSITE** state

privilege NOUN

Club members enjoy special privileges.
advantage, benefit, concession, right, entitlement

privileged ADJECTIVE

1 *coming from a privileged family background*
affluent, wealthy, prosperous, rich, well off, well-to-do
▌**OPPOSITES** disadvantaged, poor

a
b
c
d
e
f
g
h
i
j
k
l
m
n
o
p
q
r
s
t
u
v
w
x
y
z

》

435

2 *I feel privileged to be here.*
honoured, fortunate, lucky, favoured

prize *NOUN*

winning a prize in the raffle
award, reward, trophy

▶ Money that you win as a prize is your **winnings**.

▶ Prize money that keeps increasing until someone wins it is a **jackpot**.

prize *VERB*

This ancient people prized silver above gold.
treasure, value, cherish, hold dear, esteem, revere

❙ IDIOM set great store by

❙ OPPOSITE disdain

probable *ADJECTIVE*

the most probable cause of the accident
likely, feasible, possible, expected, predictable

❙ OPPOSITE improbable

probe *VERB*

1 *a mission to probe the outer solar system*
explore, penetrate, see into, plumb

2 *an inquiry to probe the handling of the murder case*
investigate, inquire into, examine, study, scrutinize, look into, go into in depth

problem *NOUN*

1 *I'm having problems with my computer.*
difficulty, trouble, complication, snag, hitch, hiccup, setback
(informal) headache

2 *a complicated maths problem*
puzzle, question, riddle, conundrum
(informal) brain-teaser, poser

problematic *ADJECTIVE*

Building intelligent robots has proved problematic.
troublesome, difficult, awkward, complex, tricky

procedure *NOUN*

What is the procedure for buying a domain name?
method, process, system, mechanism, practice, routine, technique, way

proceed *VERB*

1 *The winds forced us to proceed slowly.*
go forward, move forward, make your way, advance, progress

2 *NASA has decided to proceed with the launch.*
go ahead, carry on, continue, get on, press on, push on

3 *The stranger proceeded to tell me his life story.*
go on to, move on to, begin to, start to

proceedings *PLURAL NOUN*

A heckler in the audience interrupted proceedings.
events, happenings, activities, affairs
(informal) goings-on

proceeds *PLURAL NOUN*

the proceeds from the charity auction
income, takings, money, earnings, profit, revenue, yield, returns

process *NOUN*

a new process for storing solar energy
method, procedure, operation, system, technique, way, means

process *VERB*

We are still processing your application.
deal with, attend to, see to, handle, treat, prepare

procession *NOUN*

The procession made its way slowly down the hill.
parade, march, column, line

▶ A procession of mourners at a funeral is a **cortège**.

❙ SEE ALSO parade

proclaim VERB

Two teams were proclaimed joint winners of the title.
declare, announce, pronounce, state, publish, broadcast

prod VERB

1 *Jesse prodded the worm to see if it was alive.*
poke, dig, jab, nudge, push

2 *The council has finally been prodded into action.*
stimulate, rouse, prompt, spur, push, galvanize

produce VERB

1 *producing too many greenhouse gases*
create, generate, emit, give out, yield

2 *a company which produces computer games*
make, manufacture, construct, fabricate, put together, assemble, turn out

3 *The writers have produced an award-winning comedy.*
create, compose, invent, think up, come up with

4 *His remarks have produced mixed reactions.*
provoke, arouse, stimulate, prompt, give rise to, result in, occasion, trigger

5 *Mr Gray produced a letter from his pocket.*
bring out, pull out, fish out, extract, present, show, reveal

produce NOUN

a shop which sells organic produce
food, foodstuffs, crops, fruit and vegetables

product NOUN

1 *launching a new range of beauty products*
article, commodity, merchandise, goods, -ware

2 *The famine is the product of years of drought.*
result, consequence, outcome, upshot

production NOUN

1 *the production of handmade paper*
manufacture, making, construction, creation, assembly, building, fabrication

2 *reducing the production of household waste*
generation, output, yield

3 *a new production of 'Oliver'*
performance, show, staging, presentation

productive ADJECTIVE

1 *a long and productive literary career*
prolific, creative, inventive, fruitful, fertile

2 *It wasn't a very productive meeting.*
useful, valuable, worthwhile, constructive, profitable
❙ **OPPOSITE** unproductive

profession NOUN

Why did you choose acting as a profession?
career, job, occupation, vocation, business, trade, line of work

professional ADJECTIVE

1 *His ambition is to be a professional footballer.*
paid, full-time
❙ **OPPOSITES** amateur, non-professional

2 *The plans were drawn by a professional architect.*
qualified, chartered, skilled, trained, experienced

3 *This is a very professional piece of work.*
skilled, expert, proficient, accomplished, competent, polished
❙ **OPPOSITE** incompetent

proficient ADJECTIVE

It takes years to become proficient in judo.
skilful, skilled, accomplished, capable, expert, able
❙ **OPPOSITE** incompetent

a
b
c
d
e
f
g
h
i
j
k
l
m
n
o
p
q
r
s
t
u
v
w
x
y
z

profile NOUN
> SEE **portrait**

profit NOUN
> 1 *Did you make any profit from your first CD?*
> gain, surplus, excess
> ▶ The extra money you get on your savings is **interest**.
> **OPPOSITE** loss
> 2 *I could see little profit in arguing.*
> advantage, benefit, gain, reward, value, use
> *(informal)* mileage
> **OPPOSITE** disadvantage

profound ADJECTIVE
> 1 *a profound sense of relief*
> deep, intense, keen, acute, extreme, heartfelt
> 2 *a profound analysis of modern society*
> insightful, thoughtful, intelligent, penetrating, perceptive

programme NOUN
> 1 *an exciting concert programme*
> plan, schedule, timetable, calendar, line-up
> ▶ A list of things to be done at a meeting is an **agenda**.
> ▶ A list of places to visit on a journey is an **itinerary**.
> 2 *a cable TV programme*
> broadcast, show, production, transmission

progress NOUN
> 1 *monitoring the progress of the hurricane*
> journey, route, movement, travels
> 2 *I'm not making much progress with the trumpet.*
> advance, development, improvement, growth, headway, step forward
> ▶ An important piece of progress is a **breakthrough**.

progress VERB
> 1 *You can now progress to the next level of the game.*

go forward, move forward, proceed, advance
> 2 *The chicks are progressing at a steady rate.*
> develop, grow, improve
> *(informal)* come along

prohibit VERB
> *Taking photographs is prohibited here.*
> ban, forbid, proscribe, disallow, outlaw, rule out, veto
> **OPPOSITES** permit, allow

project NOUN
> 1 *the project to map the human genome*
> plan, scheme, undertaking, enterprise, venture, proposal, bid
> 2 *an art history project on Matisse*
> assignment, task, activity

project VERB
> 1 *A narrow ledge projects from the cliff.*
> extend, protrude, stick out, jut out, overhang
> 2 *The laser projects a narrow beam of light.*
> emit, throw out, cast, shine
> 3 *projecting the wrong kind of image*
> give out, send out, convey, communicate

prolific ADJECTIVE
> SEE **productive**

prolong VERB
> *There is no point in prolonging the argument.*
> extend, lengthen, protract, stretch out, draw out, drag out, spin out
> **OPPOSITES** shorten, curtail

prominent ADJECTIVE
> 1 *an elderly gentleman with prominent eyebrows*
> noticeable, conspicuous, striking, eye-catching, protruding, protuberant
> **OPPOSITE** inconspicuous
> 2 *a prominent TV personality*

well-known, famous, celebrated, major, leading, notable, distinguished, eminent

OPPOSITES unknown, obscure

promise *NOUN*

1 *We had promises of help from many people.*
assurance, pledge, guarantee, commitment, vow, oath, word of honour

2 *a young actor who shows great promise*
potential, talent, ability, aptitude

promise *VERB*

1 *Do you promise not to tell anyone?*
give your word, guarantee, swear, take an oath, vow, pledge

2 *I promise you I'll be there.*
assure, swear to, give your word to

promising *ADJECTIVE*

1 *The weather looks promising for tomorrow.*
encouraging, hopeful, favourable, auspicious, rosy

2 *a promising young singer*
talented, gifted, potential, budding, aspiring
(*informal*) up-and-coming

promote *VERB*

1 *Ray has been promoted to captain.*
move up, advance, upgrade, elevate

2 *The band are here to promote their new CD.*
advertise, publicize, market, push
(*informal*) plug, hype

3 *a campaign to promote healthy eating*
encourage, foster, advocate, back, support, boost

prompt *ADJECTIVE*

I received a prompt reply to my email.
quick, speedy, swift, rapid, punctual, immediate, instant, direct

OPPOSITES late, belated

prompt *VERB*

What prompted you to take up yoga?
induce, lead, cause, motivate, persuade, inspire, stimulate, encourage, provoke, spur

prone *ADJECTIVE*

1 *Sharon is prone to exaggerate things.*
inclined, apt, liable, likely, disposed, given

2 *The victim was lying prone on the floor.*
face down, on the front
► To lie face upwards is to be **supine**.

pronounce *VERB*

1 *Try to pronounce the words clearly.*
say, speak, utter, articulate, enunciate, sound

2 *The man was pronounced dead on arrival.*
declare, announce, proclaim, judge
(*formal*) deem

pronounced *ADJECTIVE*

a pronounced Australian accent
marked, strong, clear, distinct, definite, noticeable, obvious, striking, unmistakable, prominent

OPPOSITE imperceptible

proof *NOUN*

Do you have any proof of your identity?
evidence, confirmation, verification, authentication, certification

prop *NOUN*

The tunnel roof is supported by metal props.
support, strut, pole, post, upright
► A stick used to support an injured leg is a **crutch**.
► Part of a building which props up a wall is a **buttress**.

prop *VERB*

I propped my bike against the railing.
lean, rest, stand, balance

                                  》

a b c d e f g h i j k l m n o p q r s t u v w x y z

▷ **prop something up**
trying to prop up a failing economy
support, hold up, reinforce, shore up, underpin

propel VERB
a tram car propelled by electricity
power, push, drive, move forward

proper ADJECTIVE
1 *the proper way to set a table*
correct, right, accepted, established, conventional, appropriate, suitable
┃ OPPOSITES wrong, incorrect
2 *He looks just like a proper movie star.*
real, actual, genuine, true, bona fide
┃ OPPOSITE fake
3 *I could do with a proper meal.*
good, decent, adequate, substantial
┃ OPPOSITE inadequate
4 *Her whole family is very proper and polite.*
formal, correct, respectable, conventional, polite, punctilious
┃ OPPOSITES informal, unconventional
5 *(informal) I must have looked a proper idiot!*
complete, total, utter, absolute, thorough, downright

property NOUN
1 *This box contains lost property.*
belongings, possessions, goods, personal effects
2 *a list of property for sale*
buildings, houses, land, premises
(North American) real estate
3 *Many herbs have healing properties.*
quality, characteristic, feature, attribute, trait

prophecy NOUN
a hero whose birth was foretold in an ancient prophecy
prediction, forecast, divination, prognostication

prophesy VERB
The witches prophesy that Macbeth will be king.
predict, forecast, foresee, foretell, divine, prognosticate

proportion NOUN
1 *a large proportion of the population*
part, section, portion, segment, share, fraction, percentage
2 *measuring the proportion of weight to height*
ratio, distribution, relationship
▷ **proportions**
a room of large proportions
size, dimensions, measurements, area, expanse

proposal NOUN
a proposal to build a skate park
plan, project, scheme, suggestion, proposition, recommendation

propose VERB
1 *We are proposing a change in the rules.*
suggest, ask for, put forward, submit, recommend
2 *How do you propose to pay for this?*
intend, mean, plan, aim
3 *Patrick finally found the courage to propose.*
ask for someone's hand in marriage
(informal) pop the question

proprietor NOUN
the proprietor of the hotel
manager, owner, landlord or landlady
(informal) boss

prosecute VERB
Anyone caught shoplifting will be prosecuted.
charge, take to court, bring to trial, indict
▶ To take someone to court to try to get money from them is to **sue** them.

prospect NOUN
1 *lured by the prospect of fame and fortune*
chance, hope, promise, expectation, likelihood, possibility, probability
2 *an open terrace with a prospect over the sea*
outlook, view, vista, panorama

a b c d e f g h i j k l m n o p q r s t u v w x y z

prosper VERB

Over time, the settlement prospered.
do well, be successful, flourish, thrive, grow, progress, boom
❙ OPPOSITES fail, flounder

prosperity NOUN

Tourism has brought prosperity to the region.
wealth, affluence, growth, success

prosperous ADJECTIVE

the growth of a prosperous merchant class
wealthy, rich, well-off, well-to-do, affluent, successful, thriving, booming
❙ OPPOSITE poor

protect VERB

1 *a magpie protecting its nest*
guard, defend, keep safe, safeguard, secure, keep from harm
❙ OPPOSITE neglect

2 *Sunscreen will protect your skin from harmful rays*
shield, shade, shelter, screen, insulate
❙ OPPOSITE expose

protection NOUN

The shell provides protection for the growing chick.
shelter, cover, defence, insulation, security, refuge, sanctuary

protest NOUN

1 *There were protests at the plan to close the cinema.*
complaint, objection, remonstrance
▶ A general protest is an **outcry**.

2 *Supporters staged a protest outside parliament.*
demonstration, march, rally, sit-in
(informal) demo

protest VERB

1 *Hundreds of viewers protested about the programme.*
complain, make a protest, object (to), take exception (to), take issue (with),

express disapproval (of), remonstrate
(informal) kick up a fuss

2 *He has always protested his innocence.*
insist on, maintain, assert, declare, proclaim, profess, affirm

protrude VERB

Two fangs protruded from the vampire's mouth.
stick out, poke out, bulge, swell, project, stand out, jut out

proud ADJECTIVE

1 *You should be proud of your work this year.*
delighted (with), pleased (with), satisfied, gratified
❙ OPPOSITE ashamed (of)

2 *He's too proud to admit his mistakes.*
conceited, arrogant, vain, haughty, superior, self-important, pompous, supercilious
(informal) stuck-up, big-headed
❙ OPPOSITE humble

prove VERB

1 *Can you prove you were at home on the night of the murder?*
demonstrate, provide proof, provide evidence, establish, confirm, verify, substantiate
❙ OPPOSITE disprove

2 *The idea proved unpopular with the public.*
turn out to be, be found to be

proverb NOUN

SEE**saying**

provide VERB

1 *We'll provide the tea and coffee.*
supply, contribute, arrange for, lay on, come up with
▶ To provide food and drink for people is to **cater** for them.

2 *The library is provided with Internet access.*
equip, supply, furnish, issue, provision, fit out, kit out

a
b
c
d
e
f
g
h
i
j
k
l
m
n
o
p
q
r
s
t
u
v
w
x
y
z

provisions *PLURAL NOUN*

  We have enough provisions for a week.
  supplies, food and drink, rations, stores

provoke *VERB*

  1 *Rattlesnakes are dangerous if provoked.*
  annoy, irritate, anger, enrage, incense, infuriate, exasperate, madden, nettle, rile, taunt, goad
  (informal) wind up
  IDIOM rub up the wrong way
  OPPOSITE pacify

  2 *The decision provoked anger from the crowd.*
  arouse, produce, prompt, cause, generate, instigate, induce, stimulate, trigger, kindle, spark off, stir up

prowl *VERB*

  the sound of someone prowling in the basement
  creep, sneak, slink, steal, skulk

prudent *ADJECTIVE*

  1 *It would be prudent to start saving now.*
  wise, sensible, shrewd, politic, judicious
  OPPOSITES unwise, rash

  2 *being prudent with your spending*
  careful, cautious, thrifty, economical, circumspect
  OPPOSITES wasteful, reckless

prune *VERB*

  Roses should be pruned every spring.
  cut back, trim, clip, shear

pry *VERB*

  I didn't mean to pry.
  be curious, be inquisitive, interfere
  (informal) be nosy, nose around, snoop

  ▷ **pry into something**
  always prying into other people's affairs
  interfere in, meddle in, spy on

IDIOM *(informal)* poke your nose into

psychic *ADJECTIVE*

  The card reader claimed to have psychic powers.
  telepathic, clairvoyant, supernatural, paranormal

psychological *ADJECTIVE*

  suffering from a psychological disorder
  mental, emotional
  OPPOSITE physical

public *ADJECTIVE*

  1 *The public entrance is at the front.*
  common, communal, general, open, shared, collective
  OPPOSITE private

  2 *These facts are now public knowledge.*
  known, acknowledged, published, available, open, general, universal
  OPPOSITE secret

public *NOUN*

  ▷ **the public**
  This part of the house is not open to the public.
  people, everyone, the community, society, the nation

publication *NOUN*

  1 *the publication of her first novel*
  issuing, printing, production, appearance

  2 *a list of our recent publications*
  book, newspaper, magazine, periodical

publicity *NOUN*

  1 *some free publicity for their latest album*
  advertising, advertisements, promotion
  (informal) hype, build-up

  2 *an actor who shies away from publicity*
  attention, exposure, the limelight
  IDIOM the public eye

publish *VERB*

1 *The magazine is published twice a year.*

issue, print, produce, bring out, release, circulate

2 *When will they publish the results?*

announce, declare, disclose, make known, make public, report, reveal

▶ To publish information on radio or TV is to **broadcast** it.

pudding *NOUN*

There is raspberry sorbet for pudding.

dessert, sweet

(informal) afters

puff *NOUN*

1 *A puff of wind caught his hat.*

gust, draught, breath, flurry

2 *A puff of smoke rose from the chimney.*

cloud, whiff, waft, wisp

puff *VERB*

1 *a volcanic island puffing ash and smoke*

blow out, send out, emit, belch

2 *A red-faced man stood puffing in the doorway.*

breathe heavily, pant, gasp, wheeze

3 *The sails puffed out as the wind rose.*

become inflated, billow, swell

pull *VERB*

1 *Can you pull your chair a bit closer?*

drag, draw, haul, lug, trail, tow

❙ OPPOSITE push

2 *Be careful, you nearly pulled my arm off!*

tug, rip, wrench, jerk, pluck

(informal) yank

▷ **pull off**

They've pulled off an amazing stunt.

achieve, accomplish, manage, fulfil, bring off

▷ **pull out**

1 *Pull out the bee sting with a pair of tweezers.*

extract, take out, remove

2 *One team had to pull out of the race.*

back out, withdraw, retire, step down, bow out

(informal) quit

▷ **pull through**

Do you expect the patient to pull through?

get better, recover, revive, rally, recuperate, survive

▷ **pull up**

A taxi pulled up at the door.

draw up, stop, halt

pulse *NOUN*

1 *the pulse of Brazilian samba music*

beat, rhythm, drumming

2 *See if you can feel your own pulse.*

heartbeat, heart rate

pulse *VERB*

Lennie felt the blood pulsing in his head.

throb, pulsate, pound, drum

pump *VERB*

pumping water out of a coal mine

drain, draw off, empty

▶ To move liquid between containers through a tube is to **siphon** it.

▷ **pump up**

pumping up a flat tyre

inflate, blow up

❙ OPPOSITES deflate, let down

punch *VERB*

1 *I felt like punching Campbell on the nose.*

strike, hit, jab, poke, prod, thump, smash

(informal) biff, slug, sock

❙ SEE ALSO hit

2 *punching a hole through the wall*

bore, pierce, puncture

punch *NOUN*

a punch on the nose

blow, hit, box, jab, poke, prod, thump, smash

(informal) biff, slug, sock

punctual *ADJECTIVE*

Please be punctual so we can start early.

prompt, on time, on schedule, in
good time
❙ **OPPOSITE** late

punctuate VERB
*Her words were punctuated with
heavy sighs.*
break up, interrupt, intersperse, dot,
sprinkle, pepper

punctuation NOUN

 WORD WEB

punctuation marks
apostrophe, brackets, colon,
comma, dash, exclamation
mark, full stop, hyphen, question
mark, quotation marks or
speech marks, semicolon, square
brackets

other marks used in writing
accent, asterisk, at sign, bullet
point, capital letters, emoticon,
forward slash
**FOR TIPS ON USING PUNCTUATION SEE
Writer's Toolkit**

puncture NOUN
I found the puncture in my tyre.
hole, perforation, rupture, leak

puncture VERB
A nail must have punctured the tyre.
perforate, pierce, rupture

punish VERB
*Offenders used to be punished by
being put in the stocks.*
penalize, discipline, chastise

punishment NOUN
*The punishment for dropping litter
is a fine.*
penalty, sanction, sentence
▶ Punishing someone by taking
their life is **capital punishment** or
execution.

puny ADJECTIVE
Preston was rather a puny child.
delicate, weak, feeble, frail, slight,
undersized

(informal) weedy
❙ **OPPOSITES** strong, sturdy

pupil NOUN
How many pupils are in the class?
schoolchild, student, learner, scholar
▶ Someone who follows a great
teacher is a **disciple**.

puppet NOUN
*a short film made with shadow
puppets*
▶ A puppet worked by strings or wires
is a **marionette**.
▶ A person who operates puppets is a
puppeteer.

puppy NOUN
SEE **dog**

purchase VERB
purchasing a plot of land
buy, pay for, get, obtain, acquire,
procure, invest in

purchase NOUN
1 *Keep the receipt as proof of your
purchase.*
acquisition, buying, shopping
2 *I couldn't get any purchase on the
cliff face.*
grasp, grip, hold, anchorage,
leverage, traction

pure ADJECTIVE
1 *a coin made of pure gold*
solid, unadulterated, undiluted
❙ **OPPOSITES** impure, adulterated
2 *a dish made from pure ingredients*
natural, unprocessed, unrefined,
wholesome
❙ **OPPOSITE** processed
3 *a breath of pure mountain air*
clean, clear, fresh, unpolluted,
uncontaminated
❙ **OPPOSITES** polluted, stale
4 *This book is pure nonsense.*
complete, absolute, utter, sheer,
total, out-and-out

purify VERB
a filter to purify rainwater
clean, make pure, decontaminate,
sanitize

a
b
c
d
e
f
g
h
i
j
k
l
m
n
o
p
q
r
s
t
u
v
w
x
y
z

▶ You destroy germs by **disinfecting** or **sterilizing** things.

▶ You take solid particles out of liquids by **filtering** them.

▶ To purify water by boiling it and condensing the vapour is to **distil** it.

▶ To purify crude oil is to **refine** it.

purple *ADJECTIVE, NOUN*

WORD WEB

some shades of purple
lavender, lilac, magenta, mauve, plum, violet

FOR TIPS ON DESCRIBING COLOURS
SEE **colour**

purpose *NOUN*

1 *What was your purpose in coming here?*
intention, motive, aim, objective, goal, end, target

2 *She began to feel that her life had no purpose.*
point, use, usefulness, value

▷ **on purpose**
Did you trip me up on purpose?
deliberately, intentionally, purposely, knowingly, consciously

purposeful *ADJECTIVE*

She set off with a purposeful look on her face.
determined, decisive, resolute, positive, committed
❙ OPPOSITE aimless

purse *NOUN*

I always keep some change in my purse.
money bag, pouch, wallet

pursue *VERB*

1 *a van being pursued by two police cars*
chase, follow, run after, tail, track, hunt, trail, shadow

2 *He plans to pursue a career as a musician.*
follow, undertake, practise, conduct,

take up, carry on, continue, maintain

pursuit *NOUN*

1 *a film about one man's pursuit of happiness*
hunt (for), search (for), striving (for), chase, quest

2 *Guests can enjoy a range of outdoor pursuits.*
activity, pastime, hobby, recreation, amusement, interest

push *VERB*

1 *Push any key to start.*
press, depress, hold down

2 *Push the mixture down with the back of a spoon.*
pack, press, cram, crush, compress, ram, squash, squeeze

3 *pushing the ball past a defender*
shove, thrust, drive, propel, send
❙ OPPOSITE pull

4 *pushing your way through the crowd*
force, barge, elbow, jostle

5 *I think she pushes herself too hard.*
pressurize, press, drive, urge, compel, bully
(*informal*) lean on

6 *They are really pushing the new TV series.*
promote, publicize, advertise
(*informal*) plug, hype

put *VERB*

1 *Just put the parcels at the door.*
place, set down, leave, deposit, stand
(*informal*) dump, stick, park, plonk

2 *Maria put her head on my shoulder.*
lay, lean, rest

3 *putting a picture on the wall*
attach, fasten, fix, hang

4 *Where are you planning to put the piano?*
locate, situate

5 *They always put a lifeguard on duty.*
position, post, station

6 *I'm not sure of the best way to put this.*
express, word, phrase, say, state, formulate

》

a b c d e f g h i j k l m n o **p** q r s t u v w x y z

▷ **put someone off**
The stench put me off eating.
deter, discourage, dissuade

▷ **put something off**
We can't put off the decision any longer.
delay, postpone, defer, shelve, reschedule

▌IDIOM put on ice

▷ **put something out**
It took three hours to put out the blaze.
extinguish, quench, smother, douse, snuff out

▷ **put something up**
1 *putting up a tent*
set up, construct, erect, raise
2 *putting up prices*
increase, raise, inflate

▷ **put up with something**
How do you put up with that racket?
bear, stand, tolerate, endure, stomach, abide

puzzle *NOUN*
Has anyone managed to solve the puzzle?
mystery, riddle, conundrum, problem, enigma
(informal) brain-teaser, poser

puzzle *VERB*
1 *Your response puzzled me.*
confuse, baffle, bewilder, bemuse, mystify, perplex
(informal) fox
2 *Holmes spent all night puzzling over the case.*
ponder, think, meditate, worry, brood

puzzled *ADJECTIVE*
Why are you looking so puzzled?
confused, baffled, bewildered, mystified, perplexed

puzzling *ADJECTIVE*
There was something puzzling about the photograph.
confusing, baffling, bewildering, mystifying, perplexing, mysterious, enigmatic, inexplicable
▌OPPOSITES clear, straightforward

pyramid *NOUN*
an ancient Egyptian pyramid
► A pyramid which does not have smooth sides is a **stepped pyramid**.

Qq

quaint *ADJECTIVE*

We stayed in a quaint thatched
cottage.
charming, picturesque, sweet,
old-fashioned, old-world

quake *VERB*

The whole building quaked with the
blast.
shake, shudder, tremble, quiver,
heave, rock, sway, wobble

qualification *NOUN*

1 a qualification in health care
diploma, certificate, degree, licence,
training, skill

2 I'd like to add a qualification to
what I said.
condition, reservation, limitation,
proviso, caveat

qualified *ADJECTIVE*

1 a qualified speech therapist
certified, chartered, licensed,
trained, professional
❙ OPPOSITE amateur

2 The plan has been given qualified
approval.
conditional, limited, partial,
guarded, cautious

qualify *VERB*

1 The course will qualify you to
administer first aid.
authorize, certify, license, permit,
allow, entitle

2 The first three runners will qualify
for the final.

be eligible, be entitled, get through,
pass

3 I'd like to qualify that statement.
limit, modify, restrict, moderate,
temper

quality *NOUN*

1 We only use ingredients of the
highest quality.
grade, class, standard, calibre, merit

2 all the qualities of a good detective
story
characteristic, feature, property,
attribute, trait, facet

quantity *NOUN*

1 Add a very small quantity of baking
powder.
amount, mass, volume, bulk, weight
(informal) load

2 We received a large quantity of
emails.
number, sum, total

quarrel *NOUN*

a bitter quarrel between two families
argument, disagreement, dispute,
difference of opinion, row, tiff, fight,
squabble, wrangle, clash, altercation
(informal) slanging match
▶ Continuous quarrelling is **strife**.
▶ A long-lasting quarrel is a **feud** or
vendetta.
▶ A quarrel in which people become
violent is a **brawl**.

quarrel *VERB*

What are you two quarrelling
about?
argue, disagree, fight, row,
squabble, bicker, clash, fall out
❙ IDIOMS cross swords, lock horns,
be at odds

▷ **quarrel with something**
I won't quarrel with your decision.
disagree with, object to, oppose,
take exception to, take issue with,
criticize, fault

quarry❶ *NOUN*

a limestone quarry
SEE **mine**

quarry² NOUN

> *a leopard stalking its quarry*
> prey, victim, kill

quarters PLURAL NOUN

> *The attic was originally the servants' quarters.*
> accommodation, lodging, rooms, housing

quaver VERB

> *I was so nervous my voice began to quaver.*
> shake, tremble, waver, quake, quiver, falter

quay NOUN

> *boats moored alongside the quay*
> dock, harbour, pier, wharf, jetty, landing stage

queasy ADJECTIVE

> *Long bus journeys make me feel queasy.*
> sick, nauseous, ill, unwell, groggy, green

queen NOUN

> *The infant Mary was crowned Queen of Scots.*
> monarch, sovereign, ruler
> **SEE ALSO ruler**

queer ADJECTIVE

> *There's a queer smell in here.*
> odd, peculiar, strange, unusual, abnormal, curious, funny, weird, bizarre, mysterious, puzzling
> **OPPOSITES normal, ordinary**

quench VERB

> 1 *water to quench your thirst*
> satisfy, ease, alleviate, assuage, cool
> **IDIOM** take the edge off
> **OPPOSITE intensify**
> 2 *Firefighters are struggling to quench a forest fire.*
> extinguish, put out, smother, snuff out
> **OPPOSITE kindle**

query NOUN

> *Please email your queries to this address.*

question, enquiry, problem

query VERB

> *querying the referee's decision*
> question, challenge, dispute, argue with, quarrel with, object to
> **OPPOSITE accept**

quest NOUN

> *a quest to find your ancestral roots*
> search, hunt, expedition, mission, pilgrimage, odyssey

question NOUN

> 1 *Does anyone have any questions?*
> enquiry, query
> ► A question which someone sets as a puzzle is a **brain-teaser**, **conundrum**, or **riddle**.
> ► A series of questions asked as a game is a **quiz**.
> ► A set of questions used in a survey is a **questionnaire**.
> 2 *There's some question over his fitness to play.*
> uncertainty, doubt, argument, debate, dispute
> 3 *discussing important questions of the day*
> matter, issue, topic, concern, problem, controversy

question VERB

> 1 *questioning a suspect*
> interrogate, cross-examine, interview, quiz
> *(informal)* grill, pump for information
> ► To question someone about a mission they have completed is to **debrief** them.
> 2 *questioning the referee's decision*
> query, challenge, dispute, argue with, quarrel with, object to
> **OPPOSITE accept**

queue NOUN

> *a queue of people waiting for tickets*
> line, file, column, string, procession, train
> ► A long queue of traffic on a road is a **tailback**.

queue VERB

Please queue in an orderly fashion.
line up, form a queue
(North American) wait in line

quick ADJECTIVE

1 *You need to be quick when applying the paint.*
fast, swift, rapid, speedy, snappy, brisk
(informal) nippy
❙ **OPPOSITES** slow, unhurried

2 *Do you mind if I make a quick phone call?*
short, brief, momentary, hurried, hasty, cursory, perfunctory
❙ **OPPOSITES** long, lengthy

3 *I would appreciate a quick reply.*
prompt, immediate, instant, direct
❙ **OPPOSITE** delayed

4 *I'm not feeling very quick today.*
bright, sharp, clever, acute, alert, perceptive
❙ **IDIOM** (informal) on the ball
❙ **OPPOSITES** slow, dull

quicken VERB

1 *The pace quickens as the story unfolds.*
accelerate, speed up, step up, pick up speed

2 *how to quicken the interest of your readers*
stimulate, excite, rouse, stir up, spark, kindle

quickly ADVERB

1 *Ailsa walked quickly ahead.*
fast, hurriedly, swiftly, rapidly, speedily, snappily, briskly, at speed
❙ **IDIOMS** at the double, at full tilt
❙ **OPPOSITES** slowly, unhurriedly

2 *I had to come up with a plan quickly.*
immediately, at once, right away, directly, instantly, forthwith
(informal) pronto, asap
❙ **IDIOM** in a heartbeat

quiet ADJECTIVE

1 *Suddenly the whole room went quiet.*
silent, still, noiseless, soundless, speechless, mute
❙ **OPPOSITE** noisy

2 *spoken in a quiet voice*
hushed, low, soft, faint, muted, muffled, whispered
▶ Something that is too quiet to hear clearly is **inaudible**.
❙ **OPPOSITE** loud

3 *Mel has always been a quiet child.*
shy, reserved, subdued, placid, uncommunicative, retiring, withdrawn
❙ **OPPOSITE** talkative

4 *I found a quiet place to sit and read.*
peaceful, tranquil, secluded, restful, calm, serene
❙ **OPPOSITE** busy

quieten VERB

▷ **quieten down**
Eventually the audience quietened down.
fall silent, calm down, settle

quietly ADVERB

1 *Gemma crept quietly along the corridor.*
silently, noiselessly, without a sound, inaudibly
❙ **OPPOSITE** noisily

2 *A voice whispered quietly into my ear.*
softly, faintly, in a whisper, under your breath, in an undertone
❙ **OPPOSITE** loudly

quit VERB

1 *I'm thinking of quitting my job.*
leave, give up, resign from
(informal) pack in

2 *(informal) Quit asking me all these questions!*
stop, cease, refrain from
(informal) leave off

quite ADVERB

1 *His sisters have quite different personalities.*
completely, totally, utterly, entirely, wholly, absolutely, altogether
❙ **OPPOSITE** slightly

》

a
b
c
d
e
f
g
h
i
j
k
l
m
n
o
p
q
r
s
t
u
v
w
x
y
z

2 *It's still quite dark outside.*
fairly, reasonably, moderately,
comparatively, rather, somewhat
(informal) pretty

quiver *VERB*
*The dog was wet through and
quivering with cold.*
shiver, shake, shudder, tremble,
quake, quaver, wobble

quiz *NOUN*
a general knowledge quiz
test, competition

quiz *VERB*
*Detectives quizzed him about his
missing wife.*
question, interrogate,
cross-examine, interview
(informal) grill

quota *NOUN*
*Each account has a quota of
100 megabytes.*
allocation, allowance, ration, share,
portion

quotation *NOUN*
*a famous quotation from
Shakespeare*
extract, excerpt, passage, piece
▶ A piece taken from a newspaper is a
cutting.
▶ A piece taken from a film or TV
programme is a **clip**.

quote *VERB*
1 *He ended by quoting a poem by
Kipling.*
recite, repeat
2 *Let me quote you an example.*
mention, cite, name, refer to,
point out

Rr

race① NOUN

a cross-country race
competition, contest, chase

▶ A race to decide who will take part in the final is a **heat**.

race VERB

1 *I'll race you to the corner.*
have a race with, run against, compete with

2 *I raced home to tell them the exciting news.*
run, rush, hurry, dash, sprint, fly, tear, whizz, zoom
SEE ALSO run

race② NOUN

1 *people of many different races*
ethnic group, people, nation

2 *discrimination on the grounds of race*
racial origin, ethnic origin

rack NOUN

a clothes rack
frame, framework, support, holder, stand, shelf

racket① NOUN

a tennis racket
SEE **sport**

racket② NOUN

The chickens are making a terrible racket!
noise, din, row, commotion, clamour, uproar, rumpus, hubbub

radiant ADJECTIVE

a radiant smile
bright, dazzling, happy, cheerful, joyful, warm

radiate VERB

1 *All stars radiate light.*
give off, send out, emit, discharge

2 *a woman who radiates confidence*
show, exhibit, exude, emanate, ooze

3 *petals radiating from the centre of the flower*
spread out, fan out, branch out, issue

radical ADJECTIVE

1 *making radical changes to the script*
fundamental, drastic, thorough, comprehensive, extensive, sweeping, wide-ranging, far-reaching, major, profound
OPPOSITE superficial

2 *radical views on education*
extreme, revolutionary, militant
OPPOSITE moderate

radio NOUN

FOR TERMS USED IN RADIO AND TELEVISION SEE television

rage NOUN

The cyclops let out a cry of rage.
anger, fury, wrath, temper, outrage, indignation, pique

rage VERB

1 *Naomi just sat there, raging inwardly.*
be angry, be enraged, fume, seethe, rant, rave

2 *The storm raged all evening.*
blow, storm, rampage

ragged ADJECTIVE

1 *a stranger wearing ragged clothes*
tattered, torn, frayed, threadbare, ripped, patched, shabby, worn out
(informal) tatty
(North American informal) raggedy

2 *a ragged line of trees*
irregular, uneven, rough, jagged

raid NOUN

a series of nightly bombing raids
attack, assault, strike, onslaught, storming, invasion, foray, blitz

a
b
c
d
e
f
g
h
i
j
k
l
m
n
o
p
q
r
s
t
u
v
w
x
y
z

raid VERB

   1 *The monastery was raided by Vikings in 795.*
   attack, invade, ransack, plunder, loot, pillage

   2 *Police raided the house at dawn.*
   descend on, break into, rush, storm, swoop on

rail NOUN

   a track made of steel rails
   bar, rod, spar

   ▶ A fence made of rails is also called **railings**.

railway NOUN
   SEE **transport** NOUN

rain NOUN

   a sudden shower of rain
   rainfall, raindrops, drizzle
   (formal) precipitation

   ▶ The rainy season in south and south-east Asia is the **monsoon**.

   ▶ A long period without rain is a **drought**.

   ▶ A fall of rain is a **shower** or **downpour**.

   ▶ A heavy fall of rain is a **deluge**.
   FOR TIPS ON DESCRIBING WEATHER SEE **weather**

rain VERB

   Is it still raining outside?
   pour, teem, bucket, pelt, spit, drizzle

rainbow NOUN

WORD WEB

the colours of a rainbow (in order)
red, orange, yellow, green, blue, indigo, violet

   ▶ The band of colours seen in a rainbow is the **spectrum**.
   FOR TIPS ON DESCRIBING COLOURS SEE **colour**

rainforest NOUN
   the Amazonian rainforest
   tropical forest, jungle

   ▶ The topmost part of a rainforest is the **canopy** and the lower parts are the **undergrowth** or **forest floor**.

rainy ADJECTIVE

   a cold and rainy day
   wet, showery, drizzly, damp
   (formal) inclement
   ┃ OPPOSITES dry, fine
   FOR TIPS ON DESCRIBING WEATHER SEE **weather**

raise VERB

   1 *Roxanne raised the mirror to her face.*
   lift, hold up, put up, elevate, hoist

   2 *raising the price of fuel*
   increase, put up, push up, inflate
   (informal) bump up, jack up

   3 *Can you raise the volume?*
   amplify, magnify, increase, boost

   4 *raising money for charity*
   collect, gather, take in, make

   5 *trying to raise a family*
   bring up, care for, look after, nurture, rear

   6 *Several objections have been raised.*
   put forward, bring up, mention, present, submit, table, air

   7 *The letter raised some doubts in my mind.*
   produce, create, give rise to, prompt, engender

   8 *I don't want to raise your hopes.*
   encourage, build up, arouse

rake VERB

   1 *raking fallen leaves into a heap*
   gather, collect, scrape

   2 *raking through the debris for evidence*
   rummage, search, hunt, sift

rally NOUN

   1 *holding a rally in the town square*
   demonstration, meeting, march, protest
   (informal) demo

   2 *a rally in house prices*
   recovery, revival, improvement, resurgence, upturn, upswing

OPPOSITES slump, downturn

rally *VERB*
1 *trying to rally support for their cause*
gather, collect, amass, raise
2 *The dollar began to rally against the euro.*
recover, revive, improve, pick up, bounce back, perk up
OPPOSITES slump, slide

ram *VERB*
1 *Abel rammed a fist into the man's side.*
thrust, force, push, jam, stuff, plunge, dig, stick, jab
2 *The car skidded and rammed into a lamp-post.*
hit, strike, bump, crash into, collide with, smash into

ramble *VERB*
1 *We both enjoy rambling in the countryside.*
walk, hike, trek, backpack, roam, rove, range
2 *The speaker rambled on for hours.*
chatter, babble, prattle, drift
(British informal) rabbit, witter

rambling *ADJECTIVE*
1 *a rambling speech*
confused, disorganized, unfocused, roundabout, meandering, winding
OPPOSITE focused
2 *an old rambling farmhouse*
sprawling, spread out, straggly
OPPOSITE compact

rampage *VERB*
Mobs went rampaging through the city.
run riot, run amok, go berserk, storm, charge

random *ADJECTIVE*
a random selection of music
arbitrary, unplanned, haphazard, chance, casual, indiscriminate
OPPOSITE deliberate

range *NOUN*
1 *selling a range of electrical items*
variety, assortment, mixture, collection, selection, choice
2 *What is your target age range?*
span, scope, spectrum, compass, sweep, field
3 *a range of low hills*
chain, line, row, series, string

range *VERB*
1 *Prices range from fifteen to twenty pounds.*
vary, differ, extend, run, fluctuate
2 *Jars of preserves were ranged on the shelf.*
arrange, order, lay out, set out, line up
3 *Wild deer range over the hills.*
wander, ramble, roam, rove, stray

rank *NOUN*
1 *a rank of police officers*
row, line, file, column
2 *A black belt is the highest rank in judo.*
grade, level, position, status
▶ To raise someone to a higher rank is to **promote** them.
▶ To reduce someone to a lower rank is to **demote** them.

ransack *VERB*
1 *ransacking the wardrobe for something to wear*
search, scour, rummage through, comb
(informal) turn upside down
2 *Thieves had ransacked the building.*
loot, pillage, plunder, rob, wreck

rap *VERB*
1 *The detective rapped his knuckles on the desk.*
strike, hit, drum
2 *Someone rapped urgently on the door.*
knock, tap

rapid *ADJECTIVE*
the sound of rapid footsteps
fast, quick, speedy, swift, brisk
OPPOSITE slow

a
b
c
d
e
f
g
h
i
j
k
l
m
n
o
p
q
r
s
t
u
v
w
x
y
z

rare ADJECTIVE

1 *a rare species of orchid*
uncommon, unusual, infrequent, scarce, sparse

❚ OPPOSITE common

2 *a rare talent for storytelling*
exceptional, remarkable, outstanding, special, unrivalled

rarely ADVERB

Phil was rarely awake before noon.
seldom, infrequently, hardly ever

❚ OPPOSITE often

rash❶ ADJECTIVE

making a rash promise
reckless, foolhardy, hasty, hurried, impulsive, impetuous, unthinking, ill-considered

❚ OPPOSITES prudent, considered

rash❷ NOUN

1 *an itchy red rash*
spots, eruption

2 *a rash of UFO sightings*
series, succession, wave, flurry, outbreak, flood, spate

rate NOUN

1 *pedalling at a furious rate*
speed, pace, velocity, tempo

2 *charging a fixed hourly rate*
charge, cost, fee, payment, price, figure, amount

rate VERB

1 *How do you rate your chances of winning?*
assess, judge, estimate, evaluate, gauge, weigh up

2 *a film which rates among the all-time greats*
be considered, be regarded

rather ADVERB

1 *It's rather chilly today.*
slightly, fairly, moderately, somewhat, quite, a bit, a little

2 *I'd rather not discuss it on the phone.*
preferably, sooner, by preference, by choice

▷ **rather than**
We decided to walk rather than wait for the bus.
as opposed to, instead of

ratio NOUN

a ratio of three parts oil to one part vinegar
proportion, balance

▶ You can express a ratio as a **percentage**.

ration NOUN

a daily ration of water
allowance, allocation, quota, share, portion, helping, measure

▷ **rations**
buying rations for a camping trip
provisions, food, supplies, stores

ration VERB

Food had to be rationed during the war.
limit, restrict, share out, allocate, allot

rational ADJECTIVE

There was no rational explanation for what had happened.
logical, reasonable, sensible, sane, common-sense

❚ OPPOSITE irrational

rattle VERB

1 *Something rattled inside the parcel.*
clatter, clink, clunk

FOR TIPS ON DESCRIBING SOUNDS SEE **sound❶**

2 *The news had rattled her badly.*
unnerve, disturb, disconcert, perturb, fluster, shake, throw
(informal) faze

ravage VERB

a country ravaged by war
lay waste, devastate, destroy, blight, wreak havoc on

rave VERB

1 *Liz started raving at me down the phone.*
rage, rant, storm, fume, shout, yell

2 *Everyone is raving about the new book.*
enthuse, be excited, talk wildly

ravenous *ADJECTIVE*
SEE **hungry**

raw *ADJECTIVE*
1 *a salad of raw vegetables*
uncooked
▎**OPPOSITE** cooked
2 *importing raw materials*
unprocessed, crude, natural, unrefined, untreated
▎**OPPOSITES** manufactured, processed
3 *She started as a raw trainee reporter.*
inexperienced, untrained, new, green
▎**OPPOSITE** experienced
4 *a patch of raw skin*
red, rough, sore, tender, inflamed
5 *a raw north-east wind*
bitter, cold, chilly, biting, freezing, piercing

ray *NOUN*
a ray of sunlight
beam, shaft, stream

reach *VERB*
1 *Do you think humans will ever reach Mars?*
arrive at, go as far as, get to, make, end up at
2 *The appeal fund has reached its target.*
achieve, attain, hit
▎**OPPOSITES** miss, fall short of
3 *I can't reach the top shelf.*
get hold of, grasp, touch
4 *You can reach me on my mobile.*
contact, get in touch with, get through to, speak to, get hold of
▷ **reach out**
The zombie reached out its arms towards us.
extend, hold out, stretch out, thrust out, stick out

reach *NOUN*
1 *The lower branches were just out of my reach.*
grasp, range, stretch
2 *an island within easy reach of the mainland*
distance, range

react *VERB*
The woman reacted oddly when I gave my name.
respond, behave, answer, reply

reaction *NOUN*
What was your immediate reaction to the news?
response, answer, reply

read *VERB*
1 *Can you read this signature?*
make out, understand, decipher
2 *I read through my notes again quickly.*
look over, study, scan, leaf through, peruse
▎**IDIOM** cast your eye over
▶ To read through something very quickly is to **skim through** it.
▶ To read here and there in a book is to **dip into** it.
▶ To read something intently is to **pore over** it.

readily *ADVERB*
1 *Murray readily agreed to publish the book.*
willingly, gladly, happily, eagerly, unhesitatingly
▎**OPPOSITES** reluctantly, grudgingly
2 *All the ingredients are readily available.*
easily, conveniently, without any difficulty

ready *ADJECTIVE*
1 *When will tea be ready?*
prepared, all set, done, organized, arranged, available, in place
▎**OPPOSITE** not ready
2 *always ready to help a friend*
willing, glad, pleased, happy, keen, eager

a
b
c
d
e
f
g
h
i
j
k
l
m
n
o
p
q
r
s
t
u
v
w
x
y
z

》

OPPOSITES reluctant, unwilling

3 *Adam had a ready answer for everything.*
prompt, swift, immediate, unhesitating
OPPOSITE slow

4 *a ready supply of firewood*
available, accessible, handy, convenient, on hand

real ADJECTIVE

1 *The play is based on a real story.*
actual, true, factual, verifiable
OPPOSITES fictitious, imaginary

2 *Is that a real diamond?*
genuine, authentic, bona fide, natural
OPPOSITES artificial, imitation

3 *You can tell her emotion is real.*
sincere, honest, genuine, true, heartfelt, unfeigned
OPPOSITES insincere, put on

realistic ADJECTIVE

1 *Try to make the dialogue realistic.*
lifelike, true to life, faithful, authentic, convincing, natural
OPPOSITES inauthentic, fanciful

2 *It's not realistic to expect to lose weight overnight.*
feasible, practical, sensible, possible, workable
(informal) doable
OPPOSITES unrealistic, impractical

reality NOUN

Margot had begun to lose her grip on reality.
real life, the real world, the facts, the truth
OPPOSITE fantasy

realize VERB

1 *Don't you realize what this means?*
understand, appreciate, comprehend, perceive, recognize, grasp, see
(informal) catch on to, tumble to, twig

2 *realizing a lifelong ambition*
fulfil, achieve, accomplish,

attain, bring to fruition

really ADVERB

1 *Can there really be life on other planets?*
actually, definitely, genuinely, honestly, certainly, truly, in fact, in truth, in reality

2 *I thought that was a really good film.*
very, extremely, exceptionally

realm NOUN

1 *the mythical realm of Middle-earth*
country, kingdom, domain, empire

2 *in the realm of pure mathematics*
sphere, domain, field, area

rear❶ NOUN

The buffet car is at the rear of the train.
back, end, tail end
▶ The rear of a ship is the **stern**.
OPPOSITES front, head

rear ADJECTIVE

the rear coach of the train
back, end, last
▶ The rear legs of an animal are its **hind** legs.
OPPOSITES front, leading

rear❷ VERB

1 *rearing a large family*
bring up, raise, nurture

2 *Ahead of us reared the Himalayas.*
rise up, tower, loom, soar

3 *a cobra rearing its head*
hold up, lift, raise

rearrange VERB

1 *rearranging your desktop*
reorganize, reorder, reposition
(informal) rejig

2 *Let's rearrange our meeting.*
reschedule

reason NOUN

1 *What was the reason for the delay?*
cause, grounds, explanation, motive, justification, basis, rationale, excuse

2 *a man who never listens to reason*
sense, common sense, logic, rationality

3 *It was clear that Captain Nemo had lost his reason.*
sanity, mind, senses, wits
(*informal*) marbles

reason *VERB*

▷ **reason with someone**
It's no use reasoning with him.
argue with, persuade, talk round

reasonable *ADJECTIVE*

1 *It's perfectly reasonable to fear the unknown.*
sensible, intelligent, realistic, rational, logical, sane, sound, valid
❚ **OPPOSITES** irrational, illogical

2 *a reasonable price for a camera*
fair, moderate, affordable, respectable, acceptable
❚ **OPPOSITES** excessive, exorbitant

3 *The bike is in reasonable condition.*
satisfactory, acceptable, adequate, average, tolerable, passable, not bad, fairly good
(*informal*) OK

reassure *VERB*

She tried hard to reassure us.
calm, comfort, encourage, hearten, give confidence to
❚ **IDIOM** put your mind at rest
❚ **OPPOSITE** alarm

rebel *VERB*

Eventually the Aztecs rebelled against Cortés.
revolt, rise up
► To rebel against the captain of a ship is to **mutiny**.
❚ **OPPOSITE** obey

rebel *NOUN*

clashes between the government and rebels
revolutionary, insurgent, insurrectionist
► A crew member who rebels against the captain of a ship is a **mutineer**.
❚ **OPPOSITE** obey

rebellion *NOUN*

1 *showing signs of teenage rebellion*
resistance, defiance, disobedience, insubordination

2 *the Jacobite rebellion of 1715*
revolt, revolution, uprising, insurgence, insurrection
► A rebellion on a ship is a **mutiny**.

rebellious *ADJECTIVE*

My sister is going through a rebellious phase.
defiant, disobedient, insubordinate, mutinous, unruly, obstreperous, recalcitrant

rebound *VERB*

The ball rebounded off the keeper's chest.
bounce back, spring back, ricochet

rebuke *VERB*

Both players were rebuked by the referee.
reprimand, reproach, scold
(*informal*) tell off
(*British informal*) tick off
(*North American informal*) chew out

rebuke *NOUN*

issuing a sharp rebuke
reprimand, reproach, scolding
(*informal*) telling-off
(*British informal*) ticking-off

recall *VERB*

1 *Can you recall any of their names?*
remember, recollect, think back to
❚ **OPPOSITE** forget

2 *a look that recalls the style of the 60s*
bring to mind, remind you of, be reminiscent of, evoke, conjure up

recede *VERB*

1 *The footsteps receded into the night.*
go back, retreat, withdraw
❚ **OPPOSITE** advance

2 *Slowly, the pain in my head began to recede.*
lessen, diminish, decline, subside, ebb, fade, dwindle
❚ **OPPOSITES** grow, intensify

receive *VERB*

1 *receiving an Oscar for Best Actress*

a
b
c
d
e
f
g
h
i
j
k
l
m
n
o
p
q
r
s
t
u
v
w
x
y
z

be given, be presented with, be awarded, take, accept, collect

❙ **OPPOSITES** give, present

2 *Some passengers received minor injuries.*
experience, suffer, undergo, sustain
❙ **OPPOSITE** inflict

3 *How did he receive the news?*
react to, respond to

4 *The family will not be receiving visitors.*
greet, meet, welcome

recent ADJECTIVE
keeping up with recent fashion trends
current, contemporary, new, fresh, modern, the latest, up to date, up to the minute
❙ **OPPOSITE** old

recently ADVERB
I've not heard from her recently.
lately, of late, latterly

reception NOUN
1 *The landlady gave us a frosty reception.*
greeting, welcome, treatment

2 *a wedding reception*
party, function, gathering, get-together, celebration
(*informal*) do

recipe NOUN
1 *a simple recipe for carrot cake*
directions, instructions
▶ The items you use for a recipe are the **ingredients**.

2 *a guaranteed recipe for success*
formula, blueprint, prescription

recital NOUN
1 *a recital of modern poetry*
recitation, reading

2 *a short piano recital*
concert, performance

recite VERB
reciting a poem from memory
say aloud, read out, narrate, deliver, declaim

reckless ADJECTIVE
charged with reckless driving
careless, thoughtless, rash, irresponsible, heedless, foolhardy, negligent
❙ **OPPOSITE** careful

reckon VERB
1 (*informal*) *What do you reckon?*
think, believe, guess, imagine, feel

2 *reckoning the average cost of living*
calculate, work out, add up, compute, assess, estimate
(*informal*) tot up

▷ **reckon on**
They had never reckoned on having children.
be prepared for, plan for, anticipate, foresee, expect, consider, bargain on

recline VERB
Victoria reclined lazily on the sofa.
lean back, lie back, lounge, rest, stretch out, sprawl, loll

recognize VERB
1 *I didn't recognize the voice at first.*
identify, know, distinguish, recall, recollect, put a name to, place

2 *They refuse to recognize that there is a problem.*
acknowledge, admit, accept, grant, concede, confess, realize

recoil VERB
Cloe recoiled at the sight of blood.
draw back, shrink back, flinch, quail, wince

recollect VERB
1 *Do you recollect what happened?*
remember, recall, have a memory of
❙ **OPPOSITE** forget

2 *We sat for hours recollecting the past.*
reminisce about, think back to, cast your mind back to

recommend VERB
1 *I recommend that you book in advance.*
advise, counsel, propose, suggest,

advocate, prescribe, urge
OPPOSITE advise against

2 *Would you recommend the book to teenagers?*
endorse, praise, commend, vouch for, speak favourably of
IDIOM put in a good word for

recommendation NOUN

1 *Points are awarded on the judges' recommendation.*
advice, suggestion, proposal, guidance, counsel

2 *a personal recommendation from the author*
endorsement, testimonial, good word

reconsider VERB

Would you like to reconsider your answer?
rethink, review, reassess, re-evaluate
IDIOM have second thoughts about

reconstruct VERB

1 *trying to reconstruct a Viking longboat*
rebuild, recreate, remake, reassemble, restore

2 *reconstructing the murder scene*
recreate, re-enact, act out

record NOUN

1 *keeping a record of your dreams*
account, report, register, diary, journal, log, chronicle
▶ The records of what happened at a meeting are the **minutes**.
▶ Records of historical events written year by year are **annals**.
▶ Records consisting of historical documents are **archives**.

2 *listening to some old records*
album, disc, CD

record VERB

1 *Darwin recorded his observations during the voyage.*
write down, note, document, set down, put down, enter, register, log

2 *The concert is being recorded live.*
tape, film, video

recover VERB

1 *I managed to recover most of the data.*
get back, retrieve, regain, reclaim, recoup, repossess, find, trace
OPPOSITE lose

2 *She is still recovering from her illness.*
get better, recuperate, convalesce, heal, mend, improve, pick up, revive, bounce back
OPPOSITE deteriorate

recovery NOUN

1 *making a speedy recovery*
recuperation, improvement, convalescence, healing, revival

2 *the recovery of the lost data*
retrieval, reclamation, repossession, finding, tracing

recreation NOUN

1 *What do you do for recreation around here?*
leisure, fun, relaxation, enjoyment, amusement, entertainment, pleasure, diversion, play

2 *Curling is a popular recreation in Canada.*
pastime, hobby, leisure activity

recruit NOUN

training new recruits for fire fighting
trainee, apprentice, learner, novice
▶ A recruit training to be in the armed services is a **cadet**.

recruit VERB

recruiting new members for the book club
bring in, take on, enrol, sign up, hire, engage
▶ To be recruited into the armed services is to **enlist**.

rectangle NOUN

a rectangle of fabric
▶ A rectangle with adjacent sides of unequal length is also called an **oblong**.

recur VERB

a theme which recurs throughout the play
reappear, be repeated, come back, return, reoccur

recycle VERB

recycling household waste
reuse, reprocess, salvage, reclaim

red ADJECTIVE

1 *a bright red T-shirt*
SEE **word web panel**

2 *a girl with flaming red hair*
ginger, auburn, chestnut, coppery
(informal) carroty
FOR TIPS ON DESCRIBING HAIR SEE **hair**

3 *My eyes were red from lack of sleep.*
bloodshot, inflamed, red-rimmed

4 *Lily went red with embarrassment.*
flushed, blushing, rosy, ruddy

red ADJECTIVE, NOUN

WORD WEB

some shades of red
brick red, burgundy, cardinal,
carmine, cerise, cherry, crimson,
maroon, pillar-box red, pink,
rose, ruby, scarlet, vermilion,
wine
FOR TIPS ON DESCRIBING COLOURS
SEE **colour**

reduce VERB

reducing the amount of sugar in your diet
decrease, lessen, lower, diminish, minimize, cut, cut back, slash

▶ To reduce speed is to **decelerate**.

▶ To reduce the strength of a liquid is to **dilute** it.

❙ OPPOSITE increase

▷ **reduce to**

The audience were reduced to tears.
drive to, bring to

redundant ADJECTIVE

Delete any words that are redundant.

superfluous, unnecessary, not needed

❙ OPPOSITE essential

reek VERB

The whole building reeked of damp.
smell strongly, stink
FOR TIPS ON DESCRIBING SMELLS SEE **smell** NOUN

reel NOUN

a reel of cotton thread
spool

reel VERB

1 *Harvey reeled as if he was going to faint.*
stagger, lurch, sway, rock, totter, stumble, wobble

2 *All these questions are making my head reel.*
spin, whirl, swirl, swim, feel dizzy

▷ **reel off**

reeling off a list of ingredients
recite, rattle off, fire off

refer VERB

Your doctor may refer you to a specialist.
hand over, pass on, direct, send

▷ **refer to**

1 *Which book are you referring to?*
allude to, make reference to, mention, comment on, touch on, call attention to, bring up

2 *Refer to our website for more information.*
look up, consult, go to, turn to, call up

▷ **refer to as**

Junk email is often referred to as 'spam'.
call, term, style, dub, describe as

referee NOUN

The referee blew his whistle.
umpire, adjudicator
(informal) ref

reference NOUN

1 *The speech made no reference to recent events.*

allusion, mention (of), comment (on), remark (about)

2 *You must include a list of your references.*
source, citation, credit, authority

refill *VERB*
refilling a water bottle
top up
▶ To refill a fuel tank is to **refuel**.

refine *VERB*
1 *refining oil for use in cooking*
purify, filter, process, distil

2 *refining your presentation skills*
improve, perfect, polish, hone, fine-tune

reflect *VERB*
1 *Mirrored surfaces reflect sunlight.*
send back, throw back, shine back

2 *Her love of adventure is reflected in her writing.*
show, indicate, demonstrate, exhibit, reveal

▷ **reflect on**
reflecting on the events of the past week
think about, contemplate, consider, ponder, mull over

reflection *NOUN*
1 *seeing your reflection in a mirror*
image, likeness

2 *His art is a reflection of his passion for life.*
indication, demonstration, evidence, expression, manifestation, result

3 *allowing more time for reflection*
thinking, contemplation, consideration, deliberation, meditation, musing

reform *VERB*
1 *reforming the way we live on this planet*
improve, better, rectify, revise, refine, revamp, modify, adapt
(formal) ameliorate

2 *promising to reform in the future*
change for the better, mend your ways
▌**IDIOM** turn over a new leaf

Usage Note

Note that *re-form*, spelled with a hyphen, is a different word meaning 'get back together': *The band are re-forming after twenty years.*

---

reform *NOUN*
making reforms to the school curriculum
improvement, amendment, refinement, revision, modification

refrain *VERB*
▷ **refrain from**
I found it hard to refrain from smiling.
stop yourself, avoid, hold back from, abstain from

refresh *VERB*
1 *Maybe a walk will refresh me.*
revive, revitalize, reinvigorate, restore, freshen, wake up, perk up
▌**OPPOSITE** weary

2 *Let me refresh your memory.*
jog, prompt, prod

refreshing *ADJECTIVE*
a refreshing dip in the pool
reviving, invigorating, restorative, bracing, stimulating, fortifying

refuge *NOUN*
1 *providing refuge from the storm*
shelter, cover, protection, safety

2 *a secret mountain refuge*
hideaway, hideout, retreat, haven, sanctuary

refund *VERB*
Ask them to refund your money.
repay, pay back, give back, return

refusal *NOUN*
1 *I sent them a polite refusal.*
non-acceptance, rejection, rebuff
▌**OPPOSITE** acceptance

2 *a stubborn refusal to cooperate*
unwillingness, reluctance, disinclination
▌**OPPOSITE** willingness

a
b
c
d
e
f
g
h
i
j
k
l
m
n
o
p
q
r
s
t
u
v
w
x
y
z

refuse❶ *VERB*

   1 *refusing all offers of help*
   decline, reject, turn down, say no to,
   rebuff, spurn
   (informal) pass up
   ❙ OPPOSITE accept

   2 *We were refused permission to*
   film inside.
   deny, deprive of
   ❙ OPPOSITES grant, allow

refuse❷ *NOUN*

   recycling household refuse
   rubbish, waste, litter, junk
   (North American) trash,
   garbage

regain *VERB*

   Mike slowly began to regain
   consciousness.
   get back, get back to,
   return to

regard *VERB*

   1 *I still regard it as a*
   great film.
   think of, consider, judge, value,
   estimate, rate, look on

   2 *The boy regarded us*
   suspiciously.
   look at, gaze at, stare at, eye,
   view, observe, scrutinize, watch,
   contemplate
   ❙ SEE ALSO look

regard *NOUN*

   Hitchcock is held in high regard
   as a filmmaker.
   respect, esteem, approval,
   admiration

   ▷ **regards**
   Give my regards to your family.
   best wishes, greetings,
   compliments, respects

regarding *PREPOSITION*

   some comments regarding
   Internet safety
   about, concerning, on the
   subject of, with reference to, with
   regard to, with respect to,
   in connection with, apropos

regardless *ADJECTIVE*

   ▷ **regardless of**
   I kept on reading, regardless of the
   time.
   indifferent to, heedless of, not caring
   about, unconcerned about

region *NOUN*

   a remote region of northern
   Australia
   area, district, territory,
   province, sector, quarter, zone,
   neighbourhood

register *VERB*

   1 *You need to register your username.*
   record, enter, submit, lodge, enrol

   2 *This dial registers the oven*
   temperature.
   indicate, display, read, show

   3 *The cyborg's eyes registered no*
   emotion.
   show, express, display, exhibit,
   reveal

regret *VERB*

   Do you now regret your decision?
   be sorry about, feel remorse for,
   repent, rue

regular *ADJECTIVE*

   1 *It's important to take regular screen*
   breaks.
   evenly spaced, fixed
   ❙ OPPOSITES irregular, haphazard

   2 *checking for a regular heartbeat*
   steady, even, uniform, unvarying,
   constant, consistent
   ❙ OPPOSITES irregular, erratic, uneven

   3 *Is this your regular route to school?*
   normal, usual, customary, habitual,
   ordinary, routine, standard
   ❙ OPPOSITE unusual

   4 *one of our regular customers*
   frequent, familiar, habitual,
   persistent
   ❙ OPPOSITES rare, occasional

regulate *VERB*

   1 *No single body regulates the Internet.*
   manage, direct, control, govern,
   monitor, supervise, police

a
b
c
d
e
f
g
h
i
j
k
l
m
n
o
p
q
r
s
t
u
v
w
x
y
z

2 *Turn the dial to regulate the temperature.*
control, set, adjust, alter, moderate

regulation NOUN

new regulations to combat cybercrime
rule, order, directive, law, decree, statute

rehearsal NOUN

a rehearsal for the senior musical
practice, run-through, dry run, drill

▶ A rehearsal in which the cast wear costumes is a **dress rehearsal**.

rehearse VERB

rehearsing the final scene again
go over, practise, run over, read through

reign VERB

1 *How long did Queen Victoria reign?*
be king or queen, sit on the throne, govern, rule

2 *A climate of fear reigned in the capital.*
prevail, dominate, be rife, be rampant

reinforce VERB

1 *reinforcing the flood defences*
strengthen, boost, fortify, build up, bolster up, shore up

2 *Does the title reinforce the theme of the play?*
emphasize, stress, underline, support

reject VERB

1 *Why did you reject their offer?*
decline, refuse, turn down, say no to, spurn, snub, rebuff
▐ **OPPOSITE** accept

2 *Reject any words that are unnecessary.*
discard, get rid of, throw out, scrap
▐ **OPPOSITE** keep

rejoice VERB

Everyone rejoiced when the fighting ceased.
be happy, celebrate,

delight, exult
▐ **OPPOSITE** grieve

relate VERB

This poem relates the story of Beowulf.
tell, narrate, recount, report, describe

▷ **relate to**
1 *The rest of the letter relates to her family.*
be about, refer to, have to do with, concern

2 *How does this scene relate to the rest of the play?*
fit in with, connect to, be linked to

3 *I find it hard to relate to any of the characters.*
empathize with, identify with, feel for, get on with

related ADJECTIVE

Do you think the murders are related?
connected, linked, interconnected, allied
▐ **OPPOSITES** unrelated, unconnected

relation NOUN

1 *the relation between humans and animals*
connection, relationship, association, link, bond

2 *Are you a relation of hers?*
relative, member of the family, kinsman or kinswoman
▐ **SEE ALSO family**

relationship NOUN

1 *the relationship between diet and health*
connection, relation, association, link, bond

▶ The relationship between two numbers is a **ratio**.

2 *building a good relationship with your pet*
friendship, attachment (to), understanding (of)

3 *I'm not ready for a new relationship.*
romance, love affair, liaison, fling

a
b
c
d
e
f
g
h
i
j
k
l
m
n
o
p
q
r
s
t
u
v
w
x
y
z

relative NOUN
> SEE **relation**

relax VERB
> 1 *I like to relax by listening to music.*
> unwind, rest, take it easy, de-stress
> *(informal)* chill out
>> **IDIOM** put your feet up
> 2 *A warm bath always relaxes me.*
> calm down, soothe, de-stress
> 3 *Try to relax your grip on the racket.*
> slacken, loosen, unclench, ease,
> soften
>> **OPPOSITES** tighten, tense
> 4 *relaxing restrictions on air travel*
> ease, reduce, lighten, lessen,
> decrease
> *(informal)* let up on
>> **OPPOSITE** tighten

relaxation NOUN
> 1 *Allow some time for relaxation.*
> rest, repose, respite, leisure, time off
> *(informal)* chilling out
> 2 *a relaxation of the rules*
> easing, slackening, loosening
> *(informal)* let-up

relaxed ADJECTIVE
> *a cosy cafe with a relaxed
> atmosphere*
> informal, casual, carefree, leisurely,
> easy going, peaceful, restful,
> unhurried, calm
> *(informal)* laid-back, chilled-out
>> **OPPOSITES** tense, stressful

release VERB
> 1 *All the hostages have been released.*
> free, let go, discharge, liberate,
> set free
>> **OPPOSITES** capture, imprison
> 2 *What if they release the guard dogs?*
> let loose, set loose, unfasten,
> unleash, untie
> 3 *Their new CD will be released in
> April.*
> issue, publish, put out

relent VERB
> *Dad relented and let me use
> the computer.*
> give in, give way, yield, capitulate,
> soften, weaken

relentless ADJECTIVE
> *a relentless round of questions*
> constant, continuous, never-ending,
> incessant, perpetual, persistent,
> unremitting, unwavering

relevant ADJECTIVE
> *Make sure your answer is relevant to
> the question.*
> applicable, pertinent, to the point,
> appropriate, suitable, related,
> apposite
>> **OPPOSITE** irrelevant

reliable ADJECTIVE
> 1 *a reliable ally*
> faithful, dependable, trustworthy,
> loyal, constant, devoted,
> staunch, true
> 2 *a reliable source of information*
> dependable, valid, trustworthy, safe,
> sound, steady, sure
>> **OPPOSITES** unreliable,
>> untrustworthy

relief NOUN
> 1 *The pills gave some relief from
> the pain.*
> alleviation, easing, soothing
> 2 *watching TV for light relief*
> relaxation, rest, respite, diversion
> 3 *providing relief for the refugees*
> aid, charity, assistance, help

relieve VERB
> 1 *some pills to relieve the pain*
> alleviate, ease, soothe, lessen,
> diminish, dull
>> **OPPOSITE** intensify
> 2 *We played cards to relieve the
> boredom.*
> reduce, lighten, dispel, counteract,
> mitigate

religion NOUN
> *Prayers are used in many religions.*
> faith, belief, creed, denomination,
> sect

»

WORD WEB

major world religions
Buddhism, Christianity,
Hinduism, Islam, Judaism,
Shintoism, Sikhism, Taoism, Zen

▶ The study of religion is **divinity** or
theology.

major religious festivals
(Buddhist) Buddha Day,
Nirvana Day
(Christian) Lent, Easter, Christmas
(Hindu) Holi, Diwali
(Muslim) Ramadan, Eid
(Jewish) Passover, Rosh Hashana,
Yom Kippur, Hanukkah
(Sikh) Baisakhi,
Birth of Guru Nanak

religious leaders
cleric, clergyman or
clergywoman,
(Buddhist) lama
(Christian) priest, minister, vicar,
bishop, cardinal, pope, chaplain
(Hindu or Sikh) guru
(Muslim) imam
(Jewish) rabbi

places of religious worship
temple, shrine,
(Christian) church, chapel,
cathedral
(Muslim) mosque
(Jewish) synagogue

religious *ADJECTIVE*
1 *a concert of religious music*
sacred, spiritual, holy, divine
▌OPPOSITE secular
2 *Is your family very religious?*
devout, pious, reverent, god-fearing,
churchgoing

relish *VERB*
*Many people would relish the chance
to be on TV.*
enjoy, delight in, appreciate, savour,
revel in

reluctant *ADJECTIVE*
Bruce was reluctant to admit defeat.
unwilling, disinclined, loath,
resistant, hesitant, grudging
▌OPPOSITES eager, willing

rely *VERB*
▷ **rely on**
Can I rely on you to keep a secret?
depend on, count on, have
confidence in, trust in, be sure of
(informal) bank on

remain *VERB*
1 *Little remained of Pompeii after the
disaster.*
be left, survive, endure, abide
2 *A few people remained in their seats.*
stay, wait, linger, stay put
(informal) hang about
3 *The heatwave is forecast to remain
all week.*
continue, persist, last, keep on,
carry on

remainder *NOUN*
*We watched a film for the remainder
of the afternoon.*
rest, what is left, surplus, residue

remains *PLURAL NOUN*
1 *the remains of a house destroyed by
fire*
remnants, ruins, fragments, traces,
debris
2 *the remains of our picnic*
leftovers, remnants, residue, scraps,
leavings
▶ The remains at the bottom of a cup
are **dregs**.
3 *some ancient Aztec remains*
relics, antiquities, ruins, artefacts

remark *NOUN*
*We exchanged a few remarks about
the weather.*
comment, observation, word,
statement, reflection, mention

remark *VERB*
*'Lovely morning,' remarked a
passer-by.*
say, state, comment, note, declare,

a
b
c
d
e
f
g
h
i
j
k
l
m
n
o
p
q
r
s
t
u
v
w
x
y
z

mention, observe

┃ SEE ALSO say

remarkable ADJECTIVE

1 *a remarkable stroke of good luck*
extraordinary, astonishing, amazing,
incredible, wonderful

2 *a remarkable ear for music*
exceptional, outstanding, striking,
notable, noteworthy, impressive,
phenomenal

┃ OPPOSITE ordinary

remedy NOUN

1 *a traditional remedy for colds and
sore throats*
cure, treatment, medicine,
medication, therapy

► A remedy for the effects of poison is
an **antidote**.

2 *finding the remedy to all your
problems*
solution, answer, resolution, relief

remember VERB

1 *I'll never remember all this
information.*
memorize, retain, keep in your head

2 *Can you remember what she looked
like?*
recall, recollect, recognize, place

┃ OPPOSITE forget

3 *remembering the good old days*
reminisce about, think back to, look
back on

remind VERB

Remind me to buy a newspaper.
prompt, jog someone's memory

▷ **remind you of**
What does this tune remind you of?
make you think of, be reminiscent of,
take you back to

reminder NOUN

1 *The video is a reminder of our
holiday.*
souvenir, memento

2 *I sent round a reminder about the
party.*
prompt, cue, hint, nudge

reminiscent ADJECTIVE

▷ **be reminiscent of something**
*The tune is reminiscent of an old folk
song.*
remind you of, make you think of,
call to mind, evoke, conjure up

remnants PLURAL NOUN

the last remnants of the evening sun
remains, remainder, residue, traces,
scraps, dregs

remorse NOUN

*Curtis showed no remorse for
causing the accident.*
regret, repentance, guilt, contrition,
sorrow, shame

remote ADJECTIVE

1 *an expedition to a remote part of
Brazil*
isolated, faraway, distant,
inaccessible, cut off, secluded, out of
the way, unfrequented

┃ IDIOM off the beaten track

┃ OPPOSITE accessible

2 *a very remote possibility*
unlikely, improbable, slight, slim,
faint, doubtful

┃ OPPOSITES likely, strong

remove VERB

1 *removing the outer layers of the
mummy*
take away, take off, lift off, peel off,
strip off

2 *removing a bad tooth*
extract, take out, pull out, withdraw

3 *Some protesters were removed from
the building.*
throw out, turn out, eject, expel,
evict
(informal) kick out

► To remove someone from power is
to **depose** them.

4 *removing a stubborn stain*
get rid of, delete, erase, do away
with, eliminate, abolish

render VERB

1 *Even Jonathan was rendered
speechless.*

make, leave, cause to be

2 *We are asking the public to render their support.*
give, provide, offer, furnish, supply

3 *a portrait rendered in exquisite detail*
depict, represent, portray, reproduce, picture

renew VERB

1 *The paintwork has been completely renewed.*
repair, renovate, restore, replace, rebuild, reconstruct, revamp, refurbish, overhaul
(informal) do up

2 *a snack to renew your energy*
refresh, revive, restore, replenish, revitalize, reinvigorate

3 *renewing your library card*
bring up to date, update

4 *renewing the peace process*
restart, resume, return to, recommence

renounce VERB

He renounced his former life and became a hermit.
give up, surrender, relinquish, abandon, waive, forego

renowned ADJECTIVE

Venice is renowned for its canals.
famous, celebrated, well known, famed, noted, notable, acclaimed
OPPOSITE unknown

rent VERB

We rented bikes to tour the island.
hire, charter, lease

repair VERB

Will you be able to repair the damage?
mend, fix, put right, patch up

repair NOUN

1 *The ceiling is badly in need of repair.*
restoration, renovation, mending, fixing

2 *keeping your bike in good repair*
condition, working order,

state, shape
(British informal) nick

repay VERB

1 *You can repay me later.*
pay back, refund, reimburse

2 *How can I ever repay their kindness?*
return, reciprocate

repeat VERB

1 *Could you please repeat your name?*
say again, restate, reiterate, go through again, echo

2 *We will have to repeat the experiment.*
do again, redo, replicate

repeatedly ADVERB

I knocked repeatedly, but there was no answer.
again and again, over and over, time after time, frequently, regularly, often, many times

repel VERB

1 *repelling an attack on a military base*
drive back, beat back, fight off, fend off, hold off, resist, repulse

2 *a spray to repel insects*
keep away, ward off, deter, scare off
OPPOSITE attract

3 *repelled by the sight of blood*
disgust, revolt, sicken, nauseate, offend
(informal) turn off
OPPOSITE tempt

repellent ADJECTIVE

The villain is portrayed as truly repellent.
repulsive, revolting, hideous, horrible, loathsome, vile, objectionable, offensive, foul, disgusting
OPPOSITE attractive

replace VERB

1 *Please replace books on the correct shelf.*
put back, return, restore, reinstate

2 *Who will replace the coach next season?*

follow, succeed, take over from,
take the place of
IDIOM step into someone's shoes

3 *replacing a worn-out battery*
change, renew, swap, exchange

replacement NOUN

a replacement for the injured player
substitute, standby, stand-in,
reserve

▶ Someone who can take the place of
an actor is an **understudy**.

replica NOUN

a replica of the Statue of Liberty
copy, reproduction, model,
duplicate, imitation

▶ An exact copy of a document is a
facsimile.

reply NOUN

*I got an immediate reply to my
email.*
response, answer, reaction,
acknowledgement

▶ An angry reply is a **retort**.
▶ A quick clever reply is a **riposte**.

reply VERB

▷ **reply to**
I'd better reply to her text.
answer, respond to, send a reply to,
react to, acknowledge

report VERB

1 *reporting your findings to the rest of
the group*
communicate, give an account
of, describe, announce, publish,
broadcast, disclose

2 *He threatened to report us to the
police.*
complain about, inform on,
denounce
(informal) tell on, rat on, shop

3 *Please report to reception when you
arrive.*
present yourself, make yourself
known, check in

report NOUN

1 *receiving reports of heavy casualties*
account, news, information,

word, intelligence

2 *a report on the news website*
story, article, piece, item, feature,
column, bulletin

3 *hearing the loud report of a rifle*
bang, crack, noise, explosion

reporter NOUN

a reporter for a local newspaper
journalist, correspondent, columnist

represent VERB

1 *The dove usually represents peace.*
stand for, symbolize, personify,
epitomize, embody

2 *a statue representing Zeus*
depict, portray, illustrate, picture,
show, render

3 *Authors are often represented by a
literary agent.*
speak for, appear for, speak on
someone's behalf, stand in for

reprimand NOUN

*a severe reprimand from the team
coach*
reproach, rebuke, scolding
(informal) telling-off
(British informal) ticking-off
OPPOSITE praise

reprimand VERB

being reprimanded by a teacher
reproach, rebuke, scold
(informal) tell off
(British informal) tick off
(North American informal) chew out
OPPOSITE praise

reproduce VERB

1 *a device which can reproduce human
speech*
copy, duplicate, replicate, imitate,
simulate, mimic

2 *Rats and mice reproduce quickly.*
breed, procreate, produce offspring,
multiply

▶ Fish reproduce by **spawning**.
▶ To reproduce plants is to **propagate**
them.

reproduction NOUN

1 *a reproduction of the Lewis chess set*

copy, replica, imitation, duplicate, likeness
▶ An exact reproduction of a document is a **facsimile**.
▶ A reproduction which is intended to deceive people is a **fake** or **forgery**.
2 *the cycle of animal reproduction*
breeding, procreation, propagation

reptile NOUN

WORD WEB

some animals which are reptiles

alligator, caiman, chameleon, crocodile, gecko, iguana, Komodo dragon, lizard, salamander, skink, slow-worm, snake, terrapin, tortoise, turtle
▶ A **basilisk** is a reptile found in myths and legends.
▶ Reptiles are described as **cold-blooded** because their body temperature is the same as the surrounding environment.
▶ The scientific study of amphibians and reptiles is **herpetology**.
▶ A related adjective is **reptilian**.

repulsive ADJECTIVE

the repulsive stench of rotting flesh
disgusting, revolting, offensive, repellent, disagreeable, foul, repugnant, obnoxious, sickening, nauseating, loathsome, objectionable, nasty, vile
❙ **OPPOSITE** attractive

reputation NOUN

a street artist with an international reputation
fame, celebrity, name, renown, eminence, standing, stature

request VERB

1 *players who are requesting a transfer*
ask for, appeal for, call for, seek, apply for, beg for, demand
2 *requesting the government to intervene*

ask, call on, invite, entreat, implore, beg, beseech

request NOUN

1 *a request for humanitarian aid*
appeal, plea, entreaty, call, cry, demand
▶ A request for a job or membership is an **application**.
▶ A request signed by a lot of people is a **petition**.
2 *It was her last request before she died.*
wish, desire, requirement

require VERB

1 *patients who require immediate treatment*
need, must have, demand, depend on
2 *Visitors are required to sign the register.*
instruct, oblige, request, direct, order, command
3 *Is there anything in particular that you require?*
want, desire, be short of, lack

rescue VERB

1 *rescuing survivors from the rubble*
free, liberate, release, save, set free, deliver
2 *rescuing a sunken ship*
retrieve, recover, salvage

rescue NOUN

the successful rescue of the entire crew
rescuing, release, freeing, liberation, deliverance, recovery, retrieval

resemblance NOUN

the resemblance between humans and primates
likeness, similarity, closeness, correspondence, comparability
❙ **OPPOSITES** difference, dissimilarity

resemble VERB

The structure of DNA resembles a twisted ladder.
look like, be similar to, remind you of, approximate to, echo   »

(informal) take after
⌐ **OPPOSITE** differ from

resent *VERB*

> *Many Germans resented the Treaty of Versailles.*
> feel bitter about, feel aggrieved about, take exception to, be resentful of, object to, begrudge, grudge

resentment *NOUN*

> *feeling a growing resentment*
> bitterness, dissatisfaction, discontentment, disgruntlement, rancour, acrimony

reservation *NOUN*

> 1 *a reservation for bed and breakfast*
> booking
> 2 *a wildlife reservation in Kenya*
> reserve, park, preserve, sanctuary
> 3 *I still have reservations about the idea.*
> doubt, misgiving, hesitation, qualm, scruple
> ► If you have reservations about something, you are **sceptical** about it.

reserve *VERB*

> 1 *reserving fuel for the return voyage*
> set aside, put aside, save, keep, preserve, retain, hold back
> 2 *Have you reserved your seats on the train?*
> book, order, secure

reserve *NOUN*

> 1 *a month's reserve of food*
> stock, store, supply, hoard, stockpile, pool, cache, fund
> 2 *named as a reserve for the match*
> substitute, standby, stand-in, replacement
> ► Someone who can take the place of an actor is an **understudy**.
> 3 *a wild bird reserve*
> reservation, park, preserve, sanctuary
> 4 *a natural air of reserve*
> shyness, timidity, taciturnity,

reticence, inhibition, modesty, diffidence

reserved *ADJECTIVE*

> 1 *These seats are reserved.*
> booked, set aside, ordered, taken, spoken for
> 2 *He was unusually reserved that evening.*
> shy, timid, taciturn, quiet, uncommunicative, withdrawn, reticent, inhibited, diffident
> ⌐ **OPPOSITE** outgoing

residence *NOUN*

> *the former residence of John Lennon*
> home, house, address, dwelling
> *(old use)* abode

resident *NOUN*

> *the residents of Manhattan*
> inhabitant, citizen, native, occupant, householder
> ► A temporary resident in a hotel is a **guest**.
> ► A resident in rented accommodation is a **boarder**, **lodger**, or **tenant**.

resign *VERB*

> *The team manager has been forced to resign.*
> leave, stand down, step down, give in your notice, quit, bow out
> ► A monarch who resigns from the throne is said to **abdicate**.

resist *VERB*

> 1 *your body's ability to resist disease*
> stand up to, withstand, defend yourself against, fend off, combat, oppose, defy
> ⌐ **OPPOSITES** succumb to, give in to
> 2 *Some residents are resisting the plan.*
> oppose, object to, fight against, defy
> ⌐ **OPPOSITES** agree to, welcome
> 3 *I couldn't resist taking a peek.*
> refrain from, hold back from, abstain from
> ⌐ **OPPOSITE** allow yourself to

resistance *NOUN*

> 1 *widespread resistance to the proposals*

opposition, objection, hostility, defiance

┃ OPPOSITE agreement

2 *building up resistance to disease*
immunity, defences (against)

resolution NOUN

1 *making a New Year resolution*
commitment, pledge, promise, intention

2 *a long-term resolution to the problem*
solution, answer, settlement, ending, conclusion

resolve VERB

1 *We resolved to press on until nightfall.*
decide, determine, make up your mind

2 *trying to resolve a bitter dispute*
settle, sort out, straighten out, end, overcome

resort VERB

▷ **resort to**
In the end, Dave resorted to bribery.
turn to, fall back on, stoop to

resort NOUN

trying bribery as a last resort
option, alternative, choice, course of action

resound VERB

Frantic screams resounded through the crowd.
echo, reverberate, resonate, ring, boom

resources PLURAL NOUN

1 *a country rich in natural resources*
materials, raw materials, reserves

2 *allocating more resources to health care*
funds, money, capital, assets, means, wealth

respect NOUN

1 *earning the respect of your peers*
admiration, esteem, regard, reverence, honour

2 *being treated with respect*
consideration, politeness, courtesy, civility

3 *In some respects, the book is now dated.*
aspect, way, sense, regard, detail, feature, point, particular

respect VERB

1 *He was highly respected as a songwriter.*
admire, esteem, think highly of, look up to, honour, revere

┃ OPPOSITES scorn, despise

2 *respecting other people's privacy*
show consideration for, be mindful of, have regard for

┃ OPPOSITE disregard

3 *respecting the wishes of her dead husband*
obey, follow, observe, adhere to, comply with

┃ OPPOSITES ignore, defy

respectable ADJECTIVE

1 *a respectable family background*
decent, honest, upright, honourable, reputable, worthy

2 *What would be a respectable score?*
reasonable, satisfactory, acceptable, passable, adequate, fair, tolerable

respective ADJECTIVE

The pets were returned to their respective owners.
own, personal, individual, separate, particular, specific

respite NOUN

a brief respite during a hectic day
rest, break, breathing space, relief, lull

respond VERB

▷ **respond to**
No one has responded to my email.
reply to, answer, react to, acknowledge

response NOUN

an immediate response to my text
reply, answer, reaction, acknowledgement

▶ An angry response is a **retort**.

▶ A quick clever response is a **riposte**.

a
b
c
d
e
f
g
h
i
j
k
l
m
n
o
p
q
r
s
t
u
v
w
x
y
z

responsible ADJECTIVE

1 *Miss Kumar is responsible for the school's website.*
in charge (of), in control (of)

2 *You seem to be a responsible sort of person.*
reliable, sensible, trustworthy, dependable, conscientious, dutiful
❙ OPPOSITE irresponsible

3 *a responsible position in the government*
important, serious, high-powered

4 *I hope they find whoever is responsible.*
to blame, guilty (of), at fault, culpable

rest❶ NOUN

1 *taking a short rest after lunch*
break, pause, respite, breathing space, nap, lie-down, siesta
(informal) breather

2 *Try to get as much rest as you can.*
relaxation, repose, inactivity, leisure, ease, quiet, time off

rest VERB

1 *Let's stop and rest for a while.*
have a rest, take a break, relax, have a nap, take it easy, lie down
(informal) have a breather
❙ IDIOM *(informal)* put your feet up

2 *resting a ladder against a wall*
lean, prop, stand, place, support

3 *Victor refused to let the matter rest.*
lie, be dormant

rest❷ NOUN

▷ **the rest**
I spent the rest of the money on clothes.
the remainder, the surplus, the remains, the residue, the others

restaurant NOUN

WORD WEB

some types of restaurant
bistro, brasserie, buffet, cafe, cafeteria, canteen, carvery, chip shop, coffee shop, diner, grill room, ice cream parlour, pizzeria, snack bar, steakhouse, takeaway, tea room, wine bar

restful ADJECTIVE

getting a restful night's sleep
peaceful, undisturbed, quiet, relaxing, leisurely, calm, tranquil
❙ OPPOSITES restless, disturbed

restless ADJECTIVE

1 *I'd been feeling strangely restless all morning.*
agitated, nervous, anxious, uneasy, edgy, jumpy, jittery, tense
(informal) uptight, nervy
❙ OPPOSITE relaxed

2 *Monica spent a restless night worrying.*
sleepless, wakeful, troubled, disturbed, unsettled
❙ OPPOSITES restful, peaceful

restore VERB

1 *restoring a computer to its original settings*
put back, return, reset

2 *a plan to restore trams to the city*
bring back, reinstate, re-establish

3 *restoring vintage motorcycles*
renew, repair, renovate, recondition, fix, mend, rebuild
(informal) do up

restrain VERB

1 *Dogs must be restrained on a leash.*
hold back, keep back, keep under control, restrict

2 *Patty tried to restrain her anger.*
control, check, curb, suppress, contain, hold in
❙ IDIOM keep the lid on

restrict VERB

1 *software which restricts Internet access*
control, limit, regulate, moderate, keep within bounds

2 *clothes that won't restrict your movement*

a
b
c
d
e
f
g
h
i
j
k
l
m
n
o
p
q
r
s
t
u
v
w
x
y
z

hinder, impede, obstruct, block

result *NOUN*

1 *The bush fires were the result of a long drought.*
consequence, effect, outcome, upshot, sequel (to)
OPPOSITE cause

2 *What was the result of the match?*
score, tally

result *VERB*

Poor sleep may result from a high-fat diet.
come about, develop, emerge, happen, occur, follow, ensue

▷ **result in**
The passing of the Stamp Act resulted in riots.
cause, bring about, give rise to, lead to, develop into

resume *VERB*

The class will resume after lunch.
restart, start again, recommence, proceed, continue, carry on
OPPOSITES discontinue, cease

resurgence *NOUN*

a resurgence of interest in ballroom dancing
revival, renewal, reawakening, renaissance

retain *VERB*

1 *Please retain your ticket for inspection.*
hold on to, keep, preserve, reserve, save
(informal) hang on to
OPPOSITE surrender

2 *a roof designed to retain rainwater*
hold in, keep in, hold back
OPPOSITE release

retire *VERB*

1 *planning to retire at the age of 60*
give up work, stop working, bow out
▶ To leave your job voluntarily is to **resign**.

2 *Olivia retired to her room with a headache.*
withdraw, retreat, adjourn

retort *NOUN*
SEE **reply**

retreat *VERB*

1 *We retreated to a safe distance from the bonfire.*
move back, draw back, fall back, withdraw, retire
OPPOSITE advance

2 *a snail retreating into its shell*
shrink back, recoil

retreat *NOUN*

1 *the retreat of the glacier in recent years*
withdrawal, falling back, shrinking
OPPOSITE advance

2 *a peaceful island retreat*
haven, refuge, sanctuary, hideout

retrieve *VERB*

Did you ever retrieve the stolen equipment?
get back, bring back, recover, rescue, salvage

return *VERB*

1 *I hope to return to New Zealand some day.*
go back, revisit

2 *The rest of the group returns tomorrow.*
get back, come back, come home

3 *Take these pills if the symptoms return.*
reappear, come back, recur

4 *returning a book to the library*
give back, bring back, take back, send back

5 *returning the milk to the fridge*
put back, replace, restore

return *NOUN*

1 *looking forward to my friends' return*
homecoming

2 *the safe return of the missing document*
retrieval, recovery

3 *the return of spring*
reappearance, recurrence

a
b
c
d
e
f
g
h
i
j
k
l
m
n
o
p
q
r
s
t
u
v
w
x
y
z

4 *a good return on your savings*
profit, interest, gain

reveal VERB

1 *The bookcase swung out to reveal a secret room.*
uncover, unveil, expose
OPPOSITES hide, conceal

2 *She never revealed her real identity.*
disclose, make known, divulge, confess, admit, make public, give away, let slip

revel VERB

▷ **revel in**
Leona revelled in all the attention.
enjoy, delight in, love, adore, relish, savour, lap up

revenge NOUN

seeking revenge for his father's murder
vengeance, reprisal, retribution, retaliation

▷ **take revenge on someone**
He swore to take revenge on them all.
get even with, make someone pay
(informal) get your own back on

revenge VERB

Hamlet plots to revenge his father's murder.
avenge, exact retribution for, get redress for
(informal) get your own back for

revere VERB

a graphic artist who is revered in Japan
admire, respect, esteem, think highly of, look up to, venerate
OPPOSITE despise

reverse NOUN

1 *the reverse of what I expected*
opposite, contrary, converse, antithesis, inverse

2 *a letter with a note on the reverse*
other side, back

reverse VERB

1 *reversing a digital image*
turn round, swap round, turn back to front, transpose, invert, flip

2 *reversing into a parking space*
back, move backwards, go backwards

3 *reversing their previous decision*
go back on, overturn, overrule, cancel, revoke

review NOUN

1 *a review of safety procedures*
study, survey, examination, inspection, enquiry, probe

2 *a review of the new film*
critique, commentary, report, appraisal, assessment

review VERB

1 *reviewing the available evidence*
examine, go over, study, survey, consider, assess, evaluate, weigh up, size up

2 *reviewing the latest films*
write a review of, comment on

▶ A person who reviews books or films is a **reviewer** or **critic**.

revise VERB

1 *revising my notes from last term*
go over, review, reread, study, cram

2 *You need to revise that paragraph.*
correct, amend, edit, rewrite, update

3 *revising their views on climate change*
reconsider, re-examine, rethink, modify, change, alter

revival NOUN

1 *a revival in our fortunes*
improvement, upturn, upswing, resurgence, rallying

2 *the revival of the Gaelic language*
restoration, renaissance, resurrection, comeback, re-establishment

revive VERB

1 *reviving slowly after the operation*
come round, come to, regain consciousness

2 *attempts to revive the patient*
bring round, resuscitate

3 *A cup of tea should revive you.*
refresh, restore, reinvigorate, revitalize, bring back to life

revolt *VERB*

1 *Viewers were revolted by the scenes of violence.*
disgust, repel, sicken, nauseate, offend, appal, put off
(informal) turn off
  IDIOM turn your stomach

2 *In 1641 the Irish revolted against British rule.*
rebel, riot, rise up
▶ To revolt on a ship is to **mutiny**.

revolt *NOUN*

Boudicca led a revolt against the Romans.
rebellion, riot, uprising, insurgence, insurrection, revolution
▶ A revolt on a ship is a **mutiny**.

revolting *ADJECTIVE*

What is that revolting smell?
disgusting, foul, horrible, nasty, loathsome, offensive, obnoxious, repulsive, repugnant, sickening, nauseating, vile, unpleasant
  OPPOSITES pleasant, attractive

revolution *NOUN*

1 *the Russian Revolution in 1917*
rebellion, revolt, uprising, insurrection, insurgence

2 *The 1960s saw a fashion revolution.*
change, transformation, shift, sea change
(informal) shake-up

3 *a single revolution of the Earth*
rotation, turn, circuit, cycle, orbit, lap

revolutionary *ADJECTIVE*

a revolutionary type of battery
new, novel, innovative, unconventional, unorthodox, radical, pioneering

revolve *VERB*

1 *The Earth revolves once every 24 hours.*
rotate, turn, spin

2 *The Moon revolves around the Earth.*
circle, go around, orbit

reward *NOUN*

1 *a reward for all your hard work*
recompense, bonus, award, treat
(informal) pay-off
  OPPOSITE punishment

2 *a reward for the capture of Jesse James*
payment, bounty

reward *VERB*

rewarding your pet for good behaviour
recompense, give a treat to, give a bonus to, repay
  OPPOSITE punish

rewarding *ADJECTIVE*

Doing something creative is always rewarding.
satisfying, gratifying, fulfilling, enriching, pleasing, worthwhile
  OPPOSITE thankless

rhyme *NOUN*

a book of nonsense rhymes
poem, verse
  SEE ALSO poem

rhythm *NOUN*

clapping to the rhythm of the music
beat, pulse, tempo, swing
▶ The rhythm of a poem is its **metre**.

rich *ADJECTIVE*

1 *His family were relatively rich.*
wealthy, affluent, prosperous, moneyed, well-off, well-to-do
(informal) flush, loaded, well-heeled
  OPPOSITES poor, impoverished

2 *an Elizabethan house with rich interiors*
luxurious, lavish, sumptuous, opulent, splendid, expensive, costly

3 *hair of a rich chestnut colour*
deep, strong, vivid, intense

4 *cutting down on rich foods*
fatty, creamy, heavy

5 *Plant the bulbs in moist rich soil.*

》

a
b
c
d
e
f
g
h
i
j
k
l
m
n
o
p
q
r
s
t
u
v
w
x
y
z

fertile, fruitful, productive
▷ **be rich in**
The Galapagos Islands are rich in animal and plant species.
be full of, abound in, teem with, overflow with, be well supplied with, be well stocked with

riches PLURAL NOUN
Ebenezer sat greedily counting his riches.
wealth, money, fortune, treasure, affluence, prosperity

richly ADVERB
1 richly decorated with gold leaf
luxuriously, lavishly, opulently, sumptuously, splendidly, expensively
▎OPPOSITES meanly, plainly
2 an award which is richly deserved
well, fully, thoroughly, completely, utterly, absolutely
▎OPPOSITES barely, scarcely

rickety ADJECTIVE
a rickety old step ladder
shaky, unsteady, unstable, wobbly, flimsy
▎OPPOSITES solid, firm

rid VERB
Sharks help to rid the oceans of rotting carcasses.
clear, free, empty, strip, purge
▷ **get rid of**
getting rid of unwanted emails
dispose of, throw away, throw out, discard, scrap, dump, jettison
(informal) ditch, chuck out

riddle NOUN
The Sphinx posed a riddle to passers-by.
puzzle, question, conundrum, problem, mystery
(informal) brain-teaser, poser

ride VERB
1 learning to ride a bike
control, handle, manage, steer
2 riding around on a scooter
travel, drive, cycle, run

ride NOUN
taking a ride on a snowmobile
drive, run, journey, trip
(informal) spin

ridicule VERB
Einstein was ridiculed at first.
laugh at, make fun of, mock, scoff at, jeer at, sneer at, taunt, tease, deride
▎OPPOSITE respect

ridiculous ADJECTIVE
1 I felt ridiculous wearing a frilly dress.
silly, stupid, foolish, absurd, laughable, farcical
(British informal) daft
▎OPPOSITE sensible
2 charging ridiculous prices
ludicrous, senseless, nonsensical, preposterous, outrageous, absurd, unreasonable
▎OPPOSITE reasonable

right ADJECTIVE
1 using the right side of your brain
right-hand
▶ The right side of a ship when you face forwards is the **starboard** side.
▎OPPOSITE left
2 That is the right answer.
correct, accurate, true, exact
▎OPPOSITE wrong
3 waiting for the right moment to speak
proper, appropriate, fitting, suitable, ideal, perfect
▎OPPOSITE wrong
4 It's not right to make illegal copies.
fair, honest, ethical, moral, just, honourable, decent, upright, virtuous
▎OPPOSITE wrong

right ADVERB
1 Turn right at the corner.
▎OPPOSITE left
2 Go right ahead.
directly, straight
3 We had walked right round in a circle.
all the way, completely

a b c d e f g h i j k l m n o p q r s t u v w x y z

4 *a dot right in the centre of the screen*
exactly, precisely, squarely, dead
(informal) bang

5 *Did he say the words right this time?*
correctly, properly, accurately,
perfectly

6 *(informal) I'll be right back.*
immediately, promptly, soon

right NOUN

1 *Take the exit on the right.*
OPPOSITE left

2 *the difference between right and wrong*
goodness, fairness, virtue, morality,
truth, justice
OPPOSITE wrong

3 *the right of citizens to vote*
entitlement, privilege, prerogative,
freedom, liberty, licence, power

rigid ADJECTIVE

1 *a rigid steel framework*
stiff, firm, hard, inflexible,
unbending
OPPOSITES flexible, pliable

2 *taking a rigid stance on the issue*
strict, inflexible, stringent,
uncompromising, intransigent
OPPOSITES flexible, lenient

rigorous ADJECTIVE

1 *after months of rigorous training*
strict, rigid, tough, harsh,
uncompromising

2 *a rigorous police investigation*
thorough, careful, meticulous,
painstaking, conscientious,
scrupulous

rim NOUN

the breathtaking view from the rim of the canyon
brim, edge, lip, brink

ring❶ NOUN

1 *mushrooms growing in a ring*
circle, round, loop, circuit

2 *Each bird is tagged with a metal ring.*
band, hoop

3 *Four gladiators entered the ring.*
arena, circus, enclosure

4 *uncovering a spy ring*
organization, network, syndicate,
league

ring VERB

a large compound ringed by barbed wire
surround, encircle, enclose, circle

ring❷ VERB

1 *the sound of church bells ringing*
chime, peal, toll, clang

2 *The doorbell rang unexpectedly.*
sound, buzz, jangle, tinkle

3 *The auditorium rang with applause.*
resound, echo, resonate,
reverberate

4 *Ring me later this evening.*
phone, call, telephone,
give someone a call
(informal) give someone a ring,
give someone a bell

rinse VERB

Rinse the wound carefully with clean water.
wash, clean, cleanse, bathe, swill,
sluice, flush out

riot NOUN

1 *The incident sparked a riot in the capital.*
disturbance, commotion, turmoil,
disorder, uproar, uprising

2 *In summer, the garden is a riot of colour.*
mass, profusion, splash, sea

riot VERB

Students rioted in the streets of the capital.
run riot, run wild, run amok,
rampage, revolt, rise up, rebel

rip VERB

1 *ripping the lining of your jacket*
tear, slit

2 *She ripped the letter out of my hands.*
pull, tug, wrench, snatch, tear

a
b
c
d
e
f
g
h
i
j
k
l
m
n
o
p
q
r
s
t
u
v
w
x
y
z

ripe *ADJECTIVE*

  1 *You need ripe berries for making jam.*
    mature, ready to eat
  ▶ To become ripe is to **ripen**.
  2 *I feel that the time is ripe for change.*
    ready, right, suitable, favourable, opportune

ripple *VERB*

  A light breeze rippled the tree tops.
  ruffle, stir, disturb, make waves on

rise *VERB*

  1 *A plume of smoke rose high into the air.*
    climb, mount, ascend, soar, fly up, take off, lift off
    ⌐ OPPOSITE descend
  2 *The Blue Ridge mountains rose around us.*
    tower, loom, soar, reach up
  3 *Prices are set to rise again.*
    go up, increase, escalate, jump, leap, surge
    ⌐ OPPOSITE fall
  4 *I rose to greet our visitor.*
    stand up, get up, leap up, get to your feet
    ⌐ OPPOSITE sit down
  5 *Vampires never rise before dusk.*
    awake, get up, stir
    (informal) surface
    ⌐ OPPOSITES go to bed, retire

rise *NOUN*

  1 *the rise of celebrity culture*
    ascent, growth, surge, advance
    ⌐ OPPOSITE fall
  2 *an expected rise in temperature*
    increase, jump, leap, hike
    ⌐ OPPOSITE fall
  3 *The hill fort sits at the top of a rise.*
    hill, slope, ascent, incline
    (Scottish) brae

risk *NOUN*

  1 *the risks involved in deep-sea diving*
    danger, hazard, peril
  2 *There is a risk of further delays.*
    chance, likelihood, possibility, prospect

risk *VERB*

  1 *a woman who risked her life to save others*
    endanger, put at risk, jeopardize, hazard, imperil
  2 *Erik decided to risk taking a look outside.*
    chance, dare, gamble, venture

risky *ADJECTIVE*

  Bungee jumping is a risky activity.
  dangerous, hazardous, perilous, unsafe, precarious
  (informal) dicey
  ⌐ IDIOM touch and go
  ⌐ OPPOSITE safe

ritual *NOUN*

  1 *a Native American healing ritual*
    ceremony, rite
  2 *the daily ritual of reading the paper*
    custom, practice, habit, tradition

rival *NOUN*

  The two players became friendly rivals.
  opponent, adversary, challenger, competitor, contender, antagonist

rival *VERB*

  scenery which can rival any in the world
  compete with, contend with, vie with, compare with, match, equal
  ⌐ IDIOM hold a candle to

rivalry *NOUN*

  the intense rivalry between two local clubs
  competition, competitiveness, opposition
  ⌐ OPPOSITE cooperation

river *NOUN*

  taking a ferry across the river
  stream, rivulet, brook
  (North American & Australian) creek
  (Scottish) burn
  ▶ A small river which flows into a larger river is a **tributary**.
  ▶ The place where a river begins is its **source**.
  ▶ The place where a river goes into the

a b c d e f g h i j k l m n o p q r s t u v w x y z

sea is its **mouth**.

▶ A wide river mouth is an **estuary** or (*Scottish*) **firth**.

▶ The place where the mouth of a river splits before going into the sea is a **delta**.

road NOUN

crossing a busy road
street, lane, alley, avenue, boulevard, highway, motorway, bypass

▶ A road which is closed at one end is a **dead end**.

▶ A private road up to a house is a **drive**.

roam VERB

1 *We roamed about town aimlessly.*
wander, drift, stroll, amble, traipse

2 *Herds of buffalo used to roam the plains.*
range, rove

roar NOUN

1 *the roar of a wild animal*
bellow, howl, cry

2 *the roars of the crowd*
shout, cry, yell, clamour

3 *the roar of distant thunder*
boom, crash, thunder, rumble, roll

roar VERB

The Minotaur lifted its head and roared.
bellow, cry, howl, thunder, bawl, yell

rob VERB

Masked highwaymen used to rob stagecoaches.
steal from, break into, burgle, hold up, raid, loot, ransack, rifle

▷ **be robbed of something**
We were robbed of victory in the last minute of the match.
be deprived of, be denied, be cheated out of

robber NOUN

a gang of armed robbers
thief, burglar, housebreaker, looter

robbery NOUN

a daring robbery on a jewellery store
theft, stealing, burglary, housebreaking, looting

robe NOUN

the ceremonial robes of a chief
gown, vestments, regalia

robot NOUN

In the future, housework will be done by robots.
automaton, android

▶ A robot which is part-human is a **cyborg**.

▶ The study of the design and construction of robots is **robotics**.

robust ADJECTIVE

1 *in a robust state of health*
strong, vigorous, fit, hardy, healthy, rugged

⫿ **OPPOSITE** weak

2 *Bring a robust pair of boots.*
sturdy, tough, durable, hard-wearing

⫿ **OPPOSITE** flimsy

rock NOUN

some rocks deposited by a glacier
stone, boulder, pebble

 WORD WEB

some rocks and minerals
basalt, chalk, feldspar, flint, gneiss, granite, gypsum, limestone, marble, mica, obsidian, pumice, quartz, sandstone, shale, slate

▶ Rocks which are formed by cooling magma are **igneous rocks**.

▶ Rocks which are formed by pressure are **metamorphic rocks**.

▶ Rocks which are formed by deposits of sediment are **sedimentary rocks**.

▶ Rock from which metal or valuable minerals can be extracted is **ore**.

▶ A layer of rock is a **stratum**. 》

a
b
c
d
e
f
g
h
i
j
k
l
m
n
o
p
q
r
s
t
u
v
w
x
y
z

▶ The scientific study of rocks and rock formations is **geology**.

▶ The scientific study of minerals is **mineralogy**.

SEE ALSO **fossil**, **gem**

rock *VERB*

1 *At each turn, the bus rocked from side to side.*
sway, roll, toss, lurch, pitch, tilt, reel

2 *Only last year the sport was rocked by scandal.*
stun, shock, stagger, startle, shake, disturb, take aback, disconcert

rocky❶ *ADJECTIVE*

the rocky surface of the Moon
stony, pebbly, rough, craggy, shingly

rocky❷ *ADJECTIVE*

standing on a rocky chair
unsteady, unstable, rickety, shaky, wobbly, tottery

rod *NOUN*

a metal curtain rod
bar, rail, pole, strut, shaft, stick, spoke, staff

rodent *NOUN*

 WORD WEB

> *some animals which are rodents*
> beaver, capybara, chinchilla, chipmunk, coypu, gerbil, gopher, groundhog, guinea pig, hamster, jerboa, lemming, marmot, mouse, muskrat, porcupine, prairie dog, rat, squirrel, vole, water vole or water rat

rogue *NOUN*

a hero who slowly turns out to be a rogue
rascal, scoundrel, villain, cheat, fraud, swindler

role *NOUN*

1 *Who played the lead role in the film?*
part, character

2 *Each player has an important role in the team.*
job, task, function, position, responsibility, duty

roll *VERB*

1 *Slowly the wheels began to roll.*
move round, turn, revolve, rotate, spin, whirl

2 *rolling a ribbon round your finger*
curl, wind, wrap, twist, coil, twirl

▶ To roll up a sail is to **furl** it.

3 *rolling out a piece of pastry*
flatten, level out, smooth

4 *a tiny boat rolling on the waves*
rock, sway, pitch, toss, lurch

romantic *ADJECTIVE*

1 *a romantic relationship*
amorous, loving, passionate, affectionate, tender

2 *a film with a romantic ending*
sentimental, emotional, saccharine, mawkish
(informal) soppy, mushy

3 *a romantic image of life in the past*
idealistic, unrealistic, fanciful, fairy-tale

roof *NOUN*

a shed with a sloping roof
▶ The sloping beams in the framework of a roof are **rafters**.
▶ The overhanging edges of a roof are the **eaves**.
▶ The slope or angle of a roof is its **pitch**.
▶ The triangular section of wall under a sloping roof is the **gable**.

room *NOUN*

1 *a room at the top of the stairs*
(old use) chamber

2 *Do you have room for another passenger?*
space, capacity

3 *There is still room for improvement.*
scope, opportunity

room *NOUN*

WORD WEB

some types of room

anteroom, attic, basement, bathroom, bedroom, box room, cellar, classroom, cloakroom, conservatory, dining room, dormitory, drawing room, dressing room, games room, garret, guest room, hall, kitchen, kitchenette, landing, lavatory or toilet *(British informal* loo), library, living room, lounge, music room, nursery, pantry, parlour, playroom, scullery, sitting room, spare room, staffroom, storeroom, studio, study, utility room, vault, waiting room

► A sleeping room on a ship is a **cabin**.

► A small room in a monastery or prison is a **cell**.

► A room under a church is a **crypt**.

► A set of connected rooms is a **suite**.

► Someone who shares a room with you is your **room-mate**.

roomy *ADJECTIVE*

The flat is surprisingly roomy inside.
spacious, extensive, big, sizeable, capacious, palatial

root *NOUN*

getting to the root of the problem
source, cause, basis, origin, starting point

▷ **roots**

tracing your family roots
origins, heritage, ancestry, descent, lineage, background

rope *NOUN*

a length of climbing rope
cable, cord, line

► The ropes which support a ship's mast and sails are the **rigging**.

► The ropes which hold down a tent

are the **guys** or **guy ropes**.

► A rope with a loop at one end used for catching cattle is a **lasso**.

rosy *ADJECTIVE*

   1 *rosy cheeks*
   red, flushed, blushing, ruddy, florid
   ▌**OPPOSITES** pale, wan
   FOR TIPS ON DESCRIBING FACES SEE **face**

   2 *Things are looking rosy.*
   hopeful, promising, encouraging, positive, favourable, optimistic
   ▌**OPPOSITE** bleak

rot *VERB*

   1 *Most of the timber had rotted away.*
   decay, decompose, become rotten, corrode, disintegrate, crumble

   2 *Discard any fruit that has started to rot.*
   go bad, go off, perish, spoil, putrefy

rotate *VERB*

   1 *Venus rotates in a clockwise direction.*
   revolve, turn, spin, pivot, gyrate, wheel, swivel, twirl, whirl

   2 *You can set the images to rotate automatically.*
   take turns, alternate, swap, switch over

rotten *ADJECTIVE*

   1 *replacing a rotten beam*
   decayed, decaying, decomposed, crumbling, disintegrating, corroded
   ▌**OPPOSITE** sound

   2 *the smell of rotten eggs*
   bad, mouldy, putrid, rancid, gone off
   ▌**OPPOSITE** fresh

   3 *an organization which is rotten to the core*
   corrupt, immoral, unethical, dishonest, unprincipled
   (informal) crooked
   ▌**OPPOSITES** honest, ethical

   4 *(informal) I've had a rotten week!*
   bad, unpleasant, disagreeable, awful, dreadful, terrible, abysmal
   (informal) lousy
   ▌**OPPOSITES** good, agreeable

a
b
c
d
e
f
g
h
i
j
k
l
m
n
o
p
q
r
s
t
u
v
w
x
y
z

rough ADJECTIVE

1 *boots for walking on rough ground*
uneven, irregular, rugged, bumpy, rocky, stony, pitted
❙ OPPOSITES even, level

2 *the rough texture of handmade paper*
coarse, harsh, scratchy, bristly, prickly
❙ OPPOSITES smooth, soft

3 *Lena pushed him away with a rough shove.*
hard, forceful, violent, severe, tough, brutal
❙ OPPOSITES gentle, mild

4 *a rough sea crossing*
stormy, choppy, turbulent, heaving
❙ OPPOSITES calm, smooth

5 *having a rough time*
hard, difficult, troublesome, bad, disagreeable, unpleasant
❙ OPPOSITES good, easy

6 *a rough idea of the cost*
approximate, vague, inexact, imprecise
❙ OPPOSITES exact, precise

7 *a rough draft of the first chapter*
preliminary, basic, rudimentary, unfinished, unpolished, sketchy, cursory
❙ OPPOSITES finished, final

roughly ADVERB
The cinema seats roughly a hundred people.
approximately, about, around, close to, nearly

round ADJECTIVE

1 *a round patch of dry skin*
circular, disc-shaped

2 *a cluster of small round berries*
spherical, ball-shaped, globular

round NOUN

1 *doing a morning paper round*
route, circuit, tour
▶ The regular round of a police officer is their **beat**.

2 *the first round of the competition*
stage, level, heat, game, bout, contest

round VERB
The motorcade slowly rounded the corner.
go round, travel round, turn

▷ **round something off**
We rounded off the meal with coffee and cake.
finish off, conclude, complete, end, crown, cap

▷ **round someone up**
rounding up the stragglers in the group
gather together, assemble, collect, muster, rally

roundabout ADJECTIVE
a roundabout way of answering the question
indirect, circuitous, winding, meandering, circumlocutory
❙ OPPOSITE direct

rouse VERB

1 *The doorbell roused Bridget from her daydream.*
awaken, wake up, arouse

2 *My curiosity was roused by a flashing light in the sky.*
excite, arouse, stir up, stimulate, activate, galvanize, provoke, agitate, inflame

route NOUN
taking the quickest route home
way, course, path, road, direction

routine NOUN

1 *part of my morning routine*
procedure, practice, regime, drill, pattern, programme, schedule

2 *a stand-up comedy routine*
act, programme, performance, number

row❶ NOUN

1 *a neat row of houses*
line, column, file, series, sequence, string, chain

▶ A row of people waiting for something is a **queue**.

2 *the back row of the cinema*
tier, rank

row² NOUN

1 *making a terrible row next door*
noise, din, racket, commotion, clamour, uproar, rumpus, hubbub

2 *having a row with the referee*
argument, fight, disagreement, dispute, quarrel, squabble, tiff

rowdy ADJECTIVE

a rowdy group of partygoers
noisy, unruly, wild, disorderly, boisterous, riotous
⎸ OPPOSITE quiet

royal ADJECTIVE

an ancient royal tomb
regal, kingly, queenly, princely

rub VERB

1 *Try not to rub your eyes.*
stroke, knead, massage, pat

2 *rubbing suncream on your arms*
spread, smear, apply (to), smooth

3 *I rubbed the window to see outside.*
wipe, polish, shine, buff

4 *Are the boots rubbing against your heels?*
graze, scrape, chafe

▷ **rub something out**
I just need to rub out the pencil marks.
erase, wipe out, delete, remove

rubbish NOUN

1 *recycling household rubbish*
refuse, waste, junk, litter, scrap
(North American) trash, garbage

2 *talking a lot of rubbish*
nonsense, drivel, gibberish, claptrap, garbage
(informal) gobbledegook, baloney, rot, tripe, twaddle, piffle
(British informal) cobblers, codswallop
(old use) balderdash, poppycock
⎸ OPPOSITE sense

rude ADJECTIVE

1 *The assistant was quite rude on the phone.*
impolite, discourteous, bad-mannered, impertinent, impudent, insolent, offensive, insulting, abusive
⎸ OPPOSITE polite

2 *telling a rude joke*
indecent, coarse, crude, dirty, smutty, vulgar, lewd, obscene
⎸ OPPOSITE clean

ruffle VERB

1 *A light breeze ruffled the waters of the loch.*
stir, disturb, ripple

2 *Peter's dad leaned over and ruffled his hair.*
tousle, mess up, rumple, dishevel

ruin NOUN

1 *rescuing an ancient building from ruin*
destruction, disintegration, decay, collapse

2 *facing financial ruin*
failure, loss, bankruptcy, insolvency, destitution

▷ **ruins**
the ruins of an ancient Mayan city
remains, remnants, fragments

ruin VERB

1 *A sudden rainstorm could ruin the entire harvest.*
destroy, wreck, devastate, demolish, ravage, lay waste, wipe out

2 *The ending ruined the whole film for me.*
spoil, mar, blight, mess up
(informal) scupper

3 *His family were ruined by a lengthy lawsuit.*
bankrupt, make insolvent, impoverish, cripple

rule NOUN

1 *according to the rules of play*
regulation, principle, statute, law

                 »

2 *a territory which was formerly under Spanish rule*
control, authority, command, power, government, jurisdiction

3 *The usual rule is to leave a tip.*
custom, convention, practice, habit, norm

rule *VERB*

1 *The Romans ruled a vast empire.*
govern, control, command, direct, lead, manage, run, administer

2 *Queen Victoria ruled for over 60 years.*
reign, be ruler

3 *The umpire ruled that the ball was out.*
judge, decree, pronounce, decide, determine, find

▷ **rule something out**
We can't rule out the possibility of sabotage.
eliminate, exclude, disregard, disallow

ruler *NOUN*

WORD WEB

some titles of ruler
emir, emperor, empress, governor, head of state, king, monarch, potentate, premier, president, prince, princess, queen, sovereign, viceroy

▶ A person who rules while a monarch is too young or unable to rule is a **regent**.

▶ A single ruler with unlimited power is an **autocrat** or **dictator**.

▶ A member of a small ruling faction is an **oligarch**.

historical rulers
caesar, caliph, kaiser, maharaja, maharani, pharaoh, raja, rani, shah, sultan, tsar, tsarina

rumble *VERB, NOUN*
the rumble of a passing train
FOR TIPS ON DESCRIBING SOUNDS
SEE **sound❶**

rummage *VERB*
rummaging for your keys
search, hunt, root about, ferret

rumour *NOUN*
All kinds of rumours were flying round the school.
gossip, hearsay, talk, speculation, story
(informal) tittle-tattle

run *VERB*

1 *running at full speed down the hill*
race, sprint, dash, speed, rush, hurry, tear, bolt, fly, streak, whizz, zoom, zip, pelt, hurtle, scurry, scamper, career
(informal) scoot
▶ To run at a gentle pace is to **jog**.

2 *Beads of sweat ran down Lee's face.*
stream, flow, pour, gush, flood, cascade, spill, trickle, dribble

3 *My old laptop still runs well.*
function, operate, work, go, perform

4 *Her dream is to run her own restaurant.*
manage, be in charge of, direct, control, supervise, oversee, govern, rule

5 *The river Amazon runs through seven countries.*
go, extend, pass, stretch, reach

6 *Could you please run me to the station?*
give someone a lift, drive, take, transport, convey

▷ **run away** or **off**
The boys ran off when they saw me.
flee, take flight, take off, escape, fly, bolt
(informal) make off, clear off, scarper
❚ IDIOM take to your heels

▷ **run into**

1 *Guess who I ran into at the weekend?*
meet, come across, encounter
(*informal*) bump into

2 *Two lorries nearly ran into each other.*
hit, collide with

run *NOUN*

1 *a morning run along the beach*
jog, trot, sprint, race, dash

2 *going for a run in the car*
drive, journey, ride, trip, outing, excursion
(*informal*) spin

3 *having a run of good luck*
sequence, stretch, series

4 *building a chicken run*
enclosure, pen, coop

runaway *NOUN*

a film about three teenage runaways
missing person

▶ Someone who has run away from the army is a **deserter**.

▶ Someone who is running away from the law is a **fugitive** or **outlaw**.

rundown *ADJECTIVE*

1 *feeling a bit rundown*
unwell, poorly, worn out, drained, exhausted
❚ **IDIOMS** under the weather, below par

2 *an old rundown theatre*
dilapidated, derelict, crumbling, ramshackle, tumbledown

runner *NOUN*

Over a thousand runners will take part in the marathon.
athlete, competitor, racer, sprinter, jogger

runny *ADJECTIVE*

This sauce is too runny.
watery, thin, liquid, fluid
❚ **OPPOSITE** thick

rural *ADJECTIVE*

living in a remote rural area
country, rustic, agricultural, pastoral, bucolic
❚ **OPPOSITE** urban

rush *VERB*

1 *I rushed home with the good news.*
hurry, hasten, race, run, dash, fly, bolt, charge, speed, sprint, tear, hurtle, scurry

2 *Don't rush me!*
push, hurry, press, hustle

rush *NOUN*

1 *What's the rush?*
hurry, haste, urgency

2 *a sudden rush of adrenalin*
flood, gush, spurt, stream, spate

3 *a rush for tickets*
demand, call, clamour, run (on)

rustic *ADJECTIVE*

a painting of a rustic scene
country, rural, pastoral, bucolic

rustle *VERB, NOUN*

the rustle of silk
FOR TIPS ON DESCRIBING SOUNDS SEE
sound❶

rut *NOUN*

a deep rut made by a tractor
furrow, groove, channel, trough

ruthless *ADJECTIVE*

a ruthless dictator who terrorized his people
merciless, pitiless, heartless, hard-hearted, cold-blooded, callous, cruel, vicious, brutal
❚ **OPPOSITE** merciful

Ss

sack *NOUN*

a large sack of potatoes
bag, pack, pouch

▷ **the sack**

(informal) If the boss finds out, he'll get the sack.
dismissal, discharge, redundancy
(informal) the boot, the axe

sack *VERB*

They threatened to sack the whole workforce.
dismiss, discharge, let go
(informal) fire, give someone the sack

sacred *ADJECTIVE*

1 *a concert of sacred music*
religious, holy, divine, heavenly
▌OPPOSITE secular

2 *a place which is sacred to Aboriginal people*
holy, hallowed, sanctified, blessed

sacrifice *VERB*

1 *Minnie had sacrificed everything for her family.*
give up, surrender, forfeit, go without, renounce

2 *an altar where animals were sacrificed*
offer up, slaughter, kill

sad *ADJECTIVE*

OVERUSED WORD

a sad mood, sad feeling
unhappy, sorrowful, miserable,

depressed, downcast, downhearted, despondent, crestfallen, dismal, gloomy, glum, blue, low, down, dejected, forlorn, morose, desolate, doleful, wretched, woeful, woebegone, tearful, heartbroken, broken-hearted, inconsolable
(informal) downbeat

▌IDIOMS *(informal)* down in the dumps, down in the mouth

*Rhys has been **inconsolable** since his dog died.*

▌OPPOSITES happy, cheerful

a sad situation, sad news
unfortunate, upsetting, distressing, painful, disheartening, discouraging, regrettable, lamentable, deplorable, grim, serious, grave, desperate, tragic, grievous

*I'm afraid I have some **upsetting** news.*

▌OPPOSITES fortunate, good

a sad story, sad tune
depressing, melancholy, mournful, moving, touching, heartbreaking, heart-rending, pitiful, pathetic, plaintive, wistful

*I found Nicola in her room, listening to **mournful** music.*

▌OPPOSITES cheering, uplifting

sadden *VERB*

I was saddened by how much the town had changed.
depress, upset, dispirit, dishearten, discourage, grieve

▌IDIOM break your heart
▌OPPOSITE cheer up

sadness *NOUN*

There was sadness and despair in her eyes.
unhappiness, sorrow, grief, misery, depression, dejection, despondency,

melancholy, gloom
OPPOSITES happiness, joy

safe ADJECTIVE

1 *The missing hillwalkers were found safe and well.*
unharmed, unhurt, uninjured, undamaged, unscathed, sound, intact
(informal) in one piece
OPPOSITES hurt, damaged

2 *an area that was thought to be safe from flooding*
protected, defended, secure, out of danger, out of harm's way
OPPOSITES vulnerable, insecure

3 *leaving your pet in safe hands*
reliable, trustworthy, dependable, sound
OPPOSITES dangerous, risky

4 *Is the tap water safe to drink?*
harmless, uncontaminated, innocuous, non-poisonous
OPPOSITE harmful

safety NOUN
These rules are for your own safety.
protection, security, well-being
OPPOSITE danger

sag VERB

1 *Parts of the roof sagged under the weight of snow.*
sink, slump, bulge, dip

2 *These jeans are starting to sag at the knees.*
hang down, droop, flop

sail VERB

1 *Tall ships used to sail right into the harbour.*
travel, voyage, cruise
▶ To begin a sea voyage is to **put to sea** or **set sail**.

2 *learning how to sail a yacht*
pilot, steer, navigate

3 *A few clouds sailed past overhead.*
glide, drift, float, flow, sweep, flit

sailor NOUN
a crew of experienced sailors
seaman, seafarer, mariner, hand

▶ A person who sails a yacht is a **yachtsman** or **yachtswoman**.

sake NOUN
▷ **for the sake of**
He was told to lose weight for the sake of his health.
for the good of, in the interests of, to benefit, to help

salary NOUN
Payments will be deducted from your salary.
income, pay, earnings, wages

sale NOUN
a worldwide ban on the sale of ivory
selling, dealing, trading, marketing, vending
OPPOSITE purchase

salute VERB
A plaque salutes the men and women who gave their lives.
pay tribute to, pay homage to, honour

salvage VERB
trying to salvage some shred of dignity
save, rescue, recover, retrieve, reclaim

same ADJECTIVE
▷ **the same**

1 *Frida and I like the same kinds of music.*
similar, alike, equivalent, comparable, matching, identical
▶ Words which mean the same are **synonymous**.
OPPOSITES different, contrasting

2 *Our recipe has remained the same for years.*
unaltered, unchanged, constant
OPPOSITES different, new

sample NOUN
a sample of each colour of fabric
specimen, example, illustration, snippet, taster, swatch

sample *VERB*
> Would you like to sample the
> new flavour?
> try out, test, taste

sands *PLURAL NOUN*
> a stretch of golden sands on the
> Cornish coast
> beach, shore
> ► Hills of sand along the coast are
> **dunes**.

sane *ADJECTIVE*
> the only sane member of an
> eccentric family
> sensible, rational, reasonable,
> balanced, level-headed
> **OPPOSITE insane**

sarcastic *ADJECTIVE*
> It's hard to tell if the author is
> being sarcastic.
> mocking, satirical, ironical, sneering,
> cutting

satire *NOUN*
> The work was conceived as a satire
> on modern society.
> parody, lampoon
> (informal) send-up, spoof
> ► A person who writes or creates a
> satire is a **satirist**.

satisfaction *NOUN*
> Scrooge rubbed his hands together
> with satisfaction.
> pleasure, contentment,
> enjoyment, gratification,
> fulfilment, sense of achievement,
> pride
> **OPPOSITE dissatisfaction**

satisfactory *ADJECTIVE*
> That's not a satisfactory explanation
> for UFOs.
> acceptable, adequate, passable,
> tolerable, sufficient, competent,
> good enough
> **IDIOMS up to scratch,**
> up to the mark
> **OPPOSITE unsatisfactory**

satisfied *ADJECTIVE*
> **1** Are you satisfied with your score?
> pleased, contented, happy
> **OPPOSITES dissatisfied,**
> discontented
> **2** Jackson was satisfied that the danger
> had passed.
> certain, sure, convinced

satisfy *VERB*
> **1** Some days, nothing seemed to satisfy
> him.
> please, content, gratify, appease,
> make you happy
> ► To satisfy your thirst is to **quench** or
> **slake** it.
> **OPPOSITES dissatisfy, frustrate**
> **2** I think this should satisfy your
> requirements.
> meet, fulfil, answer

saturate *VERB*
> **1** Several days of rain have saturated
> the soil.
> soak, drench, waterlog
> **2** saturating the Internet with spam
> flood, inundate, overwhelm,
> overload

saunter *VERB*
> sauntering slowly along the footpath
> amble, stroll, wander, ramble
> **SEE ALSO walk**

savage *ADJECTIVE*
> **1** a savage attack on a defenceless
> young man
> vicious, cruel, barbaric, brutal,
> bloodthirsty, pitiless, ruthless,
> merciless, inhuman
> **OPPOSITE humane**
> **2** a pack of savage dogs
> wild, feral, untamed, ferocious,
> fierce
> **OPPOSITE domesticated**

save *VERB*
> **1** Firefighters managed to save most of
> the building.
> preserve, protect, safeguard,
> recover, retrieve, reclaim, salvage

2 *You saved me from making a big mistake!*
stop, prevent, spare, deter, forestall

3 *Save some berries to use as a garnish.*
keep, reserve, set aside, retain, hold on to, store, hoard

4 *trying to save household energy*
conserve, be sparing with, use wisely

savings PLURAL NOUN

The couple have lost all of their savings.
reserves, funds, capital, resources, investments
⌐ IDIOM nest egg

savour VERB

savouring every mouthful of cake
relish, enjoy, appreciate, delight in, revel in

say VERB

1 *What exactly are you trying to say?*
express, communicate, articulate, put into words, convey

2 *I'd like to say a few words before we start.*
utter, speak, voice, recite, read

OVERUSED WORD

to say something loudly
call, cry, exclaim, bellow, bawl, shout, yell, roar
*'Not much farther to go!' Lars **yelled** above the roar of the engine.*

to say something quietly
whisper, mumble, mutter
*'Now would be a good time to leave,' I **whispered**.*

to say something casually
remark, comment, observe, note, mention, blurt out
*'Lovely morning,' a passer-by **remarked**.*

to say something strongly
state, announce, assert, declare,

pronounce, insist, maintain, profess, order, command, demand
*The wife of the accused **maintains** that he is innocent.*

to say something angrily
snap, snarl, growl, thunder, bark, rasp, rant, rave
*'I don't have time to talk to you!' **barked** the voice on the phone.*

to say something unclearly
babble, burble, gabble, stammer, stutter
*The stranger kept **babbling** about an ancient prophecy.*

to say something again
repeat, reiterate, echo
*Could you please **repeat** your email address?*

to say something in reply
answer, reply, respond, retort
*'Certainly not!' **retorted** Alice.*

saying NOUN

There is an old saying, 'look before you leap'.
proverb, motto, maxim, aphorism, phrase, expression
▶ An overused saying is a **cliché**.

scan VERB

1 *scanning the horizon for anything that moves*
search, study, survey, examine, inspect, scrutinize, scour, stare at, eye

2 *scanning the papers for interesting news*
skim, glance at, flick through, browse through
⌐ IDIOM cast your eye over

scandal NOUN

1 *He discovered a scandal in his family's past.*
disgrace, shame, embarrassment

》

a b c d e f g h i j k l m n o p q r s t u v w x y z

a
b
c
d
e
f
g
h
i
j
k
l
m
n
o
p
q
r
s
t
u
v
w
x
y
z

IDIOMS skeleton in the cupboard *(North American)* skeleton in the closet

2 *The amount of money wasted was a scandal.*
outrage, disgrace

3 *reading the latest scandal in the tabloids*
gossip, rumours, muckraking
(informal) dirt

scant *ADJECTIVE*
showing scant regard for other people
little, hardly any, negligible, minimal, insufficient, inadequate, limited
OPPOSITE ample

scanty *ADJECTIVE*
a scanty supply of fresh water
meagre, paltry, inadequate, insufficient, sparse, scarce
(informal) measly
OPPOSITES abundant, plentiful

scar *NOUN*
1 *a scar left by an old wound*
mark, blemish, lesion, disfigurement

2 *The experience left emotional scars.*
trauma, damage, impairment

scar *VERB*
The victim may be scarred for life.
mark, disfigure

scarce *ADJECTIVE*
1 *Water holes are scarce in this area.*
hard to find, in short supply, sparse, scanty
(informal) thin on the ground, few and far between
OPPOSITES plentiful, abundant

2 *a scarce species of moth*
rare, uncommon
OPPOSITE common

scarcely *ADVERB*
Nat was so tired that he could scarcely speak.
barely, hardly, only just

scare *VERB*
You scared me creeping up like that!
frighten, terrify, petrify, alarm, startle, panic, unnerve
(North American informal) spook
IDIOM *(informal)* give someone the creeps

scare *NOUN*
1 *You gave me quite a scare!*
fright, shock, start, turn

2 *the latest health scare*
alarm, panic

scared *ADJECTIVE*
Were you scared of the dark when you were little?
frightened, afraid, terrified, petrified, alarmed, fearful, panicky

scary *(informal) ADJECTIVE*
I feel like watching a scary film tonight.
frightening, terrifying, chilling, hair-raising, spine-tingling, spine-chilling, blood-curdling, eerie, sinister, nightmarish
(informal) creepy, spooky
FOR TIPS ON WRITING HORROR FICTION SEE horror

scatter *VERB*
1 *scattering bird seed on the ground*
spread, strew, distribute, sprinkle, shower, sow
OPPOSITE collect

2 *The crowd scattered in all directions.*
break up, separate, disperse, disband
OPPOSITE gather

scenario *NOUN*
Discuss one of the following scenarios.
storyline, plot, outline, situation, set of circumstances

scene *NOUN*
1 *the scene of the crime*
location, position, site, place, situation, spot

2 *rehearsing a scene from the play*
episode, part, section, sequence, extract
▶ A short scene from a film is a **clip**.

3 *a painting of a winter scene*
landscape, view, outlook, prospect,
vista, sight, spectacle, setting,
scenery, backdrop

4 *creating a scene in public*
fuss, commotion, disturbance,
quarrel, row
(*informal*) to-do, carry-on
▶ To make a scene in public is to **make
an exhibition of yourself**.

5 *the local music scene*
arena, stage, sphere, world, realm,
milieu

scenery NOUN
1 *standing to admire the scenery*
landscape, outlook, prospect, scene,
view, vista, panorama

2 *painting the scenery for the show*
set, setting, backdrop

scenic ADJECTIVE
a scenic tour of the Highlands
picturesque, panoramic, attractive,
beautiful, charming

scent NOUN
an overpowering scent of vanilla
smell, fragrance, perfume, aroma,
odour
❙ SEE ALSO **smell** NOUN

scented ADJECTIVE
a scented handkerchief
fragrant, fragranced, perfumed,
aromatic, sweet-smelling

sceptical ADJECTIVE
*Poirot was sceptical about the
pharaoh's curse.*
disbelieving, doubtful, doubting,
dubious, incredulous, unconvinced,
suspicious, cynical
❙ OPPOSITES certain, convinced

schedule NOUN
a tight production schedule
programme, timetable, plan,
calendar, diary
▶ A schedule for a meeting is an
agenda.
▶ A schedule of places to visit is an
itinerary.

schedule VERB
*Your appointment is scheduled for
ten o'clock.*
arrange, set, plan, programme,
timetable

scheme NOUN
a scheme to raise more money
plan, proposal, project, strategy,
tactic
▶ A clever or cunning scheme is a
stratagem or (*informal*) **wheeze**.

scheme VERB
*scheming to overthrow the
government*
plot, conspire, intrigue

school NOUN
1 *a school for international students*
academy, college, institute

2 *a new school of thought*
approach, style, persuasion,
doctrine, creed

science NOUN
the science of forensics
discipline, subject, field of study,
branch of knowledge

 WORD WEB

some branches of science
aeronautics, anatomy,
astronomy, biochemistry,
biology, botany, chemistry,
climatology, computer
science, cybernetics, earth
science, ecology, electronics,
engineering, environmental
science, food science, forensic
science, genetics, geography,
geology, geophysics, information
technology, mathematics,
mechanical engineering,
medical science, meteorology,
mineralogy, nanotechnology,
nuclear science, oceanography,
pathology, physics, psychology,
robotics, space technology,
toxicology, veterinary science,
zoology

a
b
c
d
e
f
g
h
i
j
k
l
m
n
o
p
q
r
s
t
u
v
w
x
y
z

science fiction NOUN

writing science fiction

The alien ship was already
thundering towards the upper
reaches of the atmosphere, on its
way out into the appalling void
which separates the very few
things there are in the Universe
from each other.
— *Douglas Adams*, Life, the Universe and
Everything

characters
alien life-form, android, artificial
life-form, astronaut, cyborg,
ufologist, robot, space tourist,
space traveller, time traveller

setting
alien planet, alternative timeline,
deep space, mother ship, outer
space, parallel universe, space
colony, spacecraft, spaceship,
space shuttle, space station,
starship, time machine

useful words & phrases
alien artefact, alternative
timeline, bionic, black hole,
cybernetic, extrasolar,
extraterrestrial, force field,
fourth or fifth dimension,
futuristic, galactic, home
planet, humanoid, hyperspace,
intelligent life, inter-galactic,
inter-planetary, inter-stellar, light
year, orbit, portal,
post-apocalyptic, singularity,
spacesuit, space-time
continuum, space walk,
subspace, suspended animation,
telepathic, teleport, time shift,
time warp, UFO, wormhole

❙ SEE ALSO moon, planet, space

scientific ADJECTIVE
*a scientific approach to studying the
paranormal*

systematic, methodical, analytical,
rational, logical

scoff VERB
▷ **scoff at**
*Some people might scoff at the idea
of horoscopes.*
mock, ridicule, sneer at, deride,
belittle, make fun of, poke fun at

scold VERB
being scolded for being late for class
reprimand, reproach
(*informal*) tell off
(*British informal*) tick off
(*North American informal*) chew out

scoop VERB
1 *scooping the pulp out of a pumpkin*
dig, gouge, scrape, excavate, hollow
2 *Sandy scooped the kitten up in her
arms.*
lift, pick, gather, take, snatch

scope NOUN
1 *allowing plenty of scope for creative
work*
opportunity, space, room, capacity,
freedom, leeway
2 *That falls outside the scope of this
essay.*
range, extent, limit, reach, span,
compass, sweep

scorch VERB
*The sand was so hot, it scorched our
feet.*
burn, singe, sear, blacken, char

score NOUN
What was your final score?
mark, points, total, tally, count,
result

score VERB
1 *scoring the winning goal*
win, get, gain, earn, make, notch up,
chalk up
(*informal*) bag
2 *Someone had scored their initials on
the tree.*
cut, gouge, notch, incise, scratch,
scrape

a
b
c
d
e
f
g
h
i
j
k
l
m
n
o
p
q
r
s
t
u
v
w
x
y
z

scorn *NOUN*

At first, the theory was met with scorn.

contempt, derision, disrespect, mockery, ridicule, sneers

❙ **OPPOSITES** admiration, respect

scour❶ *VERB*

scouring pots and pans

scrub, rub, clean, polish, burnish, buff

scour❷ *VERB*

scouring the room for clues

search, hunt through, ransack, comb, turn upside-down

scowl *VERB*

Bev scowled and folded her arms across her chest.

frown, glower

❙ **IDIOM** knit your brows

FOR FACIAL EXPRESSIONS SEE face

scramble *VERB*

1 *The quickest route is to scramble over the rocks.*

clamber, climb, crawl, scrabble

2 *Everyone scrambled to get the best seats.*

push, jostle, struggle, fight, scuffle

3 *a program which will scramble the text*

jumble, mix up, rearrange, disorder

scrap❶ *NOUN*

1 *He wrote his number on a scrap of paper.*

bit, piece, fragment, snippet, oddment

▶ Scraps of cloth are **rags** or **shreds**.

❙ **SEE ALSO bit**

2 *feeding scraps of food to the birds*

remnant, leftovers, morsel, crumb, speck

3 *a pile of old scrap in the back yard*

rubbish, waste, junk, refuse, litter, debris

scrap *VERB*

I decided to scrap the last paragraph.

discard, throw away, throw out, abandon, cancel, delete, drop

(informal) dump, ditch

scrap❷ *NOUN*

a scrap between rival fans

fight, brawl, scuffle, tussle, squabble

scrap *VERB*

The cubs enjoy scrapping with each other.

fight, brawl, tussle, scuffle

scrape *VERB*

1 *How did you manage to scrape your knee?*

graze, scratch, scuff, chafe

2 *scraping mud off your trainers*

rub, scour, scrub, clean

scrape *NOUN*

1 *the scrape of chair legs on the floor*

scratch, rasp, grating, scuffing, chaffing

2 *always getting into scrapes*

trouble, mischief

(informal) jam, pickle

scratch *VERB*

1 *Try not to scratch the paintwork.*

mark, score, scrape, gouge, graze, scuff, chafe

2 *a dog scratching at the door*

claw

scratch *NOUN*

a tiny scratch on the surface

score, line, mark, gash, groove, scrape, graze

scrawl *VERB*

scrawling a message on a notepad

jot down, scribble, write

scream *NOUN*

letting out a scream of pain

shriek, screech, shout, yell, cry, bawl, howl, wail, squeal, yelp

scream *VERB*

People screamed and ran in all directions.

shriek, screech, shout, yell, cry, bawl, howl, wail, squeal, yelp

a
b
c
d
e
f
g
h
i
j
k
l
m
n
o
p
q
r
s
t
u
v
w
x
y
z

screen NOUN

1 *one large room divided by a screen*
partition, divider, curtain

2 *Look at the image on the screen.*
monitor, display

screen VERB

1 *a blood test to screen patients*
examine, investigate, check, test, vet

2 *screening your eyes from the sun*
shield, protect, shelter, shade, cover,
hide, mask, veil

3 *The match will be screened live on
Saturday.*
show, broadcast, transmit, air,
put out

screw VERB

1 *Screw the lid on tightly.*
twist, wind, turn, tighten

2 *Nail or screw the panel to the wall.*
fasten, secure, fix, attach

scribble VERB

*scribbling ideas on the back of an
envelope*
scrawl, write, jot down, note,
dash off

▸ To scribble a rough drawing is to
doodle.

script NOUN

*The film won an award for its
original script.*

▸ The script for a film is a **screenplay**.

▸ A person who writes a script is a
scriptwriter.

▸ A handwritten or typed script is a
manuscript.

scrub VERB

1 *scrubbing the kitchen floor*
scour, rub, brush, clean, wash

2 *Let's just scrub the whole idea!*
abandon, cancel, scrap, drop, call off
(informal) dump, ditch

scruffy ADJECTIVE

*wearing an old T-shirt and scruffy
jeans*
untidy, messy, ragged, tatty,
tattered, worn-out, shabby

 OPPOSITE smart

scrutinize VERB

*They scrutinized her passport for a
few minutes.*
examine, inspect, look at, study,
peruse, investigate, explore, probe

scuffle NOUN

*A scuffle broke out between rival
fans.*
fight, brawl, tussle, scrap, squabble

sculpture NOUN

a sculpture of the artist's dog
carving, figure, statue, effigy, model

▸ A sculpture of a person's head,
shoulders, and chest is a **bust**.

▸ A small sculpture of a person is a
figurine or **statuette**.

▸ An artist who creates sculpture is a
sculptor.

 SEE ALSO art

sea NOUN

1 *70 per cent of the Earth's surface is
covered by sea.*
ocean, waves
(literary) the deep

2 *performing in front of a sea of
adoring fans*
expanse, stretch, mass, swathe,
carpet

✳ WORD WEB

▸ An area of sea partly enclosed by
land is a **bay** or **gulf**.

▸ A wide inlet of the sea is a **sound**.

▸ A wide inlet where a river joins the
sea is an **estuary**, or in Scotland
a **firth**.

▸ A narrow stretch of water linking
two seas is a **strait**.

▸ The bottom of the sea is the
seabed.

▸ The land near the sea is the **coast**
or the **seashore**.

▸ Creatures that live in the sea are
marine creatures.

▸ People who work or travel on the
sea are **seafaring** people.

creatures that live in the sea

coral, dogfish, dolphin, eel, jellyfish, killer whale, manatee or sea cow, manta ray, marine fish, narwhal, octopus, plankton, porpoise, sea anemone, sea cucumber, sea horse, seal, sea lion, sea otter, sea turtle, sea urchin, shark, squid, starfish or sea star, stingray, whale

▶ Dolphins, porpoises, and whales are all types of **cetacean**.

 ⌐SEE ALSO fish

seal VERB

1 *sealing the door of the tomb*
close, fasten, shut, secure, lock
▶ To seal a leak is to **plug** it or **stop** it.

2 *sealing a bargain*
decide, settle, conclude, finalize, secure, clinch

seam NOUN

1 *Sew a seam along the curve.*
join, stitching

2 *a rich seam of coal*
layer, stratum, vein

search VERB

1 *searching for a long-lost relative*
hunt, look, seek
 ⌐IDIOM look high and low
▶ To search for gold or other minerals is to **prospect**.

2 *searching the house for clues*
explore, scour, ransack, rummage through, go through, comb
 ⌐IDIOM turn upside down

3 *Security staff searched all the passengers.*
check, inspect, examine, scrutinize
(informal) frisk

search NOUN

the search for life on other planets
hunt, look, exploration, check
▶ A long journey in search of something is a **quest**.

seashore NOUN

a rocky stretch of seashore
seaside, beach, shore, coast

seaside NOUN

a day trip to the seaside
beach, sands, seashore

season NOUN

Autumn is traditionally the season for harvest.
period, time, time of year, term

seasoning NOUN

Add a pinch of seasoning.
salt and pepper, flavouring, herbs, spices, condiments

seat NOUN

1 *There were two empty seats in the front row.*
chair, place
▶ A long seat for more than one person is a **bench**.
▶ A long wooden seat in a church is a **pew**.

2 *the real seat of power in the country*
centre, base, location, headquarters, heart, hub

seat VERB

1 *Please seat yourselves in a circle.*
place, position, sit down, settle

2 *The theatre can seat two hundred people.*
accommodate, have room for, hold, take

secluded ADJECTIVE

a secluded spot for a picnic
quiet, isolated, private, lonely, remote, cut off, sheltered, hidden
 ⌐OPPOSITE crowded

second ADJECTIVE

1 *the second day of our visit*
following, next
▶ Someone who comes second in a competition is a **runner-up**.

2 *asking for a second helping*
another, additional, extra, further

second NOUN

I'll be with you in a second.
moment, little while, instant, flash
(informal) jiffy, tick

a
b
c
d
e
f
g
h
i
j
k
l
m
n
o
p
q
r
s
t
u
v
w
x
y
z

second VERB

Will anyone second the nomination?
support, back, approve, endorse

secondary ADJECTIVE

the secondary purpose of this experiment
lesser, minor, subordinate, subsidiary, peripheral
OPPOSITES primary, main

second-hand ADJECTIVE

a shop selling second-hand computers
used, pre-owned, handed-down, cast-off
OPPOSITE new

secret ADJECTIVE

1 *It's important to keep your password secret.*
private, confidential, personal, undisclosed, classified, restricted
IDIOM under wraps
OPPOSITE public

2 *a secret conspiracy to rule the world*
undercover, covert, clandestine
(informal) hush-hush
IDIOM cloak-and-dagger

3 *a secret entrance to an underground cave*
hidden, concealed, disguised
OPPOSITE open
FOR SECRET AGENTS SEE spy

secret NOUN

1 *I'll let you into a secret.*
confidence

2 *the secret to staying calm in a crisis*
key, solution, answer, recipe, formula

▷ **in secret**
Talks were held in secret.
in private, privately, on the quiet
IDIOM behind closed doors

secretive ADJECTIVE

Clive was very secretive about his past.
uncommunicative, reticent, reserved, tight-lipped, mysterious, quiet

(informal) cagey
OPPOSITES communicative, open

section NOUN

The website has a section on teenage health.
part, division, bit, sector, segment, portion, compartment, module, chapter
▶ A section from a piece of classical music is a **movement**.

sector NOUN

1 *a residential sector of the city*
area, part, district, region, section, zone

2 *people from all sectors of the music industry*
branch, part, division, department, area, arm

secure ADJECTIVE

1 *how to keep your computer secure against viruses*
safe, protected, defended, guarded, invulnerable
OPPOSITES insecure, vulnerable

2 *Tie the ropes together with a secure knot.*
steady, firm, solid, fixed, fast, immovable
OPPOSITE loose

3 *looking for a secure job*
permanent, regular, steady, reliable, dependable, settled

secure VERB

1 *securing your system against computer hackers*
safeguard, protect, defend

2 *The door wasn't properly secured.*
fasten, lock, seal, bolt

3 *They secured their place in the semi-final.*
make certain of, gain, acquire, obtain
(informal) land

security NOUN

1 *testing the security of your email system*
safety, protection

2 *There was increased security at the airport.*
safety measures, surveillance, policing

see VERB

1 *the best time to see the northern lights*
catch sight of, spot, sight, notice, observe, make out, distinguish, note, perceive, spy, glimpse, witness
(informal) clap eyes on
⎸ SEE ALSO **look**

2 *Did anyone see the late-night film?*
watch, look at, view, catch

3 *Have you been to see a doctor?*
consult, call on, visit, report to

4 *I see what you mean.*
understand, appreciate, comprehend, follow, grasp, realize, take in
(informal) get

5 *He sees it as a challenge to his authority.*
regard, look on, view, reckon

6 *I'll see what I can do.*
think about, consider, ponder, reflect on, weigh up

7 *Please see that the lights are switched off.*
make sure, make certain, ensure, check, verify, confirm

8 *Paula went to see what all the fuss was about.*
find out, discover, learn, establish, ascertain

9 *I'll see you to the door.*
escort, conduct, accompany, guide, lead, take

▷ **see to something**
Will you see to the invitations?
deal with, attend to, take care of, sort out

seed NOUN

the large seed of a mango
pip, stone, kernel

▶ A young plant grown from a seed is a **seedling**.

seek VERB

1 *seeking comfort from each other*
search for, hunt for, look for, try to find

2 *seeking to attract shoppers*
try, attempt, strive, want, wish, desire

seem VERB

Everything seems to be in working order.
appear, look, give the impression of being, strike you as

seep VERB

water seeping through the roof
leak, ooze, escape, drip, dribble, trickle, flow, bleed, soak, percolate

seethe VERB

1 *All these thoughts seethed in Jekyll's brain.*
boil, bubble, ferment, churn, writhe

2 *Inwardly he was seething with indignation.*
be angry, be furious, rage, storm

segment NOUN

Divide the orange into segments.
section, portion, piece, part, bit, wedge, slice

seize VERB

1 *Judi seized her coat and ran out of the house.*
grab, catch, snatch, take hold of, grasp, grip, clutch

2 *The town was seized by rebels last year.*
capture, take over, conquer, occupy, overrun

3 *Customs officers have seized thousands of pirate DVDs.*
take possession of, confiscate, impound, commandeer

▷ **seize up**
Without oil, the engine will seize up.
become jammed, become clogged, become stuck

seldom ADVERB

The band seldom performs live any more.

a
b
c
d
e
f
g
h
i
j
k
l
m
n
o
p
q
r
s
t
u
v
w
x
y
z

rarely, infrequently, hardly ever,
scarcely

IDIOM once in a blue moon
OPPOSITE often

select *VERB*

selecting a new team captain
choose, pick, decide on, opt for,
settle on, appoint, elect

select *ADJECTIVE*

1 *a small select group of friends*
chosen, special, hand-picked

2 *members of a select private club*
exclusive, privileged, elite

selection *NOUN*

1 *Have you made your selection?*
choice, option, pick, preference

2 *They stock a wide selection of CDs
and DVDs.*
range, variety, assortment, array

selfish *ADJECTIVE*

*Scrooge begins as a selfish character
who hates Christmas.*
self-centred, egocentric,
thoughtless, inconsiderate,
uncharitable, mean, miserly

OPPOSITES unselfish, altruistic,
generous

sell *VERB*

*The corner shop sells newspapers and
sweets.*
deal in, trade in, stock, market

▶ Uncomplimentary synonyms are
peddle and **hawk**.

OPPOSITE buy

send *VERB*

1 *sending a text message*
dispatch, post, mail, transmit,
forward

OPPOSITE receive

2 *sending a satellite into space*
launch, propel, direct, fire, shoot

3 *This computer is sending me crazy!*
drive, make, turn

▷ **send for someone**

I think we should send for a doctor.
call, summon, fetch

▷ **send something out**

*The device was sending out weird
noises.*
emit, discharge, give off, issue,
release

senior *ADJECTIVE*

1 *one of the senior players in the squad*
older, long-standing

OPPOSITES younger, junior

2 *a senior officer in the navy*
high-ranking, superior

OPPOSITES junior, subordinate

sensation *NOUN*

1 *a tingling sensation in your toes*
feeling, sense, perception

2 *Darwin caused a sensation when he
published his theory.*
stir, thrill, commotion, fuss, furore,
to-do

sensational *ADJECTIVE*

1 *a sensational story in the tabloids*
shocking, scandalous, lurid,
melodramatic
(informal) juicy

2 *(informal) a sensational line-up of
guest speakers*
amazing, extraordinary, stunning,
spectacular, stupendous,
tremendous, wonderful
(informal) fantastic, fabulous, terrific

sense *NOUN*

1 *using all of your five senses*
faculty, perception

▶ The five human senses are **hearing**,
sight, **smell**, **taste**, and **touch**.

2 *a good sense of rhythm*
appreciation, awareness,
consciousness, feeling (for)

3 *Desmond had the sense to keep quiet.*
common sense, wisdom, wit,
intelligence, brains
(informal) gumption
(North American informal) smarts

4 *The sense of the word is not clear.*
meaning, significance, import,
definition, tenor, nuance

▷ **make sense of something**

No one could make sense of the code.

understand, make out, interpret, decipher

sense *VERB*
1 *We sensed that we were not welcome.*
be aware, realize, perceive, feel, notice, observe
2 *a camera which senses body temperature*
detect, respond to, pick up, recognize

senseless *ADJECTIVE*
1 *a senseless act of violence*
pointless, mindless, futile, foolish, stupid, irrational, illogical, mad, crazy
❙ **OPPOSITE** sensible
2 *His attackers left him senseless on the ground.*
unconscious, knocked out
❙ **OPPOSITE** conscious

sensible *ADJECTIVE*
1 *a piece of sensible advice*
rational, reasonable, logical, sane, sound, prudent, wise, shrewd, level-headed, down-to-earth
❙ **OPPOSITES** foolish, unwise
2 *Bring a pair of sensible shoes.*
comfortable, practical
❙ **OPPOSITE** impractical

sensitive *ADJECTIVE*
1 *a cream for sensitive skin*
delicate, tender, fine, soft
2 *Don't be so sensitive!*
touchy, defensive, thin-skinned
❙ **OPPOSITES** insensitive, thick-skinned
3 *Cloning is still a sensitive issue.*
difficult, delicate, tricky, awkward, emotive
4 *a sensitive portrayal of autism*
tactful, considerate, thoughtful, sympathetic, understanding, diplomatic
❙ **OPPOSITES** insensitive, thoughtless

sentence *NOUN*
awaiting the sentence of the court
judgement, verdict, decision, ruling

sentence *VERB*
Both men were sentenced to life imprisonment.
condemn, convict

sentimental *ADJECTIVE*
1 *The song has sentimental value to me.*
emotional, nostalgic
2 *The film is spoiled by a sentimental ending.*
romantic, saccharine, mawkish *(informal)* soppy, mushy

separate *ADJECTIVE*
1 *Raw food and cooked food should be kept separate.*
apart, separated, detached, isolated, segregated
❙ **OPPOSITE** together
2 *Contestants have to cook three separate dishes.*
different, distinct, discrete, independent, unrelated
❙ **OPPOSITES** related, shared

separate *VERB*
1 *A prism separates light into its individual colours.*
divide, split, beak up, segregate, part
▶ To separate things which are tangled together is to **disentangle** them.
❙ **OPPOSITES** combine, mix
2 *Separate recyclable material from general waste.*
keep apart, set apart, isolate, partition, detach, cut off, remove
3 *The trail separates from here onwards.*
branch, fork, split, divide, diverge
❙ **OPPOSITE** merge
4 *Her parents decided to separate.*
split up, break up, part company
▶ To end a marriage legally is to **divorce**.

sequence *NOUN*
piecing together the sequence of events
order, progression, series, succession, course, flow, chain, train

serene ADJECTIVE

the serene expression on the
Buddha's face
calm, contented, untroubled,
peaceful, quiet, placid, tranquil
❚ **OPPOSITE** agitated

series NOUN

1 answering a series of questions
succession, sequence, string, set,
round, chain, train

2 a new TV drama series
**FOR TERMS USED IN RADIO AND
TELEVISION** SEE **television**

serious ADJECTIVE

1 Liam answered in a serious tone of
voice.
solemn, sombre, sober, earnest,
grave, grim, unsmiling, humourless
❚ **OPPOSITES** light-hearted, cheerful

2 having to make a serious decision
important, significant, major,
far-reaching, momentous, weighty
❚ **OPPOSITES** unimportant,
insignificant

3 a serious debate about climate
change
learned, intellectual, scholarly,
heavy, in-depth
❚ **OPPOSITES** light, casual

4 Are you serious about wanting to
help?
sincere, genuine, in earnest,
resolute, committed, wholehearted

5 recovering from a serious illness
severe, grave, bad, major, acute,
critical, dangerous
❚ **OPPOSITES** minor, trivial

seriously NOUN

1 Edna nodded seriously.
solemnly, soberly, earnestly, gravely,
grimly
❚ **OPPOSITE** cheerfully

2 Are you seriously interested?
genuinely, truly, honestly, sincerely

3 No one was seriously injured.
severely, badly, gravely, acutely,
critically
❚ **OPPOSITES** slightly, mildly

4 (informal) a seriously bad film
extremely, exceptionally,
extraordinarily

seriousness NOUN

1 I saw the seriousness in her eyes.
solemnity, gravity, sobriety,
humourlessness
❚ **OPPOSITES** cheerfulness, levity

2 You must understand the seriousness
of the situation.
gravity, severity, importance, weight

servant NOUN

A servant entered with a tray of
food.
attendant, domestic, maid, retainer,
minion

serve VERB

1 He served the school for 40 years
until his retirement.
work for, contribute to
❚ **IDIOM** do your bit for

2 Is anyone waiting to be served?
help, assist, attend to, deal with

3 Serve the rice in separate bowls.
give out, dish up, present, pass
round, distribute

4 an old crate which serves
as a table
be used, act, function, double up

service NOUN

1 Let me know if I can be of any
service.
help, assistance, aid, use, usefulness,
benefit

2 a funeral service
ceremony, ritual, rite

3 Treat your bike to an annual service.
check-up, overhaul, maintenance,
servicing

service VERB

Do you service washing machines?
maintain, check, go over, overhaul

session NOUN

1 the opening session of Parliament
meeting, sitting, assembly

2 a weekly training session
period, time

set *VERB*

1 *setting a microphone on its stand*
place, put, stand, position, lay, deposit

2 *a panel of glass set in the wall*
embed, fix, mount, insert

3 *Have they set a date for the wedding?*
appoint, specify, name, decide, determine, choose, fix, establish, settle

4 *setting your watch to the right time*
adjust, calibrate, regulate, correct

5 *The jam will set as it cools.*
become firm, solidify, harden, stiffen

6 *The sun was just beginning to set.*
go down, sink

▷ **set about something**
Eve set about making some tea.
begin, start, commence

▷ **set off**

1 *setting off on a round-the-world trip*
depart, get going, leave, set out, start out

2 *setting off the smoke alarm by mistake*
activate, start, trigger

▷ **set something out**
The information is clearly set out on the page.
lay out, arrange, display, present

▷ **set something up**

1 *We can set the tripod up over there.*
put up, erect, construct, build

2 *A few of us are setting up a film club.*
create, establish, institute, start, found

set *NOUN*

1 *a set of measuring spoons*
collection, batch, kit, series

2 *She was one of the literary set of her day.*
group, crowd, circle, clique, fraternity

3 *There is a quick change of set after Act One.*
scenery, backdrop, setting

set *ADJECTIVE*

1 *Backups are run at a set time every day.*
fixed, established, definite, predetermined
▌ **OPPOSITE** variable

2 *Everything is set for the big finale.*
ready, prepared, organized, primed

setback *NOUN*
We ran into a setback before we even started.
difficulty, problem, complication, snag, hitch, hiccup, glitch
▌ **OPPOSITE** breakthrough

setting *NOUN*
The abbey stands in a rural setting.
surroundings, location, situation, position, place, site, environment, background

settle *VERB*

1 *It's time to settle our differences.*
resolve, sort out, work out, clear up, reconcile, iron out, end

2 *I had just settled down on the sofa when the phone rang.*
sit, get comfortable, ensconce yourself

3 *A crow settled on a nearby branch.*
land, alight, perch, come to rest

4 *I need something to settle my nerves.*
calm, soothe, quiet, pacify

5 *The family settled in Canada after the war.*
emigrate (to), move (to), set up home (in)
▌ **IDIOM** put down roots

6 *Wait until the mud settles.*
sink to the bottom, clear, subside

7 *How would you like to settle your bill?*
pay, clear, square

▷ **settle on**
settling on a name for the website
agree on, decide on, choose, pick, determine, establish, fix

settlement *NOUN*

1 *a speedy settlement of the dispute*

a
b
c
d
e
f
g
h
i
j
k
l
m
n
o
p
q
r
s
t
u
v
w
x
y
z

resolution, settling, reconciliation, agreement, solution, ending

2 *the site of an old Viking settlement*
community, colony, encampment, outpost, village

settler *NOUN*

a book about early European settlers in America
colonist, immigrant, pioneer, incomer

sever *VERB*

1 *The knife had severed an artery.*
cut through, shear through

▶ To sever a limb is to **amputate** it.

2 *He threatened to sever all ties with his family.*
break off, end, terminate

several *ADJECTIVE*

I made several attempts to contact them.
a number of, many, some, a few, various

severe *ADJECTIVE*

1 *Mrs Upton gave me one of her severe looks.*
harsh, strict, stern, hard, disapproving, forbidding, withering
┃ OPPOSITES gentle, lenient

2 *a severe neck injury*
bad, serious, acute, grave
┃ OPPOSITE mild

3 *the severe climate of Siberia*
extreme, tough, harsh, hostile, sharp, intense
┃ OPPOSITE mild

4 *a building with a severe modern facade*
plain, austere, unadorned, stark, clinical, grim, dour
┃ OPPOSITE ornate

sew *VERB*

sewing a buttonhole by hand
stitch, tack, seam, hem, embroider
┃ SEE ALSO textiles

sex *NOUN*

1 *Chromosomes determine the sex of a baby.*
gender

2 *education about sex and relationships*
sexual intercourse, sexual relations, lovemaking, copulation

sexual *ADJECTIVE*

1 *the sexual parts of a flower*
reproductive, procreative

2 *The film contains scenes of a sexual nature.*
erotic, carnal, sensual

shabby *ADJECTIVE*

1 *a shabby pair of slippers*
ragged, scruffy, tattered, frayed, worn out, threadbare
(informal) tatty
(North American informal) raggedy
┃ OPPOSITE smart

2 *a room in a shabby boarding house*
dilapidated, run down, seedy, dingy, squalid, sordid

3 *That was a shabby trick!*
mean, nasty, unfair, unkind, dishonest, shameful, low, cheap

shade *NOUN*

1 *sitting in the shade of a palm tree*
shadow, cover

2 *a portable sun shade*
screen, blind, canopy, awning

▶ A type of umbrella used as a sun shade is a **parasol**.

3 *a pale shade of blue*
hue, tinge, tint, tone, colour

4 *subtle shades of meaning*
degree, gradation, nuance, undertone

shade *VERB*

1 *shading your eyes from the sun*
shield, screen, protect, hide, mask

2 *Use small pencil strokes to shade the edges.*
fill in, darken

a b c d e f g h i j k l m n o p q r s t u v w x y z

shadow *NOUN*

1 *The candlelight cast weird shadows on the wall.*
silhouette, shape, figure, outline, contour

2 *Her face was deep in shadow.*
shade, darkness, semi-darkness, gloom

3 *Not a shadow of doubt remained.*
trace, hint, flicker, suggestion, suspicion

shadow *VERB*

Police have been shadowing the suspect for weeks.
follow, pursue, stalk, track, trail
(informal) tail
IDIOM keep tabs on

shady *ADJECTIVE*

1 *a shady spot under a tree*
shaded, shadowy, sheltered, dark, sunless
OPPOSITE sunny

2 *involved in shady business deals*
dishonest, disreputable, suspicious, dubious, suspect, untrustworthy
(informal) fishy, dodgy
OPPOSITE honest

shaft *NOUN*

1 *an ice axe with a metal shaft*
handle, spine, pole, rod, stick, staff

2 *a shaft of moonlight*
beam, ray, gleam, streak

3 *an old mine shaft*
pit, tunnel, hole, duct, bore

shaggy *ADJECTIVE*

Highland cows have long shaggy coats.
bushy, woolly, fleecy, hairy, thick
FOR TIPS ON DESCRIBING HAIR SEE hair

shake *VERB*

1 *The walls and floor shook with the blast.*
quake, shudder, vibrate, rattle, rock, sway, totter, wobble, judder, convulse

2 *The driver shook his fist as he overtook us.*
wave, brandish, flourish, wield, wag, waggle, joggle

3 *The couple were visibly shaken by the news.*
shock, distress, upset, disturb, unsettle, unnerve, startle, alarm, agitate, rattle, fluster
IDIOM throw you off balance

4 *Jen was so upset that her voice was shaking.*
tremble, quaver, quiver, shiver, twitch

shaky *ADJECTIVE*

1 *a chair with shaky legs*
unsteady, wobbly, unstable, insecure, rickety
(British informal) wonky
OPPOSITES steady, stable

2 *speaking in a shaky voice*
trembling, quavering, quivering, faltering, nervous, tremulous
OPPOSITES steady, calm

3 *The season has got off to a shaky start.*
uncertain, faltering, doubtful, questionable
OPPOSITES confident, sound

shallow *ADJECTIVE*

1 *No diving in the shallow end of the pool.*
OPPOSITE deep

2 *a shallow analysis of a complex poem*
superficial, insubstantial, lightweight, frivolous, trivial, facile
OPPOSITES deep, thoughtful

sham *NOUN*

I later found out that her illness was a sham.
pretence, deception, lie, act

shame *NOUN*

1 *He said he felt no shame for his past life.*
remorse, contrition, mortification, guilt

2 *Their actions brought shame to our community.*
disgrace, dishonour, ignominy,

humiliation, embarrassment

▷ **a shame**

  It's a shame you have to leave.

  a pity, unfortunate

shameful *ADJECTIVE*

a shameful incident involving eight players

disgraceful, deplorable, reprehensible, discreditable, dishonourable, contemptible, despicable, outrageous, scandalous

❙ **OPPOSITES** admirable, honourable

shape *NOUN*

1 *a Valentine card in the shape of a heart*

form, figure, outline, silhouette, configuration, contours

2 *feeling in good shape*

condition, health, form, order, fettle, trim

(British informal) nick

WORD WEB

two-dimensional geometric shapes

circle, decagon (10 sides), diamond, ellipse, heptagon (7 sides), hexagon (6 sides), nonagon (9 sides), oblong, octagon (8 sides), oval, parallelogram, pentagon (5 sides), polygon, quadrilateral, rectangle, rhombus, ring, semicircle, square, trapezium, triangle

three-dimensional geometric shapes

cone, cube, cuboid, cylinder, hemisphere, polyhedron, prism, pyramid, sphere

shape *VERB*

Shape the dough into a round.

form, mould, fashion, make

▶ To shape metal or plaster in a mould is to **cast** it.

▷ **shape up**

My plan was shaping up nicely.

develop, evolve, advance, progress, move on

share *NOUN*

Everyone gets a fair share of computer time.

portion, quota, allocation, allowance, ration, helping

(informal) cut, whack

share *VERB*

1 *We shared the cost of a taxi between us.*

divide, split, apportion

2 *They finally got round to sharing out the prizes.*

distribute, deal out, ration out, allocate, allot

sharp *ADJECTIVE*

1 *Use a pair of sharp scissors.*

keen, sharpened, razor-sharp

❙ **OPPOSITE** blunt

2 *a species of cactus with sharp spines*

pointed, spiky, jagged

❙ **OPPOSITE** rounded

3 *feeling a sharp pain in your ankle*

acute, piercing, stabbing

❙ **OPPOSITE** dull

4 *getting a sharp image on the screen*

clear, distinct, well defined, crisp

❙ **OPPOSITE** blurred

5 *Editors need a sharp eye for detail.*

keen, observant, perceptive

❙ **OPPOSITE** unobservant

6 *a brilliant physicist with a sharp mind*

clever, quick, shrewd, perceptive

❙ **OPPOSITES** dull, slow

7 *a sharp bend in the road*

abrupt, sudden, steep

▶ A bend that doubles back on itself is a **hairpin** bend.

❙ **OPPOSITE** gradual

8 *a sharp overnight frost*

severe, extreme, intense, serious

❙ **OPPOSITES** slight, mild

9 *This salad dressing is a bit sharp.*

Column guide: a b c d e f g h i j k l m n o p q r s t u v w x y z sour, tart, bitter

OPPOSITES mild, sweet

sharpen *VERB*
> *sharpening a kitchen knife*
> make sharp, grind, whet, hone

shatter *VERB*
1. *The mirror fell and shattered into tiny shards.*
   smash, break, splinter, fracture, fragment, disintegrate
2. *Jo's dreams of being a writer were shattered.*
   destroy, wreck, ruin, demolish, crush, dash
   (informal) scupper
3. *The day's events had shattered my nerves.*
   fray, strain, rattle, upset

sheaf *NOUN*
> *He handed me a sheaf of handwritten pages.*
> bunch, bundle

sheath *NOUN*
> *Keep the thermometer in its plastic sheath.*
> casing, covering, sleeve
▶ A sheath for a sword or dagger is a **scabbard**.

shed¹ *NOUN*
> *a shed full of garden tools*
> hut, shack, outhouse, cabin

shed² *VERB*
1. *All the trees had shed their leaves.*
   drop, let fall, spill, scatter
2. *The creature sheds its human skin to emerge as a werewolf.*
   cast off, throw off, discard, moult, slough off

sheen *NOUN*
> *Alex awoke covered in a cold sheen of sweat.*
> shine, gloss, lustre, polish, patina, burnish

sheep *NOUN*
> *a flock of hill sheep*
▶ A female sheep is a **ewe**.

▶ A male sheep is a **ram**.
▶ A young sheep is a **lamb**.
▶ Meat from sheep is **mutton** or **lamb**.
▶ The woolly coat of a sheep is its **fleece**.

sheer *ADJECTIVE*
1. *That story he told was sheer nonsense.*
   complete, total, utter, absolute, pure, downright, out-and-out
2. *The path ran alongside a sheer cliff.*
   vertical, perpendicular, precipitous, steep
▶ A sheer or steep cliff face is a **precipice**.
   OPPOSITE gradual
3. *a scarf of sheer silk*
   fine, thin, transparent, see-through, diaphanous
   OPPOSITE opaque

sheet *NOUN*
1. *Start on a fresh sheet of paper.*
   page, leaf, piece
2. *fitting a new sheet of glass*
   pane, panel, plate
3. *The pond was covered with a thin sheet of ice.*
   layer, film, coating, covering, surface, crust, skin

shelf *NOUN*
> *Please put the books back on the shelf.*
> ledge, rack
▶ A shelf above a fireplace is a **mantelpiece**.

shell *NOUN*
1. *an old acorn shell*
   pod, husk, hull
2. *a kayak with a fibreglass shell*
   framework, body, casing, outside, exterior
▶ The shell of an aircraft is the **fuselage**.

a
b
c
d
e
f
g
h
i
j
k
l
m
n
o
p
q
r
s
t
u
v
w
x
y
z

shellfish NOUN

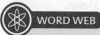 **WORD WEB**

> *some types of shellfish*
> abalone, barnacle, clam, cockle, conch, crab, crayfish, cuttlefish, langoustine, limpet, lobster, mussel, oyster, prawn, razor shell, scallop, shrimp, whelk, winkle
> ► Shellfish with legs, such as crabs, lobsters, and shrimps, are **crustaceans**.
> ► Shellfish such as clams and oysters, with soft bodies and often an external shell, are **molluscs**.

shelter NOUN

1 *The tents provide shelter from the desert winds.*
cover, protection, safety, security, refuge

2 *a shelter for homeless animals*
refuge, home, haven, sanctuary

shelter VERB

1 *An overhanging rock sheltered us from the rain.*
protect, shield, screen, guard, defend, safeguard, cushion
OPPOSITE expose

2 *They sheltered in a cave until morning.*
take shelter, take refuge, take cover

shelve VERB

The news is that the film has been shelved.
postpone, put off, put back, defer, suspend, put to one side
IDIOMS put on ice, put on the back burner

shield NOUN

The trees act as an effective wind shield.
screen, barrier, defence, guard,

protection, cover, shelter
► The part of a helmet that shields your face is the **visor**.

shield VERB

A hat will shield your eyes from the sun.
protect, screen, cover, shelter, guard, safeguard, defend, keep safe

shift VERB

1 *Do you need help to shift the furniture?*
move, rearrange, reposition

2 *a stain which is impossible to shift*
remove, get off, lift, get rid of
OPPOSITE embed

3 *Attitudes have shifted in recent years.*
change, alter, evolve, progress, move on
OPPOSITE stagnate

shine VERB

1 *A light shone from an upstairs window.*
beam, gleam, glow, glare, blaze, radiate
FOR TIPS ON DESCRIBING LIGHT SEE **light❶**

2 *the actor who really shines in this film*
excel, stand out, be outstanding

3 *Ted had forgotten to shine his shoes.*
polish, brush, buff, burnish

shiny ADJECTIVE

a marble top with a shiny surface
glossy, gleaming, glistening, polished, burnished, lustrous
OPPOSITES matt, dull

ship NOUN

a job working on a cruise ship
boat, craft, vessel
► A large passenger ship is a **liner**.
► Ships that travel long distances at sea are **ocean-going** or **seagoing** ships.
► A related adjective is **nautical**.
FOR TYPES OF BOAT OR SHIP SEE **boat**

ship VERB
Your parcel was shipped on Tuesday.
dispatch, send, post, mail, deliver

shirk VERB
shirking your fair share of the work
avoid, evade, get out of, dodge, duck

shiver VERB
A boy stood on the doorstep, shivering with cold.
tremble, quiver, shake, shudder, quake

shock NOUN
1 *News of his death came as a great shock.*
blow, surprise, fright, upset, eye-opener
▌ **IDIOMS** bolt from the blue, rude awakening

2 *The driver is still in a state of shock.*
trauma, distress, collapse

3 *The shock of the explosion was felt for miles.*
impact, jolt, reverberation

shock VERB
The whole town was shocked by the news.
horrify, appal, startle, stun, stagger, astonish, astound, shake, rock, traumatize, scandalize, outrage

shocking ADJECTIVE
1 *evidence of shocking cruelty*
appalling, horrifying, horrific, dreadful, horrendous, atrocious, abominable, horrible, terrible, distressing, sickening, revolting

2 *(informal) a shocking waste of money*
very bad, awful, terrible, deplorable, disgraceful, lamentable
(informal) abysmal

shoes PLURAL NOUN
a shop selling fancy shoes and bags
footwear

WORD WEB

some types of footwear
ankle boots, ballet shoes, baseball boots, brogues, clogs, court shoes, espadrilles, flip-flops, gym shoes, high heels, moccasins, mules, platform shoes, plimsolls, pumps, sandals, slippers, stilettos, tap shoes, tennis shoes, trainers (North American sneakers), wellingtons (informal wellies)

▶ A person who mends shoes or boots is a **cobbler**.

▶ A person who makes and fits horses' shoes is a **farrier**.

shoot VERB
1 *shooting a cannonball over a wall*
fire, discharge, launch, aim, propel

2 *It is now illegal to hunt and shoot tigers.*
fire at, hit, open fire on, gun down

3 *An ambulance shot past with its lights flashing.*
race, speed, dash, rush, tear, streak, hurtle, fly, whizz, zoom

4 *He shot the penalty into the corner of the net.*
kick, strike, hit, drive, boot

5 *Most of the film was shot in New Zealand.*
film, photograph, record

shoot NOUN
Wait till the seeds begin to put out shoots.
bud, sprout, tendril

shop NOUN
a good range of specialist shops
store, boutique, emporium, market

》

a
b
c
d
e
f
g
h
i
j
k
l
m
n
o
p
q
r
s
t
u
v
w
x
y
z

WORD WEB

some types of shop and shopkeeper

antique shop, bakery, bookshop *(North American* bookstore*)*, butcher, cheesemonger, chemist or pharmacy *(North American* drugstore*)*, clothes shop, confectioner, corner shop, delicatessen, department store, fishmonger, florist, garden centre, greengrocer, grocer, haberdasher, health-food shop, hypermarket, ironmonger *(North American* hardware store*)*, jeweller, music shop, newsagent, off-licence, pharmacy, post office, shoe shop, shopping arcade, shopping centre *(North American* shopping mall*)*, stationer, supermarket, toyshop, watchmaker

shopping NOUN
a trolley laden with shopping
goods, purchases

shore NOUN
SEE **seashore**

short ADJECTIVE
1 *a short distance from the town centre*
little, small
┃ OPPOSITE long
2 *sending a short text message*
concise, compact, brief, succinct, condensed
┃ OPPOSITES long, lengthy
3 *It was a very short visit.*
brief, quick, fleeting, hasty, cursory
┃ OPPOSITES long, lengthy
4 *Alvin was short for his age.*
small, tiny, little, diminutive, petite
▶ Someone who is short and fat is **squat** or **dumpy**.
┃ OPPOSITE tall

FOR TIPS ON DESCRIBING PEOPLE'S BODIES SEE **body**

5 *Our food supplies were getting short.*
low, meagre, scant, sparse, inadequate, insufficient
┃ OPPOSITE plentiful
6 *The receptionist was short with me.*
abrupt, rude, sharp, curt, brusque, terse, blunt, snappy
┃ OPPOSITES polite, courteous

shortage NOUN
a severe shortage of basic medicines
scarcity, deficiency, insufficiency, lack, want, dearth, shortfall
▶ A shortage of water is a **drought**.
▶ A shortage of food is a **famine**.

shortcoming NOUN
Pamela was aware of her own shortcomings.
fault, failing, imperfection, defect, flaw, weakness, limitation, weak point
┃ OPPOSITES strength, strong point

shorten VERB
a serious injury which shortened his career
cut short, curtail, truncate, reduce, trim, cut down, abbreviate, abridge, compress, condense
┃ OPPOSITE lengthen

shortly ADVERB
The guests will be arriving shortly.
soon, before long, in a little while, in no time, any minute, presently, by and by

shot NOUN
1 *We heard a noise like the shot of a rifle.*
crack, report, bang, blast
2 *Luckily the gunman was a poor shot.*
shooter, marksman
3 *a relatively easy shot at goal*
strike, kick, hit, stroke
4 *an unusual shot taken from the air*
photograph, photo, picture, snap, snapshot

5 *(informal) Can I have a shot at that?*
try, go, attempt
(informal) bash, crack, stab

shoulder VERB

1 *A woman shouldered her way to the front.*
push, shove, force, barge, elbow, jostle

2 *No one was willing to shoulder the blame.*
accept, assume, take on, bear, carry

shout VERB

Dean had to shout to be heard above the din.
call, cry out, yell, roar, bellow, bawl, raise your voice
(informal) holler
▌**OPPOSITE** whisper
▌**SEE ALSO** say

shove VERB

1 *Gemma shoved her books into her locker.*
push, thrust, force, ram, cram

2 *Stop shoving at the back!*
barge, push, elbow, jostle

show VERB

1 *You promised to show me your photos.*
present, display, exhibit, set out, put on view

2 *The cave painting shows a hunting scene.*
portray, picture, depict, illustrate, represent

3 *Can you show me what to do?*
explain to, make clear to, instruct, teach, tell

4 *Her diary shows that she was full of self-doubt.*
reveal, disclose, make plain, demonstrate, prove, confirm, verify

5 *We were shown into the waiting room.*
guide, direct, conduct, escort, accompany, usher

6 *The dots show where to put your fingers.*
indicate, point out

7 *Does my T-shirt show through the blouse?*
be seen, be visible, appear

▷ **show off**
Ignore him: he's just showing off.
boast, brag, swagger, posture
▌**IDIOMS** blow your own trumpet, put on airs

▷ **show something off**
showing off his new gadget
display, parade, flaunt, exhibit

▷ **show up**
1 *The lines don't show up on the screen.*
appear, be visible, be evident

2 *(informal) Callum showed up an hour late.*
arrive, come, appear, turn up

show NOUN

1 *a show of students' artwork*
display, exhibition, presentation

2 *tickets for tonight's show*
performance, production, entertainment

shower NOUN

a sudden shower of rain
fall, downpour, sprinkling, drizzle
FOR TIPS ON DESCRIBING WEATHER SEE **weather**

shower VERB

1 *The eruption showered a wide area with volcanic ash.*
spray, spatter, sprinkle, splash

2 *This low-budget film has been showered with praise.*
swamp, flood, inundate, overwhelm

showy ADJECTIVE

Is this tie too showy?
gaudy, flashy, bright, loud, garish, conspicuous
▌**OPPOSITES** plain, restrained

shred NOUN

There's not a shred of evidence against her.
bit, piece, scrap, trace, jot, iota

》

a
b
c
d
e
f
g
h
i
j
k
l
m
n
o
p
q
r
s
t
u
v
w
x
y
z

509

▷ **shreds**

The gale ripped the tent to shreds.
tatters, ribbons, rags, strips

shrewd *ADJECTIVE*

Doyle had been shrewd in his calculations.
clever, astute, sharp, quick-witted, intelligent, smart, canny, perceptive
❙ OPPOSITE stupid

shriek *NOUN, VERB*
SEE **scream**

shrill *ADJECTIVE*

the shrill sound of a whistle
high, high-pitched, piercing, sharp, screechy
❙ OPPOSITES low, soft

shrink *VERB*

1 *My jeans have shrunk in the wash.*
become smaller, contract, narrow, reduce, decrease
❙ OPPOSITE expand

2 *Could you shrink the image to fit the page?*
make smaller, reduce, decrease, diminish, compact, compress
❙ OPPOSITES enlarge, increase

3 *The creature shrank back instinctively from the light.*
recoil, flinch, shy away

shrivel *VERB*

Delicate plants will shrivel in the heat.
wilt, wither, droop, dry up, wrinkle, shrink

shroud *VERB*

1 *Her dark hair partly shrouded her face.*
cover, veil, mask, screen, obscure

2 *The summit was shrouded in clouds.*
wrap, envelop, blanket, cloak, hide, conceal

shrub *NOUN*

a desert shrub which grows in northern Chile
bush
▶ An area planted with shrubs is a **shrubbery**.

shudder *VERB*

Mel shuddered at the thought of being left alone.
tremble, quake, quiver, shiver, shake, judder

shuffle *VERB*

1 *A pack of zombies shuffled towards them.*
shamble, hobble, scuffle, scrape, drag your feet

2 *Did you remember to shuffle the cards?*
mix, mix up, jumble, rearrange

shut *VERB*

Please shut the door behind you.
close, fasten, seal, secure, lock, bolt, latch
▶ To shut a door with a bang is to **slam** it.

▷ **shut down**

The hotel shut down years ago.
close down, go out of business
(informal) fold
❙ OPPOSITE open up

▷ **shut something down**

the safe way to shut down a computer
switch off, shut off, close down
❙ OPPOSITE start up

▷ **shut up**

(informal) I wish those people behind us would just shut up!
be quiet, be silent, stop talking, hush up
❙ IDIOM hold your tongue

▷ **shut someone up**

1 *I hate to see animals shut up in cages.*
imprison, confine, detain

2 *(informal) This should shut them up for a while.*
silence, quieten, quiet down, hush up

shy *ADJECTIVE*

At first, Maria was too shy to say anything.
bashful, timid, coy, reserved, hesitant, self-conscious,

a
b
c
d
e
f
g
h
i
j
k
l
m
n
o
p
q
r
s
t
u
v
w
x
y
z

inhibited, modest
OPPOSITES bold, confident

sick *ADJECTIVE*
  1 *She was sick with a chest infection all last week.*
  ill, unwell, poorly, sickly, ailing, infirm, indisposed
  IDIOM under the weather
  OPPOSITES healthy, well
  2 *feeling dizzy and slightly sick*
  nauseous, queasy, bilious
  3 *a sick sense of humour*
  tasteless, macabre, morbid, ghoulish
  ▷ **be sick**
  Mo suddenly felt he was going to be sick.
  vomit, heave
  (informal) throw up, puke
  ▷ **be sick of**
  I'm sick of all this gloomy news.
  be fed up with, be tired of, be weary of, have had enough of

sicken *VERB*
  1 *The crew began to sicken from hunger and fatigue.*
  fall ill, become sick
  2 *Some audience members were sickened by the violence in the film.*
  disgust, revolt, repel, nauseate, make you sick
  IDIOM turn your stomach

sickening *ADJECTIVE*
  the sickening sight and smell of blood
  nauseating, stomach-turning, repulsive, revolting, disgusting, distasteful
  (informal) gross

sickly *ADJECTIVE*
  1 *Toby had always been a sickly child.*
  unhealthy, weak, delicate, frail
  OPPOSITES healthy, strong
  2 *the sweet, slightly sickly scent of molasses*
  nauseating, sickening, stomach-turning

sickness *NOUN*
  1 *A deadly sickness swept across the continent.*
  illness, disease, ailment, malady, infection, virus
  (informal) bug
  2 *A sudden wave of sickness came over her.*
  nausea, queasiness, biliousness, vomiting

side *NOUN*
  1 *the opposite sides of a cube*
  face, surface
  2 *a scar on the right side of his face*
  half, part
  3 *a ditch at the side of the road*
  edge, border, boundary, fringe, perimeter, verge, margin
  4 *seeing both sides of the argument*
  point of view, viewpoint, standpoint, position, perspective, angle, slant
  5 *the best side in the league*
  team, squad, line-up

side *VERB*
  ▷ **side with someone**
  Italy sided with Germany and Japan in World War II.
  support, take the side of, ally yourself with, back, favour, stand by, be loyal to

siege *NOUN*
  the story of the siege of Troy
  blockade

sift *VERB*
  Sift the flour to get rid of any lumps.
  sieve, strain, filter
  ▷ **sift through something**
  sifting through some old emails
  look through, examine, inspect, pore over, analyse, scrutinize, review

sigh *NOUN, VERB*
  FOR TIPS ON DESCRIBING SOUNDS SEE **sound❶**

sight *NOUN*
  1 *Owls have sharp sight and excellent hearing.*
  eyesight, vision, eyes

》

a
b
c
d
e
f
g
h
i
j
k
l
m
n
o
p
q
r
s
t
u
v
w
x
y
z

▶ Related adjectives are **optical** and **visual**.

2 *It was Corey's first sight of snow.*
view, glimpse, look (at)

3 *Niagara Falls is a breathtaking sight.*
spectacle, display, show, scene

4 *seeing the sights of New York*
attraction, landmark, wonder

▷ **be in sight**

1 *Not a single person was in sight.*
be visible, be in view, be in range

2 *At last the end is in sight.*
approach, loom, be imminent

sight *VERB*

After eight days at sea we sighted land.
see, catch sight of, spot, spy, glimpse, make out, notice, observe, distinguish, recognize

sign *NOUN*

1 *looking for any signs of life*
indication, mark, symptom, clue, hint, suggestion

2 *A sign pointed to the exit.*
notice, placard, poster, signpost

▶ The sign belonging to a particular business or organization is a **logo**.

▶ The sign on a particular brand of goods is a **trademark**.

3 *I'll give you the sign when I'm ready.*
signal, gesture, cue, reminder

FOR SIGNS OF THE ZODIAC SEE **zodiac**

sign *VERB*

1 *She signed to us that the baby was asleep.*
signal, indicate, gesture, motion

2 *Please sign your name here.*
write, inscribe, autograph

3 *signing new players for next season*
take on, engage, recruit, enrol

signal *NOUN*

1 *Don't move until I give the signal.*
sign, gesture, cue, reminder

2 *the first signal that something was wrong*
indication, clue, hint, suggestion, warning

signal *VERB*

The photographer signalled that she was ready.
give a sign, indicate, gesture, motion

significance *NOUN*

1 *The significance of these carvings is not clear.*
meaning, message, import, importance, point, relevance

2 *Their discovery was of major significance.*
importance, consequence, seriousness, magnitude, gravity, weight

❙ **OPPOSITE** insignificance

significant *ADJECTIVE*

1 *the significant events in our country's history*
important, major, noteworthy, notable, influential, of consequence

❙ **OPPOSITES** insignificant, minor

2 *Climate change is having a significant effect on wildlife.*
noticeable, considerable, substantial, perceptible, appreciable, striking, salient

❙ **OPPOSITE** negligible

signify *VERB*

1 *A red light signifies danger.*
indicate, denote, mean, symbolize, represent, stand for

2 *Everyone nodded to signify agreement.*
show, express, indicate, communicate, convey

silence *NOUN*

An eerie silence filled the room.
quiet, quietness, hush, stillness, calm, peace, tranquillity

❙ **OPPOSITE** noise

silence *VERB*

Tilly silenced the children with a single look.
quieten, quiet, hush, muffle

▶ To silence someone by putting something in or over their mouth is to **gag** them.

silent *ADJECTIVE*

  1 *Outside, the night was cold and silent.*

  quiet, noiseless, soundless, still, hushed

  ▶ A sound you cannot hear is **inaudible**.

  OPPOSITE noisy

  2 *Conrad was silent for a few minutes.*

  speechless, unspeaking, quiet, mute *(informal)* mum

  ▶ To be too shy to speak is to be **tongue-tied**.

  OPPOSITE talkative

silky *ADJECTIVE*

  a breed of rabbit with long silky fur

  smooth, soft, fine, sleek, velvety

silly *ADJECTIVE*

  That was a really silly idea!

  foolish, stupid, idiotic, foolhardy, senseless, brainless, thoughtless, unwise, unintelligent, half-witted, hare-brained, scatterbrained *(British informal)* daft

  OPPOSITE sensible

similar *ADJECTIVE*

  The two patterns are very similar.

  alike, nearly the same, comparable

  IDIOM *(informal)* much of a muchness

  OPPOSITES dissimilar, different

  ▷ **similar to**

  The flavour of mace is similar to nutmeg.

  like, close to, comparable to, reminiscent of

  OPPOSITES unlike, different from

similarity *NOUN*

  Notice the similarity between the paintings.

  likeness, resemblance, correspondence, parallel

  OPPOSITE difference

simple *ADJECTIVE*

  1 *answering a simple question*

  easy, elementary, straightforward

  OPPOSITE difficult

  2 *written in simple language*

  clear, plain, uncomplicated, understandable, intelligible

  OPPOSITE complicated

  3 *wearing a simple cotton dress*

  plain, undecorated, unadorned

  OPPOSITES elaborate, showy

  4 *enjoying simple pleasures*

  ordinary, unsophisticated, humble, modest, homely

  OPPOSITE sophisticated

simply *ADVERB*

  1 *I'll try to put it simply.*

  clearly, plainly, straightforwardly, in simple terms

  2 *It is simply the best book I've ever read.*

  absolutely, wholly, completely, totally, utterly

  3 *She was silenced simply for telling the truth.*

  only, just, merely, purely, solely

sin *NOUN*

  They believed that the plague was a punishment for their sins.

  wrong, evil, wickedness, wrongdoing, immorality, vice

sincere *ADJECTIVE*

  Please accept our sincere apologies.

  genuine, honest, true, real, earnest, wholehearted, heartfelt

  OPPOSITE insincere

sing *VERB*

  1 *singing an old folk song*

  chant, croon, chorus

  FOR TYPES OF SINGING VOICE SEE song

  2 *a kookaburra singing outside the window*

  chirp, trill, warble

singe *VERB*

  The flames singed the inside of the roof.

  burn, scorch, sear, blacken, char

singer *NOUN*

  The band comprises two guitarists and a singer.

  vocalist

a
b
c
d
e
f
g
h
i
j
k
l
m
n
o
p
q
r
s
t
u
v
w
x
y
z

»

► A singer who sings alone is a **soloist**.

► A group of singers is a **choir** or **chorus**.

► A member of a church choir is a **chorister**.

SEE ALSO music, song

single ADJECTIVE

1 *A single tree stood out against the sky.*
solitary, isolated, sole, lone

► When only a single example of something exists, it is **unique**.

2 *the personal details of every single customer*
individual, distinct, separate

3 *accommodation for single students*
unmarried
(old use) unwed

► An unmarried man is a **bachelor**.

► An old-fashioned word for an unmarried woman is a **spinster**.

OPPOSITE married

4 *a single ticket to Amsterdam*
one-way

OPPOSITE return

single VERB

▷ **single someone out**
The best players were quickly singled out.
pick out, select, choose, identify, earmark, target

sinister ADJECTIVE

The culprit is revealed to be the sinister housekeeper.
menacing, threatening, malevolent, dark, evil, disturbing, unsettling, eerie
(informal) creepy

sink VERB

1 *a Spanish galleon that sank off the coast of Florida*
submerge, go down, founder

► To sink a ship deliberately by letting in water is to **scuttle** or **scupper** it.

2 *The sun began to sink below the horizon.*
go down, fall, drop, dip, descend, subside, set

3 *Jessica sank back in her chair.*
slump, flop, collapse

4 *Sink each pot into the ground.*
insert, embed, plant, push, dig, drive

sip VERB

sipping a glass of lemonade
drink, taste, sample

SEE ALSO drink

sister NOUN

a younger sister
(informal) sis

► A formal name for a sister or brother is a **sibling**.

FOR OTHER MEMBERS OF A FAMILY SEE **family**

sit VERB

1 *Mollie sat on the sofa reading a magazine.*
be seated, take a seat, settle down, rest, perch, be ensconced

IDIOM take the weight off your feet

► To sit on your heels is to **squat**.

► To sit for a photograph or portrait is to **pose**.

2 *Don't sit the vase on top of the television.*
put, place, set, stand, lay, rest, deposit

3 *When are you sitting your music exam?*
take
(informal) go in for

site NOUN

This is the site of an ancient burial ground.
location, place, position, situation, setting, whereabouts, venue

site VERB

plans to site a new skate park nearby
place, put, locate, position, situate

situated ADJECTIVE

▷ **be situated**
This small village is situated in a valley.
be located, be positioned, sit in

situation NOUN

1 *The property is in a quiet situation.*

location, locality, place, position,
setting, site, spot

2 *I found myself in an awkward
situation.*
position, circumstances, condition,
state of affairs

▶ A bad situation is a **plight** or
predicament.

3 *applying for a situation in
advertising*
job, post, position,
appointment

size NOUN

1 *attempts to measure the size of the
universe*
dimensions, proportions,
measurements, area, extent

2 *Don't underestimate the size of the
task ahead.*
scale, magnitude, immensity

sizeable ADJECTIVE

*The bullet left a sizeable hole in the
wall.*
large, considerable,
substantial, fair-sized, appreciable,
noticeable

❚ **OPPOSITES** small, unnoticeable

sizzle VERB

Heat the oil until it begins to sizzle.
crackle, sputter, spit, hiss

skeleton NOUN

1 *parts of a human skeleton*
SEE **bone**

2 *The model shows the skeleton of the
building.*
frame, framework, shell

❚ **IDIOM** bare bones

sketch NOUN

1 *an early sketch of the
costume design*
drawing, outline, plan, draft, doodle

2 *a short comic sketch*
play, scene, skit, routine

sketch VERB

*Sketch your design on a piece of
paper first.*
draw, draft, outline, rough out

skid VERB

*Watch you don't skid on
the wet floor.*
slide, slip

skilful ADJECTIVE

a skilful writer of detective stories
expert, skilled, accomplished, able,
capable, talented, brilliant, clever,
masterly, deft, dexterous
(informal) crack

▶ A person who is skilled at something
is an **ace**.
Sean is an ace at anything technical.
❚ **OPPOSITE** incompetent

skill NOUN

*Balancing on a snowboard requires
considerable skill.*
expertise, ability, accomplishment,
talent, competence, proficiency,
mastery, deftness, dexterity,
prowess, artistry

skilled ADJECTIVE
SEE **skilful**

skim VERB

1 *Dragonflies skimmed across the still
water.*
glide, slide, slip, flit, dart

2 *I only had time to skim the papers.*
scan, glance through, flick through,
leaf through
❚ **IDIOM** cast your eye over

skin NOUN

1 *Drinking water is good for your skin.*
▶ The appearance of the skin of your
face is your **complexion**.
▶ A related adjective is **dermal**.
▶ The branch of medicine which treats
skin disorders is **dermatology**.
FOR TIPS ON DESCRIBING FACES SEE **face**

2 *The drums were originally made
from animal skins.*
hide, pelt, fur

3 *peeling a banana skin*
peel, rind

4 *When it cools the mixture will form
a skin.*
film, coating, membrane, crust

skin VERB

1 *Skin and deseed the tomatoes.*
peel, pare

2 *Billy had fallen and skinned his knees.*
graze, scrape, chafe

skinny ADJECTIVE

A skinny girl in bare feet answered the door.
thin, lean, bony, gaunt, lanky, gangly, scrawny, scraggy
❘ **OPPOSITE** plump
FOR TIPS ON DESCRIBING PEOPLE'S BODIES SEE **body**

skip VERB

1 *skipping along the pavement*
hop, jump, leap, bound, caper, dance, prance

2 *I skipped most of the first chapter.*
pass over, miss out, ignore, omit, leave out

skirt VERB

The bike trail skirts the east side of the lake.
go past, go round, border, edge, flank

sky NOUN

a kestrel flying high in the sky
air, heavens, atmosphere
❘ **IDIOM** (literary) blue yonder
❘ **SEE ALSO** weather

slab NOUN

an inscription on a slab of marble
block, piece, tablet, slice, chunk, hunk, lump

slack ADJECTIVE

1 *Suddenly the rope went slack.*
loose, limp, sagging, flabby
❘ **OPPOSITES** tight, taut

2 *This is usually a slack time of year.*
slow, quiet, sluggish, stagnant
❘ **OPPOSITES** busy, hectic

3 *slack standards of food hygiene*
lax, careless, negligent, slapdash, sloppy
❘ **OPPOSITE** strict

slacken VERB

1 *Dixon undid his collar and slackened his tie.*
loosen, relax, release, ease off
❘ **OPPOSITE** tighten

2 *The front runners slackened their pace a little.*
lessen, reduce, decrease, slow down
❘ **OPPOSITE** increase

slam VERB

1 *The door slammed shut behind her.*
bang, shut loudly

2 *an asteroid which slammed into the Earth*
crash, smash, ram, plough, run, collide (with)

slant VERB

1 *Italic text usually slants to the right.*
lean, slope, tilt, incline, be at an angle, be angled
▶ A boat or ship which leans over to one side is said to **list**.

2 *They slanted the story to suit themselves.*
skew, twist, distort, bias, weight

slant NOUN

1 *Here, the graph shows a steep slant upwards.*
slope, angle, tilt, incline, gradient
▶ The slant of a roof is its **pitch**.

2 *a show which offers a humorous slant on the news*
point of view, angle, viewpoint, perspective, stance, bias

slap VERB

The rider slapped the horse's side with the reins.
smack, strike, hit, spank, clout, cuff
(informal) whack

slap NOUN

The cold air hit me like a slap in the face.
smack, blow, spank, clout, cuff
(informal) whack

slash VERB

1 *Several cars had their tyres slashed overnight.*

a b c d e f g h i j k l m n o p q r s t u v w x y z

cut, gash, slit, knife, lacerate, nick

2 *Shops are slashing prices even further.*
reduce, lower, cut, drop, bring down

slash NOUN
Make a slash in the top of the loaf before baking.
cut, gash, slit, notch, nick, laceration

slaughter VERB
Waves of soldiers were slaughtered as they advanced.
kill, butcher, massacre, cull
(literary) slay

slaughter NOUN
the terrible slaughter of the trenches
massacre, killing, bloodshed, butchery, carnage, bloodbath
(literary) slaying

slave NOUN
Most of the work on the plantation was done by slaves.
▶ To make someone a slave is to **enslave** them.
┌ OPPOSITE freeman or freewoman

slave VERB
I was tired of slaving away at a dead-end job.
work hard, labour, toil, grind, sweat
(informal) slog
┌ IDIOM work like a dog

slavery NOUN
The central character is kidnapped and sold into slavery.
captivity, bondage, enslavement, servitude
┌ OPPOSITE freedom

sledge NOUN
a sledge pulled by a team of huskies
toboggan, sleigh
(North American) sled
▶ A sledge used in winter sports is a **bobsleigh**.

sleek ADJECTIVE
Seal pups are born with sleek coats.
smooth, glossy, shiny, silky, silken
┌ OPPOSITES coarse, matted

sleep NOUN
He usually has a short sleep after lunch.
nap, rest, doze, catnap, siesta
(informal) snooze
(literary) slumber
┌ IDIOM (informal) forty winks

▷ **go to sleep**
That night I was too restless to go to sleep.
fall asleep, doze, drop off, nod off

sleep VERB
The baby is sleeping in the next room.
be asleep, doze, take a nap, have a siesta
(informal) snooze
(literary) slumber
┌ IDIOM (informal) catch forty winks

sleepless ADJECTIVE
We spent a sleepless night waiting for news.
restless, wakeful, troubled, disturbed
▶ The formal name for sleeplessness is **insomnia**.
┌ OPPOSITE restful

sleepy ADJECTIVE
Does reading in bed make you feel sleepy?
drowsy, tired, lethargic, heavy-eyed
(informal) dopey
▶ Something that makes you feel sleepy is **soporific**.
the soporific warmth of the fire
┌ OPPOSITE wide awake

slender ADJECTIVE
1 *the slender silhouette of a young woman*
slim, lean, slight, thin, trim, svelte, willowy
┌ OPPOSITE fat
FOR TIPS ON DESCRIBING PEOPLE'S BODIES SEE **body**

2 *dangling on a slender rope*
thin, fine, fragile, delicate, flimsy
┌ OPPOSITE thick

》

a
b
c
d
e
f
g
h
i
j
k
l
m
n
o
p
q
r
s
t
u
v
w
x
y
z

3 *a slender chance of success*
poor, slight, slim, faint, negligible, remote

▌ **OPPOSITES** good, strong

4 *winning by a slender margin*
narrow, small, slim

▌ **OPPOSITE** wide

slice *NOUN*

a slice of cheesecake
piece, bit, wedge, slab, portion

▶ A thin slice is a **sliver**.

▌ **SEE ALSO bit**

slice *VERB*

Slice the vegetables into thick chunks.
cut, carve, chop

▌ **SEE ALSO cut**

slick *ADJECTIVE*

1 *That was a slick move on his part.*
skilful, artful, clever, cunning, smooth, deft, adroit

▌ **OPPOSITE** clumsy

2 *In places the pavement was slick with ice.*
slippery, slithery, smooth, glassy
(*informal*) slippy, slidey

slide *VERB*

Slide your cursor over an image to see it change.
glide, slip, slither, skim, skate, skid

slight *ADJECTIVE*

1 *a very slight dent on the surface*
small, minute, minor, unnoticeable, negligible, insignificant

▌ **OPPOSITES** large, noticeable

2 *There was a slight pause before anyone spoke.*
short, brief, fleeting

▌ **OPPOSITE** long

3 *a slight chance of rain tomorrow*
slim, slender, faint, remote

▌ **OPPOSITE** strong

4 *A slight figure emerged from the shadows.*
slender, slim, petite, delicate, fragile, frail

▌ **OPPOSITE** stout

slightly *ADVERB*

Kelly was slightly annoyed at not being invited.
a little, a bit, somewhat, rather, vaguely, faintly

▌ **OPPOSITES** very, seriously

slim *ADJECTIVE*

1 *sensible ways to get and stay slim*
slender, thin, lean, spare, trim, svelte

▌ **OPPOSITES** fat, plump

FOR TIPS ON DESCRIBING PEOPLE'S BODIES SEE body

2 *Their chances of winning are slim at best.*
poor, faint, slight, slender, negligible, remote

▌ **OPPOSITES** good, strong

3 *He won the election by a slim margin.*
narrow, small, slender

▌ **OPPOSITE** wide

slim *VERB*

exercises to help you slim
lose weight, get thinner

▌ **OPPOSITE** put on weight

slimy *ADJECTIVE*

a layer of slimy green algae
slippery, slithery, sticky, oozy
(*informal*) gooey, icky

sling *VERB*

1 *Pierre slung his rucksack over his shoulder.*
swing, hang, suspend, string

2 *(informal) He slung the paper away in disgust.*
throw, fling, hurl, cast, toss, pitch, lob
(*informal*) chuck

slink *VERB*

I tried to slink away from the party unnoticed.
slip, sneak, steal, creep, edge, sidle

slip *VERB*

1 *slipping on a patch of ice*
skid, slide, slither, lose your balance

2 *One by one, the seals slipped into the water.*

slip

glide, slide

3 *Jacob slipped out while the others were talking.*
sneak, steal, slink, sidle, creep, tiptoe

slip NOUN

1 *The rehearsal went off without any slips.*
mistake, error, fault, blunder, gaffe, lapse, false step

2 *a name written on a slip of paper*
piece, scrap, sliver

▷ **give someone the slip**
It won't be easy to give your friends the slip.
escape from, get away from, run away from, leave behind

slippery ADJECTIVE

The stone steps were worn and slippery.
slithery, slick, smooth, glassy, slimy, greasy, oily
(*informal*) slippy, slidey

slit NOUN

Daylight shone through a slit in the tent.
cut, split, tear, gash, rent, chink, gap, opening, slot

slit VERB

She used her nail to slit open the envelope.
cut, split, slice, slash, gash

slither VERB

Una imagined she heard creatures slithering in the dark.
slip, slide, glide, slink

sliver NOUN

a sliver of broken glass
shard, fragment, piece, strip

slogan NOUN

We need a catchy slogan for the poster.
motto, catchphrase, jingle

slope VERB

Below them the ground sloped down to the sea.
tilt, slant, incline, fall, drop, rise,
climb, bank, shelve

slope NOUN

1 *pushing a bike up a slope*
hill, rise, bank, ramp
(*Scottish*) brae

▶ An upward slope is an **ascent** and a downward slope is a **descent**.

2 *a roof with a steep slope*
tilt, slant, pitch, gradient, incline

sloppy ADJECTIVE

1 *The batter should have a sloppy texture.*
runny, watery, liquid, slushy, mushy
(*informal*) gloopy
▌ **OPPOSITE** stiff

2 *a sloppy style of writing*
careless, slapdash, slack, messy, untidy, slovenly, slipshod
▌ **OPPOSITES** careful, neat

slot NOUN

1 *Insert a coin or token in the slot.*
slit, opening, aperture, chink, gap

2 *The show has been moved to a late-night slot.*
time, spot, space, place, niche

slouch VERB

Enid sat slouched over her laptop.
hunch, stoop, slump, droop, flop

slow ADJECTIVE

1 *Theo read his lines in a slow deliberate voice.*
unhurried, leisurely, steady, sedate, plodding, dawdling, sluggish

2 *Erosion is usually a slow process.*
lengthy, prolonged, protracted, gradual, drawn-out, time-consuming

3 *She's often slow to reply to emails.*
tardy, late, behindhand, sluggish, hesitant, reluctant
▌ **OPPOSITE** quick

slow VERB

▷ **slow down**

1 *The boat slowed down as it approached the island.*
go slower, reduce speed, brake, decelerate

OPPOSITES speed up, accelerate

2 *Viruses can slow down your computer.*
make slower, retard, delay, hold up, impede, set back

slowly ADVERB

Breathe out slowly through your mouth.
unhurriedly, gradually, steadily, at a leisurely pace

IDIOM at a snail's pace

OPPOSITES quickly, hurriedly

sludge NOUN

clearing sludge from a drainpipe
muck, mud, ooze, slime
(informal) gunge, gunk

slump VERB

1 *CD sales continue to slump.*
fall, decline, drop, plummet, tumble, plunge, nosedive

2 *I slumped exhausted into an armchair.*
flop, collapse, sink, sag, slouch

slump NOUN

a slump in CD sales
collapse, drop, fall, decline, downturn, slide

▶ A general slump in trade is a **depression** or **recession**.

OPPOSITE boom

sly ADJECTIVE

1 *Foxes are traditionally portrayed as sly creatures.*
crafty, cunning, artful, clever, wily, tricky, sneaky, devious, furtive, secretive, stealthy, underhand

OPPOSITES straightforward, honest

2 *Roy looked up with a sly grin on his face.*
mischievous, playful, impish, roguish, knowing, arch

smack VERB

Ike groaned and smacked his forehead in dismay.
slap, strike, hit, cuff, clip, spank
(informal) whack

SEE ALSO hit

small ADJECTIVE

OVERUSED WORD

small in size, scale
little, tiny, minute, compact, miniature, microscopic, minuscule, mini, baby
(informal) teeny, titchy, dinky
(Scottish) wee

*Archie spotted a **minuscule** speck of dirt on his collar.*

OPPOSITES big, large

a small person, creature
little, short, squat, petite, dainty, diminutive, miniature, undersized
(informal) pint-sized

▶ A small species of animal or plant is also known as a **dwarf** species.
a rare type of dwarf orchid
*The fossil belonged to a **diminutive** species of dinosaur.*

OPPOSITES giant, tall, well-built
FOR TIPS ON DESCRIBING PEOPLE'S BODIES SEE body

small inside
cramped, confined, restricted, narrow, poky
*The cabin was a bit **cramped** for three people plus luggage.*

OPPOSITES spacious, roomy

a small amount, small portion
meagre, inadequate, insufficient, paltry, scanty, skimpy, mean, stingy
(informal) measly
*My old computer had a **paltry** 4GB of storage space.*

OPPOSITES ample, substantial

a small change, small problem
minor, slight, unimportant, insignificant, trivial, trifling, negligible

> *May I suggest some **minor** changes to the script?*
> ❙**OPPOSITES** major, significant

smart *ADJECTIVE*

1 *Carol looked smart in a simple black dress.*
well-dressed, elegant, stylish, fashionable, chic, spruce, neat, dapper, well-groomed
(informal) natty

▶ To make yourself smart is to **smarten up**.
❙**OPPOSITE** scruffy

2 *a smart restaurant in the city centre*
fashionable, upmarket, high-class, exclusive, fancy
(informal) posh, swanky, swish

3 *That was a very smart move!*
clever, ingenious, intelligent, shrewd, astute, crafty
❙**OPPOSITE** stupid

4 *Will set off at a smart pace towards the village.*
fast, quick, rapid, speedy, swift, brisk, vigorous
(informal) cracking
❙**OPPOSITES** slow, gentle

smart *VERB*

Chopping onions makes my eyes smart.
sting, prick, prickle, tingle, burn

smash *VERB*

1 *Every window in the building had been smashed.*
break, crush, shatter, splinter, crack

2 *I had to tell her I had smashed her bike.*
crash, wreck
(informal) total

3 *Hayes smashed the ball past the keeper.*
hit, strike, kick, shoot, drive, slam, power

smear *VERB*

1 *Smear butter over the inside of the dish.*
spread, rub, wipe, plaster, smother, coat, smudge, dab, daub

2 *He began a campaign to smear his rivals.*
malign, defame, damage, tarnish, sully, blacken, slander, libel
❙**IDIOM** drag through the mud

smear *NOUN*

a smear of blood on the carpet
streak, smudge, daub, patch, splodge, mark, blotch

smell *VERB*

1 *I could smell something baking in the oven.*
scent, sniff, get a sniff of, detect
(informal) get a whiff of

2 *The river was so polluted it began to smell.*
stink, reek
(British informal) pong

smell *NOUN*

1 *Don't you love the smell of fresh popcorn?*
scent, aroma, perfume, fragrance, bouquet

▶ A related adjective is **olfactory**.
olfactory organs

2 *What is that awful smell?*
odour, stench, stink, reek, whiff
(British informal) pong, niff

 WRITING TIPS

describing smells

There was the usual boiled-cabbage smell, common to the whole building, but it was shot through by a sharper reek of sweat, which — one knew this at the first sniff, though it was hard to say how — was the sweat of some person not present at the moment.

— *George Orwell, 1984*

pleasant
aromatic, delicate, fragrant,   »

a
b
c
d
e
f
g
h
i
j
k
l
m
n
o
p
q
r
s
t
u
v
w
x
y
z

perfumed, scented, sweet-smelling

unpleasant
acrid, evil-smelling, fetid, foul, foul-smelling, malodorous, musty, nauseating, noisome, odorous, (British informal) pongy, rancid, rank, reeking, rotten, sickly, smelly, stinking, (informal) stinky, (informal) whiffy

strong
choking, clawing, heady, pervasive, pungent, overpowering, rich, sharp

smile VERB, NOUN

Connie smiled and waved at us from the window.
grin, beam
▶ To smile in a silly way is to **simper**.
▶ To smile in a self-satisfied way is to **smirk**.
▶ To smile in an insulting way is to **sneer**.
FOR TIPS ON DESCRIBING FACIAL EXPRESSIONS SEE **face**

smoke NOUN

Thick acrid smoke billowed from the roof.
fumes
▶ The smoke given out by a vehicle is **exhaust**.
▶ A mixture of smoke and fog is **smog**.

smoke VERB

1 The bonfire was still smoking next morning.
smoulder
2 A man stood silently smoking a cigar.
puff at

smooth ADJECTIVE

1 Roll out the dough on a smooth surface.
flat, even, level
OPPOSITE uneven
2 windsurfing on the smooth waters of the bay
calm, still, unruffled, undisturbed, glassy
OPPOSITE rough
3 a type of guinea pig with short smooth hair
silky, sleek, velvety
OPPOSITE coarse
4 Blend the mixture until it is smooth.
creamy, velvety, silky
OPPOSITE lumpy
5 The take-off was surprisingly smooth.
comfortable, steady
OPPOSITES bumpy, rocky
6 an aromatic coffee with a smooth taste
mild, mellow, light
OPPOSITE harsh
7 Installing the software was quick and smooth.
straightforward, easy, effortless, trouble-free
OPPOSITES difficult, troublesome

smooth VERB

You can use a rake to smooth the soil.
flatten, level, even out
▶ To smooth cloth you can **iron** or **press** it.
▶ To smooth wood you can **plane** or **sand** it.

smother VERB

1 Pythons smother their prey to death.
suffocate, asphyxiate, choke, stifle
2 Rescuers tried to smother the flames.
extinguish, put out, snuff out, douse
3 Her whole face was smothered in make-up.
cover, coat, spread, smear, daub
4 Erik sat patiently and smothered a yawn.
suppress, stifle, muffle, hold back, conceal

smoulder VERB
SEE **burn**

smudge NOUN

There were smudges of ink all over the page.
smear, blot, streak, stain, mark, splodge

522

smug ADJECTIVE

Why are you looking so smug all of a sudden?
self-satisfied, pleased with yourself, complacent, superior

snack NOUN

stopping for a midday snack
refreshments, bite to eat
(*informal*) nibbles
▶ A mid-morning snack is sometimes called **elevenses**.

snag NOUN

Our holiday plans have hit a snag.
problem, difficulty, obstacle, hitch, complication, setback, catch
(*informal*) hiccup, glitch

snake NOUN

 WORD WEB

some types of snake

adder, anaconda, asp, boa constrictor, bushmaster, cobra, copperhead, coral snake, garter snake, grass snake, mamba, puff adder, python, rattlesnake, sand snake, sea snake, sidewinder, viper, water moccasin or cottonmouth

▶ Snakes which kill their prey by injecting them with venom are **venomous** snakes.
▶ A literary word for a snake is a **serpent**.

snap VERB

1 *One of the cables snapped under the strain.*
break, crack, fracture, splinter, split

2 *These turtles will snap at anything that moves.*
bite, nip

3 *'Leave me alone!' the boy snapped.*
snarl, bark, retort

snare NOUN

a rabbit caught in a snare
trap, gin, wire, net

▶ To catch an animal in a snare is to **ensnare** or **snare** it.

snarl VERB

1 *A guard dog snarled as we approached.*
growl, bare its teeth

2 *'What do you want?' snarled a voice.*
snap, bark, growl, thunder

snatch VERB

She snatched the letter from my hand.
grab, seize, grasp, pluck, wrench away, wrest away

snatch NOUN

I only heard snatches of the conversation.
fragment, bit, snippet, scrap, extract, excerpt

sneak VERB

1 *I managed to sneak in without anyone noticing.*
slip, steal, creep, slink, tiptoe, sidle, skulk

2 (*informal*) *Debbie sneaked a look at her notes.*
steal, take

sneaky ADJECTIVE

They use sneaky tactics to get your email address.
sly, underhand, cunning, crafty, devious, furtive, dishonest
OPPOSITE honest

sneer VERB

▷ **sneer at**

Louis didn't care if people sneered at him.
make fun of, mock, ridicule, scoff at, jeer at, deride

sniff NOUN, VERB

FOR TIPS ON DESCRIBING SOUNDS SEE
sound❶

snigger VERB

Someone sniggered at the back of the room.
giggle, titter, chuckle, laugh

a
b
c
d
e
f
g
h
i
j
k
l
m
n
o
p
q
r
s
t
u
v
w
x
y
z

snip _VERB_

Snip the hem to get the right length.
cut, clip, trim, chop

snivel _VERB_

We were all snivelling by the end of the film.
cry, sob, weep, sniff, whimper, whine

snobbish _ADJECTIVE_

I didn't like the snobbish atmosphere in the club.
arrogant, pompous, superior, haughty, supercilious
(informal) stuck-up, snooty
(British informal) toffee-nosed
┃ **IDIOM** high and mighty
┃ **OPPOSITE** humble

snoop _VERB_

A man was seen snooping round the building at night.
sneak, pry, poke, rummage, spy

snort _NOUN, VERB_

FOR TIPS ON DESCRIBING SOUNDS SEE
sound❶

snout _NOUN_

Aardvarks have long, narrow snouts.
muzzle, nose

snub _VERB_

Isla felt snubbed by not being invited.
insult, offend, slight, spurn, brush off
┃ **IDIOM** give you the cold shoulder

snug _ADJECTIVE_

1 _These boots will keep your feet snug through the winter._
cosy, comfortable, warm, relaxed
(informal) comfy

2 _Choose a smaller size for a snug fit._
tight, close-fitting, figure-hugging
┃ **OPPOSITES** loose, roomy

soak _VERB_

1 _You'll get soaked without a raincoat!_
wet throroughly, drench, saturate, make waterlogged

2 _Leave the beans to soak in water overnight._
steep, immerse, submerge

▷ **soak something up**

The roots act like a sponge, soaking up rainwater.
take in, absorb, suck up

soaking _ADJECTIVE_

They arrived at the campsite soaking and exhausted.
wet through, drenched, dripping, wringing, saturated, sodden, sopping, soggy
▶ Ground that has been soaked by rain is **waterlogged**.

soar _VERB_

1 _a tiny plane soaring up into the clouds_
climb, rise, ascend, fly up

2 _The number of complaints has soared recently._
go up, rise, increase, escalate, shoot up
┃ **IDIOMS** go through the roof, go sky-high
┃ **OPPOSITE** plummet

sob _VERB_

She threw herself on the bed, sobbing uncontrollably.
cry, weep, bawl, snivel, shed tears
(informal) blubber

sober _ADJECTIVE_

1 _You mustn't drive unless you're sober._
clear-headed
┃ **OPPOSITE** drunk

2 _The funeral was a sober occasion._
serious, solemn, sombre, grave, dignified, sedate, subdued
┃ **OPPOSITES** light-hearted, frivolous

sociable _ADJECTIVE_

living in a very sociable community
friendly, outgoing, gregarious, hospitable, neighbourly, amiable, cordial
┃ **OPPOSITE** unfriendly

social _ADJECTIVE_

1 _Chimpanzees live in social groups._
communal, collective, community, group

    OPPOSITES individual, solitary

  2 *a list of forthcoming social events*
    recreational, leisure
    OPPOSITE work-related

society *NOUN*

  1 *a close-knit society*
    community, culture, civilization,
    people

  2 *the local music society*
    association, group, organization,
    club, league, union, guild

  3 *He shunned the society of his fellow
    students.*
    company, companionship,
    fellowship, friendship

soft *ADJECTIVE*

  1 *a soft pillow*
    supple, pliable, springy, spongy,
    yielding, flexible, squashy
    OPPOSITES firm, hard

  2 *soft woollen fabric*
    smooth, silky, velvety, fleecy,
    feathery, downy
    OPPOSITES coarse, rough

  3 *the soft light of early morning*
    pale, muted, subdued, dim, low
    OPPOSITES bright, dazzling

  4 *We spoke in soft whispers.*
    quiet, muted, muffled, hushed, low,
    faint
    OPPOSITE loud

  5 *a warm soft breeze*
    gentle, light, mild, delicate
    OPPOSITES strong, forceful

  6 *You're being too soft with that
    puppy.*
    lenient, easy-going, tolerant,
    indulgent, lax
    OPPOSITES strict, tough

soggy *ADJECTIVE*

  The pitch was still soggy underfoot.
  wet, moist, soaked, saturated,
  sodden, drenched, waterlogged
  OPPOSITE dry

soil *NOUN*

  1 *These plants grow best in
    well-drained soil.*

    earth, ground, land
  ▶ Good fertile soil is **loam**.
  ▶ The upper layer of soil is **topsoil**.

  2 *We were glad to be back on
    home soil.*
    territory, turf, ground, country,
    domain

soiled *ADJECTIVE*

  a pile of soiled bandages
  dirty, stained, foul, unclean, muddy,
  tarnished

solar *ADJECTIVE*
  SEE **sun**

soldier *NOUN*

  *Two soldiers stood guard outside the
  gate.*
  serviceman or servicewoman,
  warrior
  ▶ A soldier paid to fight for a foreign
    country is a **mercenary**.
  ▶ Soldiers who use large guns are
    artillery.
  ▶ Soldiers who fight on horseback or
    in armoured vehicles are **cavalry**.
  ▶ Soldiers who fight on foot are
    infantry.
    SEE ALSO army

sole *ADJECTIVE*

  the sole inhabitant of the lighthouse
  only, single, one, solitary, lone,
  unique, exclusive

solemn *ADJECTIVE*

  1 *Both men wore a solemn expression.*
    serious, grave, sober, sombre,
    unsmiling, grim, dour
    OPPOSITE cheerful

  2 *Graduation is a solemn occasion.*
    formal, dignified, ceremonial, grand,
    stately, majestic
    OPPOSITE frivolous

solid *ADJECTIVE*

  1 *a solid chocolate egg*
    OPPOSITE hollow

  2 *Leave the plaster to turn solid.*
    hard, firm, dense, compact, rigid,
    unyielding
    OPPOSITES soft, liquid

a
b
c
d
e
f
g
h
i
j
k
l
m
n
o
p
q
r
s
t
u
v
w
x
y
z

»

3 *He slept for a solid nine hours.*
continuous, uninterrupted, unbroken

4 *a medal made of solid gold*
pure, genuine

5 *a racket with a solid feel and good control*
firm, robust, sound, strong, stable, sturdy

OPPOSITES weak, flimsy

6 *the solid support of her team mates*
firm, reliable, dependable, united, unanimous

OPPOSITES weak, divided

solidify *VERB*

The lava solidifies as it cools.
harden, become solid, set, stiffen

OPPOSITES soften, liquefy

solitary *ADJECTIVE*

1 *choosing to live a solitary life*
unaccompanied, on your own, reclusive, withdrawn, isolated, friendless, unsociable

OPPOSITE sociable

2 *a solitary light in the distance*
single, sole, lone, individual, one, only

solitude *NOUN*

a place where you can find peace and solitude
privacy, seclusion, isolation, loneliness

solve *VERB*

trying to solve a murder mystery
interpret, explain, answer, work out, find the solution to, unravel, decipher
(*informal*) crack

sombre *ADJECTIVE*

1 *painted in sombre shades of grey*
dark, dull, dim, dismal, dingy, drab, cheerless
(*Scottish*) dreich

OPPOSITE bright

2 *Everyone was in a sombre mood that night.*
gloomy, serious, sober, grave, grim,

sad, melancholy, mournful

OPPOSITE cheerful

song *NOUN*

WORD WEB

some types of song
anthem, aria, ballad, calypso, carol, chant, ditty, folk song, hymn, jingle, lament, lay, love song, lullaby, madrigal, nursery rhyme, pop song, psalm, rap, round, shanty, spiritual

► A play or film that includes many songs is a **musical**.

► A song from a musical is a **number**.

► The words for a song are the **lyrics**.

types of singing voice
alto, baritone, bass, contralto, soprano, tenor, treble

FOR OTHER MUSICAL TERMS SEE music

soon *ADVERB*

The others will be back soon.
before long, in a minute, shortly, presently, quickly

soothe *VERB*

1 *some music to soothe your nerves*
calm, comfort, settle, quieten, pacify, relax

2 *remedies to soothe a sore throat*
ease, alleviate, relieve, lessen, reduce

soothing *ADJECTIVE*

some soothing background music
calming, relaxing, restful, peaceful, gentle, tranquil

sophisticated *ADJECTIVE*

1 *Dee looks quite sophisticated with her hair up.*
grown-up, mature, cultivated, cultured, refined

OPPOSITE naive

2 *a sophisticated knowledge of computers*

advanced, high-level, complex,
intricate, elaborate
❙ **OPPOSITES** simple, basic

sore ADJECTIVE

My muscles are sore from exercising.
painful, aching, hurting, smarting,
throbbing, tender, sensitive,
inflamed, raw

sore NOUN

a dog with a sore on its paw
wound, lesion, inflammation,
swelling, boil, ulcer

sorrow NOUN

1 *The song expresses the sorrow of
parting.*
sadness, unhappiness, misery,
woe, grief, anguish, heartache,
heartbreak, melancholy, gloom,
wretchedness, despair
▶ Sorrow because of someone's death
is **mourning**.
▶ Sorrow at being away from home is
homesickness.
❙ **OPPOSITES** happiness, joy
2 *feeling sorrow for their past actions*
regret, remorse, repentance,
apologies

sorry ADJECTIVE

I'm sorry if I upset you in any way.
apologetic, regretful, remorseful,
contrite, ashamed (of), repentant
❙ **OPPOSITE** unapologetic
▷ **feel sorry for someone**
I actually began to feel sorry for him.
sympathize with, pity, feel
compassion for

sort NOUN

What sort of music do you like?
kind, type, variety, style, form, class,
category, genre, species

sort VERB

1 *The books are sorted according to
size.*
arrange, organize, class, group,
categorize, classify
❙ **OPPOSITE** mix
2 *Have you sorted the problem yet?*

resolve, settle, deal with, put right,
fix, clear up, straighten out

sound❶ NOUN

the sound of approaching footsteps
noise, tone
▶ A loud, harsh sound is a **din** or
racket.
▶ The loudness of sound is measured
in **decibels**.
▶ Related adjectives are **acoustic** and
sonic.
sonic waves

 WRITING TIPS

describing sounds

The air was full of sound, a
deafening and confusing conflict
of noises — the clangorous din of
the Martians, the crash of falling
houses, the thud of trees, fences,
sheds flashing into flame, and
the crackling and roaring of fire.
— *H. G. Wells, The War of the Worlds*

types of sound

bang, beep, blare, bleep, boom,
buzz, chime, chug, clang, clank,
clap, clash, clatter, click, clink,
clunk, crack, crackle, crash,
creak, crunch, ding, drone, drum,
fizz, gurgle, jangle, jingle, hiss,
honk, hoot, knock, patter, peal,
ping, plop, pop, putter, rap, rasp,
rattle, ring, roar, rumble, rustle,
scrape, scrunch, sizzle, snap,
sputter, squeak, squelch, swish,
tap, thud, thunder, tick, tinkle,
toot, trill, twang, whirr, whistle,
whoosh

sounds made by people

bawl, bellow, boo, boom, cackle,
chortle, croak, cry, gasp, groan,
hiccup, hiss, howl, hum, moan,
murmur, puff, scream, shout,
shriek, sigh, sing, sniff, snort,
sob, splutter, squeal, stammer,
stutter, wail, wheeze, whimper,
whine, whisper, whoop, yell,
yodel   》

adjectives
blaring, brittle, clangorous, croaky, deafening, discordant, droning, dulcet, ear-splitting, grating, gruff, harmonious, harsh, high-pitched, hoarse, husky, jarring, lilting, mellifluous, melodious, piercing, piping, rasping, raucous, shrill, soporific, squeaky, stentorian, sweet, thin, throaty, tinny

sound VERB

A siren sounds when a shark is spotted.
make a noise, resound, go off, be heard

sound② ADJECTIVE

1 Parts of the outer wall are still sound.
firm, solid, stable, safe, secure, intact, undamaged, in good condition
▎**OPPOSITES** unsound, unstable

2 The travellers returned safe and sound.
well, fit, healthy, in good shape
▎**IDIOM** in fine fettle
▎**OPPOSITES** unhealthy, unfit

3 a piece of sound advice
good, sensible, wise, reasonable, reliable, trustworthy, valid
▎**OPPOSITES** unwise, unreliable

4 a sound night's sleep
thorough, deep, peaceful, restful, undisturbed
▎**OPPOSITES** broken, fitful

sour ADJECTIVE

1 These apples are a bit sour.
tart, bitter, sharp, acidic
▎**OPPOSITE** sweet

2 milk which has gone sour
bad, off, rancid, curdled
▎**OPPOSITE** fresh

3 The assistant made a sour face and retreated.
cross, bad-tempered, grumpy, peevish, resentful, bitter

source NOUN

They've found the source of the infection.
origin, start, starting point, root, cause, head
▶ The source of a river or stream is usually a **spring**.

south NOUN, ADJECTIVE, ADVERB

Portugal is in the south of Europe.
▶ The parts of a country or continent in the south are the **southern** parts.
▶ To travel towards the south is to travel **southward** or **southwards**.
▶ A wind from the south is a **southerly** wind.
▶ A person who lives in the south of a country is a **southerner**.

sow VERB

sowing seed for next year's crop
plant, scatter, disperse, strew
▶ To sow an area of ground with seeds is to **seed** it.

space NOUN

1 a mission to explore deep space
outer space, the cosmos, the universe

2 freeing up space on your hard disk
room, capacity, area, volume, expanse

3 crawling through a space in the wall
gap, hole, opening, aperture, cavity, niche
▶ A space without any air in it is a **vacuum**.

4 in a short space of time
period, span, interval, duration, stretch

 WORD WEB

natural objects found in space
asteroid or planetoid, black hole, comet, constellation, dwarf planet, galaxy, meteor (informal shooting star), meteoroid, meteor shower,

Milky Way, moon, nebula, nova, planet, pulsar, red dwarf, red giant, solar system, star, sun, supernova

SEE ALSO planet, moon

► A related adjective is **cosmic**.
cosmic rays

► The scientific study of natural objects in space is **astronomy**.

► The scientific study of the universe as a whole is **cosmology**.

terms used in space exploration
astronaut, heat shield, intergalactic, interplanetary, interstellar, launch, mission, orbit, orbiter, probe, re-entry, rover, satellite, spacecraft, space shuttle, space station, spacesuit, spacewalk

FOR TIPS ON WRITING SCIENCE FICTION SEE science fiction

spacious *ADJECTIVE*
a bright and spacious front room
big, large, roomy, sizeable, capacious, commodious
OPPOSITES small, cramped
SEE ALSO big

span *NOUN*
1 *a bridge with a span of 200 metres*
breadth, length, width, extent, distance, reach
► The length between the wing tips of a bird or aircraft is its **wingspan**.
2 *published over a long span of years*
period, time, space, interval, duration, stretch

span *VERB*
1 *A rickety footbridge spanned the river.*
cross, extend across, pass over, stretch over, straddle, bridge, traverse
2 *a career which spanned over forty years*
last, extend, cover,

stretch, spread over

spare *VERB*
1 *Can you spare any money for a good cause?*
afford, part with, give, provide, do without, manage without
2 *He begged his captors to spare his life.*
pardon, have mercy on, reprieve, let off, release, free

spare *ADJECTIVE*
1 *The spare tyre is in the boot.*
additional, extra, supplementary, reserve, standby, backup, relief, substitute
2 *Have you any spare change?*
surplus, leftover, unused, unwanted, excess, superfluous
3 *Old Mr Lloyd was a spare skeleton of a man.*
lean, thin, skinny, gaunt, spindly

spark *NOUN*
1 *One firework exploded in a shower of sparks.*
flash, gleam, glint, flicker, twinkle, sparkle
2 *showing no spark of enthusiasm*
trace, hint, sign, flicker

sparkle *VERB, NOUN*
Her earrings sparkled in the lamplight.
glitter, glisten, glint, flash, twinkle, shimmer
FOR TIPS ON DESCRIBING LIGHT SEE light❶

sparse *ADJECTIVE*
Vegetation is more sparse in the dry season.
scarce, scanty, patchy, thinly scattered
(informal) thin on the ground
OPPOSITES plentiful, abundant

spatter *VERB*
Sea spray spattered our faces and clothes.
splash, spray, sprinkle, scatter, shower

a
b
c
d
e
f
g
h
i
j
k
l
m
n
o
p
q
r
s
t
u
v
w
x
y
z

speak *VERB*

1 *Michael was too nervous to speak.*
talk, communicate, say something,
express yourself

2 *Speak the words clearly into the microphone.*
say, utter, voice, pronounce,
articulate, enunciate

speaker *NOUN*

a line-up of guest speakers
lecturer, talker

▶ A person who makes formal
speeches is an **orator**.

▶ A person who speaks on behalf of an
organization is a **spokesperson**.

spear *NOUN*

a gladiator armed with a spear and shield
lance, javelin

▶ A spear attached to a rope used to
catch fish is a **harpoon**.

special *ADJECTIVE*

1 *celebrating a special occasion*
important, significant, memorable,
noteworthy, momentous, historic,
out-of-the-ordinary

OPPOSITES ordinary, everyday

2 *Early autumn has its own special beauty.*
unique, individual, characteristic,
distinctive, peculiar

3 *You need a special camera to film underwater.*
specific, particular, specialized,
tailor-made, purpose-built

speciality *NOUN*

1 *an actor whose speciality is playing villains*
strength, strong point, expertise,
forte

2 *Curd cheese is a local speciality.*
delicacy

specific *ADJECTIVE*

Can you give us some specific examples?
detailed, particular, definite, precise,
exact, explicit, clear-cut, express

OPPOSITES general, vague

specify *VERB*

Please specify your shoe size.
state, identify, name, detail, define,
stipulate

specimen *NOUN*

a specimen of each typeface
sample, example, illustration,
instance, model

speck *NOUN*

He brushed a speck of dust from his shoes.
bit, dot, spot, fleck, grain, particle,
trace

SEE ALSO bit

spectacle *NOUN*

1 *The Mardi Gras parade is a colourful spectacle.*
display, show, sight, performance,
exhibition, extravaganza

2 *As usual, they made a spectacle of themselves.*
fool, embarrassment, disgrace

spectacles *PLURAL NOUN*
SEE **glasses**

spectacular *ADJECTIVE*

1 *The film opens with a spectacular action sequence.*
dramatic, exciting, impressive,
thrilling, breathtaking, sensational

2 *a spectacular display of autumn foliage*
eye-catching, showy, striking,
stunning, glorious, magnificent

spectator *NOUN*

Spectators watched the ceremony on giant TV screens.
watcher, viewer, observer, onlooker

▶ The spectators at a show are the
audience.

▶ The spectators at a sporting event
are the **crowd**.

▶ A person who sees an accident or
crime is a **witness** or **eyewitness**.

a b c d e f g h i j k l m n o p q r s t u v w x y z

speech *NOUN*

1 *a computer which imitates human speech*
speaking, talking, articulation, pronunciation, enunciation, diction

2 *giving an after-dinner speech*
talk, address, lecture, discourse, oration

▶ A talk given as part of a religious service is a **sermon**.

▶ The art of making speeches in public is **oratory**.

3 *reciting a speech from Shakespeare*

▶ Speech between actors in a play is **dialogue**.

▶ A speech delivered by a single actor is a **monologue**.

▶ A speech in which a character reveals their inner thoughts is a **soliloquy**.

speechless *ADJECTIVE*

Lena was speechless with surprise.
dumbstruck, dumbfounded, tongue-tied

speed *NOUN*

1 *travelling at the speed of light*
pace, rate, velocity

▶ The speed of a piece of music is its **tempo**.

▶ To increase speed is to **accelerate**.

▶ To reduce speed is to **decelerate**.

2 *The rumour spread with astonishing speed.*
quickness, rapidity, swiftness, alacrity

❘ OPPOSITE slowness

speed *VERB*

He sped across the finish line with seconds to spare.
race, rush, dash, dart, hurry, hurtle, career, fly, streak, tear, shoot, zoom, zip

▷ **speed up**
The car behind us started to speed up.
go faster, hurry up, accelerate, pick up speed

❘ OPPOSITE slow down

speedy *ADJECTIVE*

We wish you a speedy recovery.
fast, quick, swift, rapid, prompt, brisk, hasty

❘ OPPOSITE slow

spell❶ *NOUN*

a spell believed to ward off evil
charm, incantation, formula

▷ **put a spell on someone**
An evil sorcerer had put a spell on her.
enchant, bewitch, put a hex on

spell❷ *NOUN*

a spell of dry weather
period, interval, time, stretch, run

spelling *NOUN*

The website uses American spelling.
orthography

▶ Words which have the same spelling but mean different things are **homographs**.

▶ Words which have different spellings but sound the same are **homophones**.

spend *VERB*

1 *How much money do you spend on clothes?*
pay out, use up, expend, get through
(informal) fork out, shell out

▶ To spend money extravagantly is to *(informal)* **splurge** it.

▶ To spend money unwisely is to **waste** or **squander** it.

❘ OPPOSITE save

2 *Ike spent the whole day working on the script.*
pass, occupy, fill, while away, fritter away

sphere *NOUN*

1 *Comets are spheres of gas and dust.*
ball, globe, orb

2 *She is an expert in her own sphere.*
subject, area, field, arena, realm, domain

spherical *ADJECTIVE*

a spherical pudding mould
round, ball-shaped, globe-shaped

spice NOUN

WORD WEB

spices used in cooking
allspice, aniseed, bay leaf, black pepper, caraway, cardamom, cayenne, chilli, cinnamon, cloves, coriander, cumin, curry powder, fennel seed, fenugreek, garam masala, ginger, juniper, mace, mustard, nigella, nutmeg, paprika, pimento, saffron, sesame, star anise, turmeric, white pepper

spicy ADJECTIVE

a spicy vegetable curry
hot, peppery, fiery, piquant
❙ **OPPOSITE** mild
FOR TIPS ON DESCRIBING TASTE SEE taste

spider NOUN

WORD WEB

some types of spider
black widow, house spider, money spider, tarantula
► Spiders and scorpions are types of **arachnid**.
► A young or immature spider is a **spiderling**.
► The organ with which a spider spins silk is a **spinneret**.
► Fear of spiders is **arachnophobia**.

spike NOUN

Crampons have spikes which grip the ice.
point, prong, spear, skewer, stake, barb, thorn

spill VERB

1 *Irene spilled a cup of tea over her dress.*
overturn, upset, tip over

2 *Diesel fuel spilled onto the roadway.*
overflow, pour, splash, slop, slosh

3 *The party spilled out onto the street.*
pour, stream, flood, swarm, surge

spin VERB

The pull of the magnet makes the coil spin.
revolve, rotate, go round, turn, whirl, twirl

spin NOUN

1 *a single spin of the wheel*
revolution, rotation, turn, whirl, twirl

2 *putting a positive spin on the news*
slant, bias, angle, twist

spine NOUN

1 *an X-ray of the patient's spine*
backbone, spinal column
► The bones in your spine are your **vertebrae**.

2 *Each fin is equipped with sharp spines.*
spike, prickle, barb, quill, needle, thorn, bristle

spiral NOUN

a snake curled in a tight spiral
coil, twist, corkscrew, helix, whorl
► A tight spiral of swirling air or water is a **vortex**.

spirit NOUN

1 *feeling refreshed in mind, body, and spirit*
soul

2 *The house is haunted by the spirit of a murdered poet.*
ghost, phantom, spectre, ghoul, demon

3 *a lively piece of music performed with great spirit*
energy, liveliness, enthusiasm, vigour, zest, zeal, fire

4 *in a spirit of friendship and cooperation*
feeling, mood, atmosphere

spiritual ADJECTIVE

1 *the spiritual part of your being*
inner, non-material, incorporeal, metaphysical
❙ **OPPOSITE** physical

a
b
c
d
e
f
g
h
i
j
k
l
m
n
o
p
q
r
s
t
u
v
w
x
y
z

2 *the spiritual leader of Tibetan Buddhism*
religious, holy, sacred
▎**OPPOSITES** secular, worldly

spite NOUN
Someone wrote the email out of spite.
malice, malevolence, ill will, meanness, spitefulness, vindictiveness, nastiness, venom

▷ **in spite of**
In spite of its name, the dogfish is a type of shark.
despite, notwithstanding, regardless of

spiteful ADJECTIVE
Any spiteful comments will be deleted.
malicious, malevolent, vindictive, hateful, venomous, mean, nasty, unkind
▎**OPPOSITE** kind

splash VERB
1 *splashing cold water on your face*
shower, spray, squirt, slop, spill
(informal) slosh
2 *splashing through the puddles*
wade, paddle, wallow
(informal) slosh

splash NOUN
1 *a splash of cold water*
shower, spray, squirt
(informal) slosh
2 *a splash of sunlight*
patch, burst, streak

splendid ADJECTIVE
1 *a splendid baroque palace*
magnificent, lavish, luxurious, grand, imposing, rich, sumptuous, gorgeous, glorious, resplendent, dazzling
2 *That's a splendid idea!*
excellent, first-class, admirable, superb, wonderful, marvellous
(informal) brilliant, fantastic, terrific

splendour NOUN
the splendour of Moorish architecture
magnificence, grandeur, richness,

sumptuousness, glory, resplendence

splinter NOUN
tiny splinters of broken glass
fragment, sliver, shard, chip, flake

splinter VERB
The meteor splintered as it entered the atmosphere.
shatter, smash, fracture, crack, split
▎**IDIOM** *(informal)* smash to smithereens

split VERB
1 *One ice floe split into several pieces.*
break apart, crack open, fracture, rupture, splinter, snap
2 *She split the class into two groups.*
divide, separate, part
3 *We split the money between us.*
distribute, share out, divide up, carve up, parcel out

▷ **split up**
The band announced they were splitting up.
break up, separate, part company, go your separate ways

split NOUN
1 *a split in the Earth's crust*
crack, break, breach, fracture, fissure, rupture
2 *a split in a trouser seam*
tear, rip, slash, slit, cut, rent
3 *a bitter split between rival factions*
division, rift, schism
4 *The couple have remained close since their split.*
break-up, separation, parting, estrangement

spoil VERB
1 *If I tell you, it'll spoil the surprise.*
ruin, wreck, destroy, upset, mess up, scupper
(informal) muck up
▶ Someone who spoils other people's enjoyment is a **spoilsport**.
2 *Overcooking will spoil the flavour of the fish.*
damage, impair, mar, blight
▶ To spoil the look of something is to **disfigure** or **deface** it.

》 533

3 *Maybe he was spoilt as a child.*
indulge, pamper, cosset, make a
fuss of

spoke *PAST TENSE*
SEE **speak**

spoken *ADJECTIVE*
a long section of spoken dialogue
oral, unwritten
▌**OPPOSITE** written

spontaneous *ADJECTIVE*
*The audience broke into spontaneous
applause.*
unplanned, impromptu,
unpremeditated, unrehearsed,
impulsive, instinctive
▌**IDIOMS** off-the-cuff,
spur-of-the-moment
▶ An action done without any
conscious thought is a **reflex** action.

sport *NOUN*

 WORD WEB

some team sports
American football, baseball,
basketball, bobsleigh, bowls,
cricket, curling, football or
soccer, hockey, ice hockey,
lacrosse, netball, polo, rounders,
rugby, volleyball, water polo

some individual sports
angling, archery, athletics,
badminton, billiards, bowling,
boxing, canoeing, climbing,
croquet, cross-country running,
cycling, darts, diving, fencing,
golf, gymnastics, horse racing,
ice skating, jogging, judo,
karate, luge, motor racing,
mountaineering, orienteering,
pool, rowing, sailing,
showjumping, skiing, snooker,
snowboarding, speed skating,
squash, surfing, swimming,
table tennis, tae kwon do, tennis,
waterskiing, weightlifting,
windsurfing, wrestling

▶ Someone who takes part
in sport is a **sportsman** or
sportswoman.
▌**SEE ALSO** athletics

 WRITING TIPS

writing about sport

Tibbut, dribbling in fast, pushed
the ball between Mr Sugden's
legs, ran round him and
delivered the ball out to his right
winger, who took it in his stride,
beat his Full Back and centred for
Tibbut, who had continued his
run, to outjump Mr Sugden and
head the ball firmly into the top
right-hand corner of the goal.
— *Barry Hines, A Kestrel for a Knave*

useful words & phrases
amateur, arena, champion,
coach, commentator, cup tie,
draw, extra time, final whistle,
first half, foul, full time,
game plan, half time, hat trick,
heats, highlights, injury time,
in play, key player, kick-off, man
or woman of the match, offside,
off target, onside, on target,
opponents, out of bounds,
penalty, player, possession,
professional, qualifying round,
quarter-final, referee, score
sheet, second half, semi-final,
sending off, squad, stadium,
substitute, supporters, tactics,
team captain, teammate,
turning point

verbs
arc, bowl, catch, chip, curl, dive,
dribble, drive, field, flick, head,
hurl, kick, lob, miss, pass, pitch,
power, save, scoop, score, shoot,
slam, smash, spin, strike, swerve,
swing, swipe, tap, throw, toss,
trickle, volley, weave
▌**SEE ALSO** football

sporting *ADJECTIVE*

setting an example of sporting
behaviour
sportsmanlike, fair, generous,
honourable

OPPOSITE unsporting

spot *NOUN*

1 a few spots of rust here and there
mark, patch, fleck, speck, dot, blot,
stain, blotch, splodge

▶ Spots on a bird's egg or plumage are
speckles.

2 skin that is prone to spots
pimple, blackhead
(informal) zit

▶ An area of spots on your skin is a
rash.

3 a good spot for a photograph
place, position, location, site,
situation, setting, venue

4 The first spots of rain began to fall.
drop, blob, bead

spot *VERB*

1 Did you spot your friends in the
crowd?
see, sight, spy, catch sight of, notice,
observe, make out, recognize,
detect

2 My best coat was all spotted with
mud.
mark, stain, blot, spatter, fleck, dot,
speckle, mottle

spotless *ADJECTIVE*

The house was spotless from top to
bottom.
clean, unmarked, immaculate,
gleaming

OPPOSITES dirty, grubby

spouse *NOUN*

rooms for married students and their
spouses
husband or wife, partner

▶ The spouse of a reigning monarch is
a **consort**.

spout *VERB*

Molten lava spouted far into the air.
gush, spew, pour, stream, spurt,
squirt, jet

sprawl *VERB*

1 We found him asleep, sprawling on
the sofa.
stretch out, spread out, lean back,
loll, lounge, slouch, slump

2 Some pencil marks were sprawled
over the page.
spread, stretch, scatter, strew

spray❶ *VERB*

A burst pipe was spraying water
everywhere.
shower, spatter, sprinkle, splash,
squirt, scatter

spray *NOUN*

1 Give the plants a daily spray of
water.
shower, sprinkling, squirt, mist

2 a perfume spray
aerosol, sprinkler, atomizer,
mister

spray❷ *NOUN*

a spray of spring flowers
bunch, posy

spread *VERB*

1 Just spread the map on
the table.
lay out, open out, fan out, unfold,
unfurl, unroll

2 Newspapers were spread all over the
floor.
scatter, strew

3 spreading butter on toast
smear, plaster, daub

4 A big grin spread across Ellen's face.
expand, extend, stretch, broaden,
enlarge, swell

5 spreading malicious rumours
communicate, circulate, distribute,
transmit, disseminate, make known,
pass round

spread *NOUN*

1 the rapid spread of information
communication, circulation,
distribution, transmission,
dissemination

2 a spread of several metres
span, width, extent, stretch, reach

a
b
c
d
e
f
g
h
i
j
k
l
m
n
o
p
q
r
s
t
u
v
w
x
y
z

535

a
b
c
d
e
f
g
h
i
j
k
l
m
n
o
p
q
r
s
t
u
v
w
x
y
z

sprightly ADJECTIVE

She still looks sprightly for her age.
lively, energetic, active, agile,
nimble, frisky, spry

OPPOSITE inactive

spring VERB

1 *Josie sprang to her feet in alarm.*
jump, leap, bound, hop, vault,
pounce

2 *Where did the idea for the character
spring from?*
originate, arise, derive, stem,
emanate

▷ **spring up**
*Weeds are springing up all over the
garden.*
appear, develop, emerge, shoot up,
sprout

springy ADJECTIVE

a springy mattress
bouncy, elastic, stretchy, flexible,
pliable

OPPOSITE rigid

sprinkle VERB

1 *sprinkling perfume on a handkerchief*
spray, shower, splash, drizzle

2 *sprinkling icing sugar on a cake*
scatter, strew, dust, dredge

sprout VERB

1 *Leave the seeds in a warm place to
sprout.*
grow, germinate, put out shoots

2 *Sites like this are sprouting all over
the Internet.*
spring up, appear, develop, emerge

spruce ADJECTIVE

*looking unusually spruce in a shirt
and tie*
smart, well-dressed, well-groomed,
elegant, neat, trim

OPPOSITE scruffy

spur VERB

▷ **spur someone on**
*We were spurred on by the thought
of adventure.*
encourage, stimulate, motivate,
inspire, prompt, galvanize, urge on,
egg on

spurt VERB

Dirty water spurted from the pipe.
gush, spout, shoot out, stream,
squirt, jet

spy NOUN

*working as a spy during the Cold
War*
agent, secret agent, mole

▶ A spy who works for two rival
organizations is a **double agent**.

WRITING TIPS

writing spy fiction

I've got the corpses of a Japanese
cipher expert in New York and
a Norwegian double agent in
Stockholm to thank for being a
Double O. Probably quite decent
people. They just got caught up
in the gale of the world.
— *Ian Fleming, Casino Royale*

characters

agent, code-breaker
(*informal* code-cracker),
code-maker, controller,
cryptographer, double agent,
mole, operative, secret agent,
sleeper, spy catcher, spymaster

useful words & phrases

behind enemy lines, briefing,
CIA, cipher, clandestine
operation, counter-espionage,
counter-intelligence, code book,
code-breaking
(*informal* code-cracking),
clandestine, covert, debriefing,
decode, decryption, deep cover,
defection, disinformation,
encode, encryption, espionage,
false identity, FBI, headquarters,
hidden camera, infiltration,
intelligence, listening device
(*informal* bug), MI5, MI6, mission,
password, recruitment,

secret service, special operations, spying, surveillance, transmitting device, under cover

spy VERB

I thought I spied a familiar face.
see, sight, spot, catch sight of, notice, observe, make out, detect

squabble VERB

Those two are always squabbling!
argue, fight, quarrel, bicker, wrangle

squad NOUN

a clean-up squad
team, crew, gang, force, unit, detail

squalid ADJECTIVE

living in squalid refugee camps
dirty, filthy, foul, dingy, degrading, nasty, unpleasant
OPPOSITE clean

squander VERB

He squandered his fortune in gambling.
waste, throw away, fritter away, misuse
(informal) blow
OPPOSITE save

square ADJECTIVE

a square floor tile
right-angled
▶ A pattern of squares is a **chequered** pattern.
SEE ALSO shape NOUN

squarely ADVERB

The ball hit him squarely in the face.
directly, straight, head on
OPPOSITE obliquely

squash VERB

1 *The cake got a bit squashed in my bag.*
crush, flatten, press, compress, mangle, mash, pulp
(informal) squish

2 *Just squash everything into the suitcase.*
force, stuff, squeeze, cram, jam, pack, ram, wedge

squat VERB

We squatted by the fire, trying to keep warm.
crouch, huddle, sit on your heels

squat ADJECTIVE

a squat little man with a reddish face
dumpy, stocky, plump, podgy, portly

squeak, squeal NOUN, VERB

FOR TIPS ON DESCRIBING SOUNDS SEE **sound❶**

squeeze VERB

1 *Aisha squeezed my hand tightly.*
press, compress, crush, grip, clasp, pinch, nip

2 *squeezing juice from a lemon*
extract, press, express, force, wring

3 *Five of us squeezed into the back of the car.*
squash, cram, crowd, stuff, jam, push, ram, shove, wedge

squeeze NOUN

1 *She gave my hand a squeeze.*
press, grip, clasp, pinch, nip

2 *It was a tight squeeze in the back seat.*
squash, crush, jam

squirm VERB

A rabbit had squirmed through a hole in the fence.
wriggle, writhe, twist

squirt VERB

Tap water squirted all over the floor.
spurt, spray, shower, gush, spout, shoot, jet

stab VERB

1 *The victim had been stabbed in the chest.*
knife, spear, jab, pierce, impale, run through, skewer

2 *A man was shouting and stabbing a finger in the air.*
stick, thrust, push, jab

stab NOUN

1 *a sudden stab of pain*
pang, twinge, prick, sting

》

a
b
c
d
e
f
g
h
i
j
k
l
m
n
o
p
q
r
s
t
u
v
w
x
y
z

2 *(informal) Why don't you have a stab at filming?*
try, go, attempt
(informal) bash, shot, crack

stable ADJECTIVE

1 *The wide wheels make the bike stable.*
steady, secure, firm, balanced, solid, fixed
❙ OPPOSITES unstable, wobbly

2 *building a stable relationship*
steady, established, lasting, durable, strong
❙ OPPOSITES casual, temporary

stack NOUN

a stack of unanswered letters
pile, heap, mound, mountain, tower
▶ A stack of hay is also called a **rick** of hay.

stack VERB

Just stack the dishes in the sink.
heap up, pile up

staff NOUN

the staff of the local library
workers, employees, personnel, workforce, team
▶ The staff on a ship or aircraft are the **crew**.

stage NOUN

1 *standing on a stage before a large crowd*
platform, podium, dais, rostrum

2 *the final stage of our journey*
part, leg, step, phase, portion, section, stretch

3 *a crucial stage in a child's development*
point, time, juncture, period, phase

stagger VERB

1 *John staggered in carrying a huge parcel.*
reel, stumble, lurch, totter, teeter, sway, waver, wobble

2 *I was staggered at the price of the tickets.*
amaze, astonish, astound, surprise, stun, startle, dumbfound

(informal) flabbergast

stagnant ADJECTIVE

a pool of stagnant water
still, motionless, static
❙ OPPOSITES flowing, fresh

stain NOUN

1 *a few coffee stains on the tablecloth*
mark, spot, blot, blotch, smear, smudge

2 *a stain on an otherwise brilliant career.*
blemish, taint, blot, flaw, fault

stain VERB

1 *The bird's feathers were stained with blood.*
discolour, mark, smear, smudge, soil, dirty, blacken, tarnish

2 *The wood can be stained a darker shade.*
dye, colour, tint, tinge

stairs PLURAL NOUN

the back stairs into the house
step
▶ A set of stairs from one floor to another is a **flight** of stairs, or a **staircase** or **stairway**.
▶ A moving staircase is an **escalator**.
▶ A handrail at the side of a staircase is a **banister**.
▶ The space in a building which contains the stairs is the **stairwell**.

stake NOUN

1 *To kill a vampire you must drive a stake into its heart.*
pole, post, stick, spike, stave, pile

2 *playing for high stakes*
bet, wager

3 *a major stake in the business*
share, interest, involvement

stale ADJECTIVE

1 *some stale crusts of bread*
old, dry, hard, mouldy, musty, rancid
❙ OPPOSITE fresh

2 *the same old stale ideas*
overused, tired, hackneyed, banal, clichéd
❙ OPPOSITES original, fresh

stalk❶ NOUN

a dandelion stalk
stem, shoot, twig
FOR PARTS OF A PLANT SEE plant

stalk❷ VERB

1 *a panther stalking its prey*
hunt, pursue, track, trail, follow,
shadow, tail

2 *Viv turned and stalked out of the
room.*
stride, strut, march, stomp
▮ SEE ALSO walk

stall NOUN

1 *a stall selling selling home-made jam*
stand, table, counter, kiosk, booth

2 *a cattle stall*
pen, enclosure, compartment

stall VERB

1 *I could tell the assistant was stalling.*
play for time, delay, procrastinate,
hedge

2 *See if you can stall them for a few
days.*
delay, detain, hold off, hold back

stamina NOUN

*Do you have the stamina to run a
marathon?*
endurance, staying power,
toughness, grit

stammer VERB

He stammered over his opening lines.
stutter, falter, stumble, splutter

stamp NOUN

a first-class stamp
▶ A person who studies or collects
stamps is a **philatelist**.

stamp VERB

1 *Please don't stamp on the flowers.*
step, tread, trample, crush, flatten

2 *stamping our feet to get warm*
tramp, stomp, clump

3 *stamping your name on an envelope*
print, impress, emboss
▶ To stamp a postmark on a letter is to
frank it.
▶ To stamp a mark on cattle with a hot
iron is to **brand** them.

stance NOUN

1 *keeping a relaxed stance*
posture, position, pose

2 *What is your stance on nuclear
power?*
opinion, attitude, standpoint,
position, policy, line

stand VERB

1 *Please stand when your name is
called.*
get up, get to your feet, rise

2 *Stand the ladder against the wall.*
put, place, set, prop, position,
station, erect

3 *The invitation still stands.*
be valid, remain in force, apply,
continue, hold

4 *How can you stand the noise?*
bear, abide, endure, put up with,
tolerate, withstand

▷ **stand for something**

1 *What do these initials stand for?*
mean, indicate, signify, represent

2 *We won't stand for their lies any
longer.*
put up with, tolerate, accept, allow,
permit

▷ **stand out**
The lettering really stands out.
catch your eye, leap out, be
noticeable, be prominent

▷ **stand up for someone**
She always stands up for her friends.
support, defend, side with, speak
up for
(informal) stick up for

stand NOUN

a trophy on a wooden stand
base, rest, pedestal, plinth
▶ A three-legged stand for a camera or
telescope is a **tripod**.

standard NOUN

1 *a high standard of workmanship*
grade, level, quality, calibre

2 *The timing is good by any standard.*
criterion, measure, model, guide,
benchmark, yardstick

»

a
b
c
d
e
f
g
h
i
j
k
l
m
n
o
p
q
r
s
t
u
v
w
x
y
z

3 *a regimental standard*
colours, flag, banner

standard *ADJECTIVE*

1 *the standard way to make an omelette*
normal, usual, common, conventional, typical, customary, established, accepted, orthodox, regular, traditional
OPPOSITES unusual, unorthodox

2 *the standard guide to North American birds*
definitive, authoritative, classic, ultimate, best, approved

standing *NOUN*

1 *their current standing in the polls*
position, place, ranking

2 *people of good standing in society*
status, stature, reputation, rank, importance, eminence

standstill *NOUN*

▷ **come to a standstill**
Traffic had come to a standstill.
stop moving, draw up, halt, stop
IDIOM grind to a halt

staple *ADJECTIVE*
Rice is the staple food in many countries.
chief, main, principal, standard, basic

star *NOUN*

1 *mapping the stars in the night sky*
celestial body, heavenly body
▶ The scientific study of stars is **astronomy**.
▶ Related adjectives are **sidereal** and **stellar**.
a sidereal astronomer
a stellar halo
FOR NATURAL OBJECTS IN SPACE SEE space

2 *a star of Bollywood movies*
celebrity, idol, superstar
(informal) celeb
FOR STAR SIGNS SEE zodiac

stare *VERB*
The eyes in the portrait were

staring straight at me.
gaze, gape, peer, look
(informal) gawk, gawp
▶ To stare angrily at someone is to **glare** at them.
SEE ALSO look

stark *ADJECTIVE*

1 *in stark contrast to the rest of the region*
complete, utter, unmistakable, sharp, distinct

2 *a stark lunar landscape*
desolate, barren, bare, empty, bleak

start *VERB*

1 *The new series will start in the autumn.*
begin, commence, get under way, get going
(informal) kick off
OPPOSITES finish, end

2 *Modern ice hockey started in Canada.*
originate, arise, begin, be born, come into being
OPPOSITE stop

3 *We're planning to start a film club.*
establish, set up, create, found, institute, initiate, inaugurate, launch
OPPOSITES close down, wind up

4 *Press here to start the computer.*
switch on, activate, fire up, boot up
OPPOSITES shut down, deactivate

5 *Patsy started when the phone rang.*
jump, flinch, jerk, twitch, wince

start *NOUN*

1 *Try not to miss the start of the film.*
beginning, opening, introduction, commencement
OPPOSITES end, close, finish

2 *the very start of life on Earth*
origin, inception, onset, emergence, birth, dawn

3 *Her voice gave me a nasty start.*
jump, jolt, shock, surprise

startle *VERB*
A sudden noise startled the horses.
alarm, panic, frighten, scare, surprise, take someone by surprise,

make someone jump

starve VERB
People were left to starve in freezing conditions.
die of starvation, go hungry
▶ To choose to go without food is to **fast**.

starving (informal) ADJECTIVE
By teatime we were all starving.
hungry, famished, ravenous

state NOUN
1 *Much of the building is in a rundown state.*
condition, shape, order
2 *a league of independent states*
country, nation, kingdom, realm
3 (informal) *getting in a state about nothing*
panic, fluster
(informal) flap

state VERB
The sign states that photography is allowed.
declare, announce, say, express, report, proclaim, pronounce, communicate

stately ADJECTIVE
The funeral service was a stately affair.
dignified, grand, formal, ceremonious, imposing, majestic, noble

statement NOUN
making a statement to the press
announcement, declaration, communication, report, testimony, communiqué

station NOUN
1 *Does the train stop at the next station?*
▶ The station at the end of a line is the **terminus**.
2 *the nearest police station*
depot, office, base, headquarters
3 *a local radio station*
channel, wavelength

station VERB
Two guards were stationed at the entrance.
post, position, situate, locate, base, deploy
▶ A body of troops stationed in a town or fort is a **garrison**.

stationary ADJECTIVE
Try to keep the cursor stationary.
still, static, unmoving, immobile, motionless, standing, at rest
❙ OPPOSITE moving

statue NOUN
a life-size statue of Abraham Lincoln
figure, sculpture, carving
▶ A small statue is a **statuette**.

status NOUN
1 *the status of women in Victorian society*
rank, level, position, grade, place
2 *a family of wealth and status*
importance, prestige, stature, standing, kudos

staunch ADJECTIVE
a staunch ally of the President
firm, strong, faithful, loyal, true, reliable, dependable, steadfast, trusty
❙ OPPOSITES disloyal, unreliable

stay VERB
1 *I'll stay here until you get back.*
wait, remain, hang on, linger
(informal) hang about
❙ OPPOSITES leave, depart
2 *Please try to stay calm.*
keep, remain, carry on being
3 *Do you plan to stay here long?*
visit, lodge, stop, stop over

stay NOUN
Our friends are here for a short stay.
visit, stopover, holiday, break

steady ADJECTIVE
1 *Keep a steady grip on the handle.*
stable, secure, fixed, firm, fast, solid, balanced
❙ OPPOSITES unsteady, shaky

》

2 *a steady stream of visitors*
continuous, uninterrupted,
non-stop, constant, consistent,
reliable

▌**OPPOSITE** intermittent

3 *jogging at a steady pace*
regular, constant, even, smooth,
settled, rhythmic, unvarying

▌**OPPOSITE** irregular

steady *VERB*

You can use a tripod to steady the camera.
balance, stabilize, hold steady

steal *VERB*

1 *The World Cup was stolen while on display in London.*
take, snatch, pilfer
(informal) swipe, lift, make off with
(British informal) nick, pinch

2 *We both stole quietly out of the room.*
creep, sneak, tiptoe, slip, slink, slope

stealing *NOUN*

found guilty of cheating and stealing
robbery, theft

▶ Stealing from a private house is **burglary** or **housebreaking**.

▶ Stealing small goods from a shop is **shoplifting**.

▶ Stealing things of little value is **pilfering**.

stealthy *ADJECTIVE*

advancing with slow, stealthy movements
furtive, secretive, surreptitious, sly,
sneaky, underhand

▌**OPPOSITES** conspicuous, open

steam *NOUN*

steam from a boiling kettle
vapour, mist, haze

▶ Steam on a cold window is **condensation**.

steamy *ADJECTIVE*

1 *the warm, steamy atmosphere of the greenhouse*
humid, muggy, close, damp, moist

2 *wiping a steamy mirror*
misty, hazy, cloudy

steep *ADJECTIVE*

1 *a dangerously steep cliff*
abrupt, sharp, precipitous

▶ A cliff or drop which is straight up
and down is **sheer** or **vertical**.

▌**OPPOSITES** gradual, gentle

2 *(informal) charging steep prices*
high, overpriced, inflated,
exorbitant, extortionate

steer *VERB*

steering a shopping trolley
guide, direct, manoeuvre, drive,
navigate, pilot

▶ A person who steers a ship is a
steersman or **steerswoman**.

stem❶ *NOUN*

a plant with a woody stem
stalk, shoot, twig

stem *VERB*

▷ **stem from**

Her love of writing stems from childhood.
come from, arise from, spring from,
derive from, originate in, have its
origins in

stem❷ *VERB*

trying to stem the flow of blood
stop, check, hold back, curb, staunch

step *NOUN*

1 *We each took a step closer to the door.*
pace, stride

2 *the sound of heavy steps outside*
footstep, tread, footfall

3 *Mind the step as you go in.*
doorstep, stair, tread

▶ The steps of a ladder are the **rungs**.

4 *the last step in installing the software*
stage, phase, action, operation,
move

step *VERB*

Don't step on the broken glass.
tread, walk, stamp, trample, stride,
pace

▷ **step down**

He's stepping down at the end of the season.

resign, stand down, quit, bow out

▷ **step in**
The referee was forced to step in.
intervene, intercede, become involved

▷ **step something up**
stepping up security at the airport
increase, intensify, strengthen, boost

sterile ADJECTIVE
1 Mars appears to be a sterile frozen desert.
barren, dry, arid, infertile, lifeless
❗ OPPOSITE fertile
2 a sterile bandage
disinfected, uncontaminated, clean, hygienic, germ-free, antiseptic
❗ OPPOSITE contaminated

stern ADJECTIVE
Marley issues a stern warning to Scrooge.
severe, strict, hard, harsh, grim, austere, forbidding, disapproving
❗ OPPOSITES kindly, lenient

stew VERB
SEE **cook**

stick❶ NOUN
1 collecting dry sticks to make a fire
twig, branch, stalk
2 a stout walking stick
cane, rod, staff, pole, stake
▶ A stick used by a conductor is a **baton**.
▶ A stick carried by a police officer is a **truncheon**.
▶ A stick used as a weapon is a **club** or **cudgel**.

stick❷ VERB
1 sticking drawing pins into the wall
poke, prod, stab, thrust, dig, jab
2 Stick the label on the front of the parcel.
attach, affix, fasten, fix, paste, glue, tape
3 The crystals stick together to form blocks of ice.
adhere, cling, bond, join

4 The rear wheels stuck fast in the mud.
jam, wedge, catch, get trapped
5 (informal) I can't stick it here any longer.
endure, tolerate, stand, bear, abide, put up with

▷ **stick out**
1 The battery sticks out at the back of the unit.
jut out, poke out, project, protrude
2 One man in particular stuck out from the crowd.
stand out, be noticeable, leap out, catch your eye

▷ **stick up for**
(informal) Thanks for sticking up for me.
support, stand up for, side with, speak up for, defend

sticky ADJECTIVE
1 a sticky blob of chewing gum
tacky, gummy, gluey
(informal) gooey, icky
2 a hot sticky climate
humid, muggy, clammy, close, steamy, sultry
❗ OPPOSITE dry
3 (informal) The hero finds himself in a sticky situation.
awkward, difficult, tricky, ticklish
(informal) hairy

stiff ADJECTIVE
1 Use a stiff piece of cardboard as a base.
rigid, inflexible, firm
❗ OPPOSITES flexible, pliable
2 Add flour to make a stiff dough.
thick, solid, firm, viscous
❗ OPPOSITES soft, loose
3 My legs were stiff from crouching.
aching, achy, painful, taut, tight
❗ OPPOSITE supple
4 They face stiff opposition in the final.
strong, powerful, vigorous, difficult, tough, dogged, determined
❗ OPPOSITE weak

》

543

5 *There are stiff penalties for dropping litter.*
harsh, severe, tough, strict, stringent, heavy
❙ **OPPOSITES** lenient, mild

6 *The writing style is stiff and old-fashioned.*
formal, awkward, wooden, strained, stilted
❙ **OPPOSITES** informal, casual, relaxed

stifle *VERB*
1 *We were nearly stifled by the midday heat.*
suffocate, smother, choke
2 *She tried to stifle a yawn.*
suppress, muffle, hold back, repress, restrain
❙ **OPPOSITE** let out

still *ADJECTIVE*
1 *Logan stood still and held his breath.*
motionless, unmoving, immobile, stationary, static, inert
❙ **IDIOM** rooted to the spot
2 *It was a crisp still morning.*
quiet, silent, peaceful, tranquil, calm, serene, noiseless, windless

still *VERB*
Yoga teaches you to still your mind.
calm, quieten, settle, silence, hush, lull
❙ **OPPOSITES** stir, disturb

stillness *NOUN*
the stillness of the early morning
calmness, quiet, silence, noiselessness, hush, peace, serenity, tranquillity

stimulate *VERB*
1 *music with the power to stimulate your imagination*
encourage, inspire, excite, stir up, galvanize, kindle, fire
❙ **OPPOSITE** dampen
2 *What stimulated your interest in science?*
arouse, prompt, provoke, trigger

sting *VERB*
1 *being stung by a wasp*
bite, nip
2 *The smoke made our eyes sting.*
smart, burn, prick, prickle, tingle

stingy *(informal) ADJECTIVE*
They're a bit stingy with their portions.
mean, miserly, penny-pinching *(informal)* tight-fisted
❙ **OPPOSITE** generous

stink *NOUN*
the stink of sweaty feet
reek, stench, odour, smell *(British informal)* pong

stink *VERB*
The cabin stank of unwashed bodies.
reek, smell

stir *VERB*
1 *Stir the mixture until it is smooth.*
mix, beat, blend, whisk
2 *Something stirred in the bushes behind us.*
move slightly, shift, rustle
3 *His words stirred a generation to fight for change.*
stimulate, excite, inspire, encourage, prompt, rouse, spur, provoke

stir *NOUN*
The book caused an immediate stir.
fuss, commotion, excitement, furore, to-do

stock *NOUN*
1 *a large stock of spare parts*
supply, store, reserve, hoard, stockpile
2 *waiting for new stock to arrive*
goods, merchandise, wares
3 *Most of the population is of European stock.*
descent, ancestry, origin, lineage, family, pedigree, line

stock *VERB*
Many supermarkets now stock organic food.
sell, carry, trade in, deal in, keep in stock

stocky *ADJECTIVE*

The striped skunk has short, stocky legs.

dumpy, squat, thickset, solid, sturdy, stubby

❙ **OPPOSITE** thin

FOR TIPS ON DESCRIBING PEOPLE'S BODIES SEE body

stodgy *ADJECTIVE*

1 *a stodgy meal*
heavy, solid, starchy, filling
❙ **OPPOSITE** light

2 *a stodgy reference book*
dull, boring, uninteresting, slow, tedious
❙ **OPPOSITES** lively, interesting

stole *PAST TENSE*

SEE **steal**

stomach *NOUN*

exercises to tone your stomach
belly, abdomen, gut
(informal) tummy

▶ A large rounded stomach is a **paunch**.

▶ A related adjective is **abdominal**.
abdominal exercises

stomach *VERB*

She found it hard to stomach the truth.

stand, bear, take, accept, tolerate, put up with, endure

stone *NOUN*

1 *throwing stones into the sea*
rock, pebble, boulder

▶ A mixture of sand and small stones is **gravel**.

▶ Pebbles on the beach are **shingle**.

▶ Round stones used to pave a path are **cobbles**.

FOR TYPES OF ROCK AND MINERALS SEE rock

2 *removing plum stones*
kernel, pip, seed
(North American) pit

stony *ADJECTIVE*

1 *a stony footpath*
pebbly, rocky, shingly

❙ **OPPOSITES** smooth, sandy

2 *We were greeted with stony silence.*
unfriendly, cold, hostile, frosty, icy
❙ **OPPOSITES** warm, friendly

stoop *VERB*

She stooped to pick up the newspaper.
bend, duck, bow, crouch

stop *VERB*

1 *There was no sign of the rain stopping.*
come to an end, end, finish, cease, conclude, terminate
❙ **OPPOSITE** start

2 *How do you stop the DVD recorder?*
switch off, shut down, halt, terminate, deactivate, immobilize

3 *Please stop asking me questions.*
give up, cease, discontinue, suspend, leave off, break off
(informal) knock off, pack in, quit
❙ **OPPOSITES** continue, resume

4 *The bus will stop at the front gates.*
come to a stop, halt, pull up, draw up, come to rest

5 *The doorman tried to stop them leaving.*
prevent, obstruct, bar, block, hinder

6 *stopping a gap in a window frame*
close, plug, seal, block up, bung up

stop *NOUN*

1 *Everything suddenly came to a stop.*
end, finish, conclusion, halt, standstill

2 *after a short stop for lunch*
break, pause, rest, stay, stopover

store *NOUN*

1 *a large store of canned goods*
hoard, supply, quantity, stock, stockpile, reserve

2 *an underground book store for the library*
storeroom, storehouse, repository, vault

▶ A store for food is a **larder** or **pantry**.

▶ A store for weapons is an **armoury** or **arsenal**.

                                     »

a
b
c
d
e
f
g
h
i
j
k
l
m
n
o
p
q
r
s
t
u
v
w
x
y
z

3 *a local grocery store*
SEE **shop**

store VERB

Yucca plants store water in their roots.
save, reserve, set aside, stow away, hoard, stockpile
(informal) stash

storey NOUN

There is a restaurant on the top storey.
floor, level, tier

storm NOUN

1 *Heavy storms are forecast throughout the country.*
squall, blizzard, gale, thunderstorm, snowstorm, hurricane, typhoon
(literary) tempest

▶ When a storm begins to develop it is **brewing**.
FOR TIPS ON DESCRIBING THE WEATHER SEE **weather**

2 *a storm of public protest*
outburst, outcry, uproar, clamour, fuss, furore

storm VERB

1 *Scarlett stormed out in a temper.*
march, stride, stalk, stomp, flounce

2 *Police stormed the building.*
charge at, rush at, swoop on, attack

stormy ADJECTIVE

1 *a wild and stormy night*
blustery, squally, windy, gusty, blowy, thundery, tempestuous
OPPOSITE calm

2 *the end of a stormy meeting*
angry, heated, turbulent, violent, passionate

story NOUN

1 *Do you know any good ghost stories?*
tale, narrative, anecdote
(informal) yarn
SEE ALSO fiction

2 *The book tells the story of her childhood.*
account, history, narrative, saga, plot

▶ The story of a person's life is their **biography**.

▶ The story which a person writes of their own life is their **autobiography**.

3 *the front-page story in all the papers*
article, item, feature, report, piece

4 *Stories have been flying around for months.*
rumour, gossip, whisper, speculation

stout ADJECTIVE

1 *a rather stout lady dressed in black*
fat, plump, dumpy, tubby, portly, podgy, rotund
OPPOSITE thin
SEE ALSO fat

2 *a pair of stout walking boots*
strong, sturdy, tough, robust, hard-wearing, durable
OPPOSITE flimsy

3 *putting up a stout defence*
brave, courageous, spirited, plucky, determined, resolute, firm
OPPOSITE weak

stow VERB

We stowed the decorations away for another year.
store, put away, pack, hoard

straight ADJECTIVE

1 *a straight section of motorway*
direct, unbending, unswerving
OPPOSITE winding

2 *Does that hem look straight to you?*
level, even, aligned, horizontal, vertical, upright
OPPOSITE crooked

3 *It took ages to get the room straight.*
neat, orderly, tidy, in order, shipshape
OPPOSITE untidy

4 *I just want a straight answer.*
honest, plain, frank, direct, straightforward, candid
OPPOSITES indirect, evasive

straight ADVERB

1 *Its eyes looked straight through me.*
right, directly

2 *They left straight after breakfast.*
immediately, promptly, right

straight away ADVERB

She replied to my text straight away.
immediately, at once, right away,
without delay, instantly, promptly

straightforward ADJECTIVE

1 *The recipe is quite straightforward.*
uncomplicated, simple, easy, clear
> **IDIOM** plain sailing
> **OPPOSITE** complicated

2 *I found him straightforward to deal with.*
frank, honest, straight, direct,
plain, candid
> **OPPOSITE** evasive

strain❶ VERB

1 *I think I've strained a muscle.*
sprain, injure, pull, twist, wrench

2 *Our team of huskies strained on the ropes.*
pull, tug, stretch

3 *Take it easy and don't strain yourself.*
overtax, overreach, exhaust, wear
out, tire out

4 *Strain the liquid to get rid of any lumps.*
sieve, sift, filter

strain NOUN

1 *The ropes creaked under the strain.*
tension, tightness, tautness,
stretch

2 *The strain was beginning to tell on us all.*
stress, tension, worry, anxiety,
pressure

strain❷ NOUN

1 *a deadly strain of the virus*
variety, type, sort, kind

2 *A strain of humour runs through her writing.*
quality, element, trace, vein

strand NOUN

a strand of embroidery thread
thread, filament, fibre

stranded ADJECTIVE

1 *A whale lay stranded on the beach.*
run aground, beached, marooned

2 *She found herself stranded without any money.*
abandoned, deserted, helpless, lost,
adrift
> **IDIOM** high and dry

strange ADJECTIVE

1 *A strange thing happened last night.*
unusual, odd, peculiar, funny,
abnormal, curious, mysterious,
weird, bizarre
> **OPPOSITES** ordinary, normal

2 *I woke up in a strange room.*
unfamiliar, unknown, new, alien
> **OPPOSITE** familiar

stranger NOUN

welcoming strangers to our city
newcomer, outsider, visitor,
foreigner

strangle VERB

The victim had been strangled with his tie.
throttle, choke, garrotte

strap NOUN

a leather watch strap
belt, band, tie, thong

strategy NOUN

a strategy to deal with bullying
plan, policy, procedure, approach,
scheme, programme

stray VERB

Don't stray too far from the shore.
wander off, drift, roam

streak NOUN

1 *a streak of bright light in the sky*
band, line, stripe, strip, slash

2 *streaks of mud on the floor*
smear, stain, mark

3 *There is a streak of vanity in his character.*
element, trace, strain, vein

streak VERB

1 *Her face was streaked with mascara.*
smear, smudge, stain, mark, line

»

2 *A group of motorbikes streaked past.*
rush, speed, dash, fly, hurtle, flash, tear, zoom

stream NOUN

1 *a clear mountain stream*
brook, rivulet
(North American & Australian) creek
(Scottish) burn

2 *a stream of molten lava*
flow, gush, jet, flood, rush, torrent, cataract, cascade

3 *answering a stream of emails*
series, string, line, succession

stream VERB

1 *Water streamed down the basement walls.*
pour, flow, run, gush, spill, cascade

2 *Thousands of fans streamed through the gates.*
swarm, surge, pile, pour, flood

street NOUN
SEE **road**

strength NOUN

1 *Hercules was said to have enormous strength.*
power, might, muscle, brawn, force, vigour

2 *testing the strength of the roof*
toughness, sturdiness, robustness, firmness, solidity, resilience

3 *The real strength of the team is in defence.*
strong point, asset, advantage, forte, speciality
❙ OPPOSITE weakness

strengthen VERB

1 *Regular exercise strengthens your muscles.*
make stronger, build up

2 *Steel is used to strengthen concrete.*
fortify, reinforce, stiffen, harden, toughen
❙ OPPOSITE weaken

strenuous ADJECTIVE

1 *avoiding strenuous exercise*
hard, tough, difficult, demanding, tiring, taxing, exhausting, gruelling

❙ OPPOSITE easy

2 *making strenuous efforts to save energy*
determined, strong, intense, vigorous, energetic, spirited, resolute, dogged
❙ OPPOSITE feeble

stress NOUN

1 *coping with the stress of exams*
strain, pressure, tension, worry, anxiety

2 *laying too much stress on appearances*
emphasis, importance, weight

stress VERB

He stressed the need for absolute secrecy.
emphasize, draw attention to, highlight, underline

stressed ADJECTIVE

feeling stressed and overworked
harassed, overwrought, fraught, tense
❙ IDIOM at the end of your tether

stretch VERB

1 *stretching a piece of elastic*
extend, draw out, pull out, elongate, lengthen, expand

2 *The spectre stretched out a bony arm.*
reach out, hold out, straighten, spread out

3 *The sand dunes stretch for miles.*
continue, extend, go on

stretch NOUN

1 *a vast stretch of open country*
area, expanse, tract, sweep

2 *a dangerous stretch of the river*
section, length, piece

3 *after a brief stretch in art college*
spell, period, time, stint

strict ADJECTIVE

1 *The sisters were brought up in a strict household.*
harsh, severe, stern, firm, rigid, authoritarian
❙ OPPOSITE lenient

2 *He left strict instructions in his will.*
precise, exact, careful, meticulous
❙ **OPPOSITES** vague, loose

3 *Please treat this in strict confidence.*
absolute, complete, total, utter

stride *VERB*
Mrs Scott strode across the hall to greet us.
march, step, pace

stride *NOUN*
Derek took a stride towards the door.
pace, step, tread

strike *VERB*
1 *I struck my head on something hard.*
hit, knock, bang, bash, bump, beat, thump
(informal) wallop, whack

2 *The driver lost control and struck a lamp post.*
collide with, crash into, bang into, run into, hit

3 *Suddenly, the idea struck me.*
occur to, hit, dawn on, spring to mind

4 *The clock struck midnight.*
chime, ring out, sound

striking *ADJECTIVE*
1 *a striking display of technical wizardry*
impressive, stunning, spectacular, outstanding, extraordinary, remarkable, astonishing, memorable, breathtaking
❙ **OPPOSITE** unremarkable

2 *There is a striking resemblance between the signatures.*
conspicuous, noticeable, marked, obvious, strong, prominent, unmistakable
❙ **OPPOSITE** inconspicuous

string *NOUN*
1 *a label tied on with string*
rope, cord, twine
FOR STRINGED INSTRUMENTS SEE **music**

2 *an endless string of complaints*
series, succession, chain, sequence, run

string *VERB*
stringing paper lanterns from the ceiling
hang, suspend, sling, thread, loop

stringy *ADJECTIVE*
a stringy piece of meat
chewy, fibrous, tough
❙ **OPPOSITE** tender

strip❶ *VERB*
1 *Deer had stripped the bark off the trees.*
peel, remove, scrape
❙ **OPPOSITES** cover, wrap

2 *He stripped and got into the bath.*
get undressed, undress
(formal) disrobe
❙ **OPPOSITE** dress

3 *They were disqualified and stripped of their medals.*
deprive, divest, relieve

strip❷ *NOUN*
Tear the paper into narrow strips.
band, length, ribbon, piece, bit

stripe *NOUN*
a pattern of blue and white stripes
line, strip, band, bar

strive *VERB*
striving to do the best you can
try hard, aim, attempt, endeavour

stroke❶ *NOUN*
1 *the stroke of a hammer*
blow, hit

2 *learning to row with even strokes*
movement, motion
FOR SWIMMING STROKES SEE **swim**

3 *rubbing out the pencil strokes*
line, mark

4 *a masterful stroke of publicity*
action, feat, effort, exploit

stroke❷ *VERB*
Cats like to be stroked under the chin.
pat, caress, fondle, pet, touch, rub

a
b
c
d
e
f
g
h
i
j
k
l
m
n
o
p
q
r
s
t
u
v
w
x
y
z

stroll VERB

After lunch, we strolled along the beach.

walk slowly, amble, saunter, promenade

SEE ALSO walk

strong ADJECTIVE

OVERUSED WORD

a strong person, strong body

powerful, muscular, well-built, beefy, brawny, burly, strapping, athletic, vigorous, lusty
(literary) mighty

*Swimmers need to develop **powerful** shoulder muscles.*

OPPOSITES weak, puny

FOR TIPS ON DESCRIBING PEOPLE'S BODIES SEE body

strong material

robust, sturdy, tough, hard-wearing, heavy-duty, durable, long-lasting, stout, substantial

*The drumsticks are made from **hard-wearing** maple.*

OPPOSITES fragile, flimsy

a strong light, strong colour

bright, brilliant, dazzling, glaring, intense

*Angus looked nervous under the **glaring** camera lights.*

OPPOSITES faint, dim, pale

a strong flavour, strong smell

intense, pronounced, overpowering, pungent, piquant, tangy, concentrated, undiluted

*Insects dislike the **pungent** aroma of eucalyptus oil.*

OPPOSITES faint, mild, subtle

SEE ALSO smell NOUN, taste

a strong argument, strong case

convincing, persuasive, effective, forceful, compelling, sound, solid, valid, cogent

*Could this be **solid** evidence of extraterrestrial life?*

OPPOSITES weak, feeble, flimsy

a strong interest, strong supporter

enthusiastic, keen, eager, passionate, fervent, avid, zealous

*I've been an **avid** fan of the band since their debut CD.*

OPPOSITES slight, casual

structure NOUN

1 *The Hoover Dam is a massive concrete structure.*
building, construction, erection, edifice

2 *the delicate structure of a spider's web*
construction, design, plan, framework, shape, form, arrangement, organization

struggle VERB

1 *People struggled to get some air.*
wrestle, tussle, fight, battle, grapple

2 *struggling along with a heavy suitcase*
stagger, stumble, labour, flounder

3 *I struggled to make sense of the letter.*
try hard, strive, strain, make every effort

struggle NOUN

1 *There were some signs of a struggle.*
fight, tussle, scuffle, brawl, clash, conflict

2 *the struggle to get the vote for women*
campaign, battle, crusade, drive, push

3 *I found the language a struggle at first.*
effort, exertion, problem, difficulty

stubborn ADJECTIVE

1 *Lizzie can be stubborn when she wants to be.*
obstinate, headstrong, strong-willed, wilful, uncooperative, inflexible, pig-headed
⎸ **OPPOSITE** compliant

2 *removing stubborn stains*
persistent, resistant, tenacious
▶ A mark or stain that is impossible to remove is **indelible**.
⎸ **OPPOSITE** removable

stuck ADJECTIVE

1 *I found a note stuck on my computer screen.*
fixed, fastened, attached, glued, pasted, pinned

2 *The bottom drawer is stuck.*
jammed, immovable
▶ You can also say that something that is stuck **will not budge**.

3 *I'm completely stuck on the last question.*
baffled, beaten, stumped, at a loss

stud VERB

▷ **studded with**
a costume studded with sequins and jewels
inlaid with, dotted with, encrusted with

student NOUN

1 *a former student of this school*
pupil, schoolboy, schoolgirl

2 *a medical student*
undergraduate
▶ A person who has been awarded a university degree is a **graduate**.
▶ A student who is studying for a second degree is a **postgraduate**.

studious ADJECTIVE

Sadiq is a quiet, studious boy.
hard-working, diligent, scholarly, academic, bookish

study VERB

1 *She spent a year abroad studying French.*
learn about, read, be taught

2 *Scientists are studying the effects of acid rain.*
research, investigate, examine, analyse, survey, review

3 *studying for your exams*
revise, cram
(British informal) swot

4 *Holmes studied the handwriting carefully.*
examine, inspect, scrutinize, look closely at, peer at

study NOUN

1 *after four long years of study*
learning, education, schooling, tuition, research

2 *a new study of reading habits*
investigation, examination, analysis, review, survey, enquiry (into)

3 *Darwin used this room as his study.*
workroom, office, studio

Usage Note

Words which mean 'the scientific study' of a subject often end with **-logy** or **-ology**, for example *cosmology*, *criminology*, and *mineralogy*.

stuff NOUN

1 *little spots of sticky stuff*
material, substance, matter

2 *a cupboard crammed full of stuff*
things, odds and ends, bits and pieces, paraphernalia

3 *(informal) Where can I put my stuff?*
belongings, possessions, things
(informal) gear

stuff VERB

1 *The cushions are stuffed with foam rubber.*
fill, pad, upholster

2 *Sam stuffed all the papers into a drawer.*
shove, push, thrust, force, squeeze, jam, pack, ram

stuffing NOUN

pillows with hypo-allergenic stuffing
filling, padding, wadding

a
b
c
d
e
f
g
h
i
j
k
l
m
n
o
p
q
r
s
t
u
v
w
x
y
z

stuffy *ADJECTIVE*

  1 *a stuffy room with no windows*
airless, close, humid, stifling, musty, unventilated
    OPPOSITE airy

  2 *I find the writing style a bit stuffy.*
pompous, starchy, staid, old-fashioned, dull, dreary
    OPPOSITES lively, fresh

stumble *VERB*

  1 *Nat stumbled backwards and fell over a chair.*
trip, lose your footing, stagger, totter, flounder, lurch

  2 *She stumbled over her opening lines.*
stammer, stutter, falter, hesitate

  ▷ **stumble across something**
I stumbled across some old photos.
come across, find, unearth, discover, happen on

stumped *ADJECTIVE*

  Detective Inspector Riley was totally stumped.
baffled, bewildered, puzzled, perplexed, mystified, at a loss
(informal) flummoxed

stun *VERB*

  1 *Scorpions use their venom to stun their prey.*
daze, make unconscious, knock out, knock senseless

  2 *The whole town was stunned by the news.*
amaze, astonish, astound, shock, stagger, stupefy, bewilder, dumbfound

stunning *ADJECTIVE*

  stunning images of the Earth from space
spectacular, breathtaking, glorious, magnificent, gorgeous, superb, sublime, awesome

stunt *NOUN*

  a breathtaking acrobatic stunt
feat, exploit, act, trick

stupid *ADJECTIVE*

  1 *I'm feeling particularly stupid today.*
dense, dim, dim-witted, brainless, unintelligent, slow, dopey, dull, simple, feeble-minded, half-witted
(informal) thick
    OPPOSITE intelligent

  2 *It was a stupid idea anyway.*
foolish, silly, idiotic, senseless, mindless, foolhardy, unwise, ill-advised, mad, crazy, hare-brained
(British informal) daft
    OPPOSITE sensible

sturdy *ADJECTIVE*

  1 *Clem was tall and sturdy for his age.*
well-built, strapping, muscular, strong, robust, brawny, burly, powerful, solid
    OPPOSITES weak, puny

  2 *a pair of sturdy walking boots*
robust, strong, tough, stout, hard-wearing, durable, substantial
    OPPOSITE flimsy

stutter *VERB*

  He tends to stutter when he's nervous.
stammer, stumble, falter

style *NOUN*

  1 *What style of shoes are you looking for?*
design, pattern, fashion

  2 *The author's style is quite readable.*
manner, tone, technique, wording

  3 *She always dresses with great style.*
elegance, stylishness, taste, sophistication, flair

stylish *ADJECTIVE*

  Warren always manages to look stylish.
fashionable, elegant, chic, smart, sophisticated, tasteful, dapper
(informal) trendy, natty, snazzy
    OPPOSITES unfashionable, dowdy

subdue *VERB*

  1 *The aim in judo is to subdue your opponent without harm.*
conquer, defeat, overcome,

overpower, beat, vanquish,
subjugate

2 *She struggled to subdue her true
feelings.*
suppress, restrain, repress, check,
hold back, curb, control

subject NOUN

1 *discussing an important subject*
matter, issue, question, point,
theme, topic, concern

2 *a new subject of scientific study*
area, field, discipline, topic

3 *the rights of foreign subjects*
citizen, national

subject ADJECTIVE

▷ **be subject to**
an island that is subject to hurricanes
be prone to, be given to, be affected
by, be liable to

subject VERB

▷ **subject someone to**
*All recruits are subjected to rigorous
training.*
put through, force to undergo,
expose to, lay open to

submerge VERB

1 *The shark cages can submerge to a
depth of 40 feet.*
go under water, go down, sink, dive,
plunge
OPPOSITE surface

2 *The land bridge was submerged after
the Ice Age.*
flood, engulf, immerse, inundate,
swallow up, swamp

submit VERB

1 *Most of the Celtic tribes were forced
to submit.*
surrender, give in, yield, capitulate

2 *submitting an application form*
put forward, hand in, present, enter,
offer, propose

▷ **submit to someone**
*The colonists were unwilling to
submit to British rule.*
be governed by, abide by, comply
with, consent to

subordinate ADJECTIVE

a subordinate place in the food chain
lesser, lower, inferior, junior
OPPOSITES superior, higher

subscribe VERB

▷ **subscribe to something**

1 *How do you subscribe to the mailing
list?*
become a member of, sign up to,
enlist in
OPPOSITE unsubscribe

2 *I no longer subscribe to that view.*
support, endorse, go along with

subsequent ADJECTIVE

*the novel and the subsequent film
version*
following, later, succeeding,
ensuing, next
OPPOSITE previous

subside VERB

1 *Venice is slowly subsiding into the
lagoon.*
sink, settle, give way, collapse

2 *The flood waters will eventually
subside.*
recede, ebb, go down, fall, decline

3 *The pain should subside in a day or
two.*
decrease, diminish, lessen, ease, die
down, dwindle

substance NOUN

1 *A diamond is the hardest substance
on Earth.*
material, matter, stuff

2 *There are a few changes in the
substance of the book.*
content, subject matter, essence,
gist

substantial ADJECTIVE

1 *making substantial changes to the
script*
considerable, significant, sizeable,
important, major, real, appreciable,
sweeping, generous, worthwhile
OPPOSITES minor, insignificant

2 *a substantial door of solid wood*
strong, sturdy, solid, robust, stout,

a
b
c
d
e
f
g
h
i
j
k
l
m
n
o
p
q
r
s
t
u
v
w
x
y
z

hefty, durable, sound, well-built
OPPOSITE flimsy

substitute NOUN

He came on as a substitute in extra time.
replacement, reserve, standby, stand-in
(informal) sub
▶ Someone who can take the place of an actor is an **understudy**.

substitute VERB

Try substituting sugar with honey.
exchange, replace, swap, switch
▷ **substitute for someone**
Other players may substitute for an injured teammate.
stand in for, take the place of, deputize for, cover for

subtle ADJECTIVE

1 a subtle shade of grey
faint, delicate, soft, gentle, pale, mild, subdued, muted
OPPOSITES strong, bright
2 detecting subtle changes in the atmosphere
slight, gradual, negligible, minute, fine
OPPOSITE pronounced
3 I tried to give her a subtle hint.
gentle, tactful, indirect
OPPOSITE obvious

subtract VERB

Subtract this number from your final score.
take away, deduct, remove
OPPOSITE add

suburbs PLURAL NOUN

living in the suburbs of Melbourne
outskirts, outer areas, fringes, suburbia
▶ People who live in the suburbs are **suburbanites**.

succeed VERB

1 Somehow he never managed to succeed in life.
be successful, do well, prosper,

flourish, thrive
(informal) make it
2 No one thought the plan would succeed.
be effective, work out, turn out well
(informal) come off
OPPOSITE fail
3 the question of who would succeed the president
come after, follow, take over from, replace
OPPOSITE precede

success NOUN

1 She talked about her success as an author.
achievement, attainment, fame
2 an incredible run of success
victory, win, triumph
3 The success of the mission depends on us.
effectiveness, successful outcome
OPPOSITE failure
4 The show was a runaway success.
hit, best-seller, winner
(informal) smash, smash hit

successful ADJECTIVE

1 He owns a successful chain of restaurants.
thriving, flourishing, booming, prosperous, profitable, lucrative, popular
2 A trophy is awarded to the successful team.
winning, victorious, triumphant
OPPOSITE unsuccessful

succession NOUN

a succession of hoax emails
series, sequence, run, string, chain, trail

successive ADJECTIVE

aiming for a third successive win
consecutive, uninterrupted, in succession, in a row, running

suck VERB

1 Salt tends to suck moisture from the air.
soak up, draw up, absorb

2 *being sucked into a black hole*
pull in, draw in
OPPOSITE push out

sudden *ADJECTIVE*

1 *a sudden urge to burst into song*
unexpected, unforeseen, impulsive,
rash, quick
OPPOSITE expected

2 *The bus came to a sudden halt.*
abrupt, sharp, rapid, swift
OPPOSITE gradual

suffer *VERB*

1 *I hate to see animals suffer.*
be in pain, hurt, be in distress

2 *The team suffered a humiliating
defeat.*
experience, undergo, go through, be
subjected to, endure, face

3 *The quality of her work has suffered.*
be damaged, be impaired, diminish,
decline, dip

▷ **suffer from something**
He suffers from a severe nut allergy.
be afflicted by, be troubled with,
have

suffering *NOUN*

*a story of wartime suffering and
courage*
hardship, deprivation, misery,
anguish, pain, distress, affliction,
trauma

sufficient *ADJECTIVE*

Make sure you get sufficient sleep.
enough, adequate, ample, plenty of
OPPOSITE insufficient

suffix *NOUN*

a list of common English suffixes
OPPOSITE prefix

suffocate *VERB*

*Most of the casualties were
suffocated by smoke.*
choke, asphyxiate, stifle, smother

suggest *VERB*

1 *asking viewers to suggest a name for
the show*
propose, put forward, nominate,
recommend, advocate, advise

2 *Readings suggest that the volcano is
still active.*
indicate, signify, show, imply, hint

suggestion *NOUN*

1 *Does anyone have an alternative
suggestion?*
proposal, plan, idea, proposition,
recommendation

2 *There was no suggestion of foul play.*
indication, sign, hint, trace,
suspicion, implication

suit *VERB*

1 *Which date would suit you best?*
be convenient for, be suitable for,
please, satisfy
OPPOSITE displease

2 *That colour really suits you.*
look good on, become, flatter

suitable *ADJECTIVE*

1 *films suitable for a teenage audience*
appropriate, apt, fitting, fit, suited
(to), right
OPPOSITE unsuitable

2 *finding a suitable time to meet*
convenient, acceptable, satisfactory
OPPOSITE inconvenient

sulk *VERB*

*Sara was still sulking and wouldn't
join in.*
be sullen, mope, brood, pout

sulky *ADJECTIVE*

*Josh was turning into a sulky
teenager.*
moody, sullen, brooding, moping,
grumpy

sullen *ADJECTIVE*

The rest of us ate in sullen silence.
sulky, moody, bad-tempered, surly,
sour
OPPOSITES cheerful,
good-tempered

sum *NOUN*

1 *the sum of the remaining numbers*
total, tally, aggregate

2 *doing a complicated sum in your
head*

calculation, addition, problem

3 *spending vast sums of money*
amount, quantity

❙ **SEE ALSO mathematics**

sum VERB

▷ **sum up**
*Let me sum up the situation as
I see it.*
summarize, outline, review
(informal) recap

summarize VERB

*Can you summarize the main points
of the story?*
sum up, outline, condense, abridge

❙ **IDIOM** put in a nutshell

summary NOUN

Give a brief summary of your idea.
synopsis, precis, abstract, outline,
overview, rundown

summit NOUN

the summit of Mount Kilimanjaro
top, peak, crown, cap, tip, apex

❙ **OPPOSITE** base

summon VERB

1 *The king summoned Beowulf to the
great hall.*
call for, send for, ask for,
bid to come

2 *I finally summoned the courage to
phone.*
gather, rally, muster

sun NOUN

Lizards bask in the sun to get warm.
sunshine, sunlight

▶ To sit or lie in the sun is to **sunbathe**.

⚛ WORD WEB

▶ The centre of the Sun is called the
core and the surface layer is the
photosphere.

▶ Dark spots which form on the
Sun's surface are **sunspots**.

▶ A related adjective is **solar**.
solar energy

▶ An explosion of hot gas from the
Sun is a **solar flare** and streams of
gas flowing out from the Sun are
solar wind.

▶ The **solstice** occurs twice a year,
when the Sun is at its furthest
point north or south of the
equator.

▶ The **equinox** occurs twice a
year, when the Sun is positioned
vertically above the equator.

❙ **SEE ALSO planet, space**

sunlight NOUN

plants which need a lot of sunlight
daylight, sun, sunshine

▶ Rays of light from the sun are
sunbeams.

sunny ADJECTIVE

1 *a sunny afternoon*
bright, clear, cloudless, fine

❙ **OPPOSITES** dull, overcast

**FOR TIPS ON DESCRIBING WEATHER SEE
weather**

2 *a sunny spot in the garden*
sunlit, sun-baked, sun-drenched,
sun-kissed

❙ **OPPOSITE** shady

3 *a naturally sunny nature*
cheerful, happy, bright, joyful,
merry, jolly
(informal) upbeat

❙ **OPPOSITES** sad, melancholy

sunrise NOUN

*At sunrise the werewolf will revert to
human form.*
dawn, daybreak, first light
(literary) break of day
(North American) sunup

❙ **OPPOSITE** sunset

sunset NOUN

*At sunset the cliffs are tinted red and
gold.*
nightfall, dusk, twilight, close of day
(North American) sundown

❙ **OPPOSITE** sunrise

superb ADJECTIVE

The Brazilian scored a superb late goal.

excellent, outstanding, exceptional, tremendous, marvellous, wonderful, fine, superior, superlative, top-notch *(informal)* brilliant, fantastic, terrific, fabulous, sensational, super

OPPOSITES bad, terrible

superficial ADJECTIVE

1 *a superficial scratch on the paintwork*

on the surface, shallow, slight

OPPOSITE deep

2 *a superficial discussion of race and gender*

trivial, lightweight, shallow, frivolous, casual, facile

OPPOSITES thorough, profound

superfluous ADJECTIVE

Get rid of any superfluous words.

excess, unnecessary, redundant, surplus, spare, unwanted

OPPOSITE necessary

superior ADJECTIVE

1 *a superior officer*

senior, higher-ranking

OPPOSITES inferior, junior

2 *a superior standard of accommodation*

first-class, first-rate, top, top-notch, choice, select, finest, best

OPPOSITES inferior, substandard

3 *I don't like his superior attitude.*

arrogant, haughty, snobbish, self-important, supercilious *(informal)* snooty, stuck-up

IDIOM high and mighty

supernatural ADJECTIVE

The runes are said to have supernatural power.

magic, magical, miraculous, mystical, paranormal, occult

OPPOSITE natural

supersede VERB

Will robots ever supersede humans?

replace, take over from, supplant, succeed

supervise VERB

Miss Williams was left to supervise the class.

oversee, superintend, watch over, be in charge of, be responsible for, direct, manage, preside over

IDIOM keep an eye on

▶ To supervise candidates in an exam is to **invigilate**.

supple ADJECTIVE

1 *shoes made of supple leather*

flexible, pliable, soft

OPPOSITES stiff, rigid

2 *keeping your body supple*

agile, nimble, flexible, lithe

supplement NOUN

1 *a dietary supplement*

add-on, extra, addition, adjunct

2 *This edition includes a special supplement.*

appendix, addendum, insert, pull-out

supplement VERB

taking vitamins to supplement your diet

add to, top up, augment, increase, enlarge, boost

supply VERB

1 *The aqueduct supplied Rome with water.*

provide, furnish, endow, equip

▶ To supply someone with weapons is to **arm** them.

2 *They grow enough food to supply their needs.*

satisfy, meet, fulfil, cater for

supply NOUN

a good supply of fuel for the winter

quantity, stock, store, reserve, cache, hoard

▷ **supplies**

I bought some supplies for the trip.

provisions, stores, rations, food, necessities

support VERB

1 *Timber beams support the roof.*
hold up, prop up, underpin, buttress, reinforce

2 *How much weight will the bridge support?*
bear, carry, stand

3 *Many Highland clans supported the Jacobite cause.*
back, favour, advocate, champion, promote, endorse, espouse

4 *a charity which supports children in need*
help, aid, assist, stand by, rally round

5 *the need to support a growing family*
provide for, maintain, keep, sustain

support NOUN

1 *She thanked her family for their support.*
backing, encouragement, aid, help, assistance

2 *The stadium was built with support from the Lottery.*
donations, contributions, sponsorship, subsidy, funds

3 *The shelves rest on wooden supports.*
prop, brace, bracket, strut, upright, post

▶ A support built against a wall is a **buttress**.

▶ A support put under a board to make a table is a **trestle**.

supporter NOUN

1 *a crowd of home supporters*
fan, follower

2 *a well-known supporter of animal rights*
champion, advocate, backer, defender, upholder, promoter

suppose VERB

1 *I suppose you're wondering why I'm here.*
expect, presume, assume, guess
┃ IDIOMS I take it, I dare say

2 *Suppose you could travel back in time.*
imagine, pretend, let's say

▷ **be supposed to do something**
Traditionally, ghosts are not supposed to speak.
be meant to, be expected to, be due to, ought to, should

suppress VERB

1 *a dictator who ruthlessly suppressed all opposition*
crush, quash, quell, curb, put down, stamp out, crack down on

2 *Charlotte could not suppress a smile.*
check, hold back, stifle, restrain, repress, bottle up, contain

▶ To suppress ideas for political or moral reasons is to **censor** them.

supreme ADJECTIVE

1 *the supreme commander of the armed forces*
highest, superior, chief, head, top, principal, foremost, prime

2 *Catherine made a supreme effort to stay awake.*
extreme, enormous, very great, exceptional, extraordinary, remarkable

sure ADJECTIVE

1 *Are you sure this is the right address?*
certain, positive, confident, definite, convinced, satisfied
┃ OPPOSITES unsure, uncertain

2 *She's sure to find out eventually.*
bound, likely, certain
┃ OPPOSITE unlikely

3 *a sure sign of an approaching storm*
clear, definite, certain, reliable, undeniable, unambiguous
┃ OPPOSITES unclear, doubtful

surface NOUN

1 *The marble is given a highly polished surface.*
exterior, outside, top, finish

▶ A thin surface of good wood on furniture is a **veneer**.
┃ OPPOSITES inside, interior

2 *the four surfaces of a cube*
face, side

surface VERB

1 *a road surfaced with loose chippings*
cover, coat, finish

2 *A dolphin surfaced a few feet away.*
rise to the surface, come up, emerge
(informal) pop up

surge VERB

1 *Huge waves surged over the sea wall.*
rise, roll, heave, billow, sweep, burst

2 *Without warning, the crowd surged forward.*
rush, push, sweep

surge NOUN

1 *feeling a surge of emotion*
rush, wave, sweep, torrent

2 *an unexpected surge in sales*
rise, increase, growth, escalation, upswing

surly ADJECTIVE

The landlord muttered a surly greeting.
bad-tempered, unfriendly, sullen, sulky, grumpy, churlish

surpass VERB

This trip has surpassed all my expectations.
beat, better, exceed, do better than, improve on, outdo, outshine, eclipse

surplus NOUN

We have a surplus of tomatoes from our garden.
excess, surfeit, glut, oversupply, superfluity
▎**OPPOSITES** shortage, dearth

surplus ADJECTIVE

The body stores surplus food as fat.
excess, superfluous, spare, unneeded, unwanted, leftover

surprise NOUN

1 *The news came as a complete surprise.*
revelation, shock
(informal) bombshell, eye-opener
▎**IDIOM** bolt from the blue

2 *To my surprise, I passed the audition.*
amazement, astonishment, bewilderment, disbelief

surprised ADJECTIVE

They seemed genuinely surprised to see me.
amazed, astonished, astounded, taken aback, startled, stunned, dumbfounded
(informal) flabbergasted

surprising ADJECTIVE

Our experiment produced a surprising result.
unexpected, unforeseen, extraordinary, astonishing, remarkable, incredible, staggering, startling
▎**OPPOSITES** expected, predictable

surrender VERB

1 *The British army was forced to surrender at Yorktown.*
admit defeat, give in, yield, submit, capitulate

2 *He was asked to surrender his passport to the authorities.*
give, hand over, relinquish

surround VERB

1 *The vineyard is surrounded by a dry stone wall.*
enclose, fence in, wall in

2 *Armed police have surrounded the building.*
encircle, ring, hem in, besiege

surrounding ADJECTIVE

people from the surrounding villages
neighbouring, nearby, adjoining, adjacent

surroundings PLURAL NOUN

These new robots can adapt to their surroundings.
environment, setting, location, habitat

survey NOUN

1 *a survey of local opinion*
review, enquiry, poll, investigation, study

▶ A survey to count the population of an area is a **census**.

»

2 *a detailed survey of the house*
inspection, examination

survey VERB

1 *Connie stood at the door, surveying the mess.*
view, look over, look at, gaze at, scan, observe, contemplate

2 *The team will survey the Antarctic coastline.*
inspect, examine, explore, scrutinize, study, map out

▶ Surveying an area in search of minerals is **prospecting**.

survive VERB

1 *A queen bee can survive for up to five years.*
stay alive, live, last, keep going, carry on, hold out, pull through
OPPOSITE die

2 *plants which can survive drought*
endure, withstand, cope with, live through, weather

3 *Few of the ancient traditions survive.*
remain, continue, persist, endure, abide

4 *She survived her husband by ten years.*
outlive, outlast

suspect VERB

1 *No one could possibly suspect him.*
doubt, mistrust, have suspicions about, have misgivings about, have qualms about

2 *I suspect we may never know the truth.*
have a feeling, think, imagine, presume, guess, sense, fancy

suspend VERB

1 *The tree house seemed to be suspended in mid-air.*
hang, dangle, sling, swing

2 *Play was suspended until the next day.*
adjourn, break off, discontinue, interrupt

suspense NOUN

The suspense will have you on the edge of your seat.

tension, uncertainty, anticipation, expectancy, drama, excitement

suspicion NOUN

1 *Something she said aroused my suspicions.*
distrust, doubt, misgiving, qualm, reservation

2 *Ted had a suspicion that something was wrong.*
feeling, hunch, inkling, intuition, impression, notion, fancy
IDIOM gut feeling

suspicious ADJECTIVE

1 *The two men became deeply suspicious of each other.*
doubtful, distrustful, mistrustful, unsure, uneasy, wary
OPPOSITE trusting

2 *There's something suspicious about this email.*
questionable, suspect, dubious, irregular, funny, shady
(informal) fishy

sustain VERB

1 *Bears need body fat to sustain them through their winter.*
keep alive, keep going, nurture, nourish, provide for

2 *Somehow the film manages to sustain your interest.*
maintain, preserve, keep up, hold onto, retain, prolong

3 *The driver sustained only minor injuries.*
suffer, receive, experience, undergo

4 *How much weight will the roof sustain?*
support, bear, carry, stand

swagger VERB

The lead guitarist swaggered about on stage.
strut, parade

swallow VERB

Pythons can swallow a whole goat or sheep.
gulp down
SEE ALSO eat, drink

▷ **swallow something up**

The summit was soon swallowed up by clouds.

envelop, engulf, cover over, absorb

swamp NOUN

The area around the lake used to be a swamp.

marsh, bog, mire, fen, quicksand, quagmire

swamp VERB

1 *Their boat was swamped by heavy waves.*

flood, engulf, inundate, deluge, submerge

2 *Our phone lines have been swamped with calls.*

overwhelm, bombard, inundate, deluge, snow under

swan NOUN

a flock of migrating swans

▶ A male swan is a **cob**.

▶ A young swan is a **cygnet**.

⌐ SEE ALSO **bird**

swap or **swop** (informal) VERB

I swapped my ticket with a friend.

exchange, switch, trade, substitute

▶ To exchange goods for other goods without using money is to **barter**.

swarm NOUN

a swarm of eager reporters

crowd, mob, army, pack, throng

swarm VERB

Fans and photographers swarmed around her.

crowd, flock, mob, throng, cluster

▷ **swarm with**

The city centre was swarming with tourists.

be overrun by, teem with, be inundated with, be crawling with

sway VERB

1 *swaying to the rhythm of the music*

move to and fro, swing, rock, wave, undulate

2 *trying to sway public opinion*

influence, affect, manipulate, bias

swear VERB

1 *Do you swear never to tell anyone?*

promise, pledge, vow, give your word, take an oath

2 *Mr Uttley muttered and swore under his breath.*

curse, blaspheme, use bad language

sweat NOUN

A bead of sweat trickled down her nose.

perspiration

sweat VERB

I began to sweat in the heat of the bus.

perspire

sweaty ADJECTIVE

The dance floor was packed with sweaty bodies.

sweating, perspiring, clammy, sticky, moist

sweep VERB

1 *sweeping the flagstones with a broom*

brush, clean, dust

2 *the dangers of being swept out to sea*

carry, pull, drag, tow

3 *The President's motorcade swept past.*

speed, shoot, zoom, glide, breeze

4 *A series of wildfires swept the continent.*

spread across, engulf

▷ **sweep something away**

The floods swept away roads and bridges.

carry off, clear away, remove, get rid of

sweet ADJECTIVE

1 *Would you prefer sweet or salty popcorn?*

sugary, sugared, sweetened, syrupy

▶ Something that is overly sweet is **sickly** or **cloying**.

▶ To make food sweet is to **sweeten** it.

⌐ OPPOSITES sour, savoury

2 *the sweet smell of magnolia*

fragrant, aromatic,

perfumed, pleasant
❙ OPPOSITE foul

3 *the sweet sound of a saxophone*
mellow, melodious, soft, pleasant,
soothing, tuneful, dulcet
❙ OPPOSITES harsh, ugly

4 *Baby elephants are so sweet!*
charming, delightful, lovable,
adorable, endearing, cuddly
(informal) cute

sweet NOUN

1 *a packet of sweets*
(informal) sweetie
(North American) candy
▶ Sweets in general are **confectionery**
and a person who makes or sells
sweets is a **confectioner**.

2 *There is apple pie for sweet.*
dessert, pudding
(informal) afters

swell VERB

1 *Yeast causes the dough to rise and
swell.*
expand, bulge, distend, dilate,
inflate, puff up, fill out, balloon,
billow
❙ OPPOSITE shrink

2 *as the population of the world has
swollen*
grow, increase, expand, enlarge, rise,
escalate, mushroom
❙ OPPOSITE shrink

swelling NOUN

a painful swelling on the horse's leg
inflammation, lump, bump, growth,
tumour

swerve VERB

*The car swerved to avoid a
pedestrian.*
turn aside, veer, dodge, swing

swift ADJECTIVE

1 *a system which allows swift web
browsing*
fast, quick, rapid, speedy, brisk,
lively
❙ OPPOSITES slow, unhurried

2 *Her reply was swift and to the point*

prompt, quick, immediate, instant,
speedy, snappy
❙ OPPOSITES slow, tardy

swim VERB

swimming in the deep end of the pool
go swimming, bathe, take a dip
▶ A person who is unable to swim is a
non-swimmer.

 WORD WEB

common swimming strokes

backstroke, breaststroke,
butterfly or fly, dog paddle or
doggy paddle, freestyle, front
crawl, sculling, sidestroke,
treading water

swindle VERB

*They were swindled out of their life
savings.*
cheat, trick, dupe, fleece
(informal) con, diddle

swing VERB

1 *A rusty old sign swung and creaked
in the wind.*
sway, move to and fro, flap, rock,
swivel, pivot, oscillate

2 *She swung her bag over her shoulder
and walked away.*
sling, hang, suspend, string

3 *The road swings sharply to the right.*
bend, curve, turn, twist, veer,
swerve, deviate

swing NOUN

1 *measuring the swing of a pendulum*
swaying, oscillation

2 *a climate with wide swings in
temperature*
change, variation, fluctuation

swipe VERB

1 *The crocodile nearly swiped us with
its tail.*
slash, lash, hit, strike, swing at

2 *(informal) Who swiped my pen?*
steal, snatch
(informal) make off with
(British informal) nick, pinch

swirl VERB
The tide was now swirling around their knees.
whirl, spin, twirl, churn, eddy

switch VERB
1 *How do you switch off your phone?*
turn
2 *a story in which two men switch identities*
exchange, swap, change, shift

swivel VERB
Dr Wallace swivelled round in her chair.
spin, turn, twirl, pivot, revolve, rotate

swollen ADJECTIVE
Erin's eyes were swollen from crying.
inflamed, bloated, puffed up, puffy

swoop VERB
1 *a heron swooping down to catch a fish*
dive, plunge, plummet, pounce, descend
2 *Police swooped on the house in the early hours.*
raid, attack, storm

swop VERB
SEE **swap**

sword NOUN
an ancient Samurai sword
blade, foil, rapier, sabre
▶ Fighting with swords is **fencing** or **swordsmanship**.
⌐ SEE ALSO **weapon**

symbol NOUN
1 *A heart is a symbol of love.*
sign, emblem, image, representation, token
2 *the symbol of the United Nations*
emblem, insignia, badge, crest, logo
3 *a stone covered in runic symbols*
character, letter, mark
▶ The symbols used in ancient Egyptian writing were **hieroglyphics**.

symbolize VERB
What does the rose symbolize in the poem?
represent, stand for, signify, indicate, mean, denote

sympathetic ADJECTIVE
1 *I longed to hear a sympathetic voice.*
understanding, compassionate, concerned, caring, comforting, kind, supportive
⌐ OPPOSITE unsympathetic
2 *Is the main character portrayed as sympathetic?*
likeable, appealing, agreeable, congenial, amiable
⌐ OPPOSITE unsympathetic

sympathize VERB
▷ **sympathize with**
You could at least sympathize with me!
feel sorry for, feel for, commiserate with

sympathy NOUN
It's hard to feel sympathy for any of the characters.
compassion, understanding, concern, fellow-feeling

synonym NOUN
'Inter' is a synonym of 'bury'.
⌐ OPPOSITE antonym

synthetic ADJECTIVE
nylon and other synthetic fabrics
artificial, man-made, manufactured, imitation
⌐ OPPOSITE natural

system NOUN
1 *a modern and efficient railway system*
network, organization, structure, framework, arrangement, complex
(informal) set-up
2 *using a new cataloguing system*
method, procedure, process, scheme, technique, routine, plan

a
b
c
d
e
f
g
h
i
j
k
l
m
n
o
p
q
r
s
t
u
v
w
x
y
z

systematic *ADJECTIVE*

a systematic search of the crime scene
methodical, orderly, structured,
organized, logical, scientific
| **OPPOSITE** unsystematic

Tt

table *NOUN*
> *Here is the full table of results.*
> chart, plan, list

tablet *NOUN*
> 1 *a glucose tablet*
> pill, capsule, pellet
> 2 *The Epic of Gilgamesh was carved on stone tablets.*
> slab, plaque

tack *VERB*
> 1 *tacking down a loose carpet*
> nail, pin
> 2 *tacking up the hem of a skirt*
> sew, stitch, baste
> ▷ **tack something on**
> *a conservatory tacked onto the house*
> add, attach, append, join on, tag on

tackle *VERB*
> 1 *Four jets of water were used to tackle the blaze.*
> deal with, attend to, handle, manage, grapple with
> 2 *a play which tackles the issue of bullying*
> address, look at, engage with
> ▌ **IDIOM** get to grips with
> 3 *You can only tackle a player with the ball.*
> challenge, intercept, take on

tackle *NOUN*
> 1 *a box of fishing tackle*
> gear, equipment, apparatus, kit
> 2 *The player was sent off for a late tackle.*
> challenge, interception

tactful *ADJECTIVE*
> *I tried to think of a tactful way to say no.*
> subtle, discreet, delicate, diplomatic, sensitive, thoughtful
> ▌ **OPPOSITE** tactless

tactics *PLURAL NOUN*
> *The other team changed tactics at half-time.*
> strategy, moves, manoeuvres, plan of action

tag *NOUN*
> *removing the price tag*
> label, sticker, ticket, tab

tag *VERB*
> *Every item is tagged with a bar code.*
> label, mark, identify, flag
> ▷ **tag along with someone**
> *Susie tagged along with us for a while.*
> accompany, follow, go with, join
> ▷ **tag something on**
> *How do I tag a signature onto an email?*
> add, attach, append, join on, tack on

tail *NOUN*
> *You'll have to join the tail of the queue.*
> end, back, rear
> ▌ **OPPOSITES** front, head

tail *VERB*
> *(informal) They tailed the suspect to this address.*
> follow, pursue, track, trail, shadow, stalk
> ▷ **tail off**
> *Audiences slowly began to tail off.*
> decrease, decline, lessen, diminish, dwindle, wane

taint *VERB*
> *He was forever after tainted with suspicion.*
> tarnish, stain, sully, blot, blight, damage, spoil, mar

a
b
c
d
e
f
g
h
i
j
k
l
m
n
o
p
q
r
s
t
u
v
w
x
y
z

take *VERB*

1 *Clara took her sister's hand.*
clutch, clasp, take hold of, grasp, grip, seize, snatch, grab

2 *Thousands of Africans were taken as slaves.*
capture, seize, detain

3 *Morgan took an envelope from his pocket.*
remove, withdraw, pull, extract

4 *Has someone taken my calculator?*
steal
(informal) swipe, make off with
(British informal) nick, pinch

5 *I'll take you upstairs to your room.*
conduct, escort, lead, accompany, guide, show, usher

6 *Would you like me to take your luggage?*
carry, convey, bring, bear, transport, ferry

7 *Take any seat you like.*
pick, choose, select

8 *Each cable car can take eight passengers.*
hold, contain, accommodate, have room for

9 *Are you taking any exams this year?*
sit
(informal) go in for

10 *I can't take much more of this.*
bear, put up with, stand, endure, tolerate, suffer, stomach

11 *It'll take decades for the forest to recover.*
need, require

12 *Let me take you name and phone number.*
make a note of, record, register, write down, jot down

13 *Take the total sum from the original number.*
subtract, take away, deduct, discount

▷ **take after someone**
Do you think she takes after her mother?
resemble, look like, remind someone of

▷ **IDIOMS** be the spitting image of, be a dead ringer for

▷ **take someone in**
No one was taken in by his story.
fool, deceive, trick, cheat, dupe, hoodwink

▷ **take something in**
I was too tired to take it all in.
understand, comprehend, grasp, absorb, follow

▷ **take off**

1 *Our plane took off on time.*
lift off, blast off, depart

2 *Social networking has really taken off.*
become popular, catch on, do well, prosper

▷ **take something off**
Please take off your coats.
remove, strip off, peel off

▷ **take part in something**
Everyone has to take part in the show.
participate in, be involved in, join in

▷ **take place**
Where exactly did the accident take place?
happen, occur, come about

▷ **take to something**
How are you taking to life in the city?
like, cope with, get on with

▷ **take something up**

1 *I hear you've taken up judo.*
begin to do, start learning

2 *This software takes up a lot of space.*
use up, fill up, occupy, require

3 *I decided to take up their offer.*
accept, agree to, say yes to

tale *NOUN*

a tale of love and betrayal
story, narrative, account, legend, fable, saga
(informal) yarn

talent *NOUN*

She shows a real talent for drawing.
gift, ability, aptitude, skill, flair, knack, forte

a b c d e f g h i j k l m n o p q r s t u v w x y z

▶ Unusually great talent is **genius**.

talented *ADJECTIVE*

> *He's a very talented actor.*
> gifted, able, accomplished, capable, skilled, skilful, brilliant, expert

▶ Someone who is talented in several ways is said to be **versatile**.

⌐ **OPPOSITE** inept

talk *VERB*

1 *One day computers will be able to talk.*
speak, say things, communicate, express yourself

2 *You two must have a lot to talk about.*
discuss, converse, chat, chatter, gossip
(British informal) natter

3 *The prisoner refused to talk.*
give information, confess

⌐ **SEE ALSO say**

talk *NOUN*

1 *I need to have a talk with you soon.*
conversation, discussion, chat, tête-à-tête
(informal) confab
(British informal) chinwag

▶ Talk between characters in a play, film, or novel is **dialogue**.

2 *a series of lunchtime talks*
lecture, presentation, speech, address

3 *There was talk of witchcraft in the village.*
rumour, gossip

talkative *ADJECTIVE*

> *You're not very talkative this morning.*
chatty, communicative, vocal, forthcoming, loquacious, garrulous

⌐ **OPPOSITE** taciturn

tall *ADJECTIVE*

1 *Hazel is tall for her age.*
big, giant, towering

▶ Someone who is awkwardly tall and thin is **lanky** or **gangling**.

⌐ **OPPOSITE** short

FOR TIPS ON DESCRIBING BODIES SEE **body**

2 *Singapore has many tall buildings.*
high, lofty, towering, soaring, giant

▶ Buildings with many floors are **high-rise** or **multi-storey** buildings.

⌐ **OPPOSITE** low

tally *VERB*

▷ **tally with**
This doesn't tally with your previous answer.
agree with, correspond with, match

tame *ADJECTIVE*

1 *These guinea pigs are tame and do not bite.*
domesticated, broken in, docile, gentle, manageable, trained

⌐ **OPPOSITE** wild

2 *The film seems very tame nowadays.*
dull, unexciting, unadventurous, boring, bland, insipid, humdrum

⌐ **OPPOSITES** exciting, adventurous

tame *VERB*

1 *trying to tame a wild horse*
domesticate, break in, subdue, master

2 *learning how to tame your fears*
control, restrain, curb, subdue, temper, discipline

tamper *VERB*

▷ **tamper with something**
accused of tampering with the evidence
meddle with, tinker with, interfere with, doctor

tang *NOUN*

> *the salty tang of sea air*
sharpness, zest, zing

tangle *VERB*

1 *The tree roots were tangled into a solid mass.*
entangle, twist, knot, jumble, muddle

▶ Tangled hair is **dishevelled** or **matted** hair.

»

a
b
c
d
e
f
g
h
i
j
k
l
m
n
o
p
q
r
s
t
u
v
w
x
y
z

2 *Dolphins can get tangled in fishing nets.*
catch, trap, ensnare

tangle NOUN
a tangle of electric cables
muddle, jumble, knot, twist, confusion

tap❶ NOUN
Turn the tap to the off position.
valve, stopcock

tap VERB
He claims that his phone is being tapped.
bug, record, monitor, intercept

tap❷ NOUN
I thought I heard a tap on the window.
knock, rap, pat, strike

tap VERB
Chris tapped out a rhythm on the table.
knock, strike, rap, pat, drum

tape NOUN
1 *a piece of elastic tape*
band, ribbon, braid, binding, string
2 *I accidentally wiped over the tape.*
recording, video, audio cassette

tape VERB
1 *A note was taped to the window.*
stick, attach, fix, glue, bind
2 *Did you remember to tape the programme?*
record, video

target NOUN
1 *Our target is to raise £5000.*
goal, aim, objective, intention, purpose, hope, ambition
2 *the target of a hate campaign*
object, victim, butt, focus, recipient

tarnish VERB
1 *The mirror had tarnished with age.*
discolour, corrode, rust
2 *The scandal tarnished his reputation.*
stain, taint, sully, blot, blacken, spoil, mar, damage

tart❶ NOUN
a slice of lemon tart
flan, pie, pastry

tart❷ ADJECTIVE
1 *the tart flavour of cranberries*
sharp, sour, acid, tangy
> **OPPOSITE** sweet
> **FOR TIPS ON DESCRIBING TASTE** SEE **taste**
2 *a tart reply*
sarcastic, biting, cutting, caustic

task NOUN
1 *The robot can carry out simple tasks.*
job, chore, errand, exercise
2 *Your task is to design a logo for the company.*
assignment, mission, duty, charge, undertaking

taste NOUN
1 *the sweet taste of roasted garlic*
flavour, savour, tang
2 *James Bond dresses with impeccable taste.*
style, elegance, discrimination, judgement
3 *She has always had a taste for adventure.*
liking, love, fondness, desire, inclination, penchant
4 *Would you like a taste of our new recipe?*
mouthful, sample, bite, bit, morsel, nibble, sip, drop

> **WRITING TIPS**
>
> **_describing taste_**
>
> Ravenous, and now very faint,
> I devoured a spoonful or two of
> my portion without thinking
> of its taste; but the first edge of
> hunger blunted, I perceived I had
> got in hand a nauseous mess.
> — *Charlotte Brontë, Jane Eyre*
>
> **_pleasant_**
> appetizing, delectable,
> delicious, flavoursome,

luscious, *(informal)* moreish,
mouth-watering, palatable,
(informal) scrumptious,
succulent, tasty, tempting,
(informal) yummy

unpleasant
disgusting, foul, inedible,
insipid, nauseating, nauseous,
rancid, revolting, sickening,
unappetizing, uneatable,
unpalatable

other
acidic, acrid, bitter, bland, burnt,
fiery, flavourless, fresh, fruity,
hot, juicy, mellow, metallic,
mild, nutty, peppery, piquant,
pungent, refreshing, salty,
savoury, sharp, smoky, sour,
spicy, strong, sugary, sweet,
syrupy, tangy, tart, tasteless,
vinegary, yeasty, zesty

taste *VERB*
1 *Taste the sauce before adding salt.*
sample, try, test, sip, savour
2 *Can you taste any difference in
flavour?*
perceive, distinguish, discern,
make out

tasteful *ADJECTIVE*
*decorated in a plain and tasteful
style*
refined, stylish, elegant, chic, smart,
cultured, artistic
OPPOSITE tasteless

tasteless *ADJECTIVE*
1 *telling a tasteless joke*
crude, tactless, indelicate,
inappropriate, in bad taste
2 *The fish was tasteless and
overcooked.*
flavourless, bland, insipid
OPPOSITE flavoursome

tasty *ADJECTIVE*
a tasty home-made pizza
delicious, appetizing, flavoursome

OPPOSITES flavourless, unappetizing
SEE ALSO taste

tattered *ADJECTIVE*
an old and tattered paperback
ragged, ripped, torn, frayed, tatty,
threadbare
OPPOSITE smart

taunt *VERB*
*Two sets of rival fans taunted each
other.*
jeer at, jibe, insult, sneer at,
scoff at, make fun of, tease,
mock, ridicule

taunt *NOUN*
*He had to ignore the taunts of the
crowd.*
jeer, jibe, insult, sneer

taut *ADJECTIVE*
Make sure the rope is taut.
tight, tense, stretched
OPPOSITE slack

teach *VERB*
*I'm teaching myself to play the
guitar.*
educate, instruct, tutor, coach, train,
school

teacher *NOUN*
a qualified dance teacher
tutor, instructor, trainer, coach
► A teacher at a college or university is
a **lecturer**.
► In the past, a woman who taught
children in a private household was a
governess.

team *NOUN*
1 *the senior basketball team*
side, squad, line-up
2 *a mountain rescue team*
group, force, unit, crew, detail

tear *VERB*
1 *The wind tore a hole in our tent.*
rip, split, slit, gash, rupture, shred
2 *A white van came tearing round the
corner.*
race, dash, rush, hurry,
sprint, speed

a
b
c
d
e
f
g
h
i
j
k
l
m
n
o
p
q
r
s
t
u
v
w
x
y
z

tear NOUN

a tear in the fabric of space and time
rip, split, slit, gash, rent, rupture,
hole, opening, gap

tease VERB

I knew she was only teasing me.
taunt, make fun of, poke fun at,
mock, ridicule, laugh at
❙ **IDIOM** (informal) pull someone's leg

technical ADJECTIVE

1 Lois is good with anything
technical.
technological, scientific, high-tech
2 a list of technical terms
specialist, specialized, advanced

technique NOUN

1 using modern recording techniques
method, procedure, approach,
means, system
2 a player who shows good technique
skill, expertise, proficiency, artistry,
ability

tedious ADJECTIVE

I found the opening chapter slow and
tedious.
boring, dull, dreary, tiresome,
monotonous, unexciting,
uninteresting, uninspiring, lacklustre
❙ **OPPOSITE** exciting

teem VERB

▷ **teem with**
The island's coral reefs teem
with life.
be overrun by, swarm with,
be crawling with,
be infested with

teenager NOUN

a website aimed at teenagers
adolescent, youth, young person
(informal) teen

telephone VERB
SEE **phone**

television NOUN

a new series on television
TV
(informal) telly, the box

 WORD WEB

*terms used in radio and
television*
aerial, analogue, announcer,
broadcast, cable TV, channel,
chat show (North American talk
show), commercial break,
digital audio broadcasting or
DAB, digital radio, digital TV,
documentary, editor, frequency,
game show, high definition or
HD, live broadcast, the media,
miniseries, off the air, on the
air, outside broadcast, pay-
per-view, phone-in, producer,
programme, ratings, reality
TV, reception, remake, repeat,
satellite TV, schedule, script,
scriptwriter, season, serial, series,
set-top box, situation comedy
(informal sitcom), sketch show,
soap opera (informal soap),
station, terrestrial TV, teletext,
trailer, transmission, TV licence,
watershed
❙ SEE ALSO **film**

tell VERB

1 I have something important to
tell you.
say to, make known to,
communicate to, report to,
announce to, reveal to, notify,
inform
2 The film tells the story of twelve-year-
old Yusef.
relate, narrate, recount, describe
3 The police told everyone to stand
back.
order, command, direct, instruct
4 Can you tell where we are yet?
make out, recognize, identify,
determine, perceive,
ascertain
5 It's impossible to tell one character
from another.
distinguish, differentiate

▷ **tell someone off**

(informal) We were told off for being late.

scold, reprimand, reproach
(British informal) tick off
(North American informal) chew out

temper NOUN

1 *Mr Griffith managed to keep an even temper.*

mood, humour, state of mind

2 *The chef is always flying into a temper.*

rage, fury, tantrum, fit of anger, fit of pique

▷ **lose your temper**

She loses her temper at the slightest thing.

get angry, fly into a rage, go berserk

▌ IDIOMS *(informal)* blow a fuse, blow your top, flip your lid, fly off the handle, hit the roof, lose your rag, go off the deep end

temperamental ADJECTIVE

Siamese cats can be temperamental.
moody, sensitive, touchy, volatile, unpredictable

▌ OPPOSITE even-tempered

temperature NOUN

 WORD WEB

units for measuring temperature

degrees Celsius, degrees centigrade, degrees Fahrenheit

▶ A **thermometer** is a device for measuring temperature.

▶ A **thermostat** is a device for keeping temperature steady.

temple NOUN

FOR PLACES OF RELIGIOUS WORSHIP SEE **religion**

temporary ADJECTIVE

1 *That will do for a temporary repair.*
interim, provisional, makeshift

2 *a temporary loss of hearing*
short-lived, momentary,

passing, fleeting

▌ OPPOSITE permanent

tempt VERB

Can I tempt you to try a spoonful?
coax, entice, persuade, attract, lure, inveigle

▌ OPPOSITES discourage, deter

temptation NOUN

1 *I resisted the temptation to laugh.*
urge, impulse, inclination, desire

2 *the temptation of easy money*
allure, attraction, appeal, enticement, draw

tempting ADJECTIVE

a tempting offer of free software
enticing, attractive, appealing, inviting, alluring, beguiling

▌ OPPOSITES off-putting, uninviting

tend❶ VERB

Antarctic icebergs tend to be larger than Arctic ones.
be inclined, be liable, be likely, be apt, be prone

tend❷ VERB

1 *He used to help his father tend the crops.*
take care of, look after, cultivate, manage

2 *Volunteers tended the wounded in makeshift hospitals.*
nurse, attend to, care for, minister to

3 *learning how to build and tend a fire*
watch over, maintain, keep going

▌ OPPOSITE neglect

tendency NOUN

Dan has a tendency to exaggerate.
inclination, leaning, predisposition, propensity

tender❶ ADJECTIVE

1 *Cook the meat until it is tender.*
soft, succulent, juicy

▶ Food that is tender is said to **melt in your mouth**.

▌ OPPOSITE tough

2 *Frost may damage tender plants.*
delicate, fragile, sensitive

▌ OPPOSITES hardy, strong

a
b
c
d
e
f
g
h
i
j
k
l
m
n
o
p
q
r
s
t
u
v
w
x
y
z

》

3 *My gums are still a bit tender.*
painful, sensitive, sore

4 *Rose turned to me with a tender smile.*
affectionate, kind, loving, caring, warm-hearted, compassionate, sympathetic, benevolent
▌**OPPOSITE** uncaring

tender❷ VERB
She was forced to tender her resignation.
offer, submit, proffer, present, put forward

tennis NOUN

WORD WEB

terms used in tennis
ace, advantage, backhand, ballboy or ballgirl, break point, court, deuce, double fault, doubles, drop shot, foot fault, forehand, lob, love, match point, net, racket or racquet, serve, service, set, singles, slice, smash, tiebreak or tiebreaker, umpire, volley

FOR TIPS ON WRITING ABOUT SPORT
SEE sport

tense ADJECTIVE

1 *Every muscle in my body was tense.*
taut, tight, strained, stretched

2 *Do you feel tense before a big match?*
anxious, nervous, apprehensive, edgy, on edge, jumpy, keyed up, worked up
(informal) uptight, jittery, twitchy
▌**OPPOSITE** relaxed

3 *The film ends with an incredibly tense car chase.*
nerve-racking, nail-biting, stressful, fraught

tension NOUN

1 *the tension of a guitar string*
tightness, tautness

2 *The tension in the room was unbearable.*

anxiety, nervousness, apprehension, suspense, worry, stress, strain

tent NOUN
sleeping in a tent in the desert
▶ A large tent used for a party or other event is a **marquee**.
▶ To set up a tent is to **pitch** it and to dismantle a tent is to **strike** it.

tepid ADJECTIVE
The water should be tepid, not hot.
lukewarm, hand-hot

term NOUN

1 *serving a long term in prison*
period, time, spell, stretch, stint, run

2 *a glossary of technical terms*
word, expression, phrase

terrible ADJECTIVE

1 *Mr Hyde commits a terrible crime.*
horrible, dreadful, appalling, shocking, horrific, horrendous, ghastly, atrocious, monstrous, heinous
▌**OPPOSITE** minor

2 *The first half of the show was terrible!*
very bad, awful, dreadful, appalling, dire, abysmal
(informal) rubbish, lousy, pathetic
▌**OPPOSITE** excellent
▌**SEE ALSO** bad

terribly ADVERB

1 *Many slaves suffered terribly.*
very badly, severely, intensely
▌**OPPOSITE** slightly

2 *I'm terribly sorry about this.*
very, extremely, awfully

terrific *(informal)* ADJECTIVE

1 *There was a terrific crash of lightning.*
very great, tremendous, huge, enormous, massive, immense, colossal, gigantic
▌**SEE ALSO** big

2 *She's a terrific gymnast.*
very good, excellent, first-class, first-rate, superb, marvellous, wonderful

(informal) brilliant, fantastic, fabulous

terrify *VERB*
Cody is terrified by dreams of giant insects.
frighten, scare, horrify, petrify, panic, alarm

territory *NOUN*
We were now deep in enemy territory.
land, area, ground, terrain, country, district, region, sector, zone
▶ A territory which is part of a country is a **province**.

terror *NOUN*
Queenie ran away screaming in terror.
fear, fright, horror, dread, panic, alarm

test *NOUN*
1 *an end-of-term test*
exam, examination, assessment, appraisal, evaluation
▶ A test for a job as an actor or singer is an **audition**.
2 *a new test for allergies*
trial, experiment, check, investigation, examination

test *VERB*
1 *an appointment to have your eyes tested*
examine, check, evaluate, assess, screen
2 *testing a new piece of software*
try out, experiment with, trial, sample
  IDIOM put something through its paces

text *NOUN*
1 *adding text to your web pages*
words, wording, content, script
2 *studying an ancient text*
work, book

textiles *PLURAL NOUN*
clothing made from natural textiles
fabrics, materials, cloths

WORD WEB

some textile arts
appliqué, crochet, dyeing, embroidery, felting, knitting, lacemaking, needlepoint, needlework, patchwork, quilting, sewing, spinning, tapestry, weaving
FOR TYPES OF TEXTILES SEE fabric

texture *NOUN*
a mild cheese with a waxy texture
feel, touch, consistency, quality, surface

WRITING TIPS

describing texture

Wemmick was at his desk, lunching — and crunching — on a dry hard biscuit; pieces of which he threw from time to time into his slit of a mouth, as if he were posting them.
— *Charles Dickens, Great Expectations*

rough or hard
brittle, bumpy, coarse, crumbly, firm, friable, grainy, granular, gravelly, lumpy, ruffled, sandy, scaly, wrinkled

smooth or soft
creamy, downy, feathery, fine, glassy, light, silky, velvety

wet or sticky
gelatinous, *informal* gloopy, glutinous, moist, runny, slimy, viscid, viscous, watery

other
chalky, chewy, doughy, elastic, fibrous, flaky, greasy, leathery, oily, papery, powdery, pulpy, rubbery, soupy, spongy, springy, *(informal)* squidgy, stretchy, stringy, waxy

a
b
c
d
e
f
g
h
i
j
k
l
m
n
o
p
q
r
s
t
u
v
w
x
y
z

thank VERB

How can I ever thank you enough?
say thank you to, express your gratitude to, show your appreciation to

thankful ADJECTIVE

We were thankful to be home at last.
grateful, appreciative, glad, pleased, relieved

thanks PLURAL NOUN

Please accept this token of my thanks.
gratitude, appreciation

▷ **thanks to**

People are living longer thanks to better health care.
because of, as a result of, owing to, due to, on account of, by virtue of

thaw VERB

1 *Polar ice caps are thawing at a faster rate.*
melt, dissolve, liquefy

2 *Leave frozen food to thaw before cooking.*
defrost, unfreeze

❙ **OPPOSITE** freeze

theatre NOUN

SEE **drama**

theft NOUN

reporting the theft of a mobile phone
robbery, stealing

❙ **SEE ALSO stealing**

theme NOUN

a film which explores the theme of loneliness
subject, topic, idea, argument, gist, thread, motif

theory NOUN

1 *Do you have any theories about the murder?*
hypothesis, explanation, suggestion, view, belief, contention, speculation, idea, notion

2 *studying musical theory*
principles, concepts, rules, laws

therapy NOUN

Acupuncture is an ancient therapy.

treatment, remedy

thick ADJECTIVE

1 *the thick roots of a banyan tree*
stout, chunky, heavy, solid, bulky, hefty, substantial

❙ **OPPOSITES** thin, slender

2 *The stone walls are more than a metre thick.*
wide, broad, deep

3 *a thick layer of fog and mist*
dense, close, compact, opaque, impenetrable

❙ **OPPOSITES** thin, light

4 *Her voice was thick with emotion.*
filled, loaded, packed, brimming, congested, choked

5 *a thick flour paste*
stiff, firm, heavy, doughy

❙ **OPPOSITES** thin, runny

6 *(informal) Maybe I'm just being thick.*
stupid, unintelligent, brainless, dense, dim

❙ **OPPOSITE** intelligent

thief NOUN

Thieves broke in and stole valuable equipment.
robber, burglar

▶ Someone who steals from people in the street is a **pickpocket**.
▶ Someone who steals small goods from a shop is a **shoplifter**.

thin ADJECTIVE

1 *a thin little girl with a freckled face*
lean, slim, slender, skinny, bony, gaunt, spare, slight

▶ Someone who is thin and tall is **lanky**.
▶ Someone who is thin but strong is **wiry**.
▶ Thin arms or legs are **spindly**.

❙ **OPPOSITES** fat, plump, stout

FOR TIPS ON DESCRIBING BODIES SEE **body**

2 *a kimono made of thin material*
fine, lightweight, light, delicate, flimsy, wispy, sheer, diaphanous

❙ **OPPOSITES** thick, heavy

3 *a thin crust of fragile rock*

narrow, fine

OPPOSITES thick, deep, broad

4 *Add water to make a thin paste.*
runny, watery, sloppy

OPPOSITES firm, stiff

5 *In my view, this is a thin argument.*
unconvincing, poor, weak, feeble, ineffective, implausible

OPPOSITES strong, convincing

thin VERB

Thin the mixture with a little milk.
dilute, water down, weaken

▷ **thin out**
Towards evening the crowd began to thin out.
disperse, scatter, break up, dissipate

thing NOUN

1 *Magpies are attracted by shiny things.*
object, article, item

2 *Phoebe had a lot of things to think about.*
matter, affair, detail, point, factor

3 *Odd things keep happening to me.*
event, happening, occurrence, incident

4 *I have only one thing left to do.*
job, task, act, action

▷ **things**
Put your things in one of the lockers.
belongings, possessions
(informal) stuff, gear

think VERB

1 *Stop to think before you respond.*
consider, contemplate, reflect, deliberate, meditate, ponder

2 *Do you think this is a good idea?*
believe, feel, consider, judge, conclude, be of the opinion

3 *When do you think you'll be ready?*
reckon, suppose, imagine, estimate, guess, expect, anticipate

▷ **think about something**
I've thought about what you said.
consider, reflect on, ponder on, muse on, mull over

► To keep thinking anxiously about

something is to **brood on** it.

▷ **think something up**
They thought up a good plan.
invent, make up, conceive, concoct, devise, dream up

thirst NOUN

1 *some water to quench your thirst*
dryness

2 *an insatiable thirst for adventure*
desire, craving, longing, yearning, appetite, hunger

thirsty ADJECTIVE

Exercise always makes me thirsty.
dry, parched

► Someone who has lost a lot of water from their body is **dehydrated**.

thorn NOUN

a cactus covered in tiny thorns
prickle, spike, spine, needle, barb

thorny ADJECTIVE

1 *a thorny cactus plant*
prickly, spiky, spiny, bristly

2 *discussing a thorny issue*
difficult, complicated, complex, hard, tricky, perplexing

thorough ADJECTIVE

1 *a thorough search of the crime scene*
comprehensive, full, rigorous, detailed, close, in-depth, exhaustive, careful, meticulous, systematic, methodical, painstaking

OPPOSITES superficial, cursory

2 *making a thorough nuisance of himself*
complete, total, utter, perfect, proper, absolute, downright, out-and-out

thought❶ NOUN

1 *What are your thoughts on modern art?*
opinion, belief, view, idea, notion, theory, conclusion

2 *Ursula was lost in thought for a moment.*
thinking, contemplation, reflection, meditation

»

3 *I've given some thought to the problem.*
consideration, deliberation, study

thought² *PAST TENSE*
SEE **think**

thoughtful *ADJECTIVE*

1 *Jamal looked thoughtful for a moment.*
pensive, reflective, contemplative, meditative, absorbed, preoccupied
❙ **OPPOSITES** blank, vacant

2 *a moving and thoughtful documentary*
well-thought-out, careful, conscientious, thorough
❙ **OPPOSITE** careless

3 *It was thoughtful of you to write.*
considerate, kind, caring, compassionate, sympathetic, understanding, obliging
❙ **OPPOSITE** thoughtless

thoughtless *ADJECTIVE*
It was thoughtless of me to say that.
inconsiderate, insensitive, uncaring, unthinking, negligent, ill-considered, rash
❙ **OPPOSITE** thoughtful

thrash *VERB*

1 *The owner was reported for thrashing his dog.*
hit, beat, strike, whip, flog

2 *The visitors thrashed the home side.*
beat, defeat, trounce
(*informal*) hammer, lick

3 *Dell had been thrashing about in his sleep.*
flail, writhe, toss, jerk, twitch

thread *NOUN*

1 *delicate threads of spider silk*
strand, fibre

2 *a skein of embroidery thread*
cotton, yarn, wool, silk

3 *losing the thread of the conversation*
theme, drift, direction, train, tenor

threat *NOUN*

1 *a letter containing empty threats*
warning, ultimatum

2 *The oil spill poses a threat to wildlife.*
danger, menace, hazard, risk

threaten *VERB*

1 *They tried to threaten him into paying.*
menace, intimidate, terrorize, bully, browbeat

2 *Acid rain is threatening the forests.*
endanger, jeopardize, put at risk

3 *The hazy sky threatened rain.*
warn of, indicate, signal, forecast

three *NOUN*
in groups of two or three
▶ A group of three people is a **threesome** or **trio**.
▶ A group or set of three things is a **triad**.
▶ A series of three related books, plays, or films is a **trilogy**.
▶ Three goals scored by the same player in a match is a **hat-trick**.
▶ To divide something into three equal parts is to **trisect** it.

> **Usage Note**
>
> Words which include 'three' in their meaning often begin with ***tri-***, for example *tricycle*, *trident*, and *tripod*.

thrifty *ADJECTIVE*
advice on being thrifty with your money
careful, economical, frugal, prudent, sparing
❙ **OPPOSITE** extravagant

thrill *NOUN*
the thrill of riding on a roller coaster
excitement, stimulation, sensation, tingle
(*informal*) buzz, kick

thrill *VERB*
It always thrills me to hear a live concert.
excite, exhilarate, stir, rouse, stimulate, electrify

IDIOM *(informal)* give you a buzz
OPPOSITE bore

thrilled *ADJECTIVE*
Dee was thrilled to see her name in print.
delighted, pleased, excited, overjoyed, ecstatic

thrilling *ADJECTIVE*
a thrilling action movie with a surprise ending
exciting, stirring, stimulating, electrifying, exhilarating, action-packed, gripping, riveting

thrive *VERB*
Dodos once thrived on Mauritius.
do well, flourish, prosper, succeed, boom, burgeon
OPPOSITE decline

thriving *ADJECTIVE*
a thriving tourist industry
flourishing, successful, prosperous, booming, healthy, profitable
OPPOSITE declining

throb *VERB*
Marty felt his heart throbbing in his chest.
beat, pound, pulse, pulsate, thump

throb *NOUN*
the incessant throb of the dance music
beat, pulse, pulsation, pounding, thumping

throng *NOUN*
Throngs of onlookers turned out to watch.
crowd, swarm, horde, mass, drove

throng *VERB*
Spectators thronged into the piazza.
swarm, flock, stream, crowd
▷ **thronged with**
In summer Venice is thronged with tourists.
crowded with, packed with, full of, swarming with

throttle *VERB*
This stiff collar is throttling me!
strangle, choke

throw *VERB*
1 *throwing scraps of food to the birds*
fling, toss, sling, cast, pitch, hurl, heave
(informal) bung, chuck
2 *Her question threw me for a second.*
disconcert, unsettle, unnerve, put off, rattle
(informal) faze
IDIOM throw someone off balance
3 *throwing a surprise party*
hold, host, put on
▷ **throw something away** or **out**
I'm throwing out all my old CDs.
get rid of, dispose of, discard, scrap, dump
(informal) ditch, bin

thrust *VERB*
1 *A woman thrust a leaflet into my hands.*
shove, push, force
2 *He thrust his way to the front of the queue.*
force, drive, push, shove, barge, elbow
3 *Celebrity had been thrust on him.*
force, foist, impose, inflict

thump *VERB*
1 *Mr Leach thumped his fist on the counter.*
bang, bash, pound, hit, strike, knock, hammer, punch
(informal) whack
2 *My head was thumping and I felt dizzy.*
throb, pound, pulse, hammer

thunder *NOUN*
We heard thunder in the distance.
▶ A burst of thunder is a **clap**, **crack**, **peal**, or **roll** of thunder.
SEE ALSO weather

thunder *VERB*
1 *Waves thundered against the rocks.*
boom, roar, rumble, pound

》

a
b
c
d
e
f
g
h
i
j
k
l
m
n
o
p
q
r
s
t
u
v
w
x
y
z

2 *'What do you want?' a voice
   thundered.*
   shout, roar, bellow, bark, boom

thunderous ADJECTIVE
   the sound of thunderous hooves
   deafening, loud, resounding,
   booming
   ❙ OPPOSITE quiet

tick NOUN
   1 *the tick of a clock*
      SEE **sound❶**

   2 *(informal) I'll be back in a tick.*
      moment, second, instant
      (informal) jiffy

tick VERB
   *A clock was ticking in the
   background.*
   SEE **sound❶**

   ▷ **tick someone off**
      *(British informal) being ticked off for
      being late*
      reprimand, reproach, scold
      (informal) tell off
      (North American informal) chew out

ticket NOUN
   1 *a cinema ticket*
      pass, permit, token, voucher, coupon
   2 *a price ticket*
      label, tag, sticker, tab

tide NOUN
   1 *seaweed washed up by the tide*
      current
      ▶ An incoming tide is a **flow tide**
        and an outgoing tide is an **ebb tide**.
      ▶ The tide is fully in at **high tide**
        and fully out at **low tide**.
   2 *the tide of recent events*
      course, direction, trend, drift

tidy ADJECTIVE
   trying to keep your room tidy
   neat, orderly, uncluttered, trim,
   spruce, immaculate, in good order
   ❙ IDIOM spick and span
   ❙ OPPOSITES untidy, messy

tie VERB
   1 *tying string around a parcel*
      bind, fasten, hitch, strap, loop,

knot, lace, truss
   ▶ To tie up a boat is to **moor** it.
   ▶ To tie up an animal is to **tether** it.
   ❙ OPPOSITE untie
   2 *The top two players tied with each
      other.*
      draw, be equal, be level

tie NOUN
   1 *ballet pumps with ankle ties*
      fastening, cord, lace, string
   2 *The final score was a tie.*
      draw, dead heat
   3 *maintaining close family ties*
      bond, connection, link, association,
      relationship

tier NOUN
   1 *the upper tier of the stadium*
      level, layer, storey
   2 *the back tier of seats*
      row, line, rank

tight ADJECTIVE
   1 *The lid was too tight to unscrew.*
      firm, fast, secure
      ▶ A tight seal which air cannot get
        through is **airtight**.
      ▶ A tight seal which water cannot get
        through is **watertight**.
      ❙ OPPOSITE loose
   2 *These jeans are quite tight.*
      close-fitting, snug, figure-hugging
      ❙ OPPOSITES loose, roomy
   3 *Make sure that the ropes are tight.*
      taut, tense, stretched, rigid
      ❙ OPPOSITE slack
   4 *squeezing into a tight space*
      cramped, confined, compact,
      limited, small, narrow, poky
      ❙ OPPOSITE spacious
   5 *He can be very tight with his money.*
      mean, stingy, miserly
      ❙ OPPOSITE generous

tighten VERB
   1 *tightening your grip*
      increase, strengthen, harden, stiffen
   2 *tightening your laces*
      pull tighter, stretch, make taut,
      make tense
      ❙ OPPOSITE loosen

a
b
c
d
e
f
g
h
i
j
k
l
m
n
o
p
q
r
s
t
u
v
w
x
y
z

tilt VERB

Uranus tilts on its axis at a 98 degree angle.

lean, incline, slope, slant, angle, tip

▶ When a ship tilts to one side, it **lists**.

timber NOUN

1 *furniture made from reclaimed timber*
wood
(North American) lumber

2 *the timbers of an old ship*
beam, plank, board, spar

time NOUN

1 *This is my favourite time of the year.*
phase, season, period

2 *He spent a short time living in China.*
period, while, term, spell, stretch

3 *Shakespeare lived in the time of Elizabeth I.*
era, age, days, epoch, period

4 *Is this a good time to talk?*
moment, occasion, opportunity

5 *keeping time with the music*
tempo, beat, rhythm

▷ **on time**
Please try to be on time.
punctual, prompt

✳ WORD WEB

units for measuring time
nanosecond, microsecond, millisecond, second, minute, hour, day, week, fortnight, month, quarter, year, decade, century, millennium

▶ The science of measuring time is **horology**.

▶ A region of the Earth in which a common standard time is used is a **time zone**.

▶ The time used in a particular time zone is sometimes called the **local time**.

devices used to measure time
atomic clock, calendar, chronometer, hourglass, metronome, pocket watch, quartz clock, stopwatch, sundial, timer, water clock, wristwatch

timely ADJECTIVE

a timely reminder
well-timed, opportune, convenient, expedient

timetable NOUN

a bus timetable
schedule, programme, rota, diary

timid ADJECTIVE

speaking in a timid little voice
shy, bashful, modest, nervous, fearful, shrinking, retiring, sheepish
OPPOSITES brave, confident

tinge VERB

1 *In the west the clouds were tinged with gold.*
colour, stain, tint, wash, flush

2 *His words were tinged with irony.*
flavour, colour, touch

tinge NOUN

1 *white with just a tinge of blue*
tint, colour, shade, hue, tone
FOR TIPS ON DESCRIBING COLOURS SEE **colour**

2 *There was a tinge of sadness in her voice.*
trace, note, touch, suggestion, hint, streak

tingle VERB

My ears were tingling with the cold.
prickle, sting

tingle NOUN

1 *a tingle in your toes*
prickling, stinging
IDIOM pins and needles

2 *feeling a tingle of excitement*
thrill, sensation, quiver, shiver

tinker VERB

tinkering with the insides of a computer
fiddle, play about, dabble, meddle, tamper

tint NOUN

> You can add a sepia tint to your photos.
> shade, tone, colour, hue, tinge
> ❚ SEE ALSO **colour**

tint VERB

> Have you had your hair tinted?
> colour, dye

tiny ADJECTIVE

> a tiny yellow tree frog
> very small, minute, minuscule, miniature, mini, microscopic, diminutive
> (informal) teeny, titchy
> ❚ OPPOSITES huge, giant
> ❚ SEE ALSO **little**, **small**

tip❶ NOUN

> **1** an arrow with a poisoned tip
> end, point, nib
> **2** the snowy tip of Mount Fuji
> peak, top, summit, cap, crown, pinnacle, apex

tip❷ NOUN

> **1** giving the waitress a tip
> gratuity
> **2** Here are some useful make-up tips.
> hint, suggestion, pointer, piece of advice

tip❸ VERB

> **1** Tip your head back to stop a nosebleed.
> lean, tilt, incline, slope, slant, angle
> ▶ When a ship tips slightly to one side, it **lists**.
> **2** She tipped everything onto the counter.
> empty, turn out, dump, unload
> ▷ **tip over**
> The surfboard tipped over on top of him.
> overturn, roll over, keel over, capsize
> ▷ **tip something over**
> I tipped the jug over by accident.
> knock over, overturn, topple, upset, upend

tip NOUN

> a waste and recycling tip
> dump, rubbish dump, landfill

tiptoe VERB

> SEE **walk**

tire VERB

> My legs were beginning to tire.
> get tired, weaken, flag, droop
> ❚ OPPOSITES revive, strengthen
> ▷ **tire someone out**
> The long walk home had tired her out.
> exhaust, wear out, drain, weary
> (British informal) knacker
> ❚ OPPOSITES refresh, invigorate

tired ADJECTIVE

> feeling tired after a long day
> exhausted, fatigued, weary, worn out, listless, sleepy, drowsy
> (informal) all in, whacked, bushed, dead beat
> (British informal) knackered
> (North American informal) pooped, tuckered out
> ❚ OPPOSITES energetic, refreshed
> ▷ **be tired of something**
> I'm tired of reading about celebrities.
> bored with, fed up with, sick of, weary of, have had enough of

tireless ADJECTIVE

> a tireless campaigner for human rights
> inexhaustible, indefatigable, energetic

tiresome ADJECTIVE

> It's tiresome wading through junk email.
> annoying, irritating, trying, vexing, exasperating

tiring ADJECTIVE

> Digging the garden is tiring work.
> exhausting, taxing, demanding, arduous, strenuous, laborious, gruelling, wearisome
> ❚ OPPOSITE refreshing

title NOUN

1 *a good title for a short story*
name, heading
▶ The title above a newspaper story is a **headline**.
▶ A title or description next to a picture is a **caption**.

2 *an Olympic title*
championship, crown

3 *What is your preferred title?*
form of address, designation, rank

toast VERB

Toast the bread on one side.
FOR WAYS TO COOK FOOD SEE **cook**

together ADVERB

1 *We wrote the song together.*
jointly, as a group, in collaboration, in partnership, with each other, side by side
OPPOSITES independently, separately

2 *Let's sing the first verse together.*
simultaneously, at the same time, all at once, in chorus, in unison

toil VERB

1 *toiling in the fields all day*
work hard, labour, sweat, slave
(informal) grind, slog

2 *toiling up a steep path*
struggle, trudge, plod

toilet NOUN

a downstairs toilet
lavatory, WC, bathroom
(British informal) loo
(North American) restroom
▶ A toilet in a camp or barracks is a **latrine**.

token NOUN

1 *We each received a free book token.*
voucher, coupon, ticket, note

2 *a token of our appreciation*
sign, symbol, mark, expression, indication, proof, demonstration

tolerant ADJECTIVE

Do you think that people are more tolerant nowadays?
open-minded, broad-minded, easy-going, lenient, sympathetic, understanding, indulgent, forbearing
OPPOSITE intolerant

tolerate VERB

1 *We do not tolerate plagiarism in any form.*
accept, permit, allow, put up with

2 *Some species can tolerate extreme temperatures.*
bear, endure, stand, abide, suffer, stomach

tomb NOUN

the tomb of an Egyptian pharaoh
burial chamber, crypt, grave, mausoleum, sepulchre, vault
▶ An underground passage containing several tombs is a **catacomb**.
▶ A large ancient burial ground is a **necropolis**.

tone NOUN

1 *There was an sarcastic tone to his voice.*
note, sound, quality, intonation, timbre

2 *painted in dark earthy tones*
colour, hue, shade, tint

3 *Eerie music sets the right tone for the film.*
feeling, mood, atmosphere, character, spirit

tool NOUN

a shed full of gardening tools
implement, utensil, device, gadget, instrument, appliance, contraption
(informal) gizmo

tooth NOUN

 WORD WEB

types of teeth
canine (tooth), incisor, molar, premolar, wisdom tooth
▶ Upper canine teeth are sometimes known as **eye teeth**.
▶ A child's first set of teeth are its **milk teeth** or **baby teeth**.   »

> ▶ The canine teeth of a wild animal are its **fangs**.
> ▶ The long pointed teeth of an elephant or walrus are its **tusks**.
>
> *parts of a tooth*
> cementum, dentine, enamel, pulp
>
> *common dental problems*
> cavity, plaque, tartar, tooth decay or caries
> ▐ SEE ALSO **dentist**

top *NOUN*

1 *at the top of a gentle rise*
peak, summit, tip, crown, crest, head, height, apex
▐ OPPOSITES bottom, base

2 *a folding table with a plastic top*
surface

3 *Remember to screw the top back on.*
lid, cap, cover, stopper

top *ADJECTIVE*

1 *a room on the top floor*
highest, topmost, uppermost, upper
▐ OPPOSITES bottom, lowest

2 *running at top speed*
greatest, maximum, utmost
▐ OPPOSITES minimum, lowest

3 *one of Europe's top chefs*
leading, foremost, finest, best, principal, superior
▐ OPPOSITE minor

top *VERB*

1 *Top the pizza with mozzarella cheese.*
cover, decorate, garnish, crown

2 *She is hoping to top her personal best.*
beat, better, exceed, outdo, surpass

topic *NOUN*

What was the topic of the conversation?
subject, theme, issue, matter, question, concern, talking point

topical *ADJECTIVE*

a round-up of topical news items

current, recent, contemporary, up to date, up to the minute

topple *VERB*

1 *His chair suddenly toppled backwards.*
fall, tumble, tip over, keel over, overbalance

2 *High winds toppled trees and power lines.*
knock down, push over, overturn, upset, upend

3 *a plot to topple the president*
overthrow, bring down, remove from office, oust, unseat

torment *VERB*

1 *Harvey was tormented by bad dreams.*
afflict, torture, plague, haunt, distress, harrow, rack

2 *Stop tormenting the poor animal.*
tease, taunt, harass, pester, bully
▶ To torment someone continually is to **persecute** or **victimize** them.

torrent *NOUN*

1 *a torrent of melted snow*
flood, gush, rush, stream, spate, cascade

2 *caught in a torrent of rain*
downpour, deluge, cloudburst

3 *facing a torrent of abuse*
outpouring, outburst, stream, tide, barrage

torrential *ADJECTIVE*

the torrential monsoon rains
heavy, violent, severe, driving, lashing
▐ SEE ALSO **weather**

toss *VERB*

1 *tossing a pebble into a pond*
throw, hurl, fling, cast, pitch, lob, sling
(informal) chuck

2 *We'll toss a coin to decide.*
flip, spin

3 *Bits of debris were tossing about in the waves.*
pitch, lurch, bob, roll, rock, heave

4 *She tossed and turned, unable to get to sleep.*
thrash about, flail, writhe

total ADJECTIVE

1 *What was your total score?*
complete, whole, full, entire, overall, combined
OPPOSITE partial

2 *The party was a total disaster.*
complete, utter, absolute, thorough, sheer, downright, out-and-out, unmitigated

total NOUN

A total of 5 million viewers tuned in.
sum, whole, entirety, aggregate

total VERB

So far the donations total 2000 euros.
add up to, amount to, come to, make

totally ADVERB

I totally agree with you.
completely, wholly, entirely, fully, utterly, absolutely, thoroughly, unreservedly
OPPOSITE partly

totter VERB
SEE **walk**

touch VERB

1 *Roz gently touched him on the shoulder.*
feel, handle, stroke, fondle, caress, pat, pet

2 *The ball only just touched the net.*
brush, graze, skim, contact

3 *Nothing in the room had been touched.*
move, disturb, interfere with, meddle with, tamper with

4 *Temperatures can touch 45 degrees in summer.*
reach, rise to, attain
(informal) hit

5 *I was deeply touched by her letter.*
affect, move, stir

▷ **touch on something**
You touched on the subject of money.
refer to, mention, raise, broach

touch NOUN

1 *I felt a light touch on my arm.*
pat, stroke, tap, caress, contact

2 *There's a touch of dampness in the air.*
hint, trace, suggestion, tinge

3 *She has added her own touch to the songs.*
style, feel, quality

4 *Are you still in touch with the family?*
contact, communication, correspondence

touching ADJECTIVE

a touching final scene
moving, affecting, emotional, poignant, heart-warming, tear-jerking

touchy ADJECTIVE

He's very touchy about his weight.
easily offended, sensitive, irritable

tough ADJECTIVE

1 *Fibreglass is tougher than carbon fibre.*
strong, sturdy, robust, durable, resilient, hard-wearing, stout, substantial
OPPOSITE flimsy

2 *promising to be tough on crime*
firm, strict, severe, stern, uncompromising, hard-hitting
OPPOSITES soft, lenient

3 *a tough individual who never quits*
robust, hardy, strong, resilient, rugged, hardened
OPPOSITE weak

4 *They team struggled against tough opposition.*
strong, stiff, powerful, resistant, determined, stubborn
OPPOSITES weak, feeble

5 *a tough piece of meat*
chewy, leathery, rubbery
OPPOSITE tender

》

a
b
c
d
e
f
g
h
i
j
k
l
m
n
o
p
q
r
s
t
u
v
w
x
y
z

6 *The first part of the climb is the toughest.*
demanding, strenuous, arduous, laborious, gruelling, taxing, punishing, exhausting

▎ **OPPOSITE** easy

7 *a tough question to answer*
difficult, hard, tricky, puzzling, baffling, knotty, thorny

▎ **OPPOSITES** easy, straightforward

tour NOUN

a sightseeing tour of Krakow
trip, excursion, visit, journey, expedition, outing, jaunt

tourist NOUN

The cathedral was full of tourists.
sightseer, holidaymaker, traveller, visitor

tournament NOUN

the finals of the basketball tournament
championship, competition, contest, series

tow VERB

Horses used to tow barges along the river.
pull, haul, tug, drag, draw

tower NOUN

 WORD WEB

some types of tower
barbican, belfry or bell tower, donjon, minaret, pagoda, steeple, turret, watchtower

FOR TIPS ON DESCRIBING BUILDINGS
SEE **building**

tower VERB

▷ **tower above** or **over something**
The monument towers above the landscape.
rise above, stand above, dominate, loom over, overhang, overshadow

town NOUN

a seaside town near Melbourne

► A town with its own local council is a **borough**.

► Several towns that merge into each other are a **conurbation**.

► The people who live in a town are the **townspeople**.

► Related adjectives are **municipal** and **urban**.

▎ **SEE ALSO** city

toxic ADJECTIVE

The flask contains a toxic gas.
poisonous, deadly, lethal, noxious, harmful

▎ **OPPOSITE** harmless

▎ **SEE ALSO** poison

toy NOUN

a box full of old toys and dolls
game, plaything

toy VERB

▷ **toy with something**

1 *Yvonne sat toying with her hair.*
play with, fiddle with, fidget with, twiddle

2 *I'm toying with the idea of starting a blog.*
consider, contemplate, think about, flirt with

trace NOUN

1 *Whole colonies of bees vanished without a trace.*
evidence, sign, mark, indication, hint, clue, track, trail

2 *They found traces of blood on the carpet.*
vestige, remnant, spot, speck, drop, touch

trace VERB

1 *trying to trace your family history*
track down, discover, find, uncover, unearth

2 *tracing a pattern on the windowpane*
draw, outline, mark out

track *NOUN*

1 *the tracks of a grizzly bear*
footprint, footmark, trail, scent, spoor

2 *a rough track through the bush*
path, pathway, footpath, trail

3 *a single lap around the track*
racetrack, circuit, course

4 *laying the track for a tram system*
line, rails

5 *a CD of classic tracks*
song, recording, number, piece

track *VERB*

Astronomers are tracking the comet's path.
follow, trace, trail, pursue, shadow, stalk

▷ **track someone down**
He manages to track down his old adversary.
find, discover, trace, hunt down, sniff out, run to ground

tract *NOUN*

a vast tract of frozen tundra
area, expanse, stretch

trade *NOUN*

1 *the international trade in bananas*
business, dealing, buying and selling, commerce, market

2 *He took up the same trade as his father.*
occupation, profession, work, career, business, craft

trade *VERB*

▷ **trade in something**
a company which trades in electronics
deal in, do business in, buy and sell

▶ Trading in illegal goods is **trafficking**.

tradition *NOUN*

The Moon Festival is a Chinese tradition.
custom, convention, practice, habit, ritual, observance, institution

traditional *ADJECTIVE*

1 *The Maya have preserved their traditional way of life.*
long-established, time-honoured, age-old, customary, habitual, ritual
┃ OPPOSITE non-traditional

2 *The dancers wore traditional costumes.*
folk, ethnic, national, regional, historical

3 *They chose to have a traditional wedding.*
conventional, orthodox, regular, standard, classic
┃ OPPOSITE unorthodox

tragedy *NOUN*

1 *'Romeo and Juliet' is a Shakespearean tragedy.*
┃ OPPOSITE comedy

2 *The accident at sea was a terrible tragedy.*
disaster, catastrophe, calamity, misfortune

tragic *ADJECTIVE*

1 *He died in a tragic accident.*
disastrous, catastrophic, calamitous, terrible, horrendous, appalling, dreadful, unfortunate, unlucky

2 *a tragic story of doomed love*
sad, unhappy, sorrowful, mournful, pitiful, heart-rending, wretched, pathetic
┃ OPPOSITES light-hearted, comic

trail *NOUN*

1 *the trail left by a comet*
track, stream, wake

2 *a bike trail through the woods*
path, pathway, track, route

▷ **on the trail of someone**
on the trail of a criminal mastermind
on the track of, on the hunt for, in pursuit of, following the scent of

trail *VERB*

1 *Plain-clothes officers are trailing the suspect.*
follow, track, chase, pursue, shadow, stalk

》

a
b
c
d
e
f
g
h
i
j
k
l
m
n
o
p
q
r
s
t
u
v
w
x
y
z

(informal) tail

2 *trailing your luggage behind you*
pull, tow, drag, draw, haul

3 *The party is already trailing in the polls.*
fall behind, lag, straggle

OPPOSITE lead

▷ **trail away** or **off**
Her voice began to trail away.
fade, grow faint, peter out, dwindle

train NOUN

1 *a journey by steam train*
SEE **vehicle**

2 *an unusual train of events*
sequence, series, string, chain, succession

train VERB

1 *Islanders are being trained in scuba-diving.*
coach, instruct, teach, tutor, school, drill

2 *training for the Commonwealth Games*
practise, exercise, get into shape
(informal) work out

3 *training a telescope at the Moon*
aim, point, direct, target, focus, level

trainer NOUN

1 *a professional voice trainer*
coach, instructor, teacher, tutor

2 *These trainers are for indoor use.*
SEE **shoes**

tramp NOUN

1 *sleeping rough like a tramp*
homeless person, vagrant, vagabond, down-and-out
(North American) hobo

2 *a tramp through the woods*
trek, walk, hike, ramble

3 *the tramp of marching feet*
tread, stamp, march, plod

tramp VERB

tramping across a muddy field
trudge, trek, traipse, stamp, march, plod

SEE ALSO walk

trample VERB

Don't trample the flowers!
tread on, stamp on, walk over, crush, flatten, squash

trance NOUN

The fortune-teller went into a trance.
daze, stupor, reverie, hypnotic state

tranquil ADJECTIVE

1 *the tranquil atmosphere of rural life*
calm, peaceful, quiet, restful, relaxing
(informal) laid-back

OPPOSITES busy, hectic

2 *Her face now wore a tranquil expression.*
still, calm, placid, serene, undisturbed, unruffled

transfer VERB

Some paintings were transferred to the new gallery.
move, remove, shift, relocate, convey, hand over

transform VERB

They transformed the wasteland into a park.
convert, turn, change, alter, adapt, modify, rework

translate VERB

The book has been translated into 36 languages.
interpret, convert, put, render, reword

► A person who translates a foreign language is an **interpreter** or **translator**.

► An expert in languages is a **linguist**.

transmit VERB

1 *transmitting a message in code*
send, communicate, relay, convey, dispatch

► To transmit a programme on radio or TV is to **broadcast** it.

OPPOSITE receive

2 *Can the disease be transmitted to humans?*
pass on, spread, carry

transparent ADJECTIVE

1 *a transparent jellyfish*
clear
(informal) see-through
▶ Something which is not fully
transparent, but allows light to shine
through, is **translucent**.

2 *a transparent attempt to hoodwink customers*
obvious, clear, plain, apparent,
unambiguous, unmistakable,
patent, manifest

transport VERB

Oil is transported in huge tanker ships.
carry, convey, transfer, ship, ferry,
move, shift, take, bear

transport NOUN

the transport of waste and recyclables
conveyance, shipping, shipment,
carriage, haulage, freight
**FOR TYPES OF TRANSPORT SEE aircraft,
boat, vehicle**

trap NOUN

1 *an animal caught in a trap*
snare, net, gin

2 *The email is just a trap to get your password.*
trick, deception, ruse, ploy
(informal) con, scam

trap VERB

1 *Animals can get trapped in plastic bags.*
catch, snare, ensnare, capture,
corner

2 *She was trapped into buying a fake autograph.*
trick, dupe, deceive, fool
(informal) con, sucker

trash (informal) NOUN

Sometimes I just feel like reading trash.
rubbish, drivel, nonsense, pap, trivia

traumatic ADJECTIVE

the story of a traumatic escape from Nazi Germany
disturbing, distressing, upsetting,
painful, harrowing, shocking,
devastating

travel VERB

I usually travel to school by bus.
go, journey, move along, proceed,
progress
▶ When birds travel from one country
to another they **migrate**.
▶ When people travel to another
country to live there they **emigrate**.

traveller NOUN

a busload of weary travellers
passenger, commuter, tourist,
holidaymaker, backpacker
▶ A person who travels to a religious
place is a **pilgrim**.
▶ A person who travels illegally on a
ship or plane is a **stowaway**.
▶ A person who likes travelling round
the world is a **globetrotter**.

treacherous ADJECTIVE

1 *a treacherous plot to kill Caesar*
disloyal, traitorous, unfaithful,
untrustworthy, double-crossing
▶ A treacherous act is **treachery** or
betrayal.
▶ The act of betraying your country is
treason.
OPPOSITE loyal

2 *The roads are often treacherous in winter.*
dangerous, hazardous, perilous,
unsafe, risky
OPPOSITE safe

tread VERB

Please tread carefully.
step, walk, proceed
SEE ALSO walk

▷ **tread on**
Don't tread on the wet cement!
step on, walk on, stamp on, trample,
crush, flatten, squash

treasure NOUN

1 *searching for sunken treasure*
riches, valuables, wealth, fortune
▶ A store of treasure is a **cache** or
hoard.

» 587

2 *one of the treasures of the silent cinema*
masterpiece, classic, prize, jewel, gem

treasure VERB
I will always treasure the memory.
cherish, prize, value, hold dear, set store by

treat VERB
1 *They treated me as part of the family.*
behave towards, act towards
2 *We are treating the case as murder.*
regard, view, look on, consider
3 *a novel which treats a difficult subject*
deal with, discuss, explore, handle, tackle
4 *Two people are being treated for minor injuries.*
tend, nurse, attend to
5 *Let me treat you to lunch.*
pay for, stand, buy

treat NOUN
What should I give my pet as a treat?
luxury, reward, present, gift

treatment NOUN
1 *the treatment of sick animals*
care, nursing, healing
2 *a new treatment for asthma*
remedy, therapy, medication
▶ Emergency treatment at the scene of an accident is **first aid**.
▌SEE ALSO **medicine**
3 *Old documents need careful treatment.*
handling, care, management, use

treaty NOUN
signing a peace treaty
agreement, pact, contract, settlement, entente

tree NOUN

 WORD WEB

some varieties of tree
alder, almond, apple, ash, aspen, baobab, banyan, bay or laurel, beech, birch, cedar, cherry, chestnut, cypress, elder, elm, eucalyptus, fir, flame tree, fruit tree, hawthorn, hazel, holly, jujube, juniper, larch, lime, maple or acer, monkey puzzle, oak, olive, palm, pear, pine, plane, plum, poplar, redwood, rowan or mountain ash, rubber tree, silver birch, spruce, sycamore, tamarind, willow, yew
▶ Trees which lose their leaves in winter are **deciduous**.
▶ Trees which have leaves all year round are **evergreen**.
▶ Trees which grow cones are **conifers**.
▶ A young tree is a **sapling**.
▶ A related adjective is **arboreal**. *an arboreal paradise*
▶ An area covered with trees is a **wooded** area or **woodland**.
▶ A large area covered with trees and undergrowth is a **forest** and the practice of planting and looking after forests is **forestry**.
▶ A small group of trees is a **copse** or **coppice**.
▶ A small wood is a **grove**, **spinney**, or **thicket**.
▶ An area planted with fruit trees is an **orchard**.
▶ A collection of trees for study or display is an **arboretum**.

tremble VERB
The poor dog was trembling with cold.
shake, shiver, quake, quiver, shudder

tremendous ADJECTIVE

1 *The werewolf let out a tremendous howl.*
very great, huge, enormous, massive, immense, colossal, mighty
(*informal*) terrific
⌐ SEE ALSO **big**

2 *Winning the cup would be a tremendous achievement.*
marvellous, magnificent, wonderful, superb, stupendous, extraordinary, outstanding
(*informal*) brilliant, fantastic, terrific

tremor NOUN

1 *There was the hint of a tremor in her voice.*
trembling, shaking, quavering, quivering, vibration, wobble

2 *an earth tremor*
SEE **earthquake**

trend NOUN

1 *a trend towards healthier eating*
tendency, movement, shift, leaning, inclination, drift

2 *the latest trend in footwear*
fashion, style, craze, fad, vogue

trendy (informal) NOUN

a trendy new outfit
fashionable, stylish, chic, up to date
(*informal*) hip, in
⌐ IDIOM all the rage
⌐ OPPOSITES unfashionable, out of date

trial NOUN

1 *a murder trial*
case, hearing, lawsuit, tribunal
▶ A military trial is a **court martial**.

2 *conducting trials on a new vaccine*
test, experiment, check, evaluation, appraisal

tribe NOUN

Boudicca was queen of the Iceni tribe.
people, ethnic group, clan

trick NOUN

1 *playing a trick on April Fool's Day*
joke, practical joke, prank

2 *a trick to get your log-in details*
deception, ruse, fraud, hoax, ploy
(*informal*) con, scam

trick VERB

These sites trick you into downloading a virus.
deceive, dupe, fool, hoodwink, cheat, swindle
(*informal*) con, sucker

trickle VERB

The sweat trickled down his nose.
dribble, drip, leak, seep, ooze
⌐ OPPOSITE gush

trickle NOUN

The water flow had slowed to a trickle.
dribble, drip
⌐ OPPOSITE gush

tricky ADJECTIVE

1 *I found myself in a tricky situation.*
difficult, awkward, problematic, complicated, delicate, ticklish
⌐ OPPOSITES simple, straightforward

2 *a tricky person to deal with*
crafty, cunning, sly, wily, devious

trigger VERB

Certain foods can trigger an allergic reaction.
set off, start, initiate, activate, cause, provoke, spark

trim ADJECTIVE

Use this organizer to keep your desk trim.
neat, orderly, tidy, well kept, smart, spruce
⌐ OPPOSITE untidy

trim VERB

1 *trimming a hedge*
cut, clip, shorten, crop, prune, pare, neaten, tidy

2 *a handkerchief trimmed with lace*
edge, fringe, decorate, adorn, embellish

a
b
c
d
e
f
g
h
i
j
k
l
m
n
o
p
q
r
s
t
u
v
w
x
y
z

trip *VERB*

1 *She tripped on a loose flagstone.*
catch your foot, stumble, fall, slip, stagger

2 *He tripped over his lines at the start.*
stumble, make a mistake, slip

trip *NOUN*

Win a shopping trip to New York.
journey, visit, outing, excursion, expedition, jaunt, break

triumph *NOUN*

The season ended in triumph for the team.
victory, success, win, conquest

triumphant *ADJECTIVE*

1 *a photo of the triumphant team*
winning, victorious, conquering, successful
OPPOSITE unsuccessful

2 *A triumphant look spread across her face.*
elated, exultant, joyful, gleeful, jubilant

trivial *ADJECTIVE*

Don't worry about trivial details.
unimportant, insignificant, minor, slight, trifling, negligible, petty, frivolous, footling
OPPOSITES important, significant

troop *NOUN*

a troop of strolling musicians
group, band, party, body, company

troop *VERB*

We all trooped into the main hall.
walk, march, proceed, stream, file

troops *PLURAL NOUN*
SEE **army**

trophy *NOUN*

an international tennis trophy
cup, prize, award, medal

trouble *NOUN*

1 *He and his family may be in trouble.*
difficulty, hardship, suffering, unhappiness, distress, misfortune, pain, sadness, sorrow, worry

2 *There were reports of trouble outside the ground.*
disorder, unrest, disturbance, commotion, fighting, violence

3 *The only trouble is that I'm broke!*
problem, difficulty, disadvantage, drawback

4 *Please don't go to any trouble.*
bother, inconvenience, effort, pains

trouble *VERB*

1 *Something must be troubling her.*
distress, upset, bother, worry, concern, pain, torment, perturb
IDIOM prey on your mind

2 *I don't want to trouble them at this hour.*
disturb, bother, inconvenience, impose on, put out

troublesome *ADJECTIVE*

1 *Sunscreens can cause troublesome allergies.*
annoying, irritating, trying, tiresome, bothersome, inconvenient, nagging

2 *Marley is a cute but troublesome puppy.*
difficult, awkward, unruly, unmanageable, disobedient, uncooperative

trousers *PLURAL NOUN*
SEE **clothes**

truce *NOUN*

The two sides agreed on a truce.
ceasefire, armistice, peace

true *ADJECTIVE*

1 *The film is based on a true story.*
real, factual, actual, historical
OPPOSITES fictional, made-up

2 *The play aims to present a true picture of war.*
genuine, real, faithful, authentic, accurate, proper, exact
OPPOSITES false, misleading

3 *What if the rumours are true?*
accurate, correct, right, verifiable, undeniable
OPPOSITES untrue, false

a b c d e f g h i j k l m n o p q r s **t** u v w x y z

4 *You've always been a true friend to me.*
faithful, loyal, constant, devoted, sincere, trustworthy, reliable, dependable
❙ **OPPOSITE** disloyal

trunk *NOUN*

1 *the trunk of a palm tree*
stem, stock

2 *an elephant's trunk*
proboscis, snout

3 *an old travelling trunk*
chest, case, box, crate, suitcase, coffer

4 *Try to keep your trunk straight.*
torso, body, frame

trust *VERB*

1 *I've never really trusted her.*
be sure of, have confidence in, have faith in, believe in

2 *Can I trust you to keep a secret?*
rely on, depend on, count on, bank on

3 *I trust you are well.*
hope, assume, presume, take it

trust *NOUN*

1 *His supporters began to lose trust in him.*
belief, confidence, faith

2 *I'm putting the documents in your trust.*
responsibility, safe-keeping, hands

trustworthy *ADJECTIVE*
the only trustworthy member of the crew
reliable, dependable, loyal, true, honourable, responsible
❙ **OPPOSITE** untrustworthy

truth *NOUN*

1 *They finally accepted the truth of Galileo's discovery.*
accuracy, correctness, truthfulness, reliability, validity, authenticity
(formal) veracity
❙ **OPPOSITES** inaccuracy, falseness

2 *The truth slowly began to dawn on him.*

facts, reality
❙ **OPPOSITES** lies, falsehood, fallacy

truthful *ADJECTIVE*

1 *I've not been entirely truthful with you.*
honest, frank, sincere, straight, straightforward
(informal) upfront
❙ **OPPOSITE** dishonest

2 *Please give a truthful answer.*
accurate, correct, true, proper, faithful, genuine
❙ **OPPOSITES** untrue, false

try *VERB*

1 *I'm trying to improve my technique.*
attempt, endeavour, make an effort, aim, strive

2 *Would you like to try a larger size?*
test, try out, sample, evaluate, experiment with
(informal) check out

try *NOUN*

1 *I think it's still worth a try.*
attempt, effort, go
(informal) shot, bash, crack, stab

2 *Have a try of this smoothie.*
test, trial, sample, taste

trying *ADJECTIVE*

1 *It's been a very trying day.*
difficult, demanding, stressful, frustrating, fraught
❙ **OPPOSITE** relaxing

2 *My sister can be trying at times.*
annoying, irritating, tiresome, maddening, exasperating, infuriating

tub *NOUN*
a large tub of popcorn
pot, drum, barrel, cask, vat

tube *NOUN*
Roll the paper into a tube.
cylinder, pipe
▶ A flexible tube for water is a **hose**.

tuck *VERB*
Ike tucked his shirt into his trousers.
push, insert, slip, stick, stuff

tuft NOUN

a few tufts of green grass
clump, bunch

tug VERB

1 *Jackson tugged the rope to test it.*
pull, jerk, pluck, wrench
(informal) yank

2 *We tugged the sledge up the hill.*
drag, pull, tow, haul, lug, draw,
heave

tumble VERB

1 *The whole bridge collapsed and
tumbled into the river.*
topple, fall, drop, pitch, plummet,
plunge, crash

2 *Mo tumbled into bed and fell straight
asleep.*
dive, flop, sink, slump, stumble

tumble NOUN

Prices have taken a tumble recently.
fall, drop, slump, plunge, nosedive,
crash

tumour NOUN

a dog with a tumour on its leg
lump, growth, swelling
▶ A harmful tumour is **malignant** or
cancerous.
▶ A harmless tumour is **benign**.

tumult NOUN

a tumult of angry voices
uproar, clamour, commotion, din,
racket, rumpus, hubbub

tune NOUN

learning a new tune on the guitar
melody, song, air, theme, strain
❙ SEE ALSO **music**

tunnel NOUN

*an old tunnel dug by prisoners of
war*
▶ A tunnel dug by rabbits is a **burrow**
and a system of burrows is a
warren.
▶ A tunnel beneath a road is a **subway**
or **underpass**.

tunnel VERB

*Moles tunnel in search of
earthworms.*
burrow, dig, mine, bore, excavate

turmoil NOUN

The whole continent was in turmoil.
chaos, upheaval, uproar, disorder,
unrest, commotion, disturbance,
ferment, mayhem
❙ OPPOSITES peace, order

turn VERB

1 *The Earth turns on its axis once
every 24 hours.*
go round, revolve, rotate, roll, spin,
swivel, pivot, twirl, whirl

2 *Turn left at the end of the street.*
change direction, change course,
wheel round
▶ To turn unexpectedly is to **swerve**
or **veer** off course.
▶ To turn and go back in the direction
you came from is to **do a U-turn**.

3 *Henry suddenly turned pale.*
become, go, grow

4 *They turned the attic into a spare
room.*
convert, adapt, change, alter,
modify, transform

5 *How can you tell if milk has turned?*
go bad, go off, go sour, spoil, curdle,
go rancid

▷ **turn something down**
I turned down the offer of a lift.
decline, refuse, reject, spurn, rebuff

▷ **turn something off**
*Please turn off the computer when
you leave.*
switch off, put off, shut down,
deactivate

▷ **turn something on**
How do you turn on your phone?
switch on, put on, start up, activate

▷ **turn out**
1 *Everything turned out well in the
end.*
end up, come out, work out, happen
(informal) pan out

2 *The email turned out to be a hoax.*
prove, be found

3 *Crowds turned out to line the streets.*
appear, come out, arrive, assemble,
gather

▷ **turn up**
Guess who turned up unexpectedly.
arrive, appear, drop in
(*informal*) show up

▷ **turn something up**
Can you turn up the volume?
increase, raise, amplify, intensify

turn NOUN
1 *Give the mouse wheel several turns.*
spin, rotation, revolution, twist, swivel
2 *We came to a turn in the road.*
bend, corner, curve, angle, junction, turning
▶ A sharp turn in a road is a **hairpin bend**.
3 *Whose turn is it to do the washing up?*
time, go, stint, slot, try, chance, opportunity
(*informal*) shot
4 *a stand-up comedy turn*
act, performance, scene, sketch
5 (*informal*) *You gave me quite a turn there!*
fright, scare, shock, start, surprise

turret NOUN
SEE **tower**

tutor NOUN
a professional singing tutor
teacher, instructor, trainer, coach

twig NOUN
a few twigs of rosemary or lavender
stick, stalk, stem, shoot

twilight NOUN
Vampires only start to emerge at twilight.
dusk, nightfall, sunset, close of day
(*North American*) sundown
(*poetic*) gloaming
❘ **OPPOSITE** dawn

twin NOUN
1 *Two of my cousins are twins.*
▶ Twins who look alike are **identical twins** and twins who do not look alike are **unidentical twins**.
▶ Three babies born at the same time are **triplets**.
2 *Venus was once thought to be a twin of the Earth.*
double, duplicate, look-alike, match, clone

twinkle VERB
The city lights twinkled in the distance.
sparkle, glitter, shine, glisten, glimmer, glint, gleam, flicker, wink
FOR TIPS ON DESCRIBING LIGHT SEE **light❶**

twirl VERB
1 *a man twirling his moustache*
twiddle, twist
2 *A few skaters twirled on the ice rink.*
spin, turn, whirl, revolve, rotate, pirouette

twist VERB
1 *Twist the handle to open the door.*
turn, rotate, revolve, swivel
▶ To twist off a lid or cap is to **unscrew** it.
2 *The road twists through the hills.*
wind, weave, curve, zigzag
3 *Blake twisted and turned in his sleep.*
toss, writhe, wriggle
4 *Heat can twist metal out of shape.*
bend, buckle, warp, crumple, mangle, distort
5 *Jenna twisted her hair into a knot.*
wind, loop, coil, curl, entwine

twist NOUN
1 *Give the handle a sharp twist.*
turn, spin, rotation, revolution, swivel
2 *a plot full of unexpected twists*
turning, convolution, surprise, revelation, upset
3 *a twist of lemon peel*
loop, coil, curl, spiral

twisted ADJECTIVE
the twisted trunk of a eucalyptus tree
gnarled, warped, buckled, misshapen, deformed

a
b
c
d
e
f
g
h
i
j
k
l
m
n
o
p
q
r
s
t
u
v
w
x
y
z

twitch VERB

One of the upstairs curtains twitched.
jerk, quiver, tremble, shudder, start, convulse

two NOUN

The chairs come in a set of two.
▶ Two people or things which belong together are a **couple** or a **pair**.
▶ Two musicians playing or singing together are a **duo**.
▶ A piece of music for two players or singers is a **duet**.
❙ SEE ALSO **double**, **dual**

Usage Note

Words which include 'two' in their meaning often begin with **bi-**, for example *bicycle*, *bilingual*, and *binary*.

type NOUN

1 *What type of music do you like to listen to?*
kind, sort, variety, category, class, genre, species
2 *a book printed in large type*
print, typeface, font, lettering, letters, characters

typical ADJECTIVE

1 *It began as just a typical day.*
normal, usual, standard, ordinary, average, unremarkable, run-of-the-mill
❙ OPPOSITES unusual, remarkable
2 *special effects that are typical of action movies*
characteristic, representative, classic, quintessential
❙ OPPOSITE uncharacteristic

Uu

UFO NOUN

the sighting of a UFO over Los Angeles
flying saucer, unidentified flying object

► The study of UFOs is **ufology**.
FOR TIPS ON WRITING SCIENCE FICTION SEE science fiction

ugly ADJECTIVE

1 *The view is ruined by an ugly tower block.*
unattractive, unsightly, unprepossessing, tasteless, hideous, ghastly, monstrous, grotesque
OPPOSITES beautiful, attractive

2 *The crowd was in an ugly mood.*
unfriendly, hostile, menacing, threatening, angry, dangerous, unpleasant
OPPOSITE friendly

ultimate ADJECTIVE

1 *the ultimate defeat of the Dark Wizard*
eventual, final, concluding

► Something which is last but one is **penultimate**.
the penultimate chapter
OPPOSITE initial

2 *Winning is not the ultimate aim in judo.*
supreme, highest, absolute, ideal

umpire NOUN
SEE **referee**

un- PREFIX

> **Usage Note**
> To find synonyms for words beginning with **un-** which are not listed below, try looking up the word to which un- has been added, then add *un-*, *in-*, or *not* to its synonyms. For example, to find synonyms for **unacceptable**, look up **acceptable** and then work out the synonyms, *unsatisfactory, inadequate, not good enough,* etc.

unable ADJECTIVE

▷ **unable to**
The Titanic was unable to withstand the impact.
incapable of, powerless to, inadequate to, unequipped to, unfit for

unanimous ADJECTIVE

1 *The judges came to a unanimous decision.*
united, undivided, joint, collective

► A decision where most but not all people agree is a **majority** decision.

2 *Critics have been unanimous in their praise.*
in agreement, united, in accord, of one mind

unattractive ADJECTIVE
SEE **ugly**

unavoidable ADJECTIVE

Do you believe that climate change is unavoidable?
inevitable, bound to happen, certain, predictable

unaware ADJECTIVE

▷ **unaware of**
The hero is unaware of the plot to kidnap him.
ignorant of, oblivious to, unconscious of, uninformed about
IDIOM in the dark about

a
b
c
d
e
f
g
h
i
j
k
l
m
n
o
p
q
r
s
t
u
v
w
x
y
z

unbearable ADJECTIVE

The stench in the cave was unbearable.
unendurable, intolerable, impossible to bear

unbelievable ADJECTIVE

1 *I found the plot frankly unbelievable.*
unconvincing, unlikely, far-fetched, improbable, incredible

2 *an unbelievable last-minute goal*
amazing, astonishing, extraordinary, remarkable, sensational, phenomenal, staggering, stunning

unbroken ADJECTIVE

1 *She sat in the one unbroken chair.*
undamaged, unscathed, intact, whole, sound
OPPOSITES broken, damaged

2 *an unbroken chain of events*
uninterrupted, continuous, non-stop, ongoing
OPPOSITE discontinuous

3 *His Olympic record is still unbroken.*
unbeaten, undefeated, unsurpassed

uncanny ADJECTIVE

1 *Moonlight helped to create an uncanny atmosphere.*
eerie, weird, ghostly, unearthly, other-worldly, unreal, freakish
(*informal*) creepy, spooky

2 *He bears an uncanny resemblance to Elvis Presley.*
striking, remarkable, extraordinary, incredible

uncertain ADJECTIVE

1 *Hamlet is uncertain what to do next.*
unsure, doubtful, unclear, undecided, in two minds, in a quandary
OPPOSITES certain, positive

2 *The future of the festival is still uncertain.*
indefinite, unknown, undecided, debatable, unpredictable, insecure
IDIOM touch and go
OPPOSITES definite, secure

unclean ADJECTIVE

SEE **dirty**

unclear ADJECTIVE

SEE **uncertain**

uncomfortable ADJECTIVE

1 *sleeping in an uncomfortable bed*
hard, lumpy, stiff, cramped, restrictive
OPPOSITE comfortable

2 *Evie felt uncomfortable talking about herself.*
awkward, uneasy, embarrassed, nervous, tense
OPPOSITES at ease, relaxed

uncommon ADJECTIVE

It's not uncommon to see dolphins here.
unusual, rare, strange, abnormal, atypical, exceptional, unfamiliar, unexpected

unconscious ADJECTIVE

1 *He was knocked unconscious by the fall.*
senseless, inert, knocked out
IDIOMS out cold, out for the count
▶ Someone who is unconscious for an operation is **anaesthetized**.
▶ Someone who is unconscious because of an accident or illness is **in a coma**.
OPPOSITE conscious

2 *an unconscious slip of the tongue*
accidental, unintended, unintentional
OPPOSITES deliberate, intentional
▷ **unconscious of**
unconscious of causing any offence
unaware of, insensible to, ignorant of, oblivious to
OPPOSITE aware of

uncover VERB

1 *Archaeologists have uncovered a second tomb.*
unearth, dig up, excavate, expose, reveal, disclose, unveil, lay bare

2 *uncovering the truth about his past*
discover, detect, come across,

stumble on, chance on
┃ OPPOSITES cover up, hide

undergo VERB
Guide dogs undergo rigorous training.
go through, submit to, be subjected to, experience, put up with, face, endure

underground ADJECTIVE
1 *an underground cavern*
subterranean, sunken, buried
2 *an underground operation*
secret, undercover, covert, clandestine
┃ IDIOM cloak-and-dagger

undermine VERB
Losing the race could undermine her confidence.
weaken, lessen, diminish, reduce, impair, damage, shake
┃ OPPOSITES support, boost

understand VERB
1 *Can you understand what he's saying?*
comprehend, make sense of, grasp, follow, make out, take in, interpret, fathom
┃ IDIOM make head or tail of
▶ To understand something in code is to **decode** or **decipher** it.
2 *You don't understand how hard it is for me.*
realize, appreciate, recognize, be aware of, be conscious of
3 *I understand they're moving to Sydney.*
believe, gather, hear, take it

understandable ADJECTIVE
1 *The instructions are quite understandable.*
comprehensible, intelligible, straightforward, clear, plain, lucid
2 *It's understandable that you feel upset.*
natural, reasonable, justifiable, normal, not surprising, to be expected

understanding NOUN
1 *The robot has limited powers of understanding.*
intelligence, intellect, sense, judgement
2 *a quiz to test your understanding of the topic*
comprehension, knowledge, grasp, mastery, appreciation, awareness
(informal) know-how
┃ OPPOSITE ignorance
3 *It is my understanding that the software is free.*
belief, view, perception, impression
4 *Sufferers need to be treated with understanding.*
sympathy, compassion, consideration, tolerance
┃ OPPOSITE indifference
5 *The two sides reached an understanding.*
agreement, deal, settlement, arrangement, accord

understanding ADJECTIVE
Try talking to an understanding friend.
sympathetic, compassionate, caring, kind, thoughtful, helpful, tolerant, forgiving

undertake VERB
1 *Frodo must undertake a long and dangerous journey.*
take on, accept, be responsible for, embark on, set about, tackle, attempt
2 *They undertook to pay all the costs.*
agree, consent, promise, pledge, guarantee, commit yourself

underwear NOUN
a drawer full of underwear
underclothes, underclothing, undergarments
(informal) undies
▶ Women's underclothes are **lingerie**.
┃ SEE ALSO clothes

undo VERB

1 *Norma undid the laces on her boots.*
unfasten, untie, unbutton, unhook, unlace, loosen, release
▶ To undo stitching is to **unpick** it.

2 *I slowly undid the packaging.*
open, unwrap, unfold, unwind, unroll, unfurl

3 *They say nothing can undo the curse.*
reverse, negate, cancel, annul, countermand

undoubtedly ADVERB

The carving was undoubtedly ancient.
definitely, certainly, unquestionably, undeniably, indubitably, without a doubt, doubtless, clearly

undress VERB

You can undress in the changing room.
get undressed, take off your clothes, strip
❙ OPPOSITES dress, get dressed

unearth VERB

1 *We unearthed a Roman coin in our back garden.*
dig up, excavate, uncover, turn up

2 *She unearthed some old letters in a drawer.*
find, discover, come across, hit upon, track down

uneasy ADJECTIVE

1 *Something about her made me feel uneasy.*
anxious, nervous, worried, apprehensive, troubled, unsettled, tense, on edge
❙ OPPOSITE confident

2 *There was an uneasy silence.*
uncomfortable, awkward, embarrassing, tense, strained
❙ OPPOSITE comfortable

unemployed ADJECTIVE

Millions of workers were unemployed.
out of work, jobless, laid off, redundant

(informal) on the dole
❙ OPPOSITES employed, working, in work

uneven ADJECTIVE

1 *The ground was very uneven in places.*
rough, bumpy, lumpy, rutted
❙ OPPOSITE smooth

2 *Their performance has been uneven this season.*
erratic, inconsistent, irregular, variable, unpredictable, erratic, patchy
❙ OPPOSITE consistent

3 *It was a very uneven contest.*
one-sided, unbalanced, unequal, unfair
❙ OPPOSITE balanced

unexciting ADJECTIVE

an unexciting end to the TV series
dull, boring, uninteresting, tedious, dreary, banal, humdrum
❙ OPPOSITES exciting, interesting

unexpected ADJECTIVE

Her reaction was totally unexpected.
surprising, unforeseen, unpredictable, unplanned
❙ OPPOSITE expected

unfair ADJECTIVE

1 *The colonists protested that the tax was unfair.*
unjust, unreasonable, discriminatory, imbalanced, one-sided, biased
❙ OPPOSITES fair, just

2 *I felt that her comments were unfair.*
undeserved, unmerited, uncalled-for, unjustified, out of order
❙ OPPOSITES fair, deserved

unfaithful ADJECTIVE

SEE **disloyal**

unfamiliar ADJECTIVE

We looked out on an unfamiliar landscape.
strange, unusual, curious, novel, alien

▷ **unfamiliar with**

They were unfamiliar with the local customs.

unaccustomed to, unused to, unaware of

unfit *ADJECTIVE*

He is too unfit to play tennis these days.

out of condition, out of shape, unhealthy

❙ OPPOSITE fit

▷ **unfit for**

food which is unfit for humans

unsuitable for, inappropriate for, not meant for, not designed for

unfortunate *ADJECTIVE*

1 *the ghost of an unfortunate young woman*

unlucky, poor, pitiful, wretched, unhappy, hapless, ill-fated

❙ OPPOSITES fortunate, lucky

2 *The team got off to an unfortunate start.*

unwelcome, unfavourable, unpromising, inauspicious, dismal, bad

❙ OPPOSITES good, favourable

3 *an unfortunate choice of words*

regrettable, unhappy, inappropriate, unsuitable, unwise, injudicious

unfortunately *ADVERB*

Unfortunately, there is no known antidote to the poison.

unluckily, unhappily, regrettably, sadly, alas

unfriendly *ADJECTIVE*

He is likely to get an unfriendly reception.

unwelcoming, inhospitable, unsympathetic, impolite, uncivil, hostile, cold, cool, aloof, stand-offish, unsociable, unneighbourly

❙ OPPOSITES friendly, amiable

ungrateful *ADJECTIVE*

I don't want to seem ungrateful.

unappreciative, unthankful

❙ OPPOSITE grateful

unhappy *ADJECTIVE*

1 *Mel was desperately unhappy away from home.*

sad, miserable, depressed, downhearted, despondent, gloomy, glum, downcast, forlorn, dejected, woeful, crestfallen

❙ IDIOMS *(informal)* down in the dumps, down in the mouth

❙ OPPOSITES happy, cheerful

2 *I'm still unhappy with my hair.*

dissatisfied, displeased, discontented, disgruntled, disappointed

❙ OPPOSITES satisfied, pleased

3 *by an unhappy coincidence*

unfortunate, unlucky, ill-fated, hapless

❙ OPPOSITE lucky

unhealthy *ADJECTIVE*

1 *Joseph Pilates had been an unhealthy child.*

sickly, infirm, unwell, poorly, weak, delicate, feeble, frail

❙ OPPOSITES healthy, strong

2 *an unhealthy diet of junk food*

unwholesome, harmful, unhygienic

❙ OPPOSITES healthy, wholesome

3 *an unhealthy obsession with zombies*

unnatural, abnormal, morbid, macabre, twisted, warped

unhelpful *ADJECTIVE*

The receptionist was most unhelpful.

uncooperative, unfriendly, disobliging

❙ OPPOSITE helpful

unidentified *ADJECTIVE*

1 *an unidentified eyewitness*

unnamed, unspecified, anonymous

❙ OPPOSITE named

2 *an unidentified fossil plant*

unknown, unrecognized

uniform *NOUN*

the uniform of the Canadian Mounted Police

costume, outfit, livery, regalia

(informal) get-up

a
b
c
d
e
f
g
h
i
j
k
l
m
n
o
p
q
r
s
t
u
v
w
x
y
z

uniform *ADJECTIVE*

1 *The air is kept at a uniform temperature.*
consistent, regular, even, stable, steady, unvarying, unchanging
❙ **OPPOSITE** varying

2 *Pearls are rarely uniform in size.*
identical, equal, the same, matching, consistent
❙ **OPPOSITE** different

unify *VERB*

the first emperor to unify India
unite, bring together, integrate, combine, join, merge, amalgamate
❙ **OPPOSITE** separate

unimportant *ADJECTIVE*

His life seemed suddenly unimportant.
insignificant, minor, trivial, trifling, secondary, irrelevant, slight, small, negligible, petty
❙ **OPPOSITES** important, major

uninhabited *ADJECTIVE*

The island has been uninhabited for decades.
unoccupied, empty, deserted, abandoned
❙ **OPPOSITES** inhabited, populated

uninteresting *ADJECTIVE*

The journey home was fairly uninteresting.
dull, boring, unexciting, tedious, dreary, banal, humdrum
❙ **OPPOSITES** interesting, exciting

union *NOUN*

a loose union of warring tribes
unification, joining, integration, merger, amalgamation, fusion, combination
▶ A union of two rivers is a **confluence**.

unique *ADJECTIVE*

1 *Each person's fingerprints are unique.*
distinctive, different, individual, special, peculiar

2 *a unique example of a lost language*
single, sole, lone, solitary, unrepeated
(informal) one-off

Usage Note

Take care not to use **unique** when you mean **rare**. You would say *a unique species of beetle* if it was one of a kind, but *one of the rarest species of insect.*

unit *NOUN*

The shelves are built from separate units.
piece, part, bit, section, segment, element, component, module
FOR UNITS OF MEASUREMENT SEE **measurement**

unite *VERB*

1 *Their marriage united the two kingdoms.*
combine, join, bring together, merge, unify, integrate, amalgamate
❙ **OPPOSITE** separate

2 *Local residents united to fight the plan.*
collaborate, cooperate, come together, join forces
▶ To unite to do something bad is to **conspire**.
❙ **OPPOSITE** compete

universal *ADJECTIVE*

a universal symbol of good luck
general, common, widespread, global, worldwide, international

universe *NOUN*

Are we really alone in the universe?
cosmos, space, infinity
❙ SEE ALSO **space**

unjust *ADJECTIVE*
SEE **unfair**

unkind *ADJECTIVE*

They never said an unkind word to me.
unpleasant, unfriendly, unsympathetic, inconsiderate,

a b c d e f g h i j k l m n o p q r s t u v w x y z

    uncaring, hard-hearted, mean,
harsh, cruel, thoughtless, heartless,
unfeeling, uncharitable, nasty
OPPOSITES kind, sympathetic

unknown *ADJECTIVE*

1 *The letter was in an unknown hand.*
unidentified, unrecognized
OPPOSITE known

2 *The author of the story is unknown.*
anonymous, nameless, unnamed,
unspecified
OPPOSITE named

3 *We were now entering unknown
territory.*
unfamiliar, alien, foreign,
undiscovered, unexplored,
uncharted
OPPOSITE familiar

4 *The main part is played by an
unknown actor.*
little known, unheard of, obscure
OPPOSITE famous

unlike *ADJECTIVE*

*The landscape was unlike anything I
had ever seen.*
different from, distinct from,
dissimilar to
OPPOSITE similar to

unlikely *ADJECTIVE*

an unlikely excuse
unbelievable, unconvincing,
improbable, implausible, incredible,
far-fetched
OPPOSITES believable, convincing

unlucky *ADJECTIVE*

1 *Some say that 13 is an unlucky
number.*
unfavourable, inauspicious,
ill-omened, ill-starred, jinxed

2 *the unlucky victim of a bungled
robbery*
unfortunate, hapless
OPPOSITE lucky

unmarried *ADJECTIVE*

an unmarried man
single
▶ If your marriage has been legally

ended, you are **divorced**.
▶ An unmarried man is a **bachelor**.
▶ An old-fashioned word for an
unmarried woman is a **spinster**.

unmistakable *ADJECTIVE*

an unmistakable smell of burning
distinct, distinctive, clear, obvious,
plain, telltale

unnatural *ADJECTIVE*

1 *An unnatural stillness reigned
through the house.*
unusual, abnormal, uncommon,
exceptional, irregular, odd, strange,
weird, bizarre

2 *Some of the acting was a bit
unnatural.*
stiff, stilted, unrealistic, forced,
affected, self-conscious

3 *Her hair was an unnatural orange
colour.*
artificial, synthetic, man-made,
manufactured
OPPOSITE natural

unnecessary *ADJECTIVE*

*Free up space by deleting
unnecessary files.*
inessential, non-essential,
unwanted, excessive, superfluous,
surplus, extra, redundant,
uncalled for, expendable
OPPOSITE necessary

unoccupied *ADJECTIVE*

1 *The building itself was unoccupied.*
empty, uninhabited, deserted,
unused, vacant
OPPOSITES occupied, inhabited

2 *The seat next to me was unoccupied.*
vacant, free, available
OPPOSITES taken, occupied

unpleasant *ADJECTIVE*

1 *Mr Quilp is a thoroughly unpleasant
character.*
unlikeable, disagreeable,
objectionable, obnoxious,
unfriendly, unkind, bad-tempered,
nasty, malicious, spiteful, mean

2 *an unpleasant experience*

a
b
c
d
e
f
g
h
i
j
k
l
m
n
o
p
q
r
s
t
u
v
w
x
y
z

uncomfortable, disagreeable,
upsetting, distressing, awful,
dreadful, horrible

3 *an unpleasant odour*
disgusting, foul, repulsive, revolting,
repellent, offensive
❙ **OPPOSITES** pleasant, agreeable
❙ **SEE ALSO bad**

unpopular *ADJECTIVE*
The new manager was unpopular
at first.
disliked, unwelcome, unloved,
friendless, out of favour
❙ **OPPOSITE** popular

unravel *VERB*
1 *trying to unravel a knot*
disentangle, untangle, undo,
untwist, separate out
2 *No one has yet unravelled the*
mystery.
solve, clear up, puzzle out, work out,
figure out, explain, clarify
❙ **IDIOM** get to the bottom of

unreal *ADJECTIVE*
The film score creates an unreal
atmosphere.
dream-like, fanciful, make-believe,
imaginary, fictitious
❙ **OPPOSITES** real, realistic

unrest *NOUN*
A period of political unrest followed.
disturbance, disorder, trouble,
turmoil, dissent, strife, agitation,
protest
❙ **OPPOSITES** calm, order

unsafe *ADJECTIVE*
The coastal rocks are unsafe for
climbing.
dangerous, hazardous, risky,
insecure, unsound, treacherous,
perilous
❙ **OPPOSITE** safe

unsatisfactory *ADJECTIVE*
The book comes to an unsatisfactory
conclusion.
disappointing, displeasing,

inadequate, poor, weak,
unacceptable, insufficient
❙ **OPPOSITE** satisfactory

unscrupulous *ADJECTIVE*
a gang of unscrupulous smugglers
dishonest, unprincipled,
disreputable, corrupt, immoral,
unethical, shameless, ruthless

unseen *ADJECTIVE*
SEE **invisible**

unsettling *ADJECTIVE*
The silence was unsettling.
disturbing, unnerving, disquieting,
disconcerting, perturbing, troubling

unsightly *ADJECTIVE*
Litter makes the beach look unsightly.
unattractive, ugly, unprepossessing,
unappealing, hideous, grotesque

unsociable *ADJECTIVE*
Pandas are unsociable animals.
unfriendly, unapproachable,
uncongenial, reserved, withdrawn,
retiring
❙ **OPPOSITES** sociable, gregarious

unstable or **unsteady** *ADJECTIVE*
standing on an unsteady chair
unstable, shaky, wobbly, insecure,
unbalanced, rickety
❙ **OPPOSITES** stable, steady

unsuccessful *ADJECTIVE*
an unsuccessful expedition to the
South Pole
failed, abortive, futile, ineffective,
fruitless, unproductive
❙ **OPPOSITES** successful, triumphant

unsuitable *ADJECTIVE*
The film is unsuitable for young
children.
inappropriate, unfitting,
unacceptable, ill-suited, out of place,
out of keeping
❙ **OPPOSITES** suitable, appropriate

unsure *ADJECTIVE*
She seemed unsure of what to say
or do.

uncertain, unclear, undecided,
doubtful, in two minds, in a
quandary
OPPOSITES certain, clear

untidy *ADJECTIVE*

1 *The garden is looking a bit untidy.*
messy, disorderly, cluttered,
jumbled, tangled, chaotic
(informal) higgledy-piggledy,
topsy-turvy
OPPOSITES tidy, orderly, well kept

2 *Kevin's suit was untidy and his hair
was a mess.*
dishevelled, bedraggled, rumpled,
unkempt, scruffy, slovenly

3 *Her work was untidy and full of
mistakes.*
careless, disorganized, slapdash
(informal) sloppy

untrue *ADJECTIVE*
*Almost every part of the story is
untrue.*
false, incorrect, inaccurate,
erroneous, wrong
OPPOSITES true, accurate

unused *ADJECTIVE*
an unused tin of paint
new, brand-new, unopened, fresh
OPPOSITES used, second-hand

▷ **unused to**
*Truman was unused to all this
attention.*
unaccustomed to, not used to,
unfamiliar with, a stranger to
OPPOSITE accustomed to

unusual *ADJECTIVE*

1 *The weather is unusual for this time
of year.*
abnormal, atypical, out of the
ordinary, exceptional, remarkable,
extraordinary, odd, peculiar,
singular, strange, unexpected,
irregular, unheard-of
OPPOSITES normal, typical

2 *Ebenezer is an unusual name.*
uncommon, rare, unfamiliar,
unconventional, unorthodox

OPPOSITE common

unwell *ADJECTIVE*
SEE **ill**

unwilling *ADJECTIVE*
*Claudio is unwilling to fight the old
man.*
reluctant, hesitant, disinclined,
loath, resistant
OPPOSITES willing, eager

unwillingly *ADVERB*
*Reena sat down unwillingly and
glared.*
reluctantly, hesitantly, grudgingly,
against your will
OPPOSITES willingly, eagerly

unwise *ADJECTIVE*
*It would be unwise to ignore the
prophecy.*
foolish, foolhardy, ill-advised,
senseless, stupid, silly
OPPOSITES wise, sensible

upheaval *NOUN*
the upheaval caused by the Civil War
disruption, disturbance, upset,
disorder, turbulence, turmoil

uphill *ADJECTIVE*

1 *The first half of the race is uphill.*
upward, ascending, rising, climbing
OPPOSITE downhill

2 *facing an uphill struggle*
hard, difficult, tough, strenuous,
laborious, arduous, exhausting,
gruelling, taxing

upkeep *NOUN*
*the upkeep of cycle paths across the
city*
care, maintenance, servicing,
running

upper *ADJECTIVE*
My bedroom is on the upper floor.
higher, upstairs, top
OPPOSITE lower

upright *ADJECTIVE*

1 *sitting in an upright position*
erect, perpendicular, vertical

》

a
b
c
d
e
f
g
h
i
j
k
l
m
n
o
p
q
r
s
t
u
v
w
x
y
z

OPPOSITE horizontal

2 *an upright member of the local community*
honest, honourable, respectable, reputable, law-abiding, virtuous, upstanding, principled, worthy
OPPOSITES disreputable, dishonest

uproar NOUN

The meeting ended in uproar.
chaos, disorder, commotion, confusion, turmoil, pandemonium, mayhem, rumpus, furore

upset VERB

1 *He must have said something to upset her.*
distress, trouble, disturb, unsettle, disconcert, displease, offend, dismay, perturb, fluster, bother

2 *Their arrival upset all our plans.*
disrupt, interfere with, interrupt, affect, throw out, mess up

3 *It's considered bad luck to upset a bowl of rice.*
knock over, tip over, overturn, topple, spill

upset NOUN

1 *a mild stomach upset*
illness, ailment, disorder
(informal) bug

2 *a major upset in the World Cup qualifiers*
shock, surprise, upheaval, setback
IDIOM turn-up for the books

upside-down ADJECTIVE

1 *A convex lens projects an image that is upside-down.*
inverted, upturned, wrong way up
(informal) topsy-turvy

2 *(informal) Suddenly her whole life was upside-down.*
in disarray, in disorder, in a muddle, chaotic, disorderly, jumbled up
(informal) higgledy-piggledy
OPPOSITE orderly

up to date or up-to-date ADJECTIVE

1 *Her clothes are always up to date.*
fashionable, stylish,
contemporary, modern
(informal) trendy, hip
OPPOSITE old-fashioned

2 *using up-to-date technology online*
new, recent, current, the latest, advanced, cutting-edge, state-of the art, up-to-the-minute
OPPOSITES out of date, out-of-date

3 *keeping up to date with all the gossip*
informed, acquainted, in touch
IDIOMS in the picture, up to speed
OPPOSITE out of touch

Usage Note

You write ***up-to-date*** or ***out-of-date*** before a noun: *providing up-to-date information, using an out-of-date passport.*

---

upward ADJECTIVE

The trail becomes a steep upward climb.
uphill, ascending, rising
OPPOSITE downward

urban ADJECTIVE

Most of the population live in urban areas.
built-up, municipal, metropolitan
OPPOSITE rural

urge VERB

I urge you to reconsider your decision.
advise, counsel, appeal to, beg, implore, plead with, press
▶ To urge someone to do something is also to **advocate** or **recommend** it.
OPPOSITE discourage
▷ **urge someone on**
The home crowd urged their team on.
encourage, spur on, egg on

urge NOUN

Agnes had a sudden urge to burst into song.
impulse, compulsion, desire, wish, longing, yearning, craving, hankering, itch, yen

urgent *ADJECTIVE*

  1 *I have an urgent matter to discuss.*
  pressing, serious, critical, essential, important, top-priority
  ❙ OPPOSITE unimportant

  2 *The stranger spoke in an urgent whisper.*
  anxious, insistent, earnest

usable *ADJECTIVE*

  1 *Your hard disk is not usable any more.*
  operating, working, functioning, functional
  ❙ OPPOSITE unusable

  2 *Is this voucher still usable?*
  valid, acceptable
  ❙ OPPOSITE invalid

usage *NOUN*

  1 *the increased usage of solar energy*
  use, consumption

  2 *an incorrect usage of the phrase*
  application, use, employment, utilization

use *VERB*

  1 *You may use a calculator to help you.*
  make use of, employ, utilize
  ▶ To use your knowledge is to **apply** it.
  ▶ To use people or things selfishly is to **exploit** them.

  2 *Can you show me how to use the photocopier?*
  operate, work, handle, manage
  ▶ To hold and use a weapon or tool is to **wield** it.

  3 *Please don't use all the hot water.*
  use up, go through, consume, exhaust, spend

use *NOUN*

  1 *a more efficient use of your time*
  usage, application, employment, utilization

  2 *A blog can have many different uses.*
  function, purpose, point

  3 *The money was of no use to him now.*
  help, benefit, advantage, profit, value

used *ADJECTIVE*

  buying a used computer
  second-hand, pre-owned, old, hand-me-down, cast-off
  ❙ OPPOSITES new, unused

  ▷ **used to**
  Cathy is used to getting her own way.
  accustomed to, familiar with, experienced in, versed in, no stranger to, inured to
  ❙ OPPOSITE unaccustomed to

useful *ADJECTIVE*

  1 *A webcam is useful for chatting online.*
  convenient, handy, practical, effective, efficient

  2 *The website offers some useful advice.*
  good, helpful, valuable, worthwhile, constructive, productive, fruitful
  ❙ OPPOSITES useless, unhelpful

useless *ADJECTIVE*

  1 *Most of her advice was completely useless.*
  worthless, unhelpful, pointless, futile, unprofitable, fruitless, impractical, unusable
  ❙ IDIOM of no avail
  ❙ OPPOSITES useful, helpful

  2 *(informal) I've always been useless at maths.*
  bad, poor, incompetent, incapable *(informal)* rubbish, hopeless
  ❙ OPPOSITE good

user-friendly *ADJECTIVE*

  a user-friendly guide to punctuation
  easy to use, straightforward, uncomplicated, understandable

usher *VERB*

  We were ushered into the dining hall.
  escort, conduct, guide, lead, show, take

usual *ADJECTIVE*

  1 *I'll meet you at the usual time.*
  normal, customary, familiar, habitual, regular, standard

                 »

2 *It's usual to knock before entering.*
common, accepted, conventional,
traditional

OPPOSITE unusual

usually ADVERB
I don't usually get up this early.
normally, generally, ordinarily,
customarily, habitually, as a rule

utensil NOUN
a rack of cooking utensils
tool, implement, device, gadget,
instrument, appliance
(informal) gizmo

utmost ADJECTIVE
*This message is of the utmost
importance.*
highest, greatest, supreme,
maximum, top, paramount

utter① VERB
*The girl could scarcely utter her
name.*
say, speak, express, pronounce,
articulate, voice, mouth, put into
words

SEE ALSO say

utter② ADJECTIVE
*The three of us stared in utter
amazement.*
complete, total, absolute, thorough,
sheer, downright, out-and-out

Vv

vacancy *NOUN*

a vacancy for a trainee hairdresser
opening, position, post, job,
situation

vacant *ADJECTIVE*

1 *The house next door is still vacant.*
unoccupied, empty, uninhabited,
deserted
OPPOSITE occupied

2 *The assistant gave me a vacant stare.*
blank, expressionless, emotionless,
impassive, glazed, deadpan
OPPOSITE expressive

vague *ADJECTIVE*

1 *The directions she gave were rather
vague.*
indefinite, imprecise, broad, general,
ill-defined, unclear, woolly
OPPOSITES exact, detailed

2 *I have only a vague memory of that
day.*
blurred, indistinct, obscure, dim,
hazy, shadowy
OPPOSITES definite, clear

vain *ADJECTIVE*

1 *Tyler is rather vain about his looks.*
arrogant, proud, conceited, haughty,
self-satisfied, narcissistic
OPPOSITE modest

2 *I made a vain attempt to tidy my
room.*
unsuccessful, ineffective, useless,
pointless, futile, fruitless,
unproductive
OPPOSITE successful

valid *ADJECTIVE*

1 *The ticket is valid for three months.*
current, usable, legal, authorized,
official, binding, in effect

2 *The author makes several valid
points.*
acceptable, reasonable, sound,
legitimate, genuine, justifiable,
cogent
OPPOSITE invalid

valley *NOUN*

*The village of Mirkdale lies in a deep
valley.*
vale, dale, gorge, gully, pass, ravine,
canyon
(Scottish) glen

valuable *ADJECTIVE*

1 *I believe the necklace is
very valuable.*
expensive, costly, dear, high-priced,
precious, priceless
OPPOSITE valueless

2 *He gave us some valuable advice.*
useful, helpful, good, beneficial,
constructive, worthwhile, invaluable
OPPOSITE worthless

Usage Note

The word ***invaluable*** is not the
opposite of ***valuable***: a piece of
invaluable advice is one that is
extremely valuable.

value *NOUN*

1 *the approximate value of the
painting*
price, cost, worth

2 *the value of taking regular exercise*
advantage, benefit, merit, use,
usefulness, importance

value *VERB*

1 *I have always valued her opinion.*
esteem, respect, appreciate, have a
good opinion of, think highly of
IDIOM set great store by

► To value something highly is to **prize**
or **treasure** it.

》

a
b
c
d
e
f
g
h
i
j
k
l
m
n
o
p
q
r
s
t
u
v
w
x
y
z

2 *The painting was valued at 6 million dollars.*
price, cost, rate, evaluate, assess

van NOUN
SEE **vehicle**

vanish VERB
Mr Byrne's smile vanished in an instant.
disappear, go away, fade, dissolve, disperse
| OPPOSITE appear

vanity NOUN
Her rejection was a blow to his vanity.
arrogance, pride, conceit, self-esteem, self-importance
(informal) big-headedness

vapour NOUN
At room temperature, dry ice turns into vapour.
gas, fumes, steam, smoke
▶ Vapour hanging in the air is **haze**, **fog**, **mist**, or **smog**.
▶ When something turns to vapour it **vaporizes**.

variable ADJECTIVE
The weather is variable at this time of year.
changeable, fluctuating, erratic, inconsistent, unpredictable, fluid, fickle, unstable
| OPPOSITE constant

variation NOUN
1 *extreme variations in temperature*
difference, change, fluctuation, shift
| OPPOSITE uniformity
2 *This recipe is a variation on a classic dish.*
alteration (of), modification (of), deviation (from)

varied ADJECTIVE
a large and varied group of insects
diverse, assorted, mixed, miscellaneous, wide-ranging, disparate, motley
| OPPOSITE uniform

variety NOUN
1 *a variety of shoe styles*
assortment, range, mixture, array, miscellany
2 *Try to add more variety to your writing.*
variation, diversity, change, difference
3 *We stock over thirty varieties of pasta.*
kind, sort, type, category, form, make, model, brand

various ADJECTIVE
The shoes are available in various colours.
different, several, assorted, varying, differing, a variety of, diverse, sundry

vary VERB
1 *Try varying the volume on the speakers.*
change, modify, adjust, alter
2 *The length of daylight varies with the seasons.*
change, alter, differ, fluctuate
3 *Estimates vary widely.*
differ, be dissimilar, disagree, diverge

vast ADJECTIVE
1 *accumulating a vast fortune*
huge, great, immense, enormous, massive, gigantic, colossal
| OPPOSITE tiny
| SEE ALSO **big**
2 *a vast tract of desert landscape*
broad, wide, extensive, sweeping, boundless

vault VERB
▷ **vault over something**
A few protesters vaulted over the barrier.
jump over, leap over, bound over, spring over, clear

vault NOUN
The documents are stored in an underground vault at night.
strongroom, treasury

► An underground part of a house is a **basement** or **cellar**.

► A room underneath a church is a **crypt**.

veer *VERB*

Suddenly, the car veered sharply to the left.

swerve, turn, swing, change direction, change course

vegetable *NOUN*

 WORD WEB

leaf vegetables

Brussels sprout, cabbage, cauliflower, Chinese cabbage or Chinese leaf, endive, globe artichoke, kale, lettuce, mustard greens, pak choi, spinach, Swiss chard, watercress

root vegetables

beetroot, carrot, celeriac, daikon, parsnip, radish, swede (*North American* rutabaga), sweet potato, turnip

legumes or pulses

broad beans or fava beans, butter beans or lima beans, chickpeas, French beans or green beans, kidney beans, lentils, mangetout or sugar snap peas, mung beans, peas, runner beans, snow peas, soya beans

other vegetables

asparagus, aubergine (*North American* eggplant), butternut squash, broccoli, cauliflower, celery, courgette (*North American* zucchini), garlic, Jerusalem artichoke, kohlrabi, leek, marrow, mushroom, okra, onion, pepper, potato, pumpkin, rhubarb, shallot, spaghetti squash, spring onions (*North American* scallions), sweetcorn, water chestnut, yam

vegetarian *NOUN*

Many but not all Buddhists are vegetarians.

► A person who doesn't eat any animal products is a **vegan**.

► An animal that feeds only on plants is a **herbivore**.

⌐ **OPPOSITES** carnivore, meat-eater

vegetation *NOUN*

the lush vegetation of the Amazon Basin

foliage, greenery, growth, plants, undergrowth, verdure

vehicle *NOUN*

 WORD WEB

some types of vehicle

ambulance, *informal* bendy bus, bicycle, bulldozer, bus, cab, cable car, car or motor car, caravan, coach, double-decker, fire engine, fork-lift truck, four-wheel drive, hearse, HGV or heavy goods vehicle, horsebox, jeep, lorry, minibus, minicab, motorbike or motorcycle, people carrier, pick-up truck, police car, rickshaw, scooter, skidoo, sledge, sleigh, snowplough, steamroller, tank, taxi, tractor, train, tram, tricycle, trolleybus, truck, underground, van

old horse-drawn vehicles

carriage, cart, chariot, gig, hansom cab, stagecoach, trap, wagon

FOR TRANSPORT BY AIR AND SEA SEE **aircraft**, **boat**

veil *VERB*

Her face was partly veiled by a scarf.

cover, conceal, hide, mask, shroud

vein *NOUN*

1 *blood pumping through your veins*

blood vessel

a
b
c
d
e
f
g
h
i
j
k
l
m
n
o
p
q
r
s
t
u
v
w
x
y
z

»

▶ Major blood vessels which carry blood from your heart to other parts of your body are **arteries**.

▶ Delicate hair-like blood vessels are **capillaries**.

2 *The story is told in a light-hearted vein.*
style, mood, manner, tone, character, spirit, humour

velocity NOUN
travelling at high velocity through space
speed, rate, rapidity, swiftness

vengeance NOUN
Prospero plots vengeance on his enemies.
revenge, retribution, retaliation
❙ OPPOSITE forgiveness

venomous ADJECTIVE
SEE **poisonous**

vent NOUN
Hot air escapes through vents in the roof.
outlet, opening, aperture, gap, hole, slit, duct

vent VERB
The crowd vented their frustration by booing.
express, let out, pour out, release, voice, air

venture NOUN
an exciting new sporting venture
enterprise, undertaking, project, scheme, operation, endeavour

venture VERB
footage of polar bear cubs venturing out into the snow
set out, set forth, emerge, journey

▷ **venture to do something**
I finally ventured to ask her name.
dare to, have the nerve to, be so bold as to, presume to, take the liberty of

verdict NOUN
waiting for the verdict of the jury
decision, judgement, finding, conclusion, ruling

verge NOUN
a grassy verge alongside the road
side, edge, margin

▶ A stone or concrete edging beside a road is a **kerb**.

▶ The flat strip of road beside a motorway is the **hard shoulder**.

▷ **on the verge of**
Some species are now on the verge of extinction.
on the edge of, on the point of, on the brink of, close to, approaching

verify VERB
An eyewitness verified his statement.
confirm, prove, validate, support, back up, bear out, substantiate, corroborate

versatile ADJECTIVE
1 *an extremely versatile cook*
resourceful, adaptable, flexible, multi-talented, all-round

2 *Cotton is a very versatile fabric.*
adaptable, multi-purpose, all-purpose

verse NOUN
1 *The entire play is written in verse.*
SEE **poetry**

2 *the first two verses of the poem*
stanza

version NOUN
1 *Write your own version of the story.*
account, description, report, statement

2 *the film version of 'Wuthering Heights'*
adaptation, interpretation, rendering

▶ A version of something which was originally in another language is a **translation**.

3 *a new version of the popular video game*
design, model, form, variation, edition

vertical ADJECTIVE
a deep valley with almost vertical sides

perpendicular, upright, erect, plumb
▶ A vertical drop is a **sheer** drop.
OPPOSITES horizontal, flat

very ADVERB
a very unusual kind of day
extremely, highly, exceedingly,
especially, particularly, truly,
remarkably, unusually, exceptionally,
singularly, decidedly, really,
intensely, acutely
(informal) terribly, awfully, seriously,
ultra, mega
(North American informal) real,
mighty
OPPOSITES slightly, rather

vessel NOUN
1 *a flotilla of fishing vessels*
boat, ship, craft
FOR TYPES OF BOAT OR SHIP SEE **boat**
2 *an ancient clay vessel*
pot, dish, bowl, jar, jug, container,
receptacle
FOR BLOOD VESSELS SEE **vein**

veto VERB
*They vetoed the proposal for a
skatepark.*
reject, turn down, say no to, dismiss,
disallow, ban, prohibit, forbid
OPPOSITE approve

vexed ADJECTIVE
*Maggie was vexed at herself for
blushing.*
annoyed, irritated, cross, frustrated,
exasperated

vibrant ADJECTIVE
a city with a vibrant nightlife
lively, dynamic, energetic, vigorous,
spirited
OPPOSITE lifeless

vibrate VERB
Sounds make the eardrum vibrate.
shake, tremble, quiver, quake, shiver,
shudder, judder, throb

vicious ADJECTIVE
1 *the scene of a vicious murder*
brutal, violent, savage, ferocious,

bloodthirsty, cruel, callous,
merciless, pitiless, ruthless,
inhuman, barbaric, sadistic
2 *a vicious satire on the American way
of life*
fierce, malicious, biting,
hard-hitting, savage, merciless

victim NOUN
the victims of the Asian tsunami
casualty, sufferer
▶ Victims of an accident are also **the
injured** or **the wounded**.
▶ A person who dies in an accident is
a **fatality**.

victor NOUN
*A Canadian crew came away as the
victors.*
winner, champion, conqueror

victorious ADJECTIVE
the captain of the victorious team
winning, triumphant, successful,
conquering, top
OPPOSITES defeated, losing

victory NOUN
He led his team to an unlikely victory.
win, success, triumph, conquest
OPPOSITES defeat, loss

view NOUN
1 *There's a great view from the top
floor.*
outlook, prospect, scene, scenery,
vista, panorama
2 *What are you views on animal
testing?*
opinion, thought, attitude, belief,
conviction, sentiment, idea, notion
▷ **in view of**
in view of the recent dramatic events
because of, as a result of,
considering, taking account of

view VERB
1 *Both locals and tourists come to view
the scenery.*
look at, see, observe, regard, gaze
at, eye, scan, survey, inspect,
examine, contemplate
SEE ALSO look

a
b
c
d
e
f
g
h
i
j
k
l
m
n
o
p
q
r
s
t
u
v
w
x
y
z

》

2 *Dexter viewed the newcomers with suspicion.*
think of, consider, regard, look on

viewer *NOUN*

a programme which invites viewers to phone in
▶ People who view a performance are the **audience** or **spectators**.
▶ People who view something as they happen to pass by are **bystanders** or **onlookers**.

vigilant *ADJECTIVE*

You must be vigilant when cycling in traffic.
alert, watchful, attentive, observant, wary, on the lookout, on your guard
❙ **OPPOSITE** inattentive

vigorous *ADJECTIVE*

1 *a firm believer in vigorous exercise*
active, brisk, energetic, lively, strenuous, forceful, powerful
❙ **OPPOSITES** light, gentle
2 *a vigorous man in the prime of life*
robust, strong, sturdy, healthy, fit
❙ **OPPOSITES** feeble, weak

vigour *NOUN*

Miss Christie felt young again and full of vigour.
energy, spirit, vitality, liveliness, enthusiasm, passion, dynamism, verve, gusto, zeal, zest
(informal) oomph, get-up-and-go

vile *ADJECTIVE*

1 *a vile smell of unwashed bodies*
disgusting, repulsive, revolting, foul, horrible, loathsome, offensive, repellent, sickening, nauseating
❙ **OPPOSITE** pleasant
2 *a vile act of inhuman cruelty*
dreadful, despicable, appalling, abominable, contemptible, wicked, evil

villain *NOUN*

an actor who enjoys playing villains
rogue, scoundrel, wrongdoer, miscreant, criminal

(informal) baddy, crook
❙ **OPPOSITE** hero

violate *VERB*

1 *Downloading music may violate copyright.*
break, infringe, contravene, disobey, flout, disregard, ignore
2 *Several ancient tombs had been violated and robbed.*
desecrate, profane, defile, vandalize, deface

violation *NOUN*

a serious violation of the rules
breach, breaking, infringement, contravention, flouting

violence *NOUN*

1 *The film includes scenes of graphic violence.*
fighting, physical force, aggression, brutality, savagery, barbarity
❙ **OPPOSITES** non-violence, pacifism
2 *The violence of the storm uprooted trees.*
force, power, strength, might, severity, intensity, ferocity, vehemence, fury, rage
❙ **OPPOSITES** gentleness, mildness

violent *ADJECTIVE*

1 *There were violent protests in the capital.*
aggressive, fierce, ferocious, rough, brutal, vicious, savage
2 *a violent storm in the Gulf of Alaska*
severe, strong, powerful, forceful, intense, raging, turbulent, tempestuous, wild
❙ **OPPOSITES** gentle, mild

virtually *ADVERB*

Plastics can be made into virtually any shape.
almost, nearly, practically, effectively, more or less, just about, as good as

virtue *NOUN*

1 *a play about love, fidelity, and virtue*
goodness, morality, honesty,

decency, integrity, righteousness, rectitude
OPPOSITE vice

2 *The main virtue of the book is its originality.*
merit, asset, strength, good point, advantage, benefit
OPPOSITE failing

virtuous ADJECTIVE
Jody always felt virtuous after doing some exercise.
good, worthy, upright, honourable, moral, just, pure, righteous, law-abiding
OPPOSITES wicked, immoral

visible ADJECTIVE
Green Gables was barely visible from the main road.
noticeable, observable, viewable, detectable, discernible, evident, apparent, manifest
OPPOSITE invisible

vision NOUN
1 *having problems with your vision*
eyesight, sight, eyes
▶ Related adjectives are **visual** and **optical**.
2 *a character haunted by nightmarish visions*
apparition, dream, hallucination, phantom, mirage
3 *a science fiction writer of great vision*
imagination, inspiration, creativity, inventiveness, foresight

visit VERB
1 *We're planning to visit friends in Toronto.*
call on, go to see, drop in on, look in on, stay with
2 *They'll be visiting eight European cities.*
stay in, stop over in, tour, explore

visit NOUN
1 *our first visit to Disneyland*
trip, outing, excursion, tour
2 *Some friends are coming for a short visit.*

stay, call, stopover

visitor NOUN
1 *Mrs Finch was expecting some visitors.*
guest, caller, company
2 *The city welcomes millions of visitors each year.*
tourist, holidaymaker, sightseer, traveller

visualize VERB
I tried to visualize the house as she described it.
imagine, picture, envisage, see, conjure up

vital ADJECTIVE
It is vital that we all stay together.
essential, crucial, imperative, critical, all-important, necessary, indispensable
OPPOSITE unimportant

vitality NOUN
Ginseng is said to increase vitality.
energy, life, liveliness, spirit, vigour, vivacity, zest, dynamism, exuberance
(informal) get-up-and-go

vivid ADJECTIVE
1 *an artist who loves to use vivid colours*
bright, colourful, strong, bold, intense, vibrant, rich, dazzling, brilliant, glowing
OPPOSITES dull, muted
FOR TIPS ON DESCRIBING COLOURS SEE **colour**
2 *a vivid account of her visit to China*
lively, clear, powerful, evocative, imaginative, dramatic, lifelike, realistic, graphic
OPPOSITES dull, lifeless

voice NOUN
1 *Her voice broke with emotion.*
speech, tone, way of speaking
2 *He promised to listen to the voice of the people.*
opinion, view, expression
FOR TIPS ON DESCRIBING VOICES SEE **sound**❶

a
b
c
d
e
f
g
h
i
j
k
l
m
n
o
p
q
r
s
t
u
v
w
x
y
z

voice VERB

Locals voiced their concerns at the meeting.

express, communicate, declare, state, articulate

volcano NOUN

 WORD WEB

parts of a volcano

crater, magma chamber, vent

▶ Molten rock that builds up inside a volcano is called **magma**. When the molten rock reaches the surface it is called **lava**. Lava and ash pouring from a volcano is a **volcanic eruption**.

▶ A volcano that may erupt at any time is an **active** volcano. One that may not erupt for some time is a **dormant** volcano; and a volcano that can no longer erupt is an **extinct** volcano.

▶ The scientific study of volcanoes is **volcanology** or **vulcanology**.

SEE ALSO earthquake

volume NOUN

1 coping with a huge volume of email traffic

amount, quantity, bulk, mass

2 How do you find the volume of the test tube?

capacity, mass, size, dimensions

3 a volume of modern poetry

book, tome, publication

voluntary ADJECTIVE

1 a voluntary donation to the museum

optional, discretionary, by choice

OPPOSITE compulsory

2 doing voluntary work in a charity shop

unpaid

OPPOSITE paid

volunteer VERB

I volunteered to do the washing-up.

offer, come forward, be willing

OPPOSITE refuse

vomit VERB

Symptoms include fever and vomiting.

be sick, heave, retch, spew

(informal) throw up, puke

vortex NOUN

SEE **spiral**

vote VERB

Suffragettes fought for women's right to vote.

cast your vote

▶ To choose someone by voting is to **elect** them.

vote NOUN

1 a vote to find the nation's favourite book

ballot, poll, election, referendum

2 When did women finally get the vote?

right to vote, suffrage, franchise

voucher NOUN

a voucher to get a free gift

coupon, ticket, token

vow NOUN

taking a solemn vow of secrecy

pledge, promise, oath, bond, word

vow VERB

He vowed never to reveal her identity.

pledge, promise, swear, give your word, take an oath

voyage NOUN

a hazardous voyage across the Atlantic

journey, trip, expedition, cruise, crossing, passage

vulgar ADJECTIVE

1 a vulgar display of obscene wealth

tasteless, cheap, tawdry, crass, unrefined, uncouth

(informal) tacky

OPPOSITE tasteful

2 using vulgar language

indecent, rude, offensive, coarse, crude

OPPOSITE decent

a b c d e f g h i j k l m n o p q r s t u v w x y z

vulnerable

vulnerable ADJECTIVE

The cubs are vulnerable without their mother.

unprotected, unguarded, exposed, open to attack, at risk, in danger

OPPOSITES safe, protected

▷ **vulnerable to**

Your computer may be vulnerable to viruses.

exposed to, open to, susceptible to, unprotected from, at risk from

OPPOSITES safe from, protected from

a
b
c
d
e
f
g
h
i
j
k
l
m
n
o
p
q
r
s
t
u
v
w
x
y
z

waddle *VERB*

A porcupine came waddling towards us.

toddle, totter, shuffle, shamble, wobble

| **SEE ALSO walk**

wade *VERB*

1 *The river is too deep to wade across.*
paddle, wallow, splash

2 *wading through piles of paperwork*
plough, labour, work, toil

wag *VERB*

The cyberdog can even wag its electronic tail.
move to and fro, wave, shake, swing, swish, waggle, wiggle

wage *NOUN*

earning a minimum wage
earnings, income, pay, remuneration

▶ A fixed regular wage, usually for a year's work, is a **salary**.

wage *VERB*

The abolitionists waged a long campaign against slavery.
carry on, conduct, pursue, engage in, fight

wail *VERB*

All night long the wind wailed.
howl, moan, cry, bawl, whine

wait *VERB*

I'll wait here until you get back.
stay, stay put, remain, rest, stop, pause, linger
(informal) hang about, hang around,

stick around, hold on

wait *NOUN*

There is a short wait between trains.
interval, interlude, pause, delay, stoppage, hold-up, lull, gap

wake or **waken** *VERB*

1 *waking from a deep sleep*
awake, awaken, rise, stir, wake up, come to, come round

2 *The doorbell woke me at 7.30.*
rouse, arouse, awaken, disturb

walk *VERB*

1 *Would you rather walk or take the bus?*
go on foot, travel on foot
(informal) hoof it

2 *I offered to walk her home after the party.*
escort, accompany, guide, show, lead, take

 OVERUSED WORD

to walk slowly, casually
amble, saunter, stroll, pace, step, tread

*Damon **sauntered** along the corridor, trying to look cool.*

to walk quietly
creep, pad, slink, prowl, stalk, steal, tiptoe, patter, mince
*I got up quietly and **padded** downstairs in my slippers.*

to walk heavily, loudly
stamp, pound, clump, tramp, trudge, traipse, plod, wade
*More police officers came **clumping** through the house.*

to walk smartly, proudly
march, stride, strut, parade, promenade, swagger, trot
*Sue imagined herself **strutting** down the catwalk in high heels.*

to walk unsteadily
stagger, stumble, shuffle, shamble, totter, hobble, toddle, dodder, lurch, limp, waddle, lope
*The creature **shuffled** off into the night.*

to walk a long distance
hike, trek, ramble, traipse
*Do you fancy a holiday **hiking** in the Alps?*

to walk in a group
file, troop, march, stream
*We all **trooped** into the dining room for breakfast.*

walk NOUN
1 *taking a walk in the countryside*
stroll, ramble, hike, trek, tramp, march, promenade
2 *a tall man with a shambling walk*
gait, step, stride
3 *a tree-lined walk alongside the canal*
path, trail, walkway, footpath, route

walker NOUN
The path is used used by walkers and climbers.
rambler, hiker, trekker, stroller
▶ Someone who walks along a street is a **pedestrian**.

wall NOUN
part of an ancient Roman wall
barricade, barrier, fortification, embankment
▶ A wall to hold back water is a **dam** or **dyke**.
▶ A low wall along the edge of a roof is a **parapet**.
▶ A wall built on top of a mound of earth is a **rampart**.
▶ A wall or fence made of sticks is a **stockade**.

wander VERB
1 *A few goats wandered down from the hills.*
roam, rove, range, ramble, meander, stroll

2 *We must have wandered off the path.*
stray, drift
3 *Try not to wander too far from the topic.*
digress, stray, drift, depart, deviate, get sidetracked

wander NOUN
going for a wander about town
roam, ramble, journey, walk

wane VERB
1 *as the afternoon light began to wane*
fade, fail, dim
❙ OPPOSITE brighten
2 *My enthusiasm was starting to wane.*
decline, decrease, lessen, diminish, subside, weaken, dwindle
❙ OPPOSITE strengthen
❙ SEE ALSO **moon**

want VERB
1 *He wants to be the lead guitarist in a band.*
wish, desire, long, hope
2 *Ginny had always wanted a room of her own.*
wish for, desire, fancy, crave, long for, yearn for, hanker after, pine for, hunger for, thirst for
❙ IDIOMS set your heart on, be dying for
3 *(informal) All it wants is a good wash.*
need, require, cry out for

want NOUN
1 *understanding the wants of your pet*
demand, desire, wish, need, requirement
2 *Livestock died from want of food and water.*
lack, need, absence
3 *Many families are still living in want.*
poverty, hardship, need, deprivation, destitution

wanting ADJECTIVE
▷ **wanting in**
The show is completely wanting in humour.

lacking, deficient in, without, missing

war NOUN

1 *the long war waged by Napoleon in Europe*
fighting, warfare, conflict, strife, hostilities

2 *joining the war against poverty*
campaign, struggle, effort

ward VERB

▷ **ward something off**

1 *Use sunblock to ward off the sun's rays.*
avert, block, check, deflect, turn aside, parry

2 *Garlic is said to ward off vampires.*
fend off, drive away, repel, keep away

warehouse NOUN

an old factory warehouse
storeroom, depository, depot

wares PLURAL NOUN

They make a living selling their wares to tourists.
goods, merchandise, produce, stock, commodities

warfare NOUN

a carved panel depicting scenes of warfare
fighting, combat, war, hostilities, conflict

warlike ADJECTIVE

'The War of the Worlds' portrays Martians as warlike.
aggressive, violent, hostile, militant, belligerent
► Someone who seeks to start a war is a **warmonger**.

⎸ OPPOSITES peaceful, peace-loving

warm ADJECTIVE

1 *on a warm summer evening*
mild, balmy, sultry, summery
► A climate that is neither extremely hot nor extremely cold is **temperate**.

⎸ OPPOSITES cold, chilly

2 *Use warm, not boiling, water.*
tepid, lukewarm, hand-hot

3 *a warm winter coat*
cosy, snug, thick, chunky, woolly, thermal

⎸ OPPOSITES thin, light

4 *Let's give our guests a warm welcome.*
friendly, welcoming, kind, hospitable, cordial, genial, amiable, sympathetic

⎸ OPPOSITES unfriendly, frosty

warm VERB

Come in and warm yourself by the fire.
heat, make warmer, thaw out

⎸ OPPOSITE chill

warn VERB

I warned you it was dangerous to come here.
advise, caution, counsel, alert, make someone aware
► To warn people of danger is to **raise the alarm**.

warning NOUN

1 *There was no warning of the recent earthquake.*
sign, signal, indication, advance notice
(informal) tip-off

2 *Perhaps the dream was a warning.*
omen, portent, sign, premonition, foreboding

3 *The referee let him off with a warning.*
caution, reprimand

warp VERB

1 *Heat may cause the plastic to warp.*
bend, buckle, twist, curl, bow, distort

⎸ OPPOSITE straighten

2 *Could video games really warp your view of reality?*
twist, distort, corrupt, pervert

warrior NOUN

the armour of a samurai warrior
fighter, soldier, combatant

wary ADJECTIVE

1 *Kyle took a wary step towards the creature.*
cautious, careful, watchful, attentive, vigilant, on your guard
OPPOSITE reckless

2 *Foxes are extremely wary of humans.*
distrustful, suspicious, leery, chary
OPPOSITE trusting

wash VERB

1 *I washed quickly and went downstairs.*
bathe, shower

2 *How often do you wash your hair?*
clean, cleanse, shampoo
► To wash clothes is to **launder** them.
► To wash something in clean water is to **rinse**, **sluice**, or **swill** it.

3 *Wash the floor regularly with warm water.*
mop, wipe, scrub, sponge

4 *A huge wave washed over the sea wall.*
flow, splash, lap, break, surge, roll

5 *The strong current washed the boat out to sea.*
carry, sweep

wash NOUN

1 *Put any used towels in the wash.*
laundry, washing

2 *It's time to give the dog a wash.*
clean, bath

waste VERB

Let's not waste any more time.
squander, misuse, throw away, fritter away
OPPOSITE save

waste NOUN

recycling household waste
rubbish, refuse, litter, junk
(North American) trash, garbage
► Waste food is **leftovers**.
► Waste metal is **scrap**.

wasteful ADJECTIVE

How can we be less wasteful with our energy?
extravagant, uneconomical, profligate, prodigal, lavish, spendthrift
OPPOSITES economical, thrifty

watch VERB

1 *Frankie paced up and down, watching the clock.*
look at, gaze at, stare at, peer at, view, eye, scan, scrutinize, contemplate

2 *Watch how the goalkeeper reacts.*
observe, note, take notice of, keep your eyes on, pay attention to, attend to, heed

3 *Could you watch my bag for a minute?*
keep an eye on, keep watch over, guard, mind, look after, safeguard, supervise, tend

4 *I got the feeling we were being watched.*
spy on, monitor, track, tail, keep under surveillance
(informal) keep tabs on

▷ **watch out**
Watch out! There's a wave coming!
be careful, pay attention, beware, take care, take heed

watch NOUN

1 *a new battery for my watch*
FOR DEVICES USED TO MEASURE TIME SEE time

2 *keeping a close watch on the horizon*
guard, lookout, eye, vigil

watchful ADJECTIVE

trying to escape the watchful eye of the media
alert, attentive, observant, vigilant, sharp-eyed, keen
OPPOSITE inattentive

water NOUN

How much of the Earth's surface is covered by water?
► Animals and plants which live in water are **aquatic**.
FOR AREAS OF WATER SEE landscape

water VERB

> *You can use bathwater to water your garden.*
> wet, irrigate, sprinkle, dampen, moisten, soak, drench

▷ **water something down**

1 *Some paints need to be watered down.*
dilute, thin out

2 *The story has been watered down for the film version.*
tone down, soften, tame, temper, moderate

waterproof ADJECTIVE

> *a layer of waterproof material*
> impermeable, watertight
> ▌ **OPPOSITES** permeable, porous

watery ADJECTIVE

1 *the watery surface of the eye*
wet, moist, damp

2 *My eyes were stinging and watery.*
tearful, welling up

3 *a bowl of watery, tasteless porridge*
weak, thin, runny, diluted, watered down

wave NOUN

1 *the sound of waves breaking on the beach*
breaker, roller, billow

▶ A very small wave is a **ripple**.

▶ A huge wave caused by an earthquake is a **tidal wave** or **tsunami**.

▶ A number of white waves following each other is **surf**.

▶ The rise and fall of the sea is the **swell**.

▶ The top of a wave is the **crest** or **ridge**.

2 *a recent wave of arrests*
rush, outbreak, flood, stream, surge, spate

wave VERB

1 *Sugar cane waved in the breeze.*
sway, swing, shake, undulate, move to and fro, flap, flutter, ripple

2 *a man waving a newspaper in the air*
shake, brandish, flourish, twirl, wag, waggle, wiggle

waver VERB

1 *Ghostly shadows wavered on the walls.*
flicker, quiver, tremble, shake, shiver

2 *Her new-found courage began to waver.*
falter, give way, weaken, crumble

3 *I wavered about whether to send the email.*
hesitate, dither, vacillate, be uncertain, think twice
(informal) shilly-shally
▌ **IDIOM** hum and haw

wavy ADJECTIVE

> *The quilt is stitched in a wavy pattern.*
> curly, curling, rippling, winding, zigzag
> ▌ **OPPOSITE** straight

way NOUN

1 *the best way to make an omelette*
method, procedure, process, system, technique

2 *The androids are behaving in a very odd way.*
manner, fashion, style, mode

3 *an author who has a way with words*
skill, talent, flair

4 *Is this the right way to the castle?*
direction, route, road, path

5 *We've still got a long way to go.*
distance, journey, length, stretch

6 *In some ways, he's a likeable character.*
respect, particular, feature, detail, aspect

7 *When I got there, Stan was in a bad way.*
state, condition

weak ADJECTIVE

1 *The refugees were weak from hunger and thirst.*
feeble, frail, sickly, infirm, debilitated, puny, weedy
▌ **OPPOSITES** strong, robust

a
b
c
d
e
f
g
h
i
j
k
l
m
n
o
p
q
r
s
t
u
v
w
x
y
z

2 *He proved to be a weak wartime leader.*
ineffective, powerless, timid, meek, soft, faint-hearted, spineless, indecisive
OPPOSITE powerful

3 *a weak area of the Earth's crust*
fragile, insubstantial, unsound, unstable, flimsy, rickety, shaky
OPPOSITES sound, sturdy

4 *The story is spoiled by a weak ending.*
poor, feeble, unsatisfactory, inadequate, unconvincing, implausible, lame
(informal) wishy-washy

5 *areas where the phone signal is weak*
faint, low, dim, muted, faded, diluted, indistinct
OPPOSITES strong, clear

weaken *VERB*

1 *The creature was weakened, but not dead.*
enfeeble, exhaust, debilitate, sap

2 *A poor soundtrack weakens the overall effect.*
reduce, lessen, diminish, undermine

3 *Gravity weakens as you travel away from the Earth.*
decrease, decline, fade, dwindle, die down, peter out, wane, ebb
OPPOSITE strengthen

weakness *NOUN*

1 *a feeling of weakness in the limbs*
feebleness, frailty, fragility, infirmity, instability

2 *What are the weaknesses of the main character?*
fault, flaw, defect, imperfection, shortcoming, weak point
OPPOSITE strength

3 *a weakness for chocolate cake*
liking, fondness, taste, partiality, penchant
(informal) soft spot

wealth *NOUN*
Texas built its wealth on oil and cattle.

prosperity, affluence, fortune, money, riches
OPPOSITE poverty

▷ **a wealth of**
finding a wealth of information
lots of, plenty of, a mine of, an abundance of, a profusion of
(informal) loads of, tons of

wealthy *ADJECTIVE*
He comes from a very wealthy family.
rich, affluent, prosperous, moneyed, well-off, well-to-do
(informal) flush, loaded, well-heeled
OPPOSITES poor, impoverished

weapon *NOUN*

 WORD WEB

some types of weapon
bayonet, blowpipe or blowgun, bomb, club, cudgel, dagger, dirk, flick knife
(North American switchblade), gun, hand grenade, harpoon, machete, machine gun, missile, mortar, pistol, revolver, rifle, shell, stiletto, sword, Taser™, torpedo, truncheon or nightstick

▶ Weapons in general are **weaponry** or **arms**.

▶ A collection or store of weapons is an **armoury** or **arsenal**.

weapons used in the past
battering ram, battleaxe, blunderbuss, bow and arrow, broadsword, cannon, catapult, claymore, crossbow, cutlass, javelin, katana or samurai sword, lance, longbow, musket, pike, sabre, scimitar, spear, staff, tomahawk, trebuchet, trident

wear *VERB*

1 *What are you wearing to the party?*
dress in, be dressed in, be clothed in, have on, sport

2 *Tina wore her best smile all evening.*
have on, bear, exhibit, display,

put on, assume

3 *Some of the paintwork is starting to wear.*
become worn, deteriorate, rub off, fray

4 *These boots have worn well.*
last, endure, survive

▷ **wear off**
The effects of the potion are wearing off.
fade, lessen, diminish, ease, subside, die down, dwindle

▷ **wear someone out**
All this talking has worn me out.
exhaust, tire out, fatigue, weary, drain
(informal) do in
(British informal) knacker

wear NOUN

1 *formal evening wear*
dress, clothes, attire
(informal) gear, get-up

2 *I've had a lot of wear out of this jacket.*
use, service
(informal) mileage

weary ADJECTIVE

1 *feeling weary after a hard day*
tired, worn out, exhausted, fatigued, flagging, drained, spent
(informal) all in, bushed

⎸ **IDIOM** ready to drop

2 *a long and weary journey*
tiring, exhausting, fatiguing, wearisome, taxing, arduous, demanding

weather NOUN

The weather should be fine tomorrow.
conditions, outlook, elements

▶ The regular weather conditions of a particular area is the **climate**.

▶ The scientific study of the Earth's climate is **climatology**.

▶ The study of weather patterns in order to forecast the weather is **meteorology**.

WRITING TIPS

describing the weather

It was a fine, clear, January day, wet under foot where the frost had melted, but cloudless overhead; and the Regent's park was full of winter chirrupings and sweet with Spring odours.

— *Robert Louis Stevenson, The Strange Case of Dr Jekyll and Mr Hyde*

weather conditions
blizzard, breeze, cloudburst, cyclone, deluge, downpour, drizzle, drought, fog, frost, gale, hail, *(Scottish)* haar, haze, heatwave, hurricane, mist, monsoon, rainstorm, shower, sleet, smog, snowstorm, squall, storm, sunshine, thunderstorm, tornado, torrent, tsunami, typhoon

cloudy
dull, *(Scottish)* dreich, grey, overcast, sunless

cold
arctic, bitter, chilly, crisp, freezing, frosty, icy, *(informal)* nippy, *(informal)* perishing, raw, snowy, wintry

hot
baking, close, humid, muggy, roasting, sizzling, sticky, sultry, sweltering, torrid

stormy
rough, squally, tempestuous, thundery, turbulent, violent, wild

sunny
balmy, bright, cloudless, dry, fair, fine, mild, summery, sunshiny

wet
damp, drizzly, lashing, pouring, rainy, showery, spitting,

teeming, torrential

windy
blowy, blustery, breezy, gusty

other
adverse, changeable, hostile, inclement, temperate, foggy, misty, springlike, autumnal

weather VERB
They had weathered many dangers together.
survive, withstand, endure, come through, pull through

weave VERB
1 She has woven a complex and gripping story.
construct, fabricate, put together, create, invent, spin
2 A cyclist weaved his way through the traffic.
wind, wend, thread, zigzag, dodge, twist and turn

web NOUN
a web of interconnecting tunnels
network, labyrinth, complex, lattice
▷ **the Web**
surfing the Web
the Internet, the World Wide Web
(informal) the Net
▶ To view information on the Web is to view it **online**.
FOR TERMS RELATED TO THE WEB SEE **computer**

wedding NOUN
a traditional Jewish wedding
marriage, union
(formal) nuptials
FOR WEDDING ANNIVERSARIES SEE **anniversary**

wedge VERB
1 The door was wedged open with a chair.
jam, stick
2 A large man wedged himself into the seat next to me.
force, shove, push, cram, ram, stuff

weep VERB
Sonia's eyes were red from weeping.
cry, sob, shed tears
▶ To weep noisily is to **bawl** or **blubber**.
▶ To weep in an annoying way is to **snivel** or **whimper**.

weigh VERB
▷ **weigh someone down**
1 shoppers weighed down with parcels
load, burden, lumber
2 Something was weighing him down.
bother, worry, trouble, distress, burden, depress
┃ IDIOM prey on someone's mind
▷ **weigh something up**
Miss Marple weighed up the evidence.
consider, assess, evaluate, examine, study, ponder, mull over

weight NOUN
1 measuring your height and weight
heaviness
FOR WEIGHTS AND MEASURES SEE **measure** NOUN
2 lifting a heavy weight
load, mass, burden
3 His name still carries a lot of weight.
influence, authority, power, pull, sway
(informal) clout

weighty ADJECTIVE
1 a series of weighty volumes
heavy, substantial, bulky, cumbersome
┃ OPPOSITES light, slim
2 a weighty matter to consider
important, serious, grave, significant
┃ OPPOSITES unimportant, trivial

weird ADJECTIVE
1 a weird sound like a wailing banshee
eerie, uncanny, unnatural, unearthly, other-worldly, mysterious, ghostly, surreal
(informal) spooky, creepy
┃ OPPOSITES natural, earthly
2 My sister has a weird taste in clothes.

a
b
c
d
e
f
g
h
i
j
k
l
m
n
o
p
q
r
s
t
u
v
w
x
y
z

strange, odd, peculiar, bizarre, curious, quirky, eccentric, outlandish, unconventional, unorthodox, idiosyncratic *(informal)* wacky, way-out
❙ **OPPOSITE** conventional

welcome *NOUN*
We were not expecting a warm welcome.
greeting, reception, salutation

welcome *ADJECTIVE*
1 *She makes a welcome addition to the cast.*
pleasing, agreeable, desirable, acceptable, favourable, gratifying
❙ **OPPOSITE** unwelcome
2 *You're welcome to use my laptop.*
allowed, permitted, free
❙ **OPPOSITE** forbidden

welcome *VERB*
1 *We were welcomed by the creepy housekeeper.*
greet, receive, meet, usher in
2 *I welcomed the chance to be alone for a while.*
appreciate, be glad of, be grateful for, embrace

welfare *NOUN*
You are responsible for the welfare of your pet.
well-being, health, comfort, security, good, benefit, interests

well *ADVERB*
1 *The whole team played well on Saturday.*
ably, skilfully, competently, effectively, efficiently, admirably, excellently, marvellously, wonderfully
❙ **OPPOSITE** badly
2 *Stir the mixture well and leave to cool.*
thoroughly, carefully, rigorously, properly, effectively, completely
3 *colours which go well together*
agreeably, pleasantly, harmoniously, suitably, fittingly, happily, nicely

(informal) famously
4 *I used to know her quite well.*
closely, intimately, personally
5 *This may well be his last performance.*
probably, reasonably, in all likelihood

well *ADJECTIVE*
1 *She looks surprisingly well for her age.*
healthy, fit, strong, sound, robust, vigorous, lively, hearty
❙ **OPPOSITES** unwell, poorly
2 *All was not well in the kitchen.*
right, fine, all right, in order, satisfactory, as it should be
(informal) OK or okay, hunky-dory

well-known *ADJECTIVE*
a well-known TV personality
famous, celebrated, prominent, notable, renowned, distinguished, eminent
❙ **OPPOSITES** unknown, obscure

werewolf *NOUN*
At each full moon, he changes into a werewolf.
lycanthrope, wolf man
FOR TIPS ON WRITING HORROR FICTION SEE horror

west *NOUN, ADJECTIVE, ADVERB*
Mumbai is in the west of India.
▶ The parts of a country or continent in the west are the **western** parts.
▶ To travel towards the west is to travel **westward** or **westwards**.
▶ A wind from the west is a **westerly** wind.

wet *ADJECTIVE*
1 *All our clothes were wet and covered with mud.*
damp, soaked, soaking, drenched, dripping, sopping, wringing wet
❙ **OPPOSITE** dry
2 *The pitch was too wet to play on.*
waterlogged, saturated, sodden, soggy, squelchy, muddy, boggy
3 *a patch of wet cement*
sticky, tacky, runny

a
b
c
d
e
f
g
h
i
j
k
l
m
n
o
p
q
r
s
t
u
v
w
x
y
z

4 *It was cold and wet all afternoon.*
rainy, showery, drizzly, misty,
pouring, teeming
❙ SEE ALSO **weather**

wet VERB
Wet the paper with a damp sponge.
dampen, moisten, soak, water,
douse
▶ To wet something thoroughly is to
saturate or **drench** it.
❙ OPPOSITE dry

wheel NOUN
the wheels inside a clock
▶ A small wheel under a piece of
furniture is a **caster**.
▶ The centre of a wheel is the **hub**.
▶ The outer edge of a wheel is the **rim**.

wheel VERB
1 *A group of vultures wheeled
overhead.*
circle, orbit
2 *Suddenly the whole herd wheeled to
the right.*
swing round, turn, veer, swerve

whereabouts NOUN
*a clue to the whereabouts of the
sunken ship*
location, position, site, situation

whiff NOUN
*I caught a whiff of perfume as she
passed.*
smell, scent, aroma
FOR TIPS ON DESCRIBING SMELLS SEE
smell NOUN

while NOUN
*Did you wait a long while for
a taxi?*
time, period, interval, spell, stretch

while VERB
*We told ghost stories to while away
the time.*
pass, spend, occupy, use up, kill

whimper VERB, NOUN
*I heard a little whimper in
the dark.*
cry, moan, whine

whine VERB
1 *The dogs growled and whined all
night long.*
cry, whimper, wail, howl
2 *What is he whining about now?*
complain, protest, grumble, grouse,
carp
(informal) gripe, moan
(British informal) whinge

whip VERB
1 *Slaves were whipped for minor
offences.*
beat, flog, lash, thrash, scourge
2 *I whipped round to find the creature
right behind me.*
whirl, spin, turn
3 *Whip the eggs in a separate bowl.*
whisk, beat

whirl VERB
1 *Dead leaves whirled in the autumn
wind.*
turn, twirl, spin, circle, spiral, reel,
revolve, rotate, pirouette
2 *Her mind whirled with new
questions.*
spin, reel, swim

whirl NOUN
1 *a few whirls on the dance floor*
twirl, spin, turn, reel, pirouette
2 *in a whirl of excitement*
bustle, flurry, spin, hurly-burly

whirlpool NOUN
a ship being sucked into a whirlpool
maelstrom, vortex

whisk VERB
Whisk the oil and vinegar together.
beat, whip, mix, stir

whisper VERB
What are you two whispering about?
murmur, mutter, mumble
❙ OPPOSITE shout

whistle VERB, NOUN
SEE **sound**❶

white ADJECTIVE, NOUN
1 *a piece of plain white paper*
snow-white, off-white, whitish,

a
b
c
d
e
f
g
h
i
j
k
l
m
n
o
p
q
r
s
t
u
v
w
x
y
z

ivory, pearl
▶ To make something white or pale is to **bleach** it.
▶ When someone turns white with fear they **blanch** or **turn pale**.
2 *a few wisps of white hair*
hoary, silvery, snowy, platinum

whole *ADJECTIVE*
1 *Have you read the whole trilogy?*
complete, entire, full, total, unabbreviated, unabridged
❙ **OPPOSITE** incomplete
2 *The skeleton appears to be whole.*
in one piece, intact, unbroken, undamaged, perfect
❙ **OPPOSITES** broken, in pieces

wholehearted *ADJECTIVE*
I would like to express my wholehearted support.
unconditional, unqualified, unreserved, full, complete, total
❙ **OPPOSITE** half-hearted

wholesome *ADJECTIVE*
a wholesome breakfast of porridge and fruit
healthy, nutritious, nourishing
❙ **OPPOSITE** unhealthy

wholly *ADVERB*
The acting is fresh and wholly convincing.
completely, totally, fully, entirely, utterly, thoroughly, absolutely, one hundred per cent
❙ **OPPOSITE** partly

wicked *ADJECTIVE*
1 *a greedy and wicked landowner*
cruel, vicious, villainous, evil, detestable, mean, corrupt, immoral, sinful
❙ **OPPOSITES** good, virtuous
2 *a wicked plan to brainwash the world*
evil, fiendish, diabolical, malicious, malevolent, monstrous, nefarious, vile, base
3 *a wicked sense of humour*
mischievous, playful, cheeky, impish, roguish

wide *ADJECTIVE*
1 *a wide stretch of sandy beach*
broad, expansive, extensive, vast, spacious, spread out
❙ **OPPOSITE** narrow
2 *a wide knowledge of classical music*
comprehensive, extensive, vast, wide-ranging, encyclopedic
❙ **OPPOSITE** limited

widely *ADVERB*
Organic foods are now widely available.
commonly, generally, far and wide

widen *VERB*
The river widens as it nears the bay.
broaden, open out, spread out, expand, extend, enlarge

widespread *ADJECTIVE*
1 *Overnight storms have caused widespread damage.*
extensive, wholesale
❙ **OPPOSITE** limited
2 *the widespread use of mobile phones*
general, common, universal, global, worldwide, ubiquitous, prevalent
❙ **OPPOSITE** uncommon

width *NOUN*
the width of the right-hand margin
breadth, thickness, span
▶ The distance across a circle is its **diameter**.
▶ The distance around something is its **girth**.

wield *VERB*
1 *A woman approached us wielding a clipboard.*
brandish, flourish, hold, wave
2 *He still wields influence over his fans.*
exert, exercise, command, hold, maintain

wife *NOUN*
Which goddess was the wife of Zeus?
spouse, partner, consort, bride
❙ **IDIOM** other half

a
b
c
d
e
f
g
h
i
j
k
l
m
n
o
p
q
r
s
t
u
v
w
x
y
z

wild *ADJECTIVE*

1 *a herd of wild buffalo*
undomesticated, untamed, feral
OPPOSITE tame

2 *wild flowers and grasses*
natural, uncultivated
OPPOSITE cultivated

3 *a wild and mountainous region*
rough, rugged, uncultivated,
uninhabited, desolate
OPPOSITE cultivated

4 *a night of wild celebrations*
riotous, rowdy, disorderly, unruly,
boisterous, noisy, uncontrollable,
hysterical
OPPOSITES calm, restrained

5 *a spate of wild weather*
stormy, windy, blustery, gusty,
turbulent, tempestuous
OPPOSITE calm

6 *Take a wild guess.*
unplanned, random, haphazard,
arbitrary

wilful *ADJECTIVE*

1 *dealing with a wilful toddler*
obstinate, stubborn,
strong-willed, headstrong, pig-
headed, uncooperative, recalcitrant
OPPOSITE amenable

2 *wilful damage to property*
deliberate, intentional, planned,
conscious, premeditated
OPPOSITE accidental

will *NOUN*

1 *a strong will to succeed*
determination, drive, resolve,
willpower, tenacity, commitment

2 *She was forced to marry against her
will.*
wish, desire, inclination, preference

willing *ADJECTIVE*

1 *Are you willing to try something
new?*
ready, prepared, inclined, disposed,
happy, glad, pleased
OPPOSITE unwilling

2 *a group of willing volunteers*
enthusiastic, helpful, cooperative,
obliging
OPPOSITES reluctant, grudging

willingly *ADVERB*
*Brad willingly agreed to be
interviewed.*
gladly, happily, readily
OPPOSITES unwillingly, reluctantly

willingness *NOUN*
a certain willingness to take risks
readiness, eagerness, inclination
OPPOSITES unwillingness,
reluctance

wilt *VERB*

1 *Without water the leaves will start
to wilt.*
become limp, droop, flop, sag

2 *Both players seemed to wilt in the
heat.*
flag, droop, become listless
OPPOSITES revive, perk up

wily *ADJECTIVE*
*a wily old pirate called Long John
Silver*
clever, crafty, cunning, shrewd,
scheming, artful, sly, devious

win *VERB*

1 *Which team do you think will win?*
come first, be victorious, succeed,
triumph, prevail, come out on top
OPPOSITE lose

2 *the chance to win a holiday for two*
get, receive, gain, obtain, secure
(informal) walk away with,
land, bag

win *NOUN*
*a famous win over over their old
rivals*
victory, triumph, conquest
OPPOSITE defeat

wince *VERB*
*Ralph clutched his side and winced
with pain.*
grimace, flinch
IDIOM pull a face

wind❶ _NOUN_

The whole island was buffeted by strong winds.

▶ A gentle wind is a **breath**, **breeze**, or **draught**.

▶ A violent wind is a **cyclone**, **gale**, **hurricane**, or **tornado**.

▶ A sudden unexpected wind is a **blast**, **gust**, **puff**, or **squall**.

❚ SEE ALSO **weather**

FOR WIND INSTRUMENTS SEE **music**

wind❷ _VERB_

1 _Several bike trails wind through the hills._

weave, bend, curve, twist and turn, zigzag, meander, snake

2 _Ava sat winding her hair round her fingers._

wrap, roll, coil, curl, loop, twine

❚ OPPOSITE unwind

window _NOUN_

a window looking onto the street

▶ The glass in a window is the **pane**.

▶ A semicircular window above a door is a **fanlight**.

▶ A window in a roof is a **skylight**.

▶ A decorative window with panels of coloured glass is a **stained-glass window**.

▶ A person whose job is to fit glass in windows is a **glazier**.

windy _ADJECTIVE_

1 _a windy day in autumn_

breezy, blowy, blustery, gusty, wild, squally

❚ OPPOSITES calm, still

❚ SEE ALSO **weather**

2 _standing on a windy hilltop_

windswept, exposed, draughty

❚ OPPOSITE sheltered

wink _VERB_

1 _My friend winked at me and smiled._

▶ To shut and open both eyes quickly is to **blink**.

▶ To flutter your eyelashes is to **bat** them.

2 _The lights winked on and off._

flicker, flash, sparkle, twinkle

winner _NOUN_

the winner of this week's lottery

victor, prizewinner, champion, conqueror

(informal) champ

❚ OPPOSITE loser

winning _ADJECTIVE_

1 _the winning entry in the competition_

victorious, triumphant, successful, conquering, top-scoring, champion

❚ OPPOSITE losing

2 _a winning smile_

engaging, charming, appealing, attractive, endearing, captivating, disarming

wintry _ADJECTIVE_

a calendar showing a wintry landscape

snowy, frosty, icy, freezing, cold

❚ SEE ALSO **weather**

wipe _VERB_

1 _Wipe the screen with a lens cloth._

clean, rub, polish, mop, swab, sponge

2 _I accidentally wiped the memory card._

erase, delete

▷ **wipe something out**

The dinosaurs were wiped out 65 million years ago.

destroy, annihilate, exterminate, kill off, get rid of

wire _NOUN_

a tangle of computer wires

cable, lead, flex

▶ A system of wires is **wiring**.

wisdom _NOUN_

offering some words of wisdom

sense, judgement, understanding, intelligence, sagacity, common sense, insight, reason

wise _ADJECTIVE_

1 _The alchemist was very old and wise._

intelligent, learned, knowledgeable, knowing, perceptive, rational,

thoughtful, sagacious
► A wise and respected person is a
sage.

2 *I think you made a wise decision.*
good, right, sound, sensible, astute,
shrewd
▌**OPPOSITE** foolish

wish *VERB*
*You can make as many copies as you
wish.*
want, desire, please, choose, see fit

wish *NOUN*
a lifelong wish to travel into space.
desire, want, longing, yearning,
hankering, craving, urge, fancy,
hope, ambition
(informal) yen

wit *NOUN*
1 *Holmes needed all his wit to solve
the case.*
intelligence, cleverness, sharpness,
shrewdness, astuteness, brains,
sense, judgement
2 *a screenplay which sparkles with wit*
humour, comedy, jokes, witticisms
3 *Uncle Charlie is a bit of a wit.*
joker, comedian, comic
(informal) wag

witch *NOUN*
*They say the family was cursed by a
witch's spell.*
sorceress, enchantress
► A group of witches is a **coven**.
FOR TIPS ON WRITING FANTASY FICTION
SEE fantasy

witchcraft *NOUN*
*Thousands of women were accused of
witchcraft.*
sorcery, wizardry, enchantment,
black magic, necromancy

withdraw *VERB*
1 *She withdrew a handkerchief from
her pocket.*
remove, extract, take out, pull out
▌**OPPOSITE** insert
2 *They could still withdraw their offer.*
take back, cancel, retract

▌**OPPOSITES** make, present
3 *A number of riders withdrew from
the race.*
pull out, back out, drop out
▌**OPPOSITE** enter
4 *The rebels withdrew to the hills.*
retreat, draw back, fall back, retire,
adjourn
▌**OPPOSITE** advance
5 *Troops are being withdrawn from
the city.*
call back, recall
▌**OPPOSITE** send in

withdrawal *NOUN*
1 *the withdrawal of my offer*
cancellation, retraction
2 *a massive withdrawal of troops*
recall, retreat, departure, pull-out,
evacuation

wither *VERB*
1 *Crops were withering
in the fields.*
shrivel, dry up, shrink, wilt, droop,
go limp
▌**OPPOSITE** flourish
2 *The smile withered on her lips.*
fade, shrink, evaporate, dwindle,
decline, diminish
▌**OPPOSITE** grow

withhold *VERB*
1 *He was accused of withholding
vital evidence.*
keep back, hold back, hold onto,
retain, keep secret
(informal) sit on
▌**OPPOSITES** release,
make available
2 *Hank struggled to withhold
a grin.*
suppress, restrain, hold back,
contain, control

withstand *VERB*
*buildings designed to withstand
earth tremors*
endure, stand up to, tolerate, bear,
cope with, survive, resist, brave,
weather

a
b
c
d
e
f
g
h
i
j
k
l
m
n
o
p
q
r
s
t
u
v
w
x
y
z

witness *NOUN*

Several witnesses reported seeing a UFO crash.
observer, onlooker, eyewitness, bystander, spectator, viewer

witty *ADJECTIVE*

Maurice tried to think of a witty reply.
humorous, amusing, comic, funny, entertaining, clever, droll
OPPOSITE dull

wizard *NOUN*

1 *the legendary wizard called Merlin*
magician, sorcerer, enchanter, warlock

2 *I thought you were a wizard with computers.*
expert, genius, ace, master, maestro
(informal) whizz, hotshot
(British informal) dab hand

wobble *VERB*

1 *The front wheel was wobbling all over the place.*
waver, sway, rock, totter, teeter, jiggle

2 *My voice wobbles when I'm nervous.*
shake, tremble, quake, quiver, waver, vibrate

wobbly *ADJECTIVE*

1 *feeling wobbly about the knees*
shaky, tottering, unsteady
OPPOSITE steady

2 *a shopping trolley with a wobbly wheel*
loose, rickety, rocky, unstable, unsteady
(British informal) wonky

woman *NOUN*

This event is for women only.
lady, female
▶ A woman whose husband has died is a **widow**.
▶ An old-fashioned word for an unmarried woman is a **spinster**.
▶ Words used in the past for a young unmarried woman are **maid**, **maiden**, and **damsel**.

wonder *NOUN*

1 *Leonora's eyes widened in wonder.*
admiration, awe, amazement, astonishment, reverence

2 *a wonder of modern technology*
marvel, miracle, phenomenon, sensation

wonder *VERB*

I wonder why he left in such a hurry.
be curious about, ask yourself, ponder, think about
▷ **wonder at**

1 *You can only wonder at the skill of the craftsmen.*
marvel at, admire, be amazed at, be astonished by

2 *I can't help but wonder at his motives.*
doubt, question, suspect, mistrust

wonderful *ADJECTIVE*

1 *It's wonderful what computers can do now.*
amazing, astonishing, astounding, incredible, remarkable, extraordinary, marvellous, miraculous, phenomenal

2 *We had a wonderful evening.*
excellent, splendid, great, superb, delightful
(informal) brilliant, fantastic, terrific, fabulous, super

wood *NOUN*

1 *chopping wood for the fire*
timber, logs
(North American) lumber
▶ A person whose job is to cut or carry wood is a **lumberjack**.
FOR TYPES OF WOOD SEE **tree**

2 *a trail through a pine wood*
woodland, forest, trees, grove, thicket

wooden *ADJECTIVE*

1 *a solid wooden door*
wood, timber

2 *The acting was a bit wooden at times.*
stiff, stilted, unnatural, awkward,

lifeless, unemotional, expressionless
OPPOSITE expressive

woolly *ADJECTIVE*

1 *a woolly hat with ear flaps*
wool, woollen
▶ Clothes made of wool, such as hats and scarves, are **woollens**.

2 *Seal pups are born with a woolly coat.*
thick, fleecy, shaggy, fuzzy, hairy

3 *This is not just a woolly idea.*
vague, confused, unclear, unfocused, hazy

word *NOUN*

1 *She can speak a few words of Mandarin.*
expression, term
▶ The words used in a particular subject or language are its **vocabulary**.

2 *I'll have a word with her about it.*
talk, conversation, discussion, chat
(informal) confab

3 *Do you have any words of advice?*
remark, comment, statement, observation

4 *You gave me your word.*
promise, assurance, guarantee, pledge, vow

5 *There has been no word since they left.*
news, message, information, report, communication

word *VERB*

Be careful how you word the email.
express, phrase, put into words

wording *NOUN*

I found the wording confusing at first.
phrasing, expression, language, terminology

work *NOUN*

1 *It is hard work pedalling uphill.*
effort, labour, toil, exertion, slog
(informal) graft, grind

2 *I'll got a lot of work to do this weekend.*

tasks, assignments, duties, chores, jobs, homework, housework

3 *What kind of work does she do?*
occupation, job, employment, profession, business, trade, vocation
FOR TYPES OF WORK SEE **occupation**

4 *the complete works of Shakespeare*
writing, composition, piece, text

work *VERB*

1 *You've been working at the computer all day.*
labour, toil, exert yourself, slave, slog
(informal) beaver away

2 *I used to work in a florist on Saturdays.*
be employed, have a job, go to work

3 *My watch has stopped working.*
function, go, run, operate

4 *This camera is very easy to work.*
operate, use, control, handle, run

5 *Work the dough into a ball with your hands.*
knead, press, shape, form, mould

▷ **work out**

1 *He works out several times a week.*
exercise, train

2 *Things didn't quite work out as planned.*
turn out, happen, emerge, develop

▷ **work something out**
See if you can work out the formula.
figure out, puzzle out, calculate, determine, solve, decipher, unravel

worker *NOUN*

The call centre employs around 200 workers.
employee
▶ All the workers in a business are the **staff** or **workforce**.
SEE ALSO occupation

world *NOUN*

1 *living in a remote part of the world*
earth, globe, planet

2 *It seemed like the world was watching.*
everyone, humankind, mankind, humanity

》

a
b
c
d
e
f
g
h
i
j
k
l
m
n
o
p
q
r
s
t
u
v
w
x
y
z

3 *searching for life on other worlds*
planet

4 *in the glamorous world of television*
sphere, realm, domain, field, arena,
society, circle

worldwide *ADJECTIVE*
*The award brought him worldwide
celebrity.*
global, international, universal
❘ **OPPOSITE** local

worried *ADJECTIVE*
*For once Bret sounded genuinely
worried.*
anxious, troubled, apprehensive,
uneasy, disturbed, concerned,
bothered, tense, nervous, fretful,
agitated
❘ **OPPOSITES** unconcerned, carefree

worry *VERB*
1 *Please tell me what's worrying you.*
trouble, bother, distress, concern,
upset, unsettle, disturb, make
someone anxious
❘ **IDIOM** prey on someone's mind

2 *What's the use of worrying?*
be anxious, be troubled, be
concerned, brood, fret, agonize, lose
sleep (over)

worry *NOUN*
1 *She has a permanent look of worry
on her face.*
anxiety, distress, uneasiness,
apprehension, vexation, disquiet,
agitation

2 *Money has always been a worry for
them.*
trouble, concern, burden, care,
problem, trial
(informal) headache, hassle

worsen *VERB*
1 *Anxiety can worsen an asthma
attack.*
make worse, aggravate, intensify,
exacerbate, compound, add to
❘ **OPPOSITES** alleviate, relieve

2 *Her condition worsened overnight.*
get worse, deteriorate, degenerate,

decline
❘ **IDIOM** go downhill
❘ **OPPOSITES** improve, get better

worship *VERB*
1 *The Greeks worshipped many gods
and goddesses.*
pray to, glorify, praise, venerate, pay
homage to
❘ **SEE ALSO** religion

2 *He used to worship his older brother.*
adore, be devoted to, look up to,
love, revere, idolize, esteem

worth *NOUN*
1 *a genuine antique that will increase
in worth*
value, price, cost

2 *How much worth do you place on
friendship?*
importance, significance, value,
merit

worthless *ADJECTIVE*
a worthless piece of information
useless, unusable, valueless
❘ **OPPOSITES** valuable, useful

worthwhile *ADJECTIVE*
1 *It's worthwhile hiring a bike for a
day.*
useful, valuable, beneficial,
advantageous, rewarding,
profitable, fruitful
❘ **OPPOSITE** pointless

2 *money for a worthwhile cause*
good, deserving, admirable,
commendable, respectable, worthy

worthy *ADJECTIVE*
*a worthy successor to their debut
album*
good, deserving, praiseworthy,
admirable, commendable,
respectable
❘ **OPPOSITE** unworthy

would-be *ADJECTIVE*
a would-be contender for the title
aspiring, hopeful, promising,
potential, budding
(informal) wannabe

wound NOUN

1 *being treated for a head wound*
injury, cut, gash, graze, scratch,
laceration, lesion

2 *a serious wound to his pride*
insult, blow, affront, slight, offence,
injury, hurt

wound VERB

1 *Four people were wounded in the
blast.*
injure, hurt, harm

2 *At first, he was wounded by her
words.*
hurt, insult, affront, slight, offend,
pain, grieve

wrap VERB

1 *wrapping a present in tissue paper*
cover, pack, package, enclose,
encase

2 *We wrapped ourselves in warm
blankets.*
enfold, swathe, bundle

▶ To wrap water pipes is to **insulate** or
lag them.

3 *Her death is still wrapped in
mystery.*
cloak, envelop, shroud, surround

wreath NOUN

a wreath of mistletoe and holly
garland, ring, crown

wreathe VERB

1 *The tree was wreathed in fairy lights.*
festoon, garland, drape, deck,
ornament, adorn

2 *Mount Fuji is often wreathed in
clouds.*
encircle, envelop, swathe, shroud,
surround

wreck VERB

1 *His bike was wrecked in the crash.*
demolish, destroy, crush, smash,
shatter, crumple
(informal) total

2 *This could wreck my chances of
seeing her again.*
ruin, spoil, put a stop to, shatter,
dash, scotch

(informal) scupper, put paid to

wreck NOUN

the wreck of an old Spanish galleon
remains, ruins, wreckage

wreckage NOUN

wreckage from a sunken ship
debris, fragments, pieces, remains

wrench VERB

*The wind wrenched the door off its
hinges.*
pull, tug, prise, jerk, twist, force
(informal) yank

wrench NOUN

1 *I felt a sudden wrench on my arm.*
pull, tug, jerk, twist
(informal) yank

2 *the wrench of leaving their old home*
pain, pang, trauma

wrestle VERB

1 *They wrestled the suspect to the
ground.*
grapple, tussle, fight, battle

2 *He'd been wrestling with the
problem for weeks.*
struggle, grapple, agonize (over)

wretched ADJECTIVE

1 *Gail was left feeling wretched and
alone.*
miserable, unhappy, desolate,
depressed, dejected, downcast,
forlorn, woeful

2 *forced to live in wretched conditions*
squalid, sordid, pitiful, bleak, harsh,
grim, miserable

3 *This wretched computer has frozen
again!*
annoying, maddening, exasperating,
useless

wriggle VERB

*He managed to wriggle through a
gap in the fence.*
squirm, writhe, wiggle, twist, worm
your way

▷ **wriggle out of something**
*wriggling out of doing their fair
share*

avoid, shirk, escape, dodge, duck

wring *VERB*

1 *She wrung the water out of her hair.*
press, squeeze, twist

2 *The actor paced up and down wringing his hands.*
clasp, grip, wrench, twist, squeeze

▷ **wringing wet**
These towels are wringing wet.
soaked, drenched, dripping, sopping, saturated

wrinkle *NOUN*

Her tiny hands were laced with wrinkles.
crease, fold, crinkle, pucker, furrow, line, groove, ridge

▶ Wrinkles at the corners of a person's eyes are **crow's feet**.
▌ SEE ALSO **face**

wrinkle *VERB*

Dr Corbett sighed and wrinkled his brow.
pucker, crease, crinkle, gather, crumple, rumple, scrunch up
▌ OPPOSITE smooth

write *VERB*

1 *He wrote the answer on a piece of paper.*
jot down, note, print, scrawl, scribble

▶ To write words or letters on a surface is to **inscribe** it.
▶ To write your signature on something is to **autograph** it.

2 *Anne Frank wrote a diary of her experiences.*
compile, compose, draw up, set down, pen

▶ To write a rough version of a story is to **draft** it.
▶ To write something hurriedly is to **dash it off**.

3 *I've been meaning to write to you.*
correspond (with)
▌ IDIOM *(informal)* drop someone a line

writer *NOUN*

WORD WEB

people who write
author, biographer, columnist, composer, correspondent, dramatist or playwright, journalist or reporter, novelist, poet, scribe, scriptwriter or screenwriter, speech-writer

▶ A writer of poor or unimaginative work is a **hack**.

writhe *VERB*

The snake writhed and tried to escape.
thrash about, twist, squirm, wriggle

writing *NOUN*

1 *The writing is very difficult to read.*
handwriting, script, lettering, print

▶ Writing that is engraved or carved is an **inscription**.
▶ Untidy writing is a **scrawl** or **scribble**.
▶ The art of beautiful handwriting is **calligraphy**.

2 *an anthology of crime writing*
literature, works, stories, publications, books
FOR TYPES OF WRITING SEE **fiction**

wrong *ADJECTIVE*

1 *These calculations are all wrong.*
incorrect, mistaken, inaccurate, erroneous
(informal) out
▌ OPPOSITES right, correct

2 *Richard always says the wrong thing.*
inappropriate, unsuitable, improper, unwise, ill-advised, ill-considered
▌ OPPOSITES right, appropriate

3 *Do you think it would be wrong to keep the money?*
bad, dishonest, irresponsible, immoral, unethical, unfair, unjust, corrupt, criminal, wicked, sinful
▌ OPPOSITES right, ethical

4 *There's something wrong with the TV.*
faulty, defective, amiss, awry, not right, out of order

▷ **go wrong**
Everything started to go horribly wrong.
fail, backfire
(*informal*) flop, go pear-shaped
❚ OPPOSITES go right, succeed

wrong ADVERB
Have I spelled your name wrong?
incorrectly, inaccurately, mistakenly, erroneously
❚ OPPOSITES correctly, properly

wrong NOUN
1 *knowing the difference between right and wrong*

dishonesty, immorality, injustice, corruption, evil, wickedness, villainy

2 *admitting the wrongs of the past*
misdeed, injustice, offence, injury, crime, sin, transgression

wrongdoer NOUN
Wrongdoers used to be put in the stocks.
criminal, offender, lawbreaker, felon, villain, culprit, malefactor, miscreant

wrongly ADVERB
Stanley is wrongly accused of stealing a pair of trainers.
falsely, mistakenly, erroneously, incorrectly, inaccurately, in error
❚ OPPOSITES correctly, accurately

a
b
c
d
e
f
g
h
i
j
k
l
m
n
o
p
q
r
s
t
u
v
w
x
y
z

Yy

yacht NOUN
> FOR TYPES OF BOAT OR SHIP SEE **boat**

yank (informal) VERB, NOUN
> Don't yank on the horse's reins.
> tug, jerk, pull (hard), wrench

yard NOUN
> a builders' yard full of old bricks
> court, courtyard, enclosure

year NOUN
> There are two solstices every year.
> ▶ A period of ten years is a **decade**;
> a period of a hundred years is a
> **century**, and a period of a
> thousand years is a
> **millennium**.
> ▍SEE ALSO **anniversary**

yearly ADJECTIVE
> a yearly festival held in mid-July
> annual, per annum
> ▶ A **biennial** event happens every two
> years and a **biannual** event happens
> twice a year.

yearn VERB
> ▷ **yearn for something**
> I yearned for some peace and quiet.
> long for, crave, wish for, desire,
> hunger for, pine for, hanker after
> (informal) be dying for

yell VERB
> Gordon yelled again from the
> kitchen.
> shout, call out, cry out, bawl, bellow,
> roar, howl

yell NOUN
> a loud yell of surprise
> shout, cry, bawl, bellow, roar, howl

yellow ADJECTIVE, NOUN

 WORD WEB

> *some shades of yellow*
> amber, buttery, cream, gold,
> golden, lemon, mustard, straw,
> tawny, yellow ochre
> ▶ Yellow hair is **blonde** or **fair** hair.
> **FOR TIPS ON DESCRIBING COLOURS**
> SEE **colour**

yelp VERB, NOUN
> One of the guards let out a yelp of
> pain.
> cry, howl, yowl

yield VERB
> 1 The King stubbornly refused to yield.
> give in, give way, back down,
> surrender, admit defeat, concede,
> capitulate, submit
> (informal) cave in
> 2 Even a small plot will yield a variety
> of vegetables.
> bear, produce, supply, generate,
> realize, return

yield NOUN
> a poor yield of potatoes
> crop, harvest, produce, return

young ADJECTIVE
> 1 a programme aimed at a young
> audience
> youthful, juvenile
> ▍OPPOSITES older, mature
> 2 This game is a bit young for
> teenagers.
> childish, babyish, immature, infantile
> ▍OPPOSITES adult, grown-up

young PLURAL NOUN
> All mammals feed their young on
> milk.
> offspring, children, young ones,
> family, progeny

▶ A group of young birds that hatch together is a **brood**.

▶ A group of young animals that are born together is a **litter**.

youngster NOUN
His mother left when he was just a youngster.
child, boy or girl, youth
(informal) kid

youth NOUN
1 *Picasso spent much of his youth in Barcelona.*
childhood, boyhood or girlhood, adolescence, teens

2 *sports facilities for youths and adults*
adolescent, youngster, juvenile, teenager, young adult

3 *the youth of today*
young people, the younger generation

youthful ADJECTIVE
Ella still has a youthful look about her.
young, youngish, vigorous, sprightly, young-looking

a
b
c
d
e
f
g
h
i
j
k
l
m
n
o
p
q
r
s
t
u
v
w
x
y
z

Zz

► Another word for a sign of the zodiac is a **star sign**.
► The study of the signs of the zodiac is **astrology**.
► An astrological forecast based on signs of the zodiac is a **horoscope**.

SEE ALSO fortune telling

zeal NOUN

She plays the leading role with zeal.
energy, vigour, enthusiasm, spirit, passion, verve, gusto

zero NOUN

All teams start with a score of zero.
nought, nothing, nil
► A score of zero in cricket is a **duck**, and a score of zero in tennis is **love**.

zest NOUN

Their performance has lost some of its zest.
enthusiasm, eagerness, vitality, energy, vigour, passion, fervour
(*informal*) zing

zigzag VERB

The road zigzags along the coast.
wind, twist, weave, meander, snake

zodiac NOUN

 WORD WEB

signs of the zodiac
Aquarius (or the Water Carrier)
Aries (or the Ram)
Cancer (or the Crab)
Capricorn (or the Goat)
Gemini (or the Twins)
Leo (or the Lion)
Libra (or the Scales)
Pisces (or the Fish)
Sagittarius (or the Archer)
Scorpio (or the Scorpion)
Taurus (or the Bull)
Virgo (or the Virgin)

zone NOUN

The whole state was declared a disaster zone.
area, district, region, sector, locality, territory, vicinity, neighbourhood

zoo NOUN

The zoo is enlarging its gorilla enclosure.
zoological gardens, wildlife reserve, safari park
► A small zoo is a **menagerie**.

zoom VERB

1 *A motorbike zoomed past us on the right.*
speed, race, tear, dash, streak, whizz, rush, hurtle, fly
2 *The camera zoomed in on a member of the audience.*
focus, close
► A photograph taken at close range is a **close-up**.

Writer's Toolkit

Writer's Toolkit

Writer's Toolkit

What is good writing?

Why do some pieces of writing work and others don't? Good writing should be easy to read, but it is not always easy to write. In fiction, you may want to impress your reader with a gripping storyline and memorable images. In non-fiction, you will want to get your points across clearly and concisely. Whatever type of writing you are doing, there are some common rules to follow and some general points to bear in mind if you want to write well.

Be clear

If your writing is muddled, then your meaning will not come across clearly. Make sure there is nothing in your phrasing or your punctuation (or lack of punctuation) which may confuse your readers.

Avoid clutter

If something isn't adding to your argument, or helping to advance your storyline or draw your characters, then leave it out. Try to avoid adding meaningless phrases like *by and large*; or falling into clichés like *as luck would have it* or *last but not least*.

Add variety

A piece of writing that uses the same words over and over again is boring to read – and also boring to write. There are some suggestions over the page for how to add variety in your choice of words. You could also try varying the length or type of sentences you use, especially in a piece of creative writing.

'Get to the point. And if you remove all the excess garbage and discover you can't find the point, tear up what you wrote and start all over again.'

STEPHEN KING, EVERYTHING YOU NEED TO KNOW ABOUT WRITING SUCCESSFULLY – IN TEN MINUTES

Adding variety

It is easy to fall into a pattern of using a vague word, like *great* or *amazing* to describe something you enjoyed, or to use words like *really* or *such a* for emphasis (*a really scary scene, such a creepy character*). That's fine in speaking or informal situations, but it can make for very dull reading in an essay or piece of creative writing.

Look out for the following in your writing:

▶ **Overused words**, such as *great*, *lovely*, and *nice*. Try to find more interesting alternatives.

▶ **Repeated words**: For example, you might keep repeating the word *then* in a plot summary, or the words *say* and *tell* in a character study. By varying the verbs you use, you will make your writing more interesting, as well as more precise. Depending on the situation, you could replace *say* and *tell* with verbs like *announce*, *confess*, *declare*, *demand*, *explain*, *relate*, and many others.

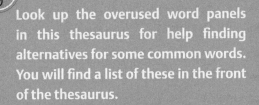

Look up the overused word panels in this thesaurus for help finding alternatives for some common words. You will find a list of these in the front of the thesaurus.

Example

Look over your final draft to check that you are not overusing words like *then*, *get*, or *tell*; or that you have not repeated a word too soon.

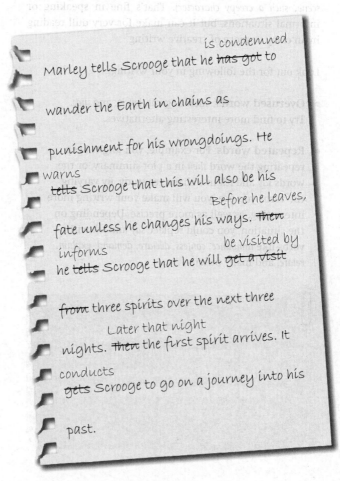

Marley tells Scrooge that he ~~has got~~ *is condemned* to

wander the Earth in chains as

punishment for his wrongdoings. He

warns
~~tells~~ Scrooge that this will also be his

Before he leaves,
fate unless he changes his ways. ~~Then~~

informs   *be visited by*
he ~~tells~~ Scrooge that he will ~~get a visit~~

~~from~~ three spirits over the next three

Later that night
nights. ~~Then~~ the first spirit arrives. It

conducts
~~gets~~ Scrooge to go on a journey into his

past.

Choosing a style

For some pieces of writing you have to use a particular style, such as a formal style for an essay. In other types of writing, such as fiction or journalism, there is more choice. A story could be written in a very poetic, descriptive style, or in the spare, hard-boiled style of some detective fiction. A magazine article could be light-hearted and chatty, or serious and technical, depending on what type of magazine it is for. Here are some pointers to help you find the right style for your writing:

▶ Choose the **right level of formality**.
  It's okay to use informal words, abbreviations, and contractions in a text or email to friends, or in a personal diary or blog; but not in a homework essay, a job application, or a letter to a stranger. There are some tips on page 649 on how to write in a formal style.

▶ Use **appropriate vocabulary**.
  If you are writing a scientific report, then use scientific terms; and if you are writing a film review, refer to the *film score* or the *soundtrack*, not just the *music*. Fictional genres, such as science fiction and crime fiction, also have their own vocabulary which helps to build and maintain a particular atmosphere.

Choosing a style

▶ Be **consistent**.

Be careful not to switch to informal language in the middle of a formal essay or letter. If you are writing fiction, give your narrator a consistent style (it could be direct and funny, or even long-winded and pompous), and make your characters speak in a style that suits them (think about their age, their personality, and where and when the story is set).

Look up the *word web* panels in this thesaurus for help finding appropriate subject vocabulary. You will find a list of these in the front of the thesaurus.

The *writing tips* panels also suggest vocabulary to use in various fictional genres. You will find a list of these in the front of the thesaurus.

Tips for formal writing

Avoid informal language

Informal language is the use of words and phrases such as *guy*, *stingy*, *freaked out*, or *tons of*. Short forms of words, like *lab* for *laboratory*, are also informal. If you are not sure whether a word is informal or not, look it up in a dictionary. You can also use your thesaurus to find alternatives for informal words. For example, *miserly* and *selfish* are more formal synonyms of *stingy*.

✗ *Scrooge is a stingy old guy.*
✓ *Scrooge is a miserly old man.*

> '*Don't use 'awful' Jo, it's slang.*'
> LOUISA MAY ALCOTT, LITTLE WOMEN

Avoid contractions

Contractions are forms such as *I'd*, *can't*, *won't*, and *you're*. These are very common in speech and informal writing, but are best avoided in formal letters or essay writing. Use the full forms instead:

I would	(not *I'd*)
can not or cannot	(not *can't*)
will not	(not *won't*)
you are	(not *you're*)

Choosing a style

Limit exclamation marks

It is tempting to use exclamation marks to add extra punch to a statement; but they look out of place in a piece of formal writing. You can emphasize your point by adding a strong word or phrase instead:

  ✗ *The film cost 180 million dollars to make!*
  ✓ *The film cost a staggering 180 million dollars to make.*

  ✗ *Some Shakespearean theatres still exist!*
  ✓ *Surprisingly, some Shakespearean theatres still exist.*

Use complete sentences

People don't always talk or write in complete sentences. For example, you might write in an informal note:

Saw the trailer for the new film. Looks good.

However, for most formal writing, you should write in complete sentences, unless you are giving a list of items or bullet points:

Having seen the trailer, I had high hopes for the new film.

Some phrases to watch

Be careful with the following phrases in formal writing:

✗ *try and do something / be sure and do something*
✓ *The correct forms are* **try to** *do and* **be sure to** *do:*

    ✗ *In this experiment, we try and prove that light rays bend.*
    ✓ *In this experiment, we try to prove that light rays bend.*

    ✗ *Be sure and turn the computer off.*
    ✓ **Be sure to** *turn the computer off.*

✗ *must of done something / should of done something*
✓ *The correct forms are* **must have** *done and* **should have** *done:*

    ✗ *The beast must of escaped.*
    ✓ *The beast* **must have** *escaped.*

    ✗ *You should of told me you were a vampire.*
    ✓ *You* **should have** *told me you were a vampire.*

Choosing a style

Example

If you are writing a formal essay or letter (such as a letter of application), take time to check that you haven't used any informal language, contractions, or incomplete sentences.

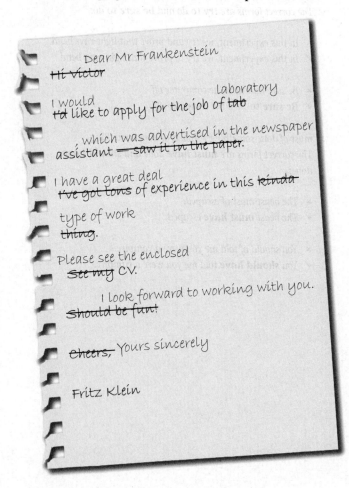

~~Hi Victor~~ Dear Mr Frankenstein

~~I'd~~ I would like to apply for the job of ~~lab~~ laboratory assistant ~~— saw it in the paper.~~ which was advertised in the newspaper

~~I've got tons~~ I have a great deal of experience in this ~~kinda~~ type of work ~~thing.~~

~~See my~~ Please see the enclosed CV.

~~Should be fun!~~ I look forward to working with you.

~~Cheers,~~ Yours sincerely

Fritz Klein

Working with sentences

Sentences are the core building blocks of any piece of writing. If your sentences are clear and well structured, you will get your meaning across; and if your sentences are varied and interesting, then your writing will be, too.

There are three main ways to build a sentence:

▶ **Simple sentences**

Simple sentences contain a single main clause (that is, a part of a sentence that has its own verb and that can stand by itself). They can be either statements or questions:

Chameleons feed mainly on insects.
Do you still play the bass guitar?

Although they have only one main clause, simple sentences do not have to be short:

Many slow-moving reptiles, such as chameleons, rely on camouflage as their main form of defence.

▶ **Compound sentences**

Compound sentences are made by joining two
or more main clauses (each of which could be a
sentence by itself). You can join the clauses with
a conjunction such as *and*, *but*, *or*, or *yet*, or with a
semicolon:

The soothsayer gave a warning, but no one listened.

Something was in the cave; I could feel its presence.

▶ **Complex sentences**

Complex sentences are made by combining at least
one main clause with a subordinate clause (that
is, a clause which cannot be a sentence by itself).
Subordinate clauses can come after conjunctions
such as *although*, *because*, *if*, *until*, *unless*, *when*, or *while*;
or after relative pronouns such as *that*, *which*, *who*, or
whose:

Although chickenpox can be dangerous, it is rarely fatal.

The camera won't work unless you switch it on.

The film is shot in digital 3D, which produces stunning images.

You can often improve a piece of writing by making a few simple changes to the wording or structure of your sentences.

▶ **Try to vary the length and type of sentences that you use**. If you use too many sentences of the same type – especially too many simple sentences – your writing may seem dull or childish to read.

▶ **Sometimes reordering a sentence can make a difference**. You can put more emphasis on a particular word or phrase, or can vary the rhythm of your writing, without changing the meaning. Compare for example:

The first country to give the vote to women was New Zealand.
New Zealand was the first country to give the vote to women.

The noises began on the stroke of midnight.
On the stroke of midnight, the noises began.

Mary Shelley wrote Frankenstein *when she was nineteen.*
Mary Shelley was nineteen when she wrote Frankenstein.
When she was nineteen, Mary Shelley wrote Frankenstein.

Working with sentences

Example

The first draft of this paragraph uses only simple and compound sentences, and only one conjunction (*and*). It is grammatically correct, but rather dull to read.

Anne Frank was a teenager at the start of the second world war. She and her family were Jewish and they lived in Amsterdam. They had to go into hiding from the Nazi authorities. Anne kept a diary of her experiences. It records her everyday thoughts <u>and</u> it is very moving and also lively and funny at times. Anne's family were eventually found and they were sent to concentration camps. Anne and her mother and sister all died in the camps. Her diary was published after the war and it became a bestseller.

The second, revised version uses a variety of sentence types and conjunctions.

Anne Frank was a teenager living in Amsterdam at the start of the second world war. Because she and her family were Jewish, they had to go into hiding from the Nazi authorities. While in hiding, Anne kept a diary of her experiences, which records her everyday thoughts. Although it is very moving, it is also lively and funny at times. Anne's family were eventually found and sent to concentration camps, where she and her mother and sister all died. After the war, her diary was published and became a bestseller.

Sentence problems

If there is a problem with your sentences, then your meaning can get lost or confused. Here are some common sentence problems – and some ways to fix them.

Run-on sentences

Be careful not to join two main clauses with only a comma. This is called a **run-on sentence**. For example:

> *Humans could not breathe on Mars, the atmosphere is too thin.*

You can fix this by making it into two sentences:

> *Humans could not breathe on Mars. The atmosphere is too thin.*

or by joining the two clauses with a colon or semi-colon, or with a conjunction:

> *Humans could not breathe on Mars: the atmosphere is too thin.*
> *Humans could not breathe on Mars, as the atmosphere is too thin.*

Sentence fragments

A sentence fragment is a bit of a sentence that cannot stand by itself. In other words, it is not a complete sentence. To make these examples work as sentences, you can either change the punctuation or reword them as follows:

- ✗ *Romeo decides to kill himself. Because he believes Juliet is dead.*
- ✓ *Romeo decides to kill himself, because he believes Juliet is dead.*

- ✗ *Romeo thinks Juliet is dead. Which is why he decides to kill himself.*
- ✓ *Romeo thinks Juliet is dead and therefore decides to kill himself.*

Although you should avoid using sentence fragments in essays or formal letters, you will see them in fiction, where writers sometimes bend the rules for stylistic effect:

'The skin was soft and withered, bent into a thousand tiny creases that clung gently to the bone underneath. Like a dried apricot, but with a puff of thick white hair standing out in a cloud around it.'
STEPHENIE MEYER, NEW MOON

Dangling clauses

A dangling clause is an opening clause that is not clearly connected to the rest of the sentence; it therefore seems to be left 'dangling'. For example:

Buried for years, archaeologists have unearthed a hidden tomb.
Running for the bus, my phone rang.

Dangling clauses are confusing to read, and are sometimes unintentionally funny. (It is not, presumably, the phone that is running for the bus.) The best way to fix this problem is to reorder the sentence, or to expand the clause that is causing the problem, so that the meaning is clear:

Archaeologists have unearthed a hidden tomb which had been buried for years.
As I was running for the bus, my phone rang.

Working with paragraphs

Nobody wants to read pages and pages of text without a break; nor do they want to be constantly distracted with short, choppy paragraphs. Getting the paragraphs right will give your writing structure and help it to flow.

▶ Make sure that each paragraph covers a single (and clear) topic or idea. If you find that you are starting a new point in your argument, or are moving into a new scene in your story, it is time to start a new paragraph.

▶ In non-fiction writing, it helps to have a **topic sentence** somewhere (usually, though not always, at the start) which sums up the point of the paragraph.

▶ **Linking words** can help your reader to follow your argument or your story. You can use linking words to sum up (*therefore*), to contrast (*however, despite this*), to add information (*in addition, also, moreover*), or to present points in order (*first, next, later, lastly*).

As with sentences, you can have more freedom in the way you use paragraphs in creative writing. Fiction writers sometimes use very short paragraphs for effect:

'Mau saw him raising his pistol as he sank, and then his expression changed to an enormous grin, with blood at the corners, and he was dragged into the swirling waters.

The sharks had arrived for dinner.'

TERRY PRATCHETT, NATION

Example

The topic of each paragraph is highlighted. The words *originally* and *later* help the flow of the second paragraph.

The Olympic Games

The first Olympic Games were held in ancient Greece in 776 BC, near the town of Olympia. In those days, there was only one event: a foot race run in the open air. Originally, women and girls were not allowed to participate in the Olympic Games. Later, they took part in a separate event, called the Herannic Games in honour of the goddess Hera.

The modern Olympic Games began in the nineteenth century, with the foundation of the International Olympic Committee (IOC). The first modern Games were held in Athens in 1896.

Using punctuation

Punctuation can help your reader understand your meaning. It can also give rhythm to your writing, by breaking up long sentences and phrases. Here are some tips for using punctuation in your writing.

Apostrophes (')

You need an apostrophe to show possession (*Mark Antony's speech* or *the murderer's fingerprints*), or to indicate a missing letter in a contraction such as *I'm* or *don't*.

However, beware of adding an apostrophe where it is not needed:

- ✗ *to discuss the planet and it's future*
- ✓ *to discuss the planet and its future*

- ✗ *That was a great idea of your's.*
- ✓ *That was a great idea of yours.*

- ✗ *the being who's face I saw*
- ✓ *the being whose face I saw*

Note that, for plural nouns, the apostrophe always goes after the plural form:

the werewolves' howling

If you are unsure where to put the apostrophe (or if the phrase sounds awkward), try rewording it so that an apostrophe is not needed:

the howling of the werewolves

You don't need an apostrophe for decades, or for plural abbreviations:
CDs, **DVDs**, and **MP3s**, *in the 1990s*

Commas (,)

Commas can make a difference to the meaning of a sentence. Compare for example:

Zombies who habitually attack people will be prosecuted.
Zombies, who habitually attack people, will be prosecuted.

In the first example, only *certain* zombies (those who habitually attack people) are to be prosecuted; in the second example, they *all* attack and are *all* to be prosecuted. The first example is called a *restrictive clause* because it *restricts* the meaning of the subject (*zombies*).

Commas tell your reader that the clause does not have a restrictive meaning. You can use them to surround clauses which begin with *who* or *which* (but not those beginning with *that*).

For example:

The filmstar, who lives in the US, was unavailable for comment.

but   *The player who scores the highest is the winner.*
                (i.e. *only* the player who scores the highest)

Mercury, which is closest to the Sun, is the smallest planet.

but   *The probe will orbit the planets which are closest*
                to the Sun.
                (i.e. *only* those planets which are closest to
                the Sun)
                The planets that are closest to the Sun are called
                the inner planets.

> If you are adding commas around a clause, be sure to add a pair of commas, not just one.

Colons (:) and semi-colons (;)

The part of a sentence after a colon should illustrate, explain, or expand on what comes before it:

In 1952 London was hit by smog: a mixture of smoke, fog, and fumes.
The book was a great success: the first edition sold out within days.

Use a colon:

▶ to introduce a list of items or a range of options:
Which do you prefer to use: email, phone, or texting?

Use a semi-colon:

▶ as a break between related or contrasting clauses:
We call it the Plough; the Americans call it the Big Dipper.

▶ to separate a series of clauses introduced by a colon:
*The witches give three prophesies: that Macbeth will be
Thane of Cawdor; that he will be Thane of Glamis; and
lastly that he will be King.*

Fiction writers sometimes use semi-colons for stylistic effect.
A series of semi-colons can give a sense of accumulating
pace to a passage. Here, the increasingly frantic pace of the
sentence reflects the frantic state of mind of the narrator:

'My life is shaken to its roots; sleep has left me; the
deadliest terror sits by me at all hours of the day
and night; I feel that my days are numbered, and
that I must die; and yet I shall die incredulous.'
ROBERT LOUIS STEVENSON, DR JEKYLL AND MR HYDE

Hyphens (-)

Some compounds words (words which are made up of more than one word) can be spelled with or without a hyphen. For example, *place name* is sometimes spelled *place-name* (with a hyphen), or *placename* (joined up). In this case, the hyphen is optional and makes no difference to the meaning of the word. But there are some places where a hyphen is required.

Always use a hyphen:

▶ if the meaning is ambiguous. For example, *a cross section of the audience* (without a hyphen) might mean an angry group of people, rather than a typical sample. But if you use a hyphen, the meaning is unambiguous: *a cross-section of the audience.*

▶ in compound numbers, like *twenty-one* and *fifty-seven*, but not for *five hundred* and *ten thousand*.

▶ in compound adjectives which come before a noun:
> *a steel-string guitar*
> *an out-of-date hairstyle*
> *a well-written autobiography*

You don't need a hyphen after adverbs that end in **-ly**, or for adjectival phrases that come after the noun:
> *a **badly** scripted film*
> *a **hairstyle** which is now out of date*

Dashes (–)

Dashes are commonly used in emails and in informal notes:

The film starts at 2 – don't be late!
Phone me later – or just send a text.

Be careful not to overuse dashes in more formal writing, where it is better to use colons, semi-colons, or full stops instead:

- ✗ *There were three Brontë sisters – Anne, Charlotte, and Emily.*
- ✓ *There were three Bronte sisters: Anne, Charlotte, and Emily.*

Question marks (?)

Only use a question mark if you are asking a direct question:

Sometimes I ask myself: has the world gone mad?

You don't use a question mark if you are reporting the question in a statement:

Sometimes I wonder if the world has gone mad.

Exclamation marks (!)

Exclamation marks are a quick way to add emphasis in informal writing or in fiction: for example, when you are writing direct speech (*'Help!' she screamed*) or a character's inner thoughts (*No! It cannot be!*); or if you want to represent a sound effect, like *Bang!* or *Thud!*

However, use them sparingly, unless you want to give an effect of heightened emotion or hysteria:

> '*Mrs Rachel felt that she had received a severe mental jolt. She thought in exclamation points. A boy! From an orphan asylum! Well, the world was certainly turning upside down! She would be surprised at nothing after this! Nothing!*'
> L. M. MONTGOMERY, ANNE OF GREEN GABLES

Writing creatively

How can you turn a run-of-the-mill piece of fiction into something more lively? Here are some things you can try to make your writing more interesting:

▶ Use **descriptive words**: for example, think about interesting shades of colour: not just white light, but *pearly* light; not just dark sky, but *inky* sky. *A frog with a mottled olive skin* will be more real to your reader than just *a green frog*.

▶ Be **specific**: how exactly does your character say something? Do they *bark* it out loudly, *blurt* it out suddenly, *splutter* it out unclearly, or *murmur* it tenderly? What are they wearing? Are their jeans *starched* and *pristine*, or *threadbare* and *baggy*?

▶ Using your **senses** can really liven up your descriptions. Think about how a place **looks** and **smells**, or how an object **feels** or **tastes**. Which of these two meals sounds more unpleasant?
The porridge was unappetizing.
The porridge had cooled to a gelatinous gloop that reminded me of frogspawn.

▶ Use **figurative language**, such as similes and metaphors.

▶ Be **creative** by making up your own words, especially for characters and settings.

Look up the *writing tips* and *word web* panels in this thesaurus for descriptive words and ideas for adding detail. You will find a list of both types of panel in the front of the thesaurus.

Example 1

Check that you are not using too many vague words. Bring your descriptions to life by being more specific and including interesting details.

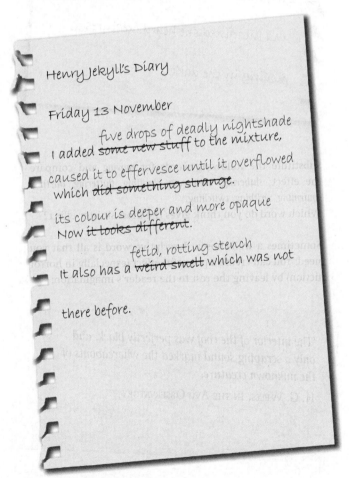

Henry Jekyll's Diary

Friday 13 November

I added ~~some new stuff~~ five drops of deadly nightshade to the mixture, caused it to effervesce until it overflowed which ~~did something strange.~~

Now ~~it looks different.~~ its colour is deeper and more opaque

It also has a ~~weird smell~~ fetid, rotting stench which was not there before.

Writing creatively

Example 2

Chapter One

Una imagined she heard creatures

moving in the dark…

Substitute the following words for *moving* and compare the effect: *slithering, lumbering, shuffling, fluttering, darting, squirming, writhing, twitching.*

Which word do you think gives the most sinister effect?

Sometimes a well-chosen descriptive word is all that you need. You can create a powerful effect (especially in horror fiction) by leaving the rest to the reader's imagination:

'The interior of the roof was perfectly black, and only a scraping sound marked the whereabouts of the unknown creature.'

H. G. WELLS, IN THE AVU OBSERVATORY

Using figurative language

What is figurative language, and how can it liven up your writing?

Figurative language concentrates on the effects which words create, rather than on their literal meaning. Here are some common types of figurative language:

▶ A **simile** is where you describe something as being **like** something else: for example, *a face like a squashed pumpkin* or *skin as rough as the bark of a gum tree.*

> 'She was horrible. Her face was the colour of a dirty pillowcase, and the corners of her mouth glistened with wet, which inched like a glacier down the deep grooves enclosing her chin.'
> HARPER LEE, TO KILL A MOCKINGBIRD

▶ A **metaphor** is where you describe something **as if it were** something else: for example, *its eyes were fathomless pools of ink.*

▶ **Personification** is where you describe an object **as if it were human or alive**: for example, *a blast of wind punched me in the face.*

► **Onomatopoeia** is where you use words which **sound like** the thing you are describing: for example, *a hundred cameras went 'click!'* or *the engines whirred into life.*

► **Alliteration** is where you use a number of words which **begin with the same sound**: for example, *grim and ghastly when he grunted.* Alliteration is mainly used in poetry, but you will also see it in advertising, and in the names of fictional characters, such *as Rowena Ravenclaw* and *Bilbo Baggins.*

Using idioms

An **idiom** is a phrase which means something other than its literal meaning. For example, if your plans *go up in smoke*, it means that they have failed completely, not that you have literally thrown them in the fire (although you might have done that, too); and if you have *a bone to pick* with someone, it means that you have reason to be annoyed with them.

'Bill is always in detention, so I guess he has a bone to pick with just about every teacher in the school, including Mr Ira.'
JEFF KINNEY, DIARY OF A WIMPY KID

You can use idioms in a piece of creative writing to make a sentence more lively or humorous, especially if you are writing in a conversational style:

> *By mid-afternoon, Duncan was still **dead to the world**.*
> *Josie looked glum. I wasn't exactly **over the moon** myself.*

Because idioms are so common in speech, they can also make written dialogue sound more natural or convincing:

> *'You're looking **full of beans**, today. What's up?'*
> *'There's no need to **lose your rag**. It was only a suggestion.'*

But be careful: your writing can look clichéd if you use too many idioms, or use the same ones over and over again.

You will find suggestions for idioms given in some entries in this thesaurus. See in particular the entries for ***angry*** and ***delighted***.

Being creative with words

What will really make your fiction writing stand out as original and creative?

Writers often make new words using parts of old words: rather like word recycling. The old parts help the reader to understand what the new word means. If you are writing a fantasy or science-fiction story, you may want to describe an object no one has ever seen before, so you will need a new word for it. For example, a four-legged artificial life-form might be a *quadriborg*, and a creature which can change shape into a lizard might be a *lizomorph*.

Some ideas for being creative with words are:

▶ Make your own **compound words** to add originality to your descriptions: for example, *a rain-slicked pavement* or *a blood-smeared pillow*. For describing a character, you could use *-faced*, *-haired*, or *-lipped*: for example *weasel-faced*, *fiery-haired*, or *cherry-lipped*.

- ▶ Make use of **prefixes** and suffixes, such as *anti-*, *multi-*, *-ful*, *-less*, and *-like*, or more unusual ones such as *hyper-*, *pan-*, *-centric*, or *-esque*: for example, a *creature with crablike arms*, or a *Tolkienesque landscape*.

- ▶ Think of interesting and original names for **characters** and **places**. Place names and personal names can convey information to your reader: for example, a character called *Mr Dankweed* is unlikely to be a cheerful person; and a place called *Mortvale* or *Corpsewood* might set the right mood for a ghost or horror story.

> *'"ProudFEET!" shouted an elderly hobbit from the back of the pavilion. His name, of course, was Proudfoot, and well merited; his feet were large, exceptionally furry, and both were on the table.'*
>
> J. R. R. TOLKIEN, THE FELLOWSHIP OF THE RING

Adding speech

Direct speech

Direct speech (when you give the actual words that a character says) adds immediate drama to a piece of creative writing. However, there are a few rules to follow when you want to use it.

▶ Start a new paragraph whenever the speaker changes. This will help your reader to identify who is speaking, and when they have finished.

▶ You don't have to include 'he said' or 'she said' after each block of speech. It will often be obvious to your reader who is speaking, especially if there are only two characters talking.

'Only one more question, Dr Mortimer. You say that before Sir Charles Baskerville's death several people saw this apparition upon the moor?'

'Three people did.'

'Did any see it after?'

'I have not heard of any.'

'Thank you. Good morning.'

SIR ARTHUR CONAN DOYLE,
THE HOUND OF THE BASKERVILLES

► Include only the actual words spoken by a character within quotations marks.

► Put final punctuation marks (full stops, question marks, or exclamation marks) within the quotation marks.

► Use the following punctuation when the name of the speaker comes before, after, or in the middle of their words:

> 'Oh, I really can't be bothered,' sighed Nora.
> Nora sighed, 'Oh, I really can't be bothered.'
> Oh,' sighed Nora, 'I really can't be bothered.'

Look up the overused word panel for *say* for some suggestions of verbs to use with direct speech.

Reported speech

When you relate what someone has said, rather than giving their exact words, it is called **reported speech**. For example:

Mark Twain once said: 'A classic is something that everybody wants to have read and nobody wants to read.'

would become in reported speech:

Mark Twain once said that a classic is something that everybody wants to have read and nobody wants to read.

When using reported speech in your writing:

▶ don't use quotation marks, as you are not giving someone's exact words.

▶ When you convert direct speech to reported speech, you sometimes need to change the pronouns and the verb tenses:

> *'My family lives under an ancient curse,' she explained. She explained that her family lived under an ancient curse.*

▶ There is no need for a question mark when you are reporting (rather than quoting) someone's question:

> *'Is there a full moon tonight?' he asked.* **[direct]**
> *He asked if there was a full moon that night.* **[reported]**

Adding speech

▶ Avoid using *how* instead of *that* after verbs like *tell*:

✗ *Pip tells Biddy how he wants to be a gentleman.*
✓ *Pip tells Biddy that he wants to be a gentleman.*

Quoting texts

When quoting from a book or other text:

▶ enclose short quotations in quotation marks, and word your sentence so that it reads naturally:

> *Macbeth hears a voice telling him to 'sleep no more'.*
or *Macbeth hears a voice crying: 'Sleep no more!'*

▶ separate longer quotations from the rest of your text by starting on a new line and indenting them (there is no need to use quotation marks). Don't try to include them within a sentence:

> *Coleridge uses alliteration throughout 'The Rime of the Ancient Mariner'. For example:*
>
> *The fair breeze blew, the white foam flew,*
> *The furrow followed free;*
> *We were the first that ever burst*
> *Into that silent sea.*

Using your own words

How do you put something you've read in a book, or found on the Internet, into your own words?

It's not enough just to substitute synonyms for a few of the words. The best way to reword something is to **condense** it first, and then **expand** it in your own words. You can keep some of the **key words**, but try to change others when you can. If possible, present the key points in a different order, as that will help you to make the argument or summary your own.

Putting something into your own words, without changing the original information, is called **paraphrasing** and it is an important skill for any writer. The key stages to good paraphrasing are:

▶ Identify the **key points** and any **key words** which you can keep. Do not copy whole phrases or sentences.

▶ Then try to **rewrite** the paragraph, without looking at the original text. Use your thesaurus to help you find alternative ways to say things.

▶ Finally, **compare** your version with the original to see if you have unconsciously copied too much of the wording.

The Origin of Species

The Origin of Species, by Charles Darwin, is one of the most important scientific books ever written. In it, Darwin argued that species evolve over many generations through a process which he called Natural Selection. He showed that the diversity of life on our planet was not planned by a divine creator, but had arisen naturally, over millions of years. Darwin's theory developed out of observations he had made on a five-year scientific voyage on HMS Beagle in the 1830s, and he worked tirelessly to accumulate further evidence over the next two decades. His ideas were controversial, because they challenged the widespread belief that humans were unique. If Darwin's theory were true, it would mean that humans were related to the rest of life on Earth. Darwin wanted his book to be read widely, not just within the scientific community. On its publication, in November 1859, it attracted huge interest and sold out within a day.

key words and points

key scientific book

Natural Selection

evolutionary process

5 years HMS Beagle

20 years research

challenged beliefs

for general audience

published November 1859

sold out in a day

Using your own words

OMNIPAEDIA (2010)

Check that you are not copying complete phrases or sentences, and that your wording is not too close to the original. You can use your thesaurus to help you find alternative words or expressions.

In November 1859, Charles Darwin

published The Origin of Species: a key

work in the history of science. The book

was written for a general audience and

~~it attracted so much~~ there was so much public interest that it sold

out in a single day. In this book, Darwin

~~argued~~ proposed that the ~~diversity of life~~ great variety of species on Earth

had developed over millions of years,

through an evolutionary process that he

called Natural Selection, rather than

being created by ~~a divine creator~~ God. It was

an idea he had first thought about in

the 1830s, during a five-year scientific

voyage on HMS Beagle. He spent

another twenty years ~~accumulating~~ gathering

~~evidence~~ data before he was ready to publish

the results. His theory ~~challenged~~ contradicted

~~widespread beliefs~~ contemporary views that humans were

different from other species, by showing

that all forms of life were related.

Some common mistakes

What are the common mistakes that you should look out for in your writing? Here are some pitfalls that you should try to avoid:

▶ Using a **confusable word**. Some pairs of confusable words are **homophones**: that is they sound the same, but they are spelled differently and have different meanings, for example *bazaar* and *bizarre*, or *retch* and *wretch*. Some common confusable pairs are listed below.

> ✗ *To kill a vampire you must drive a steak into its heart.*
> ✓ *To kill a vampire you must drive a stake into its heart.*

> ✗ *The creature was in its death **throws**.*
> ✓ *The creature was in its death **throes**.*

Using the wrong word can give your writing a meaning you did not intend. Because the wrong word (*steak* or *throws*) is spelled correctly, it will not be picked up by a spellchecking program, so it is important that you check your own writing.

▶ Mixing up **spelling systems**. Be careful not to mix American spelling with British spelling. For example, the American spelling of *favourite* is *favorite*, which you will often find on the Internet. Always check in a dictionary if you are unsure of the correct spelling. Some common American spellings are listed on page 693.

Confusable words

These pairs of words are commonly confused. It is a good idea to double-check that you have used them correctly in your final draft.

▶ **advice / advise**
advice is a noun and advise is a verb (it is never spelled with –ize):

> My **advice** is to ignore the email.
> What would you **advise**?

▶ **affect / effect**
affect is a verb meaning either 'to make a difference to' or 'to pretend':

> The law will **affect** Scotland as well as England.
> Mr Darcy **affected** indifference.

effect can be either a noun meaning 'result or consequence', or a verb meaning 'to bring about':

> the **effects** of global warming
> to **effect** a change in the law

▶ **breath / breathe**
breath is the noun, whereas breathe is the verb:

> He said these words with his dying **breath**.
> Don't **breathe** a word of this to anyone.

► **complement / compliment**

You give someone a *compliment*, but you wear a hat that *complements* your outfit.

► **especially / specially**

especially means 'particularly', whereas *specially* means 'for a special purpose' or 'solely for':

> *The film is impressive, especially the opening shot.*
> *The dress was made specially for her.*

► **historic / historical**

A *historic* event is important in history, whereas something *historical* (like a historical novel or exhibition) is about people or things in history.

► **loath / loathe**

If you are *loath* to do something, then you are unwilling to do it; but if you *loathe* something, then you despise it:

> *Stephie was loath to venture outside.*
> *Scrooge loathes everything about Christmas.*

► **passed / past**

The past tense of the verb *to pass* is *passed*. The word *past* is used for *in the past*, *past times*, or *going past your house*:

> *I passed them whispering in the corridor.*
> *She walked straight past me without speaking*

▶ **precede / proceed**
precede means 'to go before', whereas proceed means 'to go forward' or 'to go on':

> The rally was preceded by a free concert.
> Holmes proceeded to explain his theory.

▶ **principal / principle**
principal can be either an adjective meaning 'most important', or a noun meaning 'a chief or head':

> the principal characters in the play
> the principal of the college

principle is always a noun and means 'rule or law':

> the principles of good design

▶ **stationary / stationery**
stationary is an adjective meaning 'not moving', whereas stationery is a noun to describe paper and pens, etc.:

> a line of stationary vehicles
> a range of fancy stationery

Note also the difference in spelling and meaning between these pairs of words:

a guitar **chord**	a **cord** of rope
the Sahara **Desert**	a mouthwatering **dessert**
a rough **draft** of your essay	a **draught** of cold

Other words to watch

▶ **fewer** and **less**
fewer means 'smaller in number', whereas *less* means 'smaller in amount':

> There have been *fewer* sightings of UFOs.
> There is a lot *less* traffic in town today.
> I'm trying to eat *fewer* sweets and *less* stodge.

▶ **literally** and **unique**
Only use *literally* when you mean that something is *literally* true, not just to add emphasis:

✗ His argument *literally* crumbled away.
✓ Buckingham Palace is *literally* crumbling.

In the first example, you could replace *literally* with *completely* or *simply*:

> His argument *completely* crumbled away.
> His argument *simply* crumbled away.

The word *unique* means 'the only one in existence'; it is not a synonym for *rare*:

✗ one of the most *unique* types of fossil
✓ a *unique* moment in history

For the first example, you could use *rarest* or *most unusual* instead:

> one of the *rarest* types of fossil
> one of the *most unusual* types of fossil

Some common mistakes

American spelling

American spelling is often used in webpages, so it is easy to forget that it is different to British spelling. However, it is important not to muddle up the two systems by using some American spellings in the middle of a piece of writing.

Here are some common words which have a different spelling in American English:

British English	North American
amoeba	ameba
anaemia	anemia
analyse	analyze
armour	armor
behaviour	behavior
catalogue	catalog
centre	center
colour	color
defence	defense
dialogue	dialog
diarrhoea	diarrhea
favourite	favorite
fibre	fiber
flavour	flavor
fulfil	fulfill
grey	gray
harbour	harbor
honour	honor
jewellery	jewelry
labour	labor

British English	North American
manoeuvre	maneuver
meagre	meager
mould	mold
moult	molt
neighbour	neighbor
neighbourhood	neighborhood
odour	odor
offence	offense
paralyse	paralyze
programme	program
pyjamas	pajamas
skilful	skillful
spectre	specter
theatre	theater
tyre	tire
wilful	willful

Some common mistakes

The American spellings **disk** and **program** are always used in computing:

*watching a new television **programme***

but *installing a new version of the **program***

–ll– or –l–

In American English, verbs like *model* and *travel* are spelled with a single l when they add a suffix like *-ed*, *-er*, or *-ing*:

British English	North American
travelling through Time	*traveling through Time*
a Time traveller	*a Time traveler*

–ise or –ize

In American English, verbs like *criticize* and *memorize* are always spelled with *-ize*. The same is true for nouns like *civilization* and *realization*.

In British English, you can also spell these words with *-ise* or *-is*: *criticize* or *criticise*, *realization* or *realisation*.

However, the following words are *always* spelled *-ise* in both British and American English:

advertise	*comprise*	*compromise*
despise	*devise*	*enterprise*
exercise	*improvise*	*incise*
revise	*supervise*	*surprise*

Watch out also for the following pairs of words, which have different uses in British and American spelling:

licence / license

In British English, *licence* is used for the noun and *license* for the verb. American English uses *license* (with an s) for both noun and verb:

British English	North American
a driving licence	a driving license

practice / practise

In British English, *practice* is used for the noun and *practise* for the verb.

American English uses *practice* (with a c) for both noun and verb:

British English	North American
practising my guitar	practicing my guitar

Be wary of using American words like **movie** and **apartment** in formal writing:

a James Bond **movie** (*North American*)
a James Bond **film** (*British English*)

Some tricky plurals

Singular	Plural
a radio **antenna**	an insect's **antennae**
in the **appendix**	in the **appendices**
a mini **atlas**	a collection of **atlases**
the Earth's **axis**	the **axes** of the planets
her **brother-in-law**	her two **brothers-in-law**
an economic **crisis**	a series of **crises**
the only **criterion**	the following **criteria**
a **cupful** of sugar	two **cupfuls** of flour
a new **formula**	mathematical **formulae**
a slice of chocolate **gateau**	a tray of mini **gateaux**
a book with no **index**	books without **indices**
a live **larva**	the **larvae** of a wasp
in the last **millennium**	over several **millennia**
a desert **oasis**	the **oases** of central Asia
a species of **octopus**	a family of **octopuses**
a single **passerby**	a group of **passersby**
a strange **phenomenon**	unexplained **phenomena**
the **radius** of a circle	the sum of the **radii**
an ancient **sarcophagus**	painted **sarcophagi**
my **sister-in-law**	my two **sisters-in-law**
a classic TV **series**	the first of four **series**
a rare **species**	several extinct **species**
a football **stadium**	one of the Olympic **stadiums**
a **synopsis** of the plot	some short **synopses**
half a **teaspoonful**	two **teaspoonfuls**

Some common mistakes

These words have two possible plurals:

a potted **cactus**   a row of **cacti**
                or   a row of **cactusus**

a school **thesaurus**   a range of **thesauruses**
                or   a range of **thesauri**

–oes or –os?

Some words which end in –o, like *tomato* and *volcano*, add –es to form the plural. Others, like *avocado* and *piano*, just add an –s. Look it up in a dictionary if you are unsure of the plural of any word:

Some common mistakes

legendary **heroes**	ripe **avocados**
giant **mosquitoes**	classical **cellos**
boiled **potatoes**	family **photos**
sliced **tomatoes**	grand **pianos**
severe **tornadoes**	a pair of **stilettos**
active **volcanoes**	fake **tattoos**

Words which are often misspelled

an **abandoned** ship

an **accessory** to the crime

an **accidental** discovery

rented **accommodation**

your email **address**

our **annual** holiday

a **bizarre** comment

cream of **broccoli**

an advent **calendar**

a double **cappuccino**

a deserted **cemetery**

a **colossal** mistake

a definite **commitment**

contemporary art

desperate remedies

the **developing** world

a mysterious **disappearance**

a bitter **disappointment**

a jam **doughnut**

the **eighth** floor

an **embarrassing** silence

a gross **exaggeration**

an **exhilarating** ride

the first of **February**

fluorescent lighting

a temperature **gauge**

a **glamorous** lifestyle

a change of **government**

a wall of **graffiti**

a **humorous** anecdote

not very **hygienic**

an **immediate** response

a few hours of **leisure**

a **lengthy** argument

your local **library**

a bolt of **lightning**

a **miniature** model

a **minuscule** crack

necessary precautions

a **noticeable** gap

a happy **occasion**

a strange **occurrence**

parallel lines

an elected **parliament**

my favourite **pastime**

avoiding **plagiarism**

a modern **playwright**

all their **possessions**

pride and **prejudice**

a life of **privilege**

the usual **pronunciation**

psychic abilities

an online **questionnaire**

highly **recommended**

a biased **referee**

a **relevant** answer

an Italian **restaurant**

two words which **rhyme**

syncopated **rhythm**

an office **secretary**

a busy **schedule**

a pair of **scissors**

a **separate** compartment

a perfect **somersault**

a plate of **spaghetti**

superhuman **strength**

a resounding **success**

a **symmetrical** pattern

on the **threshold**

the day after **tomorrow**

a **twelfth** birthday

an **unnecessary** risk

a flu **vaccination**

a **vacuum** cleaner

a vintage **vehicle**

a **weird** experience

withholding information

a racing **yacht**

Editing your work

> 'Good writing is essentially rewriting. I am positive of this.'
> ROALD DAHL

Editing is best done in stages, or layers, especially for long essays or stories. It is a good idea to have a checklist of things to look out for, which you can work through in sequence:

Structure and flow

✓ Do you have enough paragraph breaks? Do those you have break at appropriate points?

✓ Do your paragraphs follow a logical sequence? Could you add some linking words to help your readers?

✓ Have you used whole sentences? Would your meaning be clearer if you reordered the words, or changed the punctuation?

✓ Could you vary the length and type of sentences that you use?

Language

✓ Have you used informal words or punctuation in a formal piece of work?

✓ Can you vary your choice of words to make your text more interesting or more precise?

✓ Can you add more details to bring your descriptions to life?

✓ Could you make your fiction more imaginative by using figurative language?

Details

✓ Have you corrected any errors in spelling or punctuation?

✓ Have you avoided any confusable words?

Keep writing

The best thing you can do for your writing is to practise; in other words, *keep writing*. Good writers are made, not born, and it takes time to develop your skills. So don't worry if you feel your writing isn't quite there yet: it will improve with practice. Don't forget to read, too. Reading other writers can give you new ideas and help you to develop your own style.

'You only learn to be a better writer by actually writing.'
ROALD DAHL

Editing your work